Music Radio

ALSO BY JIM COX
AND FROM McFARLAND

Rails Across Dixie: A History of Passenger Trains in the American South (2011)

American Radio Networks: A History (2009)

Sold on Radio: Advertisers in the Golden Age of Broadcasting (2008)

This Day in Network Radio: A Daily Calendar of Births, Deaths, Debuts, Cancellations and Other Events in Broadcasting History (2008)

The Great Radio Sitcoms (2007)

Radio Speakers: Narrators, News Junkies, Sports Jockeys, Tattletales, Tipsters, Toastmasters and Coffee Klatch Couples Who Verbalized the Jargon of the Aural Ether from the 1920s to the 1980s — A Biographical Dictionary (2007; paperback 2011)

The Daytime Serials of Television, 1946–1960 (2006; paperback 2010)

Mr. Keen, Tracer of Lost Persons: A Complete History and Episode Log of Radio's Most Durable Detective (2004; paperback 2011)

Frank and Anne Hummert's Radio Factory: The Programs and Personalities of Broadcasting's Most Prolific Producers (2003)

Radio Crime Fighters: More Than 300 Programs from the Golden Age (2002; paperback 2010)

Say Goodnight, Gracie: The Last Years of Network Radio (2002)

The Great Radio Audience Participation Shows: Seventeen Programs from the 1940s and 1950s (2001; paperback 2009)

The Great Radio Soap Operas (1999; paperback 2008)

Music Radio

*The Great Performers and
Programs of the 1920s
through Early 1960s*

Jim Cox

McFarland & Company, Inc., Publishers
Jefferson, North Carolina, and London

The present work is a reprint of the illustrated case bound edition of Music Radio: The Great Performers and Programs of the 1920s Through Early 1960s, *first published in 2005 by McFarland.*

All of the photographs were provided by Photofest.

LIBRARY OF CONGRESS CATALOGUING-IN-PUBLICATION DATA

Cox, Jim, 1939–
Music radio : the great performers and programs of the 1920s through early 1960s / Jim Cox.
  p.   cm.
Includes bibliographical references and index.

ISBN 978-0-7864-6085-4
softcover : 50# alkaline paper

1. Radio and music — United States. 2. Radio programs, Musical — United States. 3. Music — United States — 20th century — History and criticism. 4. Musicians — United States. 5. Disc jockeys — United States. I. Title.
ML68.C8   2011
781.5′44′097309041— dc22   2005001716

BRITISH LIBRARY CATALOGUING DATA ARE AVAILABLE

© 2005 Jim Cox. All rights reserved

No part of this book may be reproduced or transmitted in any form or by any means, electronic or mechanical, including photocopying or recording, or by any information storage and retrieval system, without permission in writing from the publisher.

Cover photograph: Musical movie starlet Jane Powell and host Gordon MacRae performing on *The Railroad Hour*

Manufactured in the United States of America

*McFarland & Company, Inc., Publishers
Box 611, Jefferson, North Carolina 28640
www.mcfarlandpub.com*

For Jimmy and Jodi,
with pride and joy!

Acknowledgments

No man writes alone, as I've expressed before. If that's true of any author, it's surely true of me. For this text there were times I was turning daily to researchers Claire Connelly (whose specialty is gathering and verifying elusive biographical records) and Ted Meland (whose broad knowledge of multiple musical genres supplied data that resulted in one-stop shopping so many times). Both did yeoman's work and a great deal of the substance of this book may be credited to them.

There were others who made significant contributions. Trusting I've not overlooked anyone, I thank Camilla Clocker, Ted Davenport, Doug Douglas, Dick Fisher, Martin Grams Jr., Jay Hickerson, Bill Knowlton, Larry Lewis, Patrick Lucanio, Elizabeth McLeod, Gary Mercer, Lee Munsick, Charles Niren, Cope Robinson, Ron Sayles, Chuck Schaden, Jim Snyder, Eric Spilker, Paul Urbahns and Shawn Wells.

Thanks also to OTR newsletter editors who, through their own journalistic pursuits, underwrite a great deal of the exposure our hobby enjoys—Bob Burchett, Jack French, Ken Krug, Patrick Lucanio, Robert Newman and more.

I cannot neglect the sacrifices of my lifelong companion, Sharon Cox, who gives me the privilege of researching and writing to my heart's content. The tedious hours I devote to those labors of love wouldn't be nearly as enjoyable without her by my side.

The OTR community at large continues to challenge me just as it mystifies me. There is a host of kindred spirits out there hungering for the material a handful of authors are providing. This one is especially grateful to so many who encourage us in everything we tackle. It's a measure of satisfaction to be able to preserve these records for the enjoyment and elucidation of readers today and tomorrow.

Contents

Acknowledgments vii
Preface 1

The Bell Telephone Hour 3
The Big Bands 16
The Bing Crosby Show 52
*The Chamber Music Society
   of Lower Basin Street* 81
Cities Service Concerts 90
The Classics 103
The Contests 127
The Disc Jockeys 144
The Fred Waring Show 164

Grand Ole Opry 177
The Horse Operas 192
The House Bands 206
The Hummert Musicales 228
The Kate Smith Show 245
The Railroad Hour 261
The Sacred Singers 271
The Vocalists 276
The Voice of Firestone 299
Your Hit Parade 317

Chapter Notes 337
Bibliography 341
Index 345

Preface

Long before the invention of "talk radio," music was filling the medium's programming — often by itself, yet also seeping in between features, filling in the background, and identifying to audiences the shows that were coming on and exiting the ether.

Quite surprisingly, with little exception, the researchers that have been responsible for providing us with comprehensive data on golden age radio have almost wholly focused their attention elsewhere, all but missing any serious investigation of radio music. While written bits and pieces on music radio can be found here and there, only a single published book is devoted to the topic (Tom DeLong, *The Mighty Music Box*, Amber Crest, 1980; see the Bibliography for this and other relevant titles).

I have with the present text intended to right what I think is an oversight in the annals of aural history. I have tried to encompass the entire range of musical programming from the early 1920s to the early 1960s. While not every series and artist is explored in depth, virtually all of the major ones are here, alongside hundreds of references to the lesser.

I hope the reader will delight in recalling the light classics, classics, pop standards, novelty numbers, dance bands, country and Western musicians, the major stars headlining their own shows, and others herein. Revisiting that era may be a pleasant reverie for millions who regularly tuned their dials to a myriad of melodic strains.

The Bell Telephone Hour

Some of radio's most beautiful music in the 1940s and 1950s emanated from the Atwater-Kents, the Crosleys and the Philcos on Monday nights. An important source was *The Bell Telephone Hour*, an acclaimed showcase of musical performances of many kinds. Over the years those lively performances filled the airwaves with no fewer than 100 gifted artists— vocalists and instrumentalists and choral ensembles— accompanied by some of the most capable musicians America had to offer. In a format that provided something for everyone, the upbeat musicale left a song in the hearts of millions. Maestro Donald Voorhees remained a common thread throughout those expositions; he was on the pedestal from its start to its finish, a versatile, yet balanced influence no matter what ambiance was required. But it was that large deputation of celebrated guests from so many walks of show business life who made *The Bell Telephone Hour* a genuinely special indulgence well worth waiting for.

Producer-Director: Wallace Magill.

Orchestra Conductor: Donald Voorhees, conducting The Bell Telephone Hour Orchestra.

Guest Stars: Licia Albanese (soprano), Fred Allen (narrator), Lucine Amara (soprano), Marian Anderson (contralto), Claudio Arrau (pianist), Jussi Bjoerling (tenor), Apollo Boys Choir, Bartlett and Robinson (twin pianists), Thomas Brookman, Christina Carroll (lyric soprano), Gaby Casadesus (pianist), Robert Casadesus (pianist), Walter Cassel (baritone), Olga Coelho (guitarist), Bing Crosby (tenor), Lucille Cummings (contralto), Clifford Curzon (pianist), Agnes Davis (pianist), Vivian della Chiesa (soprano), Victoria de los Angeles (soprano), Marilyn Dubow (violinist), Todd Duncan (baritone), Nelson Eddy (baritone), Cloe Elmo (mezzo-soprano), Lee Fairfax, Eileen Farrell (soprano), Leon Fleischer (pianist), Zino Francescatti (violinist), Nicolai Gedda (tenor), Barbara Gibson, Carroll Glenn (pianist), Benny Goodman (clarinetist), Igor Gorin (baritone), Tito Guizar (guitarist, tenor), William Hain (tenor), Nicole Harriott, Clifford Harvuot (baritone), Lansing Hatfield (baritone), Jascha Heifetz (violinist), Dame Myra Hess (pianist), Jerome Hines (bass), Josef Hoffman (pianist), Lorin Hollander (pianist), Jose Iturbi (pianist), Frederick Jagel (tenor), Helen Jepson (soprano), Raoul Jobin (tenor), Grant Johanessen (pianist), Lillian

Kallir (pianist), William Kapell (pianist), Dorothy Kirsten (soprano), Fritz Kreisler (violinist), Charles Kullmann (tenor), Marjorie Lawrence (soprano), Oscar Levant (pianist), Seymour Lipkin (pianist), George London (bass-baritone), Lauritz Melchior (tenor), James Melton (tenor), Mildred Miller (mezzo-soprano), Lorne Monroe (cellist), Grace Moore (soprano), John Nesbitt (narrator), Elena Nikolaidi (mezzo-soprano), Jarmila Novotna (soprano), Leonard Pennario (pianist), Gregor Piatigorsky (cellist), Claudia Pinza (soprano), Ezio Pinza (bass), Lily Pons (coloratura soprano), Michael Rabin (violinist), Torsten Ralf (tenor), Basil Rathbone (narrator), Artur Rubenstein (pianist), Bidu Sayao (soprano), Irmgard Seefried (soprano), Andres Segovia (guitarist), Edwin Steffe (baritone), Isaac Stern (violinist), Risë Stevens (mezzo-soprano), Polyna Stoska (soprano), Rita Streich (soprano), Brian Sullivan (tenor), Set Svanholm (tenor), Gladys Swarthout (mezzo-soprano), Ferrucio Tagliavini (tenor), Pia Tassinari (soprano), Renata Tebaldi (soprano), Alec Templeton (pianist), Dame Maggie Teyte (soprano), Blanche Thebom (mezzo-soprano), John Charles Thomas (baritone), Lawrence Tibbett (baritone), Jennie Tourel (mezzo-soprano), Giorgio Tozzi (bass), Helen Traubel (soprano), Theodor Uppman (baritone), Giuseppe Valdengo (baritone), Luben Vichey (bass), William Warfield (bass-baritone), Leonard Warren (baritone), Francia White (soprano), Yale Glee Club.

Choral Ensemble: Ken Christie Mixed Chorus.

Commentator: Floyd Mack.

Impersonations of Alexander Graham Bell: Raymond Edward Johnson.

Announcers: Tom Shirley (1940–1942), Dick Joy, Gayne Whitman.

Writers: Mort Lewis, Norman Rosten.

Theme Song: *The Bell Waltz* (Donald Voorhees).

Sponsor: Bell Telephone Company.

Ratings: High — 10.8 (tie in 1941-1942, 1942-1943 seasons); Low — 1.7 (1955-1956); Median — 7.2. (Numbers not available for 1943-1944, 1956–1958, 1968-1969.) As TV drained listeners from their radios, figures fell quickly; e.g., from 1952 to 1956 they were, progressively, 4.1, 4.5, 2.0, 1.7.

On the Air: April 29, 1940–March 30, 1942, NBC, Monday, 8:00–8:30 P.M. Eastern Time; April 6, 1942–June 30, 1958, NBC, Monday, 9:00–9:30 P.M.; *Encores from The Bell Telephone Hour*, Sept. 15, 1968–June 8, 1969, NBC, Sunday.

* * *

In its halcyon days in the late 1940s and early 1950s, *The Bell Telephone Hour* was an integral element of NBC's revered "Monday Night of Music." Across a two-hour period the chain offered a quartet of tuneful treats that millions of listeners doted on — including *The Railroad Hour* at 8:00 Eastern Time, *The Voice of Firestone* at 8:30, *The Bell Telephone Hour* at 9:00 and *The Cities Service Band of America* at 9:30. One critic credibly surmised: "*The Bell Telephone Hour* and its Monday-night sister shows addressed an audience that had been vastly underestimated by network commercialism. These were the people who attended concerts, who loved good music and plenty of it. On NBC Monday nights, they got what they wanted."

"*The Bell Telephone Hour* provided a prestigious ... showcase for fine music, always presented with elegance and style," assured another pundit. *Tune In* suitably distinguished the program as "a musical melting pot, blending the old world with the new, from Bach to Irving Berlin, from *Swanee River* to *Santa Lucia*, from Latin American folksongs to the latest in Russian opera." For nearly two decades upwards of 9 million radio listeners were enchanted by the celebrated concert series. Millions more followed it for another eight and a half years on television beyond its aural-only days.

Originating as a light classical music feature on April 29, 1940, at its inception *The Bell Telephone Hour* offered tenor James Melton and soprano Francia White backed by a 57-piece aggregate known as The Bell Symphony Orchestra, including many members of The New York Philharmonic. Interestingly, those instrumentalists crossed over to NBC each week from CBS, which aired their own orchestra's live concerts, generally on Sundays, and had done so since 1927. CBS's run of *The New York Philharmonic Orchestra* continued through 1963, a classical music series unrivaled in longevity by any program beyond the weekly Metropolitan Opera concerts. (The latter began in 1931 and persist today.)

The glory years of *The Bell Telephone Hour* were still ahead of it in the meantime. New producer-director Wallace Magill, who came on the scene two years into the run, turned it away from one limited to spotlighting the talents of a pair of vocalists (Melton and White) to signifying the abilities of many. Instituting what was called a "Great Artists" series, Magill embraced dozens of renowned concert voices and able instrumentalists deemed worthy of carrying off half-hour performances. A large contingent of those names—some who frequented the circuits of other prominent classical radio series like *The Railroad Hour* and *The Voice of Firestone* as well as many members of the Metropolitan Opera Company—made inveterate appearances beginning on April 6, 1942.

Under Magill's watchful eye, the music was carefully selected a couple of months prior to airdates with each program skillfully and painstakingly crafted. It was obvious that great care was poured into the details of every performance for little was left to chance. Monday afternoon rehearsals were intense. Guests were signed as far as a year in advance. Their repeated frequency on *The Bell Telephone Hour* sometimes after a while turned little-known names at their introduction to very familiar ones in many American households.

The impresario for the broadcasts, including hosting a year of playbacks a decade after the 18-year original series left the air, plus the extensive run on TV, was Donald Voorhees, a music prodigy who seemingly spent his life preparing for his ultimate coup. Born in Allentown, Pennsylvania, on July 26, 1903, Voorhees played piano in a local theater orchestra at 15. He advanced to a Philadelphia venue and managed to arrive on Broadway next. There he conducted pit orchestras for *Scandals and Vanities* and similar musical reviews, showing up so frequently he quickly developed as a permanent fixture.

From the Earl Carroll Theatre in 1925 he broadcast simple trial concerts over radio. His labors led to one of network radio's great early variety shows, *The Atwater Kent Hour*, which originated over New York's WEAF on October 4, 1925. It moved to the NBC network upon that chain's founding a year later. That appeared fortuitous; Voorhees had no idea that his life's work would be concentrated in directing music on the ether nor that he would make such an impact upon broadcasting.

The pencil-waving conductor joined CBS in 1927 and, according to one wag, "crowned his career as maestro for the durable *Telephone* Hour." But he had a lot of on-the-job training before he reached that pinnacle. Voorhees led orchestras for many of radio's biggest attractions during his preparatory days. They included *The Maxwell House Concerts* (1926–1932, NBC Blue), *The Fire Chief* with Ed Wynn and *The Maxwell House Showboat* (both 1932–1934, NBC), *The Castoria Program* (1933-1934, CBS), *The Joe Cook Show* (1934, NBC), *The Ford Summer Hour* (1934–1942, CBS), *The Gibson Family* (1934-1935, NBC), *The*

Cavalcade of America (1935–1939, CBS), *The Packard Hour* (1935-1936, CBS), *Tim and Irene* (1936, NBC Blue), *The Minute Men* with Stoopnagle and Budd (1936-1937, NBC Blue) and *The March of Time* (1937–1939, 1941-1942, NBC Blue; 1942–1944, NBC).

So meticulous was he in his preparation—a trait he unremittingly exhibited with *The Bell Telephone Hour*—it was confirmed that, for the E. I. duPont–sponsored historical drama series *Cavalcade of America*, "he pored over hundreds of pages of material for the right musical bridge, and sometimes composed the mood music himself." He did the same for *The Bell Telephone Hour*, penning its memorable theme, *The Bell Waltz*, while repeatedly revealing his own gifts as a composer-arranger.

Voorhees was considered "a musician's musician" and was habitually esteemed as the medium's most popular concert maestro in balloting by readers of *Musical America*. He received the Lowell Mason Award in 1955 for eminent donations to music education. He died on January 10, 1989, at Cape May Court House, New Jersey, having been one of the premier radio staff bandleaders.

The playbills for *The Bell Telephone Hour* consisted of a blend of popular and semiclassical favorites, occasionally mixed with seasonal chestnuts, stirring patriotic numbers, Negro spirituals, jazz, folk tunes and melodies drawn from other quarters. The selections and artists that comprised a half-dozen performances scattered throughout the show's long run offer an indication of the type of programming listeners could anticipate from week to week during the "Great Artists" period.

Air Date: June 8, 1942
Guest Artist: Lawrence Tibbett (baritone)
Begin the Beguine (Porter)
Golliwog's Cakewalk (Debussy)
Drink to Me Only; *Old Paint* (Traditional)
Meditation ["Thais"] (Massenet)
Standin' in the Need of Prayer ["Emperor Jones"] (Gruenberg)

Air Date: December 25, 1944
Guest Artist: Helen Traubel (soprano)
Adeste Fidelis (Traditional)
When Children Pray (Fenner)
Toyland (Herbert)
Singer's Greeting; *Wassail Song* (Williams)
Christmas Oratorio (Bach)
Die Allmacht (Schubert)

Air Date: October 13, 1947
Guest Artist: Nelson Eddy (baritone)
Oh What a Beautiful Morning (Rodgers)
Intermezzo ["Cavalleria Rusticana"] (Mascagni)
Water Boy; *Froggie Went a-Courtin'* (Traditional)
Dance of the Hours (Ponchielli)
Quand la Flamme ["Jolie Fille"] (Bizet)

Air Date: April 2, 1951
Guest Artist: Jascha Heifetz (violinist)
Czardas ["Coppelia"] (Delius)
Slavonic Dance No. 2 (Dvorak)
La Capricieuse (Elgar)
Waltz ["Eugene Onegin"] (Tchaikovsky)
Gweedore Brae (Crowther)
Scherzo Tarantelle (Wienawski)

Air Date: July 4, 1955
Guest Artist: Brian Sullivan
Great Day (Youmans)
Oh What a Beautiful Morning (Rodgers)
Legend of the Arkansas Traveler (McDonald)
Sylvia; *The Glorious Fourth—USA* (Speaks)
The Hills of Home (Fox)

Air Date: May 12, 1958
Guest Artist: William Warfield
Carousel Waltz (Rodgers)
Dichterliebe (Schumann)
An Old Love Story (MacDowell)
Go Down Moses (Burleigh)
Ride On King Jesus (Johnson)
Scherzo ["Midnight Dream"] (Mendelssohn)

Maestro Donald Voorhees (left) was preparing for his trademark assignment on the air — conducting the Bell Telephone Hour Orchestra — 15 years before it began. He remained in that pivotal spot throughout the show's long life, nearly three decades. One of the recurring "Great Artists" appearing on the Bell stage was violinist Fritz Kreisler (right).

Across *The Bell Telephone Hour*'s extensive radio run, more than 100 different artists appeared. They were among the upper crust of able performers in the circles in which they moved — the crème de la crème. While most were vocalists, and a very significant contingent were members of the Metropolitan Opera Company, there were also many instrumentalists, particularly pianists and violinists. Robert Casadesus, Clifford Curzon, Jose Iturbi, Oscar Levant and Artur Rubenstein made frequent appearances at the keyboard while Jascha Heifetz and Fritz Kreisler fiddled lots of nights away.

Those weren't the only instruments nor celebrities featured on that forum. No less than maestro Benny Goodman turned up to blow his clarinet on one 1946 outing, leading off with a Voorhees-inspired creation titled *Goodman, Goodman, Spare That Jazz*. Olga Coelho was a recurring guitarist while cellist Gregor Piatigorsky also did his thing numerous times. Twice, when the Bell Telephone Hour Orchestra performed Prokofiev's *Peter and the Wolf*, respected voices were engaged as narrators — actor Basil Rathbone in 1947 and comedian Fred Allen in 1953. And to prove, perhaps, that the program hadn't become so highbrow there wasn't anything to hold the pop crowd's interest, in 1945 the show offered Bing Crosby harmonizing on old standards, and closing out with Irving Berlin's *God Bless America*. While it wasn't Kate Smith, you got the idea.

There were also choral groups, including the program's own mixed chorus, the Apollo Boys Choir and — on a couple of occasions, in 1949 and 1953 — the Yale University Glee Club offering old standards in addition to its alma mater. The vocalists, whether singular or plural, invariably produced melodies that appealed to a veritable range of musical tastes as evidenced by the program excerpts already spelled out.

During the "Great Artists" era, between 1942 and 1958, several personalities stood out for their seasoned appearances on the *Telephone Hour* stage. An analysis of the program bills for the period produced an impressive register of the series' most frequent guests.

Jascha Heifetz, with 54 appearances, was the leader of the pack, closely followed by Lily Pons with 50 engagements, Ezio Pinza with 44, Marian Anderson with 37 and Nelson Eddy with 27. Rounding out the 10 most durable entertainers were Bidu Sayao and Blanche Thebom, tied with 26 appearances each; Helen Traubel, 23; and Eileen Farrell and Jose Iturbi, both with 22.

Several others made many stops there including James Melton, 21; George London, Brian Sullivan and John Charles Thomas, each with 17; Gladys Swarthout, 16; Mildred Miller, 14; Grace Moore, 12; and dozens more with 10 or fewer performances.

Because their names are the most familiar to listeners of the popular radio series, capsule introductions of the top 10 artists in number of appearances follow.

Jascha Heifetz was born February 2, 1901, Vilnius, Russia. He began to play on a quarter-sized violin given him by his father and at age seven debuted publicly in Dovno. At nine he was enrolled in Leopold Auer's famous class in St. Petersburg and by 12 was acclaimed as a "child prodigy of unexampled gifts." Young Heifetz played concert performances in Germany, Austria and Scandinavia. When the Russian Revolution erupted, his family immigrated to America.

On October 27, 1917, the genius performed in his premiere concert on the stage of New York's Carnegie Hall. Music critic Samuel Chotzinoff exclaimed: "The 16-year-old violinist seemed the most unconcerned of all the people in the hall as he walked out on the stage and proceeded to give an exhibition of such extraordinary virtuosity and musicianship as had not previously been heard in that historic auditorium." He was an instant sensation, making 30 public appearances in New York in his first year.

Becoming a U.S. citizen in 1925, Heifetz moved to Beverly Hills, California, in the 1940s and maintained his permanent residence there until his death on December 10, 1987, in Los Angeles. Over a lifetime he recorded more than 80 albums. For more than 60 years he mesmerized audiences the length and breadth of the world. His final public recital, in 1972, preceded several years of teaching. "Handling his students with steel-rod control tempered with humor, Heifetz instilled in them respect for discipline," an observer surmised.

The famed virtuoso asserted: "I occasionally play works by contemporary composers and for two reasons. First to discourage the composer from writing any more and secondly to remind myself how much I appreciate Beethoven." At the outset Heifetz took a dim view of radio, becoming an elitist who only focused on those who came to hear him. When later convinced that millions could be entranced by his music beyond the handful that heard him in concert halls, he changed his tune, embracing the audio medium wholeheartedly, and playing on the ether when asked. He starred on the first "Guest Artist" segment of *The Bell Telephone Hour* on April 27, 1942, and made his final appearance there on April 21, 1958, a month before the show left the air and 54 performances after he inaugurated it.

Lily Pons was born April 12, 1898, in Cannes, France, and died February 13, 1976, in Dallas, Texas. In between she became one of the most popular coloratura soprano voices in American music, performing at the Metropolitan Opera from 1931 to 1959. In 1997, long after her death, Pons was one of a quartet of the nation's distinguished vocalists to be honored with images appearing on United States postage stamps.

Her piano training won her honors at the Paris Conservatoire. In World War I she sang for wounded vets and was praised for "an extraordinary voice." She debuted in Alsace and performed now and then in the French provinces. When Pons auditioned for the Metropolitan Opera, manager Gatti-Casazza told her she had "the perfect voice." A source claimed, "She was as beautiful and charming as she was talented." On one occasion in the summer of 1939 she sang to more than 300,000 people gathered at Chicago's Grant Park. By that time her fame had long been established, then just a year shy of her first performance on *The Bell Telephone Hour*, June 15, 1942. There would be 49 more occasions like it before she left that microphone for the final time.

Pons had first broadcast on Easter Sunday in 1931 over New York's WEAF. In addition to making a trio of films between 1935 and 1937 (*I Dream Too Much, That Girl from Paris, Hitting a New High*), she recurrently sang with the orchestra of Andre Kostelanetz, who maintained a presence over CBS from 1931 to 1946 with nearly a dozen radio series. In 1938, Kostelanetz and Pons wed. Both were on hand December 25, 1937, as NBC held an inaugural gala in its huge Studio 8-H signifying the return of Maestro Arturo Toscanini to conduct the prestigious, newly formed NBC Symphony Orchestra. In addition to the *Telephone Hour*, Lily Pons was a habitual vocalist on *The Voice of Firestone* during the decade following her marriage. In 1950, she appeared briefly as herself in the celluloid production *Moments in Music*.

Ezio Pinza was born Fortunio Pinza on May 18, 1892, in Rome, Italy. He died May 9, 1957, in Stamford, Connecticut. He was also known by several other names. To many he was Don Giovanni, Figaro to others and Emile de Becque to still more, offstage as well as on. He went from carpenter to international operatic icon and never learned to read music! Everything he sang—from the most complex operatic role to the simplest popular song—was memorized laboriously, note by note. He once exclaimed, "I'm no musician. I just know how to make nice sounds."

Pinza studied at the Bologna Conservatory, interrupting a promising career in opera to serve in the military (1915–1919). Resuming his professional exploits in Rome, he later sang at La Scala in Milan. Engaged by the Metropolitan Opera Company in 1926, he performed in such theatrical revivals as Mozart's *Don Giovanni* in 1929 and—in 1939—Mussorgsky's *Boris Godunov* and Mozart's *The Marriage of Figaro*. He remained with the Met through 1948. In 1949, the bass singer took the Broadway stage, playing the male lead in *South Pacific* for which he won a Tony the following year as best actor in a musical. He also starred in three motion pictures in the early 1950s (*Mr. Imperium, Strictly Dishonorable, Tonight We Sing*). In 1953, he hosted *The Ezio Pinza Show* over NBC Radio on Saturday mornings for children.

Pinza was arrested by the Federal Bureau of Investigation in 1943, charged with being an enemy alien and held for months on Ellis Island. It appeared a jealous competitor framed him with innuendo and circumstantial evidence. Eventually cleared, Pinza never spoke publicly about his ordeal but his spouse alleged that his stress stemming from it was a contributing factor to his early demise from a stroke 14 years hence.

Marian Anderson was born on February 27, 1897, in Philadelphia, Pennsylvania. Having studied with tenor-coach Giuseppe Boghetti and singing regionally, in 1924 the contralto debuted at New York's Town Hall. Unable to establish an active career in her homeland, however, she pursued it in England, Germany and Finland the following year. For a decade she sang extensively on the continent, including a performance at an Austrian Mozart festival in 1935. When she appeared before the archbishop of Salzburg, he remarked, "Yours is a voice one hears once in a hundred years."

A recital at New York's Town Hall in 1935 was met with critical acclaim. Although she was reportedly the nation's third greatest concert box office draw, Anderson was routinely subjected to racial prejudice in restaurants, hotels and concert halls. Refused an appearance at Constitution Hall, she sang instead at the Lincoln Memorial on Easter Sunday, April 9, 1939, in a program arranged by first lady Eleanor Roosevelt. A crowd of 75,000 gathered to hear her in person while millions more tuned in by radio. On September 14, 1942, she was a guest on *The Bell Telephone Hour*. She would turn up there 36 more times in the years to follow.

The Metropolitan Opera signed Anderson in 1954. Her premiere on January 7, 1955, marked the first time an African-American had sung on that stage. She retired a decade later after a final concert in Philadelphia. Anderson died in Portland, Oregon, on April 8, 1993.

Nelson Eddy was born June 29, 1901, in Providence, Rhode Island. He will forever be known as the singing colleague of Jeanette MacDonald. There was more story there than met the eye—and ear. "America's Singing Sweethearts" of the 1930s—who starred in eight Metro-Goldwyn-Mayer hit musicals (*Bitter Sweet, The Girl of the Golden West, I Married an Angel, Maytime, Naughty Marietta, New Moon, Rose Marie, Sweethearts*) and opera and radio—had an off-screen romance, too. "Because of circumstances and Louis B. Mayer they never married each other," hints a Web site dedicated to the pair. Their motion picture appearances were branded "the most successful singing partnership in the history of the cinema."

Baritone Eddy grew up in a musical family, learning to sing by playing operatic recordings. Eventually he mastered 32 opera roles. His family moved to Philadelphia where he worked as a telephone operator, advertising salesman and copywriter. He played leading roles in Gilbert and Sullivan operettas staged by the Savoy Company before pursuing serious musical training in Europe. In 1924, he won minor parts at several New York area concert halls, including the Metropolitan Opera House. Within a few years he was also a radio vocalist. Eddy appeared in the 1933 motion picture *Broadway to Hollywood* singing *In the Garden of My Heart*. Subsequently, he was cast in bit parts in *Dancing Lady* (1933) and *Student Tour* (1934). It led to star status with MacDonald in 1935's *Naughty Marietta* and his career was assured.

Eddy starred in films without MacDonald, too (*The Chocolate Soldier, Knickerbocker Holiday, Northwest Outpost, Phantom of the Opera, Rosalie*). When his motion picture career ended in the late 1940s, he returned to the stage, sang in nightclubs and stock musicals and was a recurring voice on radio, a medium he excelled in for years. In addition to 27 appearances on *The*

Bell Telephone Hour, his gigs included *The Nelson Eddy Show* (1931, CBS), *Inside Story of Names That Make News* (1933, CBS), *Soconyland Sketches* (1933, NBC), *Vicks Open House* (1936-1937, CBS), *The Chase and Sanborn Hour* with Edgar Bergen and Charlie McCarthy (1937–1939, NBC), *The New Old Gold Show* (1942-1943, CBS), *The Electric Hour* hosted by Eddy (1944–1946, CBS) and *The Kraft Music Hall* starring Eddy (summers 1947–1949, NBC). By 1944, he was earning $5,000 per radio broadcast.

Nelson Eddy was a popular recording artist, turning out scores of discs over an extensive career. Continuing to make personal appearances, he was performing at a Miami Beach hotel when he became ill. He died in Miami on March 6, 1967. His "secret sweetheart," Jeanette MacDonald, had died a couple of years before (on January 14, 1965, in Houston) of heart failure.

Bidu Sayao was born May 11, 1902, in Rio de Janeiro, Brazil. Historiographers have left unrecorded many of the details of her professional achievements. She studied in Nice with the famous Jean De Reszke. In time, the proficient soprano diva was recognized as an operatic star in Italy, France and South America, as well as the United States. She premiered on the stage of the Metropolitan Opera House on February 13, 1937, and continued to triumph there for 14 years in soubrette roles.

Retiring from the stage in 1958, Sayao obtained American citizenship the following year. Over a long career she made many recordings as well as concert appearances with Arturo Toscanini. She appeared 26 times on *The Bell Telephone Hour* and died in Rockport, Maine, on March 12, 1999.

Blanche Thebom was born September 19, 1918, in Monessen, Pennsylvania. After studying with Margaret Matzenauer and Edyth Walker in New York City, at 23 she debuted with the Metropolitan Opera (in December 1941). For 22 years she was the Met's leading dramatic mezzo-soprano. In addition to 26 engagements for *The Bell Telephone Hour*, she turned up sporadically as a costar on *The Railroad Hour* and a singing guest on *The Voice of Firestone*, the latter on radio and television.

In 1967, after a long and illustrious career of performing in opera houses across America and Europe — including being the first American to sing at Moscow's Bolshoi Opera — Thebom was picked to lead the Southern Regional Opera Company in Atlanta. When it folded a year later she was named director of the opera workshop of San Francisco State University. Two decades later she founded a workshop in alliance with the San Francisco Girls Chorus called the Opera Arts Training Program. During the early years of the twenty-first century she continued to mentor voice students in San Francisco.

Helen Traubel was born June 16, 1899, in St. Louis, Missouri. Growing up in a German-speaking home, she began singing at an early age, making her professional debut with the St. Louis Symphony in 1923. When she performed at Lewisohn Stadium in New York three years later, she was offered a contract at the Metropolitan Opera. She refused it, however, preferring further preparation. Yet when she starred in *The Man without a Country* at the Met in 1937, she wasn't offered a permanent spot. It took public weight, in 1939, following some radio and concert performances with Dimitri Mitropoulos and Sir John Barbirolli, to impress the Met's management to acquiesce. In the next 14 years she performed with the Met 176 times, all but eight of those in Wagnerian operas. Her annual salary was $250,000.

For nearly a year, from 1936 to 1937, Traubel was featured on her own network radio series, initially over NBC Blue, then over NBC. It prepared the talented soprano for frequent singing stints on *The Bell Telephone Hour* (23 times) and occasionally on *The Voice of Firestone* well into the 1950s.

Traubel fell into disfavor with newly appointed Met manager Rudolph Bing, allegedly because she simultaneously performed in nightclubs. Forced out in 1953 in favor of Kirsten Flagstad, who had recently rejoined the Met, Traubel replaced the opera with appearances at venues like New York's Copacabana, Chicago's Chez Paree, Las Vegas's Sahara Hotel and Miami's Clover Club. She also picked up television stints on shows headlined by Jerry Lewis, Groucho Marx and Red Skelton.

Apparently none the worse for her ordeal, Traubel appeared in several films and in Rodgers and Hammerstein's revue *Pipe Dream*. She also penned a murder mystery and an autobiography (*St. Louis Woman*), owned a piece of the St. Louis Browns and was often a gossip column topic. Her indomitable spirit was characterized by a strong sense of humor. She died on July 28, 1972, in Santa Monica, California.

Eileen Farrell was born February 13, 1920, in Willimantic, Connecticut. The daughter of vaudeville vocalists, she trained with Merle Alcock and Eleanor McClellan in New York City. Imitating Rosa Ponselle, she premiered on radio on a *March of Time* broadcast. Auditioning for a radio chorus, she quickly developed as a soloist. In giving her that chance, CBS music director Davidson Taylor observed that her version of a Stephen Foster refrain brought tears to his eyes.

At 20 she was appearing regularly on the ether. She gained her own network series at 22, *Eileen Farrell Sings* (aka *The Voice of Eileen Farrell*), which ran on CBS intermittently, yet steadily, from June 5, 1942, through December 24, 1947. Concurrently she starred on *Songs of the Century* (1942, CBS), was a regular on Frank and Anne Hummert's *American Melody Hour* (1943, CBS) and on *The Prudential Family Hour* (1943–1946, CBS). In addition to 22 appearances on *The Bell Telephone Hour*, well into the 1950s she consistently turned up on simulcasts of *The Voice of Firestone*. She also appeared with *The NBC Symphony Orchestra* conducted by Arturo Toscanini and *The New York Philharmonic Orchestra* conducted by Leonard Bernstein

Simultaneously, the soprano soloist sang with several other major orchestras. As a concert singer, she toured the United States in 1947-1948 and South America in 1949. In 1956, she debuted as an operatic diva in the part of Santuzza with Tampa, Florida's San Carlo Opera. The following year she joined Chicago's Lyric Opera, and in 1958, the San Francisco Opera. She was a member of the Metropolitan Opera Company from December 1960 to 1964 and again during the 1965-1966 season. After teaching voice at Hartt School of Music in Hartford, Connecticut, Farrell became distinguished professor of music at Indiana University's School of Music in Bloomington (1971–1980). She later held the same capacity at the University of Maine in Orono (1983–1985). She made many recordings and sang the blues on CDs late in her career. Her autobiography, *Can't Help Singing*, was published in 1999. Eileen Farrell died March 23, 2002, in Bergen, New Jersey.

Jose Iturbi was born November 28, 1895, in Valencia, Spain. The son of a gas company employee who supplemented his income by tuning pianos, and of opera singer Teresa Baguena, he was readily inspired to pursue music. At age five he entered La Escuela de Musica de Maria Jordan (The Mary Jordan School of Music). Two years hence he earned an income tutoring and performing in silent movie theaters, at balls and recitals. He studied privately with Joaquin Malats and attended the Conservatorio de Musica locally. Seeing his ability, friends raised funds to send him to extend his training at Paris's Conservatoire de Musique.

Graduating with first honors, Iturbi moved to Zurich and played piano in a trendy café. There the Geneva Conservatory hired him to lead its piano department (1919–1923). Leaving education behind, he concentrated on performing across Europe, debuting in America in October 1929 with the Philadelphia Philharmonic Orchestra. He moved to the New York Philharmonic Orchestra in December. Iturbi later conducted an orchestra at the Teatro Hidalgo in Mexico City. Similar experiences followed in New York, Philadelphia, Detroit and other cities. He was named conductor of the Rochester Philharmonic Orchestra in 1936. Even as his conducting eminence grew, however, Iturbi didn't relinquish his opportunities to perform as a pianist.

His supreme acclamations resulted from occasions when he combined the two. Following a concert at Carnegie Hall in February 1941, a *New York Times* columnist wrote: "Jose Iturbi ... brought down the house.... When he added to his piano duties a vivid job of leading his band he had the audience at his mercy. Mr. Iturbi did not miss a cue. If his hands were occupied he beat time with his head. If one hand was playing a fragment of music the other hand beat time or gave a cue."

Beyond his 22 performances on *The Bell Telephone Hour*, Iturbi acted in eight motion pictures, frequently as himself (*Anchors Aweigh, Holiday in Mexico, Music for Millions, A Song to Remember, That Midnight Kiss, Thousands Cheer, Three Darling Daughters, Two Sisters and a Sailor*). He composed music, mostly piano works with a Spanish twist, the best-known being *Pequena Danza Espanola*. And he sometimes earned a reputation for volatile fits. Iturbi spoke his mind that women couldn't achieve the musical performance standards of men. He refused to play a bill with Benny Goodman, rejecting a notion that classical and jazz should be mixed. He feigned surprise by the lack of respect shown by an audience "eating hot dogs too loudly" at an outdoor concert. The gifted virtuoso died in Los Angeles on June 28, 1980.

There was an Armed Forces Radio Service version of *The Bell Telephone Hour* known as *Music from America*. In 1946, the program instituted the Walter W. Naumburg Musical Foundation Awards, citing fresh, youthful and unrecognized talent. In 1949, it won a Peabody Award, considered the aural medium's ultimate trophy. Its radio broadcasts moved to Carnegie Hall in the mid–1950s where performances continued through June 30, 1958.

In the early 1950s, stereocasting became a rage in broadcasting. While the concept wasn't new — there had been laboratory experiments with stereophonic sound as far back as the start of the twentieth century — some AM stations, particularly those playing classical music — attempted dual-outlet AM stereocasting. One station broadcast the left channel, another the right. Such programs almost always featured live music, as few sources for taped or recorded stereophonic melody existed. (Stereo records weren't in widespread use until 1958.) The national networks saw a niche and seized it, albeit late in their golden age: that same year (1958) NBC aired *The Bell Telephone Hour* stereophonically on its quartet of owned-and-operated AM-FM stations. In the meantime, by combining AM radio and television, competitor ABC stereocast *The Lawrence Welk Show*. It was a fad whose time had arrived.

A decade after the radio series ended, orchestra impresario Donald Voorhees returned to the NBC microphone on Sunday nights to preside over a reprise of some of the series' highlights. It included new interviews with artists like Marian Anderson, Nicolai Gedda, Jose Iturbi and Lily Pons. From September 15, 1968, through June 8, 1969, long after radio's heyday had faded, *Encores from The Bell Telephone Hour* stirred the memories of legions of disenfranchised classical music addicts who indulged themselves with a second taste of some incredibly satisfying treats, thanks to the magic of tape recording and transcriptions.

In the interim period, meanwhile, television pacified the fans after the *Telephone Hour* left radio. On Monday, January 12, 1959, the first of a series of specials growing out of the audio series was telecast over NBC-TV. Several more exhibitions followed that spring. Beginning on Friday, October 9, 1959 — 15 months after the radio show vanished — the program reentered America's living rooms on a continuing basis, then with accompanying visuals. Between that date and Friday, April 26, 1968 — less than five months short of its radio reincarnation as *Encores from The Bell Telephone Hour* on NBC Radio — *The Bell Telephone Hour* premiered on NBC-TV. Sometimes it was offered weekly, sometimes biweekly and sometimes as irregularly scheduled specials. Another big difference was that it expanded to an hour. It appealed to the eye as well as the ear. But it displayed familiar traits, too. Donald Voorhees was once again in his customary spot on the podium. And a rotating guest list, just like in the radio days, prevailed.

A couple of television historiographers summarized the video series for their readers.[1]

> The music ranged across the spectrum from popular to jazz to classical, performed by the top names among established Broadway, Hollywood, and recording stars (no rock 'n' roll here). A different host presided over each telecast. The featured performers appearing over the years included Benny Goodman, Mahalia Jackson, Carol Lawrence, Paul Whiteman (conducting "Rhapsody in Blue"), Marge and Gower Champion, the Kingston Trio, Ray Bolger, Richard Tucker, and Bing Crosby.
> Among the classical highlights were the American TV debuts of ballet dancer Rudolf Nureyev in January 1961..., Joan Sutherland in March 1961, and pianists Albert Casadesus in February 1964 and Clifford Curzon in April 1965.
> Just as the performers tended to be standard adult favorites, so did the music. *The Bell Telephone Hour*, though certainly classy, was not overly adventuresome. During the first few seasons, popular and show music predominated, though there was usually a classical spot in each telecast. Programs were built around tributes to popular composers such as Gershwin, Berlin, and Porter, or around holiday themes or topics such as small-town shindigs. In 1966 a new format was introduced — that of filmed musical documentaries, generally of great performers — and emphasis was shifted to more classical music. Among the subjects were Van Cliburn, Pablo Casals, Zubin Mehta, Arturo Toscanini, Duke Ellington, and even George Plimpton (in his brief career as a percussionist with the New York Symphony Orchestra)....
> During the summer of 1964 the program featured some newer talent and was subtitled *The Bell Summer Theatre*.

In addition to the presence of the familiar Don Voorhees conducting the Bell Telephone Orchestra, Barry Wood was executive producer of the television series from its inception through 1967. Henry Jaffe picked up the final season in that capacity.

Altogether, *The Bell Telephone Hour*, in dual mediums and multiple incarnations, was one of the most enduring enterprises in broadcasting history. It extended from April 29, 1940, through June 8, 1969, a cumulative 29 years with only brief interruptions. The significance of its longevity is made even more impressive by all those summers its radio performances continued airing live every week without a break, especially during a time when so many other broadcast series were taking an extended sabbatical.

Very few programs of any type achieved *The Bell Telephone Hour's* durable milestone. Possibly only a quartet of musical features with pervasive influence surpassed it in live programming — the *Grand Ole Opry*, the *Metropolitan Opera* broadcasts, *Music and the Spoken Word from the Crossroads of the West* (aka *The Mormon Tabernacle Choir*) and *The Voice of Firestone*. All but the latter persist at this writing.

Voorhees and his guests combined their artistry to offer audiences a weekly potpourri of popular, semiclassical and myriad types of melody in a blend of vocal and instrumental harmony. *The Bell Telephone Hour* could be classified a bellwether triumph as it withstood the test of time.

The Big Bands

Of all the phenomena that can be credibly traced to old-time radio, none may have been more influential or have made a greater immediate impact than the big bands. For years, those purveyors of musical enchantment dominated the agendas of the four national broadcasting chains during extended hours of their daily schedules. More importantly, the great popularity of big bands, aided by radio, epitomized a nation's zeal in transitioning from the devastating effects of a Great Depression to a future laced with hope and optimism. Universal self-pity was replaced by confidence, leading the populace out of the depths of despair. Radio—and the big bands—helped to introduce that evolution.

Assuming the presidency in 1933, Franklin Delano Roosevelt was a catalyst for the resurgence. He inspired buoyancy from a resolute faith that helped most people overcome their darkest days. The country, and especially its younger folk, perceived happier times. "Joy and excitement, the sort that can be expressed so ideally through swinging music and dancing, lay ahead."[1] Surveys found that the most popular form of radio amusement in 1934 was dance music. Change was in and on the air. Energized reform in diversionary activity swept the nation, ruling American entertainment for more than a decade.

Pinpointing its beginning is relatively easy. Even the day, the place and probably the very hour that people began to cast aside lingering misgivings and to turn collectively toward promising days has been verified by music scholars. It occurred on August 21, 1935, at the Palomar Ballroom in Los Angeles during the late evening hours. It was a watershed event that altered the nation's musical tastes for the next decade and a half.

On that occasion, Benny Goodman and his band, which had achieved national recognition only a few months earlier as the result of brief radio exposure, cut loose with the kind of music that resonated with dancers, spectators and listeners at home. It was a career-boosting experience from which they never looked back. Goodman's anticipated brief engagement at the Palomar was extended to two months. His introduction of swing caught on like wildfire almost everywhere, establishing a craze that echoed across the land, fostering a new music scene that continued to thrive beyond the next world war.

Hundreds of bands emerged to entertain a demanding public hungry for boisterous pleasure following years of deprivation. The ascendancy of radio as many people's major avenue of entertainment coincided with the rise of the bands and dance music, in particular, as a welcomed diversionary tactic. A natural partnership resulted, accommodating both trades. The collaborating partnership that resulted was mutually beneficial for years to come.

Even though the big band era dates its heritage from that auspicious occasion in late summer 1935, the seeds for it had been sown much earlier. Dancing did not become popular in this country merely overnight. Its origins may date from the arrival of the very first inhabitants from distant shores, when immigrants—mostly Europeans—brought with them the traditions that had been practiced for centuries in their homelands.

Most students of the sphere submit that the first broadcast of a dance band was likely aired over Detroit's station WWJ on September 14, 1920. It featured a rather obscure Paul Specht's six-piece outfit. Dixieland and ragtime had already migrated up the Mississippi delta from New Orleans to Memphis, advancing to Kansas City and Chicago and to a myriad of Midwestern hamlets. At Lafayette, Indiana, along that state's famous Wabash River, violinist Specht had cultivated a jazz style that he casually dubbed "rhythmic symphonic syncopation." In a few years, from his humble handful of musicians, emerged still better recognized bandmasters, among them Vincent Lopez, Russ Morgan and Artie Shaw. That achievement notwithstanding, in many ways Specht became the grandfather of the big bands' connection to the radio airwaves.

On November 27, 1921, just 14 months after the ethereal debut of his mentor Specht, Lopez and an instrumental ensemble occupied a 90-minute slot over New York's WJZ Radio (which was renamed WABC in 1953). Lopez was soon providing remotes from the Hotel Pennsylvania. By 1924, the band was so important to that establishment that it was duly signified as the Hotel Pennsylvania Orchestra. Standing on the precipice of a professional career that would continue for decades, the maestro's unseen audience was already beginning to recognize his introduction by the tranquil salutation "Lopez speaking!" It was one the new medium's very first slogans, in fact.

In the meantime, in 1922 WJZ had added to its roster of airtime personalities another nascent bandleader destined for eminent success, the self-proclaimed "king of jazz," Paul Whiteman. Until it became fact, however, Whiteman's entry into radio couldn't have been predicted as a sure thing.

A historiographer opined: "Not all of those in the music business shared this early enthusiasm for having their performances heard by the radio audience. Some of them felt that it did them little good, and might even reduce the public's desire to see them in person. Whether this was the reason, or simply because he was already highly successful without it, Paul Whiteman made no early effort to broadcast."

There was another possible explanation for his initial reluctance to remain off the air. The recording industry and, in particular, its two dominant players, Victor and Columbia, grimaced over radio appearances by celebrities under contract. In 1922, with Americans purchasing 100 million phonograph discs, those firms were in a position to make their stance count. As time progressed, however, several big-name bands like Whiteman's defied them, taking to the airwaves anyway. Allowed one pundit: "By the time record manufacturers had really got around to inserting clauses into contracts prohibiting broadcasts by their artists, it was too late to do anything about it." Joining the broadcasting rush proved

Even though he was on the air by 1922, bandleader Paul Whiteman (standing) was skeptical of the benefits of broadcasting. When he later embraced radio, he did so wholeheartedly, becoming one of its most dynamic exponents, appearing relentlessly on the dial. His fame skyrocketed as did his wealth; his name was recognized everywhere.

a clever exploit by the dance bands. Within a decade — primarily as a result of the stock market crash of 1929 — record sales dwindled to their lowest ebb. Meanwhile, nearly a thousand radio stations were offering the bands plenty of chances to ply their craft. An insurgence of new bands joined a thriving business and became one of the by-products that resulted from radio's expansion.

Returning to Whiteman's early radio outing, his entourage would appeal to legions not just on remotes but on many shows under his own name, prevailing on the air as one of the most popular bands all the way to the mid–1950s. According to one wag, jazz — Whiteman's characteristic musical style — was considered "as ruinous to youth as rock was in the 1960s and rap in the 1990s." The so-called "race music" of its day "was taboo until Paul Whiteman made it respectable and then fashionable; even his last name probably helped smuggle jazz across the color line."[2]

By 1925, the first band to broadcast every weeknight, the Coon-Sanders Orchestra, wafted across the Plains via station WDAF from the storied Muehlbach Hotel in Kansas City. Seven years before, drummer Carleton Coon and pianist Joe Sanders had struck up a friendship in a music store and ultimately determined to form their own outfit. Nothing much came of their quest until radio intervened. Suddenly their little assemblage, arriving on the airwaves at midnight, was transmitted long distances by way of crystal sets. When one of the show's sidemen observed that "no one but the nighthawks are listening," the company was promptly labeled the "Coon-Sanders Nighthawks." Joe Sanders offered a sonorous "Howdja do, howdja do, you big ole radio pooblic" as each evening's performance began. The Nighthawks typically employed megaphones for duet numbers, giving a distinct (though not unique) sound.

Their prominence grew quickly, drawing the ears of Jules Stein, a Music Corporation of America (MCA) representative. Stein traveled from Chicago to Kansas City to check out the aural upstarts. So awed was he by what he witnessed there that he quickly arranged a commitment for them at the Windy City's Blackhawk Restaurant — an engagement that extended to six years! Station WGN carried on their tradition of airing their musical antics far and wide. While in Chicago the Coon-Sanders Nighthawks shared their platform with two more promising groups headed by future big bandleaders Wayne King and Ted Weems. Everybody, it seemed, was determined to get into the act!

Next, Jules Stein would gain an intro to Guy Lombardo's troupe, which had left its homeland, crossing the Canadian border and landing at a Cleveland venue, from which it broadcast regularly. This was primarily a family oriented ensemble, including Guy's brothers Carmen, Lebert and Victor, and their sister Rose Marie, who supplied the vocals. The MCA agent was instrumental in influencing Chicago's Granada Café to take on Lombardo and company and that proved another winning move. In October 1929, Stein subsequently lined up an engagement for the Lombardo clan at New York's Hotel Roosevelt Grill — one that would be aired weekly for over two years by CBS and sponsored by the Robert Burns Panatella Cigar Company.

Notice that in all of those early ventures radio played a major role. It was the airwaves, in fact, that first informed most people beyond the immediate confines of the bandstands themselves that such groups were actually performing. Parenthetically, Chicago was the early, undisputed leader in dance band development but it did not acquire all of the action. During the late 1920s, hotels and dance halls throughout the nation added "radio wires"—direct lines to transmitters that piped ballroom dance rhythms throughout a station's (or network's) coverage territory. Large hotels were especially anxious to be equipped thus, prompting many to feature dancing merely for the recognition factor connected with those broadcasts.

William S. Paley, the head of CBS, was enthralled by Guy Lombardo's sweet music tempo and readily prevailed on him to carry on a tradition Lombardo had inaugurated in 1927 over Chicago's WBBM. Paley asked him to conclude the year 1929 by entertaining over CBS from the Roosevelt Grill between 11:30 P.M. and midnight. Meanwhile, enterprising stalwarts at rival chain NBC signed Lombardo to play on its network the same evening, from midnight to 12:30 A.M. as the year 1930 kicked off. Lombardo's theme song *Auld Lang Syne* unambiguously became identified with New Year's Eve celebrations everywhere starting then, a result of its radio transmission. On that singular festive holiday occasion, Lombardo's troupe was invited to perform his signature melody on network radio (and later, television) every year for decades. The tune still stands out in most Americans' minds as the one invariably celebrating the approach of a new year. Lombardo is even remembered in some circles as "the man who invented New Year's Eve."

"No one was more alert to radio's potential nor more astute in making it pay off for him than Rudy Vallee" claimed one writer who chronicled the period. "When he launched his own band in 1928, he grabbed every possible minute of air time, and through his singing and announcing of his own programs quickly made himself known. By the end of 1929, he was probably the biggest box office attraction in America, a success he attributed entirely to radio. When he lined up a commercial sponsor, he became a radio personality rather than a bandleader, even though the band continued to be featured with him. This was the beginning of a long career as one of radio's biggest names."[3]

A biographer of CBS's Bill Paley describes the owner-president's "first big coup" for his fledgling chain, about 1928. Shortly after buying the network, Paley pursued Paul Whiteman's symphonic jazz band, hoping to acquire it to play for a handful of affiliates that had been amassed into a cooperative venture. The radio mogul previously determined that the fastest way to gain a hefty return on his investment was to appeal to the most listeners that he possibly could. He was convinced that would draw more commercial time purchases than any other strategy he could pursue.

Paley assiduously chased Whiteman at Chicago's Drake Hotel. He harassed the jazz musician between sets, bending Whiteman's ear well past midnight. The two men at last came to terms, Paley agreeing to compensate Whiteman at $5,000 per week and to provide another $30,000 for the band. While this radio mogul didn't ignore cultural and educational features, increasingly he populated his network with greatly acclaimed musicians and comics, plus soap operas, which he believed the bulk of listeners favored. Paley's biographer added, "Clearly he was changing the emphasis of network broadcasting."

Such radio appearances translated not only into extended bookings but—more importantly—into record sales, movie contracts (once the wave of the "silents" ended) and, especially, higher fees commanded from road tours, which consisted of long-term engagements and frequent one-night stands. It didn't take most ambitious, enterprising bandmasters who saw potential in their own outfits very long to catch the trend and covet places for themselves on the air. Even in the 1920s—several years before the onset of the big band era—radio would become a valued commodity that clearly supported the business.

Audience polls documented music as the favored choice of programming categories among more than 60 percent of radio audience members during the 1920s. "Music is the foundation upon which the structure of radio in its popular aspects rests," an American Society of Composers, Authors and Publishers (ASCAP) executive pronounced at mid-decade. Beyond that, however, reliable statistics gathered at three points during radio's golden age showed music easily leaving its competitive genres in the dust. First- and second-place preferences:

1925: Music—71.5 percent; information—11.5 percent.
1932: Music—64.1 percent; other entertainment—13.3 percent.
1946: Music—41 percent; information, 23 percent.

"Because familiarity often makes it more enjoyable, music has been an entertainment staple for centuries," astute researchers point out. "It is not 'used up' in the same way as comedy or dramatic material," partially attesting to the form's durability as well as its widespread acceptance.[4]

There were many other orchestras, of course, in the pre–big band age who pursued the track records of Specht, Morgan, Shaw, Lopez, Whiteman, Coon-Sanders, King, Weems and Lombardo, several of whom were fortunate enough to earn reputations that converted into huge followings. During this period the ether influenced all of these bandleaders to some extent, some more favorably than others: Irving Aaronson, Louis Armstrong, Gus Arnheim, Ben Bernie, Al Donahue, Duke Ellington, Shep Fields, Ted Fio Rito, Jan Garber, George Hall, Horace Heidt, Fletcher Henderson, Earl Hines, Isham Jones, Hal Kemp, Kay Kyser, Freddy Martin, Ted Lewis, Jimmie Lunceford, Clyde McCoy, Red Nichols, George Olsen, Will Osborne, Ben Pollack, B. A. Rolfe, Sammy Kaye, Fred Waring, Chick Webb.

The abolition of the Volstead Act on December 5, 1933, ended a long dry spell in the American environment. Beverage alcohol had been banned since January 16, 1920. Prohibition's repeal had immediate effects on many of the venues where dance bands played. A resurgence of public imbibing increased opportunities for remotes from downtown hotels and chic nightclubs, providing greater need for bands and available dates.

Band remotes were so widely exploited during this early period that when NBC was launched with a four-hour inaugural marathon broadcast on November 15, 1926, five orchestras were piped onto the airwaves from wide-ranging locales. Included were the combos of Ben Bernie, Vincent Lopez, George Olsen, B. A. Rolfe and Fred Waring. Could anyone doubt the long-term viability of remotes—and music—on the ether?

Enter Benny Goodman.

The son of a Russian immigrant tailor, Goodman was born in Chicago in 1909, one of a dozen kids, half of them (like the contemporary Lombardo clan) employed by the family firm — the Benny Goodman Orchestra, a little-recognized fact. (Ethel ran the office, Freddy was road manager, Gene was music coordinator, Harry was a bassist and Irving a trumpeter.) Benny took up the clarinet at age 11, eventually becoming one of that instrument's most respected prodigies. By 1926, he was playing in Ben Pollack's Californians outfit at New York's Park Central Hotel. He freelanced in pit bands, on radio and on records with groups headlined by Isham Jones, Ted Lewis, Lee Morse, Red Nichols, Ben Selvin and Donald Voorhees.

In 1932, radio was typically contributing $300 to Goodman's income every week at the apex of the Depression years. Yet he was frustrated and impatient, often playing for bandmasters with whom he found himself at odds. He gained a reputation — possibly earned — of being difficult, and saw his weekly income drop to $50 frequently. By age 25 he had had enough. He formed his own group and spent the summer playing at Billy Rose's Music Hall in New York, gaining the added exposure offered by station WMCA several times weekly. The year was 1934.

Fortune continued to smile on Goodman that year. By a single vote his fledgling outfit won a tryout for an unprecedented opportunity. The National Biscuit Company signed him to perform on the same bill with a couple of peers—one, an equally unknown assemblage headed by NBC staff musician Kel Murray (Murray Kellner's stage name), considered in music terminology a "sweet orchestra"—and a better known Latin combo (a "rumba band") led by Xavier Cugat. Goodman's forte was jazz, a "hot troupe." Goodman hired singer Helen Ward for the vocals and she turned out to be an excellent choice.

Let's Dance, the longest sponsored coast-to-coast series in the ether's history, and strongly appealing to terpsichorean types, debuted over NBC on Saturday, December 1, 1934. While the feature aired for three hours beginning at 10:30 P.M. in the East, it was actually a six-hour live epic. In order for the program to be heard in its entirety at that hour on the West Coast, it was repeated as soon as it ended at 1:30 A.M. in the East. There was no such thing as taping a performance and playing it back later in those days. So the three-hour broadcast was actually six hours long for the participants and studio audience.

For six months, through June 8, 1935, it followed a simple format. Airing from NBC's largest studio, 8H, at stage left was Benny Goodman; Kel Murray was at stage center; and Xavier Cugat was at stage right. Each of the three bands was featured for 20 minutes of every hour. Then they took a 40-minute break, during which the musicians could sit on the stage, participate in a continuous crap game in an anteroom backstage or get some liquid refreshment at nearby Hurley's Bar, a popular NBC staff hangout at Sixth Avenue and Forty-Ninth Street.

Announcer George Ansbro, whose career would span six decades on the air, provides some eyewitness impressions of those months with *Let's Dance*.[5] He recalls, for instance, that his weekly salary for that show was $25. Of course, he was interlocutor for many other programs during the same period.

> Just being in that studio on Saturday nights was an experience not to be forgotten.... In Studio 8H the first ten rows of seats were removed to accommodate dancing by the studio audience. I would often spot others kicking their heels on the floor — pages and guides off duty in mufti, dancing with their dates. Likewise off-duty hostesses and receptionists. Also an occasional NBC vice president was spotted. The party atmosphere never stopped.... [*In the anteroom backstage*] I was free to look around at the others ... and contemplate the wealth of musical talent I was privileged to rub elbows with. Benny Goodman himself, I guess for want of something better to do during those off periods, frequently dropped in for a look-see but never picked up the dice. I couldn't help but like him because of his pleasant personality, off stage as well as on. He was a nice man who was also an amazing virtuoso of the clarinet and, in my opinion, surely deserved the great success he achieved.

But *Let's Dance* was only a six-month pipe dream. Things turned sour for Goodman that summer. The Music Corporation of America (MCA) booked his entourage for a gig at the Roosevelt Grill. The Roosevelt's clientele had long been enamored with the softer, sweeter sounds of Guy Lombardo and his Royal Canadians. Goodman's loud and boisterous 14-piece jazz ensemble was an aberration they simply couldn't abide. After enough of them stridently complained to management, Benny and company were history — after only one performance.

Next, MCA arranged a cross-country tour for the body, consisting of one-night stands and brief engagements principally in medium-sized cities, yet ending with a worthy appointment at the impressive Palomar Ballroom in Los Angeles. From that expedition's inception, however, things didn't go well. Reception was tepid in early outings and as word leaked out, potential subsequent crowds along their route fell off. By the time they reached Colorado despair hung over them and there was talk of cancellations, thereby ending their journey early. An appearance at Elitch's Gardens in Denver was little short of disaster. "Goodman was dying with what was, at that moment, perhaps the best band in the nation," noted one scholar.

Despite the circumstances, the entourage pressed on. MCA officials were working feverishly behind the scenes to sustain the commitments they had previously lined up. On entering the Golden State, Goodman's band got a little better reception at Oakland. This may have been chiefly due to the fact that MCA had encouraged area radio outlets to air the troupe's phonograph records, which they did just before its personal appearance there.

Patrons were at last demonstrating some enthusiasm for Goodman and his band.

Then came the Palomar and the tour's finale. Nobody knew what to anticipate. The engagement opened on Wednesday night, August 21, 1935. Goodman gave the downbeat for the subdued fare they had been playing throughout their road appearances—definitely not the hot, rowdy stuff that had gotten them fired at the Roosevelt Grill. The customers appeared bored and unresponsive, just as others had been across the country.

Writing in his autobiography, *The Kingdom of Swing*, Goodman reminisced: "This went on for about an hour, till I decided ... if we had to flop, at least I'd do it in my own way, playing the kind of music I wanted to. For all I knew this might be our last night together, and we might as well have a good time while we had the chance. I called out some of our big Fletcher Henderson arrangements [Goodman had prevailed on Henderson, one of his jazz heroes, to produce some exclusive numbers for the group while on radio's *Let's Dance*] ... and the boys ... dug in with some of the best playing I've heard since we left New York."

The Palomar patrons were taken aback. They hesitated at first, not knowing what to expect. But momentarily they responded to the change with wild abandon, auditioning their most stunning footwork, captivated by Goodman's rowdiness. "Benny and his clarinet became a symbol," explained a convert, "a direct line of emotional and musical communication between those on the stand and those who gathered around to watch, to worship, to dance and to listen—in person, on records and over the radio." Said another: "He made history that night. The kingdom of swing had arrived and Benny Goodman was its sultan."

A big band historiographer measured Goodman's contribution at the start of the rage, the band that launched the new trend that couldn't be summarily dismissed.[6]

> Several things set Goodman's apart from all the bands that had preceded it. One, of course, was the type of music it played—a crisp, clean, driving, always swinging and exciting, always easily understood kind of music. Another was its consistently superior musicianship. And then, of course, there was Goodman himself, with the personalized excitement that he projected through his horn. He and his clarinet created a kind of identity that hadn't existed before, providing an aura of glamour and personality and excitingly superb musicianship that set the mood and the pace for a dozen glorious years.

Benny Goodman, the pied piper of swing, would lead the way—merrily, exuberantly, vigorously—toward a new era in which bands dominated the American musical scene. He was at the vanguard of a new wave that grew larger seemingly by the hour. For the impresarios and their followers—including the instrumentalists and an adoring public anxious to break from the doldrums of a contemptible past—it was surely the best of times!

Goodman accepted one appearance after another on the West Coast following his tumultuous reception at the Palomar. The Congress Hotel in Chicago booked him for the winter, where his music often resounded across the nation via radio hookups. Entertainment surveys indicated that his was the number one band in the nation by the time he signed with the Elgin Watch Company for a radio series in March 1936. Returning to New York as the "king of swing" after 10 months in Chicago, his entourage appeared nightly in the Hotel Pennsylvania's Madhattan [sic] Room. Those shows were carried three evenings a week on radio. Once a week at 9:30 P.M. they sprinted to a CBS studio for the *Camel Caravan* broadcast, sponsored by the R. J. Reynolds Tobacco Company.

Radio played an awesome role in conveying the frenzy that the big bands whipped up, bringing it to the ears of the nation's citizens in the metropolises and on the prairies, to the farmers as well as the factory laborers.

In the early 1940s—the middle of the big band era, in fact—Francis Chase Jr. offered his perspectives on the scope of the industry that supply up-close revelations of how some of it worked.[7]

> The one-night stands are, oddly enough, the bottom and the top of this business whose growth has been closely linked with that of broadcasting. The one-night stands are the jumping-off places for bands of tomorrow and the place where bands without "oomph" remain year after year. At the same time, the one-night stands are where big-name bands earn the most money. They consist mostly of the pay-as-you-enter ballrooms; civic and club functions; college proms; private dates— debutante parties, weddings, charity dances sponsored by socialites. The one-night season usually begins in April ... and runs through the summer....
>
> Often, big-name bands will play hotel engagements which permit them to barely break even for months before the one-night season opens, *providing* the hotel has a direct wire for broadcasting over an important radio station. Radio appearances play a vital part in building an unknown aggregation ... into name-band proportions. It also serves to zoom the asking price of a name band for one-night dates in the hinterlands....
>
> If a band leader survives his one-night stage — they sometimes last for years — and still has a band intact, he may arrive at ... a large ballroom with a direct wire to a radio station well known for its dance-band broadcasts. There are many such jumping-off places, but not nearly enough for the multitude of aspiring Benny Goodmans who turn up each year with a baton, a band and a prayer.

The big band mania created instant careers for some determined aspirants who had thrashed about in reticent turmoil for many years. Goodman's success resulted in similar experiences for bands headlined by Charlie Barnet, Duke Ellington, Glen Gray, Woody Herman, Hal Kemp, Claude Thornhill and dozens more. Anybody with a few extra bucks might be easily tempted to attend a one-night gig at a local roadhouse, a civic auditorium or a college gymnasium since the brunt of the Depression had then subsided. And for the stay-at-homes, one wag simplified it: "Just tune up an orchestra, turn on the radio and drop in. All you needed for dance was a floor, a punch bowl and a radio."

Glenn Miller, who in the late 1930s would be acknowledged for conducting "the most successfully commercial band," emerged from the likes of the 1920s combos that produced Benny Goodman. Yet after forming his own orchestra in 1937, Miller floundered, unknown by the masses until opportunity came knocking. An NBC microphone introduced his soothing sounds to millions as his band played the Glen Island Casino. As a result, his schedule quickly filled with 10 broadcasts every week. By 1940, Liggett & Myers Tobacco Company, from an industry that became one of big band's most reliable underwriters, initialed Miller to a multiple nightly CBS quarter-hour for Chesterfield cigarettes. That kind of exposure, to Miller and many of his contemporaries, was vital in establishing permanent careers in a highly competitive business.

Radio sought these maestros from the rigors of the road, lining up plenty of commercial programs at local stations and on national chains. All by itself NBC proudly asserted in 1939 that it was habitually offering its listeners the sounds of 49 bands over its dual networks combined. Charlie Barnet, Blue Barron, Count Basie, Larry Clinton, Jimmy and Tommy Dorsey, Horace Heidt, Woody Herman, Gene Krupa, Glenn

Miller, Jan Savitt and Artie Shaw were among them. At the same point CBS touted that it was airing another 21 signatories, including Cab Calloway, Jan Garber, Benny Goodman, Sammy Kaye, Hal Kemp, Kay Kyser, Ozzie Nelson, Jack Teagarden and Paul Whiteman.

The cumulative 70 bands in no way embodied the volume then playing on the ether. Still others were featured on the Red, Blue and CBS chains, and then there was the infinite MBS network which placed its microphones in clubs that the others often missed. Between the dinner hour and the end of the "night owl" phase (10:30 P.M. to 3 A.M.) nightly dozens of bands and orchestras collectively filled several hours of programming time on all four major chains, usually in half-hour increments.

The tobacco processors became some of the big bands' best friends. Indeed, were they attracted by the incredible sounds emanating from those aggregations, or, more presumptively, as an informant suggested, principally committed to "reach the unsullied teenage smoker"? Both Glenn Miller and Fred Waring appeared for Chesterfields, Philip Morris touted Russ Morgan, Benny Goodman and Vaughn Monroe signed with Camels, Tommy Dorsey and Harry Sosnik were on for Raleighs, Artie Shaw and Paul Whiteman for Old Golds and B. A. Rolfe and Kay Kyser for Lucky Strikes.

There were a couple of commercial enterprises that didn't manufacture cigarettes but took a pronounced interest in dance music and made sizeable contributions to the mania.

The F. W. Fitch Company underwrote the *Fitch Bandwagon* over NBC Sundays at 7:30 P.M. Eastern Time for a decade (1938–1948). Initially the series offered a weekly showcase of the nation's big bands, emphasizing newer combos during the summer months. The format altered in 1945, spotlighted Cass Daley that year and—in 1946—Phil Harris and Alice Faye, the emphasis then shifting to situation comedy. The final couple of seasons were a dress rehearsal for Harris and Faye's popular NBC feature under their own names (1948–1954).

In the meantime, the Coca-Cola Company presented *Spotlight Bands* (aka *Victory Parade of Spotlight Bands*) for listeners' pleasure. The show ran weeknights over MBS (1941–1942), weeknights over NBC Blue (1942–1945) and thrice weekly over MBS (1945–1946), the latter season alternately featuring the bands of Guy Lombardo, Xavier Cugat and Harry James. During World War II, the series frequently aired from military camps and defense plants and presented a different band on every show. The program staff traveled nearly 2 million miles to take those bands before service personnel and volunteers, becoming a morale builder as well as a band-booster. The orchestras of Tommy Dorsey, Jan Garber and Frankie Masters were called upon for the most repeat performances.

In addition to the remotes, there were several other important scheduled network radio series that featured big band music. Among them: *The Lucky Strike Dance Orchestra* (1928–1934, NBC) with the outfits of Ferde Grofe, Vincent Lopez, Jack Pearl, B. A. Rolfe and Ted Weems at varying times; *The Saturday Night Swing Club* (1936–1939, CBS) featuring the band of Bunny Berigan; and *Young Man with a Band* (1939–1940, CBS) with names like Coleman Hawkins, Wingy Manone, Hot Lips Page, Louis Prima, Jack Teagarden and Fats Waller. There were many other network features spotlighting the big bands, of course, including the *ABC Dancing Party* (1951–1956, ABC), *Bandstand USA* (1949–1959, MBS), *Let's Dance* (1934–1935, NBC) and a myriad of others which kept dance music uppermost in listeners' ears, bringing it into their homes from a variety of far-flung venues.

Big band remotes were easy to produce and relatively inexpensive. Radio offered a "package plan" that gave everybody a piece of the action. Dance music was an efficient method of filling hours of air time while simultaneously promoting a hotel or ballroom and fostering the primary business itself—the band, its singers, their records, sheet music, motion pictures and personal appearances in semi-permanent locales and one-night stands on the road, plus boosting sales of radios, phonographs and musical instruments and lessons for the latter group.

"In the very broadcasting of such music" noted a critic during the epoch, "the radio station is making it possible for the band to earn much more money on its regular engagements. For wide public interest in dance bands and their leaders, generated largely by radio, has made name-bands first-line theatrical attractions as well as dance-date fillers." Said another: "By the end of the thirties the most important thing to any bandleader was identification with a sponsored radio show. Regardless of the direct income, it was priceless in terms of boosting personal appearances. Many leaders offered fabulous bonuses to agents who could get them a sponsor. Others bought their way out of commitments to locations when these commitments interfered with a radio opportunity." And another: "Radio was the lifeline for bands ... who made their name over the airwaves, and then made their money on the road—where customers turned out because they had heard those bands on the radio." Beyond that, added bandleader Les Brown, "The record companies weren't interested in you at all unless you were on the air and you could plug your records."

Anyone who realized what the big bands were taking out of radio and personal appearances monetarily—particularly during a time of the nation's colossal economic collapse, followed by years of plodding recovery—could be sure that those individuals wouldn't be going to the poor house anytime soon. "There is no doubt that any really popular leader in the United States during the peak years of the band era would have had to be singularly reckless or inefficient as a businessman not to have made enough money to keep himself in comfort for the rest of his life," a pundit assessed.

Paul Whiteman's payroll for a week in January 1928 indicated that the lowest-paid member of his staff received $150 weekly, a sizable sum then, while four others took home $350 each. Another 33 individuals (including instrumentalists, vocalists and arrangers) divided $6,420, an average split of $195. If 38 people evenly divided the weekly $30,000 that was provided from their contract with CBS starting in 1929, each would carry home $790 from radio alone! "For the time such wages are staggeringly high," declared a historian, "but while Whiteman was both a generous payer and an immensely successful leader, there is evidence that in later years other bandleaders were able to pay wages on a similar scale."

Indeed there was. In the genre's boom years during World War II, Benny Goodman, Harry James and Artie Shaw commanded $4,000 nightly. In March 1939, Kay Kyser realized more than $10,000 from a week's outing in Cleveland. Kyser set local records for paid admissions to performances in Atlantic City, Milwaukee, Pasadena, Providence and Scranton, grossing $9,000 alone at Pasadena's Civic Auditorium. Also in 1939, Artie Shaw collected $30,000 from a week's appearances at New York's Strand Theater. Meanwhile, over at the nearby Paramount that same week, Glenn Miller's group—still virtual unknowns—saw box office receipts rise to $56,000. There's no need to feel sorry for Shaw, however—he banked $50,000 annually from records, $150,000 from radio and considered their celluloid roles as icing on the cake.

There were others whose take-home pay appeared to be a permanent bonus in an era in which the dance band business was raking in in excess of a cool $110 million annually.

In 1941, Glenn Miller's band grossed over a half-million dollars out of radio, records and personal appearances. CBS coughed up more than 50 percent of that sum for three quarter-hour broadcasts weekly (a historian-mathematician reporting the figures determined that Miller and company were earning $110 per minute — not a bad haul even if it was done today, and an absolute windfall then). Miller sold almost 3 million phonograph records on the Bluebird label that year. His ongoing gig at the Hotel Pennsylvania netted him $3,000 a week and he brought in even more from one-night stands. Going on welfare was obviously the last thing on his crew's mind.

At about the same time, 11 top-name draws were receiving between $7,000 and $8,500 weekly for their theatrical performances, commanding such fees largely in response to appearances on sustaining dance-band remote broadcasts. Included were Tommy Dorsey, Eddy Duchin, Benny Goodman, Glen Gray, Sammy Kaye, Hal Kemp, Wayne King, Ted Lewis, Guy Lombardo, Phil Spitalny and Paul Whiteman.

A yet higher-ranked level boasted five more aggregates. According to an authoritative source, their fees were set "largely upon their radio importance ... in ratio to appearances on the air." Horace Heidt, Kay Kyser, Glenn Miller, Orrin Tucker and Fred Waring drew a $12,500 guarantee plus a percentage of gross above that figure. Kyser was known to take in $18,000 a week on regular occasions.

Personal appearances were on top of commercial radio series that often compensated the bands from $1,000 to $7,000 every week.

While black bands had fewer opportunities than did their white peers, radio introduced several that achieved widespread public acclaim. Duke Ellington and Cab Calloway surfaced at the Cotton Club. Earl Hines emanated from Chicago's Grand Terrace. Out of Kansas City's Reno Club, Count (William) Basie earned a national following.

Writing in 1942 at the height of the dance band craze, an observer offered this eyewitness account.[8]

> Many of the thousands of jitterbugs who come night after night pay their admissions, not to dance — real devotees of the modern dance band and jive artists would no more think of cutting capers on the floor while a Benny Goodman was performing than the bejeweled dowagers who attend chamber music recitals would think of doing a schottische to the strains of the Hart House String Quartet — but to take up a position just before the bandstand where they listen raptly to each note and break out into violent applause at the conclusion of each number. Applause at the end of a number is grand radio stuff, and the best jumping-off places for a band are those patronized by such enthusiasts. In fact, one noted band leader was sued by a large group of New York youngsters who alleged, in their suit, that this manager had hired them to stand before the podium and applaud violently after each number for several weeks, then refused to pay off.

The quality of the big band broadcasts varied from place to place. There were some logical explanations for the differences. A great deal could be ascribed to the acoustics of a particular venue. As a rule, more exciting tones emanated from larger ballrooms. At the same time the intimacy of comparatively miniscule dining rooms in hotels and nightclubs frequently resulted in lifeless sound projection.

The engineer assigned to a remote pickup was a key ingredient in what went out over the air, too. Some appeared to have tin ears, a logical explanation for the ghastly results derived on their watch. Others were perceptibly attuned to the music and deeply involved in the end result. They recognized at what point a group of instruments should prevail and when they should not and tinkered with their dials in responsible fashion to provide better reception to the unseen audience.

Some engineers, it seemed, simply had too much work to do to be very effective. CBS and NBC assigned two individuals to travel on-site for each remote broadcast — an announcer and an engineer. MBS, on the other hand, with limited discretionary resources, combined those dual missions. "This required both a good ear and a good voice," noted a spectator. "Unfortunately very few men had both."

Not every announcer fit the unique role that was conducive to providing the type of accommodating banter preferred on those occasions, also. "If he projected enthusiasm for the music, the entire tenor of the broadcast could be uplifted," maintained a scholar. "Sometimes, though, the results were pretty ridiculous, as overzealous, underinformed announcers spieled inane jive talk and clichés in hysterical attempts to match the band's musical excitement." To head that off, numerous bandmasters wined and dined their quarry, quite anxious to hear these men respond with stirring, motivational chatter that complimented the band. Playing to positive instincts, they hoped this would cause their aggregation to be favorably received by those tuning in. It was soft-sell image building, an important move that the maestros considered critical to their future welfare.

Curiously, the apple-polishing that the bandleaders showered on the announcers was mild when compared to the incessant idol worship the impresarios received from a fawning group of professionals that turned up at their every air date. Agents commonly known as "song pluggers" or "contact men"— glorified labels for music publishers' reps—could make bandleaders utterly appear to be gods. Over the years, an orchestra leader playing a hotel from which a nightly broadcast emanated might look out across a vast throng of patrons and behold a half-dozen such representatives in the crowd. At some hallowed halls, exclusive tables were reserved for their private use.

Reaching into a quiver of darts, they would withdraw their most potent weapons to woo their targets, attempting to persuade the maestros to perform certain tunes that their employers had recently released. In cunning style they plied their prey with every imaginable trinket they could think of, offering those icons cash, liquor, jewelry, clothes, women, baseball and theater tickets, musical arrangements, resort vacations — just about anything affordably conceivable. Although many less-principled impresarios accepted their treasures, some with higher standards of integrity or, just possibly, greater stamina, resisted. The stakes were high because air plugs were incalculable in promoting new songs. No other medium — including phonograph records — rendered as much influence as broadcasting; both the publishers and the conductors were well aware of it.

As a result of those transactions, a great many tunes that had pecuniary support behind them yet weren't really all that good were heard incessantly on the air. This frequently came at the expense of some more worthy refrains without similar financial backing: those were often played once or twice and never heard from again. A few years hence, when the airwaves were virtually abandoned to the disc jockeys, the record producers picked up on the same theme and greased the palms of the DJs, who played certain records over and over ad nauseam. It was called "payola" then and some broadcasters were fired, finding themselves in court when their dealings were exposed to legal and public scrutiny. But in the 1930s and 1940s the transfer of gifts for airtime — which was also maneuvered in clandestine fashion — wasn't considered illegal, unethical or amoral by the industry. As substance changed hands, program bills heard on the air were instantly determined.

Impresario Les Brown claimed that he had a repertoire of 80 or 90 songs at the time and almost never repeated the same refrain in a given week. "But some bandleaders did the same program every night and NBC used to get madder than hell," he allowed.[9] Tommy Dorsey, meanwhile, maintained his own publishing company. "Anything he recorded or published at the same time, he had on the air, and he said 'Okay, that's on Monday, Tuesday, Wednesday, Thursday...' They raged at him, and he said, 'If you want me, that's what you get.' Because you don't have the same listeners every night."[10]

One historian insisted that the bands featured on remote broadcasts "improved before a radio microphone." He argued: "The knowledge that thousands, and sometimes millions, were listening in all over America and sometimes the world, often hones a player's technique and precision. A live mike usually kept a player alert and resulted in a better performance."

Almost every broadcast band could be identified with a specific piece of music that ushered it onto and off of the airwaves. A few of the more prominent bands and their themes are spelled out here.

Charlie Agnew — *Slow But Sure*
Ray Anthony — *The Man with the Horn*
Louis Armstrong — *When It's Sleepy Time Down South*
Gus Arnheim — *Sweet and Lovely*
Desi Arnaz — *Cuban Pete*
Smith Ballew — *Home*
Charlie Barnet — *Redskin Rumba*
Count Basie — *One O'Clock Jump*
Bunny Berigan — *I Can't Get Started with You*
Will Bradley — *Think of Me/Strange Cargo*
Les Brown — *Dance of the Blue Devils/Sentimental Journey*
Henry Busse — *Hot Lips*
Billy Butterfield — *Moonlight in Vermont*
Bobby Byrne — *Danny Boy*
Frankie Carle — *Sunrise Serenade*
Del Courtney — *Good Evenin'*
Xavier Cugat — *My Shawl*
Bernie Cummins — *Dark Eyes*
Al Donahue — *Lowdown Rhythm in a Top Hat*
Jimmy Dorsey — *Contrasts*
Tommy Dorsey — *I'm Getting Sentimental over You*
Eddy Duchin — *My Twilight Dream/Be My Lover*
Sonny Dunham — *Memories of You*
Les Elgart — *The Dancing Sound*
Duke Ellington — *East St. Louis Toodle-oo/Take the A Train*
Skinnay Ennis — *Got a Date with an Angel*
Chuck Foster — *Oh, You Beautiful Doll*
Dizzy Gillespie — *I Waited for You*
Benny Goodman — *Let's Dance/Goodbye*
Glen Gray — *Smoke Rings*
Johnny Green — *Hello, My Lover, Goodbye*
Lionel Hampton — *Flying Home*
Coleman Hawkins — *Body and Soul*
Horace Heidt — *I'll Love You in My Dreams*
Fletcher Henderson — *Christopher Columbus*
Woody Herman — *Blue Flame*
Tiny Hill — *Angry*
Earl Hines — *Deep Forest*
Les Hite — *It Must Have Been a Dream*
Harry James — *Ciribiribin*
Henry Jerome — *Nice People (with Nice Habits)*
Art Kassell — *Doodle-Doo-Doo*
Hal Kemp — *Got a Date with an Angel*
Stan Kenton — *Artistry in Rhythm*
Wayne King — *The Waltz You Saved for Me*
Andy Kirk — *Until the Real Thing Comes Along*

Bennie Krueger — *It's Getting Dark on Old Broadway*
Gene Krupa — *Apurksody/Starburst*
Sam Lanin — *A Smile Will Go a Long, Long Way*
Harlan Leonard — *Southern Fried*
Ted Lewis — *When My Baby Smiles at Me*
Guy Lombardo — *Auld Lang Syne*
Johnny Long — *In a Shanty in Old Shanty Town*
Jimmy Lunceford — *Uptown Blues*
Enrico Madriguera — *Adios*
Billy May — *Lean, Baby*
Clyde McCoy — *Sugar Blues*
Hal McIntyre — *Moon Mist*
Ray McKinley — *Howdy, Friends*
Benny Meroff — *Diane*
Johnny Messner — *Can't We Be Friends?*
Glenn Miller — *Moonlight Serenade*
Vaughn Monroe — *Racing with the Moon*
Phil Ohman — *Canadian Capers*
Ben Pollack — *Song of the Islands*
Carl Ravazza — *Vieni Su*
Freddie Rich — *I'm Always Chasing Rainbows*
Johnny Richards — *Young at Heart*
Mike Riley — *The Music Goes 'Round and 'Round*
Jan Savitt — *Quaker City Jazz/It's a Wonderful World*
Boyd Senter — *Bad Habits*
Artie Shaw — *Nightmare*
Bobby Sherwood — *The Elk's Parade*
Charlie Straight — *Mocking Bird Rag*
Claude Thornhill — *Snowfall*
Paul Tremaine — *Lonely Acres*
Orrin Tucker — *Drifting and Dreaming*
Rudy Vallee — *My Time Is Your Time*
Chick Webb — *I May Be Wrong*
Anson Weeks — *I'm Sorry Dear*
Ted Weems — *Out of the Night*
Lawrence Welk — *Bubbles in the Wine*
Bob Wills — *San Antonio Rose*

The epigraphic introductions to each orchestra also became familiar to the listeners. As a supple saxophone arrangement of *When My Baby Smiles at Me* wafted in the background, an announcer with a soothingly mellow tone offered: "Need we tell you, ladies and gentlemen, that this melody heralds the approach to the microphone of that high-hatted tragedian of song, Ted Lewis?" And the maestro himself greeted his invisible audience inquiring, "Is ev'rybody happy?" On a rival's series, the announcer remarked: "Isham Jones requests your listening attention." A radio historiographer colorfully observed: "The bands came elegantly wrapped, like an invitation to the White House."

The big band shows frequently included vocalists whose names often became as well known as those of the bandleaders. Among the hundreds who sang there: Harry Babbitt, Bonnie Baker, Gene Barry, Lee Bennett, Vivian Blaine, Anita Boyer, Betty Brownell, Art Carney, June Christy, Buddy Clark, Rosemary Clooney, Dorothy Collins, Russ Columbo, Perry Como, Doris Day, Gloria DeHaven, Ray Eberle, Billy Eckstine, Skinnay Ennis, Dale Evans, Alice Faye, Ella Fitzgerald, Helen Forrest, Kenny Gardner, Georgia Gibbs, Eydie Gorme, Betty Grable, Merv Griffin, Connie Haines, Dick Haymes, Woody Herman, Harriet Hilliard, Billie Holiday, Lena Horne, Betty Hutton, June Hutton, Marion Hutton, Herb Jeffries, Kitty Kallen, Dorothy Lamour, Abbe Lane, Frances Langford, Peggy Lee, Art Lund, Gordon MacRae, Marvel (Marilyn) Maxwell, Johnny Mercer, Tommy Mercer, Vaughn Monroe, Russ Morgan, Helen O'Connell, Anita O'Day, Patti Page, Harry Prime, Ruth Robin, Jimmy Rushing, Jane Russell, Dinah Shore, Ginny Simms, Frank Sinatra, Jo Stafford, Kay Starr, Martha Tilton, Mel Torme, Sarah Vaughan, Stuart Wade, Helen Ward, Kay Weber, Lee Wiley, Eileen Wilson and Edythe Wright.

Most stayed only a little while, some with a single band while several worked at different times with different bands. The singers' records were sometimes as popular as the instrumentals and became increasingly more so after the bands began to fade.

It was a little-known secret (certainly shielded from their adoring fans' awareness) that some of the bandleaders could be publicly perceived as gregarious and extroverted while — truth be told by industry insiders— they had all sorts of obnoxious hang-ups. Tommy Dorsey could be overtly confrontational. Tales circulated that he and Jimmy Dorsey used their fists to settle arguments in the early days of the Dorsey Brothers combo. Artie Shaw had serious bouts of nervous depression — one reviewer dubbed him "a screwball" — leading him to quit his stunningly successful 1939 band, hightail it to Mexico, return home, reorganize and disband several more times. Nobody was ever certain what he'd do next. Glenn Miller's dubious behavior kept his troupe edgy and at bay; he was characterized as "cold and distant." Benny Goodman's sidemen thought him "an ornery SOB" and found his chilly gaze, tagged by them "the Goodman ray," often a frequent preface to dismissal.

The bands infused other branches of the music business with the success they enjoyed. Record producers were convinced that dance bands and the popularity of radio's *Your Hit Parade* (see separate chapter) accounted for much of the 33 million phonograph disc sales six years after just 6 million were purchased in 1932. Simultaneously, the piano was revived as a working piece of furniture in American living rooms. In 1937, upright and baby grand sales reached 150,000, topping every year of the previous 16. Many of those were spinet models, requiring little more space than a desk. Other musical instruments were also on the upswing. Communities, clubs, schools, churches and other groups formed bands and orchestras. Most tried to imitate the pop tunes being played over the air and on jukeboxes. Sales of sheet music soared; music classes filled and private instruction lessons in assorted instruments proliferated.

A few bands appeared to defy all the odds and continue on and on. A couple of well-known outfits are worth noting. Guy Lombardo's "sweetest music this side of heaven" was considered emotionless by some critics and judged, perhaps unfairly, "the working definition of square." His Royal Canadians could be compared with Lawrence Welk's champagne music that continued for almost an eternity on television. Both bands were "much mocked but unquenchable."

In the meantime, Fred Waring and His Pennsylvanians also outlasted nearly everybody else. (See separate chapter.) His penchant for supplementing his music with diversionary tactics possibly extended his popularity for nearly as long as he lived. He retained a large staff of entertainers in addition to a versatile lot of bandsmen who turned performances into a combination variety show and jazz concert. Waring was still going strong in the 1970s, still making personal appearances, by then more than two decades after the big band era had ended.

After the big band era was unofficially over, several of its leaders joined some of the opposition that had helped to kill it, becoming network or syndicated disc jockeys. Among them: Tommy Dorsey, Duke Ellington, Benny Goodman, Jack Teagarden, Rudy Vallee and Paul Whiteman.

Things were tough all over by the time Bing Crosby launched one of his last few radio series in 1954. The Buddy Cole Trio was all he got instead of John Scott Trotter's large studio orchestra, to which he had become accustomed in mid–1937 with other bands preceding Trotter's. (See separate chapter.)

Within a year and a half of the end of World War II, the big band ballroom remotes spiraled into rapid decline. It was obvious that people were no longer as enamored by the sounds of dance music playing late into the evening (or the early hours of a new day) as they once were. American citizens didn't hang onto their amusement forms forever as new ones arrived (think showboats, circuses, vaudeville, silent films, music styles, dance crazes).

The proliferation and repetition of the dance bands had run its course. Eight of the top bands disengaged starting in December 1946. Outfits headlined by Les Brown, Benny Carter, Tommy Dorsey, Benny Goodman, Woody Herman, Ina Ray Hutton, Harry James and Jack Teagarden went out of business within a few weeks of each other. (Dorsey, forced out by a discouraging economic climate, would regroup and be touring again within a year.) Another of the greats, Glenn Miller, had been lost over the English Channel in 1944. With those departures, the foundation of the big band business shuddered unequivocally.

As television challenged radio for supremacy in the nation's living rooms a short time later, the demise of the epoch was both hastened and assured. One by one radio programs disappeared and venues that had been important to remote broadcasts went silent. The disc jockey was soon to be radio's uncontested reigning monarch.

Ironically, some bandleaders would do an about-face, having initially mocked TV. In 1951, Tommy Dorsey said he wanted no part of it, blasting it as "bad for business." He obviously changed his mind before long, turning up with his own weekly sponsored series after substituting one summer (1955) for vacationing comedian Jackie Gleason. Ray Anthony acquired his own venture on the tube, too, having earlier expressed total disinterest. Freddy Martin, on the other hand, wholly embraced the new medium. For two seasons, beginning in 1951, he hosted an all-band show that tried to meld neophyte instrumentalists into a "band of tomorrow."

Several attempts to adapt video to dance venues just as the radio remotes had done were not all that successful. Hulking equipment required for telecasting in those days hampered the dancers and didn't draw the anticipated audience response that radio remotes had enjoyed. The bandleaders themselves—accustomed to a life of ease in aural broadcasting—were genuinely dismayed by the amount of preparation TV required.

So the big band remote passed, having tapered off in the late 1940s until—by 1950—only occasional vestiges remained in diverse places, reminding patrons of the glory days before their fade. Few, if any, forms of entertainment filled as many hours on American radio as did the dance bands collectively during those halcyon days. The legacy they left has continued to influence popular music to the present. Radio—and dance music—will undoubtedly live on in the hearts and memories of old-time radio enthusiasts who lived through that era until they, too, have finally become extinct.

The Bandmasters

Fifteen of the big band era's legendary radio maestros are introduced more copiously in the pages to follow. They were selected based on their sweeping notoriety and—in almost every case—because of their bountiful on-air time. Their radio listings pertain to ongoing series alone; this data does not include those thousands of band remotes and guest appearances on aural comedy, music, variety, quiz and audience participation features, most of which have never been documented permanently.

In other portions of this volume, particularly in chapters on The Contests and

The House Bands, you will also encounter biographical vignettes on several additional impresarios who emerged from the big band tradition. For the classification purposes of this book, they have been separated because their most celebrated radio links are unmistakably identified elsewhere.

Principal sources for the data in the table that follows is taken from these authors, whose works may be found in the Bibliography near the end of the book: DeLong (1966), Dunning (1998), Hickerson, McCarthy (1974, 1982), Simon, Studwell and Baldin, Sultanof, Summers, Tracy, Leo Walker, and Woods.

XAVIER CUGAT

Born: January 1, 1900, Tirona, Spain.
Died: October 27, 1990, Barcelona, Spain.
Motto: *King of the Rumba.*
Chief Instrument: Violin.
Signature Song: *My Shawl.*
Legendary Tunes: *Brazil, The Breeze and I, The Lady in Red, Night Must Fall, Perfidia, Say Si Si.*
Vocalists: Desi Arnaz, Lina Romay, Miguelito Valdes, more.
Radio Series:
Xavier Cugat Show. October 30, 1933–June 1, 1934, NBC, Monday–Friday, 6:00–6:15 P.M.; October 15, 1934–1935, NBC, Monday–Friday, 6:00–6:15 P.M., sustaining.
Let's Dance. December 1, 1934–June 8, 1935, NBC, Saturday, 10:30 P.M.–1:30 A.M., National Biscuit Company (Nabisco foodstuffs).
Xavier Cugat Show. July 1–September 2, 1939, MBS, Saturday, 12:45–1:00 P.M., sustaining.
Xavier Cugat Show. January 9–June 19, 1941, NBC, Thursday, 7:30–8:00 P.M., R. J. Reynolds Tobacco Company (Camel cigarettes).
Xavier Cugat's Rumba Revue. June 26, 1941–January 1, 1942, NBC, Tuesday, 7:30–8:00 P.M., R. J. Reynolds Tobacco Company (Camel cigarettes).
Xavier Cugat's Rumba Revue. January 6–July 7, 1942, NBC Blue, Tuesday, 8:00–8:30 P.M., R. J. Reynolds Tobacco Company (Camel cigarettes).
Camel Comedy Caravan. July 10, 1942–January 1, 1943, CBS, Friday, 10:00–11:00 P.M.; January 8–July 2, 1943, CBS, Friday, 10:00–10:45 P.M., R. J. Reynolds Tobacco Company (Camel cigarettes).
Xavier Cugat Show. September 4–November 27, 1943, NBC Blue, Saturday, 11:00–11:30 A.M., Dubonnet.
Xavier Cugat Show. December 1, 1943–July 26, 1944, MBS, Wednesday, 8:30–9:00 P.M., Dubonnet.
Xavier Cugat Show. August 3–September 7, 1947, CBS, Sunday, 10:00–10:30 P.M., Eversharp Company (Schick razors and blades).
Xavier Cugat Show. July 7–September 22, 1948, ABC, Wednesday, 8:00–8:30 P.M., sustaining.
Synopsis:

Born in Spain and raised in Cuba, Xavier Cugat relinquished a promising career as a syndicated artist (his caricatures were distributed by King Features) to pursue his major interest, music. He trained as a classical violinist, playing in Phil Harris's band before forming one of his own. In 1933, he took the Waldorf Astoria Hotel by storm; it was his base for many years. He never regretted his ultimate career choice: "I would rather play Chiquita Banana and have my swimming pool than play Bach and starve." Attired in flaming red jackets, his entourage presented the striking music of South America in captivating style. Competition, while keen, was unable to package it with as much color and glamour as did the flamboyant Cugat. Even Rita Hayworth was a member of his band! When tangos, rumbas and congas are mentioned in connection with the big band era, Cugie still forms in many minds.

Desi Arnaz, Perez Prado and others sought to follow his Latin-American beat. Singers Abbe Lane and Charo were among Cugat's four wives. He offered his trademark salsa music in many Hollywood films and on television. Cugat's memoir, *Rumba Is My Life*, was published in 1949.

JIMMY DORSEY

Born: February 29, 1904, Shenandoah, Pennsylvania.
Died: June 12, 1957, New York, New York.
Chief Instruments: Clarinet, saxophone.
Signature Song: *Contrasts*.
Legendary Tunes: *Amapola ("Pretty Little Poppy"), Besame Mucho ("Kiss Me Much"), Blue Champagne, The Breeze and I, Green Eyes, I Get Along Without You Very Well, I Understand, I'm Glad There Is You, Is It True What They Say about Dixie?, My Prayer, Tangerine, So Rare, Star Eyes, White Cliffs of Dover*.
Arrangers: Sonny Burke, Tutti Camarata, Larry Clinton, Joe Lipman, Fud Livingston, Dave Matthews, Harold Mooney, Don Redman, Leonard Whitney, more.
Vocalists: Bob Carroll, Bob Eberle, Buddy Hughes, Vicki Joyce, Kitty Kallen, Don Matteson, Ray McKinley, Vi Mele, Ella Mae Morse, Helen O'Connell, June Richmond, Martha Tilton, Kay Weber, more.
Sidemen: Ray Bauduc, Bob Burns, Bobby Byrne, Tutti Camarata, Lou Carter, Billy Cronk, Herb Ellis, Charlie Frasier, Conrad Gozzo, Johnny Guarnieri, Herbie Haymer, Roc Hilman, Jack Jenney, Nate Kazebier, Earl Kiffe, Skip Layton, Don Matteson, Dave Matthews, Jimmie Maxwell, Ray McKinley, Ralph Muzzillo, Babe Russin, Jack Ryan, Buddy Schutz, Shorty Sherock, Freddy Slack, Bruce Squires, Jack Stacy, Charlie Teagarden, Davey Tough, Bobby Van Epps, Billy Verplanck, Leonard Whitney, more.
Radio Series:
The Ipana Troubadours. c1928, NBC, Wednesday, 9:00–9:30 P.M.; c1929, NBC Blue, Monday, 8:30–9:00 P.M., Bristol Myers, Inc. (Ipana toothpaste).
Kraft Music Hall. January 2, 1936–July 1, 1937, NBC, Thursday, 10:00–11:00 P.M., Kraft Foods Company (Kraft foodstuffs).
Jimmy Dorsey Orchestra. February 3–March 10, 1939, MBS, Friday, 8:30–9:00 P.M., sustaining.
Jimmy Dorsey Orchestra. May 28–October 22, 1939, NBC Blue, Sunday, in varying half-hour timeslots, 4:15–4:45 P.M., 5:00–5:30 P.M., 5:15–5:45 P.M., sustaining.
Jimmy Dorsey Orchestra. June 14–August 2, 1940, NBC Blue, Friday, 7:30–8:00 P.M., sustaining.
The Dorsey Brothers Orchestra. 1953–1954, CBS, twice weekly, 10:35–11:00 P.M.; 1954–1955, CBS, twice weekly, 10:30–11:00 P.M., sustaining.
Synopsis:

At the start and close of their careers, Jimmy and Tommy Dorsey worked together as the Dorsey Brothers Orchestra, "a good concept that seldom works—a single great band under two sometimes brilliant and often fiery leaders," stated one writer. Their topsy-turvy arrangement lasted from 1922 to 1935 and was often marred by verbal and physical displays. They wouldn't get back together until 1953. Separated, Tommy's career took off while Jimmy's experienced fits of grandeur and adversity. A *Variety* reporter praised Jimmy Dorsey as "a musician's musician" who—on his own—worked very hard to offer a first-rate band, frequently succeeding. By the early 1940s, his group was "at the very top" thanks to a string of hit recordings. "Jimmy really didn't want to lead; he would rather have been a sideman," said a band member. And singer Helen O'Connell confirmed: "Jimmy was the nicer of the two Dorsey brothers." TV comic Jackie Gleason was enamored with Jimmy and put the Dorseys on CBS during his 1955 summer vacation, thanks to his friendship with Jimmy. A 1947 film, *Those Fabulous Dorseys*, honored both brothers.

TOMMY DORSEY

Born: November 19, 1905, Shenandoah, Pennsylvania.
Died: November 26, 1956, Greenwich, Connecticut.
Motto: *The Sentimental Gentleman of Swing.*
Chief Instrument: Trumpet.
Signature Song: *I'm Getting Sentimental Over You.*
Legendary Tunes: *All the Things You Are, Boogie Woogie, Dolores, I'll Never Smile Again, Let's Get Away from It All, Little White Lies, Marie, Music Maestro Please, Opus One, There Are Such Things.*
Arrangers: Benny Carter, Bill Finegan, Earle Hagen, Fletcher Henderson, Dean Kincaide, Sy Oliver, Nelson Riddle, Axel Stordahl, Billy Verplanck, Paul Weston, more.
Vocalists: The Beachcombers, Anita Boyer, Connie Haines, Dick Haymes, Jack Leonard, The Pied Pipers, Lynn Roberts, The Sentimentalists, Frank Sinatra, Jo Stafford, Marlene Verplanck, Cliff Weston, Edythe Wright, more.
Sidemen: Gene Allen, Joe Bauer, Louie Bellson, Bunny Berigan, Jimmy Blake, Sid Block, Red Bone, Joe Bushkin, Pete Candoli, Billy Cronk, Buddy DeFranco, Joe Dixon, Sam Donahue, Ziggy Elman, Peewee Erwin, Andy Ferretti, Bud Freeman, Terry Gibbs, Milt Golden, Earle Hagen, Skeets Herfurt, Pee Wee Irwin, Manny Klein, Gene Krupa, Yank Lawson, Don Lodice, Mickey Mangano, Walter Mercurio, Johnny Mince, Paul Mitchell, Buddy Morrow, Abe Most, Vido Musso, Chuck Peterson, Bernie Privin, Buddy Rich, Boomie Richman, Nelson Riddle, Babe Russin, George Seberg, Charlie Shavers, Zoot Sims, Charlie Spivak, Sid Stoneburn, Fredy Stulce, Dave Tough, Johnny Van Eps, more.
Radio Series:
The Ipana Troubadours. c1928, NBC, Wednesday, 9:00–9:30 P.M.; c1929, NBC Blue, Monday, 8:30–9:00 P.M., Bristol Myers, Inc. (Ipana toothpaste).
Tommy Dorsey Orchestra. 1934, unsubstantiated network, day, time, 15 minutes, Chrysler Corporation (Chrysler-Plymouth automobile division).
Tommy Dorsey Orchestra. May 17–24, 1936, CBS, Sunday, 7:00–7:30 P.M., sustaining.
Tommy Dorsey Orchestra. August 4–25, 1936, CBS, Tuesday, 9:00–9:30 P.M., Ford Motor Company (Ford automobiles).
The Jack Pearl Show. November 9, 1936–March 8, 1937, NBC Blue, Monday, 9:30–10:00 P.M.; March 19–June 25, 1937, NBC Blue, Friday, 10:00–10:30 P.M., Brown & Williamson Tobacco Company (Raleigh cigarettes and Sir Walter Raleigh pipe tobacco).
The Raleigh-Kool Program. July 2–October 15, 1937, NBC Blue, Friday, 10:00–10:30 P.M.; October 22, 1937–January 28, 1938, NBC Blue, Friday, 9:30–10:00 P.M.; February 2, 1938–September 20, 1939, NBC, Wednesday, 8:30–9:00 P.M., Brown & Williamson Tobacco Company (Raleigh and Kool cigarettes).
Summer Pastime. June 25–September 17, 1940, NBC, Tuesday, 10:00–10:30 P.M., The Pepsodent Company (Pepsodent toothpaste).
Fame and Fortune. October 17, 1940–April 10, 1941, NBC Blue, Thursday, 8:30–9:00 P.M., Nature's Remedy.

On the Town. November 19, 1940–February 12, 1941, MBS, Tuesday/Wednesday, 7:15–7:30 P.M., sustaining.

Tommy Dorsey's Variety Show. March 8–July 5, 1942, NBC Blue, Sunday, 8:00–8:30 P.M., sustaining; June 16–September 8, 1942, NBC, Tuesday, 10:30–11:00 P.M., Brown & Williamson Tobacco Company (Raleigh cigarettes and Sir Walter Raleigh pipe tobacco).

Tommy Dorsey Orchestra. September 16, 1942–September 8, 1943, NBC, Wednesday, 8:30–9:00 P.M., Brown & Williamson Tobacco Company (Raleigh cigarettes and Sir Walter Raleigh pipe tobacco).

Tommy Dorsey Orchestra. June 3–September 30, 1945, NBC, Sunday, 8:30–9:00 P.M., Standard Brands, Inc. (Tenderleaf tea).

Tommy Dorsey Orchestra. July 22–November 25, 1945, NBC, Sunday, 4:30–5:00 P.M., Radio Corporation of America (RCA entertainment appliances).

Endorsed by Dorsey. March 20–August 7, 1946, MBS, Wednesday, 10:00–10:30 P.M., sustaining.

Tommy Dorsey's Playshop. May 17–July 12, 1946, MBS, Friday, 10:00–10:30 P.M., sustaining.

Summer Playhouse. July 22–September 30, 1946, MBS, Monday, 10:00–10:30 p.m.; August 30–October 18, 1946, MBS, Friday, 8:30–9:00 P.M., sustaining.

The Tommy Dorsey Show. July 7–September 29, 1946, NBC, Sunday, 8:30–9:00 P.M., Standard Brands, Inc. (Tenderleaf tea).

Summer Serenade. July 13–August 31, 1948, ABC, Tuesday, 10:45–11:00 P.M., sustaining.

The Dorsey Brothers Orchestra. 1953–1954, CBS, twice weekly, 10:35–11:00 P.M.; 1954–1955, CBS, twice weekly, 10:30–11:00 P.M., sustaining.

Synopsis:

After years of working together, Tommy Dorsey walked out on his brother Jimmy in the summer of 1935, taking over a band led by Joe Haymes; the Tommy Dorsey Orchestra debuted at the Blue Room of New York's Hotel Lincoln. By summer 1941, the group topped Glenn Miller on popularity charts. He created Tommy Dorsey, Inc., to book his shows, publish his music and produce his records. In 1944, he purchased the Aragon Ballroom at Ocean City, California, with several partners, including Jimmy Dorsey and Harry James, and renamed it the Casino Gardens. By 1953, with bands in jeopardy almost everywhere, he combined his outfit with brother Jimmy's. A good businessman, Tommy was exceedingly disciplined and difficult as a leader ("a sharp mind and an acid tongue," claimed one informant), to the dismay of the majority of his sidemen. Dorsey choked in his sleep after dining on Italian food and taking sleeping pills the night he died. (Jimmy died of cancer only a few months later.) In 1977, Buddy Morrow began leading a 17-piece touring Tommy Dorsey Orchestra. Traveling by bus and carrying a sound system along, as of this writing they continue to play about 275 dates annually, perpetuating a celebrated musical sensation.

EDDY DUCHIN

Born: April 1, 1909, Cambridge, Massachusetts.
Died: February 9, 1951, New York, New York.
Motto: *The 10 Magic Fingers of Radio.*
Chief Instrument: Piano.
Signature Songs: *My Twilight Dream (Chopin's Nocturne in E-flat), Be My Lover.*
Legendary Tunes: *Between the Devil and the Deep Blue Sea, I Won't Dance, Let's Fall in Love, Moon Over Miami, Three O'Clock in the Morning, Try a Little Tenderness.*

Vocalists: Jane Pickens, more.
Radio Series:
Eddy Duchin Orchestra. January 2–June 23, 1934, NBC Blue, Tuesday/Thursday/Saturday, 9:30–10:00 P.M., The Pepsodent Company (Pepsodent toothpaste).

Ed Wynn, The Fire Chief. October 2, 1934–June 4, 1935, NBC, Tuesday, 9:30–10:00 P.M., The Texas Company (Texaco gasoline, oil, automotive products and services).

The Adventures of Gracie. Summer 1936, CBS, Wednesday, 8:30–9:00 P.M., Campbell Soup Company (Campbell soups, Franco-American spaghetti and other foodstuffs).

LaSalle Style Show. November 5, 1936–January 28, 1937, NBC, Thursday, 4:00–4:30 P.M., Cadillac Motor Car Company (LaSalle automobiles).

Eddy Duchin Orchestra. September 24–December 17, 1937, NBC, Friday, 7:30–8:00 P.M., Koppers Coke Company (Koppers heating).

Arden Hour of Charm. September 29–December 22, 1937, NBC Blue, Wednesday, 8:00–8:30 P.M., Elizabeth Arden, Inc. (Elizabeth Arden cosmetics).

Hour of Romance. December 28, 1937–March 22, 1938, MBS, Tuesday, 10:00–10:30 P.M., Elizabeth Arden, Inc. (Elizabeth Arden cosmetics).

Eddy Duchin Orchestra. September 5, 1938–May 29, 1939, NBC, Monday, 9:30–10:00 P.M., American Tobacco Company (Pall Mall cigarettes).

Eddy Duchin Orchestra. October 8, 1938–January 28, 1939, CBS, Saturday, 5:30–6:00 P.M.; December 2, 1939–May 4, 1940, CBS, Saturday, 5:30–6:00 P.M.; October 26, 1940–February 1, 1941, CBS, Saturday, 5:30–6:00 P.M., sustaining.

Eddy Duchin Orchestra. September 16–November 25, 1940, MBS, Monday, 9:30–10:00 P.M., sustaining.

Kraft Music Hall. August 16, 1945–May 9, 1946, NBC, Thursday, 9:00–9:30 P.M., Kraft Foods Company (Kraft foodstuffs).

A Date with Duchin. July 14–October 6, 1947, ABC, Monday/Wednesday/Friday, 4:30–4:45 P.M., Kremel shampoo.

Synopsis:
In the 1920s, Duchin was pianist for Leo Reisman's orchestra, forming his own outfit in 1931. He mesmerized most of the ladies at concerts, being exceedingly handsome and well mannered (a pundit tagged him "a virile Liberace"). Another critic observed that Duchin primarily catered "to the tastes of the upper crust of American society in live, radio, and film appearances," noting that he generally "stayed away from jazz numbers and tended to prefer more conventional and mainstream music." Duchin's band "was perhaps designed more for listening to at supper clubs than for dancing." The ensemble went on a successful goodwill tour of South America in the early 1940s. Duchin wore a navy lieutenant's uniform in World War II, absolutely dedicated to his military ventures while relinquishing his music. He picked up where he left off on his return and died of leukemia at 41. Actor Tyrone Power was featured in the title role of the 1956 motion picture *The Eddy Duchin Story* as Carmen Cavallaro tickled the ivories. Duchin's son, Peter, emerged during the 1960s as one of the most popular society bandleaders.

DUKE ELLINGTON

Born: April 29, 1899, Washington, D.C.
Died: May 24, 1974, New York, New York.
Chief Instrument: Piano.
Signature Songs: *East St. Louis Toodle-oo, Take the A Train.*
Legendary Tunes: *Black and Tan Fantasy, Come Sunday, Cotton Tail, Don't Get Around Much Anymore, I Let a Song Go Out of My Heart, In a Senti-*

mental Mood, In My Solitude, It Don't Mean a Thing If It Ain't Got That Swing, Mood Indigo, Satin Doll, Solitude, Sophisticated Lady.
Arrangers: Louis Bellson, Duke Ellington, Billy Strayhorn, more.
Vocalists: Ivy Anderson, Kay Davis, Jean Eldridge, Maria Ellington, Al Hibbler, Herb Jeffries, Betty Roche, Joya Sherrill, more.
Sidemen: Cat Anderson, Harold Baker, Louis Bellson, Barney Bigard, Jimmy Blanton, Lawrence Brown, Harry Carney, Paul Gonsalves, Sonny Greer, Jimmie Hamilton, Toby Hardwick, Johnny Hodges, Bubber Miley, Ray Nance, Oscar Pettiford, Marshall Royal, Al Sears, Willie Smith, Rex Stewart, Billy Strayhorn, Clark Terry, Juan Tizol, Ben Webster, Cootie Williams, more.
Radio Series:
A Date with the Duke. May 5–July 22, 1943, MBS, varied days, 10:15–10:30 P.M., sustaining.
A Date with the Duke. May 16–September 19, 1943, MBS, Sunday, 7:00–7:30 P.M., sustaining.
A Date with the Duke. March 31, 1945–September 21, 1946, ABC, Saturday, 5:00 P.M. to January, returning at 4:00 P.M. in April, in varied 15- to 60-minute formats, sustaining.
A Date with the Duke. Syndicated, 15 minutes, 48 shows in circulation.
Synopsis:

Edward Kennedy Ellington's adolescent friends took titles of nobility — which is when he acquired the appellation "Duke." He took up piano at age seven and upon high school graduation was earning a full-time living as a contractor, pianist and bandleader. In 1923, he broadcast locally from New York's Kentucky Club; by 1927, he was engaged at the prestigious Cotton Club. He was treated like royalty on a 1933 European tour, returning to the continent many times. When U.S. citizens began latching onto big bands in the mid–1930s, they found sounds Ellington had been playing for a decade. His is considered the best of the predominantly black outfits, overwhelming much of its white competition, reviewers noted, though he never got the deserved radio exposure it did. It's estimated he composed over 2,000 pieces of music including jazz classics, orchestral suites, ballets, Broadway shows and religious numbers. Said one pundit: "He is arguably the greatest musical talent of the twentieth century and his influence will remain for many decades to come." A member of his troupe declared, "I found him to be like my second father." Son Mercer took up the baton as conductor of the Ellington band after his dad's passing.

BENNY GOODMAN

Born: May 30, 1909, Chicago, Illinois.
Died: June 13, 1986, New York, New York.
Motto: *The King of Swing.*
Chief Instrument: Clarinet.
Signature Songs: *Let's Dance, Goodbye.*
Legendary Tunes: *And the Angels Sing, Don't Be That Way, Goody-Goody, It's Been So Long, Jersey Bounce, Moonglow, Sing Sing Sing, Stompin' at the Savoy, Symphony, Why Don't You Do Right?*
Arrangers: Frank De Vol, Fletcher Henderson, Horace Henderson, Gerry Mulligan, Jimmy Mundy, Edgar Sampson, Eddie Sauter, more.
Vocalists: Helen Forrest, Kay Foster, Dick Haymes, Ray Hendricks, Frances Hunt, Peg LaCentra, Peggy Lee, Art Lund, Margaret McCrae, Patti Page, Tommy Taylor, Martha Tilton, Louise Tobin, Betty Van, Helen Ward, more.
Sidemen: Dave Barbour, Count Basie, George Berg, Bunny Berigan, Milt Bernhart, Artie Bernstein, Eddie Bert, Johnny Best, Jimmy Blake, Vernon Brown, Billy Butterfield, Lee Castle, Sid Catlett, Charlie Christian, Ralph Collier, Corky Cornelius, Bill Crow,

Cutty Cutshall, Al Davis, Roy Eldridge, Ziggy Elman, Nick Fatool, Bud Freeman, Chuck Gentry, Stan Getz, Harry Goodman, Irving Goodman, Wardell Gray, Buddy Greco, Chris Griffin, Johnny Guarnieri, Lionel Hampton, Bill Harris, Benny Heller, Fletcher Henderson, Teddy Hill, Peanuts Hucko, Harry James, Sonny Igoe, Jerry Jerome, Nate Kazebier, Gene Krupa, Dave Matthews, Lou McGarity, Jimmy Maxwell, Murray McEachern, Miff Mole, Toots Mondello, Tommy Morgan, Vido Musso, Ralph Ruzzillo, Clint Neagley, Red Norvo, Mel Powell, Bernie Privin, Uan Rasey, Allan Reuss, Les Robinson, Arthur Rollini, George Rose, Babe Russin, Buddy Schutz, Julie Schwartz, Hymie Shertzer, Jess Stacy, Dave Tough, Vido Musso, Ed Wasserman, Sid Weiss, Cootie Williams, Teddy Wilson, more.

Radio Series:

The Ipana Troubadours. c1928, NBC, Wednesday, 9:00–9:30 P.M.; c1929, NBC Blue, Monday, 8:30–9:00 P.M., Bristol Myers, Inc. (Ipana toothpaste).

Let's Dance. December 1, 1934–June 8, 1935, NBC, Saturday, 10:30 P.M.–1:30 A.M., National Biscuit Company (Nabisco foodstuffs).

Eddie Dowling's Elgin Revue. March 17–June 9, 1936, NBC, Tuesday, 10:00–10:30 P.M., Elgin Watch Company (Elgin timepieces).

Benny Goodman's Swing School. June 30, 1936–June 22, 1937, CBS, Tuesday, 9:30–10:30 P.M.; June 29–September 21, 1937, CBS, Tuesday, 9:30–10:00 P.M., R. J. Reynolds Tobacco Company (Camel cigarettes).

Jack Oakie's College. September 28, 1937–March 22, 1938, CBS, Tuesday, 9:30–10:00 P.M., R. J. Reynolds Tobacco Company (Camel cigarettes).

Camel Caravan. March 29, 1938–June 20, 1939, CBS, Tuesday, 9:30–10:00 P.M., R. J. Reynolds Tobacco Company (Camel cigarettes).

Benny Goodman Caravan. July 8–December 30, 1939, NBC, Saturday, 10:00–10:30 P.M., sustaining.

What's New. February 10–May 5, 1941, NBC Blue, Monday, 7:30–8:00 P.M., P. Lorillard, Inc. (Old Gold cigarettes).

Housewarming Time. July 17–August 28, 1941, NBC, Thursday, 8:00–8:30 P.M., Holland Furnace Company (Holland heating units and services).

Benny Goodman Orchestra. January 10–February 21, 1942, MBS, Saturday, 2:00–2:30 P.M., sustaining.

Benny Goodman Orchestra. July 17–August 14, 1943, CBS, Saturday, 7:30–8:00 P.M., sustaining.

Music Festival. July 1–September 2, 1946, NBC, Monday, 9:30–10:00 P.M., sustaining.

The Victor Borge Show. September 9, 1946–June 30, 1947, NBC, Monday, 9:30–10:00 P.M., Socony Oil Company (Socony gasoline, oil, automotive products and services).

Synopsis:

Goodman joined Ben Pollack's band in 1926, later freelanced for others and formed his outfit in 1934, leading to his first big gig, *Let's Dance*, on radio. Touring across the nation the next year his music was met with disdain and open hostility until he reached the Palomar Ballroom in Pismo Beach. On Aug. 21, 1935, the first inkling of a national craze erupted; Benny's repertoire of Fletcher Henderson arrangements was wildly applauded, unleashing a new swing trend that would dominate the nation's music for almost 15 years. Overnight, Benny's badgered band was the hottest thing going. Competition sprang up rapidly but his aggregate remained at the forefront of swing music. His players had a love-hate relationship with him — he was perceived as "a stern and humorless taskmaster" and very tight on paydays ("As a person, there was no humanity at all," allowed one sideman). His was the first white band to integrate black musicians, setting a trend. A lot of their musical superlatives were included in the 1956 motion picture *The Benny Goodman Story*.

WOODY HERMAN

Born: May 16, 1913, Milwaukee, Wisconsin.
Died: October 29, 1987, Los Angeles, California.
Motto: *The Band That Plays the Blues.*
Chief Instrument: Clarinet.
Signature Songs: *Blue Flame, Blue Prelude.*
Legendary Tunes: *Blues in the Night, Blues on Parade, Caledonia, Do Nothin' Till You Hear from Me, Don't You Know or Don't You Care?, Early Autumn, It's My Turn Now, Laura, Let It Snow!, Sabre Dance, Woodchopper's Ball.*
Arrangers: Joe Bishop, Gordon Jenkins, Dave Matthews, Chick Reeves, Shorty Rogers, more.
Vocalists: Jean Bowes, Dillagene (Carlson), Carolyn Grey, Woody Herman, Carol Kaye, Sharri Kaye, Kathleen Lane, Muriel Lane, Mary Ann McCall, Sue Mitchell, Anita O'Day, Billie Rogers, Lynne Stevens, Frances Wayne, more.
Sidemen: Tony Aless, Gene Ammons, Jack Archer, Harry Babasin, Billy Bauer, Sonny Berman, Bill Berry, Bob Brookmeyer, Monty Budwig, Ralph Burns, Bill Byrne, Conte Candoli, Pete Candoli, Frankie Carlson, Serge Chaloff, Al Cohn, Dick Collins, Skippy DeSair, Victor Feldman, Chuck Flores, Med Flory, Carl Fontana, Charlie Frankhauser, Stan Getz, Terry Gibbs, Jimmy Giuffre, Bernie Glow, Urbie Green, Jack Hanna, Bill Harris, Neal Hefti, Nick Hupfer, Margie Hyams, Chubby Jackson, Richie Kamuca, Ed Kiefer, Bobby Lamb, Don Lamond, Don Lanphere, John LaPorta, Cliff Leeman, Saxey Mansfield, Marky Markowitz, Sam Marowitz, Arno Marsh, Pete Mondello, Vido Musso, Sal Nistico, Fred Otis, Bill Perkins, Ralph Pfiffner, Flip Phillips, Nat Pierce, Chick Reeves, Neil Reid, Red Rodney, Elizabeth Rogers, Shorty Rogers, Ernie Royal, Sam Rubinowich, Buddy Savitt, Kermit Simmons, Zoot Sims, Earl Swope, Herbie Steward, Frank Tiberi, Cy Touff, Davey Tough, Carl Warwick, Chuck Wayne, Ray Wetzel, Clarence Willard, Ollie Wilson, Kai Winding, Walter Yoder, more.
Radio Series:
Woody Herman Orchestra. March 26–April 30, 1942, MBS, Thursday, 8:30–9:00 P.M., sustaining.
The Old Gold Show. Summer 1944, CBS, Wednesday, 8:00–8:30 P.M., P. Lorillard, Inc. (Old Gold cigarettes).
The Woody Herman Show. October 13, 1945–January 19, 1946, ABC, Saturday, 8:00–8:30 P.M.; January 25–July 5, 1946, ABC, Friday, 8:00–8:30 P.M., Wildroot Creme Oil hair tonic.
The Electric Hour. July 13–August 31, 1947, CBS, Sunday, 4:30–5:00 P.M., Local electric company cooperative association.
Woody Herman Orchestra. 1955–1956, CBS, Saturday, 10:05–10:30 P.M., sustaining.
Synopsis:
At age six Woody Herman sang and tap-danced in vaudeville. At nine he was billed as "The Boy Wonder of the Clarinet." He joined his first band at 17 and soon played for conductors Harry Sosnik, Gus Arnheim and Isham Jones. He and arranger Joe Bishop took over Jones' band in 1936 when that maestro bowed out. They debuted in the Roseland Ballroom in New York, but it was 1939 when they attracted widespread acclaim with Bishop's *Woodchopper's Ball*. Herman's was the first band

held over at the Hollywood Palladium (1943) and that year he was the first to introduce a female trumpeter, Elizabeth Rogers. Unlike most contemporaries, he relied heavily on younger men, many just out of college, expecting them to contribute heavily. He was appreciated: "No name bandleader has ever been better liked by the men who worked for him as well as those for whom he works," wrote a columnist. The group continued well past the big band era, appearing for a 40th anniversary at Carnegie Hall in 1976. Poor financial decisions left Herman owing more than a million dollars to the IRS when he died. A Woody Herman Society purposes "to keep the Blue Flame infinitely burning."

SAMMY KAYE

Born: March 13, 1910, Lakewood, Ohio.
Died: June 2, 1987, Ridgewood, New Jersey.
Motto: *Swing and Sway with Sammy Kaye.*
Chief Instrument: Clarinet.
Signature Song: *Kaye's Melody.*
Legendary Tunes: *Daddy, Harbor Lights, It Isn't Fair, Swing and Sway, Until Tomorrow.*
Arrangers: Milt Buckner, more.
Vocalists: Tony Alamo, George Brandon, Jimmy Brown, Don Cornell, Maury Cross, Marty McKenna, Tommy Ryan, Charlie Wilson, Arthur Wright, more.
Sidemen: Dale Cornell, Roy Eldridge, Ralph Flanagan, Gene Krupa, Marty Oscard, Teddy Wilson, more.
Radio Series:

Sammy Kaye Orchestra. 1937–1938, MBS, 8:30–9:00 P.M., sustaining.

Sammy Kaye Orchestra. December 17, 1938–April 29, 1939, MBS, Saturday, 5:00–5:45 P.M., sustaining.

Sammy Kaye Orchestra. December 16, 1939–April 27, 1940, MBS, Saturday, 5:00–6:00 P.M., sustaining.

Sensation and Swing. January 1–June 24, 1940, NBC, Monday, 7:30–8:00 P.M., Sensation cigarettes.

Sammy Kaye Orchestra. January 12, 1941–February 7, 1943, NBC, Sunday, time unsubstantiated, sustaining.

Sammy Kaye Orchestra. June 4–July 9, 1941, NBC, Wednesday, 7:30–8:00 P.M., sustaining.

Sammy Kaye Orchestra. November 1, 1941–January 3, 1942, NBC Blue, Saturday, 10:30–11:00 P.M., sustaining.

The New Old Gold Show. January 27, 1943–March 29, 1944, CBS, Wednesday, 8:00–8:30 P.M., P. Lorillard, Inc. (Old Gold cigarettes).

Sammy Kaye Sunday Serenade. January 2–April 30, 1944, ABC, Sunday, 1:30–2:00 P.M., sustaining.

Tangee Varieties. May 7, 1944–August 26, 1945, ABC, Sunday, 1:30–1:55 P.M., Tangee.

Tangee Varieties. August 24, 1944–February 15, 1945, MBS, Thursday, 8:30–9:00 P.M., Tangee.

Tangee Varieties. February 23–May 18, 1945, ABC, Friday, 10:00–10:30 P.M., Tangee.

Sammy Kaye Sunday Serenade. November 18, 1945–January 25, 1948, ABC, Sunday, 1:30–1:55 P.M., Rayve shampoo, Richard Hudnut home permanents and Drene shampoo.

Sammy Kaye Orchestra. January 23–June 19, 1946, ABC, Wednesday, 9:30–10:00 P.M., sustaining; June 25–August 20, 1946, ABC, Tuesday, 8:30–9:00 P.M., sustaining.

So You Want to Lead a Band. September 5–October 24, 1946, ABC, Thursday, 10:00–10:30 P.M., sustaining; November 7, 1946–January 2, 1947, ABC, Thursday, 9:30–10:00 P.M., sustaining.

Sammy Kaye Orchestra. January 6, 1947–June 7, 1948, ABC, Monday, 9:30–10:00 P.M., sustaining.

Chesterfield Supper Club. June 7–September 24, 1948, NBC, Monday–Friday,

7:00–7:15 P.M., Liggett & Myers Tobacco Company (Chesterfield cigarettes).

Sammy Kaye Orchestra. 1948–1949, 15 minutes, network, day and time unsubstantiated, Chrysler Corporation (Chrysler and Plymouth automobiles).

Sammy Kaye Sunday Serenade. November 13, 1949–February 26, 1950, CBS, Sunday, 2:00–2:30 P.M., U.S. Treasury Department.

Sammy Kaye Sunday Serenade. April 2, 1950–September 30, 1951, ABC, Sunday, 1:00–1:30 P.M., sustaining.

Sammy Kaye's Sylvania Serenade. October 7, 1951–March 30, 1952, ABC, Sunday, 5:00–5:30 P.M., Sylvania Corporation (Sylvania tubes).

Sammy Kaye Sunday Serenade. April 20, 1952–October 4, 1953, NBC, Sunday, 12 noon–12:30 P.M., sustaining.

Sammy Kaye's Cameo Room. July 13, 1953–May 7, 1954, ABC, Monday–Friday, 8:15–8:30 P.M., sustaining.

Sammy Kaye Sunday Serenade. 1953–1954, MBS, Sunday, 2:30–3:00 P.M., sustaining.

Sammy Kaye Orchestra. June 6, 1954–October 23, 1955, ABC, Sunday, 9:30–10:00 P.M., sustaining.

Sammy Kaye Orchestra. June 8, 1954–October 28, 1955, ABC, Tuesday–Friday (4 nights), 9:00–9:25 P.M., sustaining.

Sammy Kaye Orchestra. January 9, 1955–February 12, 1956, ABC, Sunday, 9:35–9:55 P.M., sustaining.

Synopsis:

Sammy Kaye organized a band while a student at Ohio State University, playing college dances. Setting up his own cluster in Cleveland, he initially became known beyond those confines via radio broadcasts, beginning over Mutual from Bill Green's Casino near Pittsburgh. He moved to the Hotel Commodore in New York City in 1938. His programs instituted all sorts of devices into performances, classifying his as a "mickey mouse" band, though that never disturbed Kaye. Perhaps his most unusual gimmick was on the program *So You Want to Lead a Band* in which he allowed volunteers from the audience to conduct his outfit. The band hammed it up on those occasions, to the complete delight of the crowd. Kaye gave away a ton of batons to aspiring impresarios. An astute businessman, he made decisions that served the band well and made himself an enormously wealthy individual. As with several other major groups of that era, a touring Sammy Kaye Orchestra continues to stage concerts across America today.

WAYNE KING

Born: February 18, 1901, Savannah, Illinois.
Died: July 16, 1985, Paradise Valley, Arizona.
Motto: *The Waltz King.*
Chief Instrument: Saxophone.
Signature Song: *The Waltz You Save for Me.*
Legendary Tunes: *Alice Blue Gown, Anniversary Waltz, Beautiful Love, Blue Danube, I'd Love to Live in Loveland (with a Girl Like You), Melody of Love, The Night Is Young and You're So Beautiful, What'll I Do?*
Radio Series:

Wayne King Orchestra. July 29, 1930–January 27, 1931, NBC, Tuesday, 8:00–8:30 P.M., Pure Oil Company (Pure gasoline, oil and other vehicle products and services).

Lady Esther Serenade. September 27, 1931–July 24, 1932, NBC, Sunday, 3:00–3:30 P.M.; September 4, 1932–April 8, 1934, NBC, Sunday, 3:00–3:30 P.M., Lady Esther Company (Lady Esther cosmetics).

Wayne King Orchestra. March 30–June 1, 1932, NBC, Wednesday, 5:30–5:45 P.M., sustaining.

Lady Esther Serenade. October 11, 1932–

Aug. 23, 1938, NBC, Tuesday, 8:30–9:00 P.M., sustaining.
Lady Esther Serenade. October 9, 1933–April 9, 1934, CBS, Monday, 10:00–10:30 P.M., Lady Esther Company (Lady Esther cosmetics).
Lady Esther Serenade. December 6, 1933–December 21, 1938, NBC, Wednesday, 8:30–9:00 P.M., Lady Esther Company (Lady Esther cosmetics).
Lady Esther Serenade. April 15, 1934–February 17, 1936, CBS, Sunday and Monday, 10:00–10:30 P.M., Lady Esther Company (Lady Esther cosmetics).
Lady Esther Serenade. February 24, 1936–October 5, 1938, CBS, Monday, 10:00–10:30 P.M., Lady Esther Company (Lady Esther cosmetics).
Wayne King Orchestra. March 15–July 19, 1936, MBS, Sunday, 6:30–7:00 P.M., sustaining.
Wayne King Orchestra. September 2–October 7, 1938, NBC, Friday, 10:00–10:30 P.M., sustaining.
Wayne King Orchestra. October 21, 1939–June 15, 1940, CBS, Saturday, 8:30–9:00 P.M.; October 5, 1940–January 25, 1941, Colgate-Palmolive-Peet, Inc. (Halo shampoo, Cashmere Bouquet soap and other personal care goods).
Wayne King Orchestra. June 7, 1941–March 21, 1942, CBS, Saturday, 7:30–8:00 P.M., Luxor.
Wayne King Orchestra. June 3–September 23, 1945, NBC, Sunday, 7:00–7:30 P.M., American Tobacco Company (Lucky Strike cigarettes).
Wayne King Orchestra. June 14–September 6, 1946, CBS, Friday, 9:30–10:00 P.M., Rexall Drug Company (Rexall drug stores).
Wayne King Orchestra. 1946–1947, ZIV syndicated quarter-hours, 78 programs in circulation.

Synopsis:

About 1927, Wayne King and his entourage broadcast regularly from the Aragon Ballroom in Chicago. Those early shows brought him fame and firmly established the Aragon as one of the nation's prominent dance palaces. King acquired a strong attachment to waltzes there, his music often dubbed "dreamy." It was usually interspersed with poetry read by Phil Stewart and later by Franklyn McCormack. All of it strongly appealed to the senior set, mostly those 65 and above, never the bobbysoxers. A brother and sister who were mixing up cosmetics at home liked King. They used him on radio to introduce their products. He was paid $500 per week at the start but the commercial venture was so successful that he was soon getting $15,000 every week! Of his Lady Esther ties a historian acknowledged: "King helped establish this struggling cosmetics company and made it one of radio's most potent advertisers." On February 9, 1964, he returned to the Aragon. As grandmas and grandpas waltzed once more, King played his "dreamy" tunes. The owners were converting the place into a roller skating rink afterward, signifying that the era of the big bands had definitely passed, never to return.

GUY LOMBARDO

Born: June 19, 1902, London, Ontario, Canada.
Died: November 5, 1977, Houston, Texas.
Motto: *The Sweetest Music This Side of Heaven.*
Signature Song: *Auld Lang Syne.*
Legendary Tunes: *Boo-Hoo, Charmaine, Easter Parade, Enjoy Yourself, Everywhere You Go, Give Me a Little Kiss, Goodnight Sweetheart, I'm Getting Sentimental Over You, The Last Round-up, Little Girl, Lost, Managua Nicaragua, Paradise, Penny Serenade, Seems Like Old Times, Stars Fell on Alabama, Sweethearts on Parade, Third Man Theme.*
Arrangers: Carmen Lombardo, more.

Vocalists: Kenny Gardner, Rose Marie Lombardo, more.

Sidemen: Mert Curtis, Ben Davies, Jim Dillon, Hugo D'Ippolito, Dudley Fosdick, George Gowans, Frances Henry, Fred "Derf" Higman, Fritz Kreitzer, Carmen Lombardo, Lebert Lombardo, Victor Lombardo, Larry Owen, more.

Radio Series:

Guy Lombardo Orchestra. December 25, 1928–1929, CBS, Tuesday, 11:00 P.M.–midnight, William J. Wrigley Company (Wrigley's Doublemint, Juicy Fruit and Spearmint gums).

Guy Lombardo Orchestra. October 1929–February 15, 1932, CBS, Monday, 10:00–10:30 P.M., General Cigar Company (Robert Burns Panatella cigars).

The George Burns and Gracie Allen Show. February 22–May 16, 1932, CBS, Monday, 10:00–10:30 P.M.; May 25, 1932–January 4, 1933, CBS, Wednesday, 9:00–9:30 P.M.; January 11, 1933–September 13, 1933, CBS, Wednesday, 9:30–10:00 P.M., General Cigar Company (Robert Burns Panatella and White Owl cigars).

Pleasure Island. July 11, 1934–July 3, 1935, NBC, Wednesday, 10:00–10:30 P.M., Plough, Inc. (health care products).

Guy Lombardo Orchestra. July 8, 1935–June 29, 1936, CBS, Monday, 8:00–8:30 P.M., Standard Oil Company (Esso gasoline, oil, other vehicle products and services).

Guy Lombardo Orchestra. September 6, 1936–August 14, 1938, CBS, Sunday, 5:30–6:00 P.M., Bond Baking Company (Bond bread).

Guy Lombardo Orchestra. 1936–1937, MBS, Thursday, 8:30–9:00 P.M., sustaining.

Guy Lombardo Orchestra. October 10, 1938–July 10, 1939, CBS, Monday, 10:00–10:30 P.M.; July 17–September 4, 1939, CBS, Monday, 9:30–10:00 P.M.; September 11, 1939–July 28, 1941, CBS, Monday, 10:00–10:30 P.M., Lady Esther Company (Lady Esther cosmetics).

Guy Lombardo Orchestra. October 14, 1938–January 26, 1940, NBC, Friday, 10:00–10:30 P.M., Lady Esther Company (Lady Esther cosmetics).

Guy Lombardo Orchestra. November 20, 1940–April 30, 1941, MBS, Wednesday, 9:30–9:55 P.M., sustaining.

Guy Lombardo Orchestra. August 2, 1941–July 11, 1942. CBS, Saturday, 8:00–8:30 P.M., Colgate-Palmolive-Peet, Inc. (Colgate toothpaste and other personal care goods).

Guy Lombardo Orchestra. March 8–December 20, 1943, CBS, Monday, 10:30 P.M.–midnight, Ballantine Brewing Company (Ballantine ale and beer).

Three Ring Time. October 19–November 23, 1943, CBS, Tuesday, 10:45–11:00 P.M., Ballantine Brewing Company (Ballantine ale and beer).

Musical Autographs. January 16–April 30, 1944, NBC Blue/ABC, Sunday, 10:30–11:00 P.M., Chelsea.

Guy Lombardo Orchestra. May 6–December 30, 1944, NBC Blue/ABC, Saturday, 10:00–10:30 P.M., sustaining.

Guy Lombardo Orchestra. January 1–May 7, 1945, ABC, Monday, 10:00–10:30 P.M., Chelsea.

Guy Lombardo Orchestra. May 15, 1945–March 26, 1946, ABC, Tuesday, 9:00–9:30 P.M., Chelsea.

Guy Lombardo Orchestra. July 2–16, 1948, CBS, Friday, 9:00–9:30 P.M., sustaining.

Lombardoland USA. October 30, 1948–May 19, 1957, MBS, Saturday, 9:30–10:00 P.M., sustaining. (moved to Sunday night in final season).

Guy Lombardo Orchestra. July 3–September 11, 1949, NBC, Sunday, 7:30–8:00 P.M., sustaining.

Guy Lombardo Orchestra. June 4–September 3, 1950, CBS, Sunday, 7:00–7:30 P.M., sustaining.

Guy Lombardo Orchestra. July 13–September 11, 1953, NBC, Monday–Friday, 7:39–8:00 P.M., sustaining.

Guy Lombardo Orchestra. November 27, 1955–July 1, 1956, CBS, Sunday, 12:30–1:00 P.M., sustaining.

Guy Lombardo Orchestra. Syndicated, produced by ZIV, 92 programs available.

Synopsis:

Lombardo & company (including four brothers) began developing their musical formula in the early 1920s at home, never altering it as they made successive stops in Cleveland, Chicago and to the eminent Roosevelt Grill in New York City. Carmen Lombardo, the group's musical director, and brothers Lebert and Guy owned the band together, but from the start Guy took leadership, earning the respect of those around him. An industry insider claimed he was "the nicest man ever in the music business." From the late 1920s until the present, Lombardo's rendition of *Auld Lang Syne* has been synonymous with ushering in every new year on the airwaves. Tom DeLong summarized the unit's technique: "The Lombardo style focused on a direct singable interpretation of easily comprehended melodies. A distinctively mellow sound, the music of Guy's Royal Canadians never fell out of favor." In later years Lombardo diversified into restaurant ownership, purchasing enterprises at Freeport, Long Island and Tampa Bay, Florida. Since 1989, Al Pierson, who earlier conducted his own ballroom dancing band, has sustained the Lombardo tradition by leading a band recreating the sound of the original.

VINCENT LOPEZ

Born: December 30, 1894, Brooklyn, New York.
Died: September 20, 1975, North Miami, Florida.
Chief Instrument: Piano.
Signature Song: *Nola.*
Legendary Tunes: *La Paloma, On the Radio.*
Vocalists: Betty Hutton, Marion Hutton, Johnny Messner, more.
Sidemen: Lou Bring, Xavier Cugat, Johnny Messner, Glenn Miller, Artie Shaw, Rudy Vallee, more.

Radio Series:

Vincent Lopez Orchestra. September 5–November 14, 1928, CBS, Wednesday, 10:00 P.M., Kolster Radio Company (Kolster radios).

Vincent Lopez Orchestra. February 5–June 25, 1933, NBC Blue, Sunday, 10:15–1045 P.M., sustaining.

Vincent Lopez Orchestra. 1934–1935, NBC Blue, twice weekly, days and time unsubstantiated; 1934–1935, NBC, Friday, time unsubstantiated, sustaining.

Vincent Lopez Orchestra. 1935–1936, CBS, Saturday, time unsubstantiated, sustaining.

The Nash Program (aka *The Speed Show*). October 3, 1936–June 26, 1937, CBS, Saturday, 9:00–9:30 P.M., Nash Motors (Nash and Lafayette automobiles and Kelvinator appliances).

Vincent Lopez Orchestra. Summer 1937, CBS, Sunday, time unsubstantiated, sustaining.

Vincent Lopez Orchestra. Summer 1939, NBC Blue, Thursday, 10:30–11:00 P.M., sustaining.

Vincent Lopez Orchestra. June 30–August 29, 1941, NBC, three to five days weekly, 1:15–1:30 P.M., sustaining.

Vincent Lopez Orchestra. September 2, 1941–May 31, 1943, NBC Blue, two days weekly, 2:00–2:30 P.M., sustaining.

Luncheon with Lopez. June 14, 1943–September 23, 1944, MBS, Monday–Saturday, 1:30–2:00 P.M.; September 25, 1944–September 21, 1946, MBS, Monday–Saturday, 1:30–1:45 P.M., sustaining.

Pick and Pat. MBS, January 18–July 18, 1944, Tuesday, 8:30–9:00 P.M., Helbros Watch Company (Helbros timepieces).

Vincent Lopez Orchestra. October 11–December 6, 1948, NBC, Monday, 7:30–7:45 P.M., sustaining.

Vincent Lopez Orchestra. 1949–1950, NBC, Monday–Friday, 1:00–1:30 P.M., sustaining.

Luncheon with Lopez. 1950–1951, MBS, Monday–Friday, 1:15–1:45 P.M.; 1951–1954, MBS, Monday–Friday, 1:30–2:00 P.M., sustaining.

Vincent Lopez Orchestra. 1950–1951, NBC, Saturday, 12:30–1:00 P.M., sustaining.

Vincent Lopez Orchestra. June 16, 1951–January 9, 1954, ABC, Saturday, 1:30–2:00 P.M., sustaining.

Luncheon with Lopez. 1954–1955, MBS, Monday–Friday, 1:30–1:55 P.M., sustaining.

Vincent Lopez Orchestra. 1954–1955, ABC, Monday–Friday, 5:45–6:00 P.M., sustaining.

Shake the Maracas. 1955–June 23, 1956, ABC, Saturday, 1:30–2:00 P.M., reduced to 1:35–1:55 P.M. by early 1956, sustaining.

Vincent Lopez Orchestra. June 29–October 26, 1955, ABC, Wednesday, 9:30–10:00 P.M., sustaining.

Luncheon with Lopez. 1955–1956, MBS, Monday–Friday, 1:30–2:00 P.M., sustaining.

Vincent Lopez Orchestra. 1955–1956, ABC, Monday–Friday, 5:45–5:55 P.M., sustaining.

Synopsis:

Long before the big band craze swept the nation, Vincent Lopez was a "name" in the business. About 1917, he gave up preparing for the priesthood in favor of a musical career. In the early 1920s, his aggregate featured his piano playing. In the 1930s and 1940s, he produced "fairly up-to-date if never distinguished or inventive music," said one critic. His was among a handful of ensembles selected for NBC's inaugural broadcast in 1926. He was scared of microphones at the outset: on his first broadcast he managed to utter just four words— "Hello everybody, Lopez speaking"—a catchphrase that followed from then on. He is recalled for seemingly thousands of broadcasts from the Grill Room of the Hotel Taft where he played for 25 years. Often that venue closed at 9 o'clock—his sidemen liked that for it allowed them to hear—and sometimes perform in—other bands that played later in the evening. "Had he featured arrangements to match, his might have been one of the era's better big bands," a music historian allowed. His memoir is appropriately titled *Lopez Speaking: My Life and How I Changed It.*

FREDDY MARTIN

Born: December 9, 1906, Cleveland, Ohio.
Died: September 30, 1983, Newport Beach, California.
Motto: *Music in the Martin Manner.*
Chief Instrument: Saxophone.
Signature Song: *Tonight We Love.*
Legendary Tunes: *The Banana Boat Song, Dream, The Hut Sut Song, I've Got a Lovely Bunch of Cocoanuts, Linger Awhile, Wabash Blues, Why Don't We Do This More Often?, Yes We Have No Bananas.*
Arrangers: Ray Austin, more.
Vocalists: Elmer Feldkamp, Merv Griffin, Russ Morgan, Terry Shand, Eddie Stone, Stuart Wade, Helen Ward, more.
Sidemen: Barclay Allen, Murray Arnold, Eddie Bergman, Jack Fina, Russ Morgan, Terry Shand, Eddie Stone, Claude Thornhill, more.
Radio Series:

Freddy Martin Orchestra. January 16–September 29, 1933, CBS, Monday/Wednesday/Friday, 7:30–7:45 P.M., Tydol Oil Company.

Going Places. 1934, 15 minutes, specific information unsubstantiated, sustaining.

Vicks Open House. October 7, 1934–March 31, 1935, CBS, Sunday, 5:00–5:30 P.M., Vick Chemical Company (Vicks healthcare goods).

Freddy Martin Orchestra. 1935–1936, MBS, Sunday, 7:15–7:30 P.M., later 7:15–7:45 P.M., Eden Liquid Dry shampoo.

Penthouse Serenade. December 13, 1936–March 21, 1937, NBC, Sunday, 4:00–4:30 P.M., International Silver Company (International silver).

Freddy Martin Orchestra. August 4–September 8, 1941, CBS, Monday, 10:00–10:30 P.M., sustaining.

Freddy Martin Orchestra. February 9–October 12, 1942, CBS, Monday, 10:00–10:30 P.M., Lady Esther Company (Lady Esther cosmetics).

Freddy Martin Orchestra. July 4–September 5, 1942, NBC, Saturday, 8:30–9:00 P.M., Procter & Gamble Company (Duz detergent).

Freddy Martin Orchestra. April 24–May 22, 1943, NBC, Saturday, 10:15–10:30 P.M., sustaining.

The Jack Carson Show. 1944 (specific dates unsubstantiated), CBS, Wednesday, 9:30–10:00 P.M., sustaining.

It's Showtime from Hollywood. c1947, ZIV quarter-hour syndicated series, 41 programs released.

Freddy Martin Orchestra. July 8–November 4, 1956, CBS, Sunday, 12:30–1:00 P.M., sustaining.

Synopsis:

Freddy Martin was raised in an orphanage. He played drums quite early and tenor saxophone in his teens. In 1931, he formed his own band with a smooth, sweet, syrupy style following the model of Guy Lombardo and his Royal Canadians. For about a half century he successfully performed in hotels, on radio, television and in motion pictures. He never changed his style, even when he was music director at Elvis Presley's initial appearance in Las Vegas. Though he never tried to be a jazz musician, jazz stars were enamored with him, many taking their cues from him. The Cocoanut Grove was his principal venue, the one to which he returned from annual tours well into the 1960s. In 1947, Martin's disc and transcription royalties reached $200,000, putting him among the five best-selling RCA Victor artists, and outdistancing such contenders as Perry Como and Vaughn Monroe. The bandleader was well liked by his peers. An MCA rep once said: "Freddy Martin is such a nice man; he's almost too nice for his own good."

GLENN MILLER

Born: March 1, 1904, Clarinda, Iowa.
Died: December 15, 1944, English Channel.
Chief Instrument: Trombone.
Signature Song: *Moonlight Serenade.*
Legendary Tunes: *At Last, Chattanooga Choo Choo, In the Mood, Juke Box Saturday Night, Pennsylvania 65000, Poinciana, Serenade in Blue, String of Pearls, Tuxedo Junction.*
Arrangers: Bill Finegan, Jerry Gray, Billy May, more.
Vocalists: Dorothy Claire, Ray Eberle, Marion Hutton, Paula Kelly and The Modernaires (Ralph Brewster, Bill Conway, Hal Dickenson, Chuck Goldstein), Kitty Lane, Gail Reese, more.
Sidemen: Trigger Alpert, Ray Anthony, Johnny Austin, Gordon "Tex" Beneke, Johnny Best, Les Biegel, Sterling Bose, Rolly Bundoc, Ernie Caceres, Frank D'Annolfo, Peewee Erwin, Irving Fazola, Jack Ferrier, Hank Freeman, Gabe Gelinas, Chuck Gentry, Freddy Guerra, Bobby Hackett, Peanuts Hucko, Jerry Jerome, Manny Klein, Al Klink, Jack Lathrop, Steve Lipkins, Chummy MacGregor, Carmen Mastren, Billy May, Dick McDonough, Hal McIntyre, Ray McKinley, Dale McMickle, Johnny Mince, Skip Nelson, Bobby Nichols,

Nat Peck, Mel Powell, Bob Price, Jimmy Priddy, Bernie Privin, Maurice "Moe" Purtill, Wilbur Schwartz, George Siravo, Howard Smith, Bob Spangler, Charlie Spivak, Steve Steck, Paul Tanner, Graham Young, Zeke Zarchy, more.

Radio Series:

Glenn Miller Orchestra. 1939, CBS, Monday–Friday, 15 minutes, sustaining.

Chesterfield Time. December 27, 1939, CBS, Wednesday, 8:30–9:00 P.M., Liggett & Myers Tobacco Company (Chesterfield cigarettes)

Chesterfield Time. January 2, 1940–Sept. 24, 1942, CBS, Tuesday/Wednesday/Thursday, 10:00–10:15 P.M., Liggett & Myers Tobacco Company (Chesterfield cigarettes).

Moonlight Serenade. Syndicated, produced by ZIV c1940, 52 shows available.

Sunset Serenade. September 6, 1941–January 3, 1942, NBC Blue, Saturday, 5:00–6:00 P.M., sustaining.

Sunset Serenade. January 10–May 30, 1942, MBS, Saturday, 5:00–6:00 P.M., sustaining.

I Sustain the Wings. July 10–September 4, 1943, CBS, Saturday, 2:05–2:30 P.M., sustaining.

I Sustain the Wings. September 18, 1943–June 10, 1944, NBC, Saturday, 11:30 P.M.–midnight, sustaining.

I Sustain the Wings. September 1–November 24, 1945, NBC, Saturday, 11:30 P.M., sustaining (featuring the Glenn Miller Orchestra conducted by Jerry Gray).

Synopsis:

After joining Ben Pollack's band in Los Angeles in 1924, Miller moved with it to Chicago and then to New York (1928). Starting his own outfit, he struggled two years, disbanded, regrouped and enjoyed a few successful years (1938–1942). Disbanding again, he joined the Army Air Force to direct the American Band in Europe in World War II. Flying from Bedford, England, to Paris, his plane vanished; neither it nor its three occupants was heard from again. Jerry Gray and Ray McKinley directed the service ensemble subsequently. After the war several impresarios conducted a reconstituted Miller entourage: Tex Beneke (1946), Ray McKinley (1956), Buddy DeFranco (1965) and Larry O'Brien (1988). A Miller aggregate, claiming ties to the most memorable unit (1938–1942), performs concerts around the globe. Actor Jimmy Stewart portrayed Miller in the 1953 film *The Glenn Miller Story* with June Allyson as his wife. Musician-journalist George Simon insisted: "Of all the outstanding popular dance bands, the one that evokes the most memories of how wonderfully romantic it all was, the one whose music people most want to hear over and over again, is the band of the late Glenn Miller."

ARTIE SHAW

Born: May 26, 1910, New York, New York.

Died: December 30, 2004, Thousand Oaks, California.

Motto: *The King of the Clarinet.*

Chief Instrument: Clarinet.

Signature Song: *Nightmare.*

Legendary Tunes: *Begin the Beguine, Bill, The Carioca, Frenesi, Lover Come Back to Me, Cross Your Heart, Keepin' Myself for You, My Heart Belongs to Daddy, Rosalie, Special Delivery Stomp, Summit Ridge Drive.*

Arrangers: Ray Conniff, Dick Jones, Joe Lipman, Harry Rodgers, Dave Rose, Claude Thornhill, more.

Vocalists: Anita Boyer, Helen Forrest, Fredda Gibson (aka Georgia Gibbs), Billie Holiday, Lena Horne, Kitty Kallen, Paula Kelly, Peg La Centra, Bonnie Lake, Tony Pastor, Mel Torme and the Mel-Tones, Bea Wain, more.

Sidemen: George Arus, George Auld, Frank Beach, Johnny Best, Claude Bowen, Russell Brown, Les Burness, Billy Butterfield, Lee Castle, Ray Conniff, Malcolm Crane, Tommy DiCarlo, Sam Donahue, Roy Eldridge, Tony Faso, Hank Freeman, Conrad Gozzo, Jerry Gray, Johnny Guarnieri, Les Jenkins, Jack Jenney, Maxie Kaminsky, Barney Kessel, Bob Kitsis, Cliff Leeman, Joe Lipman, Tommy Mace, Dodo Marmarosa, Pat McNaughton, Hot Lips Page, Tony Pastor, Ron Perry, Chuck Peterson, Pete Peterson, Bernie Privin, Buddy Rich, Les Robinson, Harry Rodgers, Claude Thornhill, Davey Tough, Sid Weiss, George Wettling, more.

Radio Series:

Melody and Madness. November 20, 1938–November 12, 1939, CBS, Sunday, 10:00–10:30 P.M., P. Lorillard, Inc. (Old Gold cigarettes).

The George Burns and Gracie Allen Show. July 1, 1940–March 24, 1941, NBC, Monday, 7:30–8:00 P.M., Hormel Company (Hormel meat products).

Synopsis:

Assessing Artie Shaw's music, an author claimed: "One of the best swing outfits ever, led by an eccentric genius who couldn't stomach the harsh light of fame." It's true. He didn't like the adulation that went with big bands, refusing to sign autographs. He was a man dispossessed — with strong indications that he, himself, was often to blame. He dispossessed himself of bands he started in 1935, 1936, 1940, 1940 again, 1941, 1942, 1943, 1944, 1949 and 1953. He suffered a rare blood disease and collapsed on more than one occasion, prompting real uncertainty. He was a talented man who was incessantly restless. He dumped one band and took off to Mexico to contemplate his circumstances. Among his eight wives were movie idols Lana Turner and Ava Gardner and also Betty Kern, composer Jerome Kern's daughter. When he quit the music business in 1954, he never looked back; his afterlife included farming, gun collecting, writing (a biography, *The Trouble with Cinderella*) and dispensing motion pictures. Sickly much of his career, ironically he outlived all of the other key bandmasters.

PAUL WHITEMAN

Born: March 28, 1890, Denver, Colorado.
Died: December 29, 1967, Doylestown, Pennsylvania.
Motto: *The King of Jazz.*
Chief Instrument: Violin.
Signature Song: *Rhapsody in Blue.*
Legendary Tunes: *At Sundown, Blue Monday, I'll Never Be the Same, Mississippi Mud, My Blue Heaven, Stairway to the Stars, Three O'Clock in the Morning, Wang Wang Blues, Whispering, Wonderful One.*
Arrangers: Tutti Camarata, Duke Ellington, Ferde Grofe, Joe Mooney, Jimmy Mundy, Don Redman, Buddy Weed, more.
Vocalists: Mildred Bailey, Morton Downey, Joan Edwards, Jack Fulton, Billie Holiday, Frank Howard, Ruth Lee, Red McKenzie, Johnny Mercer, Dolly Mitchell, The Modernaires, Ramona, The Rhythm Boys (Harry Barris, Bing Crosby, Al Rinker), Joe Venetia, more.
Sidemen: Roy Baggy, Elmer Belcher, Bix Beiderbecke, Henry Busse, Jimmy Dorsey, Tommy Dorsey, Vic Engle, Chuck Evans, Tony Giannelli, Ross Gorman, Noel Kilgen, Eddie Lang, Murray McEachern, Buss Michaels, Carl Orech, Johnny Owens, Mike Pingatore, Kit Reid, Willie Rodriguez, Bob Romeo, Artie Shapiro, Ernie Striker, Charlie Teagarden, Jack Teagarden, Frankie Trumbauer, Joe Venuti, Buddy Weed, Alvy Weisfeld (aka Alvy West), George Wettling, Joe White, Murray Williams, more.

Radio Series:

The Old Gold Hour. February 5, 1929–

May 6, 1930, CBS, Tuesday, 9:00–10:00 P.M., P. Lorillard, Inc. (Old Gold cigarettes).
Paul Whiteman Orchestra. January 27–June 9, 1931, NBC Blue, Tuesday, 8:00–8:30 P.M.; June 19, 1931–January 8, 1932, NBC Blue, Friday, 10:00–10:30 P.M., Allied Paint Company.
Pontiac Hour. January 15–July 1, 1932, NBC Blue, Friday, 10:00–10:30 P.M.; July 8–September 30, 1932, NBC, Friday, 10:00–10:30 P.M., Pontiac Motor Car Company (Pontiac automobiles).
Buick Hour. October 24, 1932–March 27, 1933, NBC, Monday, 9:30–10:00 P.M., General Motors Corporation Buick Division (Buick automobiles).
Paul Whiteman Orchestra. June 26–July 31, 1933, NBC, Monday, 2 hours, sustaining.
Kraft Music Hall. August 3, 1933–November 28, 1935, NBC, Thursday, 10:00–11:00 P.M., Kraft Foods Company (Kraft foodstuffs).
Woodbury Musical Varieties. January 5–August 9, 1936, NBC Blue, Sunday, 9:45–10:30 P.M.; August 16–December 27, 1936, NBC Blue, Sunday, 9:15–10:00 P.M., Andrew Jergens Company (Woodbury soap).
Chesterfield Presents. December 31, 1937–July 8, 1938, CBS, Friday, 8:30–9:00 P.M.; July 13, 1938–December 27, 1939, CBS, Wednesday, 8:30–9:00 P.M., Liggett & Myers Tobacco Company (Chesterfield cigarettes).
Paul Whiteman Orchestra. November 9–December 28, 1939, MBS, Thursday, 9:30–10:00 P.M., sustaining.
The George Burns and Gracie Allen Show. October 7, 1941–June 30, 1942, NBC, Tuesday, 7:30–8:00 P.M.; October 6–December 29, 1942, NBC, Tuesday, 9:00–9:30 P.M.; January 4–June 28, 1943, Monday, 8:30–9:00 P.M., Lever Brothers Company (Swan soap).
Paul Whiteman Presents. June 6–August 29, 1943, CBS, Sunday, 8:00–8:30 P.M., Standard Brands, Inc. (Chase and Sanborn coffee).
Philco Radio Hall of Fame. December 5, 1943–June 10, 1945, NBC Blue/ABC, Sunday, 6:00–7:00 P.M.; June 17, 1945–April 28, 1946, ABC, Sunday, 6:00–6:30 P.M., Philco Radio Corporation (Philco radios).
Paul Whiteman Concerts. September 5–November 14, 1944, NBC Blue, Tuesday, 11:30 P.M.–midnight, sustaining.
Forever Tops. January 21–September 23, 1946, ABC, Monday, 9:30–10:00 P.M., sustaining.
The Paul Whiteman Hour. September 29–October 27, 1946, ABC, Sunday, 8:00–9:00 P.M., sustaining.
The Paul Whiteman Program. November 3, 1946–January 5, 1947, ABC, Sunday, 8:00–8:30 P.M.; January 1–June 18, 1947, ABC, Wednesday, 9:00–9:30 P.M.; June 25–September 24, 1947, Wednesday, 8:30–9:00 P.M.; September 29–November 17, 1947, ABC, Monday, 30 minutes, sustaining.
The Paul Whiteman Record Club (aka *The Human Side of the Record*). June 30, 1947–June 25, 1948, ABC, Monday–Friday, 3:30–4:30 P.M., multiple participation.
The Paul Whiteman Program. 1949–1950, ABC, Sunday, 30 minutes, sustaining.
Paul Whiteman Presents. June 27–November 7, 1950, ABC, Tuesday, 8:00–8:30 P.M., sustaining.
Paul Whiteman's Teen Club. October 29, 1951–September 8, 1952, ABC, Monday, 9:00–10:00 P.M.; September 30, 1952–April 28, 1953, Tuesday, 8:30–9:00 P.M., sustaining.
Paul Whiteman Varieties. February 4–June 3, 1954, ABC, Thursday, 9:00–9:30 P.M.; July 14–October 20, 1954, ABC, Wednesday, 9:30–10:00 P.M., sustaining.

Synopsis:

Paul Whiteman was born early in relation to most of the bandstand greats and provided training for several. Were it not for Pops Whiteman, wrote an authority, several "would never have had an opportunity to reach an audience as broad as his." Among those owing some success to Whiteman's magnanimity were the Dorseys and the Teagardens. His outfit was the first featuring a female singer (Mildred Bailey) and a vocal trio (the Rhythm Boys, including Bing Crosby). When Whiteman played New York's Paramount Theater for two years, a proviso in his $12,500-a-week contract prevented him from featuring Crosby on solos. Management termed Bing "such a bad singer." Two years hence, Crosby returned to the Paramount with top billing. A reviewer assessed: "Paul Whiteman's music was a bland apology for what was being offered by black jazz bands of the day but he was responsible for giving jazz and other syncopated music a veneer of respectability.... Whiteman succeeded in welding an effective link between jazz and the light classics." He effectively embraced TV from the late 1940s to the mid–1950s.

The Bing Crosby Show

Bing Crosby was among a handful of radio legends that so dominated the medium that everybody in the country of even a few years of age knew who they were and what made them famous. In Crosby's case, he sang his way into the hearts of Americans who tried to put their lives back together after witnessing economic collapse, global conflagration and the anxieties from wide-reaching issues like the Cold War and the Korean conflict and domestic complexities like racial unrest and a president's assassination. It was a turbulent period when the nation's favorite crooner sang, and his voice reassured millions who tuned into his programs. Crosby persisted longer than any other vocalist on radio—and was still singing on the ether three decades after he began. This pop idol of broadcasts, records and the silver screen lulled a grateful nation with an impeccable delivery that may never have been equaled.

Producers-Directors: Burt McMurtrie (*The Woodbury Radio Program*), Cal Kuhl (*Kraft Music Hall*), Bill Morrow (*Philco Radio Time*), Murdo MacKenzie (*The Bing Crosby Chesterfield Show, The General Electric Show*).

Writers: Carroll Carroll, Stanley Davidson, Vic McLeod, Elon Packard and Leo "Ukie" Sherin (*Kraft Music Hall*), Hal Kanter (*Philco Radio Time*).

Announcers: Don Wilson, Roger Krupp, Ken Carpenter (*Kraft Music Hall*, Carpenter continuing with *Philco Radio Time, The Bing Crosby Chesterfield Show, The General Electric Show*)

Orchestra Conductors: Lennie Hayton (*Music That Satisfies*), Georgie Stoll (*The Woodbury Radio Program*), Jimmy Dorsey, John Scott Trotter (*Kraft Music Hall*, Trotter continuing with *Philco Radio Time, The Bing Crosby Chesterfield Show, The General Electric Show*), Buddy Cole (*The Bing Crosby Show*).

Vocalists: Connee Boswell, Peggy Lee, Mary Martin, Marilyn Maxwell (*Kraft Music Hall*).

Vocal Groups: The Boswell Sisters and The Mills Brothers (*The Woodbury Radio Program*), The Merry Macs (Joe, Judd and Ted McMichael and Mary Lou Cook) and The Music Maids and Hal (*Kraft Music Hall*), Jud Conlon's Rhythmaires (directed by Conlon, with Mack McLean, Loulie Jean Norman, Charlie Parlato, Gloria Wood, *Philco Radio Time*).

Featured Instrumentalists: Eddie

Lang, guitarist (*Music That Satisfies*); Jerry Colonna and Spike Jones (*Kraft Music Hall*).

Specialty Acts: Victor Borge, comic pianist; Bob Burns, comedian; Jerry Lester, comedian; and George Murphy, actor (*Kraft Music Hall*).

Theme Songs: *Just an Echo in the Valley* (*Fifteen Minutes with Bing Crosby*), *When the Blue of the Night Meets the Gold of the Day* (*Kraft Music Hall* and subsequent primetime series), *Love Came Into My Heart*, then *When the Blue of the Night Meets the Gold of the Day* (*The Bing Crosby Show*, 1954–1956), *Got the Moon in My Pocket* (*This Is Bing Crosby*), *Side by Side*, then *Don't Worry About Tomorrow* (*The Bing Crosby–Rosemary Clooney Show*).

Sponsors: Sustaining, September 2–October 31, 1931; November 2, 1931–February 27, 1932, American Cigar Company (Cremo cigars); March 2–July 27, 1932, January 4–April 15, 1933, Liggett & Myers Tobacco Company (Chesterfield cigarettes); October 16, 1933–May 28, 1934, September 18, 1934–June 11, 1935, Andrew Jergens Company (Woodbury soap); December 5, 1935–August 20, 1936, October 15, 1936–July 1, 1937, October 7, 1937–July 21, 1938, October 20, 1938–June 15, 1939, September 28, 1939–August 8, 1940, November 14, 1940–July 31, 1941, October 30, 1941–June 25, 1942, October 1, 1942–April 15, 1943, June 17, 1943–July 27, 1944, November 9, 1944–May 17, 1945, February 7–May 9, 1946, Kraft Foods Company (Kraft caramels, Kraft cheese, Kraft marshmallows, Miracle Whip salad dressing, Philadelphia cream cheese, Velveeta cheese and many other dairy-based foodstuffs); October 16, 1946–June 18, 1947, October 1, 1947–June 2, 1948, September 29, 1948–June 1, 1949, Philco Radio Corporation (Philco radios and appliance parts); November 15, 1948–October 27, 1950, Minute Maid Corporation (Minute Maid orange juice); September 21, 1949–May 24, 1950, October 11, 1950–June 27, 1951, October 3, 1951–June 25, 1952, Liggett & Myers Tobacco Company (Chesterfield cigarettes); October 9, 1952–July 2, 1953, October 25, 1953–May 30, 1954, General Electric Corporation (GE home appliances); November 22, 1954–December 28, 1956, multiple participation; 1956–1957, Ford Motor Company (Ford automobiles and trucks, parts and service); September 2, 1957–1958, February 29, 1960–September 28, 1962, multiple participation.

Ratings: High, 25.8 (1944-1945 season); low, 6.0 (1953-1954); median, 18.0. Figures are available for 20 of Crosby's 30 radio seasons, including all except 1951-1952 between 1933 and 1954. In nine of those years his ranking surpassed 20, an exceedingly high mark. It was in double digits every season but the final two posted (1952-1954). In his last full year with Kraft (1944-1945) and first full year with Philco (1946-1947), Crosby's numbers dropped 15.7 points, his deepest slide.

On the Air: *Fifteen Minutes with Bing Crosby* (aka *Presenting Bing Crosby*), September 2, 1931–October 31, 1931, CBS, Monday–Saturday, 11:00–11:15 P.M. Eastern Time; *Bing Crosby—The Cremo Singer*, November 2, 1931–February 27, 1932, CBS, Monday–Saturday, 11:00–11:15 P.M.; *Music That Satisfies*, March 2–July 27, 1932, January 4–April 15, 1933, CBS, Wednesday and Saturday, 9:00–9:15 P.M.; *The Woodbury Radio Program*, October 16, 1933–May 28, 1934, CBS, Monday, 8:30–9:00 P.M.; *The Woodbury Radio Program*, September 18, 1934–June 11, 1935, CBS, Tuesday, 9:00–9:30 P.M.; *Kraft Music Hall*, December 5, 1935–August 20, 1936, October 15, 1936–July 1, 1937, October 7, 1937–July 21, 1938, October 20, 1938–June 15, 1939, September 28, 1939–June 27 1940, NBC, Thursday, 10:00–11:00 P.M.; *Kraft Music Hall*, July 4–August 8, 1940, November 14, 1940–July 31, 1941, October 30, 1941–June 25, 1942, NBC, Thursday, 9:00–10:00 P.M.; *Kraft Music Hall*, October 1, 1942–April 15, 1943,

June 17, 1943–July 27, 1944, November 9, 1944–May 17, 1945, February 7–May 9, 1946, NBC, Thursday, 9:00–9:30 P.M.; *Philco Radio Time*, October 16, 1946–June 18, 1947, October 1, 1947–June 2, 1948, September 29, 1948–June 1, 1949, ABC, Wednesday, 10:00–10:30 P.M.; *This Is Bing Crosby*, November 15, 1948–January 21, 1949, CBS, Monday–Friday, 9:45–10:00 A.M.; *This Is Bing Crosby*, January 24–September 29, 1950, CBS, Monday–Friday, 10:00–10:15 A.M.; *This Is Bing Crosby*, October 2–27, 1950, CBS, Monday–Friday, 9:45–10:00 A.M.; *The Bing Crosby Chesterfield Show*, September 21, 1949–May 24, 1950, October 11, 1950–June 27, 1951, October 3, 1951–June 25, 1952, CBS, Wednesday, 9:30–10:00 P.M.; *The General Electric Show*, October 9, 1952–July 2, 1953, CBS, Thursday, 9:30–10:00 P.M.; *The General Electric Show*, October 25, 1953–May 30, 1954, CBS, Sunday, 8:00–8:30 P.M.; *The Bing Crosby Show*, November 22, 1954–1955, CBS, Monday–Friday, 9:15–9:30 P.M., 1955–December 28, 1956, CBS, Monday–Friday, 7:30–7:45 P.M.; *Bing Crosby*, 1956–1957, CBS, Monday–Friday, five minutes; *The Bing Crosby–Rosemary Clooney Show*, September 2, 1957–1958, CBS, Monday–Friday, 7:20–7:30 A.M.; *The Bing Crosby–Rosemary Clooney Show*, February 29, 1960–September 28, 1962, CBS, Monday–Friday, 15 minutes.

* * *

Pretend that someone asks if you could count on the fingers of one hand the irrefutable megastars of American radio during the medium's golden age. Imagine that you are also instructed to select *single* individuals with name recognition, whose presence and power clearly dominated the aural airwaves, far surpassing their nearest competitors. The restricted focus, of course, would disallow some pretty formidable celebrity duos like *Amos 'n' Andy* (Freeman Gosden and Charles Correll), Edgar Bergen and Charlie McCarthy, George Burns and Gracie Allen and *Fibber McGee and Molly* (Jim and Marian Jordan). Given those parameters, who bounds to the forefront in your opinion as a few *individual* icons?

Simply taking a wild guess, our assumption — irrespective of any alphabetical sequence — is that most listeners who lived through those halcyon days would likely pick people similar to Fred Allen, Jack Benny, Bing Crosby, Arthur Godfrey and maybe Edgar Bergen, Bob Hope, Red Skelton or another favored radio legend. Perhaps then, *just perhaps*, that group might be among the most universally admired personalities of that influential era in the nation's entertainment history.

Among singers, could there be any question about who would top practically everybody's list? In his heyday, Bing Crosby readily drew the largest and most sustained following and enjoyed the greatest renown of any vocalist to appear before a radio microphone during the 1930s, 1940s and 1950s. This isn't one man's opinion. To wit:

• Crosby's top-rated radio shows, enormously successful motion pictures, and best-selling Decca records carried crooning to a plateau of mass acceptance and solid respectability, not to mention lasting popularity.

• In the mid–1940s, Crosby was the leading film star, radio star and recording star — a feat no one before him or since has matched. Singer Tony Bennett observed: "Crosby dominated in radio like Elvis and the Beatles combined — he had *hour* shows." Other pop singers — Perry Como, Eddie Fisher, Dick Haymes, Frank Sinatra, Jack Smith, et al. — had "quickie, low-budget quarter-hour programs."

• As a radio artist, he was a top attraction from 1931 — when he did his first solo broadcast — to 1957, when he began slowly to withdraw from full-time performing in favor of a rather graceful, but not too steady, semiretirement. He was purportedly "the number one radio star in the U.S.A. for eighteen years."

• Crosby made more studio recordings than any other singer in history, including 396 discs that ascended to the hit parade during the 35-year epoch from 1927 to 1962 (an average of more than 11 chart-topping songs every year)—no other artist ever coming close by comparison.

• He appeared on 4,000 radio broadcasts, nearly 3,400 programs that he himself headlined, and was a major radio performer longer than any other individual at his level of name recognition, continuing from 1931 to 1962.

Bing Crosby was the fourth of seven children born into the Harry Lowe Crosby clan of Tacoma, Washington, near the turn of the century. Several myths surrounding the crooner's birthdate persisted throughout his life. At least one of his multiple biographers contended that even he himself was unsure of his birthdate. In one account, a protective brother allegedly attempted to make his sibling younger than he really was. Sources claim he was born as early as 1897 and as late as 1904. While no birth certificate exists, because the family was Catholic a baptismal record offers proof that Harry Lillis Crosby (later nicknamed Bing) was christened on May 31, 1903, having been born May 3, 1903. Not long afterward, the family moved across the state to Spokane where Bing grew up and was educated at Gonzaga University, intending to become a lawyer.

In the meantime as a sideline he had shown considerable interest in music. In 1925, he turned up in Los Angeles with Al Rinker, a singing chum from Gonzaga days. Billed as Two Boys and a Piano, the duo played the Boulevard Theater, toured with vaudeville shows and appeared in cinema palaces. Bandleader Paul Whiteman discovered them at Los Angeles' Metropolitan Theater in 1927 and offered them jobs with his band, which they accepted. Whiteman increased their act by one, adding Harry Barris as accompanist, and renamed them the Rhythm Boys. For nearly three years they toured with Whiteman's aggregate before returning to the West Coast in 1930 to join impresario Gus Arnheim's outfit at Los Angeles' Cocoanut Grove.

Before cutting ties with Paul Whiteman, the Rhythm Boys had appeared in a 1930 motion picture titled *The King of Jazz* starring Whiteman and his entourage. In the film Crosby introduced the tune that was to become his trademark theme, *When the Blue of the Night Meets the Gold of the Day*. Celluloid fascinated him, and he appeared in several short film productions during the period. The silver screen was to become a huge part of his income-producing revenue, and a crucial measure of his public persona and popularity. Crosby was soon seeking solo opportunities with and apart from the Rhythm Boys. Brunswick Records put him under contract and he warbled ballads like *I Found a Million-Dollar Baby*, *I'm Through with Love* and *Just One More Chance*.

That same year (1930) Crosby met Hollywood film starlet Wilma Winifred Wyatt, whose professional name was Dixie Lee. The pair fell in love. Although Dixie Lee probably correctly figured Crosby as a playboy, she married him anyway. In time they would become parents of four boys, some of them following their famous parents into entertainment.

Radio, meanwhile, had shown little interest in Crosby's voice. While he had appeared with Whiteman in rather obscure parts on the impresario's broadcasts, he never had much prospect for solo recognition. All that was about to change, however. Phonograph records would become his conduit to widespread fame.

While trekking along Broadway in

New York one day, NBC vice president John F. Royal heard a Crosby recording blaring from a record shop turntable. So impressed was he with the singer that he determined to sign the owner of that voice for his web. Crosby, already aware of some of the wiles of the world, exhibited another talent that was to epitomize him. Proving as resourceful a businessman as he was artist, the vocalist hired an attorney who rebuffed NBC's offer of several hundred dollars weekly for exposure to a nationwide audience. Instead, the lawyer stood firm at $2,000 a week and nothing less. Crosby won the skirmish but lost the war; he'd not be appearing on NBC for several years. Down the road, a single program on the chimes chain would cause his name to become a household word. Yet over a professional lifetime, Crosby would invest the bulk of his radio time at NBC's principal competitor.

Was this a propitious start to a prevailing consequence or merely an irrelevant slip-up? The solution is left to one's individual rumination.

At about the same time, in June 1931, it happened that CBS owner-chairman William S. Paley was on a voyage aboard the S.S. *Europa* bound for the ship's namesake continent, then crossing the Atlantic. Paley was treated to Crosby's captivating chords in the middle of the ocean, apparently for the very first time. On one of his daily cavorts around the deck, the customarily antsy Paley heard Crosby crooning his new Decca recording *I Surrender, Dear*, piercing the sea breeze from a portable phonograph brought on deck by somebody. Not recognizing the artist, Paley momentarily interrupted the device. On the record label below impresario Gus Arnheim's moniker there appeared, in miniscule lettering, "Chorus—Bing Crosby." It was definitely an auspicious moment, whether anyone realized it or not. Paley wasted little time cabling his office at CBS in New York with orders to deliver Crosby immediately.

The network chief's second-in-command, Edward Klauber, responded promptly, cabling back that he was working on it, and added sanguinely: "Crosby is a Pacific coast ballad sensation and appeals [to] both sexes." Confident the matter had been dispatched, Paley went on with his cruise and summer journey. Not until he returned to New York weeks later did he discover that Crosby hadn't been acquired after all. His executive staff offered explanations for their failure to act such as learning that the young crooner "had a drinking problem and was considered unreliable"[1] and that he was "a rather unpredictable young fellow, unlikely to fit in with strict broadcast schedules."[2]

Paley prevailed, nonetheless. He hastily initialed Crosby for a quarter-hour at 11 o'clock for a half-dozen nights a week at an unprecedented $1,500 every week during a time when $100 was the accepted rate. Recall that this was at the zenith of the Depression era. Cogitating over that expensive proffer some years hence, Paley admitted that he conjectured to himself "why I was doing it." No matter. Crosby became CBS's early prize catch, and that singular act appeared to work in the network's favor for much of the remainder of Crosby's show business career.[3]

In passing, singing on the radio would never be Crosby's only source of income. In reality, his compensation from it then—despite its perceived extravagance—might look like pocket change to the rising achiever. In addition to records and films, both of which would increase in volume as the years rolled by, Crosby and others—Morton Downey, the Mills Brothers, Kate Smith and Rudy Vallee among them—helped sustain vaudeville's viability for a while. In the early 1930s, performing on revue circuits twice daily, Crosby and the others reportedly carried home up to $6,000 weekly from their sideline ventures. It wasn't a bad haul for a little-known performer, or for anyone for that matter, given the times in which they were living.

Incidentally, and most surprisingly, a normally reliable source flatly stated, in reference to singer Kate Smith: "Among Kate's talent finds are crooner Bing Crosby, comedians Abbott and Costello, and radio and movie writer Jean Holloway."[4] While several scholars supply documented evidence that Smith was useful in launching comedians Bud Abbott and Lou Costello and Holloway is irrelevant here, there is no apparent proof beyond this claim that America's sweetheart of song launched the professional occupation of Bing Crosby. This would seem to be a folk legend that mistakenly made its way into print.

Bing Crosby's first nationwide broadcast was little short of a disaster. In fact, several events surrounding that performance were lacking the grace and style for which the crooner was long remembered. Even Crosby himself would feign some remorse. ("I couldn't produce a sound," he intimated.) What happened was—when it came time for his debut over CBS on Monday, August 31, 1931—the soloist simply "wasn't available." An announcer offered a brief statement to the effect that the program previously scheduled had been canceled—without added explanation. The same situation occurred the following evening as broadcast time arrived. On the third successive night of Crosby's premiering week, Wednesday, September 2, the performer turned up at last, carrying out his contractual obligations, although rather feebly, as shall be observed.

The authors of several of Crosby's biographies provided at least as many explanations for his inability to go on as scheduled. While he was reportedly ill, "The word on the show-business grapevine was that Bing was on a binge, and that Everett [Crosby, his brother, whom Bing had appointed his manager] had tracked him down and was trying to get him straightened out."[5]

From Everett's perspective, the situation was a calamity of enormous proportions. He had asked over 20 prominent journalists to observe his brother's launch on the national airwaves. By then it was much too late to prevent their arrival. When they showed up, he apologized profusely for Bing's "loss of voice," indulging them with liquor and handing each one an autographed copy of Bing's recording of *Stardust*, soon to be released in record stores.

A story was published that Bing Crosby had consulted physicians about his sudden loss of voice. The docs recommended surgery but he refused it for the medics could not assure him that it would leave his voice unaltered. They reportedly found nodes on his vocal cords and those nodes were credited with providing Crosby's unique tones. "It would be a story that would last for another half century."

As for Crosby's own explanation, given in his 1953 autobiographical *Call Me Lucky*, he admitted that his broadcast delay was the result of late-night bar-hopping, as well as an air-conditioned studio in which he rehearsed at CBS, purportedly the first AC room he had ever been in. He caught a cold from it and consequently called off the show twice, he said. "Bing might have had a cold, too, at the time of his radio debut, but everyone in the business knew that the main reason he missed those first two nights was that he had gone off on one of his three-day binges and, in fact, was reported as being still in an alcoholic fog on the night of the broadcast," a source clarified.[6] He was drinking so heavily, said another, "that he was virtually paralytic."[7]

Apparently after a couple of nights as a no-show, Bing reportedly left a handwritten message for Everett that read: "Cancel all contracts. I gave it all I had, and it's a no go." Frightened and upset, Everett Crosby dashed between speakeasies in search of his sibling. When he came upon him at last, he virtually dragged him back, browbeating him to a pulp, chastising him as "the only Crosby who ever backed away from a challenge" if he failed to make the broadcast. With that, Bing went on.

Upon reflection, he might as well have stayed away a third night. William S. Paley's biographer remembered it like this.[8]

> That evening, Paley was on Long Island in a rented home without a radio. Out in the garage, he tuned in from his car. "Crosby was awful," he recalled. Paley dashed back to the house and called the studio. Crosby was drunk, as Paley suspected, and two men were holding him up as he tried pathetically to sing. "Change the program, get him off," Paley shouted. The power he felt at this moment made him giddy; years later he would say, "Think of it. I could even change a program while it was on the air!" But Paley stubbornly refused to let Crosby go. He assigned the singer a round-the-clock guard to prevent him from drinking.

Things obviously got better. Crosby improved with age. By November, American Cigar Company signed as the singer's first national sponsor (previously the show had been sustained by the network). Touting Cremo cigars, things were looking up for Crosby and company. The star was mindful that a tobacco manufacturer's underwriting greatly offended his mother who was tuning in back in Spokane. She disliked smoking in any form and he didn't exactly wish to incur her wrath. But it was a business decision, pure and simple, and at that point it took precedence over Mom's preferences.

The following year (1932) he found time to also perform as a semiregular on a new CBS musical showcase with Raymond Paige's orchestra called *California Melodies*. Simultaneously, he launched a sideline that would ultimately make him a Paramount film idol. He starred in *The Big Broadcast* that year. Several costars appeared with him, all of them radio artists.

In the meantime, when his stogie-plugging radio series ended, Crosby became well identified with one of the country's top cigarette brands, an association that probably lingered in the public's perception long after the smoke rings abated. He signed with Liggett & Myers Tobacco Company, the manufacturer of Chesterfield cigarettes, for a twice-weekly entry in CBS's prime-time schedule. For his services he was compensated at several thousand dollars weekly and given artistic control over the program. On that show, Crosby began to fashion a programming model that he would perfect on the *Kraft Music Hall* a short while later. It consisted of employing writers and a healthy blend of music and talk (both ad-libbed and scripted) that would soon turn him into one of radio's most sought-after entertainers.

The Chesterfield series ran 21 weeks, then was off the air five months and returned for another 15-week stint. (The lapse between segments allowed Crosby to kick off his silver screen quest while visiting other radio shows as a guest.) An orchestra conducted by Lennie Hayton presented background for Crosby's singing. Guitarist Eddie Lang was a featured artist. When their brief time together ended, it's possible that Crosby was never very far from the collective minds at Liggett & Myers. They would underwrite him with a multiple-year series down the line, and he and comedian Bob Hope would instantly be acknowledged by millions as the chief spokesmen for the tobacco firm — in print advertising, on broadcasts, on billboards and in many other promotional formats.

Jumping ahead briefly, radio soap opera actress Mary Jane Higby recalled an incident with some relevance to this. In the late 1950s, shortly after joining the cast of

CBS's *This Is Nora Drake* as that serial's heroine, Higby was reminded of something that had happened to her long before. A quarter of a century earlier she was sitting by herself one day, virtually unnoticed, on the stage of a live broadcast of the *Kraft Music Hall* starring Bing Crosby. Momentarily she was to have a turn at the microphone, making a pitch for the sponsor's cheese.

Upon joining the *Drake* cast many years later, meanwhile, she was bemused to hear the drama's opening plug—then on tape—for Chesterfield cigarettes. It wasn't the sponsor that preoccupied her thoughts; it was *who* was chanting "Sound off! Sound off! Sound off for Chesterfield!" over the din of a drum and bugle corps. In the twilight of network radio's heyday, Bing Crosby and Bob Hope were trilling those commercials. In some kind of misplaced irony, she enthused, *she* was now the star and Crosby was selling the sponsor's product for *her*! Higby mused pensively for a moment: things had certainly come full circle!

Crosby's next radio venture saw him headlining a dual-season weekly half-hour musical review sponsored by the Andrew Jergens Company for Woodbury soap. Daytime serial mogul Frank Hummert had brandished that beauty bar with one of the most widely recognized epithets in advertising history when he created "For the skin you love to touch." For the first time, Crosby was flanked by a group of ongoing regulars. In addition to an orchestra conducted by Georgie Stoll, there were a couple of vocal groups—the Mills Brothers in the show's first season, and the Boswell Sisters in the second.

Burt McMurtrie, a Crosby crony from Washington State who had earlier worked on a Paul Whiteman radio show, produced the Woodbury series. McMurtrie helped Crosby overcome his reluctance to perform religious music on the ether (Crosby felt listeners would think he was profiting by religion), and got him to sing his first Christmas carol there. Strangely, within a decade, the most popular song Crosby would ever record—while not religious in scope—would be a Christmas carol!

Crosby didn't renew his CBS contract when the 1934-1935 radio season came to an end. There was a hint that he had become irritated with Jergens executives and they with him. If so, Jergens wouldn't be the last sponsor that he crossed swords with. Crosby entertained inquiries from the advertising agency representing the *Kraft Music Hall*, radio's most popular musical variety program, sponsored by the Kraft Foods Company. From the start, Kraft courted him heavily. But when they parted, they were carrying him to court. In between those decisive milestones, they would make beautiful music together—and lots of it—on their way to pleasing 50 million listeners a week and—in the process—selling umpteen billion pounds of processed cheese goods and other dairy products to American consumers.

The *Kraft Music Hall* was launched over NBC as a six-week summertime replacement to introduce a new salad dressing Kraft was then bringing onto the market called Miracle Whip. The series showcased the talents of Paul Whiteman's orchestra and several recurring artists (tenor Jack Fulton, soprano Helen Jepson, singing pianist Ramona and comical music critic Deems Taylor among them). Its warm weather stint was so successful that the program was penciled in on the fall agenda.

It returned on August 3, 1933, featuring those same talents while adding popular vocalist Al Jolson (*April Showers, California Here I Come, Mammy, Rockabye Your Baby with a Dixie Melody, Toot Toot Tootsie Goodbye*, et al.) as star. (See reference in The Vocalists chapter.) When Jolson departed a year later, the program had no obvious replacement of his stature waiting in the wings. But preliminary contacts had already been made with Crosby.

In assessing the show's format, Kraft concluded that more variety might be a good thing than Maestro Whiteman was able to provide. At that juncture, Crosby was asked to participate for four weeks in a trial effort with Whiteman. Whiteman conducted his orchestra on the live broadcast from New York while Crosby, backed by the orchestra of Jimmy Dorsey, intermittently sang from Hollywood on the same program. The "audition" series aired on December 5, 12, 19 and 26, 1935.

It was an overnight ratings smash. It led Kraft to dislodge Whiteman — who had been Crosby's superior only a half-dozen years before and had opened doors for the younger man that led him to his present status — and replace him (Whiteman) with a Crosby-Dorsey combination. For his services, Crosby was to be compensated at $3,000 weekly, a sum that would ultimately increase to $7,500. In announcing the changes, Kraft decided to permanently shift the show's origin from the East Coast to the West Coast beginning January 2, 1936.

Crosby was given free rein to call most of the shots on Kraft's most important production. In that capacity, he wasted little time expressing himself pointedly on a number of matters, indicating from the outset that he intended to have final say on key essentials that he believed in strongly. A couple of major issues that promptly surfaced pertained to studio audiences and Crosby's speaking role on the ether, including — but certainly not limited to — product endorsements. There would be some softening on his part eventually. But he was absolutely adamant on both scores at the start.

In regard to an audience, Crosby simply didn't want one. Some witnesses said he objected to observers' response that was coerced by means of hand signals given by onstage agents or hand-held or electric signs flashing the directive "Applaud." Such tactics were then integrated into every other major comedy-music-variety feature that had a studio audience. Crosby was a purist, and was allegedly offended by those shows' "phoniness." One source hypothesized that his principal objection to the studio audience was due to his baldness, however — if spectators were present, he'd have to wear his toupee, which he detested, or a hat. Yet another mentioned Crosby's presumed concern for the listeners at home who "liked the fact that other people didn't have any advantage over them." His insistence on banning an audience, for whatever the reason(s), nearly pulled the plug on his deal with Kraft, one authority confirmed.

From the era of not having a live audience, a radio historiographer assessed, "Today, listening to it [*Kraft Music Hall*] on tape, one is struck by the silence, the white space, the appreciative, pregnant lull after a brilliant performance."

When the embargo on studio audiences was lifted at last, it was accomplished by convincing Crosby that spectators' presence was critical to the show's success. Producer Cal Kuhl, employed by the J. Walter Thompson advertising agency, the series' packager, told the star: "We'll just invite family members of people affiliated with the show." It turned out that, on the first night a studio audience was added, those "family members" stood in single file all the way around the building waiting to enter prior to the performance! Crosby had been deceived but appeared to enjoy playing to a live studio audience. The barrier was compromised — and the throngs would remain.

Crosby also protested vehemently when a script called for him to have very many lines. "I'm a singer — let somebody else do the talking," he scolded. He particularly didn't like it when the sponsor wanted him to say a few words plugging its cheese and other commodities, and told them so. "That's the announcer's job," he interjected. In time he would develop an easygoing conversational style (with the assistance of writers) that allowed him to banter back-and-forth with his announcer, his orchestra leader and his guest stars. Kraft officials pushed for that, wanting to break through the crooner's exterior façade and establish a warm link to his humanity. Nevertheless, Crosby was pretty uptight on the topic when he assumed the program's reins.

Despite such matters, "It was the Kraft Music Hall that cemented Bing's relationship with his public," an observer validated. "To millions, it was the only thing on the radio that they wanted to hear. When Crosby was on the air, young couples stayed home instead of going to the movies. Older people cancelled visits to restaurants. If they were visiting, they made sure they could sit in front of their hosts' radio sets."[9] Affirmed another: "In the decade that Crosby remained with Kraft, he became the best-loved star on the American scene."[10] In 1939, the nation's newspaper editors selected the "best shows in radio," picking for their first three spots programs fronted by Jack Benny, Edgar Bergen and Bing Crosby. The crooner had the nation in the palm of his hand!

The individual who may have profoundly influenced that result more than any other was Carroll Carroll. According to one wag, Carroll "dreamed the show up week by week." He was one of radio's most adept continuity and comedy writers who had a gift for turning just the right word or phrase to make the scripts glisten on several programs, without sounding forced — so the expressions became a natural part of the informal dialogue between hosts and their guests.

In addition to *Kraft*, the busy scribe was responsible for creating charismatic copy for the *George Burns and Gracie Allen Show, The Circle, Club Fifteen, Double or Nothing*, the *Eddie Cantor Show*, the *Edgar Bergen and Charlie McCarthy Show*, the *Frank Sinatra Show, Meet Corliss Archer, NTG and His Girls* and the *Rudy Vallee Show*. He produced the *Al Jolson Show*. Carroll, also employed by J. Walter Thompson, the ad agency, had been writing the *Kraft Music Hall* in New York when it was under the auspices of Messrs. Whiteman and Jolson. When the series moved West, he went with it.

In his memoir, *My Life With*, Carroll recalled his greeting on meeting Bing Crosby for the first time: "When I arrived in the studio, somebody said, 'Bing, this is Carroll Carroll, the writer of the show.' He said, 'Hi, Carroll' and then walked away." At the time, "Bing was doping horses, with a scratch sheet in his hand," Carroll remembered. "That was our entire contact for maybe six weeks."

Carroll would rapidly discover that Crosby's cool, efficient manner infiltrated nearly everything the luminary encountered. "I figured the best thing I could do would be to write," Carroll continued, "so I wrote a script and it was sent to Bing. It came back with a couple of minor word changes—but he never talked to me. I think I wrote the show for maybe three or four months before he even really knew what my name was." Later, the pair got together for a script conference over lunch at the Brown Derby on Vine Street every week. It was the only "socializing"—if it could be called that—the two did in their near-decade of working together.

Despite the standoffishness he exuded on their first meeting, Crosby's attitude belied a tremendous esteem he developed for Carroll's aptitude. "He had a marvelous talent," said the crooner. "We used to use a lot of opera people and concert musicians—such as Heifetz, and Menuhin and Rachmaninoff.... These people would sing one song of their own genre, then we'd do some kind of little light duet together. Then we'd have some comedy dialogue, which would fit the personality of the star or his work. And Carroll would write — he really put together some marvelous little spots for those folk. They loved to be on the show; they loved to let their hair down a little and be themselves."

Those "marvelous little spots" didn't occur without some tender loving care, one might be assured. "Everybody thought Bing ad-libbed the whole script," Carroll disclosed in his life's story. "He seemed to have an ear for the way I talked," Crosby responded in *his* life's story. "He encouraged me to incorporate as many of my own words as possible into the script. He'd send a script around to my home and I'd try to rewrite the speeches he'd written for me. And I'd try to put in little jokes if I could think of any. Many of them were clumsy and pointless, but once in a while I hit something mildly amusing and Carroll wouldn't delete it if he thought it had a chance of getting a laugh.... It was the next thing to ad-libbing."

Carroll wrote the *Kraft* show by himself until 1938 when he became the head writer, supervising the dialoguing skills of Stanley Davidson, Vic McLeod, Elon Packard and Leo "Ukie" Sherin. "There were no on-air script credits, enhancing the notion that all the glib smoothness was Crosby's alone." But it was Carroll himself who knew the way Crosby talked and the results showed it. "The trademark laid-back Crosby banter and tossed-off asides were largely the work of Carroll," assured a radio historian, "who gave Bing Crosby his urbane, breezy character, an easygoing chatter that segued out of his crooning. It set the tone for other variety shows that copied its back-fence congeniality."

The key to everything appeared to be Carroll's initiative. "I usually spent Friday, Saturday, and Sunday interviewing guests," he recalled. He began writing the script on Monday morning. "Tuesday evening Bing and Bob [Burns, a comic sidekick on the show] each received his script. The guests all got sides in which they were to appear. Then I'd get okays from the guests or try to take what suggestions they had that made sense. Early Thursday morning Bing's script, with any changes *he* had, was picked up. All notes and proposed changes were made, coordinated or ignored, and a revised script was sent to mimeo to be ready for rehearsal." The live program aired Thursdays at 10 P.M. Eastern time until 1940, then at 9 P.M.

In summary, what went on the air, Carroll allowed, had a "gracious informality" appreciated by the guests. "Instead of using guests to make the star look good, we worked just the other way."

Although Carroll made Crosby sound easygoing while on the air, he observed that the show's star "was about as casual as Westminster Abbey.... He perplexed me sometimes with the changes he would make to the script," said Carroll. "He'd change a word arbitrarily. Say it was 'beautifully,' he'd change it to 'magnificently.' I'd think, well, he doesn't like 'beautifully' for some reason. So the next time I'd want to use the word I'd use 'magnificently' instead and he'd change it back to 'beautifully.'"

Another personality imported from the East Coast when *Kraft Music Hall* went transcontinental was Bob Burns, a genuine folk humorist who was discovered by Rudy Vallee. Burns had also been with the show in New York. Crosby developed an immediate affinity for Burns and his mythical recollections of life in rural Van Buren, Arkansas, where he was born. (It was reminiscent of the trappings conveyed by comedienne Minnie Pearl that brought to life her humble origins at Grinder's Switch, Tennessee, on the *Grand Ole Opry*.) Burns' narratives about country relatives like Grandpa Snazzy broke up Crosby. It ideally contradicted so many of the program's longhaired guests like classical musicians, dramatic actors, composers and operatic singers.

A Crosby biographer justified: "Burns' slow southern drawl was a perfect foil for Bing's rapid-fire, intentionally hammy and pseudosophisticated oratorical style, a mixed bag of circumlocutory polysyllable formal speech, incongruously peppered with jive talk. Some of the show's funniest moments were the dialogues between Burns and Crosby." Burns became so critical to the success of the *Kraft* show, in fact, that "he held the second chair for more than five years."

Burns also appeared with Crosby in a couple of the crooner's motion picture releases, *Rhythm on the Range* and *Waikiki Wedding*. In addition, a Rube Goldbergish musical instrument Burns patented in 1905 called the bazooka earned considerable mileage when the federal government applied its name to a rocket launcher developed by the U.S. Army during World War II. The name is so commonly used today of course, no one remembers its origins as a novelty musical device.

It was during this era that the name Ken Carpenter came to the attention of Bing Crosby. Carpenter was hired as announcer for the *Kraft Music Hall*. More importantly, of course, as anyone familiar with the Crosby shows recalls, is that the two men began an association that would continue for many years and on several subsequent series. Carpenter was to become well identified with the singer, just as his orchestra conductor would.

Born in Avon, Illinois, on August 21, 1900, Carpenter launched his network career over Los Angeles station KFI, an NBC affiliate, in 1930. He had done some broadcasting in Peoria, Illinois, earlier and had acquired some experience in advertising, so he went to the coast seeking an advertising post. Instead, fate provided a radio audition. "NBC had no studios here and any work that was done on the network for NBC, KFI did it," he recalled. "I was able to get some start on the network at that time." Carpenter was hired as a staff announcer when NBC opened its Hollywood studios in 1936. He remained in that capacity for six years, freelancing on his own after that.

His resume as an announcer would be filled with a boatload of radio series on which his highly recognizable voice could be instantly identified: *The Al Jolson Show, Command Performance, The Edgar Bergen and Charlie McCarthy Show, The General Electric Theater, The Great Gildersleeve, The Halls of Ivy, The Life of Riley, Lux Radio Theatre, Meet Corliss Archer, One Man's Family, Packard Mardi Gras, The Passing Parade* and *Three Sheets to the Wind*.

Carpenter often presided over sporting events like Rose Bowl football games and Santa Anita handicaps in addition to some prestigious Hollywood celebrations. It was during one of his sideline ventures, in fact, that he first became acquainted with Bing Crosby. At the time, in 1932, he was announcing at the Cocoanut Grove. Only a few years later, he and Crosby would be working steadily together on varied radio features. Carpenter remained a major player in series emanating from the West Coast for many, many years. He died October 16, 1984, in Santa Monica, California.

One of the innovations Carpenter routinely participated in with Crosby on the *Kraft Music Hall* was some memorable station breaks in which Carpenter played a pupil at KMH and Dr. Crosby was the school's dean. Each spot led into striking the NBC chimes (they were hit manually in those days). In the early 1940s, when the American Society of Composers, Authors and Publishers (ASCAP) yanked its music from the air, Crosby's theme song—*When the Blue of the Night Meets the Gold of the Day*, which the singer had introduced in the 1930 Paul Whiteman film *The King of*

Jazz—disappeared for a while, too. The fight song of the mythical school of the station breaks, *Hail KMH*, displaced it temporarily. John Scott Trotter, Crosby's bandleader, composed the lyrics and tune.[11]

> *Hail KMH, hail, rain and snow*
> *Onward to victory*
> *Forward we will go*
> *Stamping out our adversary*
> *Like a dauntless dromedary...*
> *Hail K ... M ... H!*

The final three notes were sung to the tune of those infamous NBC chimes. The network brass had to love it.

Ken Carpenter acknowledged that he didn't object to working before an audience but "I hated the warm-up part." If he really did, one could hardly tell it by the performance he offered. A scriptwriter recalled it.[12]

> Ken usually would walk out and start talking; gracious, no big jokes. He'd introduce John Scott Trotter and the orchestra. There'd be a lot of stuff on the stage—the orchestra, the mikes and all, and Bing would just sort of casually wander around. And usually by design at some point, Ken would do a mock "take," and say, "Why, it's the boss!" And then Bing would say, "Evening, how are ya?" and the place would come apart. Then he'd say, "Yeah, Ken, looks like a lively group. We ready to go? How are things in the booth?" Just a little chatting, nothing prepared.

John Scott Trotter has been mentioned several times. If Carpenter was Crosby's right arm, Trotter was surely his left, or possibly vice versa. In fact, Trotter and Crosby became inseparable comrades frankly because a great deal of how Crosby sounded on the air and on records and in movies was directly attributable to Trotter's painstaking skill. He was a master in his field and Crosby was quick to recognize his inimitable gifts. Before Trotter arrived on the scene, the reader will recall that Jimmy Dorsey was conducting the *Kraft Music Hall* from the inception of Crosby's ascendancy as West Coast mogul. What became of Dorsey? More than one story abounds.

One explanation is that "he thought he was losing his identity as a big band leader with only one limited radio exposure a week. Bing understood how he felt and let him go with his blessing." Another suggested the two talented virtuosos had "a clash of artistic temperament" which became the deciding factor. "Bing's solution was to get rid of Dorsey and hire a man who was more a musician than a star and who would never constitute a threat to his own billing." That source hinted that both men seemed to regard themselves as "the stars of the operation." Still another rationalization for Dorsey's departure surfaced: "Jimmy Dorsey was replaced as music director only when a reluctant Crosby could be convinced that his style of swing wasn't compatible with the classical artists who were appearing in greater numbers on his show."

No matter what was responsible for the change, Crosby's career was undoubtedly improved by it. John Scott Trotter's name would appear immediately following Crosby's on every one of the star's recordings for the next two decades. For many years, Crosby would almost never go on the air on his own series without Trotter's accompaniment. In every sense, Trotter was "a Crosby institution." A Crosby biographer put the impresario into proper perspective.[13]

> He was a large, quiet man who never said anything more threatening than a stern "Gentlemen!" Bing said he was the greatest gourmet he ever knew. But there was more to Scott Trotter than that. He was a huge musical influence on Bing; one who had a similar sort of effect on the way Crosby sang as Nelson Riddle was to have on the Sinatra performing style 16 years

later. Like Riddle with Sinatra, Trotter didn't change the Crosby voice, but rather the way he used it, his style. The orchestrations sounded different, with emphasis placed on harmonies instead of melody, and so Bing himself sounded different. He was no longer blown over by trumpets and trombones. Now, more than before, Bing was able to experiment with the songs he sang. He enjoyed his "boo-boo-be-boos" in between phrases, which allowed him to drop a register or two when he thought the occasion demanded. It would be a style that would stay with him for ever after.

"John Scott Trotter was a very fastidious man," recalled one of his eventual peers, Billy May. "Everything about him was very tasteful, and I always felt it was quite an honor to work for him. He always made sure that the music associated with Bing was of a high quality. There's a song called *I'll Be Seeing You*, and the melody had been lifted from one of the Mahler symphonies. Well, John made an arrangement of that and he used every device in the book to [let you] hear Gustav Mahler. And very few people would understand that."[14]

Trotter's relevance can be witnessed in the fact that when Crosby left *Kraft* and moved to another show, Trotter was one of the few lieutenants the crooner carried with him: "To lose Scott Trotter would have been professional suicide and Bing was in no mood to consider ending his business life," an observer confirmed.

Born in Charlotte, North Carolina, on June 14, 1908, Trotter was vacationing in California in the summer of 1936 when he agreed to orchestrate several arrangements for Crosby's motion picture *Pennies from Heaven*. A year hence, on July 8, 1937, he accepted the baton on *Kraft Music Hall*. In 1925, during his collegiate years at North Carolina, Trotter joined Hal Kemp's band as pianist and remained with that aggregate nearly a dozen years. He was credited with giving the outfit a "fresh, happy sound." Later, as Crosby's musical arranger-conductor, he left his mark on the most popular record ever sold, *White Christmas*. In 1944, *Radio Life* bestowed its distinguished achievement award on him for arranging and conducting. Even after the formal Crosby association ended, Trotter persisted on the airwaves, conducting for comic George Gobel's television series. Trotter died in Los Angeles on October 29, 1975.

Another figure associated with the *Kraft* show who became another Crosby fixture was a man whose name wouldn't be recognized by the general public, Murdo MacKenzie. MacKenzie's service as Crosby's chief engineer continued on multiple series and eventually he directed some of the singer's latter programs.

Producer Cal Kuhl, writer Carroll Carroll, comic sidekick Bob Burns, announcer Ken Carpenter, maestro Jimmy Dorsey, maestro John Scott Trotter and engineer Murdo MacKenzie all made profound contributions to the *Kraft Music Hall* during the Crosby years. Yet there were others whose recurring efforts resulted in an even better show. They included Danish comic pianist Victor Borge, who stupefied audiences with the introduction of his phonetic pronunciations, giving new meanings to commas, colons and periods; singers Connee Boswell, Peggy Lee, Mary Martin and Marilyn Maxwell; vocal ensembles the Merry Macs (Joe, Judd and Ted McMichael and Mary Lou Cook) and the Music Maids and Hal; comedian Jerry Lester; actor George Murphy; and "discovering" comic instrumentalists Jerry Colonna and Spike Jones, whose latent talents had been languishing in Trotter's orchestra.

Aside from all the "regulars" who showed up every week or every now and then, Crosby included one or more guest celebrities on each *Kraft* show, a pattern that would prevail on several subsequent Crosby aural features. Many of the big names from the airwaves, the cinema, recordings, the opera, the stage, vaudeville and other entertainment venues turned up to exchange memorable Carroll Carroll–inspired discourses with Crosby. Among their number: the Andrews Sisters, Fred Astaire, Lauren Bacall, Tallulah Bankhead, Robert Benchley, Jack Benny (Crosby's very first guest), Lionel Barrymore, Humphrey Bogart, Nat King Cole, Marlene Dietrich, Douglas Fairbanks Jr., Henry Fonda, Judy Garland, Bob Hope (a frequent visitor), Al Jolson, Frank McHugh, Ethel Merman, Pat O'Brien, Les Paul and Mary Ford, Phil Silvers, Frank Sinatra, Jimmy Stewart and many more.

Said one observer: "His [Crosby's] Kraft radio show was unusually adept at cross-pollinating Crosby with cultural blue bloods (opera stars, concert musicians, classical actors). 'Those longhairs go for humanizing in a big way,' he [Crosby] noted. 'I'd sing an aria with them and they'd sing a scat song with me.' Major stars were eager to join the nation's leading singer in a duet and a few minutes of jaunty Crosbyesque badinage; it was a stamp of pop approval. [Carroll] Carroll explained that the show's attitude was to 'treat opera as if it were baseball and baseball as if it were opera.'"[15]

Kraft Music Hall remained on the air throughout the summer seasons, although hosted by other pop idols that were tapped for specific years. Don Ameche, Bob Crosby, Nelson Eddy, Dorothy Kirsten and Frank Morgan fulfilled those honors.

One of *Kraft*'s diversionary tactics was to infiltrate many of the shows with a sideline venture that had proved successful elsewhere. The show fostered a mock feud between the star (Crosby) and another major NBC headliner on the ether, Bob Hope. Their ongoing war of words came on the heels of radio's most successful verbal tongue-lashing that pitted comedians Fred Allen and Jack Benny against one another, a farce lasting 11 seasons during the 1930s and early 1940s.

Others would get in on the fun, too, including the *Edgar Bergen and Charlie McCarthy Show* in which the wooden dummy (McCarthy) routinely sparred with frequent guest luminary W. C. Fields. *Fibber McGee and Molly*, on the other hand, saw the eccentric inventor-conniver McGee taking on a more levelheaded Doc Gamble, which became a permanent barb-trading lambaste every week for years. And *The Bickersons*, a married couple played by Don Ameche (and later, Lew Parker) and Frances Langford, wouldn't be left out — their verbal diatribes put the screws to one another. Such long-running gags would never have proliferated, of course, if they hadn't increased the size of radio audiences. The ratings invariably indicated that more listeners were tuning in when scrappy insults were introduced into the scripts.

Crosby and Hope took potshots at one another about the obvious physical liabilities and pastimes that characterized each man. Hope liked to razz Crosby about his wealth, his racehorses, his sons, his toupee and his ears. The singer retorted with quips about Hope's inability to capture an Oscar, his lack of sexual prowess, his ski-jump nose and his lagging performance as a golfer. (Crosby, by the way, was honored with an Academy Award for his performance in the movie *Going My Way*.) This greeting on one show wasn't out of the ordinary.

> CROSBY: As I live, ski snoot!
> HOPE: Mattress hip!
> CROSBY: Shovel head!
> HOPE: Scoop nose!
> CROSBY: Lard!
> HOPE: Yes, Dad!

Out of Crosby and Hope's exchanges, the on-air antics — in which one star would visit the other's show to exchange a few gibes — led to their costarring with stunning screen actress Dorothy Lamour in seven motion picture releases. The films were commonly referred to as the *Road* pictures, all for Paramount Studios except the last, for United Artists: *Road to Singapore* (1940), *Road to Zanzibar* (1941), *Road to Morocco* (1942), *Road to Utopia* (1945), *Road to Rio* (1947), *Road to Bali* (1952), *Road to Hong Kong* (1962). Crosby usually played the swain who got the girl while Hope came off in second place as a humorous also-ran.

While on the subject of filmmaking, this is perhaps as good a time as any to note that Crosby's status as a leading cinematic actor rivaled his persona as a popular radio personality. From 1934 to 1954 he scored in the top 10 box office movie attractions 15 times, with his films reaching first place five of those years. In most of Crosby's celluloid frames, particularly the musicals, he found abundant opportunities to carry a tune as well as to act. In a few features, he was solely limited to thespian duty.

At the same time, of course, in another art form he was making a profusion of recordings—more than any other vocalist, as previously noted. "About the only media that Bing did not dominate were TV (he was getting too old and really wasn't thrilled about doing TV) and concerts," mused one pundit. More will be said about his restricted foray into television. Even in the case of live performances, however, he was relatively successful. Once he began making movies, to the contrary, he effectively circumvented the personal appearance circuit almost entirely.

Among Crosby's other movies, several were well remembered by theater audiences, including: *The Big Broadcast* (1932) featuring the Boswell Sisters, George Burns and Gracie Allen, Cab Calloway, the Mills Brothers, Kate Smith, Arthur Tracy (*The Street Singer*) and many more radio stars; *Anything Goes* (1936) with Ida Lupino, Ethel Merman and others; *Holiday Inn* (1942) with Crosby flanked by Fred Astaire; *Going My Way* (1944) with costars Barry Fitzgerald and Risë Stevens; *The Bells of St. Mary's* (1945) as Crosby appeared alongside Ingrid Bergman and William Gargan; *Blue Skies* (1945) featuring Fred Astaire, Joan Caulfield and Billy De Wolfe; *The Country Girl* (1954) with Grace Kelly; *White Christmas* (1954) with Rosemary Clooney, Vera-Ellen and Danny Kaye; *Anything Goes* (1956) including Mitzi Gaynor, Phil Harris and Donald O'Connor; and *High Society* (1956), said to be Crosby's personal favorite, in which he appeared with Louis Armstrong, Celeste Holm, Grace Kelly and Frank Sinatra.

While Crosby was a major Paramount star, on a few occasions he worked for other studios, such as in *The Bells of St. Mary's* (Rainbow-RKO) and *High Society* (Metro-Goldwyn-Mayer). In all, he turned up in 114 theatrical releases between 1930's *The King of Jazz* and 1974's *That's Entertainment*, a remarkable feat by any measure. Considering the fact that an adoring public primarily perceived him as a singer rather than an actor, his accomplishments on the silver screen appear even more gargantuan.

Returning to the *Kraft Music Hall*, Crosby's performing style resonated deeply with his listeners. Particularly was this true during the war years when any light amusement was welcomed in American homes. "Crosby's effect on national morale is perhaps difficult to appreciate more than a half a century later," a critic acknowledged a few years ago. "He only had to sing a song once and the record shops worked out whether it was going to be another big hit or just an also-ran." Such possibilities testify to the colossal impact that Crosby had over millions of loyal fans and their buying habits.

A radio historiographer offered this assessment of his talent.[16]

> Crosby, of course, was only partly a singer. He was at least half a comedian, a

man who never seemed to take singing all that seriously.... It was as if he were singing for the sheer joy of it.... A song was not an art form to Crosby; it was fun — part of his persona, but not the whole of it. Pop singing can be divided roughly into "AC" and "BC": Before Crosby, singers sang at you; after Crosby and radio, they sang to you.... Crosby managed to sing into a microphone and make the mike vanish, as if it were eavesdropping on him. From his earliest films, he radiated a twinkle that told people he also didn't take his lover-boy baritone role that seriously. While Sinatra was erotic and aloof, Bing was pipe-and-slippers comfy. Bing was a kidder and, like his idol Jolson, even whistled while he worked.... He sang with great warmth and even urgency, and during the war became an early voice from home with sentimental renderings of *I'll Be Seeing You, I'll Be Home for Christmas* and, of course, *White Christmas.* He specialized in casual tunes, odes to the simple life, such as *Moonlight Bay, Ol' Buttermilk Sky, In the Cool, Cool, Cool of the Evening, Lazy, Mississippi Mud, Gone Fishin', Great Day,* and *It's a Good Day.* He sang in the sunshine, or perhaps sunbeams simply sought him out.

One of the more memorable features of each Christmas show occurred when sponsor J. L. Kraft appeared with Crosby annually to deliver a seasonal message of hope and happiness. In the background, as Kraft spoke, listeners could hear the sounds of the Kraft staff chorale singing songs of good cheer. While simplistic, it undoubtedly touched the hearts of the program's loyal fans and many purchasers of the firm's kitchen commodities.

Crosby was dubbed with a new sobriquet in that era that accompanied him everywhere from that time forward. He became "the Groaner" perhaps as much as Frank Sinatra became "Ol' Blue Eyes." Crosby's laidback style permitted him to turn up at the studio only a little while before the *Kraft* show went on the air. His producers took the broadcasts far more seriously than their star did. It was a trait that was clearly manifest in nearly every area of his life.

His tenure with the Kraft Foods Company spanned a decade and finally came to an abrupt and ignoble conclusion. The official line given to reporters was that he and his employers couldn't reach a satisfactory financial agreement. Kraft hadn't provided Crosby with a tax shelter, the Groaner complained, and he was dismayed because only about 11 or 12 percent of his proffered compensation was actually going to him. The remainder, he said, went into the coffers of the federal treasury. But there was a hidden agenda that the singer didn't want publicized out of concern that his legions of faithful followers might rebuke him if they knew it.

To wit, for some time the independent-minded Crosby had implored both his sponsor and network (NBC) to let him record his programs in advance of their airdates. His request might have had any of a number of grounds prompting it.

For one, he didn't want to be at a specific place and time every week to perform but rather preferred to record several shows early, thereby being freed up to play golf, to trout fish in Canada, to relax at his Idaho ranch or to do whatever else he preferred while he was "on the air." (A couple of radio scholars dismissed that idea's substance by hinting: "If necessity is the mother of invention, then laziness may be the mother of necessity."[17])

For another reason, Crosby's own production firm was starting to improve and market recording equipment and — being a sharp capitalist — he might have considered its demonstrated use would result in a potentially lucrative return to his future business. Other observers suggested that Crosby wanted to have the flexibility to edit out program sections he didn't like, or achieve a smoother broadcast show and schedule his rehearsals at more convenient times. Yet another motive for taping a program would have been to eliminate the necessity of rebroadcasting to the West Coast after a live show was aired for the East Coast three hours earlier — merely replay the tape for the West Coast. That way, the cast and crew could take off following the "original."

Nonetheless, the networks had collectively adopted an inviolable position against transcribing any program they carried. They held fast to that rule, and didn't appear anxious to relax it even for a popular star of Crosby's caliber. The major chains had solid reasons, also, in defending their stance.

There was a longstanding belief among radio executives that — if the immediacy of live programming were missing — broadcast quality would inevitably suffer. "You can't have one without the other," they deliberated. They said it would affect the impromptu mood of the program that listeners considered special. By airing a taped show, people would turn off their radios and sponsors would pull their money out of the medium, they theorized. If advertisers were paying for Bing Crosby, they expected to hear him and not a mechanical voice beamed from a control booth. Yet another — possibly more intimidating — rationale that radio's CEOs advanced for keeping transcriptions off the air was their very unequivocal fear that performers might try to peddle their own shows to independent stations, bypassing the networks that augmented their star status in the first place.

So a line was drawn in the sand that could not be surmounted. Unfortunately for Kraft and NBC, Crosby pulled a stunt that he had used when he became unhappy with his treatment at the Cocoanut Grove 14 years earlier (in June 1931). When things didn't go to his satisfaction, he quit — lock, stock and barrel. In June 1945, having been on the air for Kraft nine full seasons, the Groaner picked up his marbles and went home. He'd go looking for somebody who was interested in his concept of transcribing his show instead.

This wasn't out of the ordinary for Crosby. In business matters, "Crosby could be difficult and moody. Things were done his way or he walked out. He would leave a broadcast in the lurch and go play golf if something annoyed him," a radio historiographer maintained. His brother Bob, meanwhile, also a crooner, confessed: "He has no friends." He could pass through a city without calling a sibling whom he hadn't seen in years. Bob Crosby depicted "a sort of cellophane bag" in which his brother had placed himself. "He lives in this bag and opens it now and then for a little while. You can only get inside for a minute, then he shuts you out."[18]

The food processor (Kraft) as well as the network — both giant U.S. corporations — retained high-priced attorneys to do their bidding. Neither was about to let Bing Crosby off the hook simply because he didn't want to play ball with them any longer. After all, Crosby had signed a contract binding him, according to Kraft, to on-air services for that sponsor for five more seasons. He'd not be getting off without a fight, and the parties geared up for a legal battle.

Crosby countered Kraft's position by claiming that, under California law, personal contracts couldn't continue more than seven years. The warring factions quibbled for months. In the meantime, the 1945–1946 radio season kicked off without Crosby, then headlined by pianist Eddy Duchin and comic Frank Morgan with contributions by the Charioteers ensemble. The legal impasse was at last resolved in early 1946 when Crosby agreed to return to *Kraft Music Hall* to finish the final weeks of the current season. Duchin and Morgan remained on the program during that period. At that juncture, Crosby's services to Kraft and NBC were terminated and all contractual obligations were considered fulfilled.

It was an inglorious end to what had been one of the radio audience's most stimulating associations. The Kraft show, incidentally, persisted through September 22, 1949. Eddie Foy, Edward Everett Horton and Frank Morgan presided over it in 1946-1947. An earlier celebrity, Al Jolson, who served alongside Paul Whiteman, returned as singing host for the last two seasons. Although it isn't well remembered, there was a brief reprise of the Kraft program between February 27 and June 19, 1955, an hour-long musical variety marathon over CBS on Sunday nights. Making a brief comeback as its host was legendary entertainer Rudy Vallee who debuted on radio in 1924, predating Crosby by seven years. The Kraft series was to be his last steady aural-only airdate. (For more about Vallee, see The Vocalists chapter.)

Subsequently, Crosby pitched a new show, with many similarities to the old one, to anybody who would back it and allow it on the air in a prerecorded format. He didn't have to wait long before inking a deal with Philco Radio Corporation and ABC Radio. The American Broadcasting Company was established as a separate full-fledged web only a couple of years earlier (it had previously been the Blue network of NBC and ultimately was to endure as a growing competitor). It also had little to lose by attracting a star of Crosby's eminence and the luminaries he would draw as guests — why yes, of course, it would be delighted to take him on any terms, transcriptions included. ABC would even permit him to choose the programs that preceded and followed his on the air, another unprecedented inducement. In so doing, Crosby would be able to keep the airwaves free of "objectionable" programming near his own that might diminish his potential audience size. A couple of commentators averred, "One assumes that such 'offensive programs' might have included radio shows like Frank Sinatra's. Bing had his own following, but why get into a ratings fight if one can manipulate a network?"[19]

Crosby's show would be the first to transcend the recording barrier and establish a new — and permanent — trend in the industry. Others would soon follow the experiment in the wake of Crosby's persistence (Groucho Marx's *You Bet Your Life* didn't waste any time after Crosby broke the ice). But at the outset, Philco maintained uneasiness about recording those shows ahead of time. What if the quality suffered? It wouldn't be a good deal for the firm. To counter such a prospect, Philco executives included a clause in Crosby's contract stipulating that if the show's ratings fell below a 12 share over four consecutive weeks, the program would immediately institute live broadcasts.

How could Crosby possibly lose? He got the pact he wanted, an arrangement that would allow him to test out his idea and — at the same time — this sweet deal was cemented with a weekly salary of $7,500 and a commensurate budget of $22,500. (Another source reported Crosby's income at $8,000 with $35,000 for the show itself, which may have occurred in a succeeding season.) As he sang in one of his films: "Blue skies, smiling at me, nothing but blue skies do I see." Everything was surely going his way.

While he was on a roll, Crosby decided to carry things further — several hundred miles further, in fact. Even though the format was essentially a repeat, to foster a new environment Crosby transferred the budding series from Los Angeles to San Francisco. He had found L.A. studio audiences "dull" and "so blasé they wouldn't laugh as much as they should." He was convinced that the performers' reception in the City by the Bay would infuse the

Pianist Eddy Duchin headlined the *Kraft Music Hall* in a mid–1940s phase when former (and later) host Bing Crosby (standing) was in dispute with the sponsor and network. Singer Nat King Cole bantered with the pair during a lighter moment while Crosby was still at the show's helm. Crosby's laid-back style characterized his professional career.

package with extra vitality that audiences at home could clearly distinguish.

For whatever the reason, meanwhile, while occupying that favored catbird seat, Crosby made the decision not to take most of the people who had helped him become so successful on the *Kraft Music Hall* with him to *Philco Radio Time*. In effect, it was a general housecleaning of all the lower echelons, even reaching one of the individuals who had strongly influenced the charismatic personality he exuded on the air. (A source labeled the unfortunates Crosby's "victims.")

Gone would be most of the instrumentalists and recurring *Kraft* cast figures (co-medians, ensembles, vocalists). Unbelievably gone was writer Carroll Carroll, who had created the remarkably superb lines that Crosby and his guests had uttered for a decade — snippets of dialogue that personified the host as a genial, down-to-earth, happy-go-lucky fellow who got along well with everybody. In fact, the only individuals of note from his past that the Groaner would keep company with in the future were bandleader John Scott Trotter, announcer Ken Carpenter and engineer Murdo MacKenzie. Joining them (and replacing The Merry Macs and The Music Maids and Hal as singing ensembles) would be Jud Conlon's Rhythmaires, a mixed quartet conducted by its namesake leader and featuring the voices of Mack McLean, Loulie Jean Norman, Charlie Parlato and Gloria Wood.

Carroll acknowledged in his memoir that Crosby dropped him without batting an eye — no notice, no warning, no confrontation. "Very complex man" was the scribe's tactful response. The Philco scriptwriting assignment went to Hal Kanter while the crooner's fishing buddy and traveling companion, Bill Morrow, took over as producer-director.

The show itself was much like predecessor and successor Crosby features. A song followed the opening signature, then some banter with Carpenter, a commercial, a guest star and more songs and commercials — if you heard one Crosby show, you could be pretty sure that the same format was followed on all his other series under several different monikers. There was no apparent harm in that; he had found a formula (as had some other variety show hosts) that radio audiences were comfortable with, and stuck to it. If it wasn't broke, Crosby wasn't of a mind to fix it.

Crosby recalled many of the pop idols, movie stars, radio personalities and recording artists as his guests whom he had featured on the *Kraft Music Hall*. Bob Hope was the first, turning up for the debut of *Philco Radio Time* on October 16, 1946. It was a show that the network had touted heavily. ("Wednesday is Bing's day!" proclaimed extensive programming plugs.) Lured by the preshow publicity and the novelty of hearing a recorded broadcast on a national network, 24 million people tuned in that first night — enough to make Crosby the fourth-rated radio program that week. The tune-out was just as striking. By November 6, *Newsweek* reported that Crosby had lost 50 percent of his premier-week audience. Crosby's rating hovered in the low 12s, only a few fractions from the end of his coveted trial if it continued.

He recorded the first four shows with a live audience in a week about a month prior to airing. On one of those early broadcasts, when a joke fell flat, comedian Fred Allen remarked: "Okay folks, we can wait four weeks for the laughs." Guests following the launch with Hope included Spike Jones, Les Paul, Ralph Mendez and Ezio Pinza. The advertising agency pushed for celebrities with instant name recognition like Maurice Chevalier, Gary Cooper, Jimmy Durante, Judy Garland and Al Jolson. It soon got all of those and many more icons of their incredible stature in its visiting cast. Soon the ratings spiraled upward, hovering around 15 to 17, and the dubious concern about recording abated. Nevertheless, "The real tale ... in Philco's eyes," said one historian, "was the result Crosby got them in the market. The radios he touted on the air sold out nationally after each show." That was, perhaps after all, the only gauge that ever really counted.

Later, the Hooper ratings concern took a poll of listeners' attitudes in regard to recording those shows. They learned that most people were comfortable with the new arrangement, thereby squashing one of the major objections the networks had argued for years. Few in the audience blamed any loss of quality on the actual recordings but more pointedly cited the showmanship lacking.

Hal Kanter, the new show's writer, recalled those guests and their opportunities with Crosby with a great deal of affection. He also shared a poignant story about his friend that certified Crosby's compassion.[20]

> Any guest that came on had such respect for Bing; they knew that Bing would not permit or countenance poor material, or bawdy material, or inferior material.... There was a dignity about Crosby and ... a level of literacy and humor, that was pretty much unapproachable.... They [the guests] were just delighted to be on the show, to work with the man.

Some performers knew how to make the people in the radio studio their partners.... One night ... Judy Garland was the guest star ... Judy had had a lot of bad publicity and had gone through a rough time. When she finally came out of the hospital and was going to make her first public appearance on the show, at the last minute she got stage fright.... She said, "They're going to hate me; they won't be listening to me, they're going to look for the scars on my wrists...." She was an emotional mess, and Bing went in to reassure her. Then when he walked out on stage ... he said, "We have an old friend here tonight. She's been away for a while, but she's come back, and I know that you missed her because we sure did. Give her a nice welcome; make her feel — make her feel *loved*." ...She walked out on the stage and that audience just put their arms around her and hugged her and kissed her ... *relaxed* her.... It was Bing's sensitivity that dictated that. I don't know too many people who would have done that.

Crosby didn't require a great deal of rehearsal for each performance. John Scott Trotter would visit the movie studio where the Groaner was working at the moment. Between setups or rehearsals or over lunch in Crosby's dressing room, Trotter would run over Crosby's numbers on the piano. When the star arrived at the broadcast studio, the orchestra had already rehearsed and was ready. Together they'd run over the songs for the show once and Crosby was ready to record. No need to louse up a perfectly good day when one could be doing other things he preferred, the crooner believed.

For radio buffs in particular, it's important to understand that the achievements resulting from Bing Crosby's determination to record his radio programs would literally change the face of broadcasting forever. While such innovations would undoubtedly have resulted in time, it was Crosby and no one else who initially introduced the concept to the masses. *The New York Times* acclaimed it as a "portentous premier" while gushing: "Mr. Crosby has delivered a major, if not fatal, blow to the outworn and unrealistic prejudice against the recorded program." From his "experiment," not only did aural tape recording develop, the advancement eventually led to videotape recording, still in use today. In fact, it would revolutionize not only broadcasting but also the recording and film industries, too. A more comprehensive overview of the process in making those strides seems worthy at this juncture for indeed, it ultimately affected not only how thousands in the industry performed their duties — but how millions benefited from their efforts.

The recording process when *Philco Radio Time* hit the airwaves in autumn 1946 was, at best, primitive. The shows were provided on discs, requiring three of them per 30-minute performance. Then they were dispersed to network affiliates across the nation. For the very first time the local stations had the power to decide when they would air a program, in due course giving them considerably greater control over their broadcast schedules as more and more series adopted prerecording. That's how it worked in theory anyway. In practice, it was a different matter.

Bob Mott, who spent his career as a network sound effects technician, was an eyewitness to that early recording process. He discusses it in detail in one of his books. Sixteen-inch records were used and dual Fairchild turntables were required to reproduce the sound. If a station didn't own the right equipment, it had to purchase it to air programs recorded on discs. Accompanying each set of the trio of discs — each disc containing about 10 minutes of programming, resulting in the necessity for the two turntables — was a printed "Instruction and Cue Sheet." It advised: "This sheet will give your playback engineer and local announcer information about their part in the production of 'PHILCO RADIO TIME' STARRING BING CROSBY — Program #24B in the 1948-49 series."

Following that, there were specifics about the equipment, the fact that "the program has been timed out to approximately 29:30" and details in how to proceed at points where the local announcer was expected to cut into the program. Cues were provided, indicating when local announcements were to be made and for how long. It was quite complicated and required extensive concentration on the part of the engineer and announcer so the production could come off flawlessly.

Mott, a network sound tech who worked hundreds of those recording sessions, didn't readily embrace taping as the bonus some portrayed it to be. Tape machines made live radio outdated, he observed, noting that when the shows were done live, everyone gave his or her best effort to it. Tape altered that dramatically. "Just when we all resigned ourselves to that bitter pill, along came television," he lamented. Mott's impressions of those changes from an insider's point of view are particularly insightful.[21]

> With the advent of transcriptions, no one knew for sure whether what they were doing was going to be accepted for the air show....
>
> This uncertainty was especially frustrating to the seasoned radio actors accustomed to accepting roles on shows that were sometimes back-to-back with the one they were doing. When shows were live, the actors knew that, come hell or high water, they'd be off the air at a certain time.... If the show was being recorded, they had to wait until the director gave the all-clear signal. And that might not be until after they'd done two or three or even a dozen different "takes."
>
> They still had to sweat it out until the completion of the recording because the records couldn't be edited. One mistake, one cough, and the whole show had to be done over from the beginning. Even if the script was 30 pages and the mistake occurred on page 29, the whole show had to be done over....
>
> Even worse, a show redo didn't have to be caused by a mistake or cough. Directors with the luxury of safety ... agonized over whether they would accept a particular recording for broadcast. Shows that would be considered excellent by live standards were now being done over and over and over again.... Directors began setting everyone's teeth on edge with ... "That was just great, everybody, but I think we can all do just a little better."

The discs were pressed rapidly. As a consequence, the sound quality diminished. Beyond that, some local station engineers who took a nonchalant attitude toward the intricate process required in playing the discs on the air occasionally caused a show's continuity to be interrupted. These factors, in addition to guests whose names weren't always legendary, undoubtedly contributed to the new series' early ratings tumble.

Bing Crosby Enterprises was then a six-member production unit located in San Carlos, on the San Francisco peninsula. A rather enterprising but obscure technician on its staff, John Mullin, offered an innovative solution to the show's inherent transcription complexities that seemed light years ahead of prevailing methods. Serving with Britain's Royal Air Force during the Second World War, Mullin was assigned to monitor any diversionary tactics that enemy communications had developed apart from established norms. In 1942, he learned that the Germans had perfected a superior recording technology that transcended anything the industry had previously known. "Germany was on the air all night," Mullin reported. "We heard beautiful music and you'd swear there was a live orchestra playing. It went on and on without a break and it was obvious that they weren't using 78 rpm records because there was no scratching or surface noise."

Mullin couldn't determine the source of the Germans' high-quality system until the war ended, however. When the Allies marched into Frankfurt, he learned the answer: magnetic tape. Realizing the importance of that find, Mullin dismantled two Radio Frankfurt machines. He smuggled them out of the country, literally shipping the parts to himself at his home in San Francisco, accompanied by 50 rolls of plastic tape. By the time he was released from the service and returned home, his shipments were waiting for him. Mullin put the mechanisms together and demonstrated their use to the Institute of Radio Engineers in San Francisco in April 1946. Within a year he had convincingly persuaded the producers of *Philco Radio Time* to discard the antiquated system of recording the program in favor of magnetic tape. That summer (August 1947), for the very first time, a radio show was tape-recorded. It aired on October 1, 1947, over ABC at the start of Crosby's new season.

As a result, *Philco* could be recorded just about anywhere, then cut, pieced, edited and spliced. Not only that, it was preserved on tape for the very first time. Competing network engineers couldn't figure out how there was none of the normal needle scratch and surface noise they had long been accustomed to hearing. The horizons were suddenly infinite for assembling improved programming in ways that only a short time before hadn't been tried.

An investigative journalist who supplied many of these facts offered this compelling backdrop to the budding possibilities in using tape.[22]

> Bing's involvement with tape recording came some fifty years after the Danish physicist Valdemar Poulsen invented magnetic recording in 1898. Ironically, the crooner's songs of love and peace were taped on machines developed initially as weapons of war.
>
> The Germans called them Magnetophons and they had been used by the Nazi war machine to broadcast Der Fuehrer's speeches and other propaganda throughout Europe at a time when Germany was crumbling.
>
> The Gestapo had also used them for interrogation and were able, by judicious editing, to concoct confessions from tortured prisoners.
>
> So it took a Danish physicist, a German madman and an American crooner to produce the device which changed the course of broadcasting.

Those two original Magnetophon machines couldn't maintain their reliability forever, of course. Crosby's entrepreneurial instincts kicked into gear. He formed a business relationship with the Ampex Company. Mullin worked with the firm's engineers nearly nonstop to produce an even more advanced device, the Ampex 200. When it went on the market, demand for the new apparatus was instant and phenomenal. ABC, the first to buy, ordered a dozen machines — four for each of its New York, Chicago and Hollywood radio facilities. Mullin's wartime memento — cultivated by Crosby's operation — was literally spawning a multimillion-dollar commercial enterprise that was to result in a corporate behemoth known as Ampex.

That wouldn't be the end of the discoveries, however. Within four years Mullin was demonstrating a new process he called videotape recording (VTR), capable of taping and preserving television features. A short time later he was able to offer color VTR. The Crosby Research Foundation would eventually amass many patents on magnetic tape recording. By 1947, Sears, Roebuck and Company was selling a model with thin wire as the recording medium for $170, opening up progress to the domestic professional and consumer market.

While the fidelity was lacking and the price high for a time when the minimum wage was a quarter an hour, the new system — while heavy and cumbersome — was more portable than previous devices.

Bing Crosby Enterprises was standing on the precipice of still further accomplishment when a strong dose of reality set in. Ampex engineers had been working feverishly in their own experiments. By then the firm was overtaking Crosby. Mullin acknowledged: "Their system was so superior to ours that we recommended to Bing that he stop further development because we didn't stand a chance." As a result, in 1956 Crosby sold his electronics division of Bing Crosby Enterprises to the Minnesota Mining and Manufacturing Company (3M). That firm had earlier produced substitute tape for Crosby when Mullin's original supply of 50 German tapes was exhausted.

Crosby's trailblazing activity led the national radio chains to finally agree that taping programs did little to dilute their anticipated standard of excellence. In fact, sound quality could virtually be guaranteed without the nagging, costly repeats for the West Coast that tradition had dictated. Not only did Groucho Marx's producer John Guedel speedily jump aboard the recording bandwagon, others were quick to follow. Musical series fronted by Frankie Carle, Burl Ives, Wayne King, Guy Lombardo, Frank Parker, Barry Wood and Michel Piastro and The Longines Symphonette put their programs on tape weeks and even months ahead. A radio historian suggested: "To a degree, the producers of many music shows on ETs [electrical transcriptions] restricted the content to long-standing 'chestnuts.' This gave a program more mileage and greater timeliness. Although a viable transcription procedure, the ETs frequently had a format that lacked the very popular tunes needed to entice the broadest possible audience."

The same scholar described the aftermath following the introduction of several methods that allowed programs to be recorded for later broadcast.[23]

Within the broadcast industry, the choice between "live" and ET absorbed the energies of producers, advertisers, and technicians well into the 1950s. But their decision scarcely affected the ultimate ear. A listener wanted a good show. He did not much care whether Jo Stafford or Percy Faith came into his home via a simultaneous studio production or a month-old, carefully edited and processed disc or tape. Audience ratings in dozens of cities generally indicated that transcribed shows were taking the lead over "live" network fare. The listener was the one to be pleased — and he tuned in the best, "live" or "canned."

While his electronics developments would be one of Crosby's most successful business ventures (one report said he made an extra $40,000 weekly peddling his own shows to independent stations, a fear the network honchos had expressed earlier), the crooner entered many other fields as an entrepreneur, making some prudent commercial buys. Among his sideline ventures Crosby invested in atomic energy, film and TV production, oil wells, property, soft drinks and sports, to name a few. His singular noteworthy failure was his music publishing company. An observer explained that there was either too much competition already or Crosby and company didn't have the essential expertise. Nevertheless, he reportedly grossed a cool million every year during the 1940s. One could make no mistake; almost every project Crosby embarked on had the potential of turning to gold.

No one was smoother on the air than Bing Crosby. But even his professional nonchalance was tried at least once. *Philco* scribe Hal Kanter tells what happened one night during the late 1940s.[24]

We were actually taping the show and while they were on stage, I was sitting in Bing's dressing room writing the tag, the good nights. And Bill [Morrow, the producer] would come in from the control room during the musical numbers and say, "How's it going?" and "Let's see it" and "Change that" and "Fix this" and "Okay" and "Hurry up" and so forth. Finally, Ken Carpenter was doing the last commercial when Bill walked out on stage with the script and carbon copies; he had made a change in one on pencil and was literally handing copies out to Bing, to the guest star and whoever else had something to say, and then slipped Ken's carbon copy under the copy he was reading.

We never stopped doing that; it was done like a live broadcast, even though it was on tape. And they came to the tag and they read it, did the good-nights. The show was over, and I was standing out in the hall; Bing came out and fixed me with a glare. If it had been a laser beam, it would have left holes through my head and on the wall behind me, and he said, "Don't you ever do that to me again." That was the only time I ever saw that man really mad about the show. Also, I guess he and Ken were about the only two people I know who could carry a thing like that off and not be rattled by it.

During this same period with the American Broadcasting Company, Crosby was simultaneously presiding over a quarter-hour daytime disc jockey program. It aired on the Columbia Broadcasting System for the makers of Minute Maid orange juice from November 15, 1948, through October 27, 1950. The feature was Crosby's first experience broadcasting on multiple days since his association with CBS in the early 1930s and was a harbinger of things to come. Crosby's association with ABC came to an end with the close of the 1948-1949 radio season. He had been in prime time there for three years.

Meanwhile, CBS president William S. Paley, Crosby's old crony from 1931 who had given the Groaner his first shot on nationwide radio, conducted several raids on NBC's treasury of superstars in the late 1940s. Offering Freeman Gosden and Charles Correll (*Amos 'n' Andy*), Jack Benny, Edgar Bergen, George Burns and Gracie Allen and Red Skelton multimillion-dollar capital gains pacts that would allow them to keep more of their income, Paley successfully wooed them all from NBC to CBS. In addition — with the ban against transcriptions relaxed — Paley broached deals with Crosby and Groucho Marx, both at ABC. He soon scooped them up, too, to enlarge his burgeoning bevy of celebrated icons.

Paley paid $1 million for 25 percent of Crosby's company, which controlled his radio and movie performances. CBS committed itself to finding a sponsor that would sign an ironclad contract with Crosby for three years. Liggett & Myers, the manufacturer of Chesterfield cigarettes — one of Crosby's early CBS underwriters — agreed to cough up (no pun intended) $40,000 weekly for the show, or more than $1.5 million per 39-week season. (According to *Variety*, in 1950 a typical evening radio mystery series, produced at a cost of $4,000 to $7,000, reached 267 households for every dollar an advertiser spent. The trade paper contrasted those figures with other formats, stating that musical-variety shows, such as Crosby's, drew only 215 households for the same advertising dollar.)

Crosby "left like a shot for CBS." He was anxious to return to prime time on the chain that had not only treated him with such promise and respect nearly two decades before but which commanded greater prestige than ABC, reaching significantly larger audiences in additional markets. It was to be Crosby's final shift in aural webs, and his new association would persist even beyond the generally accepted conclusion of radio's golden age. It proved to be a smart move for Crosby as well as CBS.

A side note: NBC's journalistic mystery drama *The Big Story*, which was launched in the spring of 1947, leaped into a challenging race for dominant ratings with Crosby's *Philco Radio Time* on ABC. Both aired at 10 P.M. on Wednesdays. When Crosby switched to CBS, having been burned by the NBC drama during several ratings periods, he opted for a 9:30 P.M. slot, out of harm's way, giving him the ability to croon without the dangers of encountering that persistent newspaperman again.

The new series, debuting on September 21, 1949, was known as *The Bing Crosby Chesterfield Show*. With that exception, it was in many ways a carbon copy of its predecessor Crosby features, again with Ken Carpenter as announcer, John Scott Trotter as orchestra leader and weekly guests from Hollywood, radio and other venues. When Liggett & Myers' three-year contract expired in 1952, General Electric stood waiting in the wings. It underwrote *The General Electric Show* headlined by Crosby with the same cast and format intact for two more years.

Not until 1954, in fact, were there any significant changes in the Crosby lineup that listeners had become so accustomed to a couple of decades earlier. By then radio was facing some stiff economic realities. More and more programs, stars, advertisers and audiences were cashing in longstanding habits, some of them vanishing entirely as others shifted to the rapidly increasing attractiveness of television, which was siphoning off large numbers from that component quartet. Radio was moving to the critical list, and those who preferred it would have to adapt new strategies to survive. Seeking to stem the tidal wave sweeping radio out to sea, CBS programmers would fight valiantly against the current, much longer and in some ways more tenaciously than its peers were doing.

In 1954, Crosby was pulled from the prime-time schedule (a time slot when more and more people were turning to television) and offered a quarter-hour slot weekday mornings. Recall, he had filled a morning period only a brief while before. He would also lose the backing of a full orchestra as austerity set in. For the first time in decades a small instrumental ensemble, the Buddy Cole Trio, accompanied him for some of his weekday programs. Singer Rosemary Clooney, an old friend who costarred with Crosby in the 1954 motion picture release *White Christmas*, was a recurring contributor.

Buddy Cole, a rare piano talent, recalled: "I'd go in and record a basic track with Bing or Rosie with just the rhythm backing. I've done as many as twenty tunes a day with Bing. Then, two or three days later, we'd play them back and add electric guitars, organ, kettle drums, chimes, or whatever." At one point Cole had nearly 300 Crosby tunes, 200 of Clooney's and 40 duets in the can. The following year (1955) Crosby moved just ahead of the prime-time hours, again airing five days a week. He continued the weekday-weeknight pattern, morning or evening, during the remainder of his radio life.

Between 1956 and 1957, Crosby did a series of five-minute CBS Radio spots for the Ford Motor Company. On September 2, 1957, he again joined forces with Clooney, that time on an early morning 10-minute singing series over CBS that ran for several months, into 1958. In early 1960, the pair was reunited for a final program that lasted more than two and a half years. When the duo left the air on September 28, 1962, it was absolutely the end of an era. The last two survivors of CBS's long-suffering dramatic lineup (*Suspense* and *Yours Truly, Johnny Dollar*) also disappeared from the dial that weekend, never to return.

Crosby had transcended the departures of hundreds of network radio features, including every one of CBS's variety series except *Arthur Godfrey Time*. For more than three decades he made radio his permanent address, where he was more prevalent than in any other medium. Few vocalists, with the possible exception of Kate Smith, could begin to approach his durability on the national airwaves.

The writers of Bing Crosby's memoirs have all had their say in regard to his well-publicized personal life. Much of it is unflattering. He is characterized as a notorious boozer and womanizer whose frequent marital infidelities coincided with plenty of occasions when he purposely stayed away from home.[25] One author dismissed those extracurricular activities, stating: "There is something likeable about a man who sows his wild oats rather spectacularly when young and then settles down to become Mr. Respectability."[26] Most other observers vigorously disagreed. For all his adoration by a fawning public, his successes and achievements, Crosby was subject to human frailties and many of his assessors spelled them out. Said a couple of them[27]:

> Behind the scenes, he [Crosby] was viciously selfish, mistreating those around him for his driving ambitions of fortune and fame. Onstage he was every woman's dream husband, but offstage he constantly abused his legendary wife, Dixie Lee, leaving for Europe as she lay dying of cancer. Onstage he was everyone's ideal "father of the year," but offstage he was cruel and cold to his children, discarding his first family for a second one, then turning against them as well. Onstage, he was a moral, honest man of God, but offstage he was a desperate near-alcoholic, a lonely man who could betray his best friends ... for the sake of his own success.

"What very few people knew — and what it took his sons at least two generations to reveal — was that the new father would turn into a martinet," said another. "He punished the little children severely when they were naughty. As they grew older, the beatings got harder.... Bing was away more and more, making promotional tours for all those movies in which he showed what a good guy he always was....

"The one incontrovertible fact is that Bing had a cruel streak in him," that author continued. "Too many people point to that to leave the matter in doubt. Was he unhappy about his marriage? Very likely. Did he resent the fact that the boys were growing up in their mother's image? Probably. It also seems probable that the younger Crosbys were convenient dogs to kick when things were going wrong. The lungs that produced the magic voice were the engine for his lost temper."[28]

Still another reporter elaborated on Crosby's child-rearing strategy: "The boys ... at times were positively frightened of their father. Punishment came in more and more severe beatings.... If they did anything wrong, there was a stick to be produced. Even worse was the strap, which as far as they were concerned was as much a part of their father's prop collection and wardrobe as his hat and pipe....

"'I dropped my pants,' Gary remembered, 'pulled down my undershorts and bent over. Then he went at it with the belt dotted with metal studs....

"'Quite dispassionately,' he said, 'without the least display of emotion or loss of self-control, he whacked away until he drew the first drop of blood, and then he stopped.'

"All this was in such stark contrast to the lovable character the fans swooned to in darkened rooms or the one they so devoutly went to see at the movies," the scribe acknowledged.[29]

Five years following Dixie Lee's death on November 1, 1952, Crosby wed Texas-bred Olive Kathryn Grandstaff, another starlet whom he met through the cinema, on October 21, 1957, in Las Vegas. She was half his age. In one of two Crosby memoirs she penned she described herself as a "Baptist alto" and gave high marks to Dixie Lee as "an excellent singer with a trained soprano voice." She added: "During our twenty years of marriage, my greatest musical accomplishment was to sing alto to Bing's tenor, or occasionally sing the lead in barber shop harmony while Bing sang bass."[30] Kathryn Crosby bore her husband three children.

Bing Crosby made no guest appearances on television until 1951. There is strong evidence that he was never as comfortable in front of a TV camera as he was a microphone, where many of the expectations for video simply didn't exist. One of his last sponsors—General Electric—disciplined him during the 1953-1954 radio season for his unwillingness to appear on television, hastening the collapse of his long-running prime-time radio show. (It was withdrawn after 32 weeks instead of the normal 39-week season.) It was classic Crosby, doing what suited him best, regardless of what anyone thought. In this case, his unwillingness to yield apparently offended a third major sponsor.

Crosby was not oblivious to the opportunities the small screen ushered in. He merely preferred allowing others to perform there. Bing Crosby Enterprises was still operating as TV took over the nation's primary home-based amusement pursuits, and Crosby saw an open door and entered it. His production unit developed a handful of moderately successful series, including *The Gloria Swanson Show*, a 1954 syndicated dramatic anthology; *Ben Casey*, a medical drama starring Vince Edwards that ran on ABC-TV from 1961 to 1966; *Slattery's People*, a 1964–1965 CBS-TV political drama starring actor Richard Crenna; a few Bing Crosby hour-long variety show specials; and last but not least, finally, an ABC-TV sitcom titled *The Bing Crosby Show* that aired from September 14, 1964, to June 14, 1965.

The latter series concerned a character named Bing Collins and his family. An electrical engineer, Collins was an ex–pro singer who departed show business to raise his family in his new line of work. He was somehow able to heist a tune or two in every show, nonetheless. Life at home was stressful. Ellie Collins, his wife, played by actress Beverly Garland, had delusions of becoming a star herself. Their 15-year-old boy-crazy daughter, Janice, played by Carol Faylen, was in sharp contrast to their 10-year-old daughter Joyce. Diane Sherry played Joyce, an overachiever with a high IQ. The family's live-in handyman, Willie Walters (actor Frank McHugh), somehow got involved in the antics and disturbances within the family setting every week. In this father-knows-best epoch, Crosby mediated quarrels, patched up divisions and offered practical advice. It was the satisfying stuff of which 1960s sitcoms were made.

Crosby found time later on to sing once more with Rosemary Clooney. The pair went on a personal appearance tour—something Crosby seemed to loathe years before—that carried them to several major cities in the United States and Europe, where crowds continued to swell the halls.

Bing Crosby passed away on a golf course in Madrid, Spain, on October 14, 1977, doing one of the things he loved most. Throughout his extensive career he was one of the aural ether's salient idols, crooning for as long as the medium influenced America as a foremost source of amusement. In that regard, unequivocally, he had no peer.

The Chamber Music Society of Lower Basin Street

It was serious stuff, those notes blowing out of slide trombones and clarinets when the troops gathered weekly in the early 1940s and 1950s for jam sessions at *The Chamber Music Society of Lower Basin Street*. At the very same time any pretentions to culture were shredded to ribbons by intentional downsizing, courtesy of some defiant interlocutory before and after those torrid numbers. The *Chamber* entourage was unlike anything else in radio. While bluesy tunes might be spilling onto the ether elsewhere, no one else used its musical style to satarize revered institutions like the Metropolitan Opera and similar classical and semiclassical citadels. Here they did, and got away with it. The *Chamber* was routinely in danger of cancellation, but not to worry — when the network got 20,000 letters protesting its intentions on one occasion, it found there really was an audience with a bent toward eccentricity.

Directors: Tom Bennett, Dee Engelbach.
Host: Gene "Dr. Gino" Hamilton.
Announcers: Ward Byron, Milton J. Cross.
Vocalists: Diane Courtney ("the poor man's Flagstad"), Lena Horne, Kay Lorraine ("slow-burning blues chanteuse"); Jane Pickens (1950s), Dinah "Diva" Shore ("our own personal one-woman torchlight parade").
Cast: Jimmy Blair, Ernest Chappell, Jack McCarthy (Dr. Giacomo); Zero Mostel (1942).
Orchestra Conductors: Paul Lavalle (c1941–1944), Henry "Hot Lips" Levine (1950s), Jack Meakin (1940).
Creator-Writer: Welbourn Kelley.
Writers: Jack McCarthy, Jay Sommers.
Guest Artists: Richard Baldwin, Henry Brant, "Professor" Benny Carter, Tommy Dorsey, Lionel Hampton Quartet, Earl Hines, Harry James, Huddie "Leadbelly"

Ledbetter, Sylvia Marlowe, Charlie and Jack Teagarden, more.

Theme Song: *Basin Street Blues.*

Sponsor: Andrew H. Jergens Company for Woodbury soap (April 4, 1943–October 8, 1944); U.S. Army Reserve (April 12–August 2, 1952); sustained (otherwise).

Ratings: Figures have been preserved for only one season, 9.4 in 1943-1944. "The show never made a serious ripple in the ratings," a pundit observed.

On the Air: February 11–August 18, 1940, NBC Blue, Sunday, 4:30–5:00 P.M.; August 26, 1940–April 21, 1941, NBC Blue, Monday, 9:30–10:00 P.M. Eastern Time; April 28–September 22, 1941, NBC Blue, Monday, 9:00–9:30 P.M.; October 1, 1941–February 18, 1942, NBC Blue, Wednesday, 9:00–9:30 P.M.; February 25–December 30, 1942, NBC Blue, Wednesday, 10:00–10:30 P.M.; January 4–February 8, 1943, NBC Blue, Monday, 10:30–11:00 P.M.; April 4–July 11, 1943, NBC Blue, Sunday, 9:15–9:30 P.M.; July 18, 1943–October 8, 1944, NBC Blue/ABC, Sunday, 9:15–9:45 P.M.; July 8–September 30, 1950, NBC, Saturday, 10:00–10:30 P.M.; April 12–August 2, 1952, NBC, Saturday, 10:30–11:00 P.M.

* * *

Radio enjoyed a good spoof.

Comedians Bob and Ray got away with it every day — impersonating virtually everything and everybody they could think of. The "dreaded detective" Mr. Chameleon, "the man of many faces," camouflaged his appearance and altered his voice to prompt cold-blooded killers to give themselves away, and in so doing, apply a kind of double-edged sword. Edgar Bergen found the secret of lampooning an initiative or an individual could be accomplished by mouthing the words of a wooden dummy who uttered hilarious things that Bergen, himself, couldn't get away with.

The pretense of fooling a subject intrigued radio audiences and netted boatloads of satisfying outcomes. So, theorized radio writer Welbourn Kelley (whose career dissolved into penning an obscure soap opera, *King's Row*, after a stint writing publicity for the U.S. Navy), why not poke fun at all those straight-laced classical music buffs? Parodying the tunes favored by the cerebral crowd and especially the trappings in which they were offered was precisely what *The Chamber Music Society of Lower Basin Street* set out to do. That it did it so well was a tribute to all whose membership in that fraternity pulled off the charade that was fostered upon unsuspecting first-time listeners. Tongue-in-cheek, they gave the highbrow set its comeuppance, cutting it down to size in an amusing program of mirthful moments. And at the very same time they offered some pretty striking musical fare combined from several styles.

"You could imagine the concert taking place in an eighteenth-century drawing room with ornate chandeliers and candelabra," an advocate depicted. "Of course, all the musicians were wearing gorgeous cutaways and knee breeches, silver-buckled shoes and powdered wigs. The gowns on the singers were sumptuous enough for royalty." (The reviewer may have overindulged a bit.)

The program's preamble set the stage for what was to come. As it arrived on the ether, violinists, flutists and bass guitarists tuned their instruments, preparing to play. Meanwhile, Milton J. Cross, that highly respected bastion of erudition, narrator of the Metropolitan Opera's weekly radio broadcasts and link to so many scholarly features, offered this epigraph on one outing as the show's announcer, playing it totally straight, displaying not a trace of glee in his delivery:

> Good afternoon, music lovers, and also those of you who just came along for the ride. You are now tuned in to a concert of

the no-doubt world-famous *Chamber Music Society of Lower Basin Street*, the small group of musicologists which gathers every Sunday in Radio City to read the music of the three Bs—barrelhouse, boogie-woogie and the blues. The conductors of this solemn occasion are Maestro Paul Lavalle with his Woodwindy Ten, and Dr. Henry Levine with his Dixieland Little Symphony of eight men and no girls. But, there *is* a girl in the picture, however, and her name is Mademoiselle Dinah Shore, the Tennessee diva who does with the blues. But I'm being motioned to sit down and shut up, for the concert is about to begin, so the next voice you'll hear will be that of the society's chairman, Dr. Gino Hamilton.

Gene Hamilton, the host, a respected NBC staff announcer, enumerated the specific itinerary for each broadcast and acted as an interlocutor, offering conversant and invariably witty asides between numbers. "The announcements were intentionally stuffy and ridiculous, the deadpan delivery wickedly deceptive," certified a radio historiographer.

On the broadcast of May 5, 1940, Hamilton concluded his opening remarks with, "Right now I see that Dr. Levine is ready with the overture. It is the traditional Dixieland chamber reading of *When My Sugar Walks Down the Street* all the little birdies go tweet, tweet, tweet. Note particularly the tenor sax solo played by Professor Louis 'Satch' Bodie Jr."

Following the upbeat jazz number, Hamilton advised: "Those were typical Dixieland shadings and harmonies, about which critics say there is no music more subtle, unless it be a concerto for concrete mixer with a chorus of 16 steam shovels. But now we turn to the Woodwindy Ten and a nostalgic ditty, which is doubtless familiar to you all. The selection is the classic *Down Home Rag* and it is chiefly notable for the fact that it contains a piccolo duet by Professors Lewis "Freckles" Martin and John "Wings" Pepper, bringing you color to our instrumentation. And for the fact that Maestro Lavalle knocks himself out in a number of dizzy technical passages on the clarinet and basso clarinet." Everybody, it seemed, was either titled nobility on this show or had a descriptive moniker (Charles "Corn Horn" Marlowe, for instance, played trumpet with The Barefoot Philharmonic).

Hamilton's introductory discourses offered fresh material every week and thus never became staid, even as he appeared to revel in reminding listeners he was reading every word by using a distinct nuance in his pronunciation. By 1941, the show added a live audience, resulting in a nice touch, giving a reactionary sentiment with raucous laughter and applause to the jibes dished out by host Hamilton. This opening treatise, offered on June 23, 1941, was emblematic.

> Greetings, music lovers, and if we've been canceled again, and you're not hearing this, please don't tell us. This is your chairman, Dr. Gino "Long Locks" Hamilton presiding at another concert of the no-doubt world-renowned *Chamber Music Society of Lower Basin Street*, whose members are dedicated to the preservation of the three Bs—barrelhouse, boogie-woogie and the blues. Tonight we are honored to have with us a group of very famous musical classicists, all of whom are out to give culture its lumps. Our conductors are Dr. Henry "Hot Lips" Levine with his off-the-cob octet, and Maestro Paul Lavalle with his 10 sap-happy woodwinds. And tonight, by the way, they are repeating Prokofiev's *Peter and the Wolf*. The wolf, incidentally, is not Dr. Levine. Our guest commentator is Dr. Will S. Scott of Princeton.... But the house lights are fading now and Dr. Levine is mounting the podium and adjusting his spurs. The overture—*Black Eyes*.

On a typical outing on June 16, 1940, W.C. Handy, whom Hamilton identified as "the grandpappy of the blues," was the half-hour's focus. The Negro composer's music was analyzed, played and sung, and the subject himself reviewed his career. It was customary for a guest — whoever it might be — to comment on the implications of his personal involvement in musical quests during the "intermission" discussion. (It was *soooo* Metropolitan Opera!)

Radio Life certified *The Chamber Music Society of Lower Basin Street* as "one of radio's strangest offspring, a wacky, strictly hep tongue-in-cheek burlesque of opera and symphony."

The show was a direct descendant of an earlier series called *Bughouse Rhythm* that ran from September 4, 1936, through April 26, 1937, initially over NBC and later over NBC Blue. The weekly quarter hour was a satirical aberration that also nudged the more scholarly musical accoutrements and those who reveled in them. Impresario Jack Meakin, who later found his way to the rostrum of *The Chamber Music Society of Lower Basin Street*, was the swing orchestra's conductor at *Bughouse*. Apparently, he never outgrew it nor did it outgrow him.

Milton Cross was also there as the announcer, providing indubitable evidence that — while he obviously enjoyed rubbing elbows with the fashionable coterie of the operatic circuit — he could literally let his hair down and be amused by pulling off a good joke on the same lords and ladies. (On *Chamber*, Cross "added humor with nothing more than his presence," claimed an observer.) A critic also noted that *Chamber* "was ahead of its time." If that's so, *Bughouse* must have been merely a figment in somebody's imagination!

Paul Lavalle, of Cities Service fame, accepted the baton when Jack Meakin permanently moved on. Lavalle, billed as the "woodwind virtuoso" while doubling on clarinet, conducted an aggregate known as the Woodwindy Ten including many "termite-proof virgin pine woodwinds." Doubling, incidentally, ran amok on this show. Collectively, the 10 musicians were proficient on 24 instruments (which underscored their authentic abilities as musicians).

The Chamber Music Society of Lower Basin Street offered some sparkling guests. Richard Baldwin and Henry Brant, a piano duo, satisfied listeners with a rousing rendition of Haydn's *Surprise Symphony* in swing style. Harpsichordist Sylvia Marlowe favored the audience with Mozart's *Turkish March* but under the revised title *Old Man Mozart on the Mooch*. Lionel Hampton's quartet turned up on the *Chamber* dais as did bandleaders Tommy Dorsey ("Dr. Thomas Dorsey," who played "his famous trombone" and was also persuaded to "kick out on a trumpet"), Harry James, Charlie and Jack Teagarden. Comic Zero Mostel added more humor (as if it were needed) as a recurring performer beginning in April 1942. The radio series quickly projected him to Broadway and motion pictures.

Several of the *Chamber*'s alumni were slated for bigger and better things elsewhere. Three were most prominent — Milton Cross, for obvious reasons; Paul Lavalle, who conducted *Highways in Melody* which segued into *The Cities Service Band of America* and then *The Band of America* (1944–1956); and Dinah Shore, who got a boost to international prominence by way of the *Chamber* series. (Details on Cross's life and career are available in The Classics chapter; for Lavalle, see the Cities Service Concerts chapter.)

Frances Rose "Fanny" Shore, meanwhile, was born March 1, 1917, at Winchester, Tennessee, her family moving to Nashville a few years later. (Her slick rendition of *Dinah* would lead to a name change in the late 1930s.) She was to become one of the hottest gal singers ever ("Dinah Shore ranks with the best vocalists broadcasting has to offer" wrote *Variety* as early as August 23, 1939). She cornered a substantial share of the entertainment market in radio, recordings, nightclubs, television and (to a limited extent) movies. A biographer noted that, during her era, she was considered "one of the ten most admired women in the world." Said he: "She epitomized the fairy tale–like rise of a small town girl to nationwide prominence."

She loved to sing even as a child and once recalled: "I stood backstage at the Grand Ole Opry every Saturday I could escape. I only got called five or six times, but I'd be there anyway, just hoping someone would sprain a tonsil and I'd get a chance to sing." While matriculating in sociology at Vanderbilt University, Shore performed regularly over Nashville's WSM beginning about 1937.

Upon graduation in June 1938 she made her way to New York City and was invited by pioneering disc jockey Martin Block to sing on his WNEW program *Make Believe Ballroom*. (See The Disc Jockeys chapter.) The big time was suddenly beckoning. Soon she appeared commonly on a couple of big-name network shows, Ben Bernie's on CBS and Eddie Cantor's on NBC. The latter performer deftly applied her talent to institute cross-programming in the broadcast media. According to a pundit, Cantor purposely scheduled Shore's vocals to air opposite the commercials on competitor Fred Allen's CBS show to siphon audiences away to his cabaret. Shore also landed her own series in 1939 over NBC Blue. Her career in broadcasting was assured.

In addition to numerous guest appearances on nationwide hookups (*The Bob Crosby Show, Command Performance, The Railroad Hour, The Screen Guild Theater, The Spike Jones Show, Suspense, What's New?* etc.), the Tennessee-bred "diva" could lay claim to a passel of ongoing aural gigs:

Musical Mock Trial, with Ben Bernie (1939-1940, CBS)
The Dinah Shore Show (1939-1940, NBC Blue)
The Chamber Music Society of Lower Basin Street (1940, NBC Blue)
The Eddie Cantor Show (1940-1941, NBC)
Songs by Dinah Shore (1941-1942, NBC Blue)
In Person, Dinah Shore (1942-1943, NBC Blue)
The Chase and Sanborn Program (1943, NBC)
Free World Theater (1943, NBC Blue)
Paul Whiteman Presents (1943, NBC)
The Birds Eye Open House, hosted by Shore (1943-1944, CBS; 1944–1946, NBC)
The Ford Show, hosted by Shore (1946-1947, NBC)
The Carnation Contented Hour (1946–1948, NBC)
Your Hit Parade (1947, CBS)
Call for Music, hosted by Shore (1948, CBS)
The Dinah Shore Show (1948, NBC)
The Jack Smith Show (1950–1952, CBS)
The Dinah Shore Show (1953–1955, NBC radio and television)

When television emerged to rival radio for the nation's amusement attention, Shore was one of the first to leap onto the bandwagon, sensing the direction audiences were traveling. She was one of Bob Hope's guests on his first TV special in April 1950. She was among a handful of luminaries on NBC-TV's inaugural *All Star Revue* that emanated from the network's just-opened Burbank studios in California on October 4, 1952. Shore was to be as accepted in that medium as she had been in radio ("the most successful female variety series performer of the 1950s and 1960s" validated one source).

She made numerous guest appearances while presiding over no less than a sextet of her own programs: *The Dinah Shore Show*, from November 27, 1951, through

July 18, 1957, over NBC-TV, a quarter-hour twice weekly; *The Dinah Shore Chevy Show*, from October 5, 1956, through May 12, 1963, over NBC-TV, monthly specials, then a weekly prime-time hour; *Dinah's Place*, from August 3, 1970, through July 26, 1974, over NBC-TV, a weekday half-hour talk show; *Dinah!* (aka *Dinah & Friends*), 1974–1980, a syndicated weekday 90-minute talk show; *Dinah and Her New Best Friends*, from June 5, 1976, through July 31, 1976, over CBS-TV, a weekly prime-time hour; and *Conversation with Dinah*, in 1989 on cable's The Nashville Network.

The CBS series, although brief, was specifically slotted as a summer replacement for the vacationing Carol Burnett. On the *Chevy* show, Shore popularized the sponsor's product by singing its memorable theme with gusto: "See the USA in your Chevrolet!" while closing out every show with her trademark giant-sized hand-to-mouth smooch — "mwah!" Wrote a TV historian: "With her warm, down-home presence, she had the knack of looking completely at ease on television. Attractive without being overtly sexy, her girl-next-door appeal registered with men without threatening women."[1] And she peppered her network daytime series with celebrities doing the unlikeliest things — Ethel Kennedy playing piano, Burt Lancaster mixing spaghetti sauce and Joanne Woodward performing needlepoint. Nevertheless, Shore's most incredible guest undoubtedly was Burt Reynolds. Meeting for the first time on *Dinah's Place*, he and she soon became an "item" in the gossip columns (even though he was 20 years her junior), tales that persisted for several years although they never wed.

On *The Chamber Music Society of Lower Basin Street*, Milton Cross observed that Shore "starts a fire by rubbing two notes together." It was emblematic of his adroit assessment of the soloists appearing before him on that feature.

By 1940, the year she appeared there, the Scripps-Howard newspaper syndicate polled its readers, inquiring who their favorite new radio star was. An unassuming, still quite modest Shore was elected handily. A couple of years later *Radio Life* termed Shore "the most popular singing star since the rise of Kate Smith."

At least one critic suggested that it was the *Chamber* series itself that provided the push Shore needed to propel her into the limelight, distinguishing the show as "her launch pad to fame." Certainly it didn't hurt her any. (Dr. Gino Hamilton introduced her on one May 1940 broadcast by stating the deep South diva was "a good reason why boys leave home to go into radio.") With all due respect, nonetheless, it would appear that *Chamber* was part of a *progression* of good fortune that occurred in Ms. Shore's life. It seemed even a little incongruent that Eddie Cantor allegedly claimed to have "discovered" her. If so, where does WSM, Martin Block, Ben Bernie, her own early network series and *Chamber* fit into the mix, all of which preceded her "discovery" by Cantor? Her rise to glory — while meteoric — upon reflection appears at this distance to have had a myriad of components rather than a simple, defined launching pad.

An interesting sidelight occurred when, in 1941, Cantor failed to exercise his option promptly for her continued services and Edgar Bergen offered her a raise to $750 weekly to come on his show. The matter wound up before an arbitrator, who ruled in favor of Cantor, yet she still got a raise.

Like so many other entertainers, during World War II Shore went overseas to play dates at U.S. Army training camps and naval bases. The international conflagration was actually a windfall to radio performers, noted a historian, and particularly to "girl singers" like Shore and others of her ilk — Kay Armen, Connee Boswell,

Comic-singer Eddie Cantor was creative in touting his radio series. He's shown with his "discovery," diva Dinah Shore, on the proverbial bicycle built for two, garnering more traffic during a publicity stunt outside their studio. By then, Shore was a familiar voice to listeners of *The Chamber Music Society of Lower Basin Street* and other airdate venues.

Joan Edwards, Jane Froman, Georgia Gibbs, Jo Stafford and more. They were "meeting their male fans face-to-face en masse for the first time, and recording transcriptions for overseas broadcasts (the famous 'V discs')."

A music critic calculated: "Dinah Shore's wholesome voice reminded soldiers and sailors of the girl they left behind. Songs by the friendly, velvet-toned vocalist — who a year or two earlier had achieved national acclaim from NBC's *Chamber Music Society of Lower Basin Street*— went out by shortwave or transcription to every place where American boys were fighting or stationed. They inundated her with mail written during off-duty hours in barracks, tents, and foxholes— letters which asked her to sing *I'll Walk Alone* or *I'll Be Seeing You*. Many thanked her for appearing in person at camp shows."

By then Shore was already making recordings and selling them by the hundreds of thousands (*Blues in the Night, Buttons* and Bows, I'll Walk Alone, Shoofly Pie and Apple Pan Dowdy*, etc.). Meanwhile, she appeared in several motion pictures, although she believed she "bombed" there. They included: *Thank Your Lucky Stars* (1943), *Follow the Boys* (1944), *Up in Arms* (1944), *Belle of the Yukon* (1944), *Make Mine Music* (1946, voice only), *Till the Clouds Roll By* (1946), *Fun and Fancy Free* (1947, voice only), *Bongo* (1947, voice only), *Aaron Slick from Punkin Crick* (1952). It was Warner Brothers, incidentally, that suggested she become a "honey blonde" for films instead of the life-long brunette she had always been. Her updated image remained for the rest of her life.

In 1979, she appeared in a made-for-TV movie, *Death Car on the Freeway*. Personal appearances occupied her professional interests into the 1980s. She took up golf and cooking, authored triple best-selling cookbooks (*Someone's in the Kitchen with Dinah, The Dinah Shore Cookbook, Dinah Shore's American Kitchen*) and sponsored a professional golf tournament that bore her name from 1972 onward at Rancho Mirage, California. Dinah Shore died February 24, 1994, in Beverly Hills, California.

Welbourn Kelley, creator of *The Chamber Music Society of Lower Basin Street* and its lead writer, praised the feature's "superlative instrumentalists" in some published commentary in 1940. In the same piece, he distinguished the show for an announcer's "composed and analytical manner" in which he "discusses the vulgarisms of the music we hear and does so with a straight face." Kelley concludes: "His self-conscious determination to ennoble the swing phase of music by stealing the nomenclature of symphonic programs is one of the best burlesques on the air." Indeed. Kelley's continuity scripting, exactly as heard on the broadcast of May 26, 1940, is priceless, offering evidence of just how much fun he and those who lightly disparaged "grand" traditions had every week.

As you all know, fellow members of the Chamber Music Society of Lower Basin Street, we take no stock in rumors. Thus we have politely pooh-poohed those who say that Professor Joe Sullivan could not possibly play as much piano as Professor Joe Sullivan plays. For instance, one group maintains that the professor is really triplets. Another group says, no — but that he is helped out greatly by the fact that he has fingers on his feet. We recently saw Professor Sullivan playing with his band at the Café Society, here in New York, and, frankly, we couldn't tell which is correct. So we merely present him now, playing his own great work, "The Ginmill Blues."

Later, Dr. Gino Hamilton supplied this bit of information.

A statement which will come as a surprise to a lot of us is the fact that Dr. Henry Levine was a member of the Original Dixieland Jazz Band — having taken Nick La Rocca's place when that master of the trumpet went back to New Orleans. In those days Dr. Levine was known as the "long-lipped short-pants wonder," and he usually played about two bars ahead of the truant officer, at the old Cinderella Ballroom here in New York. To signalize this historic event, Dr. Levine and the Dixieland group will now play the Nick La Rocca–Larry Shields classic *Ostrich Walk*. But — and this will come as a surprise to Dr. Levine — he is now being asked to play an ad-lib, unarranged growl chorus, just as he played back in the good old days.

Finally, Milton Cross concluded the week's satire with this typical sign-off.

And so, music lovers, you rascals, you, we have come to the end of another concert by the Chamber Music Society of Lower Basin Street, no doubt. But, knowing which side my announcer's job is buttered on, I think I'd better tell you that next week is another week. Period. And that means, of course, that Mademoiselle Dinah Shore and all our regulars will be back, at which time we will present the sensational new guitarist, Professor Floyd Smith, who plays with Harlem in both hands. Right now, as Dr. Hamilton would say, it behooves me to impart to you the indubitable fact that ... this is the National Broadcasting Company, RCA Building, Radio City, New York.

(*SFX*: NBC triple chimes.)

The Chamber Music Society of Lower Basin Street offered a potpourri of jazz-boogie-bluesy numbers weekly. Just as audiences came to expect, while the stuffiness of more cultured venues was exploited, the swinging stuff was hot. The docket included *Alexander's Ragtime Band, Body and Soul, Ida, Memphis Blues, Mood Indigo, Muskrat Ramble, Old Rocking Chair, St. Louis Blues, Sophisticated Lady, Tuxedo Junction* and similar fare. Sometimes blues singer Lena Horne would belt out a classic; often it would be Henry Levine and his Dixieland Octet (under a plethora of monikers) giving it all they had — and that was a lot. Some of radio's finest jazz radiated from the *Chamber* and the listeners tuning in who found the strain to their liking could not have been more enthralled.

While the show was a novelty and all in good fun, it was also a welcome oasis in a sea of classics, semiclassics, pops, big bands and other melodic embellishments that were characteristically introduced by a stuffed shirt. The irreverent reverie at *The Chamber Music Society of Lower Basin Street* was without equal. And of all the material they played, the joke on the listener may have been the best of all. They played it every week.

Cities Service Concerts

In a span that nearly embraced the full range of radio's golden age, the Cities Service Petroleum Company underwrote a series of musicales under a quartet of unique banners. These programs brought great satisfaction to Americans seeking finer musical attainment in a broad dimensional collection. A few of the nation's most talented artists performed on the *Cities Service Concerts*. Its four gifted impresarios consistently programmed selections that were known to be listener favorites. The series' pivotal star, a legendary icon on which legions of adoring fans doted, interrupted the harmonious adulation enjoyed by the program by leaving it, some said, in unseemly fashion. The *Cities Service Concerts* hardly missed a beat, nevertheless, inspiring new generations with its brand of upbeat melodic distractions.

Producer: Benton & Bowles advertising agency

Announcers: Graham McNamee (1927–1929), Ford Bond (1930–1956).

Orchestra Conductors: Edwin Franko Goldman (Winter/Spring 1927), Rosario Bourdon (June 1927–February 1938), Frank Black (1938–1944), Paul Lavalle (1944–1956).

Vocalists: Jessica Dragonette (1930–1937), Ross Graham (1935–), Lucille Manners (1937–1947), James Melton (1933), Frank Parker (1933–1934), John Seagle (1930s), Robert Simmons (1933–).

Vocal Groups: The Cavaliers (1927–1933), The Cities Service Singers, The Green and White Quartet (1940s), The Ken Christy Chorus, The Men About Town, The Revelers (1933–).

Featured Piano Duo: Frank Banta, Milton Rittenberg.

Other Regulars: Sports journalist Grantland Rice (1933–).

Theme Songs: *Cities Service March* (Rosario Bourdon), *Cities Service Triumphal March* (Paul Lavalle).

Sponsor: Cities Service Petroleum Company (February 18, 1927–September 19, 1949); multiple participation (September 26, 1949–January 16, 1956).

Ratings: High — 23.3 (1932-1933 season); Low — 1.7 (1955-1956 season); Median — 10.0. Radio ratings weren't documented until the 1930-1931 season; no existing data has been found for three other consecutive periods, 1952–1955. Through 1934-1935 figures were at a lofty 18 and higher, falling to 10.0 in 1935-1936 and dropping to single digits thereafter.

On the Air: *Cities Service Concert*, February 18, 1927–August 2, 1940, NBC, Friday, 8 P.M. Eastern Time (60 minutes); August 9, 1940–October 20, 1944, NBC, Friday, 8 P.M. (30 minutes); *Highways in Melody*, October 27, 1944–May 28, 1948, NBC, Friday, 8 P.M. (30 minutes); *The Cities Service Band of America*, June 4, 1948–September 23, 1949, NBC, Friday, 8 P.M. (30 minutes); *The Band of America*, September 26, 1949–December 28, 1953, NBC, Monday, 9:30 P.M. (30 minutes); January 4, 1954–January 16, 1956, NBC, Monday, 9:30 P.M. (15 minutes).

* * *

As the last in the line of *Cities Service Concerts* wound to a close in the mid-1950s— then widely recognized as *The Band of America*—few in its audience were aware that they were hearing the final strains of a small trace of broadcast history with roots running incredibly deep.

But it was so.

As early as 1925 — even before there were broadcast networks— the Cities Service Petroleum Company was experimenting with music on the air as a means of selling its gas and oil products to owners of vintage American vehicles. Although its initial foray into the popular new medium was limited to trial runs in the greater New York market, that response was encouraging. In a test of *The Cities Service Salon Orchestra* airing over NBC in early 1927, the sponsor was further persuaded to launch a permanent series. Enough so, in fact, that within three months of the founding of the National Broadcasting Company, the fuel group purchased an hour a week on the fledgling chain to pitch its wares.

The *Cities Service Concert*, at its start, featured a booming brass–sounding band. Under the baton of pioneering ethereal maestro Edwin Franco Goldman, the cornet-tooting troupe favored spirited, if yet conventional, arrangements. From its very inception, the program's intent never swayed —"to present the best in music, whether it was Beethoven or Berlin." All that really changed over the years, in fact, was the cast that supplied it. And some of those very changes, a historian allowed, "made radio history."

Goldman's tenure, as it turned out, was brief. (He would soon conduct bands for *The General Motors Family Party* and *The Pure Oil Company Program* in addition to *The Goldman Band Concert* for several seasons in the mid–1930s over NBC Blue.) The legacy he initiated for Cities Service, nevertheless, would be of lasting substance. The premiering show and future performances would draw millions of fans, some of whose interests wouldn't wane until the final notes were but a memory 29 years hence. The program would establish a benchmark as one of the earliest and most enduring musical series on the air, particularly among those featuring a myriad of tune types.

That first show, on February 18, 1927, offered several guest performers. Although a blown fuse eliminated three minutes of its air time, it still broadcast a number of familiar selections played by a stirring brass band: *The William Tell Overture*, *The Mignon Overture* plus excerpts from Gounod's *Faust* and Liszt's *Second Hungarian Rhapsody*. Among its artists was clarinetist Paul Lavalle, who was destined to become the group's most stable bandmaster 17 years ahead. It was also Lavalle who steered the production back to its original heritage after it had changed courses only a few months into the run.

With the departure of Goldman after but a few months at the helm, the musical landscape altered dramatically. In June 1927, upon the arrival of a new conductor, Rosario Bourdon, the *Cities Service Concerts* transformed from a marching band into a true-life orchestra, passionately relying on classical, semiclassical, operatic and pop pieces. Bourdon would be with the program through February 1938. But even well beyond that — for the next two decades, in fact — strings would dominate brass as the majority of the 30-plus instrumentalists picked and plucked and fewer and fewer beat and blew.

Rosario Bourdon was a native of Longuereil, Quebec, born March 6, 1885. He accepted the *Cities Service* baton at age 42. Trained as a cellist at the Quebec Academy of Music, he played in European concerts, appeared with the Philadelphia Orchestra and made the very first really successful cello recordings. Before radio took off, Bourdon was an adaptable musician with the Victor Talking Machine Company. He earned an income for his work on many Victor phonograph recordings as a cellist, arranger and accompanist.

Bourdon's debut on radio occurred in 1925; by the 1931-1932 season he was contributing regularly to a series called *Great Personalities*. In his spare time, meanwhile, he conducted light opera concerts at Carnegie Hall and directed the Naumburg Orchestra when it performed in New York's Central Park. Throughout the 1930s, Bourdon directed a *Rosario Bourdon Orchestra* syndicated series on the ether. Numerous transcriptions of that show still exist. It was widely circulated, appearing on local stations like KFEQ, St. Joseph, Missouri; WGH, Newport News, Virginia; WHP, Harrisburg, Pennsylvania; and WIRE, Indianapolis, Indiana. Bourdon died in New York on April 24, 1961. He was 76.

A male quartet, The Cavaliers, joined the *Cities Service Concert* at the same time as Bourdon. This foursome was the first of a progression of ensembles that would grace the *Cities Service* stage. Perhaps the most renowned solo act emanating from The Cavaliers was baritone John Seagle. By 1929, he headlined his own NBC Blue vocal show in addition to his work as a Cavaliers confederate.

The Cavaliers left the security of the *Cities Service Concert* in 1933, superseded by an even more celebrated male quartet, The Revelers. That crew was originally introduced as The Shannon Quartet, then featuring Franklyn Baur, Wilfred Glenn, Lewis James and Elliott Shaw. Ed Smalle was soon added as pianist, arranger and bass vocalist, necessitating a name change for the assemblage. Several replacements were required in time as some members of the quartet began appearing on the *Cities Service* show in solo acts. Most used their newfound fame to bounce them to enhanced status elsewhere.

Tenor James Melton, for example, was destined to become an operatic star, joining the Met in 1942 after four years of preparing for it with opera companies in several Midwest cities. In the 15 years prior to his debut there, however, Melton distinguished himself as a very versatile singer. The Moultrie, Georgia, native, born January 2, 1904, launched his career performing light music over Nashville's WSM Radio while pursuing an education at Vanderbilt University. In 1927, he joined the cast of *Roxy and His Gang*, emanating from NBC in New York. The same year he became first tenor with The Revelers.

In a brief time he appeared intermittently on several other programs including *The House of Wrigley*, *The Palmolive Hour*, *Seiberling Singers* and *The Mobil Oil Concert*. He was soloist on *The Jack Benny Program* in 1933-1934. He starred in 55 operettas on *The Palmolive Beauty Box Theatre*. In the 1940s, he became a regular on *The Bell Telephone Hour*, *The Texaco Star Theatre* and *Harvest of Stars*. Melton took turns before *The Voice of Firestone* microphones and cameras. Supplementing his busy routine, he recorded for Columbia Records, sang on George Gershwin concert tours and appeared in Warner Brothers films. When his early 1950s TV show flopped, Melton sang on road tours and pop concert bills. He died at 57 at New York City on April 21, 1961.

Frank Parker, born Frank Ciccio on April 29, 1903, in New York, was another Revelers quartet affiliate who made the big time. Discerning the enormous promise of radio, he leapt from the safety of steady employment at varied comedy venues to the ethereal medium, still in its incubation period. The day after NBC aired its inaugural extravaganza on November 16, 1926, *The Eveready Hour*—the air's first major variety series—premiered. While Parker was by no means a headliner (as Eddie Cantor, Pablo Casals and several others appearing on it were), he was cast in a recurring troupe of singers spanning the show's quadrennial life. He also performed simultaneously on the *Evening in Paris* series. Furthermore, for eight years the *A&P Gypsies* engaged him.

Parker left the *Cities Service Concert* in 1934, becoming the vocalist on *The Jack Benny Program* for a year, a job that had been held a season earlier by former Reveler James Melton. That same year Parker became one of the *Gulf Headliners*. He hosted his own *Frank Parker Show* in 1936 (with a rising Bob Hope imparting comic relief). Parker's show returned to the air in 1947. The 1940s also saw him singing regularly on *The George Burns and Gracie Allen Show* as he gained top billing on *Golden Treasury of Song*, subbed for Thomas L. Thomas on *Manhattan Merry-Go-Round* and replaced Frank Munn on the *American Album of Familiar Music*. He sang with the Chicago Opera Company also and in 1957 briefly hosted *Bride and Groom*.

Most people today, however, likely recall Frank Parker for his duets with singer Marion Marlowe. The duo was regularly featured on some popular 1950s radio and television series hosted by entertainer Arthur Godfrey (*Arthur Godfrey Time, Arthur Godfrey Digest, Arthur Godfrey and His Friends*). The voices of Parker and Marlowe brilliantly blended in melody several times a week during Godfrey's glory days. It was, of course, before the expressive emcee virtually dismantled his operation in a peculiar twist hinting at self-destruction. In the mid–1950s, he fired Marlowe and more than a dozen other cast members who—in Godfrey's estimate—had fallen from grace.

Tenor Robert Simmons launched his airwaves career over New York's WJZ in 1929, headlining his own program. He joined the Revelers and in 1933 became a solo act on the *Cities Service Concert*.

Baritone-bass Ross Graham, yet another Revelers alumnus, was born August 8, 1905, in Benton, Arkansas, and died January 5, 1986, in Fort Worth, Texas. At age 23, employed by both a public service utility and a bank, Graham won hometown notoriety as an amateur singer over Hot Springs' KTHS Radio, broadcasting from Hot Springs National Park. A couple of years later, he represented his state and geographical territory in an Atwater Kent talent competition in San Francisco. In 1932, he joined the cast of *Roxy and His Gang*.

During radio's 1935-1936 season, Graham headlined his own NBC vocal series while at the same time joining the Revelers and the *Cities Service Concert*. In 1936 and 1937, he sang on the *Metropolitan Opera Auditions of the Air*. He performed with *The NBC Symphony Orchestra* and on *The Prudential Family Hour* before retiring professionally in 1947 to return to work at another public service utility in Texas.

Throughout much of its long run, the various *Cities Service* series maintained a proclivity for male quartets. In addition to The Cavaliers and The Revelers, other brigades were The Green and White Quartet (a 1940s clan so labeled for the sponsor's primary colors) and The Men About Town.

A couple of other ensembles, both mixed groups, included The Ken Christy Chorus and a more generic-titled Cities Service Singers. The individuals performing there didn't attain the solo recognition that some of their Cities Service predecessors became accustomed to, however.

The baton passed from Rosario Bourdon to Frank Black as the *Cities Service Concert*'s third impresario on February 5, 1938. Black would hold it for nearly seven years, until Paul Lavalle relieved him on October 27, 1944. Born in Philadelphia on November 28, 1894, Black developed an utterly diverse professional background: as a pianist, theater music director and piano roll company officer, before crossing paths with The Revelers at a recording session.

In 1928, that link spirited him into becoming NBC's music director, a post he occupied for many years. There he literally could name the orchestras he most wanted to conduct and the shows he preferred to arrange music for. Included in his repertoire were *The Edison Hour, Happy Wonder Bakers, Harvest of Stars, The Jack Benny Program, The NBC Symphony Orchestra, The NBC String Symphony, The Palmolive Hour, RCA Magic Key, RCA Radiotrons* and *Symphony of the Air*. In the early 1950s, his conducting finale occurred on *The Jane Pickens Show*.

Far in advance of each *Cities Service Concert* airdate, Black habitually settled on the music and outlined the total program. It was during his tenure, in 1940, that the show's 60-minute format was trimmed to half its accustomed time. Black died in November 1967 in Atlanta, Georgia.

The last of the permanent Cities Service maestros, Paul Lavalle, would witness a trio of name changes during his 11-plus years at that bandstand. The first, taking place in 1944, saw the new moniker *Highways in Melody* replace the *Cities Service Concert* designation. In the quadrennial following, the program focused on pop tunes as opposed to the classical and semiclassical music of the previous 15 years.

The reader may recall that Lavalle was playing clarinet with the Edwin Franko Goldman orchestra at the *Cities Service Concert*'s inception in 1927. After conducting the instrumentalists on *Highways in Melody* for four years, he returned the program to its roots, turning the final seven-plus air years onto brass music (including a whole lot of marches) instead of what had dominated the epoch between. (Incidentally, he was labeled "America's Second Sousa" because he composed so many strutting tunes, a throwback to the nation's march conductor-sovereign, John Philip Sousa.) It was during Lavalle's leadership, too—in early 1946, on the occasion of the show's 19th anniversary—that it was declared "the oldest commercial radio program on the air." It was a distinction that the industry as well as the program's faithful wouldn't take lightly.

The series' name soon changed again, this time to a more familiarly recalled *Cities Service Band of America* by those who remember the program today. In its final half-dozen years, when Cities Service no longer underwrote the feature, it was simply retitled *The Band of America*. It was also reduced to a quarter-hour weekly in its final couple of years. Before the name change, it was an aggregate of 48 instrumentalists, one artist for every state in the union at that time, a fact the petroleum company sponsoring it seized upon with glee in its advertising. Paul Lavalle, meanwhile, continued holding the show's baton through its final broadcast on January 16, 1956.

A native of Beacon, New York, Lavalle was born Joseph Usifer on September 6, 1908. He was later educated at the esteemed Julliard School of Music. His expansive professional career included playing time on *The NBC Symphony Orchestra* and conducting instrumental ensembles for *The*

Chamber Music Society of Lower Basin Street, Silhouettes in Music, The Stradivari Orchestra and — in 1934 over NBC — the *Paul Lavalle Orchestra*, all of those chores beyond his challenging Cities Service stints. In the 1940s, he was in demand as a musical arranger for several other features including *The Chesterfield Supper Club* and *Club Fifteen*. Eventually he turned to television appearances, touring and — for seven years — he directed the Radio City Music Hall Orchestra. Lavalle retired from active arranging and conducting in the early 1980s. He died on June 24, 1997.

There were lots of guest artists on the *Cities Service* programs. By the same token, there was a litany of resident, soon-to-be-luminaries (beyond James Melton, Frank Parker and others previously named). One of the more unusual types was Grantland Rice, a legendary sports columnist in his day. How he came to appear on *Cities Service* was highly atypical.

In 1933, *Cities Service* announcer Ford Bond, the series' prime interlocutor, interrupted those melodious sonnets to deliver baseball scores and comment on the games. His tête-à-têtes with the audience invoked a pattern that lingered for a long while: he regularly dialogued with nonsinging celebrities such as aviatrix Amelia Earhart, appearing in an initial interview segment on May 19, 1933. By December 8, 1933, Col. Louis McHenry Howe, President Franklin D. Roosevelt's secretary, was turning up with some regularity, discussing contemporary U.S. and global issues, and particularly the government's intent for stabilizing the nation's citizens through an innovative plan known as Depression America.

If all of this seemed incongruous to a classical-semiclassical musical program, it met with such widespread acceptance that — as the football season heated up that fall (in 1933) — the show's producers decided to tip their hats to the pigskin parade just as they had waved their caps over America's pastime earlier that summer. The magnetism of those diversionary tactics went unabated for a while. Ford Bond's baseball commentaries and sports journalist Grantland Rice's football scoreboard appealed to listeners for several years.

Bond, the durable announcer on the multiple *Cities Service* programs, is mentioned in the chapter on the Frank and Anne Hummert music series. It is noteworthy to recognize that — between 1930 and 1956 — Bond held what was regarded as "broadcasting's longest sponsor-announcer association" as the permanent voice of the Cities Service Oil Company. There may have been no one else in the history of radio and television who accomplished such a uniquely specialized triumph.

Rice, meanwhile, maintained a colorful career in pioneering media coverage of athletics. Born in Murfreesboro, Tennessee, on November 1, 1880, he launched a newspaper career with *The Tennessean* in Nashville that eventually took him to *The Atlanta Journal and Constitution* and then, in 1911, to *The New York Tribune*. He wrote a popular column titled "The Sportlight." On October 5, 1921, he provided play-by-play commentary of baseball's initial World Series broadcast over a Westinghouse station hookup. (The series featured two New York teams that year, the Giants and the Yankees.)

By 1922, he was a veteran sportscaster, again called upon for that year's World Series. When he shared those duties in 1923 with Graham McNamee, a fledgling WEAF announcer, he contributed mightily to McNamee's march to fame and ultimately to network status. (McNamee presided at the microphone on the very first *Cities Service Concert* broadcast, for example.)

From his capsule commentaries on the *Cities Service Concert*, Rice earned his own half-hour NBC series, *Sports Stories*, during the 1943–1944 season. He also appeared in one-reel sports films, although his lasting notoriety was earned from journalistic pursuits. The masses probably recall Rice for an epic poem, *Alumnus Football*, he penned in 1946. An immortal line of the classic verse cautions: "When the One Great Scorer comes to write against your name, He marks not that you won or lost but how you played the game." Rice died in New York City on July 13, 1954.

As noted, the *Cities Service Concert* and its successor titles featured numerous guests. They included many from the opera and concert halls, radio, stage and touring venues. Most had already achieved minimal notoriety while *Cities Service* helped the careers of others. Among their number were soloists Vivian Della Chiesa, Dorothy Kirsten, Thomas L. Thomas and Earl Wrightson along with pianists Frank Banta and Milton Rittenberg (that pair became semiregulars during the Rosario Bourdon years).

If *Cities Service* carried a single artist of perceived star quality, however, unmistakably it was Jessica Dragonette. In her seven years as the show's leading soprano, Dragonette thrust *Cities Service* into a prominence that neither the program — nor she — had enjoyed to that time or would ever equal. (The show's ratings tell the story.) The public absolutely fawned over the young vocalist with the lilting voice. While she brought some impressive credentials with her on joining the cast in 1930, it was there, almost overnight, that she became an entertainment icon, enthusiastically received by a significantly large and loyal following. Much and maybe most of her professional legacy can be traced to her contributions on the *Cities Service Concert*.

Dragonette's sudden, unexpected exodus from the show in 1937 briefly threw things into chaotic disarray. It also prompted an outpouring of ripostes from fans that held her in high esteem: some were deeply saddened by her departure while others railed in anger over her decision to leave. It was a crucial point in both the show's life and that of its star. And it took a toll on at least one of them.

A radio historiographer correctly persisted that the *Cities Service Concert* "truly came of age in 1930, with the arrival of Jessica Dragonette." She would be characterized by many soubriquets over an illustrious career for she was dubbed "the Jenny Lind of the air," "the girl with the smile in her voice," "the Queen of Radio," "Princess of Song" and "The Greta Garbo of the airwaves." As one reviewer allowed, she was "one of radio's true made-at-the-microphone stars." She "sang her way into radio immortality" on the *Cities Service* show. Another assessment encapsulated[1]:

> The public's devotion to this petite blonde soprano was deeper than to most early broadcasters. Perhaps more ethereal, angelic-sounding than her musical contemporaries, she inspired unusual admiration and loyalty — sort of a spiritual coupling with an airborne disembodied voice. Her worshipful fans sent her handmade quilts, scarves, afghans and dolls, designed personalized lamps, sun dials and bookplates, and named hybrid roses and prized heifers in her honor. This deification from afar actually continued beyond her active days of singing, which ended a decade before the fade out of the type of musical features she helped to introduce and popularize.

Her rise to "Queen of Radio" stemmed from seven years as star of *Cities Service Concert*, a prestigious, hour-long NBC show on which she sang popular songs, arias, folk melodies and sacred selections.

Just who was this prima donna anyway?

Jessica Dragonette was born on February 14 (Valentine's Day) of French-Italian (father) and Italian (mother) parentage in Calcutta, India. (The year isn't certain, with a variety of sources specifying at least 1904, 1908 and 1910.) She was raised in

Philadelphia where she pursued vocal training. The family was devout Catholic. Following the early deaths of her parents (father in an accident and mother from an illness) and, consequently, a quite saddened childhood, the young woman enrolled in more rigorous music curricula at Georgian Court Convent in Lakewood, New Jersey.

By 1926, she was appearing as an ingénue in a Big Apple production of *The Grand Street Follies*, having been the offstage angel in Max Reinhardt's *The Miracle* three years earlier, also produced in New York. She performed in a stock company production of *The Student Prince* in between those promising engagements.

Dragonette then sang in a tryout at New York's WEAF Radio, winning a soprano part with a light opera music company, premiering on the air on October 26, 1926. Soon she was singing anonymously as Vivian, "the Coca-Cola girl," in radio's initial dramatic musical serial, sponsored by the soft drink maker. Next came a series of pithy dramatic episodes over NBC that were adapted from Shakespearean plays— *Hamlet, Romeo and Juliet, Twelfth Night* and others. Dragonette played opposite Ben Grauer in Oscar Wilde's *The Nightingale and the Rose*, followed by recurring appearances on *The WEAF Musical Comedy Hour*. At the same time she was performing with the *Hoover Sentinels* and the *A&P Gypsies* on the air.

She acknowledged: "More and more I became thrilled by the thought that as I sang in a quiet studio, my songs were reaching out to thousands and then millions of listeners who were hungry for the kind of uplifting that only music can bring."

Her career took off in 1927 when she was tapped as the soprano star of *The Philco Hour Theatre of Memories*, a weekly series of greatly beloved operettas. Subsequently, she signed an exclusive NBC contract. Over the next two and a half years she sang in 75 different roles on that show. It was an experience that would significantly impact her career in the years to follow, and one she would have a tough time reliving in the face of mammoth odds.

Commensurate with her growing popularity, Dragonette was asked to perform for an early experimental television broadcast in 1928. While the video audience wasn't large, her selection for that singular mission was a testimony to her growing fame.

In late 1929, the *Philco* series shifted from NBC to CBS. Dragonette's pact limiting her to the chimes chain prevented her from going with it. On January 3, 1930, she debuted on the *Cities Service Concert*, bringing a host of doting fans with her that would appreciably multiply her personal base while broadly elevating the show's image.[2]

During her time with *Cities Service* her repertoire developed into more than 500 tunes; she claimed there was seldom a need to repeat a song in a period of less than six months. She thrilled listeners with pop numbers, folk tunes, familiar ballads, light opera selections and grand opera arias. She reportedly was the first singer to introduce radio audiences to the work of disparate musicians like Gordon Jenkins and Victor Herbert. Dragonette performed more of the grand melodies from around the globe in their native dialects than any other artist: she was equally conversant in English, French, German, Hungarian, Italian, Russian and Spanish, maintaining several private tutors who specialized in those languages.

In a memoir published in 1951, Dragonette reflected on those days, revealing: "I was immune to all but radio's calling. Everything else was crowded out to give way to my own artistic development, and the unfoldment of radio; for I was in the studio from morning to midnight, trying to solve the riddle of microphone personality— searching for the secret of good radio entertainment...." The late comic Bob Hope postulated: "Jessica probably has done more for radio than anyone else."

"Every performance was a new and personal challenge to meet her own standards of perfection," noted a critic. While at least 20 hours of planning and rehearsal connecting many individuals went into every single hour's performance of a *Cities Service Concert*, Dragonette exceeded that effort by many hours. She didn't use sheet music while on the air, committing every word of every song to memory. She devoted multiple hours every week to scrupulously preparing her solos, duets and ensemble melodies.

For the performances she began to dress in exquisite formal evening gowns, each appropriate to the occasion. "She had a strong sense of obligation to her studio audience," maintained Helen Strauss Cotton, then publicity director for Benton & Bowles advertising agency. "Her broadcasts always were scheduled in the largest available studio in order to accommodate as many people as possible. She ... greeted her fans after each show. They came from all over the country to see her in person, and she never let them down ... making it a memorable occasion for them and herself."

Normally Dragonette was featured in about eight out of the usual 17 selections presented on a typical *Cities Service* broadcast. This included solos, joining with first The Cavaliers and later The Revelers quartets, and duets (especially with Frank Parker, their joint singing labeled by one pundit "sensational"—Parker was replaced by others on leaving the show after the sponsor failed to pay him more than he had earned as a Revelers trouper). At the close of each hour, Dragonette pitched a hit tune of the week, a scenario she later referred to as a precursor to *Your Hit Parade*. (That show aired on radio from 1935 to 1953 and on television from 1950 to 1959. See separate chapter.)

There was no mistaking the fact that, for the most part, *Cities Service Concert*'s ratings remained remarkably high after Dragonette came aboard, reaching lofty levels seldom witnessed by other concert series. Speaking of the show's star and not the show itself, a reviewer recounted: "Her popularity by 1933 was on a plane with *Amos 'n' Andy*, Eddie Cantor and Rudy Vallee." Together with CBS's Kate Smith, "NBC's petite lyrical soprano topped the popularity polls," claimed a biographer.

Her magnetism was so strong, in fact that for a single personal appearance at Chicago's Grant Park more than 150,000 spectators showed up. Even a future impresario of the New York Philharmonic Symphony (1958–1969), Leonard Bernstein, noted that he seldom missed tuning in Dragonette's performances during his teens in Roxbury, Massachusetts. She turned up at the dedication of NBC's Radio City in 1933 and appeared in the very first issue of *Life* magazine in 1936, spotlighting the network's leading ladies and gentlemen.

Voted radio's favorite feminine star by the readers of *Radio Mirror* in 1935, Dragonette received many similar accolades. Subscribers to *Radio Guide* picked her as the publication's "star of stars" in 1937. Some personal appearances she made during World War II promoting the sale of U.S. Treasury bonds earned her an honorary colonel status in the U.S. Army.

An informed radio historiographer, writing more than a quarter of a century ago about Dragonette's aural success, surmised: "The personnel changes that occurred in the *Cities* shows, especially in the first decade, made radio history." While that allusion could include a whole lot of personalities that have been examined in this chapter already, the casting shift that resulted in extreme turmoil was the departure of Jessica Dragonette in 1937. And while the decision was ultimately the star's choice to make, it left a bitter taste in the mouths of some in the radio audience. This included many of her legions of loyal fans as well as the network, sponsor, advertising agency, spokespersons and intimates who gathered about her and — perhaps most of all — Dragonette herself.

Keep in mind that many of her followers supposed that her *Cities Service* tenure was linked with intransience. Her sudden exit would quite naturally prompt unanswered questions while creating a rift that wouldn't be advantageous to anybody. The crisis was amplified because it was aired in public media with all of the connotations of dirty linen conjuring up various misconceptions. The climax (and, possibly, the *inevitable* ending) occurred after multifaceted, unresolved issues had been brewing for a while. Actually, it had started as long as four years earlier.

Recall that Jessica Dragonette fell supremely in harmony with the format of her preceding radio series, *The Philco Hour Theatre of Memories*, an operetta feature in which she played scores of speaking and singing parts. She was ecstatic over that scenario that gave her opportunities to supply more than solely musical talent. When she joined the *Cities Service* roster, of course, she knew it was totally a concert venue. There was no chance for dialoguing there.

Even after Ford Bond launched his baseball commentaries followed by interviews with guest celebrities and Grantland Rice's football capsules were added, Dragonette received no backing that would ever encourage dramatic acting. As early as 1933, she started to insist that the program's composition be altered to include occasional operettas or provide other narrative opportunities for her. Cities Service officials turned a deaf ear to it, however, not wanting to break with the traditions the program enjoyed which they were convinced the audience appreciated and expected. A part of their rationale, they added, was that speaking parts for Dragonette would remind the fans all too pointedly of her earlier affiliation with the Philco series, a matter they simply could not condone.

There were still other dynamics that came into play.

In 1934, a determined Dragonette took up Frank Parker's cause for additional compensation to be paid to her duet colleague, although it came to no avail. That was undoubtedly a primary factor in his decision to leave the series. She became agitated when the Cities Service organization withdrew the show from West Coast audiences. The firm explained that leasing expensive telephone lines beyond Denver to pacify comparatively few listeners made the practice no longer practical. Nor had Dragonette's increasing discontent escaped the sponsor's notice. Cities Service officials soon advocated holding tryouts for promising soprano voices, yet another slap in the face of its already aggrieved star.

Everything began coming to a head when Dragonette's sister, Nadea Dragonette Loftus, acting as the vocalist's agent (one source calls her "secretary," another "business manager"), discovered that the pact her sister signed with Cities Service was devoid of a renewal option. While that may have been a purely unintentional lapse, it could have just as easily been premeditated, the pair conjectured. Whatever the reason, in the siblings' estimate, Jessica Dragonette was under no compulsion to anticipate continuance beyond the current agreement's expiration.

A timely and extremely attractive opportunity surfaced at about that same juncture, one offering the singing star a treasure she had long coveted. In late 1936, a soap manufacturer was developing a radio series that was to be billed as *The Palmolive Beauty Box Theater*. Its premise would include a revolving series of light opera, musical dramas, original aural productions, grand opera vignettes and genuine concerts. The outfit offered Dragonette $2,500 a week — twice what Cities Service paid her — to sign on as a "name" celebrity. All the firm asked was that she play it close to the vest, keeping the action under wraps until a public announcement was made at a future date. Dragonette viewed it as her dream job and wasted no time signing.

That's when everything began to unravel.

The soprano was under the mistaken impression that the Palmolive show was to air over NBC, a network to which she had devoted her singing career over the previous decade. It was, as the reader will recall, a chain that held exclusive rights to her services by way of a contract she willfully negotiated in the late 1920s.

When word of the secret deal leaked to NBC officials — before Palmolive's publicists were ready to roll the presses — all hell broke loose. The network brass was absolutely enraged. Striking back at Dragonette and her co-conspirators, they decided to release her from her obligations to NBC at once, seizing the moment to surprise the unsuspecting Palmolive planners. In so doing they churned out their own publicity missives, placing the star in a very bad light. She had been terminated, those press releases announced, because listener surveys told them she had fallen out of favor with the audience, who expressed a strong preference for some fresher voices.

"Industry scuttlebutt ignited spontaneously," penned an author. "Rumors spread that she had made outrageous contract demands and had begun believing her own press notices." By February 5, 1937, seven years after she had signed with *Cities Service*, Dragonette was gone. The public's reaction was swift, mixed and vociferous. Her fierce loyalists were outraged — they blamed Cities Service, NBC or both. Each of those organizations was the object of boycotts by Dragonette's partisans. Newspaper critics also protested. Still, some of her fans reacted in a manner that was surprisingly unanticipated: they vehemently criticized *her* for the decision she had made.

Opinion was divided for a long while as to where the blame should be situated. "The most prevalent theory," one historian deduced, "is that NBC conspired to wreck her career, a charge the network always denied."[3]

"I had worked ten years for NBC, seven for Cities Service," Dragonette would explain in her biography 14 years hence in an attempt to set the record straight. "It broke my heart to realize that every supposed friend had deserted me and fallen into the trap of intrigue. The tumult and the shouting continued unabated, during which time I never gave an explanation to the press, so sure was I that I would be cleared of 'the great misunderstanding' which had arisen between NBC and me. No attempt to clear it up was ever made."

The Palmolive Beauty Box Theater, incidentally — the series Dragonette left the *Cities Service Concert* for — turned out to be a Pandora's box, perhaps one she wished she had never opened. The new CBS show was history after the proverbial 39-week season, never attracting a large or apparently satisfied audience. Poor scripting and execution and limited time (only a half-hour when much longer was needed) dissolved into a dismal failure. Its star might also have been viewed as "damaged merchandise" as a torrent of unflattering publicity and gossip worked its magic.

Dragonette would never regain the precedent-setting image that had been hers on the *Cities Service Concert* hour. After the *Palmolive* debacle, she retired from radio, although she guested on several programs over the next few years. She relented in 1941, making another try as the focus of CBS's *Saturday Night Serenade*. That lasted four years. But it was never the same — time, and the multitude of fans who had adulated her a decade before, had by then almost completely passed her by.

On June 28, 1947, Francis Cardinal Spellman officiated when Jessica Dragonette wed a New York businessman, Nicholas M. Turner. She had earlier insisted she was "too busy" to concentrate on career and marriage simultaneously. With her career having ebbed away, she reversed her priorities. It was something her contemporary, Kate Smith — who remained single all her life — was never able to do.

Dragonette summoned up her courage in 1952 and faced some of her old detractors during a 25th anniversary celebration of the *Cities Service Concerts* staged at Carnegie Hall. She sang again and was pleasant to all. A faithful, dedicated corps of idol-worshipers that had never written her off surrounded her once more. The soprano died in New York on March 18, 1980.

Her replacement on the *Cities Service Concert* program was no stranger there, having substituted for Dragonette not long before. Soprano Lucille Manners was also an attractive, blue-eyed blonde. She would remain with the program longer than any other single star. While Manners never achieved the notoriety and entourage that Dragonette collected, she drew a group of admirers who persisted throughout her tenure.

A native of Newark, New Jersey, Manners was born May 21, 1912. After growing up she prepared for a clerical position, eventually becoming a steno for a hometown attorney. But she loved music and she made it an important part of her life. For eight years she took private voice lessons several times a week. She gained a berth in radio by spending her lunch hours singing over local station WOR. She joined a semiprofessional opera company in hopes of furthering her avocation. With the help of her voice teacher, Manners gained an audition at NBC. That landed her on some sustaining morning programs and an occasional appearance on important series like *The Voice of Firestone*. By 1935, she was headlining her own vocal series over NBC.

When *Cities Service Concert* programmers were looking for a temporary replacement for a vacationing Jessica Dragonette in the summer of 1936, they picked the "girlish soprano with a sympathetic feeling for music." Manners would return that fall to try out for a permanent spot on the program — the one she eventually acquired following the hasty departure of Jessica Dragonette. Manners remained in that exalted spot for more than 10 years, virtually until the program retreated to the brassy-sounding *Band of America* intonation in 1948. She capped her "second career" by singing in Gounod's *Faust* and Puccini's *La Boheme*, productions of the New York City Opera Company.

Guest artists, most of them soloists, were featured intermittently on the *Cities Service Concert* bills, particularly in the program's early and middle years. On August 10, 1945, *Highways in Melody* broadcast selections like *When the Boys Come Home* (a typical wartime theme), *Turkey in the Straw*, *Lucky Day*, *My Song* and *Keep Your Sunny Side Up* among its aggregate. Opera star Dorothy Kirsten was the vocal guest on that occasion. At other times, choices typically included such popular favorites as *Dixie Land*, *Listen to the Mocking Bird* and *In the Still of the Night*.

When the show got its marching orders and returned to band music, it frequently touted rousing tunes like *The Thunderer*, *The Fairest of the Fair*, *Semper Fidelis*, *The Liberty Bell*, *King Cotton*, *Hands Across the Sea*, *Stars and Stripes Forever*, *The High School Cadets*, *New York Hippodrome* and many more of that ilk. Visualize the closing parade scene in the motion picture *The Music Man* starring Robert Preston and Shirley Jones and you've got the picture.

On September 26, 1949, *The Band of America* concert, for the first time under participating (multiple) sponsorship (and thus the revised title), was pried from its hallowed 8 o'clock Friday night timeslot — one it had occupied for nearly 23 years — and shifted to a trademark programming model universally cited as NBC's "Monday Night of Music." There, preceded by *The Railroad Hour, The Voice of Firestone* and *The Bell Telephone Hour*, durable series all, *The Band of America* segued into an established track of musical favorites that routinely delighted the nation's ears for 52 weeks a year.

When *The Band of America* and the predecessor series that had been previously underwritten by the Cities Service Petroleum Company left the air for the last time on January 16, 1956, it was surely the end of an era: it marked the cessation of a continuous entertainment tradition that had extended for 29 years and presented about 1,500 weekly concerts. Those programs imbued more than a single generation with quality melody while introducing many listeners to superior tuneful options for the very first time (including many who would never have tuned in to an opera or a solely classical feature).

At the same time, the *Cities Service Concerts* fostered a resurgent love of country through the themes of its patriotic songs during a time that substantially tried men's souls — extending all the way from a national depression and its painstakingly slow recovery through two major military conflagrations plus a Cold War.

While America was experiencing upheaval in appallingly tumultuous times, it was acutely refreshing to realize that an inspiring wellspring of enduring pleasure offered a transitory alternative to man's troubles. For nearly three decades, from the embryonic days of radio's golden age until that epoch had nearly run its course, the *Cities Service Concerts*, by whatever name it was called, gave reverie that could not be easily dismissed.

The Classics

The classics included programming especially aimed at refined, cultured tastes, commonly considered among the world's most beautiful music. The conductors, instrumentalists and guest artists offered were some of the most highly skilled professionals in this nation and frequently beyond its borders. Names like Leonard Bernstein, Milton Cross, Grace Moore, Eugene Ormandy, Ezio Pinza, Risë Stevens, Gladys Swarthout, Lawrence Tibbett, Arturo Toscanini and others came to the forefront. While there were scores of aural highbrow musical features that appropriately suited the classical tradition, five of the more prestigious have been purposefully targeted in highlighting the genus. Each became a hallmark in the field, setting standards of achievement that made a distinct impact on audiences and left legacies that were seldom — if ever — equaled.

The New York Philharmonic Orchestra

Sponsors: U.S. Rubber Corporation (May 23, 1943–April 13, 1947); Socony Vacuum Oil Corporation (October 10, 1948– April 17, 1949; 1950-1951); Willys Motor Company (October 19, 1952–December 27, 1953); otherwise sustaining.

Ratings: Of 34 broadcast seasons over CBS, ratings for only seven have been preserved, providing a significantly reduced interpretation of rank. High —19.4 (1933-1934 season); Low — 2.5 (1952-1953 season); Median — 6.3.

On the Air: 1927–1929 seasons, CBS, Thursday, 8:30–10:30 P.M. (all times Eastern); 1930–1940 seasons, CBS, Sunday, 3:00–5:00 P.M.; 1940–1950 seasons, CBS, Sunday, 3:00–4:30 P.M.; 1950-1951 season, CBS, Sunday, 1:00–2:30 P.M.; 1951–1956 seasons, CBS, Sunday, 2:30–4:00 P.M.; 1956-1957 season, CBS, Sunday, 3:00 P.M.; 1957-1958 season, CBS, Sunday, 3:05 P.M.; 1958–1960 seasons, CBS, Saturday, 8:30 P.M.; 1960–1963 seasons, CBS, Saturday, 9:15 P.M.

The Metropolitan Opera

General managers: Giulio Gatti-Casazza (1908–1935), Edward Johnson (1935–1950), Rudolf Bing (1950–1972) (*limited to radio's golden age broadcast epoch*)

Sponsors: The American Tobacco Company for Lucky Strike cigarettes (December 30, 1933-1934); Lambert Pharmacal Company for Listerine mouthwash (1934-1935); The Texas Company (later Texaco Corporation, then ChevronTexaco Corporation) for its Texaco gasoline, oil and other vehicle products (December 7, 1940–April 24, 2004); otherwise sustaining.

Ratings: Figures were recorded for only eight of the first 25 seasons, netting a record that is sorely lacking. High — 5.5 (1949-1950 season); Low — 1.5 (1954-1955 season); Median — 3.5.

On the Air: December 25, 1931–present. Season data: 1931-1932 (following inaugural presentation), NBC, Saturday, 3:15–5:30 P.M. (all times Eastern); 1932-1933, NBC Blue, Saturday, 2:30–4:30 P.M.; 1933-1934, NBC and NBC Blue, Saturday, 2:00–5:15 P.M.; 1934-1935, NBC and NBC Blue, Saturday, 1:50–5:00 P.M.; 1935-1936, NBC and NBC Blue, Saturday, 1:45–5:30 P.M.; 1936-1937, NBC Blue, Saturday, 1:40–5:30 P.M.; 1937-1938, NBC Blue, Saturday, 1:55–5:00 P.M.; 1938-1939, NBC, 2:00–5:00 P.M.; 1939-1940, NBC Blue, Saturday, 2:00–5:30 P.M.; 1940-1941, NBC Blue, Saturday, 2:00–5:00 P.M.; 1941-1942, NBC Blue, Saturday, 2:00–5:30 P.M.; 1942-1943, ABC, Saturday, 2:00–3:30 P.M.; 1943-1944, ABC, Saturday, 2:00–5:00 P.M.; 1944-1945, ABC, Saturday, 2:00–5:00 P.M.; 1945-1946, ABC, Saturday, 2:00–5:30 P.M.; 1946-1947, ABC, Saturday, 2:00–5:30 P.M.; 1947-1948, ABC, Saturday, 2:00–5:00 P.M.; 1948-1949, ABC, Saturday, 2:00–5:45 P.M.; 1949-1950, ABC, Saturday, 2:00–5:00 P.M.; 1950-1951, ABC, Saturday, 2:00–5:00 P.M.; 1951-1952, ABC, Saturday, 2:00–5:15 P.M.; 1952-1953, ABC, Saturday, 2:00–5:00 P.M.; 1953-1954, ABC, Saturday, 2:00–5:00 P.M.; 1954-1955, ABC, Saturday, 2:00–5:25 P.M.; 1955-1956, ABC, Saturday, 2:00–5:15 P.M.; 1956–1958 seasons, ABC, Saturday, 2:00 P.M.; 1958–1960 seasons, CBS, Saturday, 2:00 P.M.; 1960–present, special network, Saturday, 2:00 P.M.

The Metropolitan Auditions on the Air

Theme: March from *Tannhauser* (Wagner).

Sponsors: Sherwin-Williams Company for Sherwin-Williams paint (1936–1945 seasons); Farnsworth Radio & TV, Inc. for its entertainment products (1947–1949 seasons); otherwise sustaining.

Ratings: Numbers were recorded for 10 of the 20 seasons. High — 5.0 (1941-1942 season); Low — 2.6 (1948-1949 season); Median — 3.6.

On the Air: December 22, 1935–March 29, 1936, NBC, Sunday, 3:30–4:00 P.M. (all times Eastern); October 18, 1936–March 28, 1937, NBC, Sunday, 3:00–3:30 P.M.; October 3, 1937–March 27, 1938, NBC Blue, Sunday, 5:00–5:30 P.M.; October 9, 1938–April 2, 1939, NBC Blue, Sunday, 5:00–5:30 P.M.; October 1, 1939–March 24, 1940, NBC Blue, Sunday, 5:30–6:00 P.M.; October 20, 1940–March 30, 1941, NBC, Sunday, 5:00–5:30 P.M.; October 19, 1941–March 22, 1942, NBC, Sunday, 5:00–5:30 P.M.; November 29, 1942–March 14, 1943, ABC/NBC Blue, Sunday, 6:30–7:00 P.M.; November 28, 1943–April 9, 1944, ABC/NBC Blue, Sunday, 4:30–5:00 P.M.; November 26, 1944–April 1, 1945, ABC, Sunday, 5:30–6:00 P.M.; January 4, 1948–May 16, 1948, ABC, Sunday, 4:30–5:00 P.M.; November 28, 1948–March 13, 1949, ABC, Sunday, 4:30–5:00 P.M.; [*Milton Cross Opera Album*, March 20, 1949–June 18, 1950, ABC, Sunday, 4:30–5:00 P.M.] November 14, 1950–January 16, 1951, ABC, Tuesday, 8:30–9:00 P.M.; January 23, 1951–March 27, 1951, ABC, Tuesday, 10:00–10:30 P.M.; December 25, 1951–April 8, 1952, ABC, Tuesday, 8:30–9:00 P.M.; January 12, 1953-1953, ABC, Monday, 9:00–9:30 P.M.; 1953-1954, ABC, Monday, 9:00–9:30 P.M.; 1954-1955, ABC, Monday, 9:00–9:25 P.M.; 1955–March 26, 1956, ABC, Monday, 9:00–9:25 P.M.; 1956–

1957, ABC, Sunday, time unsubstantiated; 1957-1958, ABC, Sunday, time unsubstantiated.

The NBC Symphony Orchestra

Sponsors: General Motors Corporation for GMC, Cadillac, Buick, Oldsmobile, Pontiac and Chevrolet vehicles (1943–1946 seasons); multiple participation (1950-1951 season); Socony Vacuum Oil Corporation (1953-1954 season); otherwise sustaining.

Ratings: Of 26 seasons, numbers for only five have been preserved, offering an extremely meager account of how the program fared. High — 6.4 (1950-1951, Saturday broadcast). Low — 2.1 (1953-1954). Median — 4.5.

On the Air: November 2, 1937 (dress rehearsal), NBC; November 13, 1937–June 25, 1938, NBC, Saturday, 10:00–11:30 P.M. (all times Eastern); October 15, 1938–April 22, 1939, NBC Blue, Saturday, 6:00–7:00 P.M.; October 14, 1939–April 27, 1940, NBC Blue, Saturday, 10:00–11:00 P.M.; October 12, 1940–April 19, 1941, NBC Blue, Saturday, 9:35–11:00 P.M.; October 7, 1941–April 14, 1942, NBC Blue, Tuesday, 9:30–10:30 P.M. plus Saturday, 9:00–10:30 P.M.; September 27, 1942–April 11, 1943, NBC Blue, Sunday, 5:00–6:00 P.M.; October 31, 1943–April 9, 1944, NBC, Sunday, 5:00–6:00; October 22, 1944–April 1, 1945, NBC, Sunday, 5:00–6:00 P.M.; October 28, 1945–April 7, 1946, NBC, Sunday, 5:00–6:00 P.M.; October 27, 1946–April 6, 1947, NBC, Sunday, 5:00–6:00 P.M.; October 25, 1947–April 3, 1948, NBC, Saturday, 6:30–7:30 P.M.; October 23, 1948–April 2, 1949, NBC, Saturday, 6:30–7:30 P.M.; October 29, 1949–April 8, 1950, NBC, Saturday, 6:30–7:30 P.M.; October 9, 1950–April 14, 1951, NBC, Monday, 10:00–11:00 P.M. plus NBC, Saturday, 6:30–8:00 P.M.; November 3, 1951–March 29, 1952, NBC, Saturday, 6:30–8:00 P.M.; November 1, 1952–March 28, 1953, NBC, Saturday, 6:30–8:00 P.M. (last concert of season at 5:45 P.M. due to length); November 22, 1953–April 4, 1954, NBC, Sunday, 6:30–7:30 P.M.; 1954–1963 seasons, NBC, dates and times unsubstantiated.

The Longines Symphonette

Theme: *Moonlight Sonata* (Beethoven).

Sponsor: Longines-Wittnauer Watch Company for its Longines timepieces (July 5, 1943–May 26, 1957).

Ratings: Figures for four of the Sunday afternoon seasons are available. High — 4.7 (1950-1951 season); Low — 1.5 (1954-1955 season); Median — 3.4.

On the Air: July 5, 1943–January 21, 1944, MBS, Weekdays, 10:45–11:00 P.M.; January 24, 1944–March 11, 1949, MBS, Weekdays, 10:30–11:00 P.M.; March 13, 1949–December 18, 1949, CBS, Sunday, 2:00–2:30 P.M.; April 16, 1950–June 25, 1950, CBS, Sunday, time unsubstantiated; September 3, 1950–June 8, 1952, CBS, initially 2:30–3:00 P.M., later 2:00–2:30 P.M.; September 14, 1952–April 26, 1953, CBS, Sunday, 2:00–2:30 P.M.; September 27, 1953–May 30, 1954, CBS, Sunday, 2:00–2:30 P.M.; September 5, 1954–April 17, 1955, CBS, Sunday, 2:00–2:30 P.M.; October 2, 1955–April 29, 1956, CBS, Sunday, 2:00–2:30 P.M.; September 30, 1956–May 26, 1957, Sunday, time unsubstantiated. Also: October 2, 1950–December 28, 1950, ABC, Monday–Thursday, 10:35–11:00 P.M.; November 20, 1950–July 10, 1953, NBC, Weekdays, 7:00–7:30 P.M.; September 7, 1953–February 12, 1954, NBC, Weekdays, 7:00–7:30 P.M.; March 6, 1954–June 5, 1954, CBS, Wednesday (15 minutes), Friday (15 minutes), Saturday (30 minutes), times unsubstantiated.

* * *

Radio historiographer John Dunning signifies roughly five dozen concert series that aired over extended runs during the medium's golden age. Each offered what he terms "serious music" to radio listeners. Operating expenses for such programming were enormous while top-ranking artists were at first hesitant to perform on the ether, thinking they would lower their status by appearing so gamely before the common man. Yet the concert schedules of all four national chains were "varied and rich."

Violinist Jascha Heifetz was among the performers whose perception soon altered as he grasped the fact that millions of new fans could be introduced to his talent on the air, easily exceeding the thousands of sophisticated patrons who attended his concerts in person. Simultaneously, rural Americans were hearing symphony orchestras from dozens of large- and medium-sized cities for the very first time, the result infusing the populace with a more enriching bent than it had previously been accustomed to.

Boston, Chicago, Cincinnati, Cleveland, Detroit, Indianapolis, Los Angeles, Minneapolis, New York, Oklahoma City, Philadelphia, Rochester and St. Louis were among the burgs that originated symphony concert musicales over nationwide hookups. There were orchestras under the direction of some legendary conductors like Alfredo Antonini, Howard Barlow, Frank Black, Andre Kostelanetz, Erno Rapee, Fritz Reiner, Alfred Wallenstein and more. Outstanding soloists sang with them, including Florence Easton, Kirsten Flagstad, Lotte Menuhin, Lauritz Melchior, Grace Moore, Joseph Schmidt, Richard Tauber and John Charles Thomas. They were featured on program bills with violinists Yehudi Menuhin and Erica Morini and dozens of other celebrated instrumentalists.

In truth, Americans of refined tastes—and those who longed to be identified with them—never had it so good once radio became entrenched as the nation's primary home entertainment provider. The cultural level of many citizens edged a little higher, in fact, once radio became the prevailing art form in millions of homes.

Among the most prominent radio symphony series beyond those emanating from various cities with local musicians were the *General Motors Concerts* which ran in several formats over NBC between 1929 and 1937, *The NBC String Symphony* between 1933 and 1939, NBC's *Radio City Music Hall of the Air* from 1932 to 1942, *Sinfonietta* over MBS from 1935 to 1945 and various U.S. military band concerts on all the networks between 1938 and 1956. Deeply rooted among the most durable series on the aural airwaves were the five selected to represent the species of classical music shows—*The Longines Symphonette, The Metropolitan Opera, The Metropolitan Opera Auditions on the Air, The NBC Symphony Orchestra* and *The New York Philharmonic Symphony*. No other programs might surpass this quintet in providing such urbane renderings to the nation's ears.

The history of radio as a major entertainment source is inextricably linked to the inception of music on the air. It hearkens all the way back to December 13, 1910, when radio pioneer Lee De Forest conducted an experiment from the stage of the famed Metropolitan Opera House in New York City. Placing microphones before Riccardo Martin, Enrico Caruso and Emmy Destinn, De Forest relayed a performance of *Cavalleria Rusticana* and *Pagliacci* to a virtual nonlistening audience—despite the apprehensions of Met general manager Giulio Gatti-Casazza.

Norman Finkelstein recalls: "The wireless operator on board the SS *Avon* at sea was dumbfounded. An unearthly sound of human singing was clearly coming out of his headset! For the next decade hobbyists continued playing with their electrical toys, perfecting the transmission of sound over the air. By 1917 there were over eight thousand licensed broadcasters in the United States. Most did not see any applications of wireless technology beyond broadcasting between ship and shore and communicating experimentally among themselves."

Following De Forest's test, an unmovable opera management stood resolute against subsequent broadcasts from the Met for more than two decades. In spite of that injunction, New York's radio station WEAF aired a Metropolitan Opera performance of Verdi's *Aida* on May 11, 1922, starring Leon Rothier and Rosa Ponselle. The broadcast, narrated by WEAF announcer Tommy Cowan, originated from the stage of Kingsbridge Armory in the Bronx.

Even before then, in 1921, Chicago station KYW became the first in the nation to air operas on a consistent basis. Officials there operated under the presumption that "good music" was a welcome incentive to drawing listeners. Such fare became the centerpiece of its programming format. New York's WJZ adopted a similar yet modified path two years later, offering its audiences intermittent operatic features. The station negotiated with the Manhattan Opera Company to air a series of Wagnerian operas as a focus of its increased emphasis. When the National Broadcasting Company (NBC) was founded in 1926, performances by the Chicago Civic Opera were included on its schedule, that venue quickly becoming heard beyond the reaches of the Windy City. The fledgling network introduced opera to people living in the country's cities and its hinterlands, exposing them to some fresh experiences while creating innovative traditions among music lovers.

In reality, opera was at the forefront of the inception of the nation's most formidable broadcast networks, making deliberate, forceful appearances at the inaugurals of both the National Broadcasting Company and the Columbia Broadcasting System (CBS). Those chains would prominently feature highbrow fare in the decades to come.

When NBC was launched on November 15, 1926, during a four-hour gala from the grand ballroom of New York's Waldorf Astoria Hotel, Walter Damrosch conducted the New York Symphony Orchestra while Metropolitan Opera star Tito Ruffo moved an attentive audience with arias.

When Columbia premiered a few months later, on September 18, 1927, Howard Barlow's orchestra played instrumental selections in the afternoon. That evening, broadcasting from the new net's flagship station, Manhattan's WOR, Maj. J. Andrew White — the first president of CBS — read a list of call letters of 16 Columbia stations and the cities they represented. Several gifted performers, among them tenor Rafael Diaz and soprano Marie Sundelius, appeared in *The King's Henchman* by Deems Taylor, who offered comments at fitting intervals. Hundreds of thousands of the nation's families from St. Louis to Boston heard opera for the first time in their lives.

The evening was a near disaster, however. Practically drowned out by static and running more than an hour overtime, it may have been incredible that anything was transmitted at all. The premiere was delayed by heavy thunderstorms; stations west of the Allegheny Mountains missed the first quarter-hour entirely. A men's room — the only soundproof spot available — was pressed into service as a makeshift control center for the live production. Despite those minor inconveniences, it should not be overlooked that such cultural attempts received considerable emphasis as they came to the forefront during the debuts of the country's first national broadcast hookups.

The ascendancy of music and its integration into radio specifically is a fascinating narrative with roots that can be traced back long before the origination of the aural chains that broadcast so much of it. The story of David Sarnoff, a nine-year-old Jewish lad who immigrated to this country in 1900 from the Russian province of Minsk, is unambiguously intermingled in the preponderance of highbrow music introduced to the American psyche. In adulthood, Sarnoff would become the powerful leader of the Radio Corporation of America, parent firm of the National Broadcasting Company. To overlook his personal determination to imbue the airwaves with sophistication and culture would be to miss some of the significant detail that led to a prevalence of classical music programming in this country—not only over NBC but over the other chains as well.

By age 15, David Sarnoff had acquired an intense interest in the growing technology that surrounded modern telegraphy. Hoping to become a telegraph operator, he took a job with the American Marconi Company, a recognized leader in that industry. The vital role of wireless telegraphy in the *Titanic* disaster in 1912 created growth opportunities for both Sarnoff's employer and himself. Then 21, Sarnoff visualized a role for the wireless beyond merely transmitting business messages over long distances. He was among the first to glimpse the potential of radio as an entertainment and information medium for the masses.

In 1916, he projected a "Radio Music Box" to the management of the Marconi Company. "I have in mind a plan of development that would make radio a household utility in the same sense as the piano or phonograph," said he. "The idea is to bring music into the home by wireless ... also events of importance can be simultaneously announced and received." Marconi officials weren't impressed, believing Sarnoff's concept impractical.

The fascinating tale of how an indomitable Sarnoff never discarded his dream and eventually saw it achieve fulfillment is recounted in Eugene Lyons' captivating 1966 portrayal simply titled *David Sarnoff: A Biography*. The chronicle of a boy who began life with nothing—an individual who never acquired anything with ease and who doggedly toiled for virtually everything he gained—is compelling. One is reminded again and again of Sarnoff's unrelenting preoccupation with maintaining broadcasting excellence. "If those who credit radio with raising the country's musical literacy are correct, much of the credit belongs to Sarnoff," exclaimed Lyons.

Sarnoff and his opposite, CBS owner-chairman William S. Paley, career rivals, saw things differently when it came to programming. A Paley biographer distinguished sharp contrasts between the pair.[1]

> Sarnoff lacked Paley's feel for popular culture. He adored classical music; his idea of relaxation was to sneak down to Studio 8-H in Rockefeller Center [an elaborate "floating" studio Sarnoff had constructed in the NBC headquarters building in Radio City to house its "name" orchestra] and listen to the rehearsals of the NBC Symphony. When his wife tuned into *Amos 'n' Andy*, Sarnoff left the room. He had nothing but contempt for comedians. "If comedy is the center of NBC's activities, then maybe I had better quit," he ... confided to one of his executives. Given a preference, he would have aired only symphonies and classical dramas on NBC. As one of his former executives said, "His outlook on life was simply too serious to accommodate to popular taste.... He did not understand the hunger for easy entertainment.... He saw broadcasting as a means of bridging cultural differences, bringing people together in greater understanding of one another."
>
> Paley, on the other hand, had a genius for mass programming, mainly because it mirrored his own taste. He also understood that it was the path to big money.

Paley liked popular entertainers and wooed them with his customary energy. When the actress Alice Faye came to New York, he filled her hotel room with flowers; Sarnoff never sent her a posey. Paley had a good ear for musical talent. He knew enough about dramatic structure to criticize a program intelligently. To Paley, Sarnoff was a hardware man in a software business.

To an unmistakable degree Sarnoff's mission — in his mind, at least — could be equated with an awesome sensitivity for polish, without acknowledging any personal bias. That could translate into appealing to an erudite audience, of course. "His quest for quality was explained as a search for prestige," a memoir conceded. "In truth it derived from his natural preferences. No matter how logically he justified superior programs, he was in fact responding to his own hungers for beauty, music, culture, the education he had missed."

The New York Philharmonic Orchestra was the first of the quintet of classic programs previously cited that aired regularly. It was — and is — the oldest symphony orchestra in the United States and one of the oldest in the world, playing a leading role in American musical life since its founding in 1842. The series is believed to have remained on network radio longer than any of the others of its genus. This popular feature premiered over the Columbia chain in 1927, the same year that network was founded. The program was aired by CBS for 35 of the 36 years to 1963 (exception: 1929-1930), and wasn't withdrawn from its schedule until the well-documented demise of radio's golden age arrived.

In the autumn of 1930, when Paley signed the Philharmonic to an extended contract, he hoped the symphony would draw more upscale listeners to radio. One source noted, "While NBC spent far more money to develop its cultural programs — $2 million in 1932 versus CBS's $827,000 — CBS was widely thought to be the leader."

The Philharmonic's weekend broadcasts, ranging in length between 45 and 120 minutes, featured some of classical music's most renowned permanent and guest conductors. During the epoch when CBS aired those concerts, Philharmonic conductors included (years designating permanent conductors, some of them overlapping): John Barbirolli (1936–1941), Leonard Bernstein (1958–1969), Georges Enesco, Erich Kielber, Otto Klemperer, Willem Mengelberg (1922–1930), Dimitri Mitropoulos (1949–1958), Bernadino Molinari, Artur Rodzinski (1943–1947), Leopold Stokowski (1949–1950), Igor Stravinsky, Arturo Toscanini (1928–1936) and Bruno Walter (1947–1949).

Toscanini led the Metropolitan Opera Company orchestra for seven seasons between 1908 and 1915. He picked up the Philharmonic baton in 1928 and quickly carried that musical staff to new heights. When the outcome of a dispute that erupted eight years later didn't satisfy him, the maestro — who was given to outbursts of rage — quit in a huff. He soon sailed for his native Italy, asserting that he would never conduct an American orchestra again. He would eat his words, as we shall see.

Among the Philharmonic's solo and duo artists appearing as guests during those years were Ethel Bartlett and Rae Robertson (pianists), Yasoar Cassado (cellist), Hulda Dashanska (soprano), Kirsten Flagstad (soprano), Josef Hoffman (pianist), Jose Iturbi (pianist), Marjorie Lawrence (soprano), Artur Rubinstein (pianist), Rudolph Serkin (pianist), Frank Sheridan (pianist), Joseph Sziegeti (violinist) and Efrem Zimbalist (violinist).

The program's hosts were conversant musicologists Deems Taylor, Frank Gallop and Milton Cross, who offered in-depth knowledge about any of a wide range of diverse topics under discussion.

In 1922, Taylor, a valued music critic and composer, advised readers of *The New York World* that radio would be extinct within three years. His rationale was based on a couple of considerations: audio reception was "terrible" and could never be improved, he claimed, while costs would escalate as radio artists demanded payment for their services. Fifteen years later, the pundit was eating crow. In *Of Men and Music*, a book Taylor issued in 1937, he conjectured that each broadcast of *The New York Philharmonic Orchestra* attracted 9 million listeners. Across 92 years since that symphony was formed in 1845, he pontificated that 8 million individuals had probably attended a live performance in a concert hall.[2] Taylor surmised that more people were then listening to a single broadcast than those who went to hear the orchestra in person. Therefore, he freely confessed, radio had endowed the nation with momentous cultural donations, hardly an incontestable affirmation.

A 104-piece orchestra—one of the world's largest—comprised the Philharmonic. It consisted of 36 violins, 14 violas, 12 cellos, 10 bass fiddles and an assortment of wind, brass and percussion instruments. An estimated 10 million listeners regularly tuned in on Sunday afternoons for the concerts. In addition, for nine seasons ending in 1937, *The New York Philharmonic Children's Concerts* introduced youngsters to quality musical selections for an hour over CBS at 11 o'clock on Saturday mornings. Ernest Schelling conducted the orchestra until 1935 when Rudolph Ganz succeeded him.

In time, *The New York Philharmonic Orchestra* would become the principal counter to a strong NBC concert agenda. NBC was well endowed with classical offerings, particularly on weekends, given the unmistakable approving hand of RCA chairman Sarnoff. While CBS maintained several additional programs of high musical distinction, this one secured the image and prestige that allowed Columbia to competitively bid for a large share of music lovers with refined tastes. Publicists for the orchestra presently claim it is the only U.S. symphony regularly broadcast over live radio nationwide (although no longer over CBS). In 1999, the Philharmonic performed its 13,000th concert, a milestone, the organization's press agents observed, that is "unmatched by any other orchestra."

In 1965 the New York Philharmonic Orchestra launched a series of free annual Concerts in the Parks. More than 13 million people have attended these events in the years since. The largest audience in history for a classical music concert was registered during the Philharmonic's Liberty Weekend Concert in Central Park on July 5, 1986. It drew an estimated crowd of 800,000 witnesses. The New York Philharmonic was honored by the Recording Academy with a Trustees Award in February 2003 recognizing the organization's "outstanding contributions to the industry and American culture." The 45th Annual Grammy awards ceremony, carried internationally by television from New York's Madison Square Garden, featured members of the Philharmonic. It was the first time that a major symphony orchestra had performed live during the event. In June 2003 the New York Philharmonic, under music director Maestro Lorin Maazel, was in residency at the Teatro Lirico di Cagliari in Sardinia.

If a classical series rivals (or quite possibly supersedes) *The New York Philharmonic Orchestra* today it is the concert broadcasts of *The Metropolitan Opera*, still being aired, as this is written, over an exclusive coast-to-coast hookup. Indeed, the Met is considered to have set the standard for all classical music programs. On the air continuously for nearly three-quarters of a century, the program's average season lasts about five months, from late autumn to early spring. A critic astutely observed, "The broadcasts have reached millions of listeners who might never otherwise have experienced opera in any form."

The reader may recall that early on the Met's management vigorously protested against airing its live concerts from the stage of the Metropolitan Opera House. In fact, a resolute Giulio Gatti-Casazza forbade any such attempts after Lee De Forest's previously cited experiment in 1910. Two decades elapsed before Gatti, the hard-hearted director of the Metropolitan Opera Association, finally mellowed, at last permitting broadcast performances to begin late in 1931. Why had he remained so steadfast against a well-publicized campaign to thwart his directive?

"Management believed that opera was not only a glorious musical experience but a visual spectacle as well, and that radio would undercut and cheapen it," claimed an informant. "Opera is an art that must be seen as well as heard," Gatti was fond of saying. There was also the legitimate fear that putting the Met on the ether could reduce proceeds, possibly catastrophically. Nonetheless, a couple of other reasons were publicly stated — that technical considerations could not be properly satisfied ("There's no space for a control room, microphone, and all that paraphernalia without blocking the view of the audience," Gatti argued), and airing the concerts was expressly taboo according to pacts signed by Met performers.

As early as 1922, strong opposition over management's position arose from *Radio Digest*, a trendy fanzine of the era, which led a battle to override Gatti's "hard-headed" stance. But it was not until the Met's cash flow was perilously jeopardized by the disaster of a failed stock market late in 1929 and the subsequent fallout from the national Depression — resulting in a pathetically dwindling gate for the opera — that the association finally bit the bullet it had staunchly resisted and announced it would accept an infusion of broadcast capital. The Met had little alternative to such a compromise if it intended to remain a viable entertainment venue. Its "concession," of course, would expose millions of first-time listeners to opera concerts they never had any chance to experience before. Ultimately it would also create legions of devoted fans from coast to coast that would thrill to the performances.

Before that could happen, however, yet another nip-and-tuck "war" was being played out over those broadcasts — this one largely out of public view — resulting in who would air the Metropolitan Opera concerts. As in so many instances that mattered most within the industry, this mêlée erupted into a battle royal between the principal broadcasting moguls — William Paley of CBS and David Sarnoff of NBC. Both were determined, spirited competitors, a pair of steadfast fighters who were usually accustomed to winning the prizes they wanted.

For this combative chase, on the one hand there was the flamboyant playboy Paley who would press his charm to the limit to obtain whatever he sought. He would call upon every available incentive in his well-stocked arsenal to entice a target into his web in order to satisfy his insatiable desires — sometimes simply centering on a win. On the other hand, the reader is already aware of Sarnoff's zealous resolve to generate an image for his network that could be instantly perceived in the public's mind as representing quality and prestige. In Sarnoff's descriptions of the cultural potential of radio, "grand opera had always been in the forefront," a biographer certified. At the time he could think of no better ploy than to acquire the Met and he went after it to gain the status for his chain that he so passionately felt it deserved. Yet for Sarnoff, his own deep appreciation of all that the Met represented would become something of a personal coup if he succeeded in pulling it off. It would exceed the spoils of a mere business triumph for his own unquenchable tastes were also at stake.

Presenting *his* case, Paley invited Met chairman Otto Kahn to a sound quality exhibition. The broadcast tycoon noted that Kahn was greatly moved by the presentation. Exclaimed Kahn: "Just imagine hearing that wonderful music and we don't have to look at those ugly faces!" Paley was sure that such glowing affirmation concluded the matter — that CBS had the Met in its pocket. But the thing that had provoked the opera's officials to consider radio broadcasting in the first place — its desperate need for cash — ultimately became the deciding factor and Paley's undoing.

When word leaked to NBC president Merlin H. Aylesworth, acting on behalf of his superior, that CBS was about to sign the Met, Aylesworth determined to make an offer the Met officials simply couldn't refuse. Having already tendered $60,000 to broadcast the opera company's initial season on the air, he was certain that Paley had proffered more. Aylesworth reached into the air and pulled out the number $122,000. His gambit paid off. Paley had anted-up $120,000 for the prize. A beaming Sarnoff got what he wanted for his network and himself and overwhelmed his strongest rival in the fray. While Sarnoff would lose some major wars in the years ahead, he had won an important victory that day.

Having already scored his coup with the Philharmonic in 1930, in that same year Paley had attempted to lure the Met to CBS for a series of Sunday afternoon concerts. When Sarnoff won that campaign decisively, Paley was enraged. "It was a bitter blow and one that I resented for a long time," the CBS chairman acknowledged. He consoled himself, he insisted, with the knowledge that he was paying only $35,000 annually for the Philharmonic while NBC was soon shelling out $191,000 to retain the Met.

For about two decades, beginning in 1934, Sarnoff was a member of the board of directors of the Metropolitan Opera Company. Contributions from newly minted music lovers supplemented the receipts from NBC in sustaining the costly mammoth organization. Yet there were still budget shortfalls. A method of remedying that situation was to appeal directly to the opera's millions of radio listeners.

In 1940, the Met found itself in just such a shaky position, needing a million dollars to remain solvent. Sarnoff, then chairman of the organization's radio division, went on the air to personally address the listeners. He urged each new opera lover — anyone who had been won over through nine Met broadcast seasons — to tangibly express gratitude by mailing in $1 each. More than a half-million dollars poured in from his appeal. The million-dollar goal was met by the added response of private organizations and individuals. It was a marvelous testimony to the faithfulness of the fans, the tenacity of Sarnoff and the power of radio as a compelling marketing tool.

The launch of NBC's *Metropolitan Opera* broadcasts occurred on Christmas 1931 with a traditional holiday feature, Humperdinck's *Hansel and Gretel*. It starred Queena Mario, Editha Fleischer, Dorothee Manski, Henrietta Wakefield and Gustav Schultzendorf and was picked up by 129 NBC affiliates. (While a light vehicle was offered at the inception on the ether, more formidable operas were staged as the seasons progressed. In time, nothing among the Met's repertoire was considered too heavy for the unseen Saturday afternoon audiences.)

Storyteller Tom DeLong summarized what transpired that Christmas afternoon and the aftermath to it[3]:

> Milton Cross, Deems Taylor, and two engineers handled the "remote" over the combined Red and Blue networks [both

chains owned by NBC]. Before conductor Karl Riedel stepped to the podium, Taylor delivered a brief biography of composer Humperdinck. During the opera itself, he frequently broke in with a running account of on-stage action. Both Taylor and Cross sat on high stools in the cloakroom of Box 44, peering over a hodgepodge of coils, tubes, and engineers' heads....

When the curtain fell one hour and forty minutes later, cast and crew agreed that NBC had done a marvelous thing. Gatti conceded that the Met had "abided the experience in fine fettle."

Ecstatic reviews followed. Critics called the broadcast "a beautiful Christmas gift to music lovers." One reviewer noted that "eloquence of language is lacking when it comes to ... describing the praise I feel is due the Metropolitan."

Thousands of letters poured in from all parts of the country. People who had never heard opera before talked about it. "We all agreed it was the best program we have ever been privileged to hear over the air," wrote a listener in Indianapolis. "As I listened, it created a desire to see with my own eyes the action of the stage. I will be over soon to sit before the footlights."

Opera had found a new audience.

NBC broadcast the first weekly Saturday performance from the Metropolitan on December 26, 1931, a day following the *Hansel and Gretel* premiere. *Norma* starred Rosa Ponselle. "Critics were lavish in their praise," wrote a historian. "The only real bone of contention [was] the Deems Taylor commentary, which was given over the music and drew criticisms ranging from 'idiotic' to 'unnecessary.'"

From the ether's golden age the Met was conducted by a host of well-recognized names including Maurice Abravanel, Giuseppe Antonicelli, Sir Thomas Beecham, Vincenzo Bellezza, Artur Bodanzky, Paul Breisach, Fritz Busch, Feruccio Calusio, Pietro Cimara, Emil Cooper, Louis Fourestier, Louis Hasselmans, Erich Leinsdorf, Frank Martin, Italo Montemezzi, Ettore Panizza, Gennaro Papi, Wilfred Pelletier, Jonel Perlea, Fritz Reiner, Karl Riedel, Max Rudolf, Tullio Serafin, Cesare Sodero, Frank St. Leger, Fritz Steidry, George Szell and Bruno Walter.

The Met's celebrated stars in this period were legion, among them: Lucine Amara (soprano), Rose Bampton (soprano), Mimi Benzell (coloratura soprano), Jussi Bjoerling (tenor), Karin Branzell (contralto), Eugene Conley (tenor), Nadine Conner (lyric soprano), Lisa Della Casa (soprano), Mario Del Monaco (tenor), Victoria de los Angeles (soprano), Giuseppe di Stafano (tenor), Placido Domingo (tenor), Rosalind Elias (mezzo-soprano), Eileen Farrell (soprano), Kirsten Flagstad (soprano), Jerome Hines (bass), Herbert Janssen (baritone), Helen Jepson (soprano), Dorothy Kirsten (soprano), George London (bass), Jean Madeira (mezzo-soprano), Giovanni Martinelli (tenor), Lauritz Melchior (tenor), James Melton (tenor), Robert Merrill (baritone), Zinka Milanov (soprano), Grace Moore (soprano), Patrice Munsel (soprano), Birgit Nilsson (soprano), Jan Peerce (tenor), Roberta Peters (soprano), Ezio Pinza (bass), Lily Pons (soprano), Leontyne Price (soprano), Elisabeth Rethberg (soprano), Leonie Rysanek (soprano), Bidu Sayao (soprano), Friedrich Schorr (baritone), Cesare Siepi (bass), Beverly Sills (soprano), Eleanor Steber (soprano), Risë Stevens (mezzo-soprano), Brian Sullivan (tenor), Joan Sutherland (soprano), Gladys Swarthout (mezzo-soprano), Renata Tebaldi (soprano), Blanche Thebom (mezzo-soprano), John Charles Thomas (baritone), Kerstin Thorborg (contralto), Lawrence Tibbett (baritone), Giorgio Tozzi (bass), Helen Traubel (soprano), Richard Tucker (tenor), Theodor Uppman (baritone) and Leonard Warren (baritone). There were scores of other permanent performers unnamed here. (For a complete listing, including biographies of the Met's vocal entourage during its first century, the reader

For all his straight-laced comments to the cultured, legendary "voice of the Met" Milton J. Cross was a pretty swell guy. Just check out his tongue-in-cheek annotations while poking fun at the noblemen on *The Chamber Music Society of Lower Basin Street.* In a publicity pose he oils a skate with the sponsor's product for an afternoon at the Met!

is directed to William W. Granger's text *We Proudly Sang at the Met, '83-'83*, published in 1984.)

In the early radio years *New York Times* music critic Olin Downes and impresario-conductor Boris Goldovsky hosted interviews and musical tests of knowledge during the opera's intermissions. Downes' *Opera Quiz* checked guests like pianist Oscar Levant, composer John Carlo Menotti and mezzo-soprano Risë Stevens on their ability to answer opera-related stumpers. Goldovsky's *Opera News on the Air* provided not only news but interviews with performers from the worlds of opera, the theater and public life.

Perhaps no single voice is better identified with the long-running Met series than that of Milton J. Cross, however, who—for more than four decades—spoke rather than sang to the crowd. As the opera's permanent host and commentator, he was at its inception on December 25, 1931. Eventually, with good reason, he was labeled "the voice of the Met." In a sense, he became a luminary himself. With a home audience tuning in commonly estimated at between 12 million and 15 million individuals, Cross was one of the most listened-to men in America. He stayed at his post for more than 800 broadcasts, until his death on January 3, 1975, missing only two performances in that time, both upon the passing of his wife.

"His resonant voice was an instrument in itself, one that produced a burnished announcer-profundo sound," a historian of the period confirmed. "His diction was near-flawless," another pointed out. "His pronunciation of difficult names was accurate and sure."

For about $80 in salary, Cross broadcast weekly during those years from box 44 in the Met's grand tier alongside engineer Charles C. Grey and producer Herbert Liversidge. His quintessential introductory line was a simple "Texaco presents *The Metropolitan Opera*." As each performance was about to begin, he routinely advised his listeners: "The house lights are being dimmed. In a moment, the great gold curtain will go up."

Cross was born in New York City on April 16, 1897. Enamored by opera while still a lad, he reportedly sparred for the honor of transporting butter to the home of contralto Louise Homer, who sang at the Met between 1900 and 1919. Radio fascinated him and at 24 he was hired as an announcer by station WJZ. For $40 a week he was announcing, reading comic pages to kids, singing and providing his own accompaniment via a player piano. Broadcasting from a tiny booth off the station's women's room, he soon aspired to greater heights, coveting a career for himself in music. But he was unsuccessful at it. One reviewer dubbed him "a failed tenor." Cross remained in radio—speaking instead of singing—eventually announcing or hosting a myriad of listener favorites. Several of his series were enduring to audiences. In 1929, the American Academy of Arts and Letters conferred on him its highest honors for radio announcing.

Cross is identified with more than two dozen audio features: *The A&P Gypsies, America's Town Meeting of the Air, Betty and Bob, Bughouse Rhythm, The Chamber Music Society of Lower Basin Street, The Chicago Civic Opera, Coast-to-Coast on a Bus, Don't Forget, General Motors Concerts, Information Please, The Jeddo Highlanders, The Lucky Strike Music Hall, The Magic Key, Melody Highway, The Metropolitan Opera Auditions on the Air, The Metropolitan Opera, The Milton Cross Opera Album, Musical Americana, The New York Philharmonic Symphony, The Piano Playhouse, Raising Your Parents, The Raymond Paige Orchestra, Roxy and His Gang, The Slumber Hour, This Is Your FBI*.

On the Met broadcasts he filled in the color around the music. He exhibited a colossal knowledge of story line scenarios and easily conveyed to home audiences descriptions of the sets and cast backgrounds. "Cross was a veritable talking playbill who synopsized convoluted plots and provided biographical notes, between-acts trivia, and an intermission quiz with celebrity opera buffs," a pundit affirmed. *Time* magazine characterized this well-informed, legendary operatic analyst as a "huge, humble, bespectacled music-charmed announcer, whose cultured genuflecting voice seems to come straight from NBC's artistic soul."

While *The Metropolitan Opera* concerts appeared alternately or simultaneously over both the Red and Blue networks of the National Broadcasting Company from its 1931 inception through 1939, at that juncture it became an exclusive property of the Blue chain, which was spun off into the American Broadcasting Company (ABC) a few years later. ABC aired the Met concerts until 1958 when the network bowed out and CBS had a chance to originate what it struggled for and lost back in 1931. It carried the performances only two years, however; by then, most traditional radio programming had died as audiences and advertisers turned to the newer medium of television.

There remained abiding interest among classical music lovers in the Metropolitan Opera concerts, however. The Texas Company (later Texaco Corporation), which had underwritten the Saturday afternoon series since 1940 for its Texaco brand of gasoline, oil and added vehicle products and local dealers coast to coast, agreed to continue sponsoring the weekly performances. These were most recently carried by a worldwide hookup of more than 360 public and independent radio stations in 42 countries synchronized by the Met's media department. Chevron Incorporated acquired Texaco in 2001. In the spring of 2003, the renamed successor, ChevronTexaco Corporation, announced that it would no longer bankroll the Metropolitan Opera broadcasts after the Met's 2003-2004 season ended April 24, 2004. An Associated Press agent lamented the decision as "another sign of the troubled times for classical music in the United States."

A ChevronTexaco official, Patricia E. Yarrington, vice president for public and government affairs, interpreted the firm's stance: "ChevronTexaco has had a tremendously rewarding relationship with the Metropolitan Opera, which is a world-class cultural treasure. However, as our business has evolved, we believe it is important to focus more of our resources directly with the countries and markets where we do business, with an additional emphasis on addressing pressing development needs in those communities."

News reports circulating at the time of that announcement cited "a series of setbacks for classical music" in contemporary times.

Facing an $800,000 shortfall, the Pittsburgh Symphony proposed a $10,000 salary cut for its musicians and a loss of benefits. The organization canceled a summer tour to Europe in 2004 when a $400,000 deficit from the trip was projected.

In May 2003, the Florida Philharmonic Orchestra filed for Chapter 11 bankruptcy protection after suspending operations. The group was unable to finance a half-million-dollar monthly payroll for its musicians.

The Louisville Orchestra also found itself behind in paying musicians to the tune of $800,000.

With a $250,000 indebtedness, in 2003 the Nevada Opera cut 75 percent of all full-time employees, plus some performances.

The San Jose Symphony filed for bankruptcy while the Lyric Opera of Chicago and the San Francisco Opera both announced in late 2002 that they were deleting some previously scheduled operas from their 2003-2004 seasons.

In the early years of a new century, lean economic times were irrefutably affecting the arts. Several local opera groups felt the pinch of the nation's fiscal woes in disturbing ways, some threatening their very existence as a viable discretionary form of entertainment. It was a far cry from those days when multiple opera and symphony concerts were readily available to the masses at the flick of a dial.

Returning temporarily to Texaco, when in 1990 that firm reached a half-century of sponsoring the Metropolitan Opera's weekly broadcasts, a list of the operas it had presented and how many times each had been aired was published. Between 1940 and 1990 a grand total of 133 operas was recorded. In that 50-year period, five works were cited as those most frequently broadcast, often at the request of listeners: Puccini's *La Boheme*, 36 times; Verdi's *Aida*, 33 times; Bizet's *Carmen*, 31 times; Puccini's *Tosca*, 29 times; and Verdi's *Il Trovatore*, 25 times.

There were many other popular works aired over the years: Rossini's *Il Barbiere di Siviglia* (aka *The Barber of Seville*), Offenbach's *Les Contes d'Hoffmann* (aka *The Tales of Hoffman*), Mozart's *Don Giovanni*, Gounod's *Faust*, Wagner's *Lohengrin*, Puccini's *Madama Butterfly*, Massenet's *Manon*, Thomas' *Mignon*, Mozart's *Le Nozze di Figaro* (aka *The Marriage of Figaro*), Verdi's *Otello*, Verdi's *Rigoletto*, Gounod's *Romeo et Juliette*, Wagner's *Tannhauser* and Verdi's *La Traviata* among them. "The diversity and number ... indicates the significant cultural contributions these broadcasts represented," a contemporary reviewer advanced.

As *The New York Philharmonic Symphony* offered a popular sideline feature, *The New York Philharmonic Children's Concerts*, for a spell, the Met broadcasts were supplemented by a companion series known as *The Metropolitan Opera Auditions on the Air* between 1935 and 1958. Dubbed by a pundit as "one of the classiest talent shows" in broadcasting history, the series initially gave radio and eventually television audiences (in early 1952) a chance to witness tryouts for coveted performing rights at the Met. John Dunning maintained that the feature proffered dual benefits to listeners—"the excitement of hearing brilliant new performers at the dawn of genuinely promising careers," and opportunities to acquire a basic understanding of opera more readily than by tuning into a Met broadcast and "hoping to pick up some finer points."

Dunning continued: "This was no rich man's Major Bowes [a reference to *Major Bowes' Original Amateur Hour*, perceived in some quarters as a cattle call for anybody willing to take the stage], pushing the shaggy dogs of the highbrow set." *Radio Guide* explained: "It is a serious attempt to find the most promising singers the country has produced and to make the most of their talents." Some of the aspirants had sung professionally while none of them were widely known until then. On *Auditions* they could "come within voice-range of the Met." The opera company would then extend contracts to those it deemed most talented.

Maestro Wilfred Pelletier typically auditioned as many as 800 applicants annually for the chance to sing on the *Auditions* show. Sixty-three of them actually made it onto the air. Fourteen semifinalists were eventually selected and from them six finalists were culled. During each season's finale dual winners were tapped. They were given $1,000 checks and Metropolitan Opera contracts. Operatic luminaries like Robert Merrill, Patrice Munsel, Eleanor Steber and Leonard Warren gained career breakthroughs on the *Auditions* program. Some of the losers even found permanent work in radio as a result of their appearances. Jean Dickenson, Felix Knight, Evelyn MacGregor, Marian McManus, Thomas L. Thomas and more stars of Frank and Anne Hummerts' myriad of musical shows (*The American Album of Familiar Music*, *The American Melody Hour*, *Manhattan Merry-Go-Round*, *Waltz Time*, etc.) gained their starts on *Auditions*. It wasn't a bad way to launch a professional livelihood, even if one didn't take a first prize.

In 1947, Milton Cross succeeded Edward Johnson (the Met's general manager) as host-commentator of the *Auditions* spin-off—an appointment Cross also occupied on the more prestigious original. Meanwhile, the announcing for *Auditions* was vested in the capable hands of a couple of readily identified radio voices, Howard Claney and Ben Grauer.

Claney divided his aural time fairly evenly between highbrow opera and soap opera with a few other morsels thrown in. On the one hand he announced *The American Album of Familiar Music*, *The American Melody Hour*, *The NBC Symphony Orchestra*, *The Metropolitan Opera Auditions on the Air* and *Waltz Time*; on the other, he was a familiar daily interlocutor to those tuning in to *Amanda of Honeymoon Hill*,

Backstage Wife and *Stella Dallas*. He also narrated *America's Town Meeting of the Air, Borden Special Edition, The Jack Benny Program* and *Mr. Chameleon*.

Born April 17, 1898, in Pittsburgh, Claney launched a stage career in the 1920s, playing in *Cyrano de Bergerac, Juno and the Paycock* and *Liliom*. A gifted painter and watercolorist, he augmented his income by conducting one-man shows at prestigious art galleries. Taking a job as an announcer at New York's WEAF led Claney to be hired often by radio drama and music producer Frank Hummert. (At least seven of the broadcast series for which he is best known were Hummert creations.) Ad agencies regularly engaged him for programming that featured Jack Benny, Walter Damrosch, Lawrence Tibbett and Paul Whiteman. He was advertised by NBC Artists Service as "clear-voiced, an expert in selling, psychology, and blessed with an air personality which strikes a note of genuine sincerity into his excellent delivery."

One other note on his career is worthy of mention: while Claney studied painting abroad in 1938, the European crisis erupted, allowing him to provide eyewitness reports by shortwave radio from London. He died in Charlotte, North Carolina, in April 1980.

Ben Grauer, the *Auditions*' other durable announcer, possessed a voice that was once christened "the most authoritative in the world" by the National Academy of Vocal Arts. In 1944, that organization voted him "the best NBC announcer." A radio biographer claimed: "He became as much an aural identification mark for NBC as the roar of Leo the Lion for MGM."

Having joined the network's announcing staff in 1930, Grauer regularly appeared on more than three dozen radio features, most of them NBC staples: *The Adventures of Mr. and Mrs. North, American Portraits, America's Town Meeting of the Air, Atlantic Spotlight, The Baker's Broadcast, The Battle of the Sexes, Behind the Mike, Believe It or Not, The Boston Pops Orchestra, The Chesterfield Supper Club, Circus Days, Columbia Presents Corwin, Eleanor Roosevelt, Grand Central Station, The Henry Morgan Show, Home Is What You Make It, Information Please, Kay Kyser's Kollege of Musical Knowledge, Love Notes, The Magic Key, Meet the Press, Mr. District Attorney, Mr. Keen Tracer of Lost Persons, Name the Place, The NBC Symphony Orchestra, Pot 'o' Gold, Salute to Youth, The Sealtest Sunday Night Party, Service with a Smile, Sleep No More, True Story, Twenty Thousand Years in Sing Sing, Vacation Serenade, Vox Pop, Walter Winchell's Journal, What Would You Have Done?, Your Hit Parade* and *Yvette Sings*. In his first 11 years at NBC Grauer appeared on 70 commercial series. In 1952, he hosted the short-lived daily feature *It's a Problem* on NBC-TV.

Born on Staten Island, New York, on June 2, 1908, a young Grauer became a child actor in motion pictures and on the stage. Graduating from City College of New York, he broke into radio and was soon covering ambitious ventures like the first United Nations conference from San Francisco, horse racing from Aqueduct, New Year's Eve at Times Square, the maiden flight of the blimp *Akron* and presidential inaugurations.

Grauer kept ties with Hollywood by narrating films. His best known may have been 1951's *Kon-Tiki*. Retiring from Radio City in 1974, he continued to take commercial, infrequent TV and Voice of America assignments. He died May 31, 1977, in New York City only two days shy of his 69th birthday.

A postscript to the *Auditions* series is in order: in 1948, ABC-TV began televising *The Metropolitan Opera Auditions on the Air* as an occasional special. Between January 15 and April 1, 1952, the network telecast the series live, Tuesdays in prime time between 8:30 and 9 P.M. Eastern Time.

Milton Cross was the commentator for the fleeting outing.

As has been underscored previously, David Sarnoff was committed to a persuasion that one of radio's most important functions was to imbue its listeners with healthy amounts of culture, particularly fine musical programming. It may come as no real surprise that the RCA chairman didn't rest on his laurels long, being only temporarily satisfied with the plum he had won in the battle for broadcasting rights to *The Metropolitan Opera* and the appurtenances that went with it. Sarnoff's reach extended his grasp. By 1936, he envisioned a preeminent symphony orchestra that would play the world's most beautiful melodies in the classical tradition over NBC.

The suggestion for its leader is believed to have originated with NBC programming vice president John F. Royal, although Sarnoff was quick to buy into it. There was but one man on earth, Sarnoff profoundly convinced himself, who was qualified to direct such an elite body of talented professionals. He was Arturo Toscanini, the same individual who had earlier conducted The Metropolitan Opera and The New York Philharmonic Symphony. There was just one hitch: Toscanini wasn't available.

Recall that in early 1936 Toscanini reached an impasse with Philharmonic officials that couldn't be satisfactorily resolved. He left his longtime post and went home to his native Italy, vowing never to return to conduct an American orchestra again. Toscanini intimates advised Sarnoff that it was futile to try to alter the mind of the frequently contentious maestro once he had put his foot down. But Sarnoff could put his foot down, too—recall his unbending resolve to obtain *The Metropolitan Opera* broadcasts. Whatever it took, he would settle for nothing less than Toscanini to conduct the great radio orchestra he envisioned. The doomsayers who assured him he had not a prayer never convinced him that he wouldn't prevail when push came to shove.

When cables to Toscanini met with negative replies, Sarnoff dispatched an envoy to call upon the musical genius at his home in Milan, Italy. Samuel Chotzinoff (nicknamed Chotzie), a former music critic of both *The New York Post* and *The New York World*, and eventually to become NBC's music director—and his spouse (who was the sister of violinist Jascha Heifetz)—were old chums of Arturo Toscanini and his wife Carla. Before the Chotzinoffs sailed for Italy on what Chotzie perceived was a wasted voyage, Sarnoff submitted an idea for him to use in tempting the man Sarnoff was convinced was the world's greatest conductor. "Suppose," he said tranquilly, "we offered to *create* an orchestra for him—a *radio* orchestra. Would he go for that?"

Chotzie didn't think so. NBC was already paying around 70 house musicians, some of them among the most consummate classical artists in the country. Programming chief John Royal advanced the notion that they might be put to better use if they were integrated into a prodigious staff orchestra. They could even underwrite some of their own expenses by recording for RCA Victor, the parent firm's phonograph label, he added. Sarnoff liked the idea and proposed that Chotzie tell the maestro that if the staff musicians weren't to his liking, any or all of them could be replaced with substitutes he *did* like. They could come from anywhere in the world, the expense being of no consequence. What a deal! And what an invincible CEO!

Chotzie was *still* skeptical. It took him two weeks upon his arrival in Milan, in fact, to summon the courage to broach the subject with his cherished friend about why he was there. (At least one of several Toscanini biographers accepts a tale appearing in the January 1938 issue of *Fortune* magazine that refutes Chotzie's account of his experience, one he recorded in a 1956 memoir. The alternate version argues that Chotzie introduced the purpose of his trip to the maestro on only his *second day* in Italy. As Chotzie was an eyewitness, we prefer to think of his account as the one more likely accurate.) The Chotzinoffs really weren't traveling as tourists at all, as they had intimated, but had come to persuade Toscanini to accept an offer from NBC to lead yet another symphony orchestra in a series of 10 concerts. Instead of playing for a few thousand people in a hall, Chotzie informed the 70-year-old impresario that he would be playing for millions during every performance.

The emissary relayed the provisions that his supervisor had outlined. In the end, Toscanini went for it. Despite a halting aversion to any mechanical music transmission, he would go to America once more. After 10 concerts, he reasoned, he could return to his native homeland and retire permanently.

True to the inherent tendencies found in many a perfectionist, Toscanini would also have things *his way*. He maintained that he must have veto power over all orchestra personnel; he wanted full authority over programs; and he insisted that there could be no commercial messages delivered during the concert broadcasts. (The latter proviso was rescinded when the American Tobacco Company anted up about $100,000 to opera management — in addition to buying radio time and underwriting incidental expenses.) Then, reportedly at Carla's urging, the $40,000 that Toscanini was to be paid for the 10 concerts was to be tax free — the taxes on his compensation (about $5,000) were to be paid in full by NBC. He was a shrewd operator, that one. With those stipulations satisfied, Chotzie returned to America with a signed contract.

Sarnoff determined to construct a magnificent oversized floating theater, ultimately known as Studio 8H, at NBC's Radio City headquarters, as a venue for broadcasts of *The NBC Symphony Orchestra*. (The orchestra moved to Carnegie Hall in 1950 where better acoustics abounded and bigger audiences could be accommodated, leaving studio 8H to developing live television programming.) While none of this would come cheaply, of course, it would visibly underscore the chain's unconditional commitment to its listeners to providing some large doses of refinement.

Sarnoff's biographer exclaimed: "Announcement of the prodigal conductor's impending return was the sensation of the musical world. David Sarnoff made this exorbitantly costly sustaining program his personal project. He was like a boy with a new toy, emotionally in high gear as the enterprise shaped up. The hallmark of his personal style was on the first press release: Toscanini's 'incomparable genius,' it said, 'will further stimulate and enrich musical appreciation in our country.'"

While well-wishers from all over the nation openly applauded Sarnoff and NBC on the triumph, there were few cheery responses from the firm's leading stockholders, nonetheless. Those practical-minded investors were instead surveying the bottom line. The orchestra's launch was projected at a quarter of a million dollars — with little prospect that any of its financial outlay would be recaptured. "Some of them [investors] murmured that, really, this time the man [Sarnoff] was overdoing it."

Despite such apprehension, as anticipated, the venture was used to great public relations advantage. Said one writer, who could have spoken for many: "The Toscanini concerts were, and in large measure remain, the peak against which quality productions on the airwaves are measured."[4]

In a handwritten note to Sarnoff, received shortly after Toscanini signed his initial contract, the maestro listed 92 instrumentalists he would require. With Toscanini's urging, Artur Rodzinski, Cleveland Symphony Orchestra conductor, was enlisted to secure and train the musicians for the new NBC Symphony. But it quickly became clear that the choice of Rodzinski was a mistake. He not only exhibited an abrasive personality but possessed tendencies of paranoia. A few weeks preceding Toscanini's arrival, prominent French conductor Pierre Monteux was substituted for Rodzinski to lead the first three concerts of the NBC Symphony's inaugural season.

There were further personnel problems. While an entourage of roughly 70 house musicians as reported existed within the confines of NBC, and many applied for positions in the new orchestra, only 31 of the applicants were selected. An additional 61 skilled artisans were hired outside the network's ranks. In accomplishing that task NBC frequently raided some of the most qualified talent in other cities' symphonies, an issue that netted bitter scorn from those orchestra officials. At the same time it fired some of its staff musicians in a cost-cutting endeavor, a measure that Toscanini strongly rebuked, even threatening his own withdrawal.

There was another impasse that would come back to haunt NBC in time, a matter of duplicity never mentioned to Toscanini when enlisting him. He was led to believe that the musicians he would conduct were to be *his* exclusively—at his beck and call for performances as well as rehearsals that he would schedule for as long as he needed them. What neither Chotzie, Sarnoff or anyone else told the maestro nearly torpedoed their carefully crafted arrangement once it surfaced (although that didn't happen until late 1940): Toscanini learned that *his staff* of musicians was also carrying similar duties on *other* NBC programs, some of which had *prior claims* on the individual artists' time. A major furor erupted over the deceit and Toscanini walked out on his contractual commitment for the 1941-1942 season. But that was down the road a piece.

Preceding the inaugural season of *The NBC Symphony Orchestra*, Artur Rodzinski led the entourage in an on-the-air "dress rehearsal" on November 2, 1937. The "season" officially began November 13 with Monteux holding the baton followed by a trio of performances conducted by Rodzinski. On Christmas night, the maestro himself stepped to the podium and a new era of broadcast music was launched. Ticket requests for about 1,400 available studio seats reached 50,000 monthly. Even a black market for those coveted tickets was thriving! Toscanini fulfilled his obligation by leading the orchestra 10 times. Others holding the baton during that opening term included Sir Adrian Boult, Carlos Chavez, Howard Hanson, Dimitri Mitropoulos, Bernardino Molinari, Hugh Ross and William Steinberg. Several of these participated more than once. The first full season ended June 25, 1938.

In March 1938, David Sarnoff announced that Arturo Toscanini had been persuaded to return in late 1938 to take up *The NBC Symphony Orchestra* baton again. The maestro had, in fact, signed a three-year contract extension. He would go home to Italy between seasons and conduct orchestras throughout Europe during his "free time" (an itinerary he pursued throughout his NBC commitment except during the Second World War years).

Toscanini's repertoire stressed Beethoven, Brahms, Verdi and Wagner. He sporadically scheduled broadcasts of operatic works, often those of Puccini and Verdi. Among his favorite composers were Beethoven, Haydn, Liszt, Martucci, Respighi and Wagner. Toscanini liked to spotlight soloists like Rose Bampton, Vivian Della Chiesa, Robert Merrill, Nan Merriman and Jan Peerce, in addition to the Robert Shaw Chorale.

Some say the master conductor of radio was Arturo Toscanini, who was at the helm of several important musical groups, the most notable being the one created especially for him by network brass, the NBC Symphony Orchestra. Toscanini was also a taskmaster, always expecting perfection from his musicians. By broadcast time, he often got it.

It has been mentioned already that Toscanini displayed frequent outbursts of anger. He was dubbed an "uncompromising tyrant" whose word "was law to musicians, production personnel, and network executives." "Endless anecdotes of his childlike temper tantrums" abound. Without belaboring the theme, some illustration seems in order. Eugene Lyons succinctly summarized the recurring situation in this paragraph[5]:

> The ninety-two members of the orchestra and everyone responsible for putting the show on the air — especially Chotzie — adored the "old man," but their adoration was more than matched by dread of his unpredictable temper. He rehearsed his men to near-exhaustion. His sweet patience could suddenly collapse in a Homeric rage, when he stamped on his watch, broke the baton, shrieked in anguish that he was through — through! — with music. Chotzie and his staff, as rehearsals proceeded, got regular "weather reports" on his temper, like nurses watching a fever chart.

The famed conductor would permit no clocks in his studio and his concerts frequently ran well beyond the designated time frame. *Radio Guide* reported: "Toscanini and President Roosevelt are the two people who can run long or short without being cut off by the networks." It resulted after the opening concert of the 1943-1944 season (October 31) ran long and Beethoven's Symphony No. 8 in F Major, Op. 93 was cut off the air before completion. A belligerent Toscanini was so incensed on hearing of it that a network policy quickly cascaded down preventing its reoccurrence. His programs, like the president's, were to be free of all time restrictions.

In December 1940, as hinted previously, he nearly quit the symphony for good when he discovered *his* orchestra was performing piecemeal on other NBC shows, something he undoubtedly should have known upfront. He left for the remainder of the season, Leopold Stokowski filling in for him. Sarnoff intervened, urging Toscanini to conduct a series of concerts to benefit the war bond drive. The maestro did so and returned to his accustomed place at the podium for the 1942-1943 season. He divided that term with Stokowski but increasing quarrels in 1944 ended in Stokowski's exodus from the symphony.

Toscanini could be typified by another trait throughout his lifetime. While he apparently didn't allow it to interfere with his work, in contemporary times he would be labeled a womanizer. The impresario possessed an insatiable appetite for romantic liaisons outside his marriage, including more than one Metropolitan Opera diva. As he was raised an Italian Catholic, however, he never pursued divorce from his mate.

There was an amusing incident in the Toscanini era that had potential to wreak havoc on the airwaves. It occurred during the first of five exclusive concerts Toscanini conducted to increase sales of U.S. Treasury bonds. One of radio's most seasoned directors, Richard Leonard, presided over that near fiasco on December 6, 1941. At rehearsals he advised Toscanini that — near the program's end — Deems Taylor, speaking in another studio, would give a one-minute pep talk on defense bonds. While Toscanini and his entourage would neither hear nor see Taylor, Leonard would throw the maestro a cue as Taylor concluded his speech. The orchestra was to strike up *The Star-Spangled Banner* to finish the broadcast. Author Tom DeLong remembers what happened next[6]:

> No studio audience was invited for the actual broadcast. However, in the 8H balcony sat a group of distinguished guests and government VIPs, including Secretary of the Treasury Henry Morgenthau, Jr.
>
> "The program went off without a hitch," Leonard explained, "until the very close. At that point, the engineers switched to the studio where Taylor began his short talk. But, alas, Toscanini forgot to wait for my cue. As the final notes of the last selection ... ended, he immediately plunged into the national anthem. One thing I knew: when Taylor wrapped up his talk, the Symphony would be midway into *The Star-Spangled Banner*. It would ruin the whole program.
>
> "I had to stop Toscanini before he went 'live' over the air. I rushed out of the upper-level control booth, ran down a flight of stairs and sped across the stage to the podium. I grabbed the Maestro's arm. He glared at me, resisted my grasp and continued conducting. Luckily, the orchestra knew something was wrong. One by one they stopped playing as I shouted 'Taylor's talking.'
>
> "Toscanini realized his mistake. Two seconds later, the engineer signaled to me. I signaled the Maestro to begin. This time a much chagrined conductor gave the downbeat on *The Star-Spangled Banner*. All in all, we had narrowly averted a serious *faux pas*."
>
> At a postconcert reception, Leopold Stokowski, a studio guest, cornered Richard Leonard.
>
> "The FBI is after you," Maestro Stokowski jested. "You halted the playing of the national anthem."

The whole incident, as humorous as it was, was later ascribed as a chilling scenario from Leonard's perspective. The Japanese fleet struck Pearl Harbor just 14 hours later, plummeting the United States into World War II.

What had begun for Toscanini as a single-season 10-concert agreement eventually expanded into 17 years, including videocasts starting in 1948. As each year ended the impresario argued that he was too old to continue and must be released. Then he would agree to "just one more year." By age 87, however, he — and others — realized he had reached the point of no return.

"At the end of a shaky radio-TV concert in 1954, he dropped his baton and left the podium for good," one version allowed. On March 5, 1954, he wrote Sarnoff: "And now the time has come when I must reluctantly say good-bye to my orchestra, and in leaving I want you to know that I shall carry with me rich memories of these years of music making."

Toscanini, born at Parma, Italy, on March 25, 1867, died January 16, 1957, at Riverdale, New York, becoming "a legendary high priest of music." His body was interred in his beloved Milan.

Said a radio historiographer: "His long years on the air were widely acclaimed as a high-water mark of musical history in the United States and perhaps in the world.... More than any other single program, he [Sarnoff] argued, Toscanini became a symbol of quality and culture." An informant commented: "Never before or since has a radio network or corporate entity created an orchestra of this caliber or size." That it was a tribute to one man made it all the more incredible. "With many of his NBC broadcasts recorded by RCA's highly attuned engineers," assessed the source, "they remain a widely available legacy of an almost superhuman figure from a brilliant epoch in American music."

The Longines Symphonette, the last of the quintet of classical music features to be cited here, debuted over MBS on July 5, 1943. In 14 years it eventually broadcast over all four national networks. The series offered listeners an enchanting range of light instrumental pieces that featured a magnificent ensemble of superbly gifted professionals. The Longines-Wittnauer Watch Company of Saint-Imier, Switzerland, underwrote the program, signifying its name, and the production varied between 15, 25 and 30 minutes' duration.

Smooth talking, velvet-toned Frank Knight (described by one wag as owning a voice that "bordered on the pompous with an almost cathedral formality") announced. Knight achieved some fame when the American Academy of Arts and Letters presented him with its Diction Award during the 1930s, a mark of prestige in elocution. He was also among the founding fathers of the American Guild of Radio Announcers and Producers (AGRAP), a union of CBS staff announcers whose membership eventually extended to hundreds of individuals.

Knight was seldom at a loss for words as he passionately touted the *Symphonette* and the sponsor's product, qualifying both as matchless in their respective spheres. While the instrumentalists played the program's theme, Beethoven's *Moonlight Sonata*, Knight shamelessly introduced the performance with an inveterate boast: "This is the world's most honored music program presented as a salute to Longines, the world's most honored watch. The Longines Symphonette, a group of the world's finest musicians under the distinguished leadership of Mishel Piastro, plays the world's most honored music. These beautiful melodies and Longines watches have this in common: throughout the world, where there is an appreciation of things fine and beautiful, *both* are held in the highest esteem."

The program, it turned out, was venerated by a large percentage of people whose votes actually mattered in the forum of public opinion. In August 1951, the periodical *Musical American* announced that a poll of some 800 North American music critics indicated that a majority preferred The Longines Symphonette and its conductor, Mishel Piastro, as "the finest orchestra concert ensemble in radio" for the fifth consecutive year. Perhaps Frank Knight wasn't stretching the truth after all.

Born in St. John's, Newfoundland, Canada, on May 10, 1894, Knight settled in the United States in 1920. His exposure as a radio announcer-performer was confined to a few series when compared to some of his peers. It included permanent assignments on *The Adventures of Superman, Arabesque, Author Author, The Chesterfield Quarter-Hour, Collier's Radio Review, The Choraliers, The First National Hour, Literary Digest, The Longines Symphonette, Murder Clinic, The Robert Burns Panatela Show, Uncle Don* and *The White Owl Program*. He also moderated a late evening discussion series on world affairs, *Chronoscope*, carried by CBS-TV between June 11, 1951, and April 29, 1955. Having launched his broadcast career in 1928 at New York's WABC, a station soon purchased by Columbia as its flagship outlet, Knight persisted after all of his early CBS colleagues departed. He died in New York on October 18, 1973.

In the 1960s, The Longines Symphonette Society of Larchmont, New York, released two series of multiple long-playing hi-fidelity recordings that reminisced over radio's golden age and included a multitude of top-drawer excerpts from actual broadcasts. Comedian Jack Benny and Frank Knight narrated the first of those collections called "Golden Memories of Radio." For the subsequent issue titled "I Remember Radio," Knight was the sole raconteur. The dual Longines sets prompted a wave of nostalgia-driven recordings and reel-to-reel tapes that centered on old-time radio in those pre-cassette days.

Across a 14-year span two maestros conducted *The Longines Symphonette*— Macklin Marrow, from the series' inception on July 5, 1943, through March 11, 1949, over MBS — and then Mishel Piastro, from March 13, 1949, when it switched to CBS (and later added ABC and NBC) through the end of the run on May 26, 1957.

Very little of substance on Marrow's life has been preserved. Newspaper clippings and Web sites indicate he took an active interest in his community situated in the environs of greater New York, in religious projects that included music, performing as a violinist and conducting local groups. Beyond those little else appears to have been documented. Marrow died at 53 in August 1953.

Marrow's successor as conductor for *The Longines Symphonette*, Mishel Piastro, was born June 19, 1891, in the Russian Crimea. He was a student at the St. Petersburg Conservatory and a concert violinist in Australia, New Zealand and Siam before migrating to America in 1920 where he played at Carnegie Hall. He became Toscanini's concertmaster for many years during the impresario's reign with the New York Philharmonic Orchestra. Piastro was also a frequent chess opponent of Marshall Field. In later years he introduced a violin bow that could be played on all four strings at once. He married in New York City, had a family and died there in April 1970.

The *Symphonette* frequently featured more supple fare than that which listeners were accustomed to on some of the other classical musicales. "The Longines specialty is the playing of shorter selections, or 'movements,' by the greatest composers, as well as many lighter pieces," said one journalist. "Many people commonly refer to them as the 'average man's symphony orchestra.'" Typical selections included *The March of the Marionettes, I'll Take You Home Again Kathleen, The Waltz of the Flowers, Bagatelle, The Stars Were Shining, Hungarian Comedians Overture* and the first movement from *Tchaikovsky's Fifth Symphony*. The program often featured guest instrumentalists including celebrated artists like cello virtuoso Josef Schuster and pianist Milton Kaye.

The series was prerecorded, one of the earlier aural shows to be heard by transcription. One reviewer claimed that the *Symphonette* and similar musical treats "reached audiences weeks and sometimes months after the recording session in a radio studio." He explained: "To a degree, the producers of many music shows on ET [electrical transcription] restricted the content to long-standing 'chestnuts.' This gave a program more mileage and greater timeliness. Although a viable transcription procedure, the ETs frequently had a format that lacked the very popular tunes needed to entice the broadest possible audience."

Between March 13, 1949, and April 22, 1955, CBS aired *The Choraliers*, also sponsored by the Longines-Wittnauer Watch Company. The vocal series was an outgrowth of an earlier feature with two monikers, the *Festival of Music* and the *Festival of Song*, originating over the NBC Blue network on December 11, 1938. *The Choraliers* was a musical variety program under the command of Eugene Lowell, director, with the familiar voice of Frank Knight as announcer.

There were many other radio features that incorporated music of a classical tradition within the context of their normal broadcasts. Certainly this includes a triumvirate of longstanding listener favorites — *The Railroad Hour, The Bell Telephone Hour* and *The Voice of Firestone*. These treats for the ear secured their places in the hearts of loyal fans by presenting show melodies, marches, pop tunes and other varieties of specialized fare. They also emphasized star qualities with renowned artists from assorted realms appearing as their guests. Because of their diversionary nature, each member of this programming trio is included under separate chapter titles in this volume.

Before leaving this sphere, a mention of the indomitable aural feature *The Chamber Music Society of Lower Basin Street* (1940–1944, 1950, 1952) is worth noting. (See separate chapter.) This musical satire targeted the classics. *Radio Life* aptly labeled it "a wacky, strictly hep tongue-in-cheek burlesque of opera and symphony." Perhaps surprisingly to highbrow enthusiasts, none other than Milton Cross turned up to needle the revered traditions and musicians he so righteously defended on other programs. "Good evening, lovers of fine music," he allowed at the show's opening. "Welcome to the no-doubt world-famous *Chamber Music Society of Lower Basin Street* and another concert dedicated to the perpetuation of the three Bs— barrelhouse, boogie-woogie and the blues."

He threw in humorous asides between selections that featured Dinah "Diva" Shore (the series made her name a household word), Diane Courtney (identified as "the poor man's Flagstad") and Kay Lorraine (a "slow-burning blues chanteuse"). Jack Meakin, Paul Lavalle and Henry Levine held the baton at different times before an ensemble that belted out blues as easily as it switched to swing and tossed in heavier fare on occasion, too. Host Gene Hamilton was tagged "Dr. Gino" and nearly every speaking role was assigned to a "professor" or "doctor." It was a hilarious takeoff— and hopefully the longhairs didn't lose their composure as the madcap merry-makers took them down a notch.

The classics were one of radio's greatest contributions to aural audiences. Some of the most beautiful music ever heard was presented on those series as their listeners gained introductions to refinement and culture that multitudes had never before experienced — and had precious little prospect of being exposed to but for the airwaves. There can be no doubt that this music raised the level of appreciation among American musical tastes.

The Contests

When categorized as a type of broadcast programming, the audience participation feature can be carved into multiple sectors. The form includes advice and self-help exchanges, amateur and semi-professional talent trials, brainteasers, games, giveaways, human interest, interviews, repartee between host and audiences, skill matches, songfests, quizzes and the like. In several of them, music predominates, particularly exploiting those where competition is a big underpinning. The golden age airwaves were graced by numerous melody-based contests that perked up the ears of listeners as fans pulled for favorites and underdogs, hoping people they had never met might claim cash and merchandise prizes or advance toward fame or other rewards. These musical escapades were pure and simple fun and games. And audiences, swept up by the hysteria that frequently escorted them, were seldom disappointed.

The Horace Heidt Show

Theme Songs: *I'll Love You in My Dreams, Pot o' Gold in the Air.*

Sponsors: Shell Oil Corporation for Shell gasoline, oil and other vehicle products and services (1932); Alemite (1936–1939); Lewis-Howe Company for Tums stomach distress reliever (1939–1941); Lewis-Howe Company for Tums stomach distress reliever (1940–1944); Hires Root Beer soft drink (1944–1945); Philip Morris Company for Philip Morris cigarettes (1947–1951); American Tobacco Company for Lucky Strike cigarettes (1953); otherwise sustaining.

On the Air: *Ship of Joy*, 1932, NBC Blue; *Answers by the Dancers*, 1932, NBC Blue; *Captain Dobbsie's Ship of Joy* (aka *Anniversary Night with Horace Heidt, Horace Heidt's Alemite Brigadeers*), February 26–April 23, 1935, CBS, Tuesday/Thursday, 10:30–10:45 P.M. Eastern Time; May 2–June 27, 1935, CBS, Thursday, 10:30–11:00 P.M.; *The Alemite Half-Hour*, July 6, 1936–December 20, 1937, CBS, Monday, 8:00–8:30 P.M.; December 28, 1937–July 12, 1938, NBC Blue, Tuesday, 9:00–9:30 P.M.; July 17–December 18, 1938, NBC, Sunday, 10:00–10:30 P.M.; December 19, 1938–March 6, 1939, NBC Blue, Monday, 10:30–11:00 P.M.; (concurrently) December 21, 1938–March 8, 1939, NBC Blue, Wednesday, 7:30–8:00 P.M.;

June 23–September 1, 1939, NBC Blue, Friday, 10:30–11:00 P.M.; *Pot o' Gold*, September 26, 1939–June 4, 1940, NBC, Tuesday, 8:30–9:00 P.M.; June 13–September 26, 1940, NBC Blue, Thursday, 8:30–9:00 P.M.; October 3, 1940–June 5, 1941, NBC Blue, Thursday, 8:00–8:30 P.M.; *Tum's Treasure Chest*, June 11, 1940–January 11, 1944, NBC, Tuesday, 8:30–9:00 P.M.; *Sunday Morning Revue*, July 5–October 4, 1942, ABC, Sunday, 11:05 A.M.–noon; October 11, 1942–April 25, 1943, ABC, Sunday, 1:00–2:00 P.M.; *The Horace Heidt Show*, May 8–September 25, 1943, NBC Blue, Saturday, 5:00–6:00 P.M.; *The Horace Heidt Show*, January 24, 1944–January 15, 1945, ABC, Monday, 7:00–7:30 P.M.; *The Youth Opportunity Program*, December 7, 1947–December 26, 1948, NBC, Sunday, 10:30–11:00 P.M.; January 2–April 17, 1949, NBC, Sunday, 7:00–7:30 P.M.; April 24–August 28, 1949, NBC, Sunday, 10:30–11:00 P.M.; September 4, 1949–June 24, 1951, CBS, Sunday, 9:30–10:00 P.M.; July 1–December 16, 1951, CBS, Sunday, 8:30–9:00 P.M.; *The American Way*, January 1–December 24, 1953, CBS, Thursday, 10:00–10:30 P.M.

Arthur Godfrey's Talent Scouts

Producers: Irving Mansfield, Jack Carney, Janette Davis (1956–1958, TV).
Host: Arthur Godfrey.
Orchestra Conductors: Archie Bleyer (1946–1954), Jerry Bresler (1954–1955), Will Roland and Bert Farber (1955–1958, until the TV series left the air July 21, 1958).
Vocalists: Peggy Marshall and the Holidays.
Announcer: George Bryan.
Writers: Chuck Horner, Ken Lyons, Andy Rooney.
Theme Songs: *Sing a Song of Sixpence* (with commercial jingle), *Seems Like Old Times*.

Sponsors: Sustaining (1946-1947), Thomas J. Lipton, Inc. for Lipton tea, soup mixes and other foodstuffs (August 4, 1947–1955), The Gillette Company for Toni home permanents, White Rain shampoo and other hair care preparations (1955–October 1, 1956).

Ratings: High — 22.1 (1948-1949 season); Low — 2.0 (1955-1956); Median —12.2 (based on sponsored seasons, 1947–1956). By 1951 the audio numbers were tumbling rapidly from double digits that had often topped 20, to single digits— 7.3, 5.2, 3.7 and 2.0 in the final quadrennial. TV ratings for *Talent Scouts* indicated large numbers remained fans to the end of Godfrey's run in 1958. Of a quartet of series that Godfrey hosted in tandem in the 1950s, *Talent Scouts* invariably drew the largest crowds, appearing in dual mediums.

On the Air: July 2–August 20, 1946, CBS, Tuesday, 9:00–9:30 P.M. Eastern Time; August 27–December 17, 1946, CBS, Tuesday, 10:00–10:30 P.M.; December 24, 1946–April 22, 1947, CBS, Tuesday, 9:30–10:00 P.M.; May 27–June 17, 1947, CBS, Tuesday, 9:00–9:30 P.M.; July 4–August 1, 1947, CBS, Friday, 9:30–10:00 P.M.; August 4, 1947–June 27, 1949 and August 29, 1949–October 1, 1956, CBS, Monday, 8:30–9:00 P.M.

Major Bowes' Original Amateur Hour

Theme Songs: *Stand By, There's No Business Like Show Business, A Perfect Day*.
Sponsors: Standard Brands, Inc. for Chase and Sanborn coffee (1935-1936), Chrysler Corporation for Chrysler, Plymouth, Dodge and De Soto vehicles, parts and service (1936–1945); P. Lorillard, Inc. for Old Gold cigarettes (1948-1952).
Ratings: High — 45.2 (1935-1936 season); Low — 7.2 (1944-1945); Median — 20.5 (over Bowes' 10-year span). The show

fell to single digits only once, after Bowes was no longer with it. For the four-year run fronted by Ted Mack, only in one season — the first — did the numbers peak in double digits (10.5 in 1948-1949), falling rapidly thereafter to a low in 1951-1952 of 4.9, its final radio season.

On the Air: *Capitol Theater Concert*, July 26, 1925–November 21, 1926, New York City's WEAF, Sunday; November 28, 1926–1927, NBC Blue, Sunday, 7:30–9:30 A.M. Eastern Time; *Capitol Theater Musicale* (aka *Major Bowes' Capitol Theater Concert*), 1927–1929, NBC, Sunday, 7:30–9:00 A.M.; *Major Bowes' Capitol Family*, 1929-1930, NBC, Sunday, 7:30–8:30 A.M.; 1930–March 1, 1931, NBC, Sunday, 8:00–8:30 A.M.; March 6–December 18, 1931, NBC, Friday, 8:00–8:30 P.M.; December 20, 1931–August 30, 1936, NBC, Sunday, 11:30 A.M.–12:30 P.M.; June 7, 1936–May 25, 1941, CBS, Sunday, 11:30 A.M.–12:30 P.M.; *The Amateur Hour*, 1934, New York City's WHN; *Major Bowes' Original Amateur Hour*, March 24, 1935–September 13, 1936, NBC, Sunday, 8:00–9:00 P.M.; September 17, 1936–January 15, 1942, CBS, Thursday, 9:00–10:00 P.M.; January 22, 1942–January 4, 1945, CBS, Thursday, 9:00–9:30 P.M.; *Shower of Stars*, February 8–August 30, 1945, CBS, Thursday, 9:00–9:30 P.M.; *Ted Mack's Original Amateur Hour*, September 29, 1948–July 20, 1949, ABC, Wednesday, 8:00–9:00 P.M.; July 28, 1949–September 18, 1952, Thursday, 9:00–9:45 P.M.

Kay Kyser's Kollege of Musical Knowledge

Producer: Frank O'Connor.
Directors: Ed Cashman, John Cleary, William Warwick.
Orchestra Leader-Host: Kay Kyser.
Vocalists: Harry Babbitt, Georgia Carroll, Julie Conway, Mike Douglas, Trudy Erwin, Ish Kabibble (Merwyn A. Bogue), The King Sisters (Alyce, Donna, Louise, Yvonne), Sully Mason, Lucy Ann Polk, Ginny Simms, Gloria Wood.
Organist: Rex Koury.
Announcers: Bill Forman, Bud Hiestand, Ken Niles, Verne Smith.
Theme Song: *Thinking of You*.
Sponsors: Sustaining (1932, 1934), Willys Overland Motors Company for Willys Jeep (1937), American Tobacco Company for Lucky Strike cigarettes (1938–December 20, 1944, including 1939-1940 MBS series), Colgate-Palmolive-Peet Company for Colgate dental cream, Palmolive soap and other personal care commodities (December 27, 1944–1948), Pillsbury Mills, Inc. for Pillsbury cake flour and other baking goods (1948-1949).
Ratings: High — 26.2 (1942-1943 season); Low — 3.4 (1948-1949, as the show aired in daytime); Median — 17.4. In every season but the last the series earned double-digit numbers, remaining exceedingly high throughout the first decade of its 11-year run.

On the Air: *Kay Kyser Orchestra*, 1932 and 1934, more data unsubstantiated; *Surprise Party*, May 2–July 25, 1937, MBS, Sunday, 10:00 P.M. Eastern Time; *Kay Kyser's Kollege of Musical Knowledge*, February 1–March 29, 1938, Chicago's WGN; March 30, 1938–September 11, 1946, NBC, Wednesday, 10:00–11:00 P.M.; (concurrently) June 29, 1939–May 9, 1940, MBS, Thursday, 8:00–9:00 P.M.; September 18–25, 1946, NBC, Wednesday, 10:00–10:30 P.M.; October 2, 1946–July 2, 1947, NBC, Wednesday, 10:30–11:00 P.M.; October 4, 1947–June 26, 1948, NBC, Saturday, 10:00–10:30 P.M.; November 1, 1948–January 7, 1949, ABC, Monday–Friday, 11:00–11:30 A.M.; January 10–July 29, 1949, ABC, Monday–Friday, 4:00–4:30 P.M.

Stop the Music!

Producer: Louis G. Cowan.
Director: Mark Goodson.
Masters of Ceremonies: Bert Parks, Bill Cullen, Happy Felton.
Orchestra Conductors: Harry Salter, Ray Bloch.
Vocalists: Kay Armen, Dick Brown, Jill Corey, Jack Haskell.
Announcers: Don Hancock, Douglas Browning, Hal Simms.
Theme Song: An original composition.
Sponsors: An untried formula was applied from the series' start, selling commercial time in quarter-hour segments. For three years participating sponsors underwrote the show, including Speidel watches and jewelry, P. Lorillard, Inc. for Old Gold cigarettes, American Home Products Company for Anacin pain reliever, Smith Brothers cough drops and other goods. In the show's fourth year P. Lorillard, Inc. bought it all. On returning in 1954 for an abbreviated fifth season, the program was abruptly cancelled.
Ratings: High — 20.8 (1948-1949 season); Low — 7.6 (1951-1952); Median —11.7. (Figures not available for 1954-1955 partial season).
On the Air: March 21, 1948–August 10, 1952, ABC, Sunday, 8:00–9:00 P.M. Eastern Time; August 17, 1954–February 15, 1955, CBS, Tuesday, 8:00–9:15 P.M. (originally 60 minutes but extended to 75 minutes toward end of run).

* * *

During the 1940s, a surfeit of aural features punctuated the airwaves as game, skill and stunt shows emerged as popular forms of amusement for American radio audiences. Listeners were enthralled by snappy comebacks that called forth brainpower, knack or agility to accentuate divergent series styles. Dial-tuners turned into addicts as an infusion of question-and-answer formats mesmerized legions of listeners. The folks at home became, possibly for the first time, vicariously *involved* in what they were hearing.

As the number of those shows proliferated, some durable favorites surfaced, including *Break the Bank, Dr. I. Q., Can You Top This?, Double or Nothing, Give and Take, Information Please, It Pays to Be Ignorant, People Are Funny, The Quiz Kids, Strike It Rich, Take It or Leave It* (aka *The $64 Question*), *Truth or Consequences, Twenty Questions* and *You Bet Your Life*. In all, more than 400 audience participation entries flooded the ether before network radio's swan song.

Big band leader Horace Heidt ("and His Musical Knights") was at the conception of the phenomenon. While he was responsible for the medium's most successful trial series of the type — *Pot o' Gold*, which in 1939 initiated the model of calling listeners at home, simply getting them to answer the telephone in exchange for cash awards at this early stage — still, a previous concept Heidt introduced paved the way for much that was to follow.

During a band remote at Chicago's Drake Hotel in 1932, a WGN microphone was knocked to the floor inadvertently. Heidt jumped from the platform to retrieve it from among the spectators seated below. Suddenly he found himself swapping pleasantries with the guests. The small talk set the stage for a lively discourse that followed which he titled *Answers by the Dancers*. In that human-interest feature, Heidt dialogued with entertainers who comprised his permanent cast of singers, dancers and instrumentalists. In so doing he instigated a natural give-and-take technique that resonated with the listeners at home. The innovation — the outcome of a tipped-over mike — laid a little of the groundwork for the affable interactions that would in time become commonplace on the airwaves.

While CBS's *Professor Quiz*, appearing in 1936, is generally credited as radio's first true question feature, it's obvious that Heidt, one of the most widely recognized musicians of his day, was a founding father of the new form.

Music, in fact, became an essential ingredient of radio contests and some analogous diversionary amusement. It figured as the central device for more than 50 of those 400-plus involvement-type entries mentioned earlier. And it turned up in dozens of others from time to time as a method of enhancing quiz delivery like inserting musical questions, some of them even presented in song. Such tuneful extensions arrived in many forms.

The largest segment in which melody was the axis on which a game turned could generally be classified as quiz programs that linked their common existences to it. In this group, comprising nearly half this category of tune-based series, one finds programs like *Beat the Band, Ben Bernie's Musical Quiz, Dough Re Mi, Grand Slam, Hit the Jackpot, The Texaco Opera Quiz* and *Yours for a Song*. Of this cluster, maybe *Grand Slam*—a CBS daytime entry (from 1946 to 1953) in which singing hostess Irene Beasley fired listener-submitted queries at studio contestants—and Milton Cross's *Texaco Opera Quiz*, wherein operatic veterans responded to fan-originated teasers during intermissions at Metropolitan Opera concerts on NBC/ABC from 1940 on — are better recalled than their counterparts.

Other tuneful attempts in the quiz category include titles with even less ringing familiarity like *Melody Puzzles, Musical Mock Trial, Musical Treasure Chest, Musico, Rhymo, Scripteasers, Sigmund Spaeth's Music Quiz, The Singing Bee, Singo, Songo* and more. (For brief details on all of these programs the annotated guide in the appendix of the author's text *The Great Radio Audience Participation Shows* offers a comprehensive list with descriptions.)

Another competitive breed of radio features that relied exclusively upon music for its core offered neophyte artists who were hoping to grab the brass ring and — usually through a single appearance — land in the big time. While that wasn't true in every case, it was much of the time. There were at least 22 radio series that could be clearly identified as amateur contests in one form or another, predominantly offering their listeners voluntary singing or instrument playing as their principal claim to fame. (Radio historian Gerald Nachman casually observed, "Precisely what constituted an amateur was very much open to question.") Yet there were even specialty subsets within that framework.

On 1952's *Stars in Khaki 'n' Blue* over NBC, hostess Arlene Francis presented gifted aspirants from the ranks of the armed services doing their thing onstage. At the same time, emcee Tom George of CBS's *Talent Search, Country Style* (aka *Saturday Night, Country Style*) from 1951 to 1956 introduced homegrown pickers, pluckers and wailers from rural America. And at least two programs highlighted the artistry of adolescents: *Teen Town*, a 1946 ABC entry hosted by Dick York, and *The Youth Opportunity Program*, Horace Heidt's talent-thon organized in numerous locales across the nation and carried by NBC between 1947 and 1951.

Of the quartet just named, Heidt's show was easily the most recognizable, rewarding and enduring. Recall that Heidt, born May 21, 1901, in Alameda, California, previously established a track record for integrating competitive action into some of his myriad broadcast efforts. It dated at least from *Pot o' Gold* in 1939 and he influenced the genre as early as *Answers by the Dancers* in 1932. When *The Youth Opportunity Program* premiered over NBC on December 7, 1947, Heidt was already accustomed to doing lots more than merely introducing band numbers and waving his arms.

The show, as its title indicates, focused on some talented adolescents, frequently green as gourds, who aspired to personal achievement, reward and acclaim. A radio historian likened them to Major Bowes' amateur show (which will be examined in detail presently), noting: "Heidt's troupe [was] going from town to town auditioning local accordionists, piano players, and abusers of the harmonica and holding talent contests each Sunday night." Another referenced "Hustling Horace Heidt's *Youth Opportunity Program*, with its WPA overtones, as if Heidt were providing work for roving teenage accordionists who might otherwise go astray." He admonished: "Heidt's major find was the squeeze-box virtuoso Dick Contino, whose peppy version of *Lady of Spain* remains to this day amateurism's finest hour." For that, Contino earned a $5,000 prize and a brief stay on the airwaves.

The *Youth Opportunity Program* persisted for a quadrennial, however. It shifted in midstream from NBC to CBS but continued for the same sponsor, Philip Morris. It was withdrawn on December 16, 1951. In the meantime, Heidt was headlining a similar effort on the tube. *The Horace Heidt Show*, in which talented amateurs and young professionals were showcased weekly, appeared on CBS-TV between October 2, 1950, and September 24, 1951. The maestro-turned-talent scout later returned to the cameras for NBC with *The Swift Show Wagon* from January 8 to October 1, 1955. In that one the program journeyed from city to city each week for a live performance, displaying talent culled from the nearby terrain.

Heidt, himself, had led something of a checkered career in the music business before settling on the talent competitions that proffered notoriety and stability. Studying piano as a child at his mama's command, he organized his first outfit at the age of 21. The "act" included a trained German shepherd named Lobo that interjected an unusual distraction into a dance band show. After touring awhile, the entourage folded and Heidt recruited a new one, playing Oakland's Athens Club, circa 1927. A couple of years later Heidt joined the Fanchon-Marco vaudeville circuit. He played the Drake Hotel in Chicago for six years followed by six years at the Biltmore Hotel in New York, staging *Pot o' Gold* while at the latter venue.

Heidt achieved some success in recordings, principally in the 1940s, including his theme song *I'll Love You in My Dreams* along with *Don't Fence Me In, I Don't Want to Set the World on Fire* and a single hand-clapping million-disc seller *Deep in the Heart of Texas*. He peppered his showbill with some pretty formidable rising talent, including singers Art Carney (who appeared with the vocal ensemble Donna and the Don Juans), Larry Cotton, Ronnie Kemper, The King Sisters, Fred Lowrey, Gordon MacRae, pianist Frankie Carle (who for a brief time in the early 1940s was Heidt's orchestra co-director) and trumpeter Al Hirt.

Music critic Albert McCarthy recounted some of Heidt's career ups and downs.[1]

> For years Heidt had led one of the most commercially successful but musically dismal bands in the United States, reaching a peak of popularity in the mid-'30s when his music was compounded of every gimmick in the book, from the electric guitar effects of Alvino Rey and the flashy showmanship of pianist Frankie Carle to a saxophone section that out-Lombardoed Lombardo. In 1939 the musical world was astonished when Bobby Hackett accepted an invitation to join Heidt's band, and even more surprised when several of the leader's sidemen provided adequate backing to Hackett on a number of small-group jazz recordings. Around 1942-3 Heidt totally revamped his band and style, bringing in jazz stars like Jess Stacy,

Shorty Sherock and Joe Rushton, but unfortunately this group was active during the [ASCAP — the American Society of Composers, Authors and Publishers] recording ban and so there is no recorded evidence of Heidt in a role other than that of a purveyor of musical dross.

Yet another respected authority, music journalist George Simon, painted a similar portrait of Heidt's vocation and contributions while adding a few intimate insights to his canvas.[2]

> Horace Heidt was always an enigma to me. For years he had one of the most showmanly, most corny, most successful bands in the world. And then, when those of us who liked better music had become convinced that there was no musical hope for Heidt, he suddenly began hiring some of the best swing musicians, gave them their heads, and their hearts, and wound up with a thoroughly impressive outfit.
>
> He was a difficult man for many of us to know, and the "us" included many of the musicians who worked for him.... He moved stiffly, almost clumsily. He seemed devoid of a sense of humor. He smiled a great deal, but it was seldom a complete smile, so that one wondered whether he was really happy or whether the smile was just part of an astonishingly effective cover-up for an ill-at-ease leader of one of the most formidable of all show bands.

Heidt was successful in maintaining an almost constant presence on the air. From his initial series in 1932, *Ship of Joy* on NBC Blue, through numerous successive ventures ultimately touching all the chains but MBS, he appeared to have no problem in corralling time and sponsors for his divergent musical platforms. His last on radio, from January 1 to December 24, 1953, was a weekly stint over CBS.

In the mid–1940s he surprised the industry by announcing that he was quitting as a bandleader, disbanding his orchestra and concentrating on varied commercial interests. Heidt seemed to move freely from hot to cold and probably formed more bands than the average conductor. A critic suggested: "Heidt was really more impresario–front man–organizer than musician, but had a Midas touch." Despite his seeming temporary lapses into indecision, his efforts made him extremely wealthy and allowed him to retire comfortably in the mid–1950s. A couple of years before he passed away an insider confidently acknowledged, "He is probably the wealthiest businessman of all the former bandleaders." Heidt died December 1, 1995, in Los Angeles.

There was one radio show of volunteers in which an impresario turned over his podium and baton to audience spectators and allowed them to conduct for a while — *So You Want to Lead a Band*. Big band leader Sammy Kaye presided over this engaging departure from the amateur theme between 1946 and 1948 on ABC. A $1,000 grand prize went to the "maestro" who was selected best in competitive judging.

Surprisingly, a quartet of radio features in this epoch dwelled on novice composers, too. Each series tweaked the concept a tad to distinguish it from its peers.

On *Fame and Fortune* over NBC Blue in 1940-1941, the Tommy Dorsey Orchestra and vocalists Connie Haines and Frank Sinatra performed the compositions of several amateurs. A $100 prize was awarded the tunesmith whose song was selected for top honors by the studio audience on a given show.

On *Sing It Again*, with Dan Seymour as host, novices performed new arrangements of popular melodies (CBS, 1948–1951).

A quartet of composers, meanwhile — including a trio of amateurs and a pro — performed their own works in 1944 on NBC's *A Song Is Born*. Tales of the tunes' backgrounds were recounted or dramatized and participants received $25 each for their contributions. A panel picked the best of the four numbers to be published.

Finally, in likely the best remembered of the strain, *Songs for Sale* (CBS, 1950-1951), hosts Jan Murray and Richard Hayes presided while neophytes' compositions were performed, appraised by a panel of professionals and put up for purchase.

There were no fewer than 13 amateur talent contests aired by the various networks, doubtlessly the most fertile sector among such optimistic tenderfoots. The first of those, *National Amateur Night* hosted by Ray Perkins, debuted on December 30, 1934, over CBS. It persisted for two years, airing its final 10 months over MBS.

In this classification one would find *Arthur Godfrey's Talent Scouts* (CBS, 1946–1956), purportedly presenting semi-professional artists, never the rank (and file) amateurs that other series attracted, in a show that discovered some pretty impressive finds. Among them: Tony Bennett, Pat Boone, Lenny Bruce, The Chordettes, Roy Clark, Van Cliburn, Patsy Cline, Rosemary Clooney, Wally Cox, Vic Damone, The Diamonds, Connie Francis, Robert Goulet, Betty Johnson, Steve Lawrence, Shari Lewis, Ann-Margret, Al Martino, Marian McPartland, Jose Melis, Lu Ann Simms, The McGuire Sisters, Carmel Quinn, and Leslie Uggams. (Two who were turned down from appearing on that stage for lack of appreciable talent were rock 'n' rollers Buddy Holly and Elvis Presley, by the way!)

On *Talent Scouts*, friends, business associates and even relatives would attempt to charm host Godfrey with some preliminary chitchat about the aspiring young men and women on the way up that they brought to the show. An audience applause meter gauged the reaction of the studio spectators when a handful of acts finished competing, most of those performing vocal or instrumental musical numbers. The winners not only achieved satisfaction and honor but also were invariably showcased for a week on Godfrey's daytime program, hardly a shabby reward for their night's work.

Godfrey, of course, was CBS's reigning king, presiding over *Arthur Godfrey Time* for up to 90 minutes weekdays for 27 years (1945–1972). He also had a weekly TV variety series and a transcribed recap of his best morning shows of the previous week each weekend on radio. The Old Redhead acquired a fiery reputation for dismissing some of his most talented entertainers— at least once literally while on the air. Until then, he was nearly idolized by hordes of faithful followers who appreciated his humor, his talented troupe of entertainers and his easygoing salesmanship for a long list of sponsors. At the peak of his popularity in 1953 he was seen and heard by 80 million Americans every week and was personally responsible for generating 12 percent of CBS's annual revenues, a hefty $27 million in those days.

A biographer described Godfrey "as close ... to a one-man network as radio and television ever produced." Others designated him "the most powerful man in broadcasting" and "the original and ultimate infotainer." Billed as "Red Godfrey, the Warbling Banjoist," Godfrey launched his broadcast career over Baltimore's WFBR in 1926. In the 1930s, he successively advanced to Washington, D.C.'s WRC, WMAL and WJSV (now WTOP), becoming an early morning DJ at the latter, an assignment that took him to the CBS flagship station in New York, WABC, for similar duty. He was soon knocking on the network door. Born in New York City on August 31, 1903, Godfrey succumbed to death there on March 16, 1983.

A daytime aural contender was *Live Like a Millionaire* (NBC, 1950–1952; ABC, 1952-1953). Master of ceremonies Jack McCoy welcomed the offspring of budding— though frequently lagging—artists who then presented their not-so-famous folks.

Winners, determined by a studio audience applause meter, earned a week's tax on a million dollars. Thus they lived *like* a millionaire without becoming one. Get it?

The granddaddy of the genre is indubitably *Major Bowes' Original Amateur Hour*, however, later reprised as *Ted Mack's Original Amateur Hour* (NBC, 1935-1936; CBS, 1936–1945; ABC, 1948–1952). It was claimed, rather descriptively, that for "bus fare and a harmonica" almost anyone — talented or not — could land at Bowes' venue. That certainly appeared to be the case in the show's early days. "Small-time entertainers who had wowed the local Lions Club were encouraged to sell their homes, pack up their banjos, tap shoes, washboards and cowbells and, like showbiz Okies, head east in pursuit of theatrical fame and fortune," wrote an observer. "The program was as much freak show as talent contest."[3] Despite the allegation, *OAH* was immediately designated "the most popular radio program in 1935," touched 20 million fans weekly and netted its producer-host a cool million bucks annually.

Major Edward Bowes was born in San Francisco on June 14, 1874, and claimed to have been a major in intelligence during World War I, although that appears debatable. He had already lived six decades when NBC premiered his hour-long radio masterpiece on March 24, 1935. A showman at heart (one wag labeled him "the Ziegfeld of bird-whistlers and spoon-players") and a salesman par excellence, Bowes was managing director at New York's Capitol Theater. He produced film shorts and managed a score of corps that traversed the nation fostering amateur entertainment, possibly with an eye toward resuscitating vaudeville.

Among his marketing innovations at the Capitol, however, Bowes launched a weekly radio series over a Gotham station on July 26, 1925 — even *before* there was an NBC or CBS, over which his feature later aired — that ran continuously through May 25, 1941. *Capitol Family* showcased members of Bowes' theater ensemble as well as many guest performers. By the time he debuted the *Original Amateur Hour* in 1934 over New York's WHN, he was a well-practiced stage show marvel.

The entertainment industry journal *Variety*, having checked out the debuting *Original Amateur Hour*, lavished praise on Bowes' entrepreneurial skills.

> For showmanship, deft handling, color and human interest appeal it's one of the slickest things yet effected by any of the New York stations.... If Major Bowes thinks a tyro's efforts have passed the indulgence point the latter is abruptly halted by the ringing of a gong. The gong idea here is a species of substitute for the hook of the old vaude house days. Talent that Major Bowes parades before his mike is of a highly varied assortment and well balanced.

"Every week," wrote one reporter, "the humorless Major spun his show business roulette wheel and droned in a funeral voice, 'Tonight we spin our weekly wheel of fortune for the 5,368th time. Around and around she goes, and where she stops nobody knows.' When the performers were too awful to be permitted to continue, Bowes would strike a gong, ... a gimmick later exploited by TV's *Gong Show*, a sort of subamateur hour." He was also ascribed as possessing a "mirthless chuckle" and was flanked by a bodyguard, should an unruly losing bird-caller challenge a show's outcome.

No matter. Thousands of would-be performers reportedly applied weekly for a place on that coveted stage. A few hundred were invited to audition. Of that number, about 20 actually got on the air, dispensing the leftover jobless yodelers and wineglass virtuosi to the street. Some 30,000 in the radio audience, meanwhile, responded every week to the performances, acknowledging

The chickens came home to roost (as well as everything else, apparently) when Major Edward Bowes (left) allowed almost anybody who could toot a harmonica on stage for his *Original Amateur Hour*, a radio classic. The young man beside him may be singing with gusto but one wonders if Bowes' personal bodyguard might be called upon soon.

their selections for zenith-reaching spoon-and-glass stylists by mail, telephone and telegraph. Bowes, in turn, organized aggregates of winners and runner-ups to play in theaters across the nation.

Major Bowes' Original Amateur Hour was responsible for leaving a legacy within the environs of greater New York that was less than flattering. Many of those unskilled harmonica-players arriving in the Big Apple, hoping for a shot on the road to eminence, sometimes lingered a while afterwards, significantly increasing local welfare rolls. There was an outcry from relief agencies as a result of the large influx of indigents the Bowes program was bringing in. They, too, needed some relief. In fact, when another "down-on-their-luck" radio and television series emerged in the late 1940s—*Strike It Rich*—a hue and a cry went up from several organizations. They hadn't forgotten the significantly large numbers of destitute claimants who took up temporary residence in their fair burg at the hands of Major Bowes' magnetic drawing card.

The Travelers Aid Society for one vehemently protested that *Strike It Rich* beckoned an overabundance of similar folks. When aspirants went bust on the *Original Amateur Hour*, they flocked to Travelers Aid for help in getting home. *Newsweek* reported that, in a single month in 1935, about 1,200 stranded and disappointed entertainers required emergency support. "We don't know if the successes on the show balance off against the human misery caused by it," the society's supervisor allowed. "But from what we see, I'd say it didn't.... Putting human misery on display can hardly be called right."

Another order, the Family Service Association of America, argued against a benevolent-intending *Strike It Rich*, too: "Victims of poverty, illness, and everyday misfortune should not be made a public spectacle or seemingly be put in the position of begging for charity."

Despite the ominous clouds gathering overhead, the *Original Amateur Hour* infused the nation's observers with an interest in parading those in front of them who were willing to display their talents, albeit sometimes quite small, for a fleeting chance at fame — in that day, their three minutes of it. After Bowes became too ill to continue his performances, *OAH* ended on January 4, 1945, but not without fanfare. In its absence, some winners, along with some novice talent, came before the microphones in a brief series heralded as *Major Bowes' Shower of Stars*. Morton Gould and later Donald Voorhees conducted an orchestra on the CBS feature that ran from February 8 through August 30, 1945. Bowes never returned and died at Rumson, New Jersey, on June 14, 1946.

But never say die. Bowes' idea persisted many years after him.

An equally colorless Ted Mack, who had worked alongside Bowes in directing those infamous talent tryouts, perpetuated the major's ritual by assuming the reins for an extension of the *original* idea — this time allowing folks at home to also visualize the legions of prancing neophytes lining up to strut their stuff. Starting January 18, 1948, *Ted Mack's Original Amateur Hour* became an early ratings success on Dumont Television (keep in mind that there wasn't a whole lot else to see at the time). It went downhill soon. One reviewer claimed the "niftiest act on the show" was a dancing pack of Old Gold cigarettes.

Mack, who was born Edward Maguiness at Greeley, Colorado, on February 24, 1904, blew a clarinet and a saxophone in his younger days and appeared with bands fronted by Red Nichols, Ben Pollack, Benny Goodman and Glenn Miller. When he formed his own entourage and had difficulty placing "Edward Maguiness and His Band" across theater marquees, he shortened it to "Ted Mack and His Band." He died on July 12, 1976, in Tarrytown, New York.

The revised version of the *Original Amateur Hour*, under Mack's tutelage and with Dennis James as announcer, would ultimately embrace all four major TV networks then in existence before it reached finality on September 27, 1970. Concurrently, the radio show returned, airing on ABC — its third chain — for the same TV sponsor from September 29, 1948, to September 18, 1952.

The spectacle that Major Bowes launched in 1935 was really remarkable as it lasted a cumulative 35 years, without any debate one of the most durable traditions in broadcast history. And to its credit, not all those aspiring performers fell on their faces by any count. A handful turned into celebrated legends a few years beyond their initial exposure before a national audience with Bowes or Mack. They included Mimi Benzell, Teresa Brewer, Jack Carter, Robert Merrill, Lily Pons, Beverly Sills, Frank Sinatra (who lost in his appearance on Bowes' stage) and Jerry Vale. Not all of those, surely, played the spoons.

There were still other programs of a competitive nature with music at their core in radio. Contestants actually sang the songs themselves on *Fish Pond*, *Sing for Your Dough* and *Sing for Your Money*. On *Three for the Money*, host Clayton "Bud" Collyer coaxed a trio of players to predict a studio audience's reaction to various tunes. Neither series lasted beyond a few weeks or months, incidentally.

But a final big category that did resonate with the listeners was centered on musical identifications. Of five series that can be readily included here, the inaugural one set the tone for it, albeit a blend of corn, contestants and crooners.

Kay Kyser's Kollege of Musical Knowledge was a radical departure from anything else in radio with the minor exception of an imitator that hoped to gainfully transfer Kyser's curious routine to an ethnic copy (called *Quizzical*, lasting a season, 1941-1942, over NBC Blue with Cab Calloway's band). The original, in the meantime, caught on quickly, drew legions of listeners and stuck around for more than a decade.

Kay Kyser was born James Kern Kyser on June 18, 1897, in Rocky Mount, North Carolina. It's speculated that he assumed the more artistic moniker of Kay Kyser to avail himself of the catchy-sounding matched initial letters. Kyser took an early interest in music and conducted bands as if he was a college cheerleader, his spirited zest and jaunty jests becoming an instant crowd-pleaser. While attending the University of North Carolina in Chapel Hill (where he actually *was* head cheerleader), he gathered a coterie of promising young instrumentalists, like several other bandleaders were doing starting out in the 1920s.

Kyser's troupe was soon scouring the country performing dates on college campuses and in community centers and dance halls, wherever people would pay to hear them play. Eventually making the right connections, Kyser and company landed in the big time. In March 1939, for example, they pulled in $10,000 weekly during a Cleveland engagement. But it had taken Kyser nearly a decade to discover a formula that would propel the aggregate to the widespread celebrity he sought.

In the summer of 1934, while performing at the Miramar Hotel in Santa Monica, California, Kyser instituted one of several commercial gimmicks that were to characterize his outfit. Instead of announcing the songs before they were performed, the entourage played a few bars of each tune while a vocalist warbled the title's words off key. Kyser later said the substitution served a utilitarian purpose — it saved time usually devoted ploddingly to verbal introductions, an important factor in radio, he insisted. Curiously, the band echoed a few bars of its theme, *Thinking of You*, as the maestro announced the singer's name shortly before the chorus. It was an "ingenious image-building device," a pundit allowed, and at that time was unique in the business. Kyser included the novelty as a part of his stage act when he followed another UNC alumnus, bandleader Hal Kemp, to Chicago's fabled Blackhawk Restaurant in September 1934. The gimmick soon became a permanent trademark for Kyser's team.

At the Blackhawk in 1937, the impresario introduced yet another distinctive notion that was to result in one of the ether's earliest audience participation features. *Kay Kyser's Kollege of Musical Knowledge* commenced over potent station WGN and was beamed to the nation's heartland starting February 1, 1938. It could be interpreted as Kyser's launching pad for the distinction he lacked. In less than two months it attracted a national sponsor, the American Tobacco Company, manufacturer of Lucky Strike cigarettes, and — on March 30 — was slotted into an hour at 10 P.M. Wednesdays on NBC. Kyser's opening, delivered in a Southern drawl, became familiar to admirers everywhere: "Evenin' folks, how y'all? Come on, chillun, le's dance!" It was soon upgraded with 1940s-style jive: "Greetings, Gates, let's matriculate!"

Contestants, drawn from among the patrons (the *stoodents* of his mythical institute) who came to hear the band, were interviewed before being asked to identify a number just played. "Kay's bubbly way of handling contestants and his method of practically giving answers to slow quizzes endeared him to all," wrote a reviewer. Getting it right meant a $10 bill to a lucky guesser. Kyser, meanwhile, arrayed in full academic cap-and-gown regalia, was dubbed "The Old Perfesser" and was fond of exclaiming, following a contender's incorrect response: "That's right, you're wrong!"

But for those who got it right, there was a diploma waiting, suitable for framing, similar to that given by institutions of higher learning upon satisfactory completion of course work. In a bold script flourish, the certificates read[4]:

Kay Kyser's Kollege of Musical Knowledge
This Certifies That
_____
has satisfactorily completed
the prescribed Course in
Musical Knowledge
And is hereby declared a Graduate
and is awarded this
Diploma
In witness whereof we have hereunto
set our hands and seal
Kay Kyser, Music Master
1938 Semester Broadcast over the
WGN and Mutual
Coast-to-Coast Network
From
The Blackhawk, Chicago

In between instrumental selections involving the "class" there were vocals by singers Harry Babbitt, Georgia Carroll, Sully Mason and Ginny Simms, and zany antics by Ish Kabibble (comic Merwyn Bogue). It was such a success that it made Kyser a top box office draw in theaters, ballrooms and on one-night touring stands across the country for many years. A couple of contemporary music critics later assessed: "The Kay Kyser Orchestra was a lovable group with a good sense of humor as well as the talent to offer one of the best sweet bands of the midcentury."

On the sidelines, meanwhile, gossip persisted for years that Kyser and Ginny Simms were an "item." Both were still single. She wanted to marry him but he tarried, observers said. In 1941, when he was finally persuaded to take the plunge, she was no longer attracted and hastily departed the Kyser organization. (Her trio of marriages and subsequent legal quagmire reads like a soap opera and is profiled in The Vocalists chapter.) Kyser later wed Georgia Carroll, another singer with his outfit, classified by one source as "a breathlessly beautiful, well-bred Hollywood model." Their union resulted in one of the most successful show business marriages of that day. Carroll retired professionally when their children came along, staying home to raise a family.

Overcome by patriotism at the outbreak of the Second World War, Kyser decreed that all of his personal appearance engagements for the duration of that conflict would be staged at naval stations or army camps. By the time the war ended in 1945 he had played nearly 600 service installations (one source put it at more than 700). During the same epoch, he made numerous visits to radio's *Fitch Bandwagon* and performed at the inaugural of Hollywood's Stage Door Canteen. Some of his recordings—from a farcical *Jingle, Jangle, Jingle, Three Little Fishes* and *Woody Woodpecker* to a more engaging *Praise the Lord and Pass the Ammunition* and *Who Wouldn't Love You?*—were well received by doting fans.

Between 1939 and 1944, Kyser appeared in eight major motion pictures, starring as himself in all but one: *That's Right— You're Wrong* (1939), costarring Adolphe Menjou, Lucille Ball, Dennis O'Keefe, Edward Everett Horton, Ginny Simms, Harry Babbitt, Sully Mason and Ish Kabibble; *You'll Find Out* (1940), with Peter Lorre, Boris Karloff, Bela

Participating in the zany antics integrated into *Kay Kyser's Kollege of Musical Knowledge* were (left to right) Sully Mason, Eddie Shea, Kyser, Harry Babbitt and Ish Kabibble. An infusion of humor added novelty to the very fine orchestra Kyser headlined, thrusting the group into the public limelight and giving it staying power for about as long as bands aired.

Lugosi, Dennis O'Keefe, Ginny Simms, Harry Babbitt, Ish Kabibble and Sully Mason; *Playmates* (1941), with John Barrymore, Ginny Simms, Peter Lind Hayes, Harry Babbitt, Ish Kabibble and Sully Mason; *My Favorite Spy* (1942), with Ellen Drew, Jane Wyman, William Demarest and Harry Babbitt; *Thousands Cheer* (1943), starring Kathryn Grayson, Gene Kelly, Mary Astor, Ben Blue, Frances Rafferty and in cameo appearances Mickey Rooney, Judy Garland, Red Skelton and Kyser; *Around the World* (1943), with Joan Davis, Georgia Carroll, Harry Babbitt, Ish Kabibble and Sully Mason; *Swing Fever* (1943), with Marilyn Maxwell, William Gargan, Lena Horne, Max "Slapsie Maxie" Rosenbloom, Harry Babbitt and Sully Mason; and *Carolina Blues* (1944), with Ann Miller, Georgia Carroll, Ish Kabibble, Harry Babbitt and Sully Mason.

Surprisingly, what worked well on radio failed to impress the small-screen viewers later. When his series left the air forever on July 29, 1949, Kyser tried to replicate its triumph on video. But after two insipid attempts—from December 1, 1949, to December 28, 1950, and July 4 to September 12, 1954, both over NBC-TV—he folded his tent and returned to Chapel Hill, North Carolina, for a while entering the family pharmacy business. A Christian Scientist, Kyser taught the faith's precepts and—in the 1970s—became chief of its film and broadcast ministries, thereby activating still another career. He died in Chapel Hill on July 23, 1985.

What's the Name of That Song? with emcees Dud Williamson, Bob Bence and Bill Gwinn was next in the strain, after *Kyser's Kollege* picked up steam and *Quizzical* folded. While this one debuted in 1943 over the Don Lee network on the West Coast, it gained a berth on the MBS lineup on September 24, 1944. With a 16-month break in action during 1947-1948, it completed its run on December 16, 1948. And although never as popular as predecessor or successor series of the breed, *What's the Name of That Song?* affirmed the premise Kay Kyser had promulgated, turning detection of unnamed melodies into a viable theme for a half hour. Studio contestants played the guessers. The show itself traveled about the country, appearing before local crowds while drawing regional gameplayers to its mobile stage. Largely sustained, the program drew a loyal following until it was overtaken by a much more refined tweaking of the model.

The phenomenon of title-guessing games reached its apex when a telephone was introduced into the mix. ABC flung its ball of wax into prime time against NBC's hardy laugh-getters Edgar Bergen and Fred Allen and waited expectantly for the results. They weren't long in coming. *Stop the Music!* with effusive personality Bert Parks as its master of ceremonies was an overnight ratings smash. So much so that it knocked perennial ratings leaders Bergen off the air for the remainder of the season and Allen permanently.

It so angered the latter, in fact, that before departing Allen took caustic swipes at his nemesis, parodying the show on his own comedy feature. After nearly two decades in ruling his time period, the great wit was history. "Radio actually died when *Stop the Music!* got higher ratings than Fred Allen," theorized a couple of historiographers. Humorist Henry Morgan assured everybody that such an aberration drove "the final nail in radio's coffin." In spite of that, the audience participation series "created more national excitement than any other game or contest in the country."

Stop the Music! prospered at the peril of anything that was designated as its competition. It followed a simple pretext: drawing from a huge bank of telephone directories from all over the nation, backstage ABC operators would telephone listeners at random while a musical selection was performed live onstage. Sometimes the orchestra conducted by Harry Salter (later, Ray Bloch) played alone; often, a vocalist — Kay Armen or Dick Brown at the start, Jill Corey or Jack Haskell in a later version — sang with the melody, humming a song's title to avoid giving it away. (Typical tunes: *At a Georgia Camp Meeting, The Hucklebuck, I'm Looking Over a Four-Leaf Clover, Isle of Capri, Golden Earrings, Ruby, Someone to Watch Over Me, Steam Heat.*) Seldom did they finish a number; when the studio operators connected with a listener at home, a loud telephone-sounding bell rang as Bert Parks shouted: "Stop the music!" The melody instantly halted as a frenetic suspense charged the air. From the telephone operator, Parks requested the name and location of the individual on the line, then asked the listener to identify the tune just played or sung.

More often than not the listener was often one song behind, and named the tune that had just been featured prior to the one he or she was asked to identify. It's possible the contestant was discussing that particular title with someone at home and perhaps had even written it down, but was distracted when the call came from ABC. On those occasions the emcee — never at a loss for words — punctuated the situation with some good-natured ribbing as the studio audience howled and jeered. What those in the studio failed to acknowledge, of course, was that offering the right title on cue might not have been as simple as it appeared, and especially if they were at the other end of the telephone line.

A correct response earned a listener a $50 U.S. savings bond. If the wrong title or no title was given, someone in the studio audience took a shot at the $50 bond. A correct reply on the initial tune qualified a telephone winner for a much greater opportunity. A $1,000 U.S. savings bond and a two-week all-expense-paid trip to Paris were offered at one point for merely naming the "Mystery Melody," an ongoing tune repeated at each qualifying call until a listener could identify it. If no one got it, the jackpot was enlarged with added cash or merchandise. Its prize value consistently topped $20,000 at a given time. At least once during the show's first year the jackpot surpassed $30,000.

Stop the Music! premiered on March 21, 1948, for an hour on ABC at 8 o'clock on Sunday evenings. It remained in that slot until it met the same fate Fred Allen had experienced, sharply falling ratings, and was withdrawn on August 10, 1952. CBS reprised it with Bill Cullen and eventually Happy Felton as emcee, beginning August 17, 1954, initially for 60 minutes and later for 75. It didn't fare well in its second go-round, however, and ended abruptly on February 15, 1955.

Certainly the catalyst that made the show, aside from the novelty of telephoning people at home to ask them to identify a melody, was Bert Parks, who was linked with the program for a long while even after it was over. Parks wasn't new to network radio by any means, having arrived at the CBS studios a dozen years earlier. A native Atlantan, born December 30, 1914, his radio career began on his hometown's WGST when he was only 16. Hired for the dual roles of announcer and singer, he performed pleasingly there and moved to the big time in New York a couple of years later. It was 1933 and he was earning $50 weekly as a CBS staff announcer, considerable wealth in that Depression era.

Parks' extroverted persona soon caught the attention of comedian Eddie Cantor, who put him on his show as announcer, vocalist and foil to himself. Before long the gregarious Georgian was also emceeing series for bandleaders Xavier Cugat and Benny Goodman. Parks soon acquired announcing chores on several more features: *The Adventures of Ellery Queen, Camel Caravan, Columbia Workshop, Forty-Five Minutes in Hollywood, How'm I Doin?* (an early game show), *The Kate Smith Show, Luncheon at the Waldorf, Matinee at Meadowbrook, Our Gal Sunday* and *Renfrew of the Mounted.*

Summoned in the early 1940s by Uncle Sam, he fulfilled his service requirements. Returning to radio, he picked up new announcing stints, introducing *Judy, Jill and Johnny* and *McGarry and His Mouse.* By then he could hardly be contained as a behind-the-mike narrator. Bursting on the scene as a rotating emcee, he came across as a fresh shot of adrenaline to *Break the Bank's* prime-time audience in the mid–1940s.

In 1947, Parks launched another audience participation series over station WAAT, Newark, New Jersey, called *Second Honeymoon.* It subsequently found its way to ABC. When he was picked to emcee the debuting *Stop the Music!* in 1948, Parks hosted his *third* competitive show *concurrently.* It hadn't been done previously, and may not have been done since. By then he was considered among radio's top five or six game show leaders.

Parks is recalled by nearly everybody who lived through the epoch as the vocalist with the leaping eyebrows who bellowed "There she is! Miss America!" From 1954 to 1979 he presided over the televised Miss America Pageant, requesting from the judges the envelope that contained the name of the winner. Withdrawing the name of the lucky lady who was selected and then crowned, he read her state's name aloud and crooned to her. Parks had arrived in that coveted spot from a long career as a radio and television celebrity, backed with Broadway appearances that included the title role in *The Music Man.*

During the mid–1950s he presided over a two-hour daily radio series titled *NBC Bandstand*, a half-hour of which was simulcast on TV in 1956. Previously, from 1950 to 1952, he hosted a triweekly daytime variety feature, *The Bert Parks Show*, over NBC-TV and then CBS-TV. He maintained credentials as a game show host by presiding over the tube's *Double or Nothing* (1952–1954), *County Fair* (1958-1959), *The Big Payoff* (1959) and *Yours for a Song* (1961–1963). Parks died in La Jolla, California, on February 2, 1992.

The final series in the song-identification quintet, considered a *Stop the Music!* spinoff, was NBC's answer to that extraordinary spectacle. *Name That Tune* arrived on December 20, 1952—four months after the original *Stop the Music!* was cancelled due to low ratings, presumably because the audience defected to something it preferred elsewhere. *Name That Tune* prevailed just 17 weeks before getting the ax. Reverting to the format fostered by *What's the Name of That Song?*, studio contestants—as opposed to listeners at home—attempted to answer that pivotal question. A couple of agile, lissome, sneaker-donned competitors sprinted along a 25-foot route to ring a bell to qualify them for eligibility for a melodious mystery round.

The venture, unfortunately, must have had failure written all over it from the start. It changed masters of ceremonies three times, presenting in order Red Benson, Bill Cullen, George de Witt and Tom Kennedy. Apparently poor timing finished it off. *Name That Tune* fared somewhat better as a visual entry, however, returning in several network and syndicated TV reincarnations in the 1950s and 1970s.

Fun and games seemed natural cohabitants. When music was introduced into the midst of such trifles, a new sparkle was added that made those contests appear even more amusing than they really might have been.

The Disc Jockeys

Doubtlessly displaying considerable prescience, a Philadelphia radio station started airing records in the middle of the 1920s as a part of its everyday programming format. While that outlet may not have been the very first to transmit that form of entertainment, it certainly could be considered a pioneer in the endeavor.

Not everybody was amused by those tunes cracking across the ether, however, emanating to whoever was listening through the headphones of early crystal sets or whatever apparatus or receiver had been rigged together. Among the dissatisfied were several music publishers in New York City plus a few dance band conductors, Paul Whiteman among their number. Collectively, they brought a lawsuit against the station. Their argument? That a portion of their livelihood was being delivered gratis to those tuning in — without any recompense to themselves. It was a dispute that, by extension, would be similarly fought numerous times in the years ahead.

On that occasion, nevertheless, a judge sided with the station. "A recording purchased from a proper source is no longer the property of the manufacturer or the performer," the jurist concluded. "The buyer may use it in any way he sees fit, including broadcasting its contents." (That ruling would not hold up in every case, as further investigation will reveal.)

The possibility that airing those wax discs as a tactic for boosting their sales made little, if any, impression upon those music professionals and purveyors, astonishingly. Did it ever cross anybody's mind that floating those tunes over the airwaves not only offered the very real prospect of increasing demand for the records themselves but also significantly enhancing the performing and publishing industries as a result of added exposure?

It would look like the very products that were making the individuals who produced them simultaneously famous and wealthy would also do a lot more for them, like garnering premium personal appearance bookings while increasing sheet music sales, and spawning demand for ongoing radio appearances by many artists and bands on shows that could potentially generate still more record revenue. Careers seemingly would be enhanced, not trampled, by playing an entertainer's discs on the ether. And the firms that produced the records would see bottom lines escalate. Apparently this wasn't particularly well thought out as those officials introduced their ill-fated suit in court.

It actually took them all by surprise when—as a result of broadcasting the tunes—the retail sales of said recordings soared across the City of Brotherly Love. Stations in far-flung markets, hearing of Philly's success, rapidly adopted this revolutionary pattern. The idea of an announcer playing recordings on the air was becoming firmly entrenched in some places. It offered a departure from the live music that had become a mainstay on many of the larger stations' agendas of that early radio era, a practice that was frequently unavailable to many smaller outlets.

While the permanent appellation hadn't arrived by that time, the birth of the disc jockey as a shill for record artists and publishers had. Its founding was to have ample impact on what Americans heard radiating from their radios in the decades ahead. Given time, the totalitarian of the turntables would come to dominate the airwaves, overtaking most of the hours of radio broadcasting's days and nights, placing them under his irrefutably autocratic power. (Eventually, at least one wag would classify the breed as "the scourge of postwar radio."[1])

But that was in the distance.

During radio's early years, his was merely one among many of the ether's pleasant reveries. The platter-spinner's diversionary tactics would be a sidelight held mostly in abeyance for a quarter of a century. That is not to say that there weren't gramophone gurus taking hold in many places even then. While their number and influence remained minuscule, a definite trend had been born. From the prenetwork days, the model of airing recorded music would continue to grow in substance and scale.

In due course the music publishers and probably every conductor with money to burn spent large sums on local station spinmeisters (soon to be dubbed disc jockeys) from sea to shining sea in an effort to grab and fortify support. "Some romanced disc jockeys with intense and sometimes nauseating ardor," recalled a big band critic. Cash, alcohol, sex, show and sports tickets, vacations and other conniving handouts were silently passed to DJs to reap favorable hype on the air—to guarantee a certain number of spins coupled with an avalanche of flattering chitchat in an effort to augment their record sales.

The innovation was probably originally introduced to the dance and big band conductors themselves. Individuals commonly known in the trade as "song pluggers" performed those duties then. (See The Big Bands chapter for greater detail.) Although not generally disclosed publicly, it was a fact that the music vendors plied those impresarios with similar trinkets for many years in an effort to coax them into programming specific tunes at their live venues—and particularly when those shows were broadcast over local, regional or national radio hookups. The terms weren't new when those attempts at last reached the disc jockeys—only the targets and some of the actors had been altered.

None of this might have ever become a serious problem for the DJs—although it eventually did—had the infamous television quiz show scandals of the late 1950s not erupted. By then the industry was shining its spotlights into every crack and crevice in an effort to ferret out anything that could be mildly interpreted as unethical tactics. Some of TV's dispelling experience spilled over into radio—not to its waning vestiges of quiz and contest marathons still airing, but to the province of the platter-spinners. A few details will set the stage.

By the early 1950s, the clout of the disc jockey as a record promoter was firmly established. As many new independent stations arrived with up to 24 hours per day of air time to fill, and as the networks relinquished more and more of their daily schedules in response to the clamor of their affiliates—the quickest, simplest, least costly and most profitable solution for the local outlets was to fill much of that available time with recorded music. "The jockeys became radio's stars," confirmed a source. Soon a few trade journals were suggesting, with some degree of disdain, that the platter-and-patter agents were being romanced with all sorts of trappings to curry their favor. There was a strong hint that the practice was primarily attributed to the producers of what was then called "rhythm and blues" records, a forerunner of the middle 1950s "rock 'n' roll" craze.

More disturbing concerns came to light about 1954 when an industry insider — one of the nation's premier DJs— proclaimed in a trade journal article that "the public did not determine its own preference in music, but instead was almost completely influenced to accept the music played for them by the nation's disc jockeys."[2] That revelation, coupled with the emerging indications that the DJs were being heavily wined and dined by the record companies, caused eyebrows to arch and consternation within the troops. Obviously, the rigorous efforts to influence the individuals in such pivotal spots were having a profound effect on shaping what was aired. Ultimately, that appreciably determined what was purchased in phonograph record shops across the land, influencing millions of dollars that changed hands every week. It was a lucrative prospect and its possibilities were mind-boggling. The DJs literally could make or break an artist's career, his recording's sales and his publisher's future. The decisions were enormously potent.

Music historiographer Leo Walker summarized what subsequently happened.[3]

> The subject got much additional publicity as time went along, with the climax coming in 1959. Investigation of the quiz shows on television gathered radio and the disc jockeys up in its momentum, and shook them around, too. "Payola," a word with far-reaching connotations, but actually coined many years earlier, was now in standard usage by the public in general. Yet the same public sat back and looked on with only lukewarm interest as attempts were made to prove that many of the nation's top disc jockeys had a good thing going for themselves with an under-the-table arrangement to see that the right discs were programmed....
>
> Not a great deal came of the "payola" investigation except to cast a reflection on the innocent along with those who may have been guilty.

With all due respect, some of the nation's better-known DJs were caught in the quagmire and their services promptly terminated. While a pall of gloom was shed over the innocent victims of the debacle, the loss of job and reputation was undoubtedly pretty demoralizing to those who experienced it.

Possibly no more visible scapegoat in the payola crisis can be found than the popular New York broadcaster Alan Freed, who was also affectionately known as "Moon Dog." His situation is indicative of the extent of the toxins that infiltrated the system, casting unfavorable light upon a profusion of its characters.

Freed was a native of Johnstown, Pennsylvania, born December 15, 1922. When Manhattan's powerful station WINS became the first of Gotham's outlets to succeed with a rock 'n' roll format, Freed was pried away from Cleveland's WJW to spearhead its new drive. Premiering over WINS on September 6, 1954, he not only turned adolescents in that major metropolis onto rock 'n' roll but also the teens in 60 other markets as well by way of a syndicated rocking radio series. For an hour at 4 o'clock each weekday afternoon, Freed reigned supreme over the WINS airwaves. And every night at 11 o'clock he returned to the microphone with another three hours of his rock 'n' roll beat.

In March 1956, just 18 months after Freed's arrival in the Big Apple, CBS felt enough confidence in the trendy musical fad then sweeping the nation to add a half-hour Saturday night youth-oriented bash to its TV agenda. Labeled *Rock 'n' Roll Dance Party*, it featured Freed and co-host Count Basie, who earlier was a prominent big band musician. The video series spotlighted current teen idols including The Drifters, Fats Domino, Joe Turner and The Moonglows. By all accounts Freed was one of the medium's future breed of true "stars" in thousands of towns, large and small.

While *American Bandstand* had been on local TV in Philadelphia since its inception in 1952 — and was destined to have far greater impact on the nation's youth in decades to come — it didn't debut to a national TV audience until August 1957, nearly a year and a half after Freed's launch on the tube. Until that juncture he was very possibly in a better position to influence many more of America's younger citizens than anybody else.

But Freed fell from his lofty perch in a hurry. On June 2, 1958, he switched from WINS to New York's WABC after WINS temporarily suspended him for allegedly provoking a racial riot in Boston at a rock 'n' roll festival. Not long after that — while continuing his radio contract with WABC — he also signed with WABD-TV (which was soon renamed WNEW-TV) as host of *Alan Freed's Big Beat Party*. This hour-long weekday afternoon dance marathon would quickly rival *American Bandstand* for the teenagers' loyalty in the environs of New York.

But regrettably, Freed may have become a victim of his own success.

In late November 1959 he was fired by both the New York radio and television outlets that concurrently employed him. His refusal to sign a statement that he hadn't engaged in receiving payola got him canned. In a fleeting moment his fame and fortune evaporated, while the frenzy that he had been so instrumental in crafting was left to others to propel.

"In the end, no deejays were packed off to prison, but the broad brush wielded by the investigators ruined the careers of dozens and dozens of radio disc jockeys," a critic confirmed. "The best-known deejay, Alan Freed, would be the best-known casualty. He never recovered and died both broke and broken-hearted." He passed away January 20, 1965, in Palm Springs, California.

A few scholars intimated that the root of the payola dilemma might be directly traced to the dictates of the very overbearing and powerful leader of the American Federation of Musicians (AFM), James Caesar Petrillo. In a mid–1942 ultimatum, Petrillo banned recording companies from using AFM musicians unless the production firms guaranteed that their discs would *not* be played in jukeboxes or on the air. Does this theme have a familiar ring? It's only a slight variation from the earlier gridlock encountered by the Philadelphia station airing records nearly two decades earlier. But in this not-quite-instant replay it carried the exposed teeth of a tenacious union leader who was simultaneously taking action on several fronts to protect his musicians.

Again the courts ruled that the recordmakers had no control over their releases after the discs were purchased. Instead, Petrillo's directive had the effect of actually preventing recordings from being made. "In a period when the spirit and morale of our nation needs music," Edward Wallerstein, the Columbia Records head responded, "Mr. Petrillo's edict seems particularly ill-considered and ill-timed. The American people will be deprived of enjoying great artists and fine music."

That didn't faze the musicians' arbitrator. Even when President Franklin D. Roosevelt intervened in the controversy, Petrillo refused to budge. As a result, disc jockeys on small stations were severely hit. The all-pervasive decree required that new songs be played "live" or not at all.

The major record producers stood their ground for more than two years, until late autumn 1944, in fact, before submitting to Petrillo's demands. When they finally did, they had to cough up a payment for every record and duplication of a record made by an AFM member. The fees stretched from a quarter of a cent for each 35-cent phonograph disc to a nickel for each $5 album, plus a fixed fee from all jukebox vendors. Surprisingly, no penalties were levied on radio. Petrillo felt that the collection of the prescribed sums—aimed squarely at the production houses—could generate enough income to compensate the musicians' union for its previously unsettled donations to American entertainment. He was probably right: the union coffers immediately swelled by $4 million annually.

In reference to the payola puzzle, one authority professed: "It's just possible the stand taken by the head of the Musicians Union [Petrillo] set the stage for it." The implication suggested that—in order to recover the huge payout being made to the AFM—the recording industry turned to payola to achieve it. Whether that's a proper interpretation is subject to conjecture. The fact that greasing those palms significantly inflated record sales is pretty defenseless, however.

There were other legitimate concerns of a legal nature that deeply impacted the radio DJs in the performance of their duties. One of the more discernible, occurring in the early 1940s, inculcated the business with some lasting consequences. It swirled around the American Society of Composers, Authors and Publishers (ASCAP), which licensed the stations to transmit its music.

In 1940, that auspicious group banned playing music on the airwaves that its members had created unless the stations airing it paid a handsome fee for the privilege. In essence, the body was collecting royalties on its work. No harm in that, some stations (especially many larger ones) reasoned. There wasn't unanimous acceptance of the idea, however. New York's WJZ, for one, unapologetically refused to kowtow to the stipulation and in so doing turned down the right to air copyrighted melodies proffered by ASCAP.

A pundit assessed the dilemma: "If the broadcasting choice was narrowed to the few bits of music in public domain, it would neither satisfy the majority of listeners nor encourage big-money advertisers to sponsor programs. Obviously, some degree of cooperation with ASCAP was essential to commercial broadcasting. Outright compatibility, however, was hit and miss."

Lawsuits and countersuits filled courtroom dockets in the 1920s and 1930s with reference to what could be played on the ether and what couldn't, and whether money was to change hands if it *was* permissible and if so, *how much*. Some federation officials apparently spent about as much time at the hall of justice as they did the union meeting halls. Radio stations ultimately had to comply with a basic ASCAP monetary obligation while forking over added sums that covered performance rights every time a copyrighted song aired.

Parenthetically, this author well remembers from the 1950s his initial exposure to a program manifest at a time-news-temperature station in a state capital city that primarily favored live chatter between recorded platters with little else. Visiting the studio during an evening air shift, the author was struck by the fact the DJ on duty followed a precise outline developed by others on the station's staff during the daylight hours. It specified the exact minute when a preselected tune was to be aired while naming the artists and the unions represented. It furthermore designated which commercials were to be queued up for airing and when. To this greenhorn, it was an eye-opening disclosure. Here was a permanent hard copy register of what was being broadcast. It was helpful not just in keeping track of the commercials transmitted but in verifying the music, too, in order for proper assessments to be paid to the copyright owners.

The National Association of Broadcasters (NAB), formed in the 1920s, was instituted largely to deflect the challenges imposed on its affiliates by the ASCAP. When those burdens became so great that the NAB could no longer abide them (including a contractual dispute that intended to double ASCAP's receipts to a whopping $9 million annually), the NAB created its own performance rights alliance, Broadcast Music, Inc. (BMI). Beginning January 1, 1941, ASCAP's music virtually disappeared from the networks and many local outlets after far more favorable financial transactions were negotiated with BMI.

"The American public accepted the inroads of such music without missing a beat," reported one source. "The average dial twister appeared unconcerned. Neither outpourings of protest nor picket lines vexed the 674 radio stations that had broken with ASCAP. A *Variety* poll in Philadelphia in mid–January typified the country's indifference. The overwhelming majority had not noticed any change in musical programs."

Yet when the smallest of the networks, Mutual — particularly minuscule in light of its contributions to the union's treasury — caved in, resuming a relationship with ASCAP in late spring 1941, the door was cracked for others to enter. By summer's end, new agreements acceptable to both the NAB and ASCAP had been hammered out and signed. BMI, meanwhile, remained in place and continues today, still offering a healthy alternative to ASCAP's virtual ironclad monopoly during those early confrontational days. The listeners as well as the music providers have undoubtedly come out the winners as a result of the increased competition.

Despite all the legal wrangling, there could be little doubt as to the potential influence of music on the masses in disparate dimensions. It had been that way since the inception of radio, of course, to an extent. But as the music became more prevalent, it became more prominent. A survey toward the close of the 1950s purported that American adolescent females spent $432 million annually on party food. The middle-class, early baby boom generation obviously valued revelry. Teens loved to dance and they were radio addicts. They had their own language, their own clothes and — for the first time for that age group — their very own music. Before them teens had listened to music with their parents, primarily big bands and crooners, now passé. In their collective fumbling for identity status, they found record store bins bulging with discs from a previously unrecognized source, black performers. The affections of the nation's melody-lovers were about to receive a big transfusion.

Valid documentation exists concerning the shifting preferences of America's tuneful tastes during the period.

The retail disc best sellers list for July 1940 published in *Billboard* was composed of these 10 titles and artists:

1. *I'll Never Smile Again*— Tommy Dorsey
2. *The Breeze and I*— Jimmy Dorsey
3. *Imagination*— Glenn Miller
4. *Playmates*— Kay Kyser
5. *Fools Rush In*— Glenn Miller
6. *Where Was I?*— Charlie Barnet
7. *Pennsylvania 6-5000*— Glenn Miller
8. *Imagination*— Tommy Dorsey

9. *Sierra Sue*— Bing Crosby
10. *Make Believe Island*— Mitchell Ayers

A decade later, *Billboard's* best-selling pop singles for the week ending September 1, 1950, were no longer dominated by the big bands but often by vocalists:

1. *Goodnight, Irene*— Gordon Jenkins and The Weavers
2. *Mona Lisa*— Nat King Cole
3. *Play a Simple Melody*— Gary and Bing Crosby
4. *Sam's Song*— Gary and Bing Crosby
5. *Tzena, Tzena, Tzena*— Gordon Jenkins and The Weavers
6. *Bonaparte's Retreat*— Kay Starr
7. *Can Anyone Explain?*— The Ames Brothers
8. *No Other Love*— Jo Stafford
9. *Nola*— Les Paul
10. *Count Every Star*— Hugo Winterhalter

A decade after that, not a single dance band recording could be found among the top 40 selections nominated by the nation's disc jockeys as their most requested tunes. For the week ending April 2, 1960, the Hollywood DJ powerhouse, KFWB, released this list of its favored top 10:

1. *Theme from a Summer Place*— Percy Faith
2. *Wild One*— Bobby Rydell
3. *Puppy Love*— Paul Anka
4. *Sweet Nothin's*— Brenda Lee
5. *Clementine*— Bobby Darin
6. *He'll Have to Go*— Jim Reeves
7. *Starbright*— Johnny Mathis
8. *Step by Step*— The Crests
9. *Hully Gully*— The Olympics
10. *Greenfields*— The Brothers Four

By the early 1950s, the jukebox, reliably cited as the prime band-building vehicle of the early 1940s, was replaced by the disc jockey as the foremost means of keeping dance music alive. By 1954, *Billboard* was proclaiming the rock 'n' roll DJ the "undisputed king of local radio programming." The DJ "had slowly taken over radio during the late forties, and now had it all to himself," a reviewer insisted. At that juncture, all-night DJ shows were standard fare in every major market and they obliterated whatever late-night band remotes had previously existed, turning the darkened airwaves into a protracted volley of recorded melody.

As their professional careers were drawing to a close, some of those individuals who would forever be remembered as fronts for a few of the nation's major big band outfits, laid down their batons and picked up earphones. For a while, at least, several of their number would resort to platter spinning, just like the individuals who had so recently ferreted away those same maestros' livelihoods. There in the trenches at Platterland they labored side by side.

Among them: Del Courtney (a particularly enterprising fellow who spun records on a San Francisco Bay station days and still conducted a band in nearby dance halls at night), plus no less than Tommy Dorsey, Benny Goodman, Joe Reichman, Jack Teagarden, Ted Weems and — lo and behold — Paul Whiteman himself! The man who in the 1920s had so vehemently protested airing phonograph records took a turn as a DJ a couple of decades further down the road. *The Paul Whiteman Record Club* (aka *The Human Side of the Record*) debuted over ABC for an hour weekday afternoons on June 30, 1947. One commentator shared this opinion of Whiteman's newborn occupation.[4]

Whiteman proved the ideal personality for the job. Not only did he have an extensive and first-hand knowledge of popular music, but also a long and close association with most of the country's leading singers and musicians. Ethel Merman, Mel Torme, and Guy Lombardo appeared as guests on the *Paul Whiteman Club*....

Whiteman had introduced dozens of tunes and compositions as far back as the 1920s. Playing recordings of songs he had helped to popularize now filled many hours of air time. He also had acquired an almost inexhaustible fund of stories about these works. Little-known anecdotes about *Whispering*, *Avalon*, and *Rhapsody in Blue*; facts on composers Buddy De Sylva, Ferde Grofe, and George Gershwin; backstage stories on vocalists Bing Crosby, Mildred Bailey, Morton Downey, and musicians Henry Busse, the Dorsey Brothers, and Jack Teagarden attracted major sponsors for the ABC series over 228 stations.

The show lasted a year, obviously underscoring the fact the impresario had made his peace with the opposition camp. (It was, after all, a paying job!)

In addition to the bandleaders, stars like comedienne Jane Ace (1951-1952, NBC) and singers Eddie Cantor (1951–1954, NBC), Tennessee Ernie Ford (1952-1953, ABC) and Frank Sinatra (1950-1951, CBS) turned up at the studio turntables hosting record shows, often interviewing celebrities between turns.

While one observer acknowledged, "Big names generally did not make good disc jockeys," there were still a few on various New York outlets who enjoyed moderate to substantial success in their newly acquired roles. Andre Baruch and Bea Wain (WMCA), Duke Ellington (WMCA), Ted Husing (WHN), Kate Smith and Ted Collins (WOR), Leopold Stokowski (WNBC) and Rudy Vallee (WOR) slipped confidently into air chairs.

Several fairly nondescript network DJ series emerged in this period, some headlined by moderately recognized individuals and others that went nameless. With few exceptions—which are duly noted—most surfaced over the Mutual chain: *The Two Ton Baker Show* (1948-1949), *Dunn on Discs* (1949-1950), *The Wayne Howell Show* (1950-1951, NBC), *Mert's Record Adventures* (1951-1952), *Off and On the Record* (1952-1953), *The Mac McGuire Show* (1952–1954), *Walter Preston's Show Shop* (1952–1954), *The Big Preview* (1953-1954, NBC), *The Fred Robbins Show* (1953-1954), *The National Juke Box* (1955-1956, ABC), *The National Radio Fan Club* (1955-1956, NBC), *Lucky Pierre* (1955-1956).

There were several radio competitions in which phonograph records were rated on the air, sort of veiled DJ shows. Certainly the best known was *Your Hit Parade*, which for two decades relied upon its own evaluative findings that had been determined by sheet music and record sales, song requests at dance halls and ballrooms and the like. (See separate chapter.) Lesser known was the panel-rating series *Platterbrains*, a sustaining program that appeared on ABC from 1953 to 1956 hosted by jazz critic Leonard Feather. There a panel offered its "expert opinion" of contemporary record releases.

Not very many network radio programs had their inceptions on television. A few did, nevertheless, including at least one disc jockey series. Peter Potter's *Juke Box Jury*, a CBS Saturday night entry in the dual 1954–1956 radio seasons, had already been acclimated by a six-month stint over ABC-TV on Sunday nights in 1953-1954. The West Coast–based show drew celebrities from the film, radio, recording, stage and television fraternities. Each week they formed a guest panel that rated soon-to-be-released records performed by vocalists or musical combos. A live studio audience participated in the voting, determining if a new tune would be a "hit" (signified by a "bong" sound) or a "miss" (followed by a "clunk").

Potter was by that time an old hand at introducing phonograph records, having initiated *Peter Potter's Platter Parade* over Hollywood's KFWB in 1948 and hosting a similar show over Los Angeles' KLAC in 1954. He drew heavily upon West Coast pop idols as resident experts. For his first CBS outing, the panel included actresses Mitzi Gaynor and Ann Sheridan, radio and television host Art Linkletter and actor Robert Wagner. Potter's series continued on Los Angeles TV after it was no longer available to nationwide audiences, although a syndicated version was produced in 1959 for the small screen.

One of the more unusual radio disc jockey departures can be attributed to a pair of the golden age's most resilient, brilliant and admired characters, *Amos 'n' Andy*. Their straight comedy sketches debuted over Chicago's WMAQ on March 19, 1928, joining the NBC lineup on August 19, 1929. (On January 12, 1926, the Anglo-American comedic actors posing as those blackface figures — Freeman Gosden (Amos Jones) and Charles Correll (Andrew H. Brown) — originally trotted out their hilarity as *Sam 'n' Henry* over Chicago's WGN.)

The duo became such an instant, continuous hit that they never left NBC or CBS for more than three decades. Radio historiographer John Dunning termed theirs "the most popular radio show of all time" and claimed that, at its peak, the program "held the hearts and minds of the American people as nothing did before or [has] since." In time, Gosden and Correll's early dialogue turned into one of the most captivating situation comedies on the air, lasting through May 22, 1955. There was also an unsuccessful attempt to present them on television in the 1951–1953 seasons by employing black actors. But their riotous antics didn't translate well there.

And how are they connected with disc jockeying? The pair's final network series, *The Amos 'n' Andy Music Hall*, was little short of a glorified DJ program. It ran five nights weekly over CBS in varying 20- to 45-minute time slots between September 13, 1954, and November 25, 1960. Elizabeth McLeod, an authoritative old-time radio buff who has made *Amos 'n' Andy* her principal study, claims the *Music Hall* was essentially a show "done out of necessity." McLeod described the circumstances like this.[5]

CBS had invested a huge amount of money in buying out Correll and Gosden, and needed to do something to recover as much of that investment as they could.

They paid $2.5 million to buy all rights to the property, and had expected that revenue from an *A&A* TV series would cover that outlay, basing their projections on an anticipated seven-year network run for the TV show. But the series lasted only two seasons, leaving the network desperate not to end up losing money on the deal. Added to that, even though the weekly radio series was still a ratings leader, Rexall Drug Company dropped out as sponsor in 1954, ending the revenue from that source. So the *Music Hall* was devised as something that could be produced with very little additional expenditure, and could be sold on a participating sponsorship basis, maximizing revenue.

Correll and Gosden had no creative involvement in the series — it was written and produced by Joe Connelly and Bob Mosher on a shoestring budget — and C&G's only role in the production was to come in once or twice a week to tape their inserts. The music and "simulated audience reaction" would then be spliced into the master tape. There was generally no more than 10 minutes of actual A&A dialogue in each program, with the rest taken up by recorded music and guest-star interviews.

The A&A material tended to be extremely generic — the Kingfish acted as master of ceremonies, with Amos 'n' Andy joining him in "The Grand Ballroom of the Mystic Knights of the Sea Lodge Hall." They would introduce each record with a few short comments about the song or the artist, and occasionally work in a low-key joke or two. Some programs would come up with a running-gag theme to tie the continuity together, and occasionally the newly recorded material might be supplemented by excerpts clipped from past *A&A* sitcom episodes.

In other words, it was a cut-and-paste job from start to finish, and sounded like it. But what made it work was the likeability of Correll and Gosden's characters—they were such a familiar part of the American landscape, and had been for so long, that even in this reduced form they were able to hold an audience. The series basically coasted on the familiarity of these characters up until CBS finally pulled the plug as part of the same across-the-board programming purge that killed the last soap operas [which occurred on the same day].

One amusing footnote: In 1957 a *TV-Radio Mirror* reader poll named George "Kingfish" Stevens "the most popular disc jockey in America." Gosden seemed genuinely bemused over the award but accepted it good-naturedly.

The professional critics almost universally disparaged the boys' "final act." One referred to it as a "watered-down disc jockey show," but claimed the "embarrassing" *Music Hall* didn't negate the fact that they had at one time been "a great show." Another depicted the *Music Hall* as "sterile, stilted.... It was sad."

If a vote were taken among those who recall the names of some of the more prominent disc jockeys of the aural airwaves, near or occupying the top of almost everybody's list would likely be the name of Martin Block. Possibly he more than any other single individual breathed life into the genre, popularizing it early in the nation's largest market and—for a short while—exposing listeners all over America to his brand of platter chatter. Both Block and his mentor, Al Jarvis, who ruled the airwaves at Hollywood's KFWB for many years, laid claim to coining the term *Make Believe Ballroom*. Both adopted the title for programs they each hosted on stations situated 3,000 miles apart. Block would also use the appellation for a national DJ series.

Some scholars leave the matter of originating that name to speculation. Yet there is ample evidence that Jarvis was the instigator of the inspired moniker. Both Jarvis and Block earned still more identification with it by jointly starring in a 1949 Hollywood movie titled *Make Believe Ballroom*. The film underscored the power and effect of the disc jockey on the music industry. It featured substantial footage of the bands of Charlie Barnet, Jimmy Dorsey, Jan Garber, Pee Wee Hunt, Gene Krupa and Ray McKinley. Also in that celluloid production were vocalists Nat King Cole, Frankie Laine, Jack Smith and Kay Starr.

Jarvis, who was to become a U.S. citizen, was born on America's Independence Day, July 4, in 1909 in Russia. A quarter of a century later (1934) he was spinning records over the airwaves of Warner Brothers' station KFWB in Los Angeles. His show emanated from an "imaginary" dance hall complete with audience applause and his vivid descriptions of invented dancers and musicians. It was truly the original *Make Believe Ballroom* and he would be cited in the decades ahead as "the first real disc jockey" as the idiom is defined in modern broadcasting.

The show's intent was to "create in the minds of the dialers the illusion that they are skimming across the dance floor.... Wisecrack in between numbers in the manner of an emcee," he recalled later from his proposal to station management seeking innovative program ideas. Until then, announcers playing recorded music penitently avowed, "The next song will be by phonograph record." But Jarvis, apparently well versed in timely Federal Communications Commission dictates, noted that a mere disclaimer that a program was *totally* derived from recordings was sufficient, as opposed to a repetitive assertion before each tune.

"I came up with the format for the *Make Believe Ballroom*, a program consisting of four revolving bandstands.... It wasn't very long before Bing Crosby himself would call up and ask me to spin a few," said Jarvis. He applied sound effects records for crowd noises and applause while ad-libbing the song intros and other patter. He harvested current intelligence about the musicians by consistently devouring articles in *Billboard* and *Variety*.

An innovative Jarvis would have a hand in boosting the careers of such music luminaries as Nat King Cole, Benny Goodman, Lionel Hampton, Frankie Laine and Andre Previn, while launching Betty White's television start. One of the first video disc jockeys, Jarvis premiered the West Coast's original TV teen dance show. His death occurred on April 23, 1970.

Despite the fact that Jarvis was of paramount influence on Block — a protégé serving alongside his tutor on the West Coast who was referred to by one observer as "an assistant to Al Jarvis" — it was Block who may have done more to establish the public's perception of the disc jockey than anybody else. He appeared over New York's WNEW in 1935 just as the big band epoch was taking off.

"Instead of playing a hodgepodge of discs, he broke his show into fifteen-minute segments and programmed his records, as did the networks with their 'live' music," a historiographer of the genre explained. "Block was soon giving listeners a quarter hour of Benny Goodman, then Lombardo, followed by fifteen minutes of Eddy Duchin and Glen Gray. It was almost a photocopy of the pattern Al Jarvis had originated a year before. Audiences liked Block's suave, musically informed manner and his interest-holding material, ranging from Nat Cole to Spike Jones."

Block became widely recognized and well respected for his insightful commentary on the prospects of each recording that he delivered between tunes. Habitually he conducted a competition that pitted some of the prominent bands against one another, a popularity poll among listeners to allow them to choose their favorites. For several years Glenn Miller's outfit occupied that coveted spot. But in 1941 Tommy Dorsey's orchestra overtook its rival, being succeeded in 1942 by Harry James' aggregate. Winning such a prestigious census certainly held the prospect of netting increased premium billings and escalating fees for a band.

In the meantime, Block gained such notoriety that numerous major market stations routinely sent their DJs to New York to check out WNEW's operation in a concerted effort to pattern themselves after Block and his cohorts. In time he would transfer his allegiance from WNEW to WOR and to WABC in the Big Apple.

Block was such a powerful force in the medium that he became one of only a handful of disc jockeys to gain his own nationwide show. Undoubtedly more listeners from that era still recall his *Make Believe Ballroom* than any other DJ feature. It surfaced over MBS for an hour five afternoons a week in 1947-1948. Following a lapse (while several other DJs infiltrated the national airwaves), Block returned to the microphone in 1953-1954 for a Saturday afternoon fling over MBS. During the next two seasons he was once again heard weekday afternoons, this time on ABC, occupying a 90-minute midafternoon slot.

"Block was the epitome of jocks anywhere," ascribed a partisan. "A deep, smooth, easily identifiable voice. Intelligent, convincing commercials, and a thorough knowledge of the music business made Block a standout."

When he liked something he gave it his best shot. In 1938, he introduced the Andrews Sisters, then largely unknown, who performed their new Decca recording of an old Jewish melody, *Bei Mir Bist du*

Schoen, on his program. He was so taken with the tune and the artists that he promoted the record into the ground. It was an overnight hit and gave the Andrews Sisters instant acclaim, eventually leading to their becoming one of the best recognized feminine vocal groups in entertainment history.

In 1951, Block and more than two dozen contemporaries appeared in yet another full-length motion picture based on their profession, this one simply titled *Disc Jockey*. It starred singer-actress Ginny Simms, a big name in radio in the 1940s (see chapter on The Vocalists), and Michael O'Shea. Many well-established musicians also appeared as themselves, including Tommy Dorsey, Russ Morgan, Red Nichols, Red Norvo, Ben Pollack, Sarah Vaughn and Joe Venuti.

Born in Los Angeles on February 3, 1903, Block returned to California in the mid–1940s, recording his shows for WNEW several days in advance. He purchased a small ranch at Encino but continued to play a major role in disc jockey programming on both coasts and across the nation. He died in California on September 18, 1967. A pundit summarized his extensive career as "a power unparalleled to this day among New York jockeys."

There were other DJs whose stars may not have shone quite as brightly as Block's but who achieved some distinction in that fold on their own merit. Just who were those smooth-talking, silver-tongued spinmeisters? Several from both the big chains and the far-flung locales in the hinterlands are introduced as representative of the legions comprising their renowned alliance. A cursory glance at their lives will supply an overview of how some of the more durable disc jockeys performed.

Probably the most famous name among disc jockeys was Martin Block. His reputation drew hordes of contemporaries wanting to copy his style. His *Make Believe Ballroom* had a huge following and he spawned respectability for DJs everywhere, fostering a genre that would succeed for a while after radio's actors and comedians became history.

Bob Poole may have broadcast more network hours than anybody else. His *Poole's Paradise*, heavy on the humor ("Hi there my little chickadees"), became a MBS daytime staple in the 1948–1952 quadrennial. His airtime ranged between mid- and late-morning hours to a midafternoon slot. He often did two network shows a day with a

Saturday afternoon half-hour added some of the time. Poole featured telephone quizzes along with his banter, and the joy in his voice was evocative of a happy, hasty Raymond of *Inner Sanctum* fame. Most of Poole's shows were sustaining or jointly sponsored by participating advertisers. He was among the DJs who turned up in the 1951 motion picture *Disc Jockey*. Born November 25, 1917, Poole died in March 1978.

Robert Q. Lewis may be best recalled as second banana to Arthur Godfrey on that redoubtable entertainer's CBS weekday morning series when Godfrey took annual summer sabbaticals in the late 1940s and throughout the 1950s. A comedian by trade, Lewis also gained notice in his own right as host of a few TV series (*The Show Goes On, The Robert Q. Lewis Show, Robert Q's Matinee, The Name's the Same*) and — more germane to our topic — as an inveterate disc jockey. His *Waxworks* series over CBS from 1951 to 1953 (initially three nights a week, later Saturday mornings) gave listeners a chance to revel in his wit between platters. He presided over more than a dozen CBS Radio features, many titled by his own name, and several on which he played records and conferred with guests about them. It was obvious Lewis was a DJ at heart, and a mirthful one at that.

Born in Manhattan on April 25, 1921, he was discovered "running wild" on a local New York station "theoretically handling a disc jockey's chores," *Radio Album* reported in 1948. While earlier studying dramatics at the University of Michigan, he tried his hand at the turntables of a Detroit station and found it to his liking. *TV Radio Mirror* encapsulated: "As a disc jockey, he was a natural." The quipster's snappy asides usually left listeners rollicking, turning what might otherwise have been serious stuff into trivialized fluff. He never became a major star of radio or television but seemed comfortable as temporary relief for Godfrey, Bud Collyer, Bing Crosby, Jackie Gleason, Ed Sullivan and other celebs. As such, he was considered the quintessential substitute host.

When, as Lewis informed *TV Guide* in the late 1960s, "My relaxed, easygoing format just went out of vogue," he departed Gotham, seeking his fortune in the California sun. There he found another disc jockey post and continued spinning records, which took him back to his broadcast origins. The bespectacled man with the droll wit and impish gleam died on December 11, 1993.

Eddie Gallaher had the good fortune of making a name for himself in a single market for more than half a century, one of few DJs to accomplish it. Some contend that he was the premier disc jockey in the nation's capital, airing on a succession of stations from 1947 to 2000. The native Washingtonian was born February 27, 1915. He launched his life's work at 24 over Tulsa, Oklahoma's KTUL in 1938, then moved to Minneapolis' WCCO. By 1947, he was back in his hometown, a city where he would spend the rest of his days.

Starting at the top (WTOP), filling a vacancy on the CBS affiliate's DJ staff that Arthur Godfrey had relinquished for more lucrative pastures at the network in New York, Gallaher remained at that prestigious address until it adopted a news-and-information format in 1968. At WTOP he took over Godfrey's early morning *Sundial* program and added *Moondial* to his resume, a late-night disc jockey series. Celebrities passing through the nation's capital often sought him out for interviews. He commanded tremendous respect and achieved widespread notoriety.

Willard Scott, part of Gallaher's local radio competition in those days (on NBC's outlet WRC, 1955–1972) and later an NBC-TV weatherman, attested: "He could read a phone book and make it sound good. He was incredible.... And even when he was 140 ... he sounded like he was 25 years old again!" Gallaher provided an answer to a newspaperman inquiring the secret of his dulcet-toned inflection: "I gargle with Drano," the baritone replied.

Although Gallaher initially played big band music, "he was never trapped by that format," wrote a Washington columnist. At one point the scribe portrayed Gallaher's fare as "a goulash of oldies, standards and alternative rock.

"Eddie Gallaher was not comfortable around the likes of Springsteen," said he. "Yet his voice had a smile built into it, like the voice of every great radio talent. He didn't look down on the music he was given to play. He always kept in mind that someone out there liked it — and didn't want his morning ruined by a wiseguy who disdained his favorites."

He branched beyond the turntables at WTOP, adding sportscasting for the Washington Redskins to his inventory, providing aural coverage in 1955-1956 and video coverage on WTOP-TV from 1957 to 1965. Returning to his radio roots, in 1968 Gallaher took up residence as a DJ at Washington's WASH-FM followed by WWDC in 1982. He retired from the latter station (subsequently labeled WGAY) on December 22, 2000, 62 years after entering the business. In his last couple of years on the air, station management provided helpers who read copy for him and assisted with his program. Gallaher died in Washington on November 26, 2003.

In the summers of 1954, 1955 and 1956, CBS Radio temporarily added Gallaher to its New York staff as host of a live-and-recorded music series saturating much of the network's Sunday afternoon agenda during the warm months. Typically, in June, July and August from about 2:30 until 5 o'clock — with occasional interruptions for five-minute Chevrolet-sponsored newscasts with Allan Jackson, Larry LeSueur or Robert Trout — Gallaher presided over a sterling marathon of pop and classical selections.

At the start of each portion, he'd exclaim: "Hello everybody! This is Eddie Gallaher inviting you to join us ... *On a Sunday Afternoon!*" Accenting the last four words, the show's title, the greeting was instantly followed by a resounding cut of *Summertime Is Summertime* performed by an orchestra and chorus directed by Vincent Travers. The stirring arrangement was from a recording of the Broadway stage production of Booth Tarkington's *Seventeen*.

On a Sunday Afternoon featured music by artists with familiar names from the operatic stage, singers from motion pictures and radio and television vocalists. While most of the program's melody emanated from turntables, interspersed by Gallaher's informed annotations, every show was augmented by a huge CBS staff orchestra conducted by resident impresario Alfredo Antonini. The combination of musical tastes and sources resulted in an inspired reverie for those summertime weekend matinees.

John Richbourg was the patron saint of rhythm and blues below the Mason-Dixon line. For three decades his legendary commercials for Ernie's Record Mart in Memphis reverberated across mammoth territory. But it was his choice of music that dignified him among fans who tuned in six nights a week, awaiting his trademark salutation, "This is John R. comin' at ya from way down south in Dixie."

The Anglo-American DJ spun recordings of primarily African-American musicians over the extensive reaches of the 50,000-watt Nashville CBS voice, WLAC. At the peak of his popularity in the 1950s he could count on an audience of 15 million listeners, more than many network shows of varying strains. Admirers writing to him — annually at his zenith he received a quarter of a million pieces of mail — often had difficulty spelling his name correctly. He got tons of letters addressed to "Richard Bug" and "John Are" after shortening his moniker to a simplified "John R."

Richbourg introduced scores of performers to the airwaves leading to national acclaim. Among others, he's credited with giving the following artists initial exposure to widespread audiences: Chuck Berry, James Brown, Bo Diddley, Aretha Franklin, Marvin Gaye, B. B. King, Gladys Knight, Little Richard (Penniman), Wilson Pickett, Otis Redding, Joe Simon, Joe Tex, Ike and Tina Turner, and Jackie Wilson.

At the midpoint of the twentieth century, the powerful implications of Richbourg's influence on the nation's musical preferences, and of a couple of his Nashville DJ buddies (Gene Nobles and Bill "Hoss" Allen), may be witnessed in an arresting appraisal.[6]

> In the early days of personality deejays, there were few in the country, especially among the white deejays, who could match the trio at WLAC for their selection of hot new rhythm-and-blues records, the power of their signal, the length of their broadcast day, and their ability to pitch products. They were the three kings of early rhythm-and-blues radio. When rock-'n'-roll emerged in its earliest incarnation as rhythm-and-blues played by whites, often with a strong rockabilly influence, they wouldn't have much to do with it. They generally preferred playing black artists unless their sponsors mandated otherwise. Even though they professed disdain for rock-'n'-roll, in truth Gene Nobles, John R., and Hoss Allen had everything to do with it. They opened the door.
>
> They were one wild bunch, the legendary three deejay boys of WLAC. Starting in the mid- to late 1940s, these white men played black records for an audience of blacks and whites.... John R. was the best known and the most beloved ... with a voice that sounded like every listener's closest friend, black or white....
>
> Because few other stations of such power were on as late as WLAC, Richbourg's show [from 1 to 3 A.M.] was incredibly influential. Other late-night deejays around the country tuned their radio to John R. while they were driving home from work. Musicians did the same while packing up and hitting the road from one gig to the next.

John Richbourg was born in Manning, South Carolina, on August 20, 1910. For a dozen years he pursued acting as a career. In New York City, his attempts on the stage plainly weren't celebratory and he found more promise in radio. For a while he played in dramatic roles on daytime serials like *Lorenzo Jones, Our Gal Sunday* and *Second Husband* and occasionally on nighttime series like *Gangbusters*. Deciding to try his luck in the medium nearer home, in 1941 he returned to his native South Carolina and landed a job as a newscaster at Charleston's WMTA. A year later he was reading the news four times daily as the *Esso Reporter* at Nashville's WLAC.

In 1943, he joined the Navy, returning to WLAC in 1947 to deliver news and fill in for Gene Nobles on the latter's rhythm-and-blues DJ show. Richbourg soon merited the slot that gained him his fame. A quarter of a century later, preferring to retire rather than play rock 'n' roll music as management insisted, he quit on August 1, 1973. Richbourg died in Nashville February 15, 1986. Few in the industry had held the pivotal role he did in initiating the direction recorded music took.

Kurt Webster is another Southerner who wielded substantial influence over the musical tastes of an immense portion of the nation in the 1940s. In at least one case, the all-night DJ (on *The Midnight Dance Party*) over Charlotte's powerful 50,000-watt WBT, also a CBS affiliate, figured in determining what all of America heard.

Even CBS luminary Arthur Godfrey took note of it on his nationwide morning show when Webster "played the heck out of" *Heartaches*, a reissue of a 1933 instrumental recorded by Ted Weems (with Elmo

Tanner's whistling). Webster's popular nightcap series received so many phone calls for the disc in 1947 that he spun it nightly for a while. DJs in other markets took notice and added it to their own playlists. In six weeks, more than a half-million new pressings of the old disc were purchased. Webster was attributed with single-handedly reviving the tune and making it an overnight hit.

In the mid- to late 1940s, Webster was also the announcer for a quarter-hour CBS Sunday morning series featuring the gospel-harmonizing Johnson Family Singers. The Johnsons were a popular sextet performing regionally throughout the Carolinas and adjacent states from the 1930s to the 1950s.

Interestingly, Webster left his nighttime duties with WBT in the late 1940s to become a daytime audience participation host, an innovation he pursued for about a decade. As such he emceed two popular live features every morning over WBT just before and after Godfrey's 90-minute network program. On one of those — an hour-long potpourri of contests, interviews, music and banter titled *What's Cookin'?*— Webster chose for a theme song Ted Weems' *Heartaches*. It had, after all, extended the careers of at least *two* men.

Webster's radio career included a sportscasting stint at WBIR, Knoxville, Tennessee, before he went to Charlotte and a DJ series afterward at WAVY, Portsmouth, Virginia.

Art Ford is another New York disc jockey earning some eminence as one of Gotham's premier and most memorable radio voices. Born in New York City on April 15, 1921, he continued to reside in Manhattan as this was written (early 2004). The locals probably recall him best for *Milkman's Matinee*, an all-night WNEW series on which he spun platters for a dozen years (1942–1954) before shifting to daytime. He transferred from the confines of WNEW to nearby WNTA in 1957.

In the 1950s, Ford made several forays into television. As host of the interview series *Art Ford on Broadway* over ABC-TV in spring 1950, he talked with people behind the scenes at the Great White Way. *The Art Ford Show* (aka *In Record Time*) was a 1951 NBC-TV summer insert on NBC-TV. There he presided over a trio of guest disc jockeys from all over the nation who attempted to guess composers, singers and bands on the phonograph records he played. He also presented a performing artist with a "million seller recording." The series cited humanitarian, charitable and public service works of disc jockeys, too. Ever the DJ, in the late 1950s Ford hosted a local television series over WNTA-13 from the Mosque Theater in Newark called *Rate the Records*. It was in the vein of a plethora of like shows springing up around the nation. During the same decade he also produced and hosted the *Art Ford Jazz Party* on TV under the auspices of the Westinghouse Corporation.

Officials at NBC were attracted to Ford's authoritative inflection and easygoing style and cleverly cast him as one of its communicators (later, "hosts") on the epic weekend radio programming service, *Monitor*, when a vacancy opened in the late 1960s. In four- or three-hour segments, hosts presided over a grab-bag that embraced such diversions as spinning records, interviewing guests, introducing features and events on a wide range of topics that were picked up from anywhere around the globe. Of course, they also continually reminded listeners "This is Monitor ... going places and doing things!" and "You're on the Monitor beacon!"—cues that were invariably followed by an inimitable juxtaposition of "multifreq" tones unmistakably identifying the program as they reverberated up and down the scale. Art Ford was a natural for it. He seemed particularly adept when the series was given to accents on big bands, singers and their ilk, a sphere in which he specialized.

On a classic occasion in 1973 focusing on "Crooners, Spooners and Rockers," the convivial Ford interviewed several of the veterans of that bygone era whose hits he also played. They included singers Perry Como, Doris Day, Bob Eberle, Peggy Lee, Jack Leonard, Vaughn Monroe, Dinah Shore and Frank Sinatra. He featured several of the big bands, too—with headliners Les Brown, Jimmy and Tommy Dorsey, Benny Goodman, Ted Weems and more. It was a nostalgic reminiscence, and Ford was truly its *master* of ceremonies.

When *Monitor* spelled programs like that one, the host frequently urged his listeners to write in and tell him if they enjoyed the show. Ford wanted to know if his audience had lived through the early days of popular music and the vocalists who performed it or if they might be hearing that music for the first time. He compiled the responses to determine future programming fare. It was the mark of a practiced DJ.

Gene Rayburn was another of the *Monitor* strain (of which there were many) who launched a sterling career as a DJ. In Rayburn's case, he would go on to become one of television's most successful game show hosts.

Rayburn's association with *Monitor* dealt him the distinction of becoming the program's dean—its sturdiest and possibly (as the show's biographer intimates) "most-beloved" interlocutor. Debuting there in 1961, he remained with the program for the long haul, sticking around to 1974, turning with ease into its most durable communicator. "Rayburn's sassy, irreverent, 'I'm going to be naughty' type of presentation seemed perfect," declared the historian in an introspective about that unique broadcast service.

"Rayburn was extraordinarily well-qualified to ad-lib his way around a broadcast. He had spent years doing so—first, as a mainstay on WNEW Radio in New York, where he teamed up with Jack Lescoulie [1946] and later with Dee Finch on a morning show that some say created the drive-time formula still in use at stations around the nation. Rayburn and his partners played records and ad-libbed about anything that interested them."[7]

In 1952, he joined NBC Radio and headlined yet another early morning feature. He announced, read news bulletins and performed in sketches on the premiering *Tonight Show* in 1954 over NBC-TV hosted by comedian-musician Steve Allen. But an adoring public best recalls Rayburn for the TV game shows he suavely emceed, complete with lots of funny business. They included: *The Sky's the Limit* (1954, NBC), *Make the Connection* (1955, NBC), *Choose Up Sides* (1956, NBC), *Dough Re Mi* (1958–1960, NBC), *Tic Tac Dough* (1959, NBC), *Play Your Hunch* (1962, NBC), *The Match Game* (1962–1969, NBC; 1973–1979, CBS; 1975–1981, syndication; 1983-1984, NBC; 1985, syndication); *Snap Judgment* (1969, NBC), *The Amateur's Guide to Love* (1972, CBS), and *Break the $250,000 Bank* (1985, NBC). Unequivocally, his most noteworthy vehicle was *The Match Game* and its subsequent multiple incarnations.

Gene Rayburn was born with the given name of Eugene Rubessa on December 22, 1917, in Christopher, Illinois. He lived in Gloucester, Massachusetts, when death occurred on November 29, 1999.

In the Midwest, Howard Miller is one of those DJs whose versatile broadcast legacies survive him. Chuck Schaden, a nostalgia buff who has hosted a weekly Chicago old-time radio show for decades, cites Miller as "big, big, BIG in Chicago for many years." Miller rose to fame as a WIND disc jockey, where his career extended more than two decades.

Born December 17, 1912, by the time he reached his early twenties he had convinced officials of the Federal Communications Commission to issue him a license to establish a radio station in his hometown of Galesburg, Illinois. It was an omen of things to come for he would eventually acquire ownership of a string of small radio outlets throughout the Midwest. Once Miller had his first station, he occasionally filled in for sportscasters covering local basketball games, a task he accepted with gusto. After serving in the Navy in World War II, he went to Chicago, initially linking up with station WIND as program director. His earlier experience before a microphone, though brief, caused him to jettison his executive's post in favor of announcing. Soon he drifted into spinning discs.

In the years ahead, he served at several more stations in the Windy City including WCFL, WMAQ and WJJD. By the mid–1950s, he was doing a morning show on WIND, an afternoon show on WMAQ and — in between — a quarter-hour CBS network program five mornings a week (at 11:30 A.M. ET) from the studios of the local affiliate, WBBM. Not many local DJs got a shot at a national audience, of course — Miller's stint lasted almost five years, from July 18, 1955, through January 9, 1959. On *The Howard Miller Show* he introduced the soon-to-be hits just arriving in record stores everywhere, undoubtedly often providing the impetus that boosted disc sales and turned budding artists into proverbial pop idols.

In the 1970s, Miller transitioned from that busy endeavor into a controversial talk show host over Chicago powerhouse WGN. Described by friends as "a very compassionate man," he attempted to "right the wrongs" he witnessed in government excess, taxes, crime and other concerns with sweeping impact on society. He left a sizeable mark upon many who followed his crusades. Miller died November 8, 1994, in Naples, Florida.

There were many other disc jockeys whose names became familiar to audiences far and wide, either from their work in that province or the result of some added territory that made them permanently conspicuous. In many cases their broadcasting fame began as jocks, escalating to ancillary entertainment arenas. While their numbers are legion, a handful of the most notable includes Steve Allen (KNX, Hollywood), Ted Brown (WHN and WMGM, New York), Dick Clark (WFIL, Philadelphia), Bill Cullen (WNBC, New York), Arthur Godfrey (WJSV, Washington, D.C., and WCBS, New York), Durward Kirby (WFBM, Indianapolis), Jack Lescoulie (WOR, New York), Jim Lowe (WCBS, New York), Robert W. "Wolfman Jack" Smith (KWKH, Shreveport, and XERF, Via Cuncino, Mexico), and Jack Sterling (WCBS, New York).

By the late 1950s, there was a dramatic shift in the traditional composition of disc jockey formats that radio listeners had been accustomed to, until then exploited in countless markets by the so-called personality (or name) DJs. At that juncture, the Storz-owned string of outlets scattered about the country inaugurated what came to be commonly called "top-40 radio." Owner Todd Storz devised the model after observing the same tunes in a beer joint jukebox being repeated frequently by discriminating patrons. That bit of humanity's behavior was obviously not lost on him.

Storz pondered: wouldn't the results be similar if radio listeners were granted a choice? If everything else was equal except the playlists, he hypothesized, audiences would most likely pick the station that repetitively offered the songs they most wanted to hear over — say — a station that merely played records. Consequently, the limited top-40 hit list was born and spread like wildfire from the Storz-owned stations to hundreds of others.

Interestingly, there were tradeoffs once the new design was implemented. "In dictating to deejays what they could play, the top-forty format cut off the power source for the personality disc jockeys and, many believe, led to the dilution of the power of rock-'n'-roll," an observer alleged.[8]

Referring to the "Curse of the Top-Forty Format," he opined:

> Some of the biggest radio station chains around the country were ordering their deejays to play only the top forty hit records on their shows. The same forty songs over and over and over again.... It was taking most of the fun and nearly all of the muscle out of the job. Deejays at the top-forty factories didn't get to play what they wanted anymore.... This top-forty stuff was really cramping the lifestyle to which deejays had become accustomed.
>
> More threatening were the virtue vigilantes out there who saw rock-'n'-roll and the deejays who played it as threats to every image America held dear in the 1950s.... The country preferred to view itself as it was reflected in its shiny new mirror: television. The wild gyrations of teens dancing to that heavy beat, particularly white teens under the manipulations of black musicians, ran up hard against the well-controlled lily-white world portrayed on *Father Knows Best, Ozzie and Harriet,* and *Leave It to Beaver.*

The disc jockey had a lot more to contend with than simply cueing up the next number on the turntable.

While DJs would continue to dominate what Americans heard coming out of their radios in the 1960s, by the end of that decade their influence would be significantly reduced as a new wave of radio programming entered the arena, vying for the listeners' rapt attention. Many major stations simply stopped playing music one day and adopted a news-and-information format the next. It was the precursor of today's all-talk layout. The changes were finely tuned in the 1970s and by the 1980s hundreds of outlets in metropolises and hamlets were offering little more than opinions on every issue arguable. Music, which had ruled the roost when radio's golden age faded, now found itself taking a back seat to the far more pervasive talk show programs that flooded the dial.

Let's take a moment to look back on the era when the DJ became such a dominant force in the American airwaves. In some quarters, the disc jockeys are probably blamed for usurping the radio time that for decades had fostered comedy, drama, live music, mystery, serials, adventure tales, sports, interviews and all else that purists encountered during the medium's golden age and genuinely missed beyond it. Actually, in this author's view, the turntable spinners were blameless. They weren't the instigators—they were the inheritors. They didn't take the time away from the networks. Station owners and operators did, lobbying the big chains relentlessly through concerted efforts to capture more and more of each day's schedule for their own ends.

They could sell the time in their local markets far more profitably than when they relied on the trickle-down fractions of advertising revenue they received from the networks after the chains sold the time. For years the affiliate stations lobbied their networks to relinquish greater shares of programming schedules for their specific financial gain. By the time CBS—the last holdout—finally caved in to their demands in 1960, joining ABC, MBS and NBC who had opted out before them, the disc jockeys were all over the dial. They offered a quick fix for filling all those hours the local outlets had suddenly acquired at relatively little cost. Thus, when the turntables spun, the coffers swelled.

"As audiences grew and revenues rose, broadcasters kept hands off their DJs," observed a radio historiographer. "They were money-making machines." The platter-and-patter technique was king. And the only folks with regrets were those who were addicted to other formats after decades of exposure to comedy, drama, live music, mystery, serials and the other entertainment that had faded into oblivion.

But the DJs didn't prompt the changes as much as they embraced and benefited by them. In a sense, they were little more than a means to an end.

Writing a few years ago, a perceptive author offered a fairly depressing assessment of what transpired in the *successive* era of aural broadcasting — when the disc jockeys were firmly entrenched and radio's golden days had passed.[9]

> Gradually, the DJs began to intrude on the discs, until the songs sounded more like backup music for the host's banter. This eventually gave way to robot DJs, who were just plugged into the Top 40 charts, which in turn led to today's characterless DJs and syndicated formats — the worst of all possible musical worlds.

The point is worth noting. In the observer's opinion, even such a deflated musical format would probably have been preferable to contemporary times. Today the media historiographer views radio as "stuck on a relentless treadmill of news-music-sports, interrupted for warmed-over weather, commute, and stock updates every ten minutes."

Not so in the halcyon days of the DJ. While that epoch was never as extraordinary as the golden age that preceded it by any stretch of brainpower, the phase was indubitably far better than the "babble of opinion, most of it mindless and mean-spirited, whipped on by shrill talk-show hosts" available to radio audiences today.

The interval of the local DJ has not only diminished but — in many quarters — vanished completely. Americans may not have realized just how well off they really had it until the spinmeisters disappeared from the scene.

The Fred Waring Show

I hear music, I hear melodies, Sparkling songs of love, tingle from your touch.... The lyrics of the opening bars of *The Fred Waring Show* were sung by the Waring glee club. Over multiple decades they thrilled homegrown audiences with a bill genuinely separating themselves from all other radio orchestras. They performed pop, rumba, jazz, swing and everything between. Waring and his Pennsylvanians could just as readily lace their musical style with humor as they could embrace patriotism, religiosity and collegiality, offering listeners romantic ballads and tunes favoring sentimental and seasonal subjects as well. But no characteristic was more distinctive than the glee club, forming a unique sound that widely differentiated that entourage from its peers. On Waring's show, the singing ensemble held the limelight, the instrumentalists playing softly in the shadows. And for many years, Americans tingled from the touch.

Producer-Director: Bob Banner (TV), Tom Bennett.

Writers: Jack Dolph, Mike Dutton, Dave Harmon, Jay Johnson, John Medbury (comedy routines), Frank Moore, Bob Weiskopf.

Announcers: Bill Bivens, Bob Considine, Paul Douglas, David Ross.

Orchestra Conductors: Fred Culley (assistant, 1925–1966), Fred Waring.

Choral Directors: Robert Shaw, Kay Thompson.

Vocalists: Jimmy Atkins, Gordon Berger, Daisy Bernier, Stuart Churchill (tenor), Ruth Cottingham, Don Craig, Donna Dae, Gordon Goodman (tenor), Joe Marino, Mac Perron, Harry Richman, Robert Shaw, Kay Thompson, Joanne Wheatley, Jane Wilson (soprano).

Vocal Groups: Babs and Her Brothers, aka The Smoothies (Blanche Redwine and brothers Charlie and Little Ryan), Honey and the Bees (Diane Courtney, later Daisy Bernier as Honey; Murray Kane and Hal Kanner as the Bees), The Lane Sisters (Priscilla and Rosemary), Stella and the Fellas (Stella Friend, Paul Gibbons, Craig Leitch, Roy Ringwald), Keith and Sylvia Textor, Blanche and Marian Thompson, The Three Girl Friends (Stella Friend, Ida Pierce, June Taylor), The V-8 (vocal pop swing ensemble with one girl, seven guys).

Featured Instrumentalists: Hugh "Lumpy" Brannum (bassist and violinist), Fred Buck (banjoist), Ferne Buckner (violinist), Fred Culley (violinist), George Culley (trumpeter), Johnny "Scat" Davis (trumpeter), Livingston Gearhart and Virginia Morley (piano duo), Poley McClintock (drummer), The McFarland Twins (Arthur and George, saxophonists), Les Paul (guitarist), Tom Waring (pianist).

Specialty Acts: Roy Atwell (stuttering comic), Milton Berle (comic), Hugh "Lumpy" Brannum (comic vocals), Johnny "Scat" Davis (comic vocals), George Givor (comic), Poley McClintock (frog sounds and comic vocals), J. P. Medbury (comic), Moran and Mack — The Two Black Crows (George Moran and Charles Mack, later replaced by George Searchey, Charles Sellers, Bert Swor, blackface vaudevillians), Kay Thompson (comic vocals).

Theme Songs: *I Hear Music* (opening), *Sleep* (closing).

Sponsors: Sustaining, 1931-1932, September 7, 1944–January 11, 1946, October 1, 1956–October 4, 1957; P. Lorillard, Inc. (Old Gold cigarettes), February 8, 1933–January 31, 1934; Ford Motor Company (Ford automobiles and trucks), February 4, 1934–December 29, 1936, including simultaneous series, January 17–December 25, 1936; Grove Laboratories, Inc. (Bromo-Quinine distress reliever), October 8, 1938–March 4, 1939; Liggett & Myers Tobacco Company (Chesterfield cigarettes, Granger pipe tobacco), June 19, 1939–June 9, 1944; Participating sponsors including American Meat Packers Association, Florida Citrus Growers, Illinois Glass Company, Minneapolis Valley Canning Company, January 15, 1946–July 8, 1949; S. C. Johnson & Sons (Johnson's wax and other household and vehicle cleaning compounds), summers 1946, 1947, 1948; Minneapolis Valley Canning Company, July 16, 1949–July 22, 1950; local underwriters in each market, syndicated series.

Ratings: High — 22.9 (1935-1936 season, including 14.0 Tuesday plus 8.9 Friday) — High for a single network, 17.4 (1933-1934 season); Low — 4.1 (1948-1949 season); Median — 10.7. In respectable numbers most of prime-time broadcast era through 1942-1943 season; daytime ratings hovered around 4.2, losing appreciably to serial and Arthur Godfrey audiences on competing chains. Figures not available for three seasons (1931-1932, 1945-1946, 1956-1957).

On the Air: *Roxy Theater Concert*, 1931-1932, CBS, Sunday, 9:00–9:30 P.M. Eastern Time; February 8, 1933–January 31, 1934, CBS, Wednesday, 10:00–10:30 P.M.; February 4–April 22, 1934, CBS, Sunday, 8:30–9:00 P.M.; April 29–September 30, 1934, CBS, Sunday, 9:30–10:00 P.M.; February 8–June 28, 1934, September 13–December 27, 1934, CBS, Thursday, 9:30–10:00 P.M.; January 3–June 27, 1935, CBS, Thursday, 9:00–9:30 P.M.; July 2, 1935–January 14, 1936, CBS, Tuesday, 9:30–10:30 P.M.; January 21–June 23, 1936, CBS, Tuesday, 9:30–10:00 P.M.; June 30–December 29, 1936, CBS, Tuesday, 9:00–9:30 P.M.; January 17–May 29, 1936, NBC Blue, Friday, 9:30–10:00 P.M.; June 5–December 25, 1936, NBC Blue, Friday, 9:00–9:30 P.M.; October 8, 1938–March 4, 1939, NBC, Saturday, 8:30–9:00 P.M.; *Chesterfield Time* (aka *Pleasure Time, Victory Tunes*) June 19, 1939–June 9, 1944, NBC, Monday–Friday, 7:00–7:15 P.M.; September 7–December 28, 1944, NBC Blue, Thursday, 7:00–7:30 P.M.; January 4–May 31, 1945, NBC Blue, Thursday, 10:00–10:30 P.M.; June 4, 1945–September 26, 1947, NBC, Monday–Friday, 11:00–11:30 A.M.; September 29, 1947–July 8, 1949, 10:00–10:30 A.M.; June 18–September 24, 1946, June 24–September 30, 1947, NBC, Tuesday, 9:30–10:00 P.M.; October 6, 1947–July 19, 1948, NBC, Monday, 10:30–11:00 P.M.; July 29, 1948–September 29, 1949, NBC, Thursday, 10:30–11:00 P.M.; June 8–September 28, 1948, NBC, Tuesday, 9:30–10:00 P.M.; July 16, 1949–July 22, 1950, NBC, Saturday, 10:00–10:30 A.M.; October 1, 1956–March 15, 1957, ABC, Monday–Friday, 2:00–2:30 P.M.; April 8–June

14, 1957, ABC, Monday–Friday, 9:30–10:00 P.M.; June 17–October 4, 1957, ABC, Monday–Wednesday–Friday, 10:30–11:00 P.M.; 156 half-hour ZIV syndicated shows.

* * *

Fred Waring exuded a dapper, polished showmanship style that was derived from years of practice, perfecting his aggregate's stage presence long before the big band era came into vogue. He invariably rewarded his audiences with reverie that blended instrumental and vocal melody into a menagerie of pleasant harmony. One scholar suitably christened the Waring showcase an "at-ease" performance. Waring's radio programs were not only popular but also enduring, a testimony to the gratifying performances his entourage offered virtually every time out.

Waring was, in that regard, the consummate bandleader. Among early groups, none so dominated the airwaves nor persevered for as long or as profusely as did the combination headlined by Waring. "So long as radio remained a user of live music he was on it," a critic observed. It seemed he could always be found somewhere on the radio dial, even in the twilight of an ebbing network radio epoch after his music had resonated for decades with loyal fans.

"The man who taught America how to sing," as he was lauded, was born in Tyrone, Pennsylvania, on June 9, 1900. The Keystone State has produced several prominent vocalists and conductors, although none whose allegiance has imparted greater eminence on it than his. Fred Waring took violin lessons around the age of 13 but lost interest supposedly because the school orchestra was so terrible he couldn't stand it. By his mid-teens he was playing the banjo, an instrument that was to have a profound importance in his early career.

As a high school freshman, young Waring joined the school glee club, directed by Principal J. L. Gaunt. Gaunt encouraged the youth's musical fascination with his concentration on text and articulation. Years later that devotion inspired Waring to develop Tone Syllables techniques that were revered everywhere and adopted by numerous choral leaders across the country.

When young Waring later enrolled at Pennsylvania State College (subsequently renamed University), he failed in several tries for acceptance into the institute's glee club. "Many feel that gave him the incentive to 'show them,'" acknowledged Peter T. Kiefer, coordinator of Fred Waring's America at University Park, Pennsylvania. "It stuck in his craw because he always talked about the rejection and as much said 'and look what I did,'" Kiefer elaborated.[1]

Before Waring left for college, a quartet of musically inclined chums in Tyrone formed an instrumental group that played for their own amusement and, when asked, at special events. Membership included banjoists Freddie Buck and Fred Waring, pianist Tom Waring (Fred's brother) and drummer Poley McClintock (Fred's best friend). Ask a reputable critic to name Waring's initial group and you'll likely receive more than one answer. A quintet of informed sources supplied five discrete monikers for the cluster: Waring's Banjatrazz, Waring's Banjazztra, Waring's Banjo Orchestra, Waring's Collegians and the Waring-McClintock Snap Band. On first deliberation it would appear that at least four of them got it wrong.

After further investigation, we are persuaded that, at 16, Fred Waring joined the Waring-McClintock Snap Orchestra formed by Tom Waring and neighbor Poley McClintock. The trio renamed itself the Banjazzatra Quartet (note different spelling) when Fred Buck joined. Tom Waring and McClintock would remain with Fred Waring as key members of his troupe far out into the future, incidentally.

In a short while that early quartet, by then college oriented, increased in number as several others joined its ranks. They included bassist Bill Borscher, trombonist Jim Gilliland, saxophonists Art Horn and Park Lytell and trumpeter Nelson Keller. Waring took charge of the expanded formation, bestowing it with the appellation Waring's Collegians. By then he was giving unmistakable hints of the direction he intended to take for his life's work.

Waring's Collegians principally played venues on the college and university circuits. The group's moniker would be altered in the early 1920s to the Pennsylvanians, a designation that stuck throughout Waring's career.

On at least one occasion they played a junior hop at the University of Michigan. While in the Wolverine State they were given an opportunity to perform over Detroit radio station WWJ, then in its infancy. The year was 1921. It was clearly the precursor of things to come. The youthful entourage would soon be playing dates in recording studios, Broadway musicals and on vaudeville circuits. From that very moment it stood on the precipice of imminent discovery followed by pervasive celebrity.

The early access to radio transmitted Waring's music to the perception of a wider public. Discarding both his banjo and the moniker that was heretofore applied to his fledgling group of academic music-makers, Waring took absolute control as permanent conductor, renaming them the Pennsylvanians. The new appellation and Waring's capacity for making all of the major and final decisions stuck. He would be plucking strings no longer; his cohorts hastily gathered that he intended to be pulling strings instead from that time forward.

The Pennsylvanians enjoyed tremendous success in playing at college functions. Before long they signed for an engagement at Hollywood's Metropolitan Theater.

Things were looking up. Soon Waring penned a pact with Victor to record Earl Lebieg's *Sleep*, a tune that was to become the group's most durable and recognizable theme. It turned into the proverbial smash hit. The Pennsylvanians were immediately an established commodity, by then widely known in far-flung locales. They'd not be taking a back seat to anybody's band from then on, even rivaling the inimitable Paul Whiteman's orchestra, an outfit Waring had used as a model as he developed his own.

The critics were among those who took notice. In the early 1940s, radio historiographer Francis Chase Jr. observed: "Go back a dozen years and you could count the well-known dance-band leaders of the country on the fingers of your hands and still have both thumbs to spare. Paul Whiteman, Coon-Sanders, Guy Lombardo, Paul Specht, Fred Waring and a few others dominated the popular dance-band market of the mid-twenties when the lifeblood of the industry flowed largely from the recording business."

Waring was categorically a pioneer in dance band recording. His *Collegiate* became the first record to highlight a vocal chorus backed by a dance band. The initial recording of a George Gershwin tune was Waring's release of *Nashville Nightingale*. And his arrangement of *Oh, Donna Clara* was the first in a long line of rumba recordings, further demonstrating his capacity for range.

The Pennsylvanians' not-too-distant agenda included the Broadway musical *Help Yourself* that they headlined, and an appearance in a well-received motion picture, 1929's *Syncopation*. Only a year before they took an engagement in Paris, performing at Les Ambassadeurs in an "All-American" revue. Not only did they earn critical acclaim, it was also a lucrative endeavor. By 1930, the entourage was appearing onstage in *The New Yorkers*, a Big Apple musical farce featuring a Cole Porter score.

The group's stock would continue to rise. Waring committed his 55-member troupe for a series of live Sunday night performances at New York's Roxy Theater, to be broadcast over the full reaches of the Columbia network. The "experiment" resulted in a six-month stand during radio's 1931-1932 season. With that added standing, Waring's name had become a household word virtually everywhere. It wouldn't be forgotten in most places in half a century.

By 1937, the Pennsylvanians were appearing in the Warner Brothers film production *Variety Show* starring Dick Powell. Their stock had risen; they found themselves in demand in many places simultaneously.

What was it that set Waring's music apart from many of its contemporaries, making it the beneficiary of adulation rather early, respect that wasn't always bestowed on every other musical entourage by a fickle public? There is more than one answer to the question.

For openers, Waring insisted that his staff proffer a distinctive quality. To accomplish that, he injected the human voice into the mix—not just an occasional vocalist or two as some other bandleaders were already doing, but literally turning the whole tribe into a congregation of spirited singers! Beyond that "unique approach of singing the music as well as playing it," Waring purposely developed a glee club harmony that harkened back to his high school days. The Waring chorus was accentuated at each performance, intentionally removing the limelight from the instrumentalists. Instead, that 18-member aggregate became the centerpiece of every revue.

Waring's lifelong interest in vocalizing grew out of his personal familiarity with it acquired from his mother, who rehearsed the local choir in the parlor of their home. When he joined his high school glee club that confirmed his growing passion for singing. His fervent participation there characterized the kind of show he offered audiences on stage and on radio and television throughout his life. Singing, more than anything else, became the Waring band's most notable asset, taking precedence over the orchestration itself and breaking with tradition, placing the emphasis squarely on the human voice.

The stress on singing wasn't universally accepted, however, at least not by potential commercial underwriters. Because the idea was such a radical departure from traditional band instrumental programming, most would-be sponsors fled. Waring and company tolerated 32 tryouts before finding one (P. Lorillard, Inc.) that accepted the accent on a mammoth vocal ensemble. "That choir singing is good only for Sunday morning. It would flop on an evening show," one firm's ad contact lamented.

"Without the glee club, the Pennsylvanians would be just another band," Waring interposed. "Take all or nothing." Most rejected it. When one finally said "yes" and the notion became an immediate hit, other advertisers clamored for the enhancement of similar vocal groups to their own programs.

By the mid–1930s, Waring's paramount accent was on singing, the instrumentalists becoming ancillary to the vocalists and choirs. The impresario didn't limit the singing to that body alone, however. There were often smaller ensembles—duos and trios—as well as multiple soloists who were regularly featured on all of his playbills.

Parenthetically, Paul Whiteman fronted another outfit that introduced choral music into his performances. The innovation begun by Waring and Whiteman in the early 1930s actually developed into a fad by the close of the decade.

Another distinguishing factor separating Waring's music from other groups was its sound. It was clearly opposite that of the handful of orchestras offering more than passing stress on vocalization. As one introspective fittingly put it, the choristers could be characterized by "startling phrasing, sudden changes of volume and tempo, and long hums on traditional and jazz tunes alike." There were cleverly arranged vocal numbers that set the Waring programs apart from all others on the air and at public appearance venues. Irrefutably, "His sound became an audio trademark."

Waring's impact on the nation's music—recall that he was dubbed "The Man Who Made America Sing"—went well beyond the radio studios and performing venues where he collected acclaim. Music historiographer Tom DeLong spells out still further contributions.[2]

> As Waring's glee club demonstrated new styles in choral singing to a receptive public, more and more groups in schools, colleges, and churches began to follow his lead. Youngsters, especially, began to get more fun out of the tunes a teacher assigned to them by demanding they be taught to "sing like the Pennsylvanians." Inevitably, Fred Waring became the hero of school glee clubbers; and when he began supplying arrangements for music teachers and singing groups, they also became his "fans." By 1947 more than eight hundred of them were using his methods and arrangements, while hundreds more were enrolling in his summer courses for choral conductors that were held at his spacious ninety-five room Shawnee-on-the-Delaware Inn near Stroudsburg, Pa.

Waring's own voice came to be readily identified by his steadily growing stream of radio listeners for—without fanfare—he tempered the order of programs by introducing each number in an informed fashion, often adding some brief detail about a song's setting or history, while the melody was already playing quietly behind him. This contrasted sharply with the traditional style then in vogue on most other orchestral series on the ether. Elsewhere, an announcer deftly gave the name of the piece and perhaps named its composer but with little else before or following its airing, most often to a background occupied by silence. One wag cited the "brisk pacing which made for almost continuous music" an "outstanding" element of the Waring programs.[3]

Incidentally, Waring had an unusual technique for opening and closing his broadcast shows. Presented by an announcer at their start, he'd state, matter-of-factly: "Hello everybody, and thanks for coming!" The latter phrase was repeated at the conclusion of the broadcasts, a kind of trademark signature in addition to his launching and ending themes—*I Hear Music* at the start and *Sleep* at the close. "The program was so relaxing," a critic observed, possibly tongue-in-cheek, "that most of his listeners probably hit the sack long before the last bars of the theme were over."

When the Ford Motor Company sponsored Waring's series in the mid–1930s, it capitalized on the firm's then-current advertising catchphrase "Watch the Fords Go By." The Pennsylvanians played and sang the melody *Breezing Along with the Breeze* to underscore the slogan. With Chesterfields as a later sponsor, the product was exploited by the theme *A Cigarette, Sweet Music, and You* sung by the glee club.

The fact that Waring himself was his program's interlocutor, offering brief asides of relevant patter between musical selections—invariably after each refrain started—underscored the fact that he was the unquestioned power from start to finish.

As the strains of the clip-clop of a donkey trot issued in the background, Waring serenely inquired of his radio audience on August 27, 1946: "What is this? *The Song of India*. Paul Whiteman's famous recording…" he continued interpreting the tune's history. The same bill included a soprano warbling *I'm Always Chasing*

Rainbows and a jazzy instrumental number, *The Russian Rag*—the maestro insisting it was "the first serious music played for dancing," adapted from Sergei Rachmaninoff's *Prelude in C-sharp minor*, the composer's "most popular music."

"Do you realize how many of the pops come from the classics?" he pondered. Not waiting for the answer, he introduced a theme based on Rachmaninoff's *Second Piano Concerto*. Under its contemporary title, *Full Moon and Empty Arms*, the full Waring chorus and a baritone soloist performed.

It was archetypal Waring. This was the kind of offering he gave his listeners week in and week out and they responded enthusiastically, keeping him on the airwaves year after year, hardly letting him miss a beat. The variety of his programs—including novelty numbers and even some comic routines—increasingly set this show apart from its contemporaries. Together it indelibly left marks on the singing hearts of vast audiences across the land that were privileged to tune in week after week and year after year.

In August 1966, Waring told a *New York Times* correspondent: "We don't sing music, we sing songs." One source correctly claimed Waring "understood and exploited the tastes of the great American public," calling his approach "the common man's."

One of the variations in style the impresario flaunted as far back as 1939 was in introducing specially written alma maters and pep songs, touting colleges and universities that were his shows' focal points during the Chesterfield-sponsored era. Those shows were commonly known as "Friday Smokers." The sidelights were enthusiastically received by the masses of young people tuning in. In 1942, Waring staged a national competition involving collegiate glee clubs from all over the nation. The University of Rochester commandeered first place as "best vocal group."

Over the decades, Waring's coterie featured several sterling talents who became famous in their own rights. Among the more famous of his alumni were comic Milton Berle; bassist and violinist and comic vocalist Lumpy Brannum, better known as Mr. Green Jeans on the long-running *Captain Kangaroo* juvenile daytime CBS-TV series; movie stars Priscilla and Rosemary Lane; celebrated guitarist Les Paul; Robert Shaw, who rehearsed and conducted the Waring glee-clubbers before forming his own chorale; and choral director Kay Thompson.

Waring quickly earned a reputation as a perfectionist, even so describing himself as such, a label frequently assigned to certain professional musicians and other skilled artists. "This [perfectionist] care was illustrated by his thorough preparation upon accepting an offer in 1930 to make regular broadcasts," suggested one authority. "He hired a sound studio and in seven days the band produced something like two hundred transcriptions for him to study balance, blending of sounds, and many other aspects of radio transmission." Despite the tendencies, some viewed his obsessions as misplaced and a waste of talent, hinting: "Throughout his career Waring's perfectionist criteria were applied to what was essentially trivial material." A second source underscored: "Waring ... labored long and mightily on material which was seldom worthy of the care he lavished upon it."

Waring maintained a low tolerance for shallowness and inattention. His neurotic compulsions did not endear him to some of his subordinates. As a reputed taskmaster, he was not "a man who inspired much affection in his musicians," noted one observer. There were reports that he sometimes pushed them beyond belief, frequently rehearsing them up to eight hours daily. Painstakingly preparing every detail before performances, he'd bellow to the

Could maestro Fred Waring get blood out of a turnip? He had a reputation for endless rehearsing. He appears to be urging his musicians to "give me all you've got." Or else? The results usually proved sufficient for Waring and his entourage was able to perform on stage at full throttle long past the traditionally accepted finale of radio's golden age.

troops: "You'd better be on your toes tonight or I'll be on yours tomorrow."

"He drove his men and women hard," reported a music journalist with a working knowledge of the business' internal operations. "Some hated him; many admired him; few ever really knew him.... He could be utterly charming as well as frustratingly condescending and brutally dictatorial." The critic acknowledged that Waring might have possessed "the most dictatorial attitude I'd ever witnessed on the part of any bandleader."[4] Those forcible machinations notwithstanding, he surmised: "His [Waring's] strong will, plus his love and respect for good musicianship, paid off."

On the other hand, Peter Kiefer, an insider who was well acquainted with the Waring clan, confirmed: "Yes he was a taskmaster, demanded your best at all times. He had his idiosyncrasies, a temper when things weren't going the way he wanted. Some found it hard to put up with but the majority found him an awesome person to work for. He was loyal to the nth degree to those who were loyal to him. The longevity of so many of his singers and instrumentalists testify to that."[5]

Waring's intense, at-times surreal convictions can be illustrated in the matter of making — and not making — phonograph recordings over an extensive time frame. While many discs carried the warning "Not licensed for radio broadcast," artists had little or no recourse preventing such outlets from airing their commercially released recordings. Leo Walker offers some discerning background.[6]

> After the mid-twenties, radio began to hit its stride, and by bringing the sound of live entertainment into the home, reduced the interest in recorded music, taking a heavy toll in record sales. Smaller stations unable to program live entertainment were broadcasting recorded music, although the announcers who spun platters had not yet been given the title of disc jockeys. In some cases the manner in which these numbers were announced gave, at least by implication, the impression that the listener was hearing a live broadcast.
>
> In 1928, the Federal Radio Commission stepped into the picture and instructed broadcasters to identify recorded music as such when it was used, or at least desist from practices which might fool the listening public. A year later the artists' Protective Society initiated a suit which was indicative of the stand the artists themselves intended to take in the matter. Contending that the broadcasting of phonograph records had contributed to a heavy decline in record sales, they asked that the stations playing them be forced to pay royalties to the artist whose record was thus used. Recording companies joined in supporting this action. Fred Waring took a still firmer stand, refusing to make any records at all unless a compensation arrangement with radio broadcasters could be enforced. He maintained this position for some ten or twelve years before he once again signed a contract with a recording company.

Some authorities speculate that Waring's long holdout against recording may have been prompted by his own prosperity. He was already generally acknowledged as the highest earning bandleader in radio and theater by 1933. That factor was likely influential in his decision to stand firm against what he perceived as unnecessarily lost income to the radio stations that were spinning his songs without any remuneration. Never mind that those spins routinely translated into greater fame for musical troupes. In addition to boosting its image, that exposure increased a group's public demand for stage bookings, radio shows and record sales. As one radio disc-spinner later remembered, "The record manufacturers began to sponsor programs as a showcase for their new releases and started to pay for what in the past they had objected to receiving gratis." But Waring stood firm on his principles. It was late 1941 before he finally relented and recorded with Decca.

In the meantime, he had also sued for performance costs for each of his records played on the air. The precedent-setting case, filed in Pennsylvania, was successfully argued on his behalf in court. As a result, radio stations in the Keystone State dispensed with recordings he had made in the 1920s and early 1930s during his "silent" period.

In 1945, Waring became part of an NBC trial to bring nighttime quality to daytime radio. His abundantly orchestrated prime-time series was transferred to the daytime programming agenda and aired five weekday mornings for several years. While the ratings he amassed there could never top the appeal of *Arthur Godfrey Time* nor the soap operas on other networks—and didn't come close to the numbers he acquired in prime time—the class he injected into the sunshine hours bespoke volumes of commitment by his network to uplifting the listening habits of the nation's homemakers.

In its halcyon days, the composition of the Waring entourage was variously estimated to include in excess of 100 instrumentalists, vocalists, arrangers, assistant conductors, production specialists and staff aides. From time to time the number of glee club members varied from 18 to 36 members. It was, without doubt, one of the largest such entertainment amalgamations in the business. While Waring taught some of those choral members to read music, a great many of the men and women comprising it boasted college musical preparation.

The Pennsylvanians premiered on the tube in January 1944 on a one-time exposition over the Dumont Television's New York City outlet. Five years later they were the first "name" orchestra to be featured in a continuing video series. *The Fred Waring Show* debuted over CBS-TV on April 17, 1949, for an hour on Sunday nights (9:00–10:00 Eastern time). In January 1952 it was reduced to a half-hour (9:00–9:30) and, by 1953, it alternated weeks with *General Electric Theater* half-hour dramas. The Waring show left the air on May 30, 1954, having performed before live audiences in its first and final TV seasons and from a studio without spectators the other three years. The small-screen series produced and directed by Bob Banner typically included about 65 singers and instrumentalists. Dancing, light musical sketches and fairy tale interpretations were regular parts of the program.

When the weekday *Garry Moore Show* took a summer hiatus from CBS-TV in 1957, Waring's entourage was tapped to replace it. The show ran from July 22 through August 30, from 10:00–10:30 A.M. Monday-through-Thursday and 10:00–11:30 A.M. Friday. Airing live from Shawnee-on-the-Delaware, his Pennsylvania country club, it marked the last regular appearance of Waring's group on television. After that the maestro (sometimes with his entourage) turned up on the small screen for infrequent guest appearances.

Waring was a shrewd businessman who learned how to turn performing opportunities into highly profitable results. In addition, he was far-sighted in discovering and seizing other moneymaking possibilities, significantly adding to his own personal net worth.

His experiences in radio indicate just how good a manager he was. In 1934, after a year of broadcasting for P. Lorillard, Inc., the maker of Old Gold cigarettes, Waring balked when Lorillard proffered a $3,300-a-week renewal contract. (The original contract, under which he was then laboring, was for $3,250.) The conductor had recently padded his staff with a couple of extra performers and anticipated significantly more cash to cover them. Lorillard returned with a revised offer of $3,500. An intemperate, determined Waring turned thumbs down. Just at that juncture the Ford Motor Company appeared with a bid of $10,000 weekly. Waring signed and the vehicle manufacturer underwrote the program for nearly three years.

From 1939 to 1944, Waring's entourage appeared on radio for another cigarette maker, Liggett & Myers Tobacco Co. and its Chesterfield brand. At the start of that association, the Pennsylvanians were netting almost $20,000 every week for a quarter-hour show Monday-through-Friday evenings, an outrageous sum to many. As one historiographer confirmed, "More than half a hundred Pennsylvanians" added up — Waring's show was clearly one of radio's most expensive.

The numbers continued spiraling upward. When the group moved to airing in the daylight in 1945, the orchestra itself was dividing $18,000 weekly. The program was confidently acknowledged as "the highest-priced daytime show ever." During some of this feature's quadrennial, Waring was also working on nighttime series for other sponsors. And — dare we suggest? — laughing all the way to the bank.

Meanwhile, outside the radio studio, Warning wasn't faring poorly, either. By the start of the 1940s, he was among a handful of bandleaders on the public appearance circuit (including outfits fronted by Horace Heidt, Kay Kyser, Glenn Miller and Orrin Tucker) who were guaranteed at least $12,500 per one-night stand, plus a percentage of the gross above the guarantee.

Compared to their contemporaries, all these groups were doing exceptionally well.

Waring didn't rely on the performing venues to provide all of his income, however. An imaginative entrepreneur with a keen eye on the bottom line, the impresario significantly extended his reach, diversifying his interests into several moneymaking measures linked with — as well as unrelated to — the music industry. Through his highly profitable music-publishing firm, Words and Music Inc., reportedly the largest enterprise like it then on the planet, he marketed millions of copies of hundreds of specially written band and choral arrangements. Beginning in 1942, he published a highly successful monthly periodical, *Music Journal*, to thousands of subscribers, principally consisting of music teachers and performers.

In 1944, along with a couple of business partners, he purchased a 95-room resort known as Buckwood Inn, situated on 600 acres in the Pocono Mountains of Pennsylvania at Shawnee-on-Delaware, near Stroudsburg and Delaware Water Gap. With Waring's penchant for renaming things, the place was soon called the Shawnee Inn and Golf Resort. He was to have an interest in it for nearly three decades, until it was sold in 1973 to a land developer, who later sold it to its present owner, land developer Charles Kirkwood.

The Shawnee property was to play a colossal role during the years of Waring's affiliation with it, however. In 1946, his educational consultant director, Ennis Davis, convinced Waring to invite to Shawnee several of the choral directors who had been continually asking permission to attend Waring's rehearsals to see "how he did it." An invitation was extended to about 100 individuals and each one was told it would be permissible to bring along a friend. Three hundred people showed up. The sessions were moved to the ballroom of the Astor Hotel. Some of the clinicians, in addition to Waring, included Irving Berlin, Richard Rodgers and Robert Shaw.

By 1947, Fred Waring Choral Workshops were held annually at Shawnee Inn and Golf Resort, and continued every year through Waring's death in 1984. Sessions specifically geared toward high school and collegiate singers were added. They became some of the most coveted vocal training experiences offered in America as thousands embarked on a mission of acquiring Waring's time-tested Tone Syllables choral techniques.

His clever business acumen assisted him in marketing several inventions. In 1937, he purchased the patents on a mixing machine, contracting with a Toledo manufacturing plant to produce it. The Waring Blender became a prominent fixture in home and commercial kitchens everywhere. He also turned a profit on the Aluron steam iron, another case of somebody else's idea going nowhere until Waring got involved. He later leased those commodities to an outfit still in operation, currently known as Waring Products, Inc.

Waring's business interests completely filled the 10th floor of an office edifice at 1697 Broadway in New York. Words and Music's marketing activities were housed in the forward half of the occupied territory. The rear was subdivided into several sectors including separate capacious studios for the orchestra and glee club, cubicles designated for a half-dozen music arrangers and a control room in which radio broadcasts were prerecorded. For several hours daily the 10th floor resonated with echoing Waring rehearsals. There was also a suite for Waring's personal use, affording him a generous office, totally equipped kitchen and shower room.

This volume's author attended a live Waring road concert in the early 1960s and was impressed by the conductor's shock of white hair (a departure from earlier pictures), his smooth stage presence and the blended voices of the glee club harmony — still the defining trademark of the Waring coterie. Those road trips were important to the impresario. He would continue doing them for another couple of decades. By the 1980s, covering about 40,000 miles via bus across 40 states each fall and winter, the Waring entourage still played about 150 dates annually, principally on college campuses, in performing arts centers of major American cities and at community venues in smaller locales. In Waring's final "performance" — only hours before his death — he conducted a youth choral group convening at his beloved alma mater, Penn State. Fred Waring died July 29, 1984, at Danville, Pennsylvania. He was 84.

After Waring's death the annual workshops ceased. For six summers, between 1986 and 1991, Penn State hosted a 100-voice Fred Waring U.S. Chorus in part conducted by Virginia Waring, the late orchestra leader's widow and herself a former member of the famous musical entourage. She authored his biography, *Fred Waring and the Pennsylvanians*, published by the University of Illinois Press. While the Tyrone (Pennsylvania) Historical Society displays some Waring memorabilia, a Fred Waring Room is designated at the Pennsylvania State University Library, where Waring archives are maintained.

Appraising Waring's place in American entertainment, one assessor proclaimed: "Waring and his aggregation became an American institution. They moved musically with the times from swing to rock 'n' roll. Perhaps their finest moments drew upon patriotic and devotional songs during the war years.... Waring left the selection of many numbers to servicemen. A frequently requested presentation was the stirring *Battle Hymn of the Republic*."

Some other tunes favored by Waring audiences included *Ain't Misbehavin', April Showers, The Continental, Dry Bones, Give Me Your Tired— Your Poor, Here I'll Stay, I Can't Give You Anything But Love Baby, I Feel a Song Comin' On, I Hear Music, I Only Have Eyes for You, It's Only a Paper Moon, The Lord's Prayer, Love for Sale, Love Is on the Air Tonight, Moonlight and Roses, Riders in the Sky, The Rosary, Sentimental Journey, Sleep, Some Enchanted Evening, Somebody Loves Me, Someone to Watch Over Me, Stardust, Temptation* and *White Christmas*. "No other musical aggregation on radio gave listeners so much variety," a scholar maintained.

Waring often featured a refrain that was played as intended, then repeated as a march, grand opera and a swing melody. His programs took unusual twists with premises like Colorado, The Constitution, manufacturing, the open highway, home and the U.S. Marines.

While Fred Waring's influence would be felt in the recording industry, motion pictures, Broadway and local stages around the nation, television, marketing, publishing, schoolrooms and wherever choral and instrumental groups assembled, and in industrial production, in reality — as is so often the case — most of that might never have transpired without the advent of radio.

In the 1930s, the aural airwaves translated his name into a household word in millions of the nation's homes. Before then he was known only by a few thousand who had been seated in audiences where he played, or watched him in a movie or purchased an early recording of one of his tunes. Radio was the key to his public awareness. More than any other medium, it made him and his Pennsylvanians stars. By the 1960s, Waring and company had aired more than 5,000 broadcasts, and did so while maintaining a fairly high Nielsen rating across several decades on the ether.

A pundit characterized Lawrence Welk as "the Fred Waring of TV." Welk demonstrated the staying power that affixed Fred Waring in the minds and hearts of legions of adoring fans. As contemporaries, both sustained the ability to linger longer than most others in the mediums they conquered. As a result, both remained active entertainers, their names readily recognizable in millions of American homes into the 1980s.

Grand Ole Opry

The most durable broadcasting enterprise to cross the airwaves continues more than three-quarters of a century after it began. The *Grand Ole Opry* in Nashville, Tennessee, has registered more than 4,100 consecutive weekend performances to date and shows no signs of impending suspension. Its humble beginnings, traceable to songs the Scottish settlers brought with them to America, are gripping. Yet the mark that the *Opry* makes on global entertainment is even more imposing. At mid-twentieth century, the little country show with roots in a simple lifestyle was beamed over a coast-to-coast hookup. Even when it wasn't chain-fed, inhabitants of 38 states and Canada could tune in as a 50,000-watt clear channel transmitter pushed it across the ether. The *Opry* proved the most resilient of a myriad of hillbilly features popping up at local stations. By any criteria, it remains today a veritable epic in the annals of broadcasting.

Producers: Ott Devine, Jack Stapp.

Directors: Kenneth W. MacGregor, Vito Pellettieri.

Writers: Noel Digby, Dave Murray, Cliff Thomas.

Announcers (network portion era): Louie Buck, David Cobb, T. Tommy Cutrer, Tom Hanserd, George D. Hay ("The Solemn Old Judge"), Bill Randall, David Stone, Grant Turner.

Hosts/Masters of Ceremonies (network portion era): Benjamin Francis "Whitey" Ford ("The Duke of Paducah"), Roy Acuff ("The King of Country Music"), Clyde Julian "Red" Foley.

Performers (network portion era): Roy Acuff ("The King of Country Music") and The Smoky Mountain Boys, Bill Anderson, Eddy Arnold ("The Tennessee Plowboy"), Chet Atkins ("Mr. Guitar"), Rod Leon Brasfield ("The Hohenwald Flash"), "Jumping" Bill Carlisle and the Carlisles, Martha Carson, June Carter, Mother Maybelle Carter and the Carter Sisters, Johnny Cash ("The Man in Black"), Patsy Cline, Wilma Lee and Stoney Cooper, Lloyd T. "Cowboy" Copas, The Crook Brothers (instrumentalists), Skeeter Davis, Little Jimmy Dickens, Lester Flatt and Earl Scruggs and the Foggy Mountain Boys, Clyde Julian "Red" Foley, Benjamin Francis "Whitey" Ford ("The Duke of Paducah"), Wally Fowler, William Orville "Lefty" Frizzell, The Fruit Jar Drinkers (instrumentalists), Harold F. "Hawkshaw" Hawkins, Homer

(Harry Haynes) and Jethro (Kenneth C. Burns), Randy Hughes, Ferlin Huskey, Stonewall Jackson, Cousin (James C. Summey) Jody, Johnny (Wright) and Jack (Anglin), George Jones, Louis M. "Grandpa" Jones, The Jordanaires (Hoyt Hawkins, Neal Matthews, Gordon Stoker, Ray Walker), Wyatt Merle Kilgore, PeeWee Frank King, Brenda Lee, Lonzo (Johnny Sullivan) and Oscar (Rollin Sullivan), The Louvin Brothers (Charlie and Ira), Lulu Belle (Myrtle Eleanor Cooper Wiseman), Sam and Kirk McGee ("From Sunny Tennessee"), Uncle Dave ("The Dixie Dewdrop"), Bill Monroe ("The Father of Bluegrass"), George Morgan, Moon Mullican ("King of the Ivories"), Jimmy C. Newman, The Old Hickory Singers (who sang the commercial jingle for Prince Albert), The Osborne Brothers (Sonny and Bob), Cousin Minnie Pearl (Sarah Ophelia Colley Cannon), Luther Monroe Perkins, Webb Pierce, Ray Price ("The Cherokee Cowboy"), James Travis "Jim" Reeves, Don Reno, Marty Robbins, Jean Shepard, Carl Smith, Clarence Eugene "Hank" Snow ("The Singing Ranger") and the Rainbow Ranch Boys, The Stony Mountain Cloggers (square dancers), Stringbean (David Akeman, "The Kentucky Wonder"), The Tennessee Travelers (square dancers), Henry William "Hank" Thompson, Ernest Dale Tubb and the Texas Troubadors, Justin Wayne Tubb, Leroy Van Dyke, Porter Wagoner and the Wagon Masters, Charlie Walker, Kitty Wells ("The Queen of Country Music"), Otis Dewey "Slim" Whitman Jr., The Wilburn Brothers (Doyle, Leslie, Lester, Teddy), Hank Williams, The Willis Brothers (Guy, Skeeter and Vic), Mac Wiseman, Del Wood (Adelaide Hazelwood, "Queen of the Ragtime Pianists"), Faron Young, more.

Sponsor: R. J. Reynolds Tobacco Company for Prince Albert pipe tobacco (network portion only).

Ratings: High — 13.7 (1949-1950 season); Low — 4.1 (1952-1953); Median — 9.6 (numbers available for 11 of 17 network seasons only, excluding 1939–1941, 1947-1948, 1954–1957). When chain figures are compared with the *National Barn Dance*, the *Opry's* predecessor and longest-running rival, that show's median is 9.2 for six head-to-head seasons against 11.2 for the *Opry*, indicating a preference for the latter among network listeners.

On the Air: *WSM Barn Dance* through September 24, 1927, *Grand Ole Opry* thereafter. November 28, 1925–present, Nashville's WSM, Saturday nights at varying times between 6:30 P.M. and 12 midnight Central Time, also Friday nights since late 1940s, plus certain added spring and summer nights and matinees since 1980s. In addition to WSM broadcasts, live portions integrated into the network schedule: October 14, 1939–September 29, 1951, NBC, Saturday, 10:30–11:00 P.M. Eastern Time; October 6, 1951–July 25, 1953 and September 25, 1954–December 28, 1957, NBC, Saturday, 9:30–10:00 P.M. Eastern Time.

* * *

It's the only radio program in the world that has never had a summer replacement, never had an intermission and never missed a performance since it started in 1925.[1] The *Grand Ole Opry* is in a class by itself when it comes to measuring longevity against everything else on the ether. It's positively remarkable that a radio series could be approaching the start of its ninth decade on the air (in November 2005) and still be as vibrant as it was years earlier. Nothing compares to its durability or its style. One really has to witness the legendary country music spectacle in person to properly appreciate its unique import in American entertainment.

In this revered shrine frequently referred to as "the mother church of country music" a pundit fittingly observed: "A singer had not arrived in country music until being granted an audience on the broadcast." That was a reality *then* and it appears little is changing as the decades roll on. Nashville's temple is the Mecca at which all true country music lovers worship.

It started in 1925 when George D. Hay, hailed as the Solemn Old Judge, scoured the countryside in search of local fiddlers, pickers and singers for a Saturday night barn dance he intended to host over WSM. He found them "in churches, barbershops, gas stations, farms, front porch swings, and back-roads radio stations," a critic said. Once he put them on the air, Nashville's standing as an erudite "Athens of the South" was in jeopardy, the cultured upper crust of that municipality complaining vociferously. Their protestations to the contrary, Hay persisted in his quest. Before long a tradition was entrenched, the hills and hollows of middle Tennessee, southern Kentucky and northern Alabama emptying out on Saturday nights as a backwater brigade made its way to Nashville to pay their respects to Hay's innovation.

No one, of course, could have predicted the far-reaching implications that phenomenon would ultimately touch. An unalterable fact is that the *Grand Ole Opry's* tentacles have for a long time extended in many directions far beyond the original radio program. What began in 1925 has resulted in the capacity to influence much of the music that people listen to in their homes, their vehicles, their workplaces and wherever they are, whether it's country, pop, gospel or some other derivative of melody.

The impact of Nashville's Music Row — a conglomerate of major and minor recording studios compressed within a few square city blocks — has a powerful bearing on what is released to the nation's ears. And Nashville's industry has been at the forefront of that movement for many years. The city's ascension as a premier recording center is a credit not only to the radio show from which it materialized but to the skills and dedication of artists and executives who recognized its enormous possibilities and helped it secure such a strategic position. In so doing, they created what has become known as the "Nashville Sound," a distinct quality that has permeated millions of discs and has been broadcast around the globe.

The *Opry's* origins predate the widespread use of radio. George Dewey Hay, the father of country music, was born November 9, 1895, at Attica, Indiana. He was exposed to the South when he went to Camp Gordon, Georgia, for training during World War I and found himself enchanted by his experiences with southerners. After completing his tour of duty, he was hired by *The Commercial Appeal* in Memphis as a news reporter. Assigned to the police beat, he covered 137 murders in a single year. "It was the human interest in it that I loved," he remarked.

In time Hay was given his own column which he titled "Howdy Judge." (The nickname "Judge" was substituted for "George" during his childhood and stuck — hence, "The Solemn Old Judge" later.) In 1923, when the newspaper inaugurated radio station WMC, Hay was designated the radio editor and given a nightly hour to chat on the air about his encounters as a reporter.

During his time at Memphis, Hay once took an excursion on muleback into the foothills of the Ozark Mountains in northern Arkansas around Mammoth Spring. There he encountered homesteaders who lived such simple existences that most of their customs extended from the interval of the American Revolution. Hay was taken with their earthy characteristics, and especially found beguiling the primitive mountain sounds people enjoyed at dances and socials. Following a hoedown in a log cabin lit by coal oil lamps, he recalled, "No one has ever had more fun than those Ozark mountaineers had that night."

He became an exponent of their music, something he would never overcome, which was to influence him profoundly a few years later.

In early 1924, an exceptional opportunity materialized when Sears, Roebuck & Company launched its own radio station, WLS ("World's Largest Store") at its Chicago headquarters. Hay was invited to join its staff where he could not only renew his unshakable attraction for boondocks rhythm but also share it with thousands more by way of a novel broadcasting application. The outlet's ownership wooed him to host a Saturday night shindig that would feature instrumentalists and singers of the persuasion that had appealed to him during his trek to the Ozarks in 1919. He set his fee at $75 weekly, thinking WLS would surely turn him down. The station didn't flinch, and only later he learned it would have paid him $100 if he had asked for it. Hay was enamored with the South but, reluctantly, went to the Windy City, convinced it was too promising a prospect to pass up.

The *WLS Barn Dance*, as it was then called, debuted on April 19, 1924, beamed to much of the nation's upper middle section. It became a programming staple, so much so that NBC Blue picked it up on September 30, 1933, renaming it the *National Barn Dance*, and carried it to June 22, 1940. The following week, June 29, 1940, the program shifted to NBC Red where it persisted to September 28, 1946. Miles Laboratories, Inc. underwrote both NBC series for Alka-Seltzer distress reliever. The show aired over ABC for Sterling Drugs, Inc. and its Phillips Milk of Magnesia laxative brand from March 19, 1949, through March 11, 1950. The following week, March 18, 1950, it continued locally over Chicago's WLW until it was cancelled on April 30, 1960, some 36 years after its inception.

While he was at WLS, readers of *Radio Digest* picked Hay as "the most popular announcer in the United States." He garnered more than 120,000 votes in a write-in competition. That would bode well for him in the days ahead.

In the meantime, in Nashville, Tennessee, Edwin Craig, vice president of the National Life and Accident Insurance Company, had been lobbying the firm's owners to establish their own radio station. In the mid-1920s he convinced them that radio would be advantageous in promoting insurance policy sales in the 21 states where the firm's agents worked. The new station, with the call letters WSM (for National Life's slogan "We Shield Millions") was to be the second in the South (after Atlanta's WSB) to operate at an initial power of 1,000 watts. This seems diminutive today and compared with WSM's 50,000-watt clear channel acquired in 1932 is small, yet there was no interference then due to there being so few stations on the air so signals traveled extensive distances.

When the station went on the air on October 5, 1925, its formal opening ceremonies attracted Tennessee political dignitaries, local entertainers and a few well-known radio personalities from major markets. Among the latter group was the man who so recently had been voted the nation's "most popular announcer," George D. Hay. The occasion turned out to be providential. In an exchange with Edwin Craig, Hay discovered that station officials were seeking something that would translate into national identification. Because of the celebrity Hay had already achieved, he was offered a post with WSM. Possibly, Craig suggested, he might be able to start a "hillbilly music show" akin to the *WLS Barn Dance* he was then hosting. (Note: Country music has acquired copious labels that extend across the breadth of its history, going beyond hillbilly to encompass bluegrass, contemporary, folk, gospel, mountain, pop, rockabilly, rural, western and several other descriptive designations.)

A biographer recounted: "A discussion of folk music between Craig and Hay was a meeting of like minds. The thirty-four-year-old insurance executive had played a mandolin in a string band at school, and he liked the music played by rural people. He knew its heritage, once remarking that the folk music in the central South had derived from North Carolina camp meetings and that the camp meetings preserved songs brought to America from Scotland."[2]

Music critic John S. Wilson proffered: "Much of the appeal of country music ... is in its simplicity, the down-to-earth quality of its lyrics. Country music deals with human emotions, frequently centered around sin, guilt, and pain. Its words have a tradition of heartfelt simplicity and homespun reality. Among all musical idioms, it is durable, perhaps ageless."

Hay believed "that rural people deserved the chance to hear their own music on the radio, rather than having to accept programs dictated exclusively by urban tastes." His ideas and those of Craig were a good match. Hay accepted the offer for what has been estimated as a starting salary of $250 to $300 monthly. "He seems to have done so for love rather than money," wrote an observer.

It began as the *WSM Barn Dance*, a title similar to that used on Hay's previous show in Chicago. But a couple of years later it acquired the inscription that would seemingly remain for its lifetime. On a Saturday night in 1927, an unplanned ad-lib by the infamous Solemn Old Judge provided a distinctive moniker. After an hour-long broadcast of the *Music Appreciation Hour* directed by the eminent composer-conductor Walter Damrosch, Hay declared to his radio listeners: "For the past hour, we have been listening to music taken largely from Grand Opera. But from now on, we will present the Grand Ole Opry." The handle stuck.

For many years, Hay opened each show with a long blast on an old steamboat whistle, then cried: "All right, let'er go, boys!" And the rustic music began.

After sawing his fiddle for an hour on the *Opry's* first performance, told his time was up, 83-year-old dirt farmer Uncle Jimmy Thompson, a Civil War veteran, exclaimed, "Shucks, a man can't get warmed up in an hour!" Hay asked him to return the following week and to bring with him some of his banjo-picking friends.

Thompson didn't last long. On a subsequent occasion, he totally passed out, plunging to the floor in front of the mike without warning. "Uncle Jimmy isn't feeling very well tonight" was Hay's understated explanation.

To the program itself, listener reaction was swift. Nashville's elite termed the exhibit "awful," convinced that — if it persisted — the city's cultural standing would be ruined. Even Mrs. Hay, who intended to climb the ladder of Nashville society, turned a deaf ear to her spouse's profession, calling his subjects "dreadful hillbillies." (The couple would later divorce.) But within a matter of days hundreds of letters of affirmation flowed in to WSM, and not only from rural areas but from large hubs like Atlanta, Cincinnati, Memphis and St. Louis, all of which still maintained some semblance of refinement. Praising the show because it reflected the life of sincere, humble folk, city dwellers with roots deep in rural soil acknowledged their support of a country hoedown over the airwaves and begged for more.

"Soon the mountain folk began to swarm into the studio, bringing with them unwritten songs that had been passed from generation to generation," a historian divulged. "Some walked down; some came on mules and in wagons.... None could read music; they just scraped and sawed away by ear, turning out the closest thing to pure Americana ever heard on the air." Tunes like *Brown's Ferry Blues*, *Greenback Dollar* and *Rabbit in the Flea Patch* were among the most frequently repeated in those days. Southern folk melodies dominated the early agenda. Some of the initial acts included Uncle Ed Poplin and His Old Timers, Arthur Smith and His Dixie Liners, Paul Warmack and His Gully Jumpers and the Brinkley Brothers and Their Clod Hoppers.

The Tennessean, a leading newspaper of that city, took note of the show's inception in its December 27, 1925, edition, a month after the launch.

> Old tunes like old lovers are the best at least judging from the applause which the new Saturday night features at WSM receive from listeners from all parts of the country. Jazz has not completely turned the tables on such tunes as *Turkey in the Straw* and *Pop Goes the Weasel*. America may not be swinging its partners at a barndance, but it seems to have the habit of clamping on earphones and patting its feet as gaily as it ever did when the old-time fiddlers get going.

Most of the early music was instrumental. But by 1926, a banjo-picking singing star appeared, Uncle Dave Macon. Wearing a wide-brimmed black felt hat and an unbuttoned double-breasted waistcoat, he would set the pace for what was to follow. For 15 years "The Dixie Dewdrop," as he was affectionately christened, was to be the show's single biggest attraction. He made the performance a regional phenomenon while his "successor," Roy Acuff, who joined the cast in 1938, made it a national treasure. By 1941, there were nearly 100 performers in the *Opry* entourage and the exhibition was already becoming established as a country music institution, extending well beyond the confines of Nashville. Even in its early years WSM was reaching into 30 states, and later to 38 states and Canada. People from as far away as Alaska were regularly penning its fan mail.

The crowds turning out for the live Saturday night performances soon overflowed WSM's small fifth-floor studio at the National Life Building facing Nashville's central square downtown, in front of the Tennessee Capitol Building. That little studio accommodated only about 75 spectators. But in no time there were already at least 50 performers! Something had to give. National Life responded by constructing Studio C, an auditorium facility with a stage at its far end and a capacity to seat 500 people. It contained the burgeoning onlookers for a while (and indeed, was still being used to air the *Friday Night Opry* (originally, *Friday Night Frolics*) from the late 1940s through the early 1960s.

The stars and their backup players ambled down a long middle aisle to get to and from the platform, stopping along the route to talk with fawning fans and generously signing autographs. The shows had no separate entrances or elevators for talent in those days. This author clearly remembers that anybody could mix freely with stars that had earned national reputations while on those elevator rides, in hallways and in seats along the middle aisle. The *Opry* performers related to their audiences so intimately perhaps because their roots were so firmly planted in the rural areas from which many of their fans emanated. Even in contemporary times many of the stars welcome their admirers rather than shun them, not separated by bodyguards and other security measures that celebrities elsewhere expect. This was especially characteristic of the Opryland U.S.A. theme park, where big-name artists strolled nonchalantly through the grounds greeting admirers, answering questions and signing autographs for any who asked.

The day at last came when the *Grand Ole Opry* outgrew Studio C. The increasing demand for seats continued unabated.

The *Opry* was forced to seek larger facilities. Subsequently, in 1934 it moved to the 750-seat Hillsboro Theater on Belcourt Avenue on the city's southern perimeter, then in 1936 to the Dixie Tabernacle on Fatherland Street in east Nashville that accommodated about 2,000 patrons on crude bench seats. In July 1939, the program shifted back downtown to the 2,200-seat War Memorial Auditorium opposite the National Life headquarters building. That's where it was when it began broadcasting on a nationwide hookup. In 1941, it moved a few blocks away to the 4,000-seat Ryman Auditorium, the structure it would occupy for more than three decades and a name that was to become synonymous with the *Opry*.

Eventually, the Saturday night four-and-a-half-hour performance was split into two two-and-a-half-hour shows to accommodate more people. In 1974, the *Opry* moved into gleaming new quarters erected especially for it, called the Grand Ole Opry House, seating 4,340 spectators, on the city's eastern border. Not only did the dual performances on Saturday night continue, a second show was added on Friday nights during the peak (summer) tourist season along with performances on other weeknights and matinee shows as needed to accommodate the crowds. In recent years, the *Opry* has returned to the confines of the Ryman Auditorium every winter to perpetuate the tradition so many fans associate with that historic facility.

Parenthetically, in the 1930s, WSM began feeding the National Broadcasting Company, the chain with which it had long been affiliated, regular programming for airing across the nation. Nashville native Jack Stapp, who became program director at Atlanta's WGST and hired singer Bert Parks while there, moved with Parks to CBS in New York where the entertainer became a popular radio announcer and Stapp moved up as acting production manager for the network. After five years in the Big Apple, in the mid-1930s, WSM offered him a position as its second in command. Stapp jumped at it. Before leaving New York, he contacted NBC officials, telling them he hoped to feed them some programs from Nashville, and got a favorable response.

Within a few weeks of his return to Nashville, Stapp organized an 18-piece staff orchestra and started producing several polished hour-long musical shows for the network. NBC accepted them when its schedule contained openings. Calling his first trial *Sunday Down South*, a series of Sunday afternoon features, Stapp exposed pop singers Snooky Lanson and Dinah Shore to national audiences there. Many other series would follow in its train. (WSM, incidentally, is one of a handful of local stations within the nation's heartland that maintained a live studio orchestra throughout most of the 1980s, which it called upon daily for performances on both radio and television.)

It would not be an unbelievable stretch, then, for WSM to seek to air its Saturday night hoedown beyond the territory its own transmitter could grasp. On October 14, 1939, with a large contingent of network executives watching from the audience, the *Grand Ole Opry* went nationwide, carried coast-to-coast by the National Broadcasting Company. While the premiering network show didn't encompass NBC's full reaches at first — affiliates in some large metropolitan markets preferred not to air it for a while — the show was available to them and was beamed from outlets on both coasts.

It was a momentous occasion brought about by the perseverance of the radio director at New York's William Esty advertising agency, Dick Marvin. He devoted a year to convincing the network and an advertiser. Among Esty's clients was the R. J. Reynolds Tobacco Company of Winston-Salem, North Carolina. Marvin was finally able to sell a half-hour portion of the *Opry* to Reynolds for live transmission over NBC on Saturday nights on behalf of the firm's Prince Albert pipe tobacco brand. "That sale turned out to be the most important in the Opry's history," said a historiographer.

Anyone who has attended the *Opry* in person knows that the performances tend to run rather loose. They are, for the most part, unscripted and — throughout the show's history, until contemporary times, at least — pickers and singers wandered on and off the stage at will. When their names were called ushering them to a microphone to perform, they were often already in plain view of the spectators, having possibly been there for some time. This was especially true in the years before the program shifted to the Grand Ole Opry House. Thus, there were people wandering all over the stage, carrying on private conversations with one another, while the program progressed. It gave the appearance of disorganized confusion.

A podium to one side of the stage with a lamp nearby was for the announcer who introduced the various segments and ushered them off the air, plus for reading the commercial copy, about the only thing that wasn't written down on the back of an envelope. The show was sold in quarter-hour and half-hour segments to local, regional and national sponsors. When it originated at the Ryman Auditorium — as the big red curtains temporarily closed between segments — a backdrop featuring the next advertiser's products was rolled down at the rear of the stage or a billboard was shoved into view or some other props provided to indicate who the sponsor was for the benefit of the live audience. It might be the Coca-Cola Company, W. E. Stephens Manufacturing Company (work clothes), Martha White Foods (flour, cornbread and biscuit mixes), Standard Candy Company (Goo-Goo candy bars), Pet Milk Company, Cracker Barrel Old Country Store, Procter & Gamble Company (Lava soap), W. K. Kellogg Company (cereals), Ralston Purina Company (cereals), Jamison Bedding Company (mattresses), Jefferson Island salt or any of dozens of other manufacturers or retailers that purchased segments of the show. There has seldom been an advertising opening that hasn't been quickly filled.

The show's timing, while important, has always been a variable on the *Opry*. As long as a segment began or ended within a couple of minutes either way of its scheduled time period that was satisfactory to the program's clients, performers and patrons. The advertisers understand that, if their portion runs a little over one week, it might run a mite under its allotted time the following week. But when the network decided to include the *Opry* on its Saturday night agenda, that laid-back system had to be altered for obvious reasons.

"Heretofore, we had not made any attempt to produce the show, in the accepted sense of the word," according to George D. Hay. "We had to be snatched off the air at the end of our thirty minutes [when the show went on the network], but with that exception, the half hour went over pretty well. Before the next week rolled around, we had timed our opening and closing and had no further difficulty."

This author became a veteran eyewitness to many of the *Opry* performances, including some of the network programs. Lester Flatt and Earl Scruggs (who may be recalled as the music-makers picking and singing *The Beverly Hillbillies* TV show theme) headlined the half-hour immediately prior to the network feature in its later years. They *had* to get off the air before 8:29 P.M. Central Time in order for their portion to properly conclude and allow time for required commercials and station ID before the next portion began at straight up 8:30:00. Thus, they broke into their final number well before that.

Meanwhile, along about 8:25 there was a noticeable change in the tempo around and behind them as instrumentalists accompanying the headliner for the next half-hour arrived on stage to set up shop. In this scribe's memory, portable stands were temporarily added at several floor microphones across the front of the platform and sheaves of paper stacked on them, the audience spectators discovering soon enough that those were scripts. For that one half-hour, every word spoken into the microphones had been typed out, surpassing the commercials to include all introductions and jokes and banter between on-air personalities during the Prince Albert show. It had been timed and rehearsed earlier, too, the only segment to get that specialized treatment on the *Opry*.

The heavy curtain was lowered and Flatt and Scruggs and their accompanying instrumentalists, the Foggy Mountain Boys, exited the stage. The Martha White flour backdrop behind the performers was raised and replaced with one for Prince Albert pipe tobacco. The audience could hear the commercials and other announcements, including the familiar station identification, going out over the air: "Clear Channel, 650, WSM, the broadcasting service of the National Life and Accident Insurance Company, Nashville, Tennessee, now bringing you the *Grand Ole Opry* from the stage of Ryman Auditorium in downtown Nashville."

Then there was a hush of possibly 10 seconds as the sweeping second hand of a large wall clock moved upward toward the figure 12. At that precise instant, the music resumed and announcer Grant Turner welcomed the nation to the *Grand Ole Opry*, sponsored by Prince Albert. Spectators felt a rush of adrenalin for they knew that *this* show was going out to as many as 10 million homes all over America. Transmitting a live broadcast, at that auspicious moment, was as momentous in Nashville as it was every day in New York, Chicago, Detroit and Hollywood.

On the Ryman stage, as performers read their lines and arrived at the end of a page, they quietly dropped the sheet they were reading to the floor, just the way it was done on shows fronted by Jack Benny, Edgar Bergen and Bing Crosby. By the time the half-hour was over, the stage was littered in 8½ × 11 sheets that were swept up and removed after the big curtain fell between half-hour segments. The only distinguishing difference between the *Opry* and the variety shows emanating from the coasts, in fact, appeared to be that this music was lowdown hoedown rather than sophisticated strings that backed pop stars.

After 8:59, when the network show ended, everything on the *Opry* stage resumed its typical casual personality. Segments ran long or short, the scripts and portable stands were gone, cast members and stagehands milled about the platform in idle chatter, seemingly oblivious to the 4,000 pairs of eyes fixed on them, a decidedly more relaxed state than the network show had allowed. Now they could "be themselves" again. While nobody had changed wardrobes, bib overalls and colorful checkered shirts and gingham dresses were once again in vogue.

That was part of the beauty of the *Opry* in the years before it moved to a more stylish Grand Ole Opry House, and especially in the pretelevision era. A segment of the show is presently beamed to a nationwide TV audience every Saturday night with some of the same parameters of the live NBC show that prevailed (except for a 14-month break in 1953-1954) to December 28, 1957.

The Prince Albert network portion produced several "stars" that appeared on it every week. Roy Acuff, who in later years would be designated "The King of Country Music," was the show's headliner during the early years. Comedienne Cousin

Minnie Pearl (Sarah Ophelia Colley Cannon), "The Gossip of Grinder's Switch," was also permanently entrenched in that half hour, keeping a rollicking audience fulfilled with her humorous tales of mythical relatives.

In 1942, Benjamin Francis "Whitey" Ford, the widely-touted "Duke of Paducah," was enticed from the predecessor *National Barn Dance* in Chicago, joining the Prince Albert troupe as a comedian. One wag termed him "slick, polished, citywise," the result of broad experience in big-time amusement with Otto Gray's Oklahoma Cowboys, then fronting a road show for Gene Autry and later appearing on multiple Chicago-based radio series. Ford's trademark farewell became a standard catchphrase among hillbilly music fans after he joined the Prince Albert segment: "I'm goin' back to the wagon, boys, these shoes are a-killin' me!"

In addition to Roy Acuff and Minnie Pearl and a guest or two each week from the *Opry*'s extensive cast, other talent appearing regularly on the Prince Albert show included a guitar solo by Chet Atkins; an occasional piano number by Moon Mullican; a square dance featuring the Stony Mountain Cloggers or the Tennessee Travelers and backed by a longstanding *Opry* instrumental unit such as the Crook Brothers or the Fruit Jar Drinkers; and choral backup by the Old Hickory Singers who—while gathered around Mullican's piano—cut loose every week with the commercial jingle after an announcer's spirited proclamations favoring the tobacco sponsor.

> *Roll your own with good P. A.*
> *And take a puff, or two...*
> *You'll get that extra smoking joy*
> *Prince Albert ... brings to you!*

In October 1943, NBC started airing the Prince Albert portion of the show on its full coast-to-coast network, then comprised of more than 125 affiliates. The program had, unmistakably, for the first time acquired national — and permanent — attention. It would be a significantly influential force within the music industry's many facets forever more.

In 1946, the soon-to-be legendary Roy Acuff got into a contractual dispute with R. J. Reynolds officials that couldn't be resolved to both parties' satisfaction. As a result Acuff left the Prince Albert show, though not the *Opry* itself. Esty, Reynolds' New York ad agency, once again summoned a performer from the *National Barn Dance*. A native Kentuckian, baritone Clyde Julian "Red" Foley, one of the Chicago-based radio series' most popular personalities, was picked to follow Acuff in the coveted Prince Albert spot. Foley soon brought in Chet Atkins as featured guitarist. Some time hence Esty decided to eliminate Atkins from the lineup and the gifted instrumentalist left Nashville for a while, returning to the city down the road.

There were still more changes coming in the network portion's lineup. In 1948, Whitey Ford, Esty's handpicked comedian plucked from Chicago six years earlier, had his own dispute with the sponsor which also couldn't be satisfactorily resolved. He was sent packing, literally headed "back to the wagon." His replacement was a Hohenwald, Tennessee, comedian named Rod Brasfield (calling himself "The Hohenwald Flash") whom audiences instantly loved.

Over the course of his time with the *Opry* he and Minnie Pearl worked up dozens of verbal routines that they performed weekly to the delight of audiences at the Ryman as well as those tuning in across the nation. She would play the "straight man" and he would come across as a country fool. "It scared her badly sometimes when they did it on the network show, because she could never be sure what Brasfield was going to do, especially if he had had a drink," a critic recounted. Minnie, herself, claimed: "Sometimes on the network he

Cousin Minnie Pearl, she of the price-tagged blooming bonnet, never really knew what to expect from comedian Rod Brasfield, especially when he was a little tipsy and left the script behind for their NBC portion of the *Grand Ole Opry*. The pair tickled the nation's funnybone at midtwentieth century as folks at the Ryman and across America rollicked.

would get me way off the routine we were supposed to be doing, just for the fun of gradually pulling me back into it again."

The success of the limited network broadcast attracted yet another national advertiser. In January 1943, the Ralston Purina Company began to underwrite a similar half-hour broadcast of the *Opry*, sending the show to stations in the South and Southwest.

In the meantime, and as early as 1934, the WSM staff began booking and promoting road show appearances of *Opry* acts, charging 15 percent for its services. Organized by Judge Hay, the Artist's Service Bureau was a profitable sideline for the station. In succeeding years it went through several permutations to remain a viable means of assisting members of the *Opry* family.

In the spring of 1940, in Hollywood, Republic Pictures filmed a movie titled *Grand Ole Opry* featuring the legendary radio series. The production was completed in a two-week period by the same outfit responsible for putting singing cowboys Gene Autry and Roy Rogers in scores of Western films. The *Opry* motion picture premiered that year at a gala at Nashville's Paramount Theater and included many of the motion picture's featured acts.

WSM, nevertheless, was determined to be at the forefront of the music business growing up around the Opry. As historiographer Jack Hurst demonstrates, this was not always a simple task.[3]

> In 1948, [Eddy] Arnold threatened to leave the Opry unless he received a percentage of the gate receipts. WSM refused to make such an arrangement. All Opry stars were paid the same amount — the "scale" set by the musicians' union for pay to a leader of a group in Nashville — although some received special pay from advertisers on whose portions of the show they appeared.
>
> Arnold's manager ... sold a series of transcribed Arnold half-hour shows to Ralston Purina. These were then offered to WSM for airing on Saturday nights. WSM refused to take them because doing so would mean breaking up the Opry broadcast. The shows were then offered to another Nashville station [WLAC] for use on Friday nights.
>
> Irving Waugh ... WSM's sales director ... heard about the offer to the other station, [and] he flew to St. Louis to the Ralston Purina vice-president in charge of advertising....
>
> "I told them that if they put the Eddy Arnold show in this market it had to go on WSM, because we were the country station," Waugh says....
>
> "I told him that if he went on the other station on Friday night, we would put a live country music show against him, and in front of him, and behind him," Waugh recalls....
>
> "He finally said, 'You can have it, but you'll have to do what you say you would do if the show went on the other station — you'll have to build a live show in front of it and behind it.'"

That situation prompted the launch of *The Friday Night Frolics* (later *Friday Night Opry*) in 1949. But even that didn't come about easily. Edwin Craig, Waugh's superior, "kept me upstairs for three and a half hours" over it on his return to Nashville, Waugh remembered. Craig complained that the overexposure by adding a second night's performance would dilute the program. Waugh reasoned that putting on the Friday night show was in line with Craig's perpetual instructions: try to make friends for the parent company, deliver the biggest audience we can, and make a dollar if possible. "This will do all of those things," Waugh assured him. Craig finally let it go and the Friday night series was born. It continues today, thriving more than a half-century later.

For all intents and purposes the Friday night performance is a duplication of the Saturday night show. While the sponsors are different, the format is integrated into quarter-hour and half-hour segments presenting the same performers and often the same songs as on Saturday night. Craig's worry about overexposure seems unfounded given these years of perspective. During the peak travel season, for instance, tickets must be ordered for either night (two shows nightly) months in advance. While the cost as this is written hovers close to $40 a seat for much of the year (a slight increase from the 25 cents instituted to "control the crowd" years ago!), there are plenty of patrons willing to cough it up.

In the autumn of 1947, George D. Hay, who started it all, suffered an emotional collapse. While he remained with WSM for another decade, his duties were largely confined to a trio of appearances on the Saturday night shows and a quarter-hour Saturday morning entry called *Strictly Personal* on which he discussed *Opry* stars. One of his Saturday night duties was the sign-off spot for the hoedown, reprising a classical routine he introduced many years earlier. It may have been heartrending for those who tuned in for a very long time, particularly in Hay's declining years.

That's all for now friends,
Because the tall pines pine,
And the pawpaws pause,
And the bumblebees bumble all around....
The grasshoppers hop,
And the eavesdroppers drop,
While, gently, the ole cow slips away...
George D. Hay saying so long for now.

Hay was elected to the Country Music Hall of Fame in 1966, another direct descendant of the *Opry* itself. He died at Virginia Beach, Virginia on May 7, 1968. Today the George D. Hay Foundation at Mammoth Spring, Arkansas, perpetuates his legacy. This is the same hamlet where Hay initially encountered rustic mountain music during an all-night hoedown in 1919, with the community now linking itself to the *Grand Ole Opry* as a direct contributor. A museum honoring the patron saint of country music has been established and, as of early 2004, the George D. Hay Music Hall of Fame Theater scheduled a local band to perform every Saturday night.

In 1952, the *Opry* began to observe a "Grand Ole Opry Birthday Celebration" every October. Disc jockeys from all over the nation who spun platters made by *Opry* stars were feted during the annual festivities. The commemoration is still marked today.

Over the years the stars came and went and the music styles were updated. The music business surrounding the *Opry* has mushroomed many fold from radio to records, sheet music, personal appearances, books and other printed materials, merchandising, television, motion pictures, theme parks, Web sites, videos, cassettes, DVDs and to many other diverse areas of American entertainment. All of that is an outgrowth of a simple radio show that cast a lasting impetus over the nation's amusement choices.

Of course, simultaneously, there were many other hillbilly-oriented or country music shows emanating from local radio stations across the country while the *Grand Ole Opry* was rising to the forefront of the industry. Some of those shindigs rivaled the Nashville hoedown for a while. According to *Opry* historians, WSM officials were not only mindful of their existence but regularly assessed whatever real or perceived threats to their own show's existence the others projected. At times this resulted in overtures to top stars elsewhere, allaying the executives' fears for their survival by adding promising new talent to the permanent *Opry* roster.

The following is a partial list of the leading country music series originated by local stations during this period. Portions of a handful of these were also carried on national networks at varying times:

Badger State Barn Dance— WRJN, Milwaukee, Wisconsin
Barnyard Frolics— KLRA, Little Rock, Arkansas
Big D Jamboree— KRLD, Dallas, Texas
Brush Creek Follies— KMBC, Kansas City, Missouri
Carolina Hayride— WBT, Charlotte, North Carolina
Hayloft Jamboree— WCOP, Boston, Massachusetts
Hometown Jamboree— KXLA, Pasadena, California
Hometown Jamboree— WAMO, Pittsburgh, Pennsylvania
Hometown Jamboree— WHIL, Medford, Massachusetts
Louisiana Hayride— KWKH, Shreveport, Louisiana
Midwestern Hayride— WLW, Cincinnati, Ohio
National Barn Dance— WLS, WGN, Chicago, Illinois
Old Dominion Barn Dance— WRVA, Richmond, Virginia
Old Kentucky Barn Dance— WHAS, Louisville, Kentucky
Ozark Jubilee (aka *Jubilee USA*)— KWTO, Springfield, Missouri
Renfro Valley Barn Dance— WHAS, Louisville, Kentucky; WLW, Cincinnati, Ohio
Saturday Nite Shindig— WFAA, Dallas, Texas
Tennessee Barn Dance— WNOX, Knoxville, Tennessee
Texas Barn Dance— KWBU, Corpus Christi, Texas
WCKY Jamboree— WCKY, Cincinnati, Ohio
WJR Barn Dance— WJR, Detroit, Michigan
WSB Barn Dance— WSB, Atlanta, Georgia
WWVA Jamboree (aka *Jamboree USA*)— WWVA, Wheeling, West Virginia

A connoisseur of acoustic old-time country and bluegrass music, Bill Knowlton, who hosts *The Bluegrass Ramble* that airs on WCNY-FM, Syracuse-Utica-Watertown, New York, exclaims: "Sad to say, only *Jamboree USA* remains, but only a shadow of its former mountain music self. WWVA first airs it *live* early on Saturday night before its 50kw clear channel output sets in, but they do repeat it later in the evening. Although there are occasional bluegrass bands, *Jamboree USA* is mostly extreme modern country with relatively unknown acts serving as window dressing for a big out-of-town country music guest."[4]

Not particularly good news for anybody who recalls *when*— and misses what isn't broadcast most places any more.

Still dreaming big, in 1972 an innovative WSM opened a 110-acre amusement park known as Opryland U.S.A. on Nashville's eastern edge. In addition to numerous thrill rides and other attractions appealing to every member of the family, strong emphasis was placed on music as the core of the park's operation. More than a dozen live shows highlighting various musical genres were staged daily. The 1.4 million visitors attending that first year exceeded WSM's utmost expectations. The park proved a popular tourist destination for a quarter of a century, until new *Opry* owners decided to move in an altogether different direction, replacing the theme park with a shopping mall a few years ago.

The Grand Ole Opry House, a shiny new $15 million home for an American entertainment tradition, opened at Opryland U.S.A. in 1974. President Richard Nixon played piano onstage during the inaugural performance in the unsullied digs of the world's most durable country music show. There to greet him were Roy Acuff, Minnie Pearl and legions of the faithful who had come to worship at a new shrine. The *Opry* was an incredible "institution" then — and is even more so now when measured against everything else on the air. Although the Solemn Old Judge would have difficulty recognizing much of the music, the instruments and performers at that venue today, it succeeded where all the others failed. Hay once referred to it as "a good-natured riot." It never was anything less.

The Horse Operas

When Harold Gray's popular comic strip character Little Orphan Annie was adapted to a serialized radio format in 1930 — the first adventure thriller to be targeted at younger listeners — a new wave of radio programming was introduced. The profound focus of most of the new features was in righting wrongs, overcoming evil and meting out justice. Enter the action heroes of the Old West who first appeared in silent movies, made their way to talkies and then into radio. Shortly after the inception of sound motion pictures, a new idol appeared on the screen — the singing cowboy. It wasn't long before he was also turning up on the ether. Although the number was limited, a couple of vocalist-thespians became icons in more than one medium. While the small fry found desirable models, they were well received by older generations, too, who liked their acting, approved their moral lifestyles and hummed along as they sang.

Gene Autry's Melody Ranch

Producer-Director: Bill Burch.
Director: Fletcher Markle.

Host-Star: Gene Autry.
Musicians: Johnny Bond (comic vocalist), the Cass County Boys (trio — Bert Dobson, Fred Martin, Jerry Scroggins), Carl Cotner (steel guitarist), Eddie Dean; Mary Ford (vocalist), the Gene Autry Blue Jeans (ensemble), Jerry Hausner, the King Sisters (quartet — Alyce, Donna, Louise, Yvonne), Harry Lang, Frankie Marvin (instrumentalist), Jack Mather, the Melody Ranch Six (sextet), Horace Murphy, the Pinafores (ensemble), Alvino Rey (guitarist), Paul Sills (bandmaster), Jimmy Wakely (vocalist).
Support Roles: Sara Berner (actress), Jim Boles, Pat Buttram (comedian), Scotty Harrel, Wally Maher, Frank Mahoney, Nancy Mason, Tyler McVey (actor).
Announcers: Lou Crosby, Tom Hanlon, Charles Lyon, Wendell Niles.
Writers: George Anderson, Irwin Ashkenazy, Carroll Carroll, Doris Gilbert, Ed James.
Sound Effects Techs: Gus Bayz, Ray Erlenborn, David Light, Jerry McCarty, Gene Twombly.
Theme Song: *Back in the Saddle Again* (Gene Autry, Ray Whitley).
Sponsor: William J. Wrigley Company

for Doublemint chewing gum (all performances).

Ratings: High—15.2 (1949-1950 season); Low—3.2 (1955-1956); Median—8.8 (all seasons included except 1954-1955). Numbers in double digits in five of 14 seasons represented an excellent mark for a prime-time series that drew many adolescents.

On the Air: January 7, 1940–August 1, 1943, CBS, Sunday, 6:30–7:00 P.M. Eastern Time (expanded to 6:30–7:15 P.M. for 1941-1942 season); September 23, 1945–June 9, 1946, CBS, Sunday, 5:30–6:00 P.M.; June 16, 1946–December 19, 1948, CBS, Sunday, 7:00–7:30 P.M.; December 25, 1948–June 24, 1950, CBS, Saturday, 8:00–8:30 P.M.; July 29, 1950–June 30, 1951, CBS, Saturday, 8:00–8:30 P.M.; August 4, 1951–July 25, 1953, CBS, Saturday, 8:00–8:30 P.M.; August 2, 1953–May 13, 1956, CBS, Sunday, 6:00– or 6:05–6:30 P.M.

The Roy Rogers Show

Producer-Director: Tom Hargis.
Producer: Art Rush.
Directors: Fran Van Hartesfeldt, Ralph Rose.
Host-Star: Roy Rogers.
Musicians: Perry Botkin (orchestra), Milton Charles (orchestra), Pat Friday (vocalist), the Mello Men (vocal ensemble), Riders of the Purple Sage (vocal ensemble), Frank Smith (orchestra), the Sons of the Pioneers (vocal ensemble, at varying times including Ken Dawson, Hugh Farr, Bob Nolan and Tim Spenser), the Whipporwills (vocal ensemble), Foy Willing (vocalist), Frank Worth (orchestra).
Support Roles: Pat Brady, Pat Buttram, Herb Butterfield, Leo Curley, Dale Evans, Gabby Hayes, Frank Hemingway, Forrest Lewis, Pat McGeehan, Marvin Miller, Ralph Moody, Ken Peters, Stan Waxman.
Announcers: Lou Crosby, Verne Smith.
Dramatic Narrator: Frank Hemingway.
Writers: Ralph Rose, Ray Wilson.
Sound Effects Tech: Bob Conan.
Theme Songs: *Smiles Are Made Out of Sunshine, It's Roundup Time on the Double R Bar, Happy Trails to You* (the latter by Dale Evans).
Sponsors: Goodyear Tire and Rubber Company for Goodyear tires and other vehicle products (November 21, 1944–May 15, 1945), Miles Laboratories, Inc. for Alka-Seltzer stomach distress reliever and other health care products (October 5, 1946–March 29, 1947), Quaker Oats Company for various breakfast cereals (August 29, 1948–May 13, 1951), General Foods, Inc. for various Post brand breakfast cereals (October 5, 1951–August 20, 1953), October 1–December 24, 1953), sustained (August 25–September 29, 1953), Chrysler Corporation for Dodge automobiles and trucks, parts and service (January 28, 1954–July 21, 1955).

Ratings: High—12.1 (1949-1950 season); Low—3.3 (1954-1955); Median—7.3 (all seasons included in tally except 1953-1954). In only one of the series' eight seasons for which data exists did the numbers climb to double digits.

On the Air: *The Roy Rogers Show* (aka *Roy Rogers*), November 21, 1944–May 15, 1945, MBS, Tuesday, 8:30–9:00 P.M. Eastern Time; October 5, 1946–March 29, 1947, NBC, Saturday, 9:00–9:30 P.M.; August 29, 1948–June 25, 1950, MBS, Sunday, 6:00–6:30 P.M.; August 6, 1950–May 13, 1951, MBS, Sunday, 6:00–6:30 P.M.; October 5, 1951–June 27, 1952, NBC, Friday, 8:00–8:30 P.M.; August 28, 1952–August 20, 1953, NBC, Thursday, 8:00–8:25 P.M.; August 25–September 29, 1953, NBC, Tuesday, 6:00–6:30 P.M.; October 1–December 24, 1953, NBC, Thursday, 8:00–8:25 P.M.; *The Roy Rogers Radio Show* (aka *Roy Rogers*), January 28,

1954–July 21, 1955, NBC, Thursday, 8:00–8:30 P.M.

* * *

On a Saturday night in 1927, an unplanned ad-lib over Nashville's WSM Radio by the famous Solemn Old Judge, George D. Hay, provided a distinctive moniker for what subsequently became America's longest-running ethereal tradition. After an hour-long broadcast of the *Music Appreciation Hour* directed by the eminent composer-conductor Walter Damrosch, Hay declared to his radio listeners: "For the past hour, we have been listening to music taken largely from Grand Opera. But from now on, we will present the Grand Ole Opry." The appellation stuck. A new ritual was christened, and it became the archetypical phenomenon of the breed. (See the *Grand Ole Opry* chapter for further details.)

The *Grand Ole Opry* was not to be the only radio feature gaining stature from an operatic label by any means. *Soap operas* were next, arriving in 1930 — those dainty dishpan dramas that occupied milady with sagas of domestic disunity while she performed her household chores throughout the day. That model's designation was derived from the principal soapmaking concerns that underwrote a profusion of washboard weepers at their air-life inception.

Finally, there was yet another programming trend that exploited the term — becoming affectionately known in some circles as "horse operas." These action-oriented dramatic narratives could be identified by their setting, on the Western plains during the days of America's continental settlement. Most were further characterized by a relentless pursuit of lawlessness as one or more heroic figures emerged to tame the frontier by disparaging any who employed illegal methods of self-aggrandizement.

One's choices were hardly limited when looking for idols that matched personal values and interests. In its heyday, radio gave audiences a steady diet of the good guy vs. bad guy syndrome in the form of *Bobby Benson and the B-Bar-B Riders, The Cisco Kid, Frontier Town, Gene Autry's Melody Ranch, Hashknife Hartley, Hawk Larabee, Hoofbeats, Hopalong Cassidy, Law West of the Pecos, Lightning Jim, The Lone Ranger, Maverick Jim, Red Ryder, The Roy Rogers Show, The Sheriff, Six Gun Justice, Straight Arrow, Tennessee Jed, Tom Mix, Wild Bill Hickok* and *The Zane Grey Show.*

In the 1950s, the medium added several adult-oriented Westerns where chaos still reigned including *Dr. Sixgun, Gunsmoke, Have Gun — Will Travel, Luke Slaughter of Tombstone* and *The Six Shooter.* Anyone looking for a good "shoot-em-up" could find it in several places on the golden-age ether.

Of those 26 features, a handful took on traits of the movie idols on which some of them were based. In the early 1930s, a new breed of pictures infiltrated the silver screen that focused on the singing cowboy. A handful of rising professionals who could both act and sing were signed to play in Western films in which music was integrated into the plotlines. Thus a hero might be out on the prairie, riding horseback while chasing thieves, murderers, stagecoach bandits and cattle rustlers and — during a lull in the action — be overcome with a sudden compulsion to hoist a tune. The boys riding with him, consistently possessing equally trained tonal abilities, chimed in, harmonizing on a chorus or two of *Let the Rest of the World Go By* or whatever melodic notion had impulsively stricken the protagonist. (It always seemed a mystery to this observer that whatever number the hero selected the ranch hands invariably knew all its words. Did they practice in between roping the steers, mending the fences and baling the hay, perhaps?)

Before long, radio took advantage of the new trend that the celluloid producers had established in theaters, populating some of their aural offerings with singing cowboys, too. A pair of personalities virtually dominated the terrain while a few "also rans" will be mentioned in due course. Gene Autry and Roy Rogers became the most widely known headliners on several fronts. Both men attracted large followings not only in movies and on radio but also on records, at personal stage-show appearances and championship rodeos and other venues and as mass merchandising marketers and, in time, television stars. Each was a gifted actor and singer and wore well with multiple generations of fans.

Gene Autry's Melody Ranch sometimes went by other titles like *The Gene Autry Show* or a more simplistic *Melody Ranch*. Under either moniker, it was a combination of several elements designed to content the tykes and preteens while their parents hummed along. The sweet balladeer dubbed "America's Favorite Cowboy" rolled out some picturesque Western tunes—*Tumbling Tumbleweeds*, *I'm an Old Cowhand*, *Cool Water*, *Don't Fence Me In* and of course his signature *Back in the Saddle Again*.

Between numbers, which were frequently backed by the soothing accompaniment of the Cass County Boys, "the boss man himself" swapped humorous lines with other members of the *Melody Ranch* troupe—froggy-voiced sidekick Pat Buttram, comic Johnny Bond and other "cowpokes" whose names often went unregistered but who did a credible job making it sound as if a large crowd had gathered. A mythical campfire outside Autry's cattle farm in the San Fernando Mountains of southern California was the normal setting for each week's show. Announcer Charlie Lyon as well as host Autry offered lots of reasons every week to stock up on "healthful, refreshing, delicious Doublemint chewing gum."

And just when you didn't think you could stand one more bit of harmony or another corny joke, along came the treat that the kids had been waiting for—about a 12-minute dramatic adventure in which good triumphed over evil. Autry narrated those tales as if he were sharing them with the "hands," but the audience at home got the benefit of it, too, as they eavesdropped on his stories of skill, bravery and perseverance. Autry might recall an incident in which he tracked down an owlhoot who had wronged somebody. Think cattle rustler, bank robber, horse thief, stagecoach bandit, arsonist or even murderer—pick one. A supporting cast of dramatic players acted out the brief improvisations. And like other radio heroes of his day, Autry got his man without killing him—wounding him only if absolutely necessary, preferably relying only on his fists. It was, after all, a kinder, gentler epoch in which he settled a score.

Usually there would be a moral bromide growing out of the tale that the legendary cowboy dispensed, tailored especially for his younger listeners as he brought his narrative to a close. His personal "Cowboy Code" was infrequently recalled: "A cowboy never betrays a trust; a cowboy is kind to small children, animals and old folks; a cowboy is clean about his person, and in thought, word and deed; a cowboy is a patriot...." It was the stuff parents absolutely adored from a source the kids strongly admired.

Those lessons "took" with at least one of the era's chroniclers, and most likely with millions of other youngsters.[1]

> Heroes were important in those days. They were something you thought about consciously. You talked about them or at least thought about them every day. You pretended that you were them when you could, certainly when you were alone. I'm sure I didn't analyze my hero worship for the Lone Ranger or Gene Autry during

those years; I just accepted that they were what they were to me, and I wanted to grow up to be just like them. Oh, I don't mean the adventure part of it. I knew that could never be — I mean the personal characteristics of my heroes: the honesty, friendliness, bravery, kindliness, integrity — all of those things we value so highly, but rarely talk about in connection with our adult selves for fear of embarrassment, or, perhaps, melancholia.

After the story, Autry would contribute a final ballad. Lyon reminded everybody to pick up a pack of Doublemint as the chorus returned to harmonize on a final few bars of melody. Autry expressed a farewell and lustily broke into familiar strains about being back in the saddle again.

It made no difference to listeners in the final half of the series' long life that Lyons often prefaced and concluded the feature with the tagline "This program came to you transcribed from Hollywood." (Dozens of shows did that, for sure.) Legions of loyal fans paid little attention to the disclaimer. In the theater of the mind, it was utterly believable that Autry and company were gathered *right then* in front of a campfire underneath the stars on the Autry spread with a backdrop of coyotes howling in the distance and sparks from burning timbers flying through the air. It didn't matter than the cast was really on a stage in a soundproof studio in downtown L.A., dozens of miles from anybody's ranch and had recorded that show several weeks earlier. That was the beauty of transcriptions, of course, and nobody was about to burst the imagery — and the imagination — stirred by fictitious cowpokes on the plains.

Another point worth mentioning about the taping is that longtime sponsor William J. Wrigley took a hard line against the practice. It's been speculated that the show might have continued beyond 1956 had Autry and Wrigley officials not reached an impasse on it (similar to the stalemate Bing Crosby and Kraft Foods Company officials encountered a decade before — for a fuller introspective into how shows came to be recorded, breaking a decades-old ban that forbade it, check out the Crosby chapter). Wrigley consented only when Autry's rodeo tours and one-night stands kept him from the studios.

Leonard Maltin proclaimed: "Gene Autry spent much of the year making personal appearances around the country, but wherever he was, by week's end he would have to check in to the nearest major CBS station in order to prepare and broadcast his *Melody Ranch* program. As it happened, many of his radio costars also appeared in his touring show, but those who didn't would have to make their way to Chicago or St. Louis or Minneapolis in order to be part of the broadcast."

Kenneth M. Johnson, who performed with the Johnson Family Singers over Charlotte's WBT as well as CBS Radio, recalled from his youth an incident that occurred as Autry and company appeared there on January 18, 1948. "When Gene Autry came to town, my brothers and I were hired as back-up singers to augment the music on his Sunday evening program, *Melody Ranch*, over CBS. That six-thirty appearance proved to be not only musically challenging but also financially helpful, with a large talent check going into the family account for our services. My brother Bob remembers Autry giving each of us a new bicycle as a bonus."[2] The singing cowboy, it seems, could be generous, too.

Autry had gone "from cowpoke to potentate," a source confirmed. By 1948, he was running a multimillion-dollar business empire called Gene Autry, Inc. requiring his habitual oversight. It was comprised of five ranches, five radio stations, a couple of television stations, a couple of music publishing houses and part interest in a Phoenix newspaper. He was, by then, a media mogul and his holdings would expand as the years progressed, eventually owning the California Angels professional baseball club.

Gene Autry was a native of Tioga, Texas, born September 29, 1907. Working on his dad's ranch as a cowpuncher, he sang in the church choir where his granddaddy preached and also performed at community socials. Later, he toured with a medicine show. When he grew older, he took a post as an Oklahoma telegraph operator, sometimes passing the time singing humorist Will Rogers, a Ziegfeld Follies star, overheard this and urged him to seek a job in radio. Autry did just that and was hired by Tulsa's KVOO. He was soon on the air billed as "The Oklahoma Yodeling Cowboy." Before long he scored a big recording hit with *That Silver-Haired Daddy of Mine* on the Vocalian label and from then on he never looked back.

Subsequently singing for Sears, Roebuck & Company's Conqueror records, Autry came to the attention of the large station owned by the giant retailer and catalog house, Chicago's WLS. In 1930, he was summoned to the Windy City to appear on WLS's *Conqueror Record Time* (1930–1931) and the WLS *Barn Dance* (1930–1934), which was to become NBC's *National Barn Dance* in 1933, along with infrequent appearances on the network's *National Farm and Home Hour*. He met comic actor-singer Smiley Burnette while there and the two formed a lasting friendship, partnering in radio and movies. "He [Autry] was a natural, untrained performer," noted a music critic, "and made no pretense of being, or wanting to be, anything other than himself — a simple cowhand with a pleasant singing voice. By 1934 he was unquestionably the most popular country-and-Western singer on the air."[3]

In 1935, he appeared in his first serialized film release, *The Phantom Empire*, and landed a contract to star in the new strain of film features just then coming into vogue that were identified as the musical Western.

Five years later — having already starred in many films — he was approached by CBS with an offer to host his own weekly audio series highlighting that developing screen innovation. He signed on the dotted line. *Gene Autry's Melody Ranch* was devised as a vehicle to feature the ex-cowpuncher and his vocals. It debuted on the ether January 7, 1940.

Autry remained with it for three and a half years before ending the show himself. In 1942, he joined the Army Air Corps. By mid-1943 it was clear that he couldn't pursue that call and do the show. While on the air one evening in July 1943, the 35-year-old star was administered an official oath of duty. The military probably saw that occasion as a propitious platform for encouraging others to follow in his train. The show itself was disbanded on August 1, 1943. Autry became a flight officer, flying Air Transport Command craft to North Africa and China. He was stationed overseas for two years.

When he returned from his tour of duty it was like déjà vu transpired. CBS immediately found a slot on its evening weekend schedule for him, and his earlier sponsor, the William J. Wrigley Company, once again stepped up to the plate. Wrigley, in fact, underwrote *Melody Ranch* for the duration of the series' radio life, nearly 15 years between early 1940 and mid-1956, omitting the time the show was off the air. It was one of the most enduring star-sponsor pacts in the annals of evening broadcasting.

Gene Autry's Melody Ranch resumed on September 23, 1945, and always appeared on a Saturday or Sunday night at an hour early enough for millions of juveniles to be in its audience. They were, after all, some of Autry's most fanatic fans. The series survived through May 13, 1956.

A custom before each broadcast — included for the benefit of the studio audience — depicted how Champion, Autry's fabled mount, was to be imitated for the sensitive microphones. A sound-effects technician armed with a coconut shell in each hand and a flat surface appeared as props. Autry and the soundman provided an actual demonstration for the spectators so they would know what to anticipate once the show was on the air. It was the producers' intent that any urge to emit titters upon seeing the "horse" walk, clomp, trot or race during the performance would be muffled and, preferably, nonexistent. Stifling such natural responses was sometimes troublesome. Viewing "fistfights" in which actors stood grimacing and grunting at microphones as sound specialists huffed and puffed and pounded leather-upholstered pillows was usually a big risk if the audience wasn't primed in advance.

Director Fletcher Markle acknowledged: "I simply had to adjust to the fact that this was unalterable, and therefore, we made part of the warm-up to these fifteen to eighteen hundred people ... how sound effects are manufactured, if there was any danger of them being laughed at. We simply demonstrated if horses' hooves were being done with half-coconut shells, or if someone was receiving a lethal blow by a hammer going into a cantaloupe, or whatever. It was done for them so they could laugh at it before we went on the air."

By the way, according to Robert L. Mott, one of network radio's proficient soundmen, Gene Autry trusted but one person to provide the snorts and whinnies of his horse Champion. It was Dave Light, a Mott peer who worked the *Melody Ranch* programs after 1942. Light was so good at contriving realistic animal sounds that Judy Garland insisted he alone be responsible for the dog barks for Toto each time she appeared on a radio production of *The Wizard of Oz*.

On other fronts, Autry resumed making films and recordings and eventually entered television. Careerwise, from 1934 to 1953 he is credited with 95 motion pictures (nearly five a year). He starred in all but three of them and played himself in all but a handful. A few of the titles of his B-movie features, most for Republic Pictures, are representative: *Melody Trail* (1935), *Red River Valley* (1936), *The Singing Cowboy* (1936), *Yodelin' Kid from Pine Ridge* (1937), *Man from Music Mountain* (1938), *Mexicali Rose* (1939), *Melody Ranch* (1940), *Back in the Saddle* (1941), *Cowboy Serenade* (1942), *The Last Round-Up* (1947), *The Cowboys and Indians* (1949), *Gene Autry and the Mounties* (1951), *Night Stage to Galveston* (1952), *On Top of Old Smoky* (1953), *Last of the Pony Riders* (1953).

On CBS Television between July 23, 1950, and August 7, 1956, *The Gene Autry Show* offered 104 half-hour episodes in which the singing cowboy tamed the West by catching outlaws while in the company of his radio sidekick Pat Buttram. The series was so successful that it fostered a couple of spinoffs — the syndicated *Annie Oakley*, video's initial Western heroine (from 1952 to 1956), and *The Adventures of Champion*, featuring Autry's horse (CBS-TV, September 30, 1955–February 3, 1956).

Occasionally, an out-of-the ordinary opportunity came Autry's way. On March 10, 1939, he co-starred with Frances Langford on a *Texaco Star Theater* production *Sheriff Goes a' Callin'*. On January 20, 1941, displaying a flair for novelty casting, the *Lux Radio Theater* tapped him for the silver screen role that actor Gary Cooper originated in *The Cowboy and the Lady*.

Autry also turned out to be a rather prolific writer of the type of songs he sang in various media. His hits often bridged the gap between pure country and Western ballads to cross over into popular selections. Among those scoring big were *Have I Told You Lately That I Love You?*, *Tears on*

My Pillow and *Yesterday's Roses*. While the Western tunes he recorded continued to be strong sellers, it was a Christmas novelty tune he introduced in 1949 that topped all of the charts and remained a solid favorite for many holiday seasons afterward, *Rudolph, the Red-Nosed Reindeer*. It became the second-best-selling record of all time, after Bing Crosby's *White Christmas*.

Gene Autry died October 2, 1998, at Studio City in Los Angeles. Today the Gene Autry Oklahoma Museum at Gene Autry, Oklahoma (until 1941, Berwyn, "the town named for a legend," according to publicists), continues to perpetuate the legacy of the cowboy singer. The museum contains memorabilia honoring many country and Western artists in several mediums. Since 1993, a Gene Autry Film and Music Festival has been staged annually in late September. From 1939 to 1946, Autry owned a 1,200-acre ranch just west of Berwyn where he kept hundreds of cattle and horses for a rodeo road show. He owned similar operations at Dublin, Texas, and Florence, Arizona.

A profiler gave Autry high marks on his contributions to the music industry, possibly higher than anyone anticipated.[4]

> Perhaps more than any other performer in this category of music, Gene Autry was responsible for bringing cowboy and country music into the nation's homes and establishing it in the mainstream of American musical culture. At first his yodeling type of singing had been considered by top radio executives to be no more than a passing fad. But it endured. Listeners remained loyal and increased in numbers. The cowboy ballad, the Appalachian lament, and the yodeling blues grew in popularity, eventually outlasting the generation that had first embraced these folklore melodies, and creating in America a staple musical syndrome that was deep-rooted and perennial. Along the way Gene Autry also blazed a trail for other singing cowboys who swiftly followed in his bootsteps.

One of those cowboys who crooned to the cattle and nearby "hands" was Roy Rogers who became Autry's hardiest rival for the enviable spot of chief sagebrush singer — in radio, on records, in motion pictures, on television and in comic books and other merchandising ventures.

Born Leonard Slye on November 5, 1911, in Cincinnati, Ohio — a Mecca not generally associated with Western culture — he learned to play the guitar and yodel Western tunes while a youngster. In 1929, at 17, he moved to California and found a job as a fruit picker. But he aspired to something greater. Changing his name to Dick Weston, he and a couple of pals formed the Sons of the Pioneers, an instrumental-vocal trio, in 1934. The following year they appeared in a film titled *Slightly Static*. The Sons of the Pioneers were featured in a half-dozen movies successively.

In the meantime, a recording they made of *The Last Roundup* propelled them into the forefront among prominent Western performers. And independently, Slye-Weston, who was changing his moniker erratically, drifting back and forth between them, sang *Hi-Yo Silver* for Vocalian records (Gene Autry's initial label), a long-forgotten ditty linked to *The Lone Ranger's* radio and film escapades. In 1938, having already appeared in a dozen movies under various appellations, Leonard Slye-Dick Weston burst from the limitations of his past and emerged as Roy Rogers in *Under Western Stars*. From that time forward he would forever be recognized as Rogers, star of Republic Pictures' musical Westerns. Once again, it was the same production house that had employed Gene Autry. Rogers, too, would never have occasion to look back.

In the twenty-first century, longtime network radio broadcaster John Rayburn was still repeating a hilarious story about Rogers' imposing claim to fame. Rayburn loved to share the tale with vintage hobbyists who gathered at old-time radio conventions scattered across the country every year. He said that about 10 years after Rogers left Cincinnati and earned widespread notoriety under his newly assumed professional identity and was a major star of screen, records and radio, Rogers was riding a train to his hometown of Cincinnati when an old high school chum boarded. As his friend came down the aisle of the coach and recognized the familiar face, he shook the star's hand excitedly, exclaiming: "Well Leonard Slye! What have you been doing with yourself lately?"

While Gene Autry was labeled "America's Favorite Cowboy," Roy Rogers resonated with essentially the same audience as "The King of the Cowboys." Both wore white hats and rode great steeds (Autry saddled Champion while Rogers mounted Trigger—Rogers also had a dog named Bullet) and both men were on the side of the law, vigilantly pursuing evildoers. But there were some distinguishing differences in the pair.

For one, while Autry might sing to a different charming senorita in every film, much of the time Rogers had his eyes affixed on the same girl, the one he married on December 31, 1947, Dale Evans. Evans became Rogers' second wife after Arlene, his first, died in 1946. Evans was the self-dubbed "Queen of the West" and often rode with him and his "boys" in pursuit of fleeing ruffians. (One wag observed: "Alongside such nonsense, *The Lone Ranger* seemed very much the real thing.") Both Rogers and Evans were singers; the Sons of the Pioneers normally accompanied their solos and duets. It was the same group that Rogers had launched his career with years before. But by 1948, Riders of the Purple Sage supplanted the Pioneers with the backup harmony.

While they were rivals on the screen, Autry and Rogers became competitors for similar audiences on radio, too. Autry established a foothold in the aural medium nearly five years before Rogers premiered on November 21, 1944, over MBS Tuesdays at 8:30 P.M. (Incidentally, just before that first broadcast, Rogers experienced a severe case of mike fright, and never totally lost his fear of the microphone, even though he became a veteran of it.) Taking nothing away from Rogers' personal performance, *The Roy Rogers Show* had several strikes against it when compared with *Gene Autry's Melody Ranch*.

For one thing, MBS did not normally attract as many listeners as CBS because its affiliates were often less powerful (and thereby less prestigious) and were frequently situated in smaller markets. In four of Rogers' nine seasons on the ether his show aired over MBS while a far superior CBS beamed Autry's songfest to many more listeners during all of his 15 broadcast seasons.

Then there was the matter of timing. Recall that Autry was off the air for two consecutive years while serving overseas. Rogers, regrettably, met with numerous scheduling conflicts, apparently not of his own making, that must have left fans frustrated in trying to find him. Upon leaving the airwaves for a break in the action, the Rogers program might return on a different night at a different hour. Not only was it off the air during long summer lapses and for an occasional month here and there, it experienced only abbreviated seasons in 1944-1945 and 1946-1947. And no chain picked it up during the 1945-1946 and 1947-1948 broadcast seasons. Under those conditions, establishing any lasting continuity was a daunting challenge. An audience habitually had to be "found" again after each interruption.

At the time Rogers' series premiered in late 1944, Autry was away in military service. It was an auspicious opportunity to make significant inroads into the territory that "America's favorite cowboy" had previously carved out. Although he had no serious contemporaries among singing cowboys then, Rogers lasted only six months and was cancelled. Returning to the ether 17 months later, he found Autry again firmly entrenched. Autry had been home for a year and reconnected with his faithful followers. Autry would simply never feel Rogers gaining on him in Radioland.

Rogers' schedulers couldn't seem to get it right. His debuting series appeared on Tuesday, a school night for many of the hero's followers. The 8:30 broadcast hour arrived after bedtime for many youngsters along the Eastern seaboard who were his fans. Some subsequent planning—in the series' final quadrennial—had Rogers airing on Tuesday, Thursday or Friday nights instead of weekends, not particularly great times to attract a large influx of adolescent listeners.

The ratings told the story. Rogers' five highest recorded figures were 12.1, 9.2 (twice), 8.5 and 6.0. His combined average for eight aural seasons for which there are records was 7.3. Autry, on the other hand—consistently airing on the weekends on CBS—garnered far more striking numbers: 15.2, 12.9, 12.4, 10.7, 10.5. His median for 14 documented seasons reached 8.8. Comparatively speaking, the programming strategists appeared to smile on Autry. Rogers, conversely, was never able to overcome the handicaps meted out to him.

While Autry's show was about evenly divided between music and mayhem (those 12-minute dramatic vignettes mentioned earlier), the Rogers program differed in that its mystery thriller plots tended to predominate, particularly in the final two seasons on the air, with only minimal singing on the side. In that period, under the title *The Roy Rogers Radio Show*, those weekly visits opened with Roy and Dale singing a few bars of a duet that invariably recalled for them an adventure from the past.

The narrative that followed was recounted in dramatic action with a flashback technique. Rogers went after the bad guys with a vengeance, concentrating more than two-thirds of the half hour on a myriad of malcontents. He was pointedly appealing to adults, too, who would be buying the commodities that brought him to the airwaves—Goodyear tires, Alka-Seltzer, Quaker Oats, Post cereals and Dodge cars and trucks. There wasn't any chewing gum in his commercial inventory! When the tale was concluded, he and Dale would blend their voices on the song they had begun singing earlier, this time finishing it.

The sketches were almost always based on the good guys vs. bad guys motif, the former finally subduing the latter. *Radio Life*, in 1948, called it "typical Western drammer," suggesting that Rogers and *his* funnyman sidekicks, Gabby Hayes and Pat Brady (who were like Autry's Smiley Burnette and Pat Buttram), would almost always "meet villainous adversity, save Miss Evans' ranch-home, or her father, or her younger brother, and ride off in a swirl of dust."

It seemed every cowboy had a familiar line for leaving his admirers each week. Rogers' was simply: "To all of you from all of us, goodbye, good luck and may the good Lord take a likin' to ya." Then, with gusto, he and Dale erupted into a sweet-sounding blend on the theme song she had penned for just that occasion, "Happy Trails."

The Rogers show may have extended the margins of the traditional radio Western to its uttermost limits. The dramatic plots in the 1954-1955 season focused on "the adversities encountered by Roy and Dale Evans when they visited Washington, D.C.; prospecting for uranium with Geiger counters; investigating a stolen stamp collection; resolving the tensions that arose at a roadside diner during a tornado; and breaking a smuggling ring which used railroad refrigerator cars to transport diamonds from Mexico." A radio historiographer observed that the program might have moved from a traditional Western format to a detective series in its quest for more mature listeners.

The Roy Rogers Show, including Rogers, Evans, Pat Brady and the Sons of the Pioneers, premiered on NBC-TV on December 30, 1951, nearly a year and a half following Gene Autry's foray to the tube. Rogers would persist there for a single season beyond Autry's run. Staged by Roy Rogers Productions, the series became a Sunday evening staple that lasted through June 23, 1957, with only a brief hiatus in the summer of 1952. It was seen in reruns on CBS-TV's Saturday morning schedule between January 1961 and September 1964.

A later attempt to capitalize on Rogers' reputation wasn't as successful in video. *The Roy Rogers and Dale Evans Show*, a musical variety entry, debuted on September 29, 1962, over ABC-TV for an hour on Saturday nights. It included Pat Brady, the Sons of the Pioneers, Cliff Arquette playing his popular Charley Weaver comedic character, the Ralph Carmichael Orchestra and a handful of lesser knowns. Circus and horse acts were regulars on the show's bill. Authorities have been unable to agree on when the program was withdrawn, some suggesting it was as early as December 29, 1962, while others opt for December 22, 1963. In either case, the variety series didn't sustain the interest of the viewers as Rogers' previous show had, but the competition for people's time was probably greater in the 1960s. There were also many more attractive choices to select from on television by then.

Rogers' B-movie Westerns were similar to those made by Gene Autry. Between 1938 and 1952 he starred in 86 films, in all but one as Roy Rogers. Altogether over his movie career he appeared in 103 motion pictures, exceeding Autry's aggregate by eight. Typical titles: *Shine On Harvest Moon* (1938), *Rough Riders' Round-Up* (1939), *Saga of Death Valley* (1939), *The Ranger and the Lady* (1940), *Sons of the Pioneers* (1942), *Sunset Serenade* (1942), *The Man from Music Mountain* (1943), *The Yellow Rose of Texas* (1944), *Along the Navajo Trail* (1945), *Don't Fence Me In* (1945), *Eyes of Texas* (1948), *Spoilers of the Plains* (1951).

Throughout his radio career Rogers made frequent appearances on shows other than his own. He was often a guest of other NBC headliners where he usually sang a few cowboy ballads. Occasionally he was featured in dramatic parts on assorted series. He reprised the starring role from the film *In Old Oklahoma* in a *Lux Radio Theater* production on CBS March 13, 1944, with co-stars Albert Dekker and Martha Scott. The movie producers plugged it as "two-fisted action in the new oil fields of the Indian territory."

On June 29, 1944, Rogers sang with Bing Crosby on NBC's *Kraft Music Hall*. The cowboy singer yodeled and called a square dance while his and Crosby's horses purportedly chatted. Rogers turned up as a guest on NBC's *Edgar Bergen and Charlie McCarthy Show* on March 31, 1946, and December 7, 1947, and appeared on that network's *Bob Hope Show* on June 10, 1952.

Rogers joined a luminary-laden cast of Western players on *The Hallmark Hall of Fame* January 3, 1954, for a saga about one of its own, the late Tom Mix, who died in 1940. In a yarn titled *The True Story of Tom Mix*, the legendary cowboy captured a couple of murderers by remaining awake for four days as a blizzard raged about him. Appearing in that celebrated cast of radio and film actors were Gene Autry, Harry Bartell, William Boyd (aka Hopalong Cassidy), John Dehner, Larry Dobkin, Jack

Edwards, Clark Gable, Vic Perrin, Roy Rogers and Will Rogers Jr.

Roy Rogers died on his ranch in San Bernadino, California, on July 6, 1998. His family later moved a Rogers museum from southern California, its site for many years, to Branson, Missouri, where it continues in operation at this writing.

While Gene Autry and Roy Rogers predominated the genre of the singing cowboy, there were a few other minor figures who contributed to the strain.

John I. White, a name long forgotten, is credited as the first singing cowboy. The Washington, D.C., native visited some Arizona cousins and "fell in love with cowboy songs." He introduced them to radio listeners in 1926 as he launched a singing career over New York City's WEAF, the flagship station of the NBC Red chain. Moving over to local station WOR, White was billed as "The Lonesome Cowboy." In 1930, he was selected as a vocalist for NBC's debuting dramatic series *Death Valley Days*. A folio of cowboy songs White collected was published and made available to fans that sent in a box top from one of the sponsor's products. It was one of the earliest premiums to be offered on a coast-to-coast hookup.

Tex Ritter, who became a major box office attraction in Western films, left a radio job in Houston to gain singing experience on Chicago and New York radio. *Tex Ritter's Camp Fire* was an early airwaves feature, airing prior to his Hollywood endeavors.

Bob Wills, later dubbed the "King of Western Swing," played violin on Fort Worth and Tulsa stations before joining *The Texas Playboys* on radio, later performing in Western pictures.

Eddy Arnold, a yodeler and cowboy singer labeled "The Tennessee Plowboy," initially appeared on the air in the Volunteer State with Pee Wee King's band. He soon headlined a show of his own in Nashville and joined the *Grand Ole Opry* on WSM and NBC. In the late 1940s, he replaced Roy Acuff as the top-selling country-recording star.

Curt Massey debuted in 1930 over Kansas City's KMBC as a hillbilly crooner, leading to Chicago and the *National Barn Dance* in 1933. A short while later he was fiddling (literally) in The Westerners family entourage on *Showboat* from New York and joined them in a 1938 Tex Ritter film, *Where the Buffalo Roam*. He replaced hillbilly singer Red Foley on *Avalon Time*, leading to singing radio series of his own. Massey later became musical director of two TV hits, *Petticoat Junction* and *The Beverly Hillbillies*. (See details of his career achievements in The Vocalists chapter.)

Bobby Benson and the B-Bar-B Riders, an action adventure series popular with the juvenile set and appearing under various monikers between 1932 and 1955, not only offered a dramatic tale of suspense but — in the early 1950s, under the title *Songs of the B-Bar-B* — presented a five-minute matinee musicale featuring cowboy and Western ballads. Purportedly sung around a campfire setting, it was like *Gene Autry's Melody Ranch* without the narrative (presented earlier on a separate show). Cowboy singer Tex Ritter was a member of the cast while actor Clyde Campbell (pseudonym for Clive Rice) was playing the title role at that time.

Beyond Autry and Rogers, vocalist-thespian Curley Bradley may have come closer to carrying the cowboy singer torch better than anyone else. He is best recalled as the star of a single radio series, *Tom Mix*, but he was an understudy for the role for seven years before gaining that part.

Born Raymond George Courtney in Coalgate, Oklahoma, on September 18, 1910, Bradley and two brothers worked as range cowboys for their true pioneering parents. In those days, he observed some of the last Western gun duels from beneath the local courthouse steps. In the 1920s, he went to Hollywood, one of the last places a cowboy could still ride and rope for a living.

At 16, Bradley was hired as a stunt rider for silent films starring actors Hoot Gibson, Buck Jones and Tom Mix, and was involved in chases, horse falls, fistfights and similar escapades. But he preferred Western singing to being a stuntman and minor film actor. "I didn't like having one arm stuck up in the air, and one leg tied down, while broken bones healed up," he said. "I enjoyed singing. I didn't enjoy being busted into bits."

Most of his professional singing experience occurred with the Ranch Boys trio, formed while he was a stuntman, and included a couple of contemporaries. Jack Ross became the group's leader. He and Bradley sang Western ballads while Shorty Carson picked guitar. (The latter was renamed Ken Carson later, appeared in several John Wayne movies and became a permanent soloist on the daytime Garry Moore radio and TV shows in the 1950s.) The threesome left stunts to make personal appearances, Decca records and acquire better film opportunities. Bradley was the featured lead soloist on about half of their recordings. The Ranch Boys appeared in the movie *It Happened One Night* and in the Gene Autry film *In Old Monterey*.

When Ralston Purina officials saw Bradley perform as a member of the Ranch Boys, they picked him for the *Tom Mix* radio drama that they sponsored. (Mix was a legendary Hollywood cowboy actor who lent his name to the radio series but never appeared in it. According to Pat Buttram, Mix didn't care at all for musical Westerns, either.) Due to Bradley's inexperience, the cereal-makers put him in the lesser role of Pecos Williams, assuring him he would be shifted to the lead in due course. Bradley didn't accept the assignment before they agreed to employ the other members of the Ranch Boys trio, too.

"On the air Curley Bradley's own personality took over, and Pecos became a good-natured, loyal young cowboy who liked to sing," a pundit noted. His "temporary" role as Pecos lasted seven years (1935–1942) and then the show was cancelled! It was 1944, upon the series' resumption, that Bradley finally got the part he was promised.

As a publicity stunt, in May 1938, the Ranch Boys began a three-month trek on horseback from Los Angeles to Chicago, a 2,875-mile journey. En route they performed on 36 broadcasts from remote locations and posed for pictures and signed autographs for fans.

The Sons of the Pioneers, the group Roy Rogers sang with which accompanied him in movies, on records and broadcasts, offered Bradley a starting annual compensation of $10,000 to join them. By then he was earning more than $30,000 on multiple radio series in Chicago. He was a vocalist on *The National Farm and Home Hour*, appeared as a cowboy on *Mr. First Nighter*, substituted for host Don McNeill on *The Breakfast Club*, and was a singer on Garry Moore's *Club Matinee*, on *Road to Danger* and *Ranch-House Jim*. In the latter he played a singing cowboy-detective. His highest salary on *Tom Mix*, by the way, was $550 weekly.

Bradley, who died June 3, 1985, in Long Beach, California, also made records on his own, including "The Tom Mix Album" comprised of ballads sung on the show. A critic noted that his opportunities for singing on radio series were few and far between. Only an occasional lyrical interlude — maybe once every few months—fell from his lips, with the daily exception of the sponsor's familiar commercial jingle, sung to the tune of *When It's Round-Up Time in Texas and the Bloom is on the Sage*.

Shredded Ralston for your breakfast
Starts your day off shining bright;
Gives you lots of cowboy energy

With a flavor that's just right;
It's delicious and nutritious,
Bite-size and ready to eat;
So take a tip from Tom…
Go and tell your Mom…
Shredded Ralston can't be beat!

The singing cowboys could be considered an anomaly among the considerably substantial species of Western adventures, on the big and small screens and — because their numbers were so small — in radio especially. Nevertheless, they developed mass appeal to people of all ages who enjoyed their courageous dramatic exploits and who enjoyed a little melody tossed in on the side.

The House Bands

All four of the national hookups maintained what was commonly known in radio parlance as house bands. The aggregates of varying sizes were also called by a multiplicity of monikers: backup, resident, staff, studio and other common expressions referring to a cluster of musicians whose livelihoods often depended as much on their agility to respond quickly when summoned as it rested on their ability to meet performance quality expectations in a myriad of situations.

Out of this pool of talent a chain could pluck one or more individuals as called for in a script (a harpist or a clarinetist, for instance), a small string ensemble, a jazz combo, a brassy-sounding band or a very large orchestra, as the dictates of a program demanded. By having such trained musicians available, under the tutelage of conductors and musical directors with whom they were familiar, a lot of ongoing requirements that cropped up in producing live entertainment every day were satisfactorily answered. Networks simply couldn't operate by merely keeping a few staff or freelance organists around to provide musical bridges and theme songs for soap operas. The big national chains, and even many large radio stations in metropolitan areas throughout the country, maintained a paid corps of staff musicians to supply all sorts of melodious necessities.

The members of such a clan usually rehearsed in advance for specific programming features on which music was to be heard. At the same time, they knew they were standby talent, too. On rare occasions they might be unpredictably pressed into service. With little more than a moment's notice, they appeared before the microphones to fill in an unanticipated hole that spoiled the day's agenda. This happened when a program failed to materialize (as in the circumstance of a key personality's delayed arrival or — possibly in extreme cases — even a figure's sudden disappearance or death). The house band was useful when — wonder of wonders — "due to technical difficulties beyond our control" a remote pickup or mechanical adversity within the confines of the broadcast facility netted dead air (as in a sudden lapse in a transcription device, for example).

For radio, dead air was an absolutely calamitous plight that had to be remedied at once lest the audience turn elsewhere. More often than not, those occasions of silent lapses occurred at local outlets where some poor devil inadvertently disconnected the power or lightning knocked out a line or a piece of equipment. Yet, if a band or an ensemble or even a pianist and soloist were on standby, the airwaves didn't remain hushed long. While the broadcast chains were better able to deflect a catastrophe, they didn't totally escape such maladies, particularly in the earliest days of radio's golden age.

In their normal day-in-and-day-out assignments, when they knew what to expect in advance, however, the house bands could be called upon to supply a mixture of obligations. They usually played the opening and closing themes of a given show, plus any bridge music to distinguish between scenes in dramatic series. They also provided whatever a sponsor required in the way of melody during some commercial pitches. (In the early decades of broadcasting, you recall, everything was performed live on network radio following edicts handed down from policymakers banning prerecording.) Normally, such music was practiced in advance of the actual broadcasts.

On music and variety series, plus some comedy and quiz programs, the house bands' involvement was even more extensive. In some shows outside the realm of typical musical fare one or more compositions were played (and sometimes also sung by a vocalist or vocal ensemble). Thus, the scope of the resident musicians' work was wide-ranging. Versatility as well as talent became the order of the day.

Studio bands proliferated during what was commonly known as the big band era. Some acquired the names of sponsors and touted them as their own, to the delight of their underwriters, e.g., Harry Horlick and the A&P Gypsies (for the Great Atlantic & Pacific Tea Company), Sam Lanin and the Ipana Troubadors (for Bristol Myers' Ipana toothpaste) and Harry Reser and the Cliquot Club Eskimos (a popular brand of ginger ale). Such appellations were assigned in radio's incubation days when commercials weren't yet permitted. Bands and ensembles typically assumed the names of the firms that subsidized them.

A few of the more prominent studio musicians eventually fled the security of those confines to strike out on their own, often carrying with them enough cronies to launch an outfit which they themselves headlined. Among their number: Jimmy and Tommy Dorsey, Benny Goodman, Glenn Miller, Artie Shaw and Claude Thornhill.

But back at the ranch, enough artists stayed put (and some came in off the road, a reversal of the aforementioned design) to furnish a plethora of commercial orchestra ventures. Some of the more notable conductors included Alfredo Antonini, Victor Arden, Robert Armbruster, Mitchell Ayers, Eddie Ballantine, Paul Baron, Howard Barlow, Frank Black, Archie Bleyer, Les Brown, Frank De Vol, Lud Gluskin, Al Goodman, Morton Gould, Jerry Gray, Gus Haenschen, Wilbur Hatch, Gordon Jenkins, Rex Koury, Abe Lyman, Muzzy Marcellino, Jack Miller, Billy Mills, Ozzie Nelson, Ray Noble, Raymond Paige, Charles Paul, Jacques Renard, Al Rickey, Nelson Riddle, Willard Robison, David Rose, Walter Schumann, Vladimir Selinsky, Ben Selvin, Jack and Nat Shilkret, Harry Sosnik, Leith Stevens, Peter Van Steeden, Donald Voorhees, Paul Weston, Meredith Willson, Victor Young and many others.

A music historiographer provides impressions of the environment in which the house bands operated.[1]

> Most of their music was different from that of the big dance bands. Much of it was strictly background for singers. A good deal consisted of uninspired readings of mundane arrangements. And almost all of it was constricted by the penny-pinching of network executives who allowed

their studio bands a minimum of rehearsal time and personnel, by the old-fashioned attitudes of some leaders who were coasting on their reputations, and by insecure, hard-shelled advertising agency executives, who constantly kept quashing creativity lest anything outside the norm offend their clients. Much of the radio network programming of the thirties and forties rivaled that of television of the sixties in the vastness of its wasteland.

Once in a while a studio band with a distinctive, musical sound would emerge. Raymond Scott fronted an outstanding outfit in New York. And Philadelphia produced three topflight bands: Jan Savitt's, Joey Kearns's and Elliot Lawrence's.

But by far the most exciting sounds came from the established dance bands, some during their commercial programs but many more during their broadcasts direct from where the bands were playing....

Anecdotes surrounding the staff bands are legion.

When news of D-Day broke out about 1 o'clock in the morning, network affiliates wanted to remain on the air with live late-breaking news bulletins. But big gaps between those reports were anticipated. NBC solved its dilemma by telephoning members of the NBC Orchestra, getting them out of bed and commanding them to rush to the studios and be ready to play whenever called upon. No recorded music was allowed then.

In an era in which prerecorded music still remained anathema, in the early 1950s the Western dramatic CBS series *Gunsmoke* taped its narrative dialogue in advance of each airing. But the staff musicians for it, led by conductor Rex Koury, were required to perform in the studio at the time of each "live" broadcast.

One of the best-intended uses of the house musicians occurred when NBC decided to create a new musical assemblage for impresario Arturo Toscanini, perceived as "the world's greatest conductor," in an attempt to lure him to that network. They hoped he would conduct an impending NBC Symphony Orchestra. [See more details in The Classics chapter.] With about 70 house musicians on its staff, an NBC official believed they might be integrated into the symphony combine.

Radio Corporation of America (RCA) chairman David Sarnoff (RCA was NBC's parent firm) proposed that—should any of the staff musicians dismay Toscanini— he could replace any or all of them. (Only 31 were eventually tapped for the new symphony; an additional 62 musicians from outside NBC were engaged for the orchestra. Some remaining staff musicians were fired, eliciting a strong rebuke from Toscanini.)

What Sarnoff didn't tell the maestro before his hire was that *his* orchestra's members would continue to play for other NBC programs, though he had a quite different impression. They silently slipped out of his rehearsals for other broadcast commitments. Somehow Toscanini didn't uncover the duplicity for a few years. When he did, he became enraged and stalked off, walking out on his contract for the following season.

Nila Mack, the creator and longtime director of CBS's children's fairly tale series *Let's Pretend*, recalled some of the foibles she encountered when launching that series' lesser remembered predecessor, *The Adventures of Helen and Mary*, in 1930:[2]

> As for the music — we had to be a little resourceful there.... Emery Deutsch and his ensemble were available — but only for the air show, since they were doing programs like crazy all over the place. In order to get them, Emery, in Studio 5, would sign off the ensemble program while Sidney Raphael, the pianist, would tear into Studio 3 and whip up the opening for our show. About the third musical bridge we were a complete unit.
>
> Of course I never had a dress rehearsal

and had to devise some quaint way of timing strictly by ear.

Concerning the successor series, cast member Arthur Anderson explained:[3]

> From the first, music was an essential part of *Let's Pretend*. For the program's entire life, starting with the *Helen and Mary* days, there was always a six-piece string ensemble consisting of first violin, second violin, cello, viola, bass, and piano. (The only exception was during a short period in 1938 when a 20-piece orchestra, led by Alexander Semmler, provided the music. They were probably all on salary, and assigned by CBS to our show because they had little or nothing else to do at the time. The orchestra's size was rather overwhelming, though, and it detracted greatly from the program's charm.)
>
> The music chosen for the theme and for bridges between scenes was light classical, or what was termed slightly contemptuously "parlor music" by serious musicians. However, these pieces were ideal for a children's radio program. They were simple and bright, and a definite melodic theme was established within their opening bars, or 15 or 20 seconds, which was all the time there was for each music cue.

There were also instances when networks removed their house musicians from the air. One such case surrounded the launch of a budding trend in programming begun by ABC in 1948 when it attacked its competition, principally NBC's lineup of firmly entrenched Sunday night comedies. For years, ABC had been hit over the head by rival chains and it was desperately searching for a ratings coup d'état. At the 8 o'clock hour it was meandering along in third place behind CBS, offering listeners one of many guest musical aggregates from far-flung locales. At that juncture it was presenting the Detroit Symphony Orchestra, supplanted by ABC's own in-house musicians during periods when no guest symphony was available. NBC, meanwhile, was beating the socks off ABC with the *Edgar Bergen–Charlie McCarthy Show* at 8 P.M. followed by the *Fred Allen Show* at 8:30.

When ABC replaced the symphony and its house band with a fast-paced musical quiz integrating the listeners at home— *Stop the Music!*, hosted by an effervescent bundle of joy named Bert Parks—everybody's standings changed. Overnight ABC became number one in that hour. Bergen quit for a year and Allen was knocked out of the water completely. Indeed, *Stop the Music!* is recalled as "the show that ended Fred Allen's radio career" after 17 consecutive seasons. In that instance, kicking out a house band and a guest symphony significantly altered a distressed network's fortunes.

At its inception, *The Breakfast Club* early morning radio show boasted a 12-piece orchestra drawn from the roster of musicians on NBC's Chicago staff. In his introspective into the program, John Doolittle pursued the reaction of those instrumentalists designated for that early morning duty at its start. "When [host Don] McNeill first took over the show it was obvious that musicians saw the assignment as tantamount to punishment, since they were required to show up for 7:00 A.M. rehearsals," said Doolittle. But when they realized the show was all about fun, "This attitude began to change, and soon orchestra members started requesting assignment to the *Breakfast Club*." A few of them stayed for the duration, which lasted more than 35 years!

Such accounts from the inside are legendary among the annals of network house musical aggregations.

A fascinating aspect, alluded to previously, concerned the pacing of music comedy series in the 1930s. Furthermore, by the 1950s music was still being introduced into programs that could generally be considered comedies (or possibly situation comedies) by common labels. By then some shows that focused on laughter had abandoned the variety format that had dominated radio's earliest days.

In that era a staff orchestra, often combined with a soloist or vocal group, was added to the substance of many programs to unmistakably define segments within a half-hour or hour-long performance. Doing so allowed the scriptwriters to create single, episodic or separate, disjointed plotlines or sketches. The music added diversity to a series, linking it to a thriving variety show format of popular features like *The Collier Hour*, Fleischman's *Rudy Vallee Show* and the Maxwell House *Showboat*. Some big names were among the bandmasters playing behind the radio comedians: Ferde Grofe (Fred Allen's *Hellman's Salad Bowl Revue* and *Sal Hepatica Revue*), Eddy Duchin, Jan Garber, Glen Gray, Ferde Grofe, Guy Lombardo, Ray Noble, Artie Shaw and Paul Whiteman (all appearing with *George Burns and Gracie Allen* at varying times), Ozzie Nelson (*The Joe Penner Show*), Jimmy Dorsey and Paul Whiteman (*Kraft Music Hall*) and Mildred Bailey (*The George Jessel Show*).

There were occasions when the orchestra leaders were incorporated into the plots of the shows, too, becoming running cast members just as vital to a show's success there as they were in conducting the band. Several of those just mentioned performed double duties. One of the most memorable in that capacity, appearing later in the golden age, was Phil Harris, who often became a stooge or foil for his perceived taskmaster, Jack Benny. Their lighthearted exchanges, and the persona created for Harris as an inveterate inebriate, instilled raucous laughter into that show every week in the late 1940s.

From the beginnings of radio, it was traditional to "interrupt" the pace of such series with one or more musical selections. Sometimes only the band was featured; at other times, a vocal would be accompanied by the band, performed by singers like Tony Martin (*George Burns and Gracie Allen Show*), Deanna Durbin (*Eddie Cantor Show*), Gene Austin (*Joe Penner Show*) or Frank Parker and Dennis Day (*Jack Benny Program*). Radio historian Fred MacDonald outlined a sample program format from a Fred Allen *Linit Bath Club Revue* that aired in 1932.

1. Announcer opens the program
2. Orchestra plays full song
3. Monologue by Allen — intro first scene of skit
4. Vocal solo by Charles Carlile [*sic*]
5. Second scene in skit — Portland Hoffa enters
6. First commercial
7. Musical interlude
8. Third scene of skit
9. Orchestra and vocalist — portions of two songs
10. Second commercial
11. Closing comments from Allen

Throughout *Fibber McGee & Molly's* half-hour series, extending from 1935 to 1953, the house musicians operating there invariably divided the inane banter between the McGees and their friends of Wistful Vista into triple segments. A typical McGee program — presenting a common theme in its humorous sketches on a given broadcast — would be formatted like this:

1. Announcer introduces the show ("The Johnson's Wax Program, with Fibber McGee and Molly," for most of the run)
2. Orchestra launches theme song
3. First commercial — announcer
4. Orchestral bridge music
5. Announcer sets the scene for the comedic plot; audience applauds

6. First comedy scenario (situation established)

7. First musical number — either by Billy Mills and his orchestra or The Kings Men vocal quartet backed by the orchestra

8. Second comedy scenario (situation progresses with second commercial integrated into plot and delivered by announcer)

9. Second musical number — reverse participation from the first musical number

10. Third comedy scenario (situation resolved)

11. Third commercial — announcer

12. Orchestra launches theme song as McGee and Molly bid "goodnight"

13. Closing comments by announcer

Here's a thought worth pondering: Did Billy Mills even *have* an orchestra? Or was he merely conducting a group selected from the aggregate of resident staff musicians available at NBC? It's logical to speculate, as some observers have, that such outfits didn't embrace the same individuals every week.

"I would imagine that there were some broadcasts which required specific instrumentation for some mood or another one week, but a different combination for another," one music historian contended.[4] "A pool seems to me to be the only logical way they could always have available just what was needed." If true, it would reaffirm the beauty of a selective system. The composition of house bands could be tailored to fit the requirements of specific broadcasts. Of course, the major chains maintained enough talented artists for every instrument that just the right number of musicians could be secured without tying up extra people. The ability to customize translated into significantly reducing expenses for many shows.

What happened to the house bands? As the prosperity of radio began to ebb in the 1950s, the future livelihoods of those musicians dimmed, at least under traditional arrangements, as fewer and fewer were needed. More and more programming disappeared from the aural airwaves, diminishing the necessity for large and versatile instrumental staffs. Bing Crosby is a good example.

For decades, an assemblage of scores of professional talents provided background for his singing. But by late 1954, Crosby could lay claim to nothing more than a minuscule cluster of accompanists, a common situation experienced by most radio vocalists. Adding to the artists' dilemma, by the early 1950s CBS — the chain that persevered longer than the others against great odds by stubbornly embracing dramatic series as a popular form of entertainment — began eliminating the posts of studio musicians entirely.

By then CBS had gathered a capacious collection of stock music from musicians on its payroll. Most of the studio's programming was no longer dependent upon live performances. (The ban against transcribed music had been lifted a few years before this.) Thus, programs like *Mr. and Mrs. North, Suspense, Yours Truly Johnny Dollar, Gunsmoke, Mr. Keen Tracer of Lost Persons, The FBI in Peace and War, The Whistler* and others of that ilk no longer relied on the presence of large orchestras, including rehearsals with musicians on a grand scale. Producers were permitted to borrow appropriate prerecorded material from the CBS archives for their own radio and television series.

This led to union protests from the musicians who were by then scrambling for work. "The matter went *very* public by the late 1950s when the same practice was applied to television," explained researcher Martin Grams. "The matter went to court where the eventual ruling was that the network had to hire musicians to compose and conduct music for a minimum of 13 television episodes per season. All other broadcasts could feature stock music."5 Even those rules would be relaxed eventually. Producer Himan Brown was able to draw at will from the CBS library for all 1,600-plus episodes of his 1970s series *The CBS Radio Mystery Theater*, without employing an ensemble or so much as an organist.

The passing of time had made the house musicians totally irrelevant at all the major networks. Parenthetically, today's prime-time TV producers usually hire the same musicians to compose and conduct the melodies heard on all the episodes of a given series, almost never surrendering to the temptation to exploit stock music.

In radio's halcyon days, the house musicians rendered essential support to hundreds of programs of several differing genres. The shows would have been absolutely bereft of much of their substance and meaning without the contributions of those behind-the-scenes, frequently unrecognized artists. In truth, most listeners probably wouldn't have noticed their work at all unless it hadn't been there.

The Bandmasters

The remainder of the chapter includes brief introductions of some of the principal house band conductors who performed regularly on ongoing radio shows. Each trained and directed artists who were adapted from the studio pools, melding them into superior entertainers able to supply just the right musical intonations that each show required.

While well-known names among the big bands were often thrust into the limelight, it goes without saying that the music the in-house impresarios provided was some of the most essential to cross the ether. Most of these probably never achieved their just due, missing the public adulation that the big bandleaders gained from a fawning following. From that standpoint, this is an attempt to right a wrong while concurrently documenting much of their work.

A random sampling of several prominent, durable and possibly familiar house bandmasters has been selected for citation. In addition to the 18 maestros presented here, at least another eight are introduced in other chapters of this text where their contributions are more appropriately adapted. Included: Victor Arden, Gus Haenschen and Abe Lyman (*The Hummert Musicales*), Frank Black (*The Cities Service Concerts*), Howard Barlow (*The Voice of Firestone*), Jack Miller (*The Kate Smith Show*), John Scott Trotter (*The Bing Crosby Show*) and Donald Voorhees (*The Bell Telephone Hour*).

A disclaimer is in order. More definitive information isn't included on radio broadcast dates and times because the preponderance of published sources of such data (indeed, there are several) is often in conflict with each other, especially regarding actual beginning and ending dates. Given those parameters, it seems best to provide the years, networks and sponsors but to avoid material that isn't documented somewhere. Transcriptions would be required to accomplish that feat and, regrettably, certain critical information appears to exist no longer.

ROBERT ARMBRUSTER

Born: October 9, 1897, Philadelphia, Pennsylvania.
Died: June 20, 1994.
Highlights: Debuted with Philadelphia Orchestra as an eight-year-old pianist; at 19, played at a White House diplomatic event; accompanied the inaugural of NBC, November 15, 1926; became a pianist for that network and later a house

bandleader; gained Hollywood radio and film work in the early 1940s, conducting the NBC Hollywood Orchestra frequently.

Radio Shows:

Enna Jettick Melodies. 1928–1933, NBC Blue, Enna Jettick shoes.

The Cuckoo Hour. 1930–1932, 1934, 1935-1936, NBC Blue, sustaining, except for two months in summer 1934, NBC, AC Delco Corporation (AC spark plugs).

The Natural Bridge Revue. 1930-1931, NBC Blue, Natural Bridge shoes.

Lux Radio Theater. 1936, CBS, Lever Brothers Company (Lux toilet soap).

Coronet on the Air. 1937, NBC Blue, *Coronet* magazine.

Gladys Swarthout. 1937, NBC, National Ice Advertising Company.

The Chase & Sanborn Hour. 1937–1939, NBC, Sunday, 8:00–9:00 P.M., Standard Brands, Inc. (Chase & Sanborn coffee, Royal gelatin and puddings).

Red Ryder. 1942–1951, NBC Blue (initially), MBS, Langendorf bread.

The New Old Gold Show. 1942-1943, CBS, P. Lorillard, Inc. (Old Gold cigarettes).

The Groucho Marx Show. 1943, CBS, sustaining.

Blue Ribbon Town. 1943-1944, CBS, Pabst Brewing Company (Pabst Blue Ribbon beer).

The Judy Canova Show. c1943–c1953, CBS (initial season), NBC (all others), Colgate-Palmolive-Peet Company (various personal care commodities) 1943–1951, sustaining (1951-1952), multiple participation (1952-1953).

The Electric Hour. 1944–1946, CBS, consortium of 170 regional electric companies (utility image building).

Blue Ribbon Time. 1944-1947, CBS, Pabst Brewing Company (Pabst Blue Ribbon beer).

The Eternal Light. 1944–1981 (a portion of this run), NBC, Jewish Theological Seminary and NBC (joint goodwill venture).

The Cavalcade of America. 1945–1947, NBC, E. I. Dupont Company (solutions to home and industrial challenges).

A Day in the Life of Dennis Day. 1946–1951 (a portion of this run), NBC, Colgate-Palmolive-Peet Company (Lustre Crème shampoo and other personal care goods).

Kraft Music Hall. c1947–1949, NBC, Kraft Foods Company (Kraft cheese and other foodstuffs).

Nightbeat. 1950–1952 (a portion of this run), NBC, sustaining.

Sara's Private Caper. 1950, NBC, General Mills, Inc. (Wheaties cereal).

The Cass Daley Show. 1950, NBC, sustaining.

Western Caravan. 1950, NBC, sustaining.

The Great Gildersleeve. c1950–1957, NBC, Kraft Foods Company (Kraft cheese and other foodstuffs) through 1954; multiple participation thereafter.

The Adventures of Sam Spade. 1950-1951, NBC, sustaining.

Dangerous Assignment. 1950–1952, NBC, sustaining.

Cousin Willie. 1953, NBC, Tuesday, sustaining,

Hawthorne TBA. 1953, NBC, sustaining.

Two in the Balcony. 1954-1955, no further information.

MITCHELL AYERS

Born: December 24, 1910, Milwaukee, Wisconsin.

Died: September 5, 1969, Las Vegas, Nevada.

Highlights: Signature song — *You Go to My Head*; best recalled as singer Perry Como's radio, television, recording and stage musical conductor beginning in the late 1940s, continuing for many years, after disbanding his own outfit in 1948; also assumed the post of music director for Columbia Records.

Radio Shows:

Dunninger, the Mentalist (aka *The Dunninger*

Show). 1943-1944, NBC Blue, Sherwin-Williams paints; 1945, 1946, NBC, Lever Brothers Company (Rinso detergent).

The Jack Pepper Show. 1944, CBS, Lever Brothers Company (Swan soap).

The Chesterfield Supper Club. 1948-1949, NBC, Liggett & Myers Tobacco Company (Chesterfield cigarettes).

Let's Go to Town. 1950s, AFRS, 82 quarter-hour transcribed shows.

The Perry Como Show. 1954-1955, CBS (simulcast of CBS-TV series), Liggett & Myers Tobacco Company (Chesterfield cigarettes).

ARCHIE BLEYER

Born: June 12, 1909, Corona, New York.

Died: March 20, 1989, Sheboygan, Wisconsin.

Highlights: CBS house bandleader after 1939 who had a stylish band of his own earlier; created a distinctive musical sound and played venues like Earl Carroll's Club in Hollywood; gained fame in the 1940s and 1950s as conductor for entertainer Arthur Godfrey, appearing multiple times weekly on Godfrey radio and television shows; one of many staffers dismissed in highly visible firings as Godfrey's public adulation dropped sharply ("I think the show went steadily downhill after Archie left ... he was the brains behind ... what made the show successful" — longtime sideman Remo Palmieri); Bleyer enjoyed further success heading his own recording label (Cadence).

Radio Shows:

Archie Bleyer Orchestra. 1934, NBC, sustaining (launched over Philadelphia's WIP).

Archie Bleyer and His Commodore Hotel Orchestra. 1939, CBS, sustaining (continuing a run that began over New York's WMCA in 1934).

Fifty-One East Fifty-First (aka *Kay Thompson Show*). 1941-1942, CBS, sustaining.

The Charlie Ruggles Show. 1943–1945, half-hour in syndication.

Casey, Crime Photographer (aka *Flashgun Casey*; *Casey, Press Photographer*; *Crime Photographer*). c1943–c1948, CBS, American Hocking Glass Corporation (Anchor Hocking glassware), 1946–1948, otherwise sustaining.

The Joan Brooks Show. 1944, CBS, sustaining.

The Gordon MacRae Show. 1945-1946, CBS, sustaining.

The Patti Clayton Show. 1945–1947, CBS, sustaining.

Skyline Roof. 1946, CBS, sustaining.

The Janette Davis Show. 1946–c1948, ABC, sustaining.

Arthur Godfrey Time. 1946–1953, CBS, Bristol-Myers, Inc. (Ban deodorant, Bufferin pain reliever, Ipana toothpaste, Vitalis hair preparation, others), General Foods Corporation (Post Bran Flakes cereal), Gold Seal Company (Glasswax window and Gold Seal wood cleaning agents), Kimberly-Clark, Inc. (Kleenex tissues), Lever Brothers Company (Lux toilet soap, Rinso detergent), Monarch, Inc. (Monarch jams, jellies and preserves), National Biscuit Company (Nabisco Saltine and Ritz crackers, other foodstuffs), Liggett & Myers Tobacco Company (Chesterfield cigarettes), Pillsbury Mills, Inc. (Pillsbury flour and cake mixes), Staley Corporation (Sta-Puf laundry starch, fabric softener, other goods), Sterling Drugs, Inc. (Bayer aspirin), Thomas J. Lipton, Inc. (Lipton tea, soup mixes, main dishes and other foodstuffs), many more.

Arthur Godfrey's Talent Scouts. 1946–1953, CBS, sustaining (first year), Thomas J. Lipton, Inc. (Lipton tea, soup mixes, main dishes and other foodstuffs).

Danny O'Neil and His Guests (aka *Danny O'Neal Show*). 1946-1947, CBS, sponsorship unsubstantiated.

Arthur Godfrey Digest (aka *Arthur Godfrey*

Round Table). 1950–1953, CBS, taped highlight repeats from weekly *Arthur Godfrey Time* broadcasts with some of the same sponsors.

LES BROWN

Born: March 14, 1912, Reinerton, Pennsylvania.

Died: January 4, 2001, Los Angeles, California.

Highlights: Signature songs for "Les Brown and His Band of Renown" were *Dance of the Blue Devils* and *Leap Frog*; played the Glen Island Casino, New Rochelle, New York, early in his career, featuring vocals by a young Doris Day; soared to prominence with Bob Hope, accompanying him for two decades on radio, TV, records, global tours of military bases, stage appearances and film; named 1953 Best Dance Band of the Year by *Downbeat* fanzine.

Radio Shows:

Les Brown Orchestra. 1935, MBS, sustaining; continued in 1937 and 1942 over Cleveland, Ohio's WTAM.

The Fitch Bandwagon. 1944, NBC, F. W. Fitch Company (Fitch shampoo).

The Bob Hope Show. 1947–1958, NBC, The Pepsodent Company (Pepsodent toothpaste, 1947-1948), Lever Brothers Company (Swan soap, 1948–1950), Liggett & Myers Tobacco Company (Chesterfield cigarettes, 1950–1952), General Foods Corporation (Jell-O gelatin, puddings and other foodstuffs) 1952–1954, American Dairy (simultaneous overlapping series, 1953–1955), multiple participation (taped repeats, 1956–1958).

A Dream Comes True. 1948-1949, half-hour syndicated series, local sponsorship.

The Doris Day Show. 1952-1953, CBS, Columbia Recording Company (Columbia records).

FRANK DE VOL

Born: September 20, 1911, Moundsville, West Virginia.

Died: October 27, 1999, Lafayette, California.

Highlights: Alto sax player and prolific arranger in bands headlined by Horace Heidt, George Olsen and Alvino Rey in the 1930s; wrote scores for several film and TV productions including *Cat Ballou, My Three Sons, Pillow Talk*; Columbia Records executive; moved to television with Dinah Shore.

Radio Shows:

Adventures in Rhythm. 1940s, Don Lee network, unsubstantiated sponsorship.

California Melodies. At unspecified times between 1944 and 1947, MBS, unsubstantiated sponsorship.

The Rudy Vallee Show. 1944-1945, NBC, Drene shampoo.

The Ginny Simms Show. 1945–1947, CBS, The Borden Company (Borden dairy products).

Tommy Riggs and Betty Lou. 1946, CBS, The Borden Company (Borden dairy products).

The Sealtest Village Store. c1945–1948, NBC, Sealtest Corporation (Sealtest dairy products).

The Jack Smith Show. 1945–1952, CBS, Procter & Gamble Company (Oxydol detergent, 1945–1950; Tide detergent, 1951-1952).

The Dinah Shore Show. 1953–1955, NBC, General Motors Corporation (Chevrolet automobiles and trucks).

LUD (LUDWIG) GLUSKIN

Born: December 16, 1898, New York, New York.

Died: October 13, 1989, Palm Springs, California.

Highlights: Signature song *On the Air*; drummer with Paul Whiteman in the

1920s, followed by lengthy stint conducting The Playboys jazz band in Berlin and Paris, European radio broadcasts and hundreds of recordings; hired by CBS in 1934, became its music director in 1936 and music director of CBS-TV, 1948–1958.

Radio Shows:

I Was There. 1935–late 1930s, CBS West Coast, Mobil Oil Company (Mobil gasoline, oil, other vehicle products and services).

Lud Gluskin Orchestra. 1935-1936, CBS, sustaining.

World Dances (aka *Fiesta*). 1936-1937, CBS, sustaining.

The Al Jolson Show (aka *The Lifebuoy Program, The Rinso Program, The Tuesday Night Party*). 1936–1939, CBS, Lever Brothers Company (Lifebuoy soap, Rinso detergent).

The Ken Murray Program. 1937, CBS, Campbell Soup Company (Campbell juices and soups, Franco-American spaghetti and macaroni and other foodstuffs).

The Campbell's Tomato Juice Program. 1937, CBS, Campbell Soup Company (Campbell's tomato juice).

Hollywood Showcase. 1937-1938, 1941-1942, 1948, CBS, sustaining (1937-1938, 1948), Richard Hudnut, Inc. (Richard Hudnut hair care products, 1941-1942).

Melody and Madness (aka *The Old Gold Program*). c1938-1939, CBS, P. Lorillard, Inc. (Old Gold cigarettes).

Lud Gluskin Orchestra. 1940, CBS, sustaining.

Columbia Presents Corwin. 1941, CBS, sustaining.

Southern Cruise (aka *American Cruise*). 1941, CBS, sustaining.

Ceiling Unlimited. 1942-1943, CBS, Lockheed Corporation (Lockheed Vega aircraft).

Grapevine Rancho. 1943, CBS, Roma Wine Company (Roma wines).

Passport for Adams. 1943, CBS, sustaining.

Campana Serenade. 1943-1944, CBS, Campana cosmetics.

The Open House (aka *The Ona Munson Show*). 1943–1946, CBS, sustaining.

The Orson Welles Theater (aka *Orson Welles' Almanac*). 1944, CBS West Coast, Mobil Oil Company (Mobil gasoline, oil and other vehicle products and services).

The Amos 'n' Andy Show. 1943-1947, NBC, Lever Brothers Company (Rinso detergent).

The Sea Has a Story (aka *The Story of the Sea*). 1945, CBS, sustaining.

The Jack Kirkwood Show. 1946, CBS, sustaining.

Intrigue. 1946, CBS, sustaining.

The Sweeney and March Program. c1946 or 1947, CBS, sustaining.

The Amazing Mr. Smith. 1946-1947, CBS, sustaining.

Suspense. c1946-1947, CBS, Roma Wine Company (Roma wines) 1946–mid 1947, sustaining (1947).

Joanie's Tea Room (aka *Joan Davis Time*). c1946-1947, Lever Brothers Company (Swan soap).

My Friend Irma. 1947–1954, CBS, The Pepsodent Company (Pepsodent toothpaste, 1947–1951), Pearson Company (Ennds [sic] Chlorophyll Tablets breath mints, other personal care goods) 1951-1952, R. J. Reynolds Tobacco Company (Camel cigarettes) 1952-1953, multiple participation (1953-1954).

The Amazing Mr. Tutt. 1948, CBS, sustaining.

The Philip Morris Playhouse. 1948-1949, CBS, Philip Morris Company (Philip Morris cigarettes).

The Adventures of Sam Spade. 1949-1950, NBC, Wildroot Crème Oil men's hair preparation.

Life with Luigi. c1950–1953, 1954, CBS, William J. Wrigley Company (Wrigley's Doublemint, Juicy Fruit and Spearmint chewing gums) 1950–1952, sustaining (1952-1953, 1954).

The Frank Fontaine Show. 1952, CBS, sustaining.
My Little Margie. 1952–1955, CBS, Philip Morris Company (Philip Morris cigarettes).
Rogers of the Gazette. 1953, CBS, sustaining.
Cathy and Elliott Lewis on Stage. 1953-1954, CBS, sustaining.
The Amos 'n' Andy Show. 1954-1955, CBS, sustaining.

AL GOODMAN

Born: August 5, 1890, Nikopol, Russia.
Died: January 10, 1972, New York, New York.
Highlights: Collaborated with Earl Carroll in writing his first hit show, *So Long Letty*, in 1916; launched a string of successes as a pit bandleader, including for Al Jolson's *Sinbad*; numerous RCA Victor recordings; one of the early maestros for *Your Hit Parade* (1935–1938) while breaking in comic Bob Hope on his first network outing, plus a lengthy run with comic Fred Allen.
Radio Shows:
The Ziegfeld Follies of the Air. 1932, CBS, Chrysler Corporation (Chrysler-Plymouth automotive division).
Lucky Strike Dance Orchestra. 1933, NBC, American Tobacco Company (Lucky Strike cigarettes).
Gulf Headliners. 1933-1934, NBC Blue, Gulf Oil Corporation (Gulf gasoline, oil and other vehicle products and services).
The Joe Cook Show. 1934, NBC, Colgate-Palmolive-Peet Company (Colgate dental cream, Palmolive soap and other personal care products).
The Intimate Revue (aka *Bob Hope Show*). 1935, NBC Blue, Emerson Drug Company (Bromo Seltzer pain reliever, Bromo Quinine distress tonic).
Rhythm at Eight (aka *The Ethel Merman Show*). 1935, CBS, Lehn & Fink Products (Lysol sanitizing cleansers).
The Palmolive Beauty Box Theater. 1935, NBC Blue; 1936, 1937, CBS, Colgate-Palmolive-Peet Company (Palmolive soap and other personal care products).
Music by Goodman. 1935, NBC, Food Industries of Philadelphia (Ludens cough drops and confections).
Your Hit Parade. 1935–1938, NBC, American Tobacco Company (Lucky Strike cigarettes).
The Ziegfeld Follies of the Air. 1936, CBS, Colgate-Palmolive-Peet Company (Palmolive soap and other personal care products).
Showboat (aka *The Maxwell House Showboat*). 1936-1937, NBC, General Foods Corporation (Maxwell House coffee).
Your Hollywood Parade. 1938, NBC, American Tobacco Company (Lucky Strike cigarettes).
The Fred Allen Show (aka *The Texaco Star Theater*). 1940–1944, CBS, The Texas Company (Texaco gasoline, oil and other vehicle products and services, 1940–1944); 1945–1949, NBC, Standard Brands, Inc. (Tenderleaf tea and other foodstuffs) 1945–1947, Ford Motor Company (Ford automobiles and trucks) 1948-1949.
The Prudential Family Hour. 1941–1948, CBS, Prudential Insurance Company (Prudential insurance).
Treasury Star Parade. 1942–1944, transcribed quarter-hour, U. S. Treasury Department (war bonds).
The James Melton Show (aka *The Texaco Star Theater*). 1943, 1944–1946, CBS, The Texas Company (Texaco gasoline, oil and other vehicle products and services).
Hit the Jackpot. 1948-1949, CBS, sustaining (first six broadcasts), Chrysler Corporation (Chrysler-Plymouth automobile division).
Al Goodman's Musical Album. 1951–1953, NBC, sustaining.

Morton Gould

Born: December 10, 1913, Richmond Hill, New York.

Died: February 21, 1996, Orlando, Florida.

Highlights: Pianist in vaudeville, cinemas and radio, appearing on Newark's WOR at 12; teamed with pianist Bert Shefter on NBC and Radio City Music Hall staff; hired by MBS as conductor-arranger (1936); composing at age six, he gained notice supplying scores for some of Meredith Willson's radio shows and for symphonies, movies, Broadway shows and ballets; conducted orchestras on 100 record albums; president of the American Society of Composers, Authors & Publishers (ASCAP) from 1986 to 1994.

Radio Shows:

The Jack Pearl Show. 1932, CBS, Chrysler Corporation (Chrysler-Plymouth automobile division).

The Lucky Strike Hour (aka *The Jack Pearl Show*). 1932-1933, NBC, American Tobacco Company (Lucky Strike cigarettes).

The Jack Pearl Show. 1934, NBC, Standard Brands, Inc. (Royal gelatin, puddings and pie fillings).

Family Hotel. 1935, CBS, Frigidaire home appliances.

The Raleigh and Kool Program. 1936-1937, NBC, Brown & Williamson Tobacco Company (Raleigh and Kool cigarettes and Sir Walter Raleigh pipe tobacco).

Music for Today (aka *Morton Gould Orchestra*). 1936-1937, 1937-1938, 1938–1940, 1940 (three series beginning and ending in 1940), 1940–1942, 1942 (two series beginning and ending in 1942), MBS, sustaining.

Keep 'em Rolling. 1941-1942, MBS, U. S. Office of Emergency Management (home-front morale-boosting).

The Cresta Blanca Carnival of Music (aka *The Carnival of Musical Contrasts*). 1942-1943, MBS; 1943-1944, CBS, Cresta Blanca wines.

Shower of Stars. 1945, CBS, Chrysler Corporation (Chrysler-Plymouth automobile division).

Wilbur Hatch

Born: May 24, 1902, Moken, Illinois

Died: December 22, 1969, Studio City, California

Highlights: A pianist on Chicago's KYW in 1922; became a company man for CBS in its earliest days, almost to the exclusion of other chains; a prolific lyricist who created eerie music for *The Whistler* and penned scores for numerous other series; conducted for several aural features over very long runs (*Meet Corliss Archer, My Favorite Husband, Our Miss Brooks, The Screen Guild Theater, The Whistler*); never a big bandleader, thus missed the public acclaim that frequently was assigned to that turf.

Radio Shows:

Calling All Cars. 1933–1939, CBS West Coast, Rio Grande Oil Company (Rio Grande gasoline, oil and other vehicle products and services).

Design for Happiness (aka *The Buddy Clark Show*). 1938, MBS, American Tobacco Company (Lucky Strike cigarettes).

The Buddy Clark Show, 1938-1939, CBS, sustaining.

Man about Hollywood. 1939, CBS, Lever Brothers Company (Lux toilet soap); 1940, CBS, General Foods Corporation (Grape Nuts cereal and other foodstuffs).

Gateway to Hollywood. 1939, CBS, William J. Wrigley Company (Wrigley's Doublemint, Juicy Fruit and Spearmint chewing gums).

Suspense. 1940, CBS, sustaining.

The Whistler. 1942–1955, CBS West Coast, sustaining (1942-1943), Signal Oil Company (Signal gasoline, oil and other vehicle products and services) 1943–1954; 1946, CBS, Campbell Soup Company (Campbell juices and soups, Franco-

American spaghetti and macaroni and other foodstuffs); 1947-1948, CBS, Household Finance Corporation (Household lending services); 1955, CBS West Coast, Lever Brothers Company (personal care products), then sustaining.

The Lady Esther Screen Guild Theater. 1942–1947, CBS, Lady Esther Cosmetics Company (Lady Esther cosmetics).

Meet Corliss Archer. 1943, 1944-1945, 1946, 1947-1948, CBS, sustaining (1943), Anchor Hocking Glass Company (Anchor Hocking glass) 1944-1945, Campbell Soup Company (Campbell's juices and soups, Franco-American spaghetti and macaroni and other foodstuffs) 1946–1948, sustaining (1948); 1948, NBC, The Pepsodent Company (Pepsodent toothpaste); 1949–1952, CBS, local electric companies cooperative; 1952-1953, ABC, local electric companies cooperative; 1954, CBS, Gillette Company (Toni home permanents and other hair preparations) and Carter Company (Carter's health care goods); 1956, CBS, sustaining.

America — Ceiling Unlimited. 1943-1944, CBS, Lockheed Corporation (Lockheed Vega aircraft).

Broadway Matinee. 1943, CBS, Owens-Illinois Glass Company (Owens glass).

Spotlight on Music. 1944, CBS, sustaining.

Twelve Players. 1945, CBS, sustaining.

Hawk Durango (aka *Hawk Larabee*). 1946–1948, CBS, sustaining.

The Sweeney and March Program. 1946–c1947, CBS, sustaining.

The City. 1947, CBS West Coast, sustaining.

The Camel Screen Guild Players. 1947-1948, CBS; 1948–1950, NBC, R. J. Reynolds Tobacco Company (Camel cigarettes).

It's a Great Life. 1948, CBS West Coast, General Mills, Inc. (Wheaties cereal and Bisquick biscuit mix).

Life with Luigi. 1948, CBS, William J. Wrigley Company (Wrigley's Doublemint, Juicy Fruit and Spearmint chewing gums).

My Favorite Husband. 1948–1951, CBS, General Foods Corporation (Sanka instant coffee, Jell-O desserts, LaFrance bleach, Swans Down cake mixes and other foodstuffs).

Our Miss Brooks. 1948–1957, CBS, sustaining (1948), Colgate-Palmolive-Peet Company (Lustre Crème shampoo, Palmolive brushless shaving cream, Colgate dental cream and other personal care products) 1948–1954, American Home Products (Anacin pain reliever, Kolynos toothpaste and other health care products) and The Gillette Company (Toni home permanents, White Rain shampoo, Deep Magic facial lotion and other personal care products) 1954–1956, multiple participation (1957).

Escape. cLate 1940s–early 1950s, CBS, sustaining and Richfield Oil Company, spring-summer 1950 only (Atlantic gasoline, oil and automotive products and services).

Broadway Is My Beat. 1949–early 1950s, CBS, sustaining and multiple participation — Lever Brothers Company (Lux toilet soap), William J. Wrigley Company (Wrigley's Doublemint, Juicy Fruit and Spearmint chewing gum), others.

Fiesta. 1951, CBS, sustaining.

I Love Lucy. 1952, CBS, Philip Morris, Inc. (Philip Morris cigarettes). [*A radio audition show of the popular TV series that was never aired.*]

December Bride. 1952-1953, CBS, sustaining.

The General Electric Theater. 1953, CBS, General Electric Company (GE home appliances).

Rogers of the Gazette. 1953-1954, CBS, sustaining.

On a Sunday Afternoon. 1955-1956, CBS, sustaining.

Frontier Gentleman. 1958, CBS, sustaining.

Luke Slaughter of Tombstone. 1958, CBS, sustaining.

Gordon Jenkins

Born: May 12, 1910, Webster Groves, Missouri.

Died: May 1, 1984, Malibu, California.

Highlights: At 17, opened St. Louis' KMOX daily, accompanying his own vocals on organ, piano, accordion, ukulele and banjo; created arrangements for bandleaders Isham Jones, Benny Goodman, Lennie Hayton, Vincent Lopez and Paul Whiteman; became NBC's West Coast music director in the 1930s; a Decca records conductor and music director in the 1940s, showcasing The Andrews Sisters, Louis Armstrong, Dick Haymes, Peggy Lee and The Weavers; penned several chart-topping tunes like *My Foolish Heart* and *P.S. I Love You*; won a Grammy in 1967 for Frank Sinatra's *September of My Years* album.

Radio Shows:

Gordon Jenkins Orchestra, 1935, NBC, sustaining.

Hall of Fun. 1938-1939, NBC, sustaining.

The Signal Carnival. cLate 1930s–1941, NBC West Coast, Signal Oil Company (gasoline, oil and other vehicle products and services).

Little Ol' Hollywood. 1939–1942, NBC Blue, sustaining.

Everyman's Theater. 1940-1941, NBC, Procter & Gamble Company (Oxydol detergent).

The Fred Brady Show (aka *That's Life*). 1941, CBS, sustaining; 1943, NBC, Lever Brothers Company (various household cleaning and personal care products).

Gordon Jenkins Orchestra. 1941, NBC, sustaining; 1941, NBC Blue, sustaining.

Hap Hazard. 1941, NBC, S. C. Johnson and Sons (Johnson's wax and other household and automotive cleaning compounds).

Sweet and Rhythmic. 1941, NBC Blue, sustaining.

Plays for Americans. 1942, NBC, sustaining.

In Person, Dinah Shore. 1942-1943, NBC Blue, Bristol-Myers, Inc. (Ipana toothpaste and other personal care products).

Eyes Aloft. 1942-1943, NBC West Coast, sustaining.

The Colgate Program (aka *The Al Jolson Show*). 1942-1943, CBS, Colgate-Palmolive-Peet Company (Colgate dental cream, Palmolive soap and other personal care products).

Free World Theater. 1943, NBC Blue, sustaining.

Mayor of the Town. c1943–1945, CBS, Lever Brothers Company (household cleansing and personal care products) 1943, Noxzema (personal care products) 1944-1945.

The Man Called X. 1944, CBS, Lockheed Corporation (Lockheed aircraft).

Everything for the Boys. 1944-1945, NBC, Electric Autolite Company (Autolite batteries, headlights, spark plugs and other vehicle power supplies).

The Dick Haymes Show. 1945–1948, CBS, Electric Autolite Company (Autolite batteries, headlights, spark plugs and other vehicle power supplies).

The Bob Burns Show. 1944–1946, NBC, Lever Brothers Company (Lifebuoy soap, Rinso detergent and other household and personal care products).

The Judy Canova Show. c1951–1953, NBC, sustaining (to mid 1952), multiple participation (including Emerson Drug Company, General Motors Corporation and Smith Brothers, 1952-1953).

Rex Koury

Born: 1911, London, England.

Highlights: At 14, accompanied silent movies as a house organist at cinemas, securing a gig at New York's Roxy Theater; a few years later landed on Los Angeles' KFI, became staff organist for NBC Hollywood and penned freelance compositions for CBS Radio; named music director of ABC Hollywood; in the 1930s gained notoriety as pianist on *Fibber McGee & Molly*; major radio contributions as an organist-arranger; most famous triumph writing *Gunsmoke's* signature song *The Old Trail* in 1952, a radio–TV classic (it came to Koury while shaving and he completed it in 10 minutes); penned music for other shows on the tube including *The Amazing Mr. Malone* and *The Fugitive*; composed church music after retiring in 1980; Organist of the Year of the American Theatre Organ Society in 1982 and the fraternity's president (1983–1985).

Radio Shows:

Fibber McGee & Molly. 1935–1938, NBC, S. C. Johnson and Sons (Johnson's wax and other household and automotive cleaning compounds).

Kay Kyser's Kollege of Musical Knowledge. 1938, MBS, sustaining; 1938–1944, NBC, American Tobacco Company (Lucky Strike cigarettes); 1944–1948, NBC, Colgate-Palmolive-Peet Company (various personal care products); 1948-1949, ABC, Pillsbury Mills, Inc. (Pillsbury cake flour and other baking goods). Partial simultaneous run: 1939-1940, MBS, sustaining.

The Hermit's Cave. 1940–1944, Los Angeles' WMPC, sustaining.

Murder and Mr. Malone. ABC, Guild Wines Company.

The Adventures of Ellery Queen. 1947-1948, ABC, sustaining.

I Love Adventure. 1948, ABC, sustaining.

The Lone Wolf. 1948-1949, MBS, sustaining.

We Care. 1948-1949, ABC, CARE human relief services.

The Croupier. 1949, ABC, sustaining.

Defense Attorney. 1951-1952, ABC, Clorets breath mints (1951-1952), General Mills, Inc. (Kix cereal) and Goodyear Tire and Rubber Company (Goodyear tires), both 1952.

Gunsmoke. 1952–1961, CBS, sustaining (1952-1953), General Foods Corporation (Post Toasties cereal) 1953, Liggett & Myers Tobacco Company (Chesterfield and L&M cigarettes) 1954–1957, sustaining and multiple participation (1957–1961). [*Theme song continued on CBS-TV series of same title, 1955–1975.*]

BILLY MILLS

Born: September 6, 1894, Flint, Michigan.

Died: October 20, 1971, Glendale, California.

Highlights: Similarities to Rex Koury; theater pianist, church soloist, military bandleader and arranger for Isham Jones in the 1920s prior to forming an orchestra; arranger, staff conductor and general music supervisor for CBS Chicago (1932–1937); transferred to NBC in 1938, hired by S. C. Johnson and Sons as music director for *Fibber McGee & Molly*, his most durable and infamous legacy, a program connection continuing 15 years.

Radio Shows:

Poetic Melodies. 1932-1933, NBC Blue, sustaining; 1935, CBS, sustaining; 1935-1936, NBC, sustaining; 1936–1938, CBS, William J. Wrigley Company (Wrigley's Doublemint, Juicy Fruit and Spearmint chewing gums).

Myrt and Marge. 1934–1936, CBS, William J. Wrigley Company (Wrigley's Doublemint, Juicy Fruit and Spearmint chewing gums).

Billy Mills Orchestra. 1935-1936, CBS, sustaining.

Stars of the Milky Way. 1936-1937, MBS, Milk Foundation, Inc. (milk's benefits).

Fibber McGee & Molly. 1938–1953, NBC, S. C. Johnson and Sons (Johnson's wax and other household and automotive cleaning compounds) 1938–1950, Pet Milk Company (Pet evaporated milk) 1950–1952, Reynolds Metals Company (Reynolds aluminum tin foil) 1952-1953).

Alec Templeton Time. 1939, NBC, S. C. Johnson and Sons (Johnson's wax and other household and automotive cleaning compounds).

Hap Hazard. 1941, NBC, S. C. Johnson and Sons (Johnson's wax and other household and automotive cleaning compounds).

The Great Gildersleeve. 1941-1942, NBC, Kraft Foods Company (Kraft cheese and other foodstuffs).

The Amos 'n' Andy Show. 1944-1945, NBC, Lever Brothers Company (Rinso detergent).

Ice Box Follies. 1945, ABC, Hires root beer.

The Victor Borge Show. 1945, NBC, S. C. Johnson and Sons (Johnson's wax and other household and automotive cleaning compounds).

RAYMOND PAIGE

Born: May 18, 1900, Wausau, Wisconsin.

Died: August 7, 1965, Larchmont, New York.

Highlights: Violinist in Los Angeles theater pits during silent movie era, becoming conductor at the Paramount Theater, a job ending when talkies arrived; Don Lee hired him as music director of his 13-station chain (1930); conducted the Hollywood Bowl Orchestra, Los Angeles Philharmonic, NBC Symphony and Pittsburgh Symphony, music director of Radio City Music Hall (1950–1965).

Radio Shows:

Hildegarde. 1930s, syndicated five-minute transcriptions, U. S. Tire and Rubber Company.

Louella Parsons. 1931, CBS, Sunkist Growers (Sunkist oranges), Charis Corset Company (Charis foundational undergarments).

California Melodies. 1932–1936, CBS, sustaining.

Chandu, the Magician. c1934–1935, Don Lee/MBS/syndicated, White King granulated soap (Western hookup), Adams Gum Company (Beech Nut chewing gum, Eastern stations).

Hollywood Hotel. 1934–1938, CBS, Campbell Soup Company (Campbell's juices and soups, Franco-American spaghetti and macaroni and other foodstuffs).

The Marx Brothers. 1937, NBC, sustaining.

The Packard Hour (aka *Hollywood Mardi Gras*). 1937-1938, NBC, Packard Motor Car Company (Packard automobiles).

The Circle. 1939, NBC, W. K. Kellogg Company (Kellogg's cereals).

Ninety-Nine Men and a Girl. 1939, CBS, U. S. Tire and Rubber Company.

Raymond Paige Orchestra. 1940, NBC, sustaining.

Musical Americana. 1940, NBC Blue; 1940-1941, NBC, Westinghouse, Inc. (Westinghouse home appliances).

Star-Spangled Vaudeville. 1942, NBC, Standard Brands, Inc. (Chase & Sanborn coffee).

Stage Door Canteen. 1942–1945, CBS, Corn Products Refining Company.

Salute to Youth. 1943-1944, NBC, Electric Autolite Company (Autolite batteries, headlights, spark plugs and other vehicle power supplies).

Kraft Music Hall (aka *The Edward Everett Horton Show*). 1945, NBC, Kraft Foods Company (Kraft cheese and other foodstuffs).

Music America Loves Best (aka *The RCA Victor Show*). 1945–c1946, NBC, Radio Corporation of America (RCA Victor phonographs, radios, recordings).

Musicomedy (aka *The Silver Summer Revue*). 1948, CBS, International Silver Company (International silverware).

DAVID ROSE

Born: June 15, 1910, London, England.

Died: August 23, 1990, Burbank, California.

Highlights: Pianist with the band of Ted Fio Rito; member of NBC Chicago's staff orchestra (1930–1938), four years as arranger; music director at MBS; established a career headlining an orchestra for Red Skelton, appearing with the comedian four years on radio (1947–1951) and two decades on television (1951–1971); composed scores for numerous TV series and motion pictures including Skelton's theme *Holiday for Strings*; nominated for an Oscar for the score of *Wonder Man*, 1945 film starring Danny Kaye.

Radio Shows:

David Rose Orchestra. 1936, NBC; 1940, MBS; 1941-1942, MBS, sustaining.

I Want a Divorce. 1940-1941, MBS, sustaining.

California Melodies. 1940–1943, MBS, sustaining.

The David Rose Show. 1940–1942, MBS, sustaining.

The Ginny Simms Show (aka *Purple Heart*). 1942–c1945, NBC, Philip Morris Company (Philip Morris cigarettes).

Guest Star. 1943-date unsubstantiated, quarter-hour transcribed, U. S. Treasury Department (U. S. savings bonds).

Holiday for Music (aka *The Curt Massey Show*). 1946, CBS, Nash Motors (Kelvinator home appliances).

Blue Ribbon Music Time. 1947, NBC, Pabst Brewing Company (Pabst Blue Ribbon beer).

The Raleigh Cigarette Program (aka *The Red Skelton Show*). 1947–1949, NBC, Brown & Williamson Tobacco Company (Avalon and Raleigh cigarettes, Sir Walter Raleigh pipe tobacco).

The Red Skelton Show. 1949–1951, CBS, Procter & Gamble Company (Tide detergent); 1951-1952, CBS, Norge home appliances; 1952-1953, NBC, multiple sponsorship (Blue Star razor blades, others).

The David Rose Show. 1950, CBS, Procter & Gamble Company (Tide detergent).

Hallmark Playhouse. cEarly 1950s–1953, CBS, Hallmark Greeting Card Company (Hallmark cards).

Bold Venture. 1951-1952, 78 ZIV syndicated half-hour transcriptions, local sponsorship.

NAT SHILKRET
(NATHANIEL SCHILDKRAUT)

Born: December 25, 1889, Queens, New York.

Died: February 18, 1982, Long Island, New York.

Highlights: Instrumentalist with E. F. Goldman, Arthur Pryor and John Philip Sousa bands, the Metropolitan Opera and the New York Philharmonic Symphony; at 23, was RCA Victor's musical director, then managed the label's recordings abroad, directing operations in 35 nations; conducted what may have been the first permanent series on any major chain, launching *The Eveready Hour* the day after NBC's inaugural performance November 15, 1926; successfully combined careers in recording and radio; directed broadcast orchestras in several Northeastern cities, including Boston's WBZ (1935), Baltimore's WFBR (1936), Harrisburg's WHP (1937), Washington's WMAL (1938), Providence's WPRO (1939); led several Hollywood film studio bands.

Radio Shows:

The Eveready Hour. 1923, New York's WEAF; 1924–c1926, WEAF, Providence's WJAR and Buffalo's WRG; 1926–1930, NBC, National Carbon Company (Eveready batteries and other vehicle products).

Victor Salon Orchestra (aka *International Novelty Orchestra, Victor Hour*). 1925, New York's WEAF; 1926, NBC, (RCA Victor phonographs, radios, recordings).

Maxwell House Concert. c1927–1932, NBC Blue, General Foods Corporation (Maxwell House coffee).

General Electric Hour. 1929, NBC West Coast, sustaining; 1929-1930, NBC, General Electric Company (GE home appliances).

General Motors Concert (aka *General Motors Family Party*). c1919–c1931, NBC, General Motors Corporation (GM cars and trucks).

Music That Satisfies (aka *The Chesterfield Quarter Hour, The Ruth Etting Show*). 1931-1932, CBS, Liggett & Myers Tobacco Company (Chesterfield cigarettes).

An Evening in Paris. 1931-1932, CBS, Bourjois Company (Evening in Paris fragrances).

The Kodak Weekend Hour. 1932, CBS, Kodak Company (Kodak cameras, film and other photographic supplies).

Wheeler and Woolsey. 1933-1934, NBC Blue, sustaining.

Songs You Love (aka *The Smith Brothers Program, Trade and Mark*). 1932–1935, CBS, Smith Brothers cough drops.

The Palmolive Beauty Box Theater. 1934-1935, NBC, Colgate-Palmolive-Peet Company (Palmolive soap and brushless shave cream, other personal care products).

Camel Caravan. c1935–c1939, CBS, R. J. Reynolds Tobacco Company (Camel cigarettes).

The Carmen Miranda Show. 1939, NBC, sustaining.

The Magic Key. 1939, NBC Blue, Radio Corporation of America (RCA Victor phonographs, radios, recordings).

Let's Be Charming. c1943–1944, MBS, sustaining.

HARRY SOSNIK

Born: July 13, 1906, Chicago, Illinois.
Died: March 22, 1996, Bronx, New York.
Highlights: Pianist on Chicago's WEBH in 1925, accompanying Jack Crawford's orchestra over the Windy City's WBBM a year later; played band remotes, forming own outfit in the early 1930s (signature song *Lazy Rhapsody*), appearing at esteemed venues like the Chicago World's Fair and Edgewater Beach Hotel; conducted orchestra during *Your Hit Parade's* radio incubation (1936), returning as its final conductor on television (1958-1959); played numerous radio shows with eminent headliners; Decca Records musical director; same post at Ted Bates advertising agency; music VP at ABC (late 1960s).

Radio Shows:

Al Pearce and His Gang (aka *The Al Pearce Show, Fun Valley, The Happy-Go-Lucky Hour, Here Comes Elmer, Watch the Fun Go By*). 1928–1932, San Francisco's KFRC, sponsorship unsubstantiated; 1934-1935, NBC Blue, sustaining; 1935-1936, NBC or NBC Blue (alternating), The Pepsodent Company (Pepsodent toothpaste); 1937-1938, CBS, Ford Motor Company (Ford automobiles); 1938-1939, NBC, General Foods Corporation (Grape Nuts cereals); 1939-1940, CBS, Dole Cannery (Dole pineapple foodstuffs); 1940–1942, CBS, R. J. Reynolds Tobacco Company (Camel cigarettes); 1942, NBC, R. J. Reynolds Tobacco Company (Camel cigarettes); 1944, NBC Blue, Dr [sic] Pepper Bottling Company (Dr Pepper soft drink); 1944-1945, CBS, Lewis Howe Company; 1945-1946, 1947, ABC, sustaining.

The Penzoil Program. 1932, CBS, Penzoil (Penzoil automotive products).

Olsen and Johnson. 1933-1934, CBS, Swift & Company (Swift's meat packing foodstuffs).

Harry Sosnik Orchestra. 1934, NBC, sustaining.

Red Horse Tavern. 1935-1936, CBS, Socony Oil Company (Socony gasoline, oil and other vehicle products and services).

Harry Sosnik Orchestra. 1936, CBS, sustaining.

Your Hit Parade. 1936, CBS, American Tobacco Company (Lucky Strike cigarettes).

The Realsilk Program. 1936-1937, NBC Blue, Realsilk Hosiery Mills (Realsilk hosiery).

Hollywood Playhouse. 1937–1939, NBC Blue, Andrew Jergens Company (Jergens lotion, Woodbury soap).

Hobby Lobby. 1937-1938, CBS, Hudson Company (Hudson automobiles); 1938, NBC, General Foods Corporation (Jell-O desserts); 1938-1939, NBC Blue and 1939-1940, CBS, Fels Naphtha (laundry products); 1941–1943, CBS, Colgate-Palmolive-Peet Company (various personal care goods); 1945-1946, CBS, sustaining; 1949, MBS, sustaining. [*Sosnik was not the sole impresario on this series.*]

The Joe E. Brown Show. 1938-1939, CBS, General Foods Corporation (Post Toasties cereal).

Promoting Priscilla. 1940, CBS, Andrew Jergens Company (Jergens lotion, Woodbury soap).

The Gracie Fields Show (aka *The Gracie Fields Victory Show*). 1942-1943, NBC Blue; 1943-1944, both series for American Tobacco Company (Pall Mall cigarettes); 1944-1945, Bristol Myers, Inc. (various health care goods); 1952-1953, MBS, sustaining. [*Sosnik was not the sole impresario on this series.*]

The Adventures of the Falcoln. 1943, NBC Blue; 1945–1947, Gem blades and razors; 1948–1950, MBS, Anahist antihistamine spray and other health care goods (1950 only); 1950–1952, NBC, Kraft Foods Company (Kraft cheese and other foodstuffs) 1950-1951 only; 1952, MBS; 1952, NBC; 1953-1954, MBS, multiple participation, including General Mills, Inc. (various foodstuffs). [*Sustaining except where noted. Emerson Buckley (orchestra conductor) and Bob Hamilton (organist) shared the musical duties on this program. While at least 87 of several hundred episodes exist on tape, to the author's knowledge no documentation has surfaced signifying the dates on which each musical artist began or finished his connection with this series.*]

Beat the Band. 1943-1944, NBC, Brown & Williamson Tobacco Company (Raleigh cigarettes and Sir Walter Raleigh pipe tobacco), sustaining (summer 1944).

Keepsakes. 1943-1944, NBC Blue, Carter Products Company (Carter's Little Liver pills, other health commodities).

Guest Star. c1943–c1962 (dates unsubstantiated), quarter-hour transcribed, U. S. Treasury Department (U. S. savings bonds). [*Conducting shared with others.*]

Hildegarde's Raleigh Room (aka *The Raleigh Room*). 1944–1946, NBC, Brown & Williamson Tobacco Company (Raleigh cigarettes and Sir Walter Raleigh pipe tobacco).

Sunday on the N. K. Ranch. 1945, ABC, Nash Motors (Nash-Kelvinator home appliances).

Vacation with Music. 1946, NBC, sustaining.

The Danny Kaye Show (aka *Pabst Blue Ribbon Town*). c1945-1946, CBS, Pabst Brewing Company (Pabst Blue Ribbon beer).

Hildegarde's Radio Room. 1946-1947, CBS, Campbell Soup Company (Campbell's juices and soups, Franco-American spaghetti and macaroni and other foodstuffs).

The Danny Thomas Show. 1947-1948, CBS, Pabst Brewing Company (Pabst Blue Ribbon beer). [*Several orchestra leaders alternately conducted on this series.*]

Treasury of Stars. 1954, NBC, sustaining.

LEITH STEVENS

Born: September 13, 1909, Mount Moriah, Missouri.

Died: July 23, 1970, Los Angeles, California.

Highlights: A pianist accompanying Kansas City vocalists before touring with Lambert Murphy and Ernestine Schumann-Heink; CBS company man who—while serving the other chains on occasion—devoted much of his career to

CBS, as arranger in 1930 and staff conductor by 1934; composed many *Columbia Workshop* scores (1936–1947) and music for several motion pictures, including Marlon Brando's *The Wild One*; music director for TV series including *The George Burns and Gracie Allen Show* (1950–1958).

Radio Shows:

The Four Clubmen. 1932, 1935, 1938, 1940, 1941, CBS, sustaining.

Death Valley Days. 1933–1935, NBC Blue, Pacific Borax Company (Twenty Mule Team Borax and Boraxo cleansers).

Saturday Review. 1934, CBS, sustaining.

Molle Merry Minstrels (aka *Modern Minstrels*). 1934-1935, CBS, Molle shaving cream.

Leith Stevens Harmonies. 1934-1935, CBS, sustaining.

Ford Sunday Evening Hour (aka *Ford Summer Hour*). 1934–1942, CBS; 1945-1946, ABC, Ford Motor Company (Ford automobiles and trucks). [*Other conductors were also featured.*]

Stoopnagle and Budd. 1936, CBS, sustaining.

Saturday Night Swing Club. 1936–1939, CBS, Hormel, Inc. (Hormel meat packing foodstuffs).

Heinz Magazine of the Air. 1936, CBS, H. J. Heinz Company (Heinz 57 varieties of foodstuffs).

Big Town. 1937, CBS, Lever Brothers Company (Rinso detergent).

This Is New York. 1938-1939, CBS, sustaining.

The Buddy Clark Show (aka *Design for Happiness, Buddy Clark's Musical Weekly*). 1938, MBS, American Tobacco Company (Lucky Strike cigarettes); 1938-1939, CBS, sustaining. [*Orchestra leadership alternating with Frank Novak in this period.*]

Buddy Clark's Summer Colony. 1939, CBS, sustaining.

Leith Stevens Orchestra. 1939, CBS, sustaining.

The Adventures of Ellery Queen. c1939–1940, CBS, sustaining and Gulf Oil Corporation (Gulf gasoline, oil and other vehicle products and services).

The Free Company. 1941, CBS, sustaining.

The Remarkable Miss Tuttle. 1942, NBC, General Foods Corporation (Jell-O desserts).

The Abbott and Costello Show. 1942, NBC, R. J. Reynolds Tobacco Company (Camel cigarettes).

The Doctor Fights. 1945, CBS, Schenley Laboratories.

Rogue's Gallery (aka *Bandwagon Mysteries*). 1945, NBC; 1945-1946, MBS; 1946, NBC; 1947, NBC, all F. W. Fitch Company (Fitch shampoo and other hair properties).

Request Performance. 1945-1946, CBS, Campbell Soup Company (Campbell's juices and soups, Franco-American spaghetti and macaroni and other foodstuffs).

Academy Award Theater. 1946, CBS. House of Squibb (Squibb toothpaste and other health care commodities).

Lights Out. 1947, ABC, Schick blades and razors.

Escape. 1947–1954, CBS, Richfield Oil Company (Atlantic gasoline, oil and other vehicle products and services). [*Stevens shared orchestra conducting during these years with Cy Feuer and Wilbur Hatch.*]

Pursuit. 1949-1950, CBS, at varying times sustaining, Ford Motor Company (Ford automobiles), William J. Wrigley Company (Wrigley's Doublemint, Juicy Fruit and Spearmint chewing gums).

Much Ado about Doolittle. 1950, CBS, sustaining.

Yours Truly, Johnny Dollar. 1950–c1952, CBS, sustaining and William J. Wrigley Company (Wrigley's Doublemint, Juicy Fruit and Spearmint chewing gums).

The Black Book. 1952, CBS, sustaining.

The Judge. 1952, CBS, sustaining.

Biography in Sound. 1955–1958, NBC, sustaining.

MEREDITH WILLSON

Born: May 18, 1902, Mason City, Iowa.
Died: June 15, 1984, Santa Monica, California.
Highlights: Toured with John Philip Sousa's band, flutist with the New York Philharmonic under Arturo Toscanini, flutist and piccolo soloist with the CBS Symphony Orchestra; music director at NBC Hollywood (1932); in World War II director of Armed Forces Radio Service's music division; composer, arranger, impresario and disc jockey (1951); signature song *Thoughts While Strolling*; conductor on radio's purported final extravaganza, *The Big Show*, for which he penned the inspiring chorus *May the Good Lord Bless and Keep You* while responding to summons by basal-timbred star Tallulah Bankhead with "Yes, Miss Bankhead, sir?"; best recalled as composer, librettist and lyricist of *The Music Man* (1957), Broadway and motion picture epic.

Radio Shows:

The Golden State Blue Monday Jamboree. 1927, San Francisco's KFRC, segued into Don Lee/CBS West Coast hookup c1929-1930, sponsorship unsubstantiated.

Ship of Joy. 1933-1934, CBS, Del Monte Corporation (Del Monte canned fruits and vegetables).

What's New? 1935, NBC, sustaining.

Meredith Willson Orchestra. 1935 (two series), 1936-1937, NBC Blue, sustaining.

Carefree Carnival. 1935-1936, NBC Blue, Crazy Water Crystals (1935), Blue Jay Corn Plasters (1935), sustaining (1935-1936).

Songs America Sings. 1936, NBC, sustaining.

The Signal Carnival. c1936–1941, NBC West Coast, Signal Oil Company (Signal gasoline, oil and other vehicle products and services).

Good News of 1938–1940. 1937–1940, NBC, General Foods Corporation (Maxwell House coffee).

Showboat (aka *Maxwell House Showboat*). 1937, NBC, General Foods Corporation (Maxwell House coffee).

Meredith Willson's Musical Revue (aka *America Sings*). 1940, 1942, S. C. Johnson & Sons (Johnson's wax and other home and automotive cleansers).

Maxwell House Coffee Time. 1940-1944, NBC, General Foods Corporation (Maxwell House coffee).

Maxwell House Coffee Time (aka *The George Burns & Gracie Allen Show*). 1945-1948, NBC, General Foods Corporation (Maxwell House coffee).

Meredith Willson Orchestra. 1946, NBC, General Foods Corporation (Maxwell House coffee).

Sparkle Time. 1946-1947, CBS, Canada Dry Bottling Company (Canada Dry ginger ale).

The Ford Showroom. 1947, CBS, Ford Motor Company (Ford automobiles).

Meredith Willson's Music Room (aka *Meredith Willson Show*). 1948-1949, ABC, General Foods Corporation (Maxwell House coffee).

Meredith Willson Orchestra. 1949, NBC, General Foods Corporation (Jell-O desserts).

The Big Show. 1950–1952, NBC, multiple participation including American Home Products Corporation (Anacin pain reliever), Liggett & Myers Tobacco Company (Chesterfield cigarettes), Reynolds Metals Company (Reynolds aluminum tinfoil) and others.

Meredith Willson's Music Room. 1951, 1952, NBC, Radio Corporation of America (RCA Victor phonographs, radios, records and televisions).

Meredith Willson Orchestra. 1951-1952, 1952, 1953, NBC, sustaining.

Meredith Willson Orchestra. 1952, NBC, multiple participation; 1953-1954, NBC, Florida Citrus Growers Assn. (Florida grapefruit, oranges, tangerines and other fresh fruit).

Encore. 1952-1953, NBC, sustaining.

The Hummert Musicales

While their faces weren't familiar to most who heard their programs every day or week, their names were instantly recognized by zillions of American homemakers who tuned in to scores of daytime dramas (soap operas) that radiated their inspired labors five days a week. What many people never realized about Frank and Anne Hummert was that they practiced in other breeds beyond matinee misery. They introduced late afternoon juvenile adventure thrillers and prime-time detective mysteries. And they excelled in music. From the inception of their rise to become the most proficient programmers in the history of broadcasting — including radio *and* television — the Hummerts registered with several tuneful wares. Although most repetitiously drew from a single well of singers and instrumentalists, and many of their songs were familiar, the pair supplied melodies that radio audiences utterly adored.

The American Album of Familiar Music

Producers: Anne and Frank Hummert.

Director: James Haupt.

Orchestra Conductors: Gustav Haenschen, Abe Lyman.

Celebrity Leads: Frank Munn (tenor), 1931–1945; Frank Parker (tenor), 1945–1951.

Vocalists: Bernice Claire (coloratura soprano), Donald Dame (tenor), Margaret Daum (soprano), Vivian Della Chiesa (soprano), Jean Dickenson (soprano), Felix Knight (tenor), Elizabeth Lennox (contralto), Daniel Lieberfeld, Evelyn MacGregor (contralto), Lucy Monroe (soprano), Virginia Rea (soprano).

Ensemble: The Buckingham Choir.

Featured Artists: Arden and Arden (piano duo), Bernard Hirsch (violinist).

Announcers: Andre Baruch, Howard Claney, Roger Krupp.

Theme Song: *Dream Serenade* (Gustav Haenschen).

Sponsors: Sterling Drugs, Inc. for Bayer aspirin pain reliever.

Ratings: High — 17.8 (1933-1934 season); Low — 3.2 (1938-1939); Median — 10.6. In 14 of 20 seasons figures soared to double digits, an impressive showing for a musical entry without icon-status names.

On the Air: October 11, 1931–April 2, 1933, NBC, Sunday, 9:00–9:30 P.M. Eastern

Time; April 9, 1933–June 25, 1950, NBC, Sunday, 9:30–10:00 P.M.; September 3, 1950–November 19, 1950, NBC, Sunday, 9:30–10:00 P.M.; November 26, 1950–June 17, 1951, ABC, Sunday, 9:30–10:00 P.M. (In some summers the show was not broadcast.)

Manhattan Merry-Go-Round

Producers: Anne and Frank Hummert.
Director: Paul Dumont.
Orchestra Conductors: Victor Arden, Andy Sannella.
Celebrity Leads: Rachel Carlay, early in the run; Thomas L. Thomas (baritone), 1940s era.
Vocalists: Glenn Cross (tenor), Rodney McClennan, Marian McManus, Lucy Monroe (soprano), Dick O'Connor, Barry Roberts (baritone), Dennis Ryan, Conrad Thibault (baritone).
Ensembles: The Boys and Girls of Manhattan, The Jerry Mann Voices, The Men About Town.
Featured Artists: Jimmy Durante, Bert Lahr, Beatrice Lillie.
Announcers: Ford Bond, Roger Krupp.
Theme Song: *Manhattan Merry-Go-Round*.
Sponsors: Sterling Drugs, Inc. for Dr. Lyons' tooth powder dentifrice through February 27, 1949; sustaining from March 6, 1949, to the end of the run.
Ratings: High — 14.3 (1939-1940 season); Low — 5.4 (1937-1938); Median — 10.5. Numbers available for every season except 1934-1935. In 16 seasons for which figures are available the show reached double digits 10 times, a superior performance.
On the Air: November 6, 1932–April 2, 1933, NBC Blue, Sunday, 3:30–4:00 P.M. Eastern Time; April 9, 1933–April 17, 1949, NBC, Sunday, 9:00–9:30 P.M.

Waltz Time

Producers: Anne and Frank Hummert.
Orchestra Conductor: Abe Lyman.
Celebrity Leads: Frank Munn (tenor), 1931–1945; Evelyn MacGregor, (contralto), costar in 1940s; Bob Hannon (baritone), 1945–1948.
Vocalists: Lois Bennett (soprano), Bernice Claire (coloratura soprano), Mary Eastman (soprano), Lucy Monroe (soprano), Vivienne Segal (soprano).
Ensemble: The Amsterdam Chorus.
Announcers: George Ansbro, Andre Baruch, Ford Bond.
Sponsors: Sterling Drugs, Inc. for Phillips Milk of Magnesia laxative.
Ratings: High — 13.5 (1945-1946 season); Low — 6.0 (1935-1936); Median — 9.8. In 15 seasons on the air the numbers hit double digits nine times (60 percent), a healthy confirmation.
On the Air: September 27–November 29, 1933, NBC, Wednesday, 8:30–9:00 P.M. Eastern Time; December 8, 1933–September 28, 1945, NBC, Friday, 9:00–9:30 P.M.; October 5, 1945–June 25, 1948, NBC, Friday, 9:30–10:00 P.M.; July 2–16, 1948, 9:30–10:30 P.M.

American Melody Hour

Producers: Anne and Frank Hummert.
Orchestra Conductors: Victor Arden, Frank Black.
Celebrity Lead: Frank Munn (tenor).
Celebrity Lead: Vivian Della Chiesa (soprano).
Vocalists: Eileen Farrell (soprano), Bob Hannon (baritone), Evelyn MacGregor (contralto), Stanley McClelland (baritone), Conrad Thibault (baritone), Jane Pickens (soprano).

Ensemble: The Knightsbridge Chorus.

Announcers: Andre Baruch, Ford Bond, Howard Claney.

Sponsors: Sterling Drugs, Inc. for Bayer aspirin pain reliever.

Ratings: High — 10.1 (1946-1947 season); Low — 2.4 (1941-1942); Median — 7.4. Of seven seasons on the air the program reached double digits only once, not a great response.

On the Air: October 22, 1941–April 15, 1942, NBC Blue, Wednesday, 10:00–10:30 P.M. Eastern Time; April 21, 1942–June 24, 1947, CBS, Tuesday, 7:30–8:00 P.M.; July 2, 1947–July 7, 1948, CBS, Wednesday, 8:00–8:30 P.M.

* * *

Frank and Anne Hummert were doubtless broadcasting's most eccentric couple. At the same time, the entrepreneurial pair was decidedly clever—quite astute businesspeople who recognized opportunities, took risks and made openings work to their advantage. Together for a quarter of a century, the duo became a formidable presence in radio broadcasting, a powerful and intimidating influence controlling a large share of the four networks' programming schedules, a combined force unequivocally to be reckoned with.

This twosome was at the forefront of radio broadcasting. During the five years before they married in 1935 they perceived vast possibilities for entertainment offered on the ether. They correctly judged, for instance, that stay-at-home moms would embrace some diversionary amusement as they plowed through the drudgery of housekeeping chores without very many conveniences for dispatching their onerous tasks.

Edward Frank Hummert Jr. and his gifted assistant, Anne S. Ashenhurst, employed by a prominent Chicago advertising agency, got in on dishpan drama's ground floor. Together they created a string of serialized narratives—labeled *soap operas* in ensuing vernacular—to give a lift to milady's day. *Amanda of Honeymoon Hill, Backstage Wife, Chaplain Jim U.S.A., David Harum, Front Page Farrell, Just Plain Bill, Lora Lawton, Lorenzo Jones, Ma Perkins, Our Gal Sunday, The Romance of Helen Trent, Stella Dallas, Valiant Lady, Young Widder Brown* and dozens more—at least 61 washboard weepers in all—flowed from the pens of their fertile assembly line scribes. So successful was the pair in establishing matinee misery that in time they would be remembered for that input and little else. But there was more, so much more, that this inventive couple would bring to the airwaves.

The duo soon turned their attention to action thrillers for adolescents, later dubbed juvenile adventure serials. These late-afternoon entries were frequently adapted from newspaper comic strips and often targeted to preteen audiences. While their number would be small—eight total—when compared with the Hummerts' more pervasive drainboard drama category, their kids' features drew a coterie of youngsters who were as steadfast in their loyalty as were their mothers and grandmothers to their own Hummert series. Included in the mix were such winners as *Jack Armstrong the All-American Boy, Little Orphan Annie, Popeye the Sailor* and *Terry and the Pirates*.

Another genre in which the Hummerts excelled was crime detective mysteries. In these dramatic episodes, Hummert protagonists invariably confirmed that good triumphs over evil and justice is ultimately meted out to those who pursue mayhem. The strain is comprised of only 10 entries but a quartet of their number—*Hearthstone of the Death Squad, Mr. Chameleon, Mr. Keen Tracer of Lost Persons* and *Mark Sabre*—left a mark upon addicted followers. In *Keen's* case, their loyalty persisted nearly two decades, more extensive than that of any rival sleuth in the history of broadcasting, including television.

The Chicago creative team would introduce no fewer than 125 separate radio features in nine programming breeds, literally making themselves broadcasting's most prolific producers. And 37 series of that aggregate would be in music and variety, their second most fruitful field, the one that concerns our interests and a sphere that is frequently overlooked by historians who assess the Hummerts' airwaves contributions. From the earliest days of their radio careers the pair sensed enormous possibilities afforded by listeners' impassioned music tastes.

Capitalizing on it, they assumed production for the *MGM Radio Movie Club*—which had begun in 1927, and *Aunt Jemima*, which debuted in 1929. In 1931, they introduced a quartet of musical features of their own: *The American Album of Familiar Music, Hollywood Nights, Paris Night Life* and *Waves of Melody*. Within a couple of years after that, the creative duo added another quintet to a budding repertoire: *Manhattan Merry-Go-Round, Mr. Gallagher and Mr. Shean, The Musical Revue, Roxy Symphony Theater of the Stars* and *Waltz Time*.

While several of those programs came and went quickly, the innovators used their experiences to define public interest, refine their offerings and—in due course—derive a handful of musical showcases with staying power. "Hummert radio musicals tended to go on year after year," noted a reviewer. A threesome of their tune-filled properties persisted for 15 or more years while a fourth aired nearly seven years, a rewarding target for some of their peers. The fact that a single health and personal goods manufacturer (Sterling Drugs) underwrote all four of their most durable properties is yet another testament to their resourceful ingenuity.

Before examining their principal musical offerings in detail, some background on the Hummerts will prove helpful. Equipped with that knowledge, the reader will have a greater respect for what they were able to accomplish.

Both Hummert and his future bride, Ashenhurst, arrived in advertising from journalistic backgrounds.

A native of St. Louis, Hummert was born June 2, 1884, and graduated from St. Louis University. He married a neighborhood girl in St. Louis although she died in the early 1930s. Young Hummert acquired a reporting assignment on the Pulitzer Prize-winning *St. Louis Post-Dispatch*. Later he gained reportorial posts with the news journal of the Catholic Archdiocese of Chicago, *New World*, and the International News Syndicate of *The New York Times*.

While making some entrepreneurial moves, by 1920 he landed at one of the most prestigious ad agencies in New York, Lord & Thomas, where as chief copywriter he carried home $50,000 the first year. Hummert penned several slogans that gained him immense notoriety within the industry. They included a motto for Liberty Bonds he created during World War I—*Bonds or Bondage*. Another aphorism, for soapmaker Andrew Jergens' Woodbury bar, made a lasting impression—*For the Skin You Love to Touch*. His best remembered epithet, still in use today by General Mills' Wheaties cereal, was inspired during his early radio days—*Breakfast of Champions*.

Hummert left Lord & Thomas in 1927 to join Chicago's Blackett and Sample as vice president. Recognizing the awesome influence he brought to the agency, owners Hill Blackett and J. G. Sample soon changed the firm's name to Blackett-Sample-Hummert, Inc. While Hummert didn't own shares in it, as creative director he brought in lots of new business.

Ashenhurst, nee Anne Shumacher, was born in Baltimore on January 19, 1905, nearly 21 years after Hummert's birth. To help fund her way through Goucher College, she snagged a post as the school's correspondent for *The Baltimore Sun*. Upon graduating magna cum laude in 1925, she put her newly acquired reportorial skills to work for that paper full time. Before long she fell in love with her city editor, John W. Ashenhurst. In 1926, he took an appointment as a Hearst correspondent with that syndicate's Paris bureau and a starry-eyed Schumacher tagged along. There she was employed by a precursor journal of *The International Herald Tribune*.

The star-crossed pair wed in the French capital shortly after their arrival, returning to the states for the birth of their only child, a son, the next spring. Anne Ashenhurst, seeking work to help sustain her family, applied for a job at Blackett and Sample ad agency. She so impressed J. G. Sample that he commended her to Hummert as an assistant. Hummert appeared cool about employing a young newspaperwoman, yet found her "a fount of ideas and organized efficiency."

Ashenhurst's personal life rapidly unraveled about that same time. Her spouse was often inebriated and out of work and her son was shuttled back-and-forth between relatives. By 1929, she and John separated and soon divorced. Surprisingly, her ex, while showing signs of instability, became their son's custodial parent with Anne's blessing. The boy was an adolescent "problem child." His mom — weary of paying his way into costly prep schools where he was expelled or ran away — gave up on him in his upper teens. She never saw him after that and his death preceded hers by perhaps 15 years. Anne Ashenhurst, on the other hand, threw her whole self into her new occupation.

All of this came about just as radio was taking root in American homes — in households impoverished by economic devastation, among families looking for economical means of amusement, something to take their minds off their troubles. An innovative Frank Hummert and Anne Ashenhurst could hardly have met at a more auspicious moment. In 1932, Hill Blackett boasted that his firm was "handling more than 150 broadcasts a week, and have been [doing so] for some time." Much of this could be credited to Hummert and Ashenhurst. Blackett further noted that in 1931 NBC informed his agency that a third of the mail the chain received "was addressed to advertisers whose radio broadcasting we supervise." Such acknowledgement appears to remove any doubt that BSH was wading deep into the new medium quite early and indicates the depth of its commitment.

Three years following their marriage in 1935, Frank and Anne Hummert were airing 36 separate radio series while purchasing an eighth of all commercial network time at $12 million per year. Corralling a large assembly of writers, editors and directors who were beholden to them, they were already churning out 6.5 million words of dialogue annually that was aired over the various national chains.

Frank Hummert reached the summit of his profession in 1937 when he became advertising's highest paid executive. "Everyone conceded his flair and his ... brilliance in his copy layout put him up there with half a dozen of the copy greats," declared one pundit. Things were definitely looking up!

The following year the Hummerts moved to New York City to be at the nerve center of network radio, plus being near the headquarters of many of the nation's leading advertising agencies. While the couple briefly resided in luxurious digs of a fashionable Fifth Avenue apartment, later they purchased a magnificent estate that validated the aristocratic accouterments of chic Greenwich, Connecticut. Their distinctive living quarters said a lot about how they viewed themselves as compared to the hundreds of minions in their employ. It was indicative of a deep chasm they maintained throughout their professional careers separating themselves and nearly everybody else. The trappings of chauffeur-driven limousines at their constant beck and call portrayed a lifestyle that those who labored below could but dream of.

The pair retained identity with Blackett-Sample-Hummert through 1943, although one critic observed: "The relationship was clouded, another one of the innumerable secrecies in which Hummert seemed to delight." At the start of 1944, they cut the umbilical cord with BSH, formally opening their own production shop in New York called Air Features, Inc. (interchangeably dubbed Hummert Radio Features). At the same time they created a subsidiary that would amply reward them for delivering on-air talent (Featured Artist Service, Inc.).

Industry insiders soon observed a number of eccentricities in the operation of Air Features. It wasn't difficult to trace the oddball patterns to the owners themselves. At times the Hummerts flaunted "stupefying behavioral traits." Both appeared utterly heedless of the gossip swirling about them. Instead, they retreated to their own little world that visibly revolved around one another, deliberately shutting out almost anything that attempted to penetrate it.

Alleged one report: "A flagrantly callous disregard for others, at times bordering on disdain (and often surprisingly aimed at those in their employ who were helping make them wealthy) possibly overshadowed every other curious quirk they exhibited. Their seeming coldness toward the cares and concerns of others branded them as insensitive snobs and social outcasts. Yet if any of it ever bothered them, neither one let on."

There was a definite aura and mystique that constantly enveloped the Hummerts. "The couple were so secretive with everything," insisted a contemporary researcher. *Advertising Age* labeled Hummert "a man of mystery who avoided personal publicity and co-workers." Reclusive to a fault, the couple seldom made public appearances, going out of their way to avoid being seen by nearly everybody. At a favorite posh bistro on New York's Park Avenue, where they often dined over lunch, the twosome secluded themselves at a special table behind bulky fern planters where they could watch other patrons without being seen.

They were also widely characterized by peculiar business practices. They seldom had direct contact with the dozens of actors and musicians who appeared on their programs, preferring to have a staff attorney engage and terminate their services. As a rule, only when they were casting lead performers did they observe auditions, picking individuals who impressed them and notifying the program directors, seldom talking directly with their new leads.

A large stable of writers churned out dialogue required for their bevy of shows. Most of their names weren't mentioned on the air. When credit was given, it was normally assigned to Frank and Anne Hummert alone, as if they had penned the scripts themselves.

Air Features was renowned among industry insiders for upholding a surfeit of hard-and-fast policies that were inviolable. "There was a rule or set of rules laid down by the Hummerts to govern almost any contingency," claimed a couple of observers. "The Hummerts did not want their original concepts tampered with…, so they ran their shows by rules rather than inspiration," said another. Those canons were well understood by all who earned a living under the Hummert umbrella. Other production houses had no such pervasive cardinal statutes. The rules forbade unessential sound, background music or speech that might overlap dialogue, plus specifics pertaining to explicit enunciation and frequent and repetitious use of character identification. "If you displeased the Hummerts, you might be wise to consider a new line of work," asserted one radio historiographer. "They frowned on clowning around, late arrivals, or a breath of scandal."

The salaries they paid performers were strictly scale and, in general, a whole lot less than other producers were paying. "The Hummerts were extremely astute operators in terms of giving sponsors a simple, inexpensive, unobjectionable type of program, built for long runs and cumulative network discounts. The orchestras were reliable, the arrangements standard, the wages strictly scale."[1] Scale was the absolute minimum that talent received for rehearsal time and performances in compliance with union contracts. Frank and Anne Hummert earned a reputation in the industry — which they apparently wore proudly, almost like a badge of honor — for not offering their artists any recompense above scale. Money they didn't have to pay out, of course, remained in their own bank account.

Because they relied on the same individuals over and over — a singer might turn up on three, four or five of their music and variety shows weekly, just as a freelance actor might appear on a half-dozen daily serials simultaneously — their employees had an opportunity to take home decent wages anyway. It's just that their people worked long and steady hours to accomplish it, compared with most contemporaries. (A soap opera writer, for example, might earn $125 for a week's worth of five scripts for a Hummert serial while a drama writer laboring for one of the Hummerts' chief rivals, Irna Phillips, might carry home $500 for the same work.)

The Hummerts insisted that rehearsal time be kept to a minimum because that time was costly and they weren't in any mood to part with more than they had to. To their credit, or possibly because there wasn't another alternative, many half-hour musical productions were rehearsed four to five hours before going on the air. That contrasted with the maximum one-hour rehearsal time they prescribed for quarter-hour serials. It was apparent not as many corners could be cut when musicians were the stars as when a program included dialogue alone. The cast was called for weekly rehearsals of the Hummerts' most durable musical series, *The American Album of Familiar Music*, for example, Sundays at 5 o'clock in the afternoon. The show went on the air at 9:30 P.M. Practice was intense and frequently didn't end until moments before it broadcast live.

Many more of the Hummerts' idiosyncrasies are examined in detail in the author's text *Frank and Anne Hummert's Radio Factory: The Programs and Personalities of Broadcasting's Most Prolific Producers* (McFarland, 2003). Frank Hummert died in New York City on March 12, 1966, and Anne Hummert, who retired following her spouse's demise, never remarrying, remained active for years. She died in New York on July 5, 1996.

In regard to their many musical treasures, even those who listened regularly were probably unaware of the Hummerts' involvement in those programs. Unlike most features that literally bore their names in one or more on-air announcements, the pair took exception with the musical entries. That possibly bespoke of the appeal those shows had with a more erudite, dynamic and influential audience cluster than the typical fans tuning in their dramatic features.

Nor should it be a surprise that the couple so acutely investing themselves in drainboard dramas professed empathy for more cultured works. After all, Frank and Anne Hummert received quality training from prestigious institutions of higher learning. This surely exposed them to a level of refinement. A portion of Frank Hummert's own attraction to more polished pursuits may have also resulted from some ventures in his early professional life.

One of his distinguished advertising triumphs was to institute a national Brunswick New Hall of Fame for the talent on a particular recording label. He recalled that it launched new voices at opera and concert venues. Phonograph disc sales also increased while some of the label's obscure artists emerged to widespread acclaim. Hummert directly benefited from these activities: in so doing, he was introduced to and connected with the world of classical pop music. Doors opened that were to become invaluable to him once he became involved in radio entertainment.

Before advertising beckoned, Hummert was rewriting theatrical scripts. From that training he not only gained an understanding of the complexities of stage creations in multiple formats but was exposed to their producers, too. It helped him prepare for what was ahead while enlarging his vision for openings he would ultimately grab.

Although Frank and Anne Hummert had precious little time to attend opera, film or stage productions during their working careers (they routinely put in 12- to 14-hour days seven days a week), it can't be assumed they wouldn't have enjoyed those distractions. Radio, records and television sufficed while they judiciously attended to business demands.

The profusion of tune-filled features in their stable of audio series appreciably increased their bottom line. Never ones to resist lucrative potential, the Hummerts literally made beautiful music together for sizeable recompense over two full decades. That strain became a key player among the programming innovations they packaged for national networks.

Straight melodies ruled their musical productions, seldom straying from ballad or waltz tempos. A critic noted that radio and classical or semiclassical music became "natural allies" and certified that many Hummert features were "distinguished." The lyrics on their shows were marked by uncommon clarity. Complex arrangements that might obscure the listeners' quick recognition of a song simply had no place on their programs. The public embraced the formula and kept a handful of their wares on the ether for 15 to 20 years.

As with some other genres, by introducing such a large volume of musical entries it might be supposed that a lot of series wouldn't survive very long. While some didn't curry the public's favor, others never attracted sponsors or were lost in direct competition with better programming on other networks. Quite a few of their offerings were quickly discarded and forgotten including *Evening Melodies, Gems of Melody, Matinee Melodies, Melodiana, The Musical Revue, Showland Memories* and *Sweetest Love Songs Ever Sung*. Nondescript monikers were usually withdrawn after brief outings. A few series without long-term staying power even featured the performers' names in their titles like *Abe Lyman and Movieland's Favorite Band, Don Donnie's Orchestra, French Mignon Trio, Hammerstein Music Hall* and *The Imperial Hollywood Band*.

Yet when the Hummerts encountered a premise that they liked, they tended to drive it into the ground. They gave fans a glut of French-themed shows. In addition to the *French Mignon Trio* there was *La Gaiete Parisienne, Paris Night Life, Folies Bergere of the Air, Folies de Paree* and *Revue de Paree* (the latter three appellations given the same series).

But nothing surpassed their notion of visiting cabarets for the purpose of eavesdropping on mythical choral "performances" on a kind of whirlwind carousel marathon. Each series bore its own distinctive modification while the basic idea remained the same. Thus, listeners could tune in to *Broadway Merry-Go-Round, London Merry-Go-Round, Manhattan Merry-Go-Round* and *Monday Merry-Go-Round*, all of them reworking the same basic theme.

Investigative journalist Thomas Whiteside disclosed in 1947 that Anne Hummert was managing Air Features. This would have included overseeing all of the melodramatic narratives that the couple created for a wide range of programming species. Frank Hummert persisted in supervising the couple's nighttime crime thrillers in spite of Whiteside's opinion that he was "content to handle the *American Album of Familiar Music, American Melody Hour, Manhattan Merry-Go-Round* and *Waltz Time*." It was also a well-established fact that Frank Hummert was "a radio czar who reputedly could 'make or break' performers."

This quartet of Hummert musicales was the most timeless, resilient and celebrated of the 37 offerings they created. (A pundit classified *Manhattan Merry Go-Round* and *The American Album of Familiar Music* as the "elevator music of its day.") Make no mistake: the four features together made a profound contribution to radio harmony. Each will be surveyed independently before looking at some of the couple's lesser tuneful delights.

The oldest and most durable of the foursome, *The American Album of Familiar Music*, dated from October 11, 1931. It remained a continuous and popular network feature for two decades, through June 17, 1951, airing continuously except for a few summers. *Album* debuted to the theme of conductor Gustav Haenschen's *Dream Serenade*. The maestro was later followed in that post by Abe Lyman, yet another Hummert favorite. *Album* was originally introduced as "a program of supremely lovely songs and melodies that capture all hearts."

The series' most active vocalists were tenor Frank Munn, billed as "the golden voice of radio" and a fabled Hummert celebrity for many years; coloratura soprano Bernice Claire; tenors Donald Dame and Felix Knight; sopranos Margaret Daum, Vivian Della Chiesa, Jean Dickenson (dubbed "the nightingale of the airwaves"), Lucy Monroe and Virginia Rea; contraltos Elizabeth Lennox and Evelyn MacGregor; and Daniel Lieberfeld. Sporadically there were piano duets by the team of Arden and Arden; performances by a featured violinist, Bernard Hirsch; songs by a dozen-member Buckingham Choir; and a mixture of other artists who drifted in and out of the lineup. (A sharp journalist noted that — by the late 1930s — a contingent of the Hummerts' Fairfield County, Connecticut, neighbors were turning up on *Album*. They included Norwalk's Gustav Haenschen, conductor, and Westport songbirds Jean Dickenson and Elizabeth Lennox.)

While Frank and Anne Hummert oversaw every decision of any import made on all of their radio series, they dispatched James Haupt to direct this tuneful romp and he prevailed for quite a while. A progression of familiar Air Features announcers offered little in the way of monologue, thereby increasing the show's gratification for buffs. Andre Baruch, Howard Claney and Roger Krupp performed in that capacity.

Although the Hummerts often went to great lengths to hide the names of those appearing on their serials and detective crime dramas — including actors, writers, directors, sound techs and musicians — the individuals that performed on their assorted musicales were usually considered a "draw," especially when their names were recognized by audiences right away. The Hummerts had few "stars" in the proper sense of that term, yet they made an exception in their musical entries. The quality of the artists they presented was a plus in enticing listeners.

Because it was "all in the family"—including the same sponsor, announcers, producers and network—the Hummerts routinely added plugs for their evening musical fare before their matinee soap operas departed the airwaves earlier in the day. On those occasions, the artists performing on the current week's prime-time show were cited in an effort to increase listenership at night. Nobody realized, of course, that all of those series were born in the same production house. Washboard weeper-keepers probably thought of it as merely gimmicks from that chain's promotion department.

On those rare occasions when singing star Frank Munn was absent from his normal slot on *Album*, rising male vocalists, notably Frank Parker when he was available (who was labeled "America's great romantic tenor," shortly before he became an Arthur Godfrey trouper), filled in, invariably "singing for Frank Munn tonight." No one was believed capable of actually *replacing* Munn. Assigned the sobriquet "dean of the ballad singers," Munn was a legendary recording artist and radio entertainer whose ethereal career dated from the mid-1920s. (Let it be duly noted that Parker did ultimately replace Munn when the latter pulled a surprise and retired.)

Munn got such a good workout from the Hummerts that he literally savored his time away from the microphone. Unlike most of his contemporaries, he vetoed most concert tours, preferring instead a quieter subsistence. He absolutely prized his leisure time. Standing only five feet, seven inches and weighing more than 250 pounds, he was concerned about his public image. "Self-conscious of his unromantic roly-poly shape, the short and stocky singer preferred to appeal only to the ear," claimed a biographer.

Frank and Anne Hummert were incontrovertibly delighted when Munn declined guest spots on other shows. At his request they agreed to shield their feted pop idol from most studio audiences and public scrutiny. They didn't want "to dispel the illusion of listeners whose image of him as a dashing amorous troubadour had been conceived from his romantic voice." In 1938, the couple banned live theater spectators that, they claimed, distracted listeners at home. Despite it, a long-held tradition remained that required talent to appear in full evening attire, even though only the cast, production crew and sponsor (on an occasional visit) could actually see them.

Frank Munn was in demand as the star of a trio of durable Hummert series. In addition to *The American Album of Familiar Music's* Sunday night performances, he concurrently turned up on Tuesday or Wednesday nights (the day sometimes shifted) as the lead vocalist on *American Melody Hour*. He held the same duty on Friday nights on *Waltz Time*. Earlier, he starred in a couple of additional Hummert singspirations—*Lavender and Old Lace* (from 1934 to 1936) and *Sweetest Love Songs Ever Sung* (1936-1937). He not only achieved a large radio following but obviously convinced his employers of his worth, no small feat.

A determined advocate of time off from such pressing labors, in 1945 at the age of 51, Munn suddenly bowed out of all of it. His decision shocked Frank Hummert while also catching sponsor Sterling Drugs off guard and disappointing millions of fans who followed him from show to show. For nearly two decades "the golden voice of radio" was equally at ease performing popular and semiclassical works. Ranking as one of the medium's principal male vocalists, he was often cited alongside Kenny Baker, Bing Crosby, Nelson Eddy and Frank Sinatra. Only eight years later, on October 1, 1953, at Queens Village,

New York, Frank Munn suffered a fatal heart attack at age 59. He had given his audiences—and the Hummerts—an incomparable treat.

Munn, vocalists Elizabeth Lennox and Virginia Rea and impresario Gus Haenschen, regulars on *The American Album of Familiar Music*, collaborated on *The Palmolive Hour* (1927–1931) before *Album* premiered. In a gracious tribute, Munn gushed, "Everything I am in radio I owe to Gus Haenschen. It is his artistry, musicianship, and advice which have allowed me to achieve whatever success has been mine." The *Palmolive* feature was recognized as NBC's premier musical showcase of that era. Its favorable reception initiated at least seven other series including *The American Album of Familiar Music, American Melody Hour, The Contented Program, Hammerstein Music Hall, Highways in Melody, The Hour of Charm* and *The Voice of Firestone*. Three were Hummert creations (*Album, American Melody, Hammerstein*).

The popular consumer fanzine *Radio Mirror*, assessing *Album* in 1939, commented: "Not a song is sung or a melody played that hasn't first been selected and okayed by Mr. and Mrs. Hummert. The Hummerts have only one rule for the music they select, but that's a good one — it must be full of melody." Listeners to such predictable *Album* broadcasts could anticipate hearing chestnuts like *Believe Me If All Those Endearing Young Charms*, Irving Berlin's *Remember* and *The Rose of Tralee*. The last of those was a recurring Hummert staple (theme song of their matinee *Backstage Wife* serial and frequently turned up on several of their classic musical features, becoming one of their most identifying tunes).

Manhattan Merry-Go-Round was the Hummerts' second-most-durable musical creation. It debuted on November 6, 1932, and hung around through April 17, 1949. It, too, drew Sterling Drugs as sponsor and the firm hawked Dr. Lyons tooth powder there for all but its final few weeks on the air. Singer Rachel Carlay "and her French ditties," offering a Continental flair, was the big attraction in the prewar era. Baritone Conrad Thibault and other vocalists flanked Carlay. The series dabbled in variety acts early in its run, presenting comedians like Jimmy Durante, Bert Lahr and Beatrice Lillie, thus making it a truly diverse environment. After a while, the Hummerts decided to focus everything on melody, and the funny business discreetly vanished.

The Welsh-born baritone Thomas L. Thomas, beloved singer of stage and radio, was the show's featured artist during its final half-dozen years, probably its best-recalled period. (The "L" in his name was for "Llyfwny," a common identity in his homeland.) Thomas won a spot in the Metropolitan Opera auditions that led him to the Met stage in 1937. He joined a coterie of Met auditions graduates populating Hummert showcases, among them Jean Dickenson, Felix Knight, Evelyn MacGregor and Marian McManus. Between 1947 and 1954, Thomas was "the most frequently featured [voice] on [*The*] *Voice of Firestone* on radio and early television." In 1948 and 1949, he hosted a weekly Hummert musicale, *Your Song and Mine*. It included a singing cast of Mary Martha Briney, Felix Knight and Charles Meynante. Enrico Wahl conducted the orchestra and Andre Baruch announced.

Thomas L. Thomas headlined a *Manhattan* series comprised of vocalists Glenn Cross, Rodney McClennan, Marian McManus, Lucy Monroe, Dick O'Connor, Barry Roberts and Dennis Ryan. Barry Roberts, incidentally, was the pseudonym of singer Bob Hannon, who took over Frank Munn's place on *Waltz Time* when he stepped down. Hannon was already appearing on *American Melody Hour* under his own moniker at the time. The Boys and

Girls of Manhattan, The Jerry Mann Voices and The Men About Town offered choral selections.

Victor Arden and multitalented instrumentalist Andy Sannella raised the baton over a contingent of studio musicians. A radio historiographer opined: "Players with Victor Arden's house band on the Sunday night *Manhattan Merry-Go-Round* might be playing in the Campbell Soup orchestra led by Howard Lanin on Monday, Wednesday, and Thursday evenings at 7:15, and on Friday often were turning up with Abe Lyman for *Waltz Time*." This was characteristic of most Hummert players, be they musical or dramatic; many individuals regularly appeared on multiple programs produced by the couple. Paul Dumont directed *Manhattan* and the Hummert stable supplied Ford Bond and Roger Krupp as interlocutors.

The program bounced onto the airwaves with an animated chorus expelling memorably lilting lyrics with joyful exclamation. The chorus invited listeners to leap onto the merry-go-round for a musical tour of American hotspots.

Someone appositely noted that *Manhattan Merry-Go-Round* was "the Hummert version of *Your Hit Parade*, but filled with much the same musical sound as the Hummerts' other prime-time musicales." The choice of musical numbers was determined by contemporary sheet music and recording purchases, prime factors in also figuring *Your Hit Parade's* selections, hence the analogous comparison. While the sound on *Manhattan* may have echoed that which was offered week to week on *The American Album of Familiar Music*, *Manhattan's* fanciful urgency set it apart from *Album's* more traditional, repetitive melodies.

Announcer Ford Bond introduced the sprightly affair each week, utilizing the idiosyncratic staccato style for which he is well remembered on a plethora of Hummert musicales and daytime dramas: "Here's the *Manhattan Merry-Go-Round* that brings you the bright side of life ... that whirls you in music to all the big nightspots of New York town ... to hear the top songs of the week sung so clearly you can understand every word and sing them yourself!" Clarity was a mandatory Hummert trademark, recall. Ironically, a couple of the more proficient old-time radio chroniclers, having listened over and over to the lyrics that launched *Manhattan* each week, wrote: "We found it extremely difficult to decipher the third and fourth lines of the theme."[2] Given their proclivity for clarity, one can visualize Frank and Anne Hummert turning over in their graves.

The show's format took audiences on an imaginary tour of eight name clubs in Gotham where their venues were, by sheer coincidence no less, presenting the stars of the radio troupe. In reality, of course, those performers never left the NBC studio. That should have been evident from the fact that there was never any applause for anyone, there were no tinkling glasses or extraneous murmur from mythical live audiences. No matter. "Listeners were given such full ambiance that they often asked to see cast members when they came to New York and visited the actual clubs," claimed a wag. The typical bill included tunes like *Don't Fence Me In*, *Heartaches*, *Together*, *The Trolley Song* and *Whispering*.

In an industry dispute fostered by the American Society of Composers, Authors, and Publishers (ASCAP) in the early 1940s, broadcasters found themselves making adjustments in their playlists. *The American Album of Familiar Music*, *The Bell Telephone Hour*, *The Voice of Firestone* and others of that ilk fared relatively well because they stressed traditional native tunes and public domain classics. Popular music series like *The Carnation Contented Program*, *Manhattan Merry-Go-Round* and *Your Hit Parade* on the other hand were pretty hard hit by the cease-and-desist ultimatum.

The order prohibited radio from airing ASCAP-produced melodies without making pricey recompense to that organization, something the networks and independent suppliers (including the Hummerts) were loathe to do. As a consequence, *Manhattan* and its aural peers cranked out substitutes for the chart-toppers that consisted of long-forgotten tunes, disregarded classical pieces and esoteric newer melodies. The abrupt moratorium on broadcasting the customary hit parade continued until a resolution was negotiated that satisfied all sides.

Waltz Time was the third-most-durable Hummert musicale. It arrived on September 27, 1933, and stuck around through July 16, 1948, all the while underwritten by Sterling Drugs. Premiering on Wednesday nights, it soon transferred to Friday nights and became firmly entrenched in that evening's NBC lineup.

Tenor Frank Munn, that inimitable "golden voice of radio," was also the long-running star of that half-hour series. In the 1940s, contralto Evelyn MacGregor, one of the more popular Hummert artists, was elevated to costar. In 1945, another Hummert singing trouper, Bob Hannon, joined her after Munn retired. Other regulars in the company were vocalists Lois Bennett (who just happened to be the spouse of oft-recycled announcer Ford Bond), Bernice Claire, Mary Eastman, Lucy Monroe and Vivienne Segal. Most circulated through other Hummert musical series. Choral voices included the Amsterdam Chorus.

Abe Lyman's orchestra turned up here just as he did in the later run of Sunday night's *American Album* show. Actually, some of the musicians were recruited from Victor Arden's house band that played on Sunday night's *Manhattan Merry-Go-Round*. Merry-go-round seemed apropos in describing how Hummert performers approached their varied work assignments.

Andre Baruch and Ford Bond were recruited to announce *Waltz Time* while yet another Hummert stalwart, George Ansbro, delivered "hitchhike" plugs (those ads appearing between the program's close and the network system cue). Ansbro promoted Sterling Drugs goods from a vast arsenal of health and personal care commodities during those brief asides—for Astring-O-Sol mouthwash, Campho-Phenique canker sore reliever, Double Danderine shampoo, Energine cleaning fluid, Energine Shoe-White polish, Fletcher's Castoria laxative, Haley's M-O mineral emulsion oil laxative, Ironized Yeast vitamin supplement, Mulsified Coconut Oil shampoo, ZBT baby powder and dozens more. All of these men, incidentally, were pushing the same products throughout the daylight hours on Hummert soaps.

Baruch introduced the show with, "Ladies and Gentlemen, it's dance time on the air." Upon recounting the evening's performers, he acknowledged: "*Waltz Time* comes to you from the leading druggists of America who feature genuine Phillips Milk of Magnesia." The mention of the druggists seemed essential in the packaging that the Hummerts delivered for Sterling Drugs—incongruously, they even went so far as to dedicate some of their series to the nation's pharmacists!

Listeners anticipated songs like *Just a Little Bit South of North Carolina*, *The Rose of Tralee* (a recurring trademark), *Time After Time* and *Two Hearts That Pass in the Night*.

American Melody Hour was the fourth member of the enduring Hummert quartet of musical features. It bowed on October 22, 1941, over NBC Blue, later shifting to CBS where it continued through July 7, 1948, on behalf of Sterling Drugs' Bayer aspirin pain reliever. The star for two seasons was Vivian Della Chiesa. "If there existed a radio music hall of fame to enshrine the airwaves' commanding singers, conductors, and musicians, Vivian Della Chiesa and many more would qualify," said a music critic.

A short time before, Della Chiesa was the first-place winner of a vocal competition among anonymous aspiring talents staged by Chicago's WWBM Radio. She beat out 3,700 other entrants for the top honor and debuted professionally on series emanating from the Windy City. Later moving to the Big Apple, hoping to extend her career, she was requested by Frank Hummert to sing for him on an audition record for a potential new series he had in mind. In November 1940, Della Chiesa wholly beguiled him as he watched enthralled from a control booth window. On that occasion, the charming soprano dispatched every piece of music given her with absolute aplomb, ranging from *Caro Nome* to *Minnie the Moocher*. Hummert quickly signed her as a permanent addition for *The American Album of Familiar Music*.

"Only then did I actually meet Frank Hummert," she later recalled. "I was already working with two other Franks—tenor Frank Munn and conductor Frank Black. To avoid confusion, I told Hummert I'd call him Uncle Frank. He was totally disarmed. I became one of his favorites, and he called me Butch."

Nearly a year went by before Hummert created *American Melody Hour*, a midweek spin-off of *Album*, chiefly for Vivian Della Chiesa. But after two years she longed to spread her wings by performing serious music in a concert hall. The urge was so great that she finally left the stability and security of the Hummert fold.

"It was an impulsive act," she explained. "I sold Hummert short. He had fallen into a wartime sacred music syndrome, and it seemed every other week I was singing *The Rosary*. I was so 'bugged' with his choice of inspirational selections that I left all his shows. My family, too, thought I was wasting my talent by not pursuing operatic roles and concert appearances with the likes of [Arturo] Toscanini, who had engaged me for two appearances with the NBC Symphony [in January and October 1943]. Alas, if I had stayed with Hummert, I would have been heard by many more people, and, in the long run, probably performed more serious music." The earlier assessment of Hummert's czar-like power in no way shortchanged him.

In the 1960s, Della Chiesa was the singing hostess of a weekday Cincinnati TV talk show. She returned to Long Island in 1970, becoming a vocal instructor there. Born October 9, 1915, in Chicago, at this writing (early 2004) she is still living.

Paradoxically, when Toscanini signed her to perform with the NBC Symphony, Frank Hummert was pushed by one of his own staff members to mention her appearance on a Hummert series for which Della Chiesa was a participant. Hummert wasted no time rebuking the suggestion: "Does Mr. Toscanini give *me* credit on *his* programs?" Frank Hummert could display his temper when the situation, in his opinion, warranted it.

Other *American Melody Hour* regulars included soprano Eileen Farrell, baritone Bob Hannon, contralto Evelyn MacGregor, baritones Stanley McClelland and Conrad Thibault, tenor Frank Munn and soprano Jane Pickens—most of them familiar to audiences from other aural venues, and many of those Hummert musicales. The Knightsbridge Chorus and the American Melody Hour Orchestra, at separate intervals under the direction of Victor Arden and Frank Black, were also on hand.

From their bullpen of announcers the Hummerts sent Andre Baruch and Howard Claney to pitch for this one supported by Ford Bond, who delivered hitchhike plugs for Lyons toothpaste and Dr. Lyons tooth powder. One or the other of these familiar voices observed that the series was "dedicated to the druggists of America, who supply you with Bayer aspirin," surely an unconventional epigraph.

The program offered "the songs of the day so you can know them all, sing them all yourself." Typical among the selections were *I Still Get Jealous*, *Near You* and *The Whiffenpoof Song*. Knowing those words would probably have been easy for many listeners—the songs, the singers and the accompanists were, you recall, exploited several times a week.

The four series just examined predominated in the Hummerts' long history of introducing musical and variety showcases. There were also 33 more in their repertoire. Here's a synopsis of them, in alphabetical order. Regrettably, details aren't available on a few of the features.

Abe Lyman and Movieland's Favorite Band. One of a series of orchestra performances, under the baton of one of radio's most prominent and popular 1930s conductors. (1932–1934, CBS)

Album of Familiar Canadian Music. A series featuring standard compositions traditionally associated with our nation's northern neighbors. (c1933–1935)

Along the Boulevard. No details preserved. (c1940)

America the Free. No details preserved. (c1941–1942)

Aunt Jemima. Part of a variety series that extended from 1929 to 1953 highlighting the traditional southern Negro minstrel. Three white women (Tess Gardella, Hariette Widner, Vera Lane) hosted it as the stereotypical "blackface mammy" depicted on the sponsor's pancake mix box, before African-American actress Amanda Randolph acquired the role late in the run. Exaggerated black dialect plus vocalists Mary Ann Mercer, Bill Miller, William Mueller, The Mixed Chorus, The Old Plantation Sextet and Harry Walsh's Dixieland Band were featured. (1931–1933, CBS)

Broadway Merry-Go-Round. Here was a spin-off of the eminently popular *Manhattan Merry-Go-Round* sporting a distinct French flair. Fanny Brice, followed by Beatrice Lillie, was the major attraction. (1936-1937, NBC Blue)

Broadway Varieties. The orchestra of Jerry Freeman and then Victor Arden backed vocalists Fifi D'orsay, Eugene and Willie Howard, Elizabeth Lennox, Helen Morgan, Carmela Ponselle, Guy Robertson and Oscar Shaw on a program beginning as *Broadway Melodies*. Light, popular and semiclassical chestnuts were featured. (1933–1937, CBS)

California Theatre of the Air. No details preserved. (c1939)

Don Donnie's Orchestra. One of numerous lesser-known bands on the airwaves during its epoch; guest vocalists featured. (c1935)

Evening Melodies. This is one of many nondescript and seldom-recalled purveyors of tunes on the ether. (c1939)

For America We Sing. This show arrived shortly before America's involvement in World War II, promoting sales of defense and savings bonds on behalf of the U.S. Treasury Department. Frank Black conducted a 44-piece orchestra and chorus. Donating time and talent were guest vocalists Rose Bampton, Helen Jepson, Elizabeth Lennox, Dorothy Maynor, Frank Munn, Frank Parker, Lanny Ross, Gladys Swarthout and Robert Weede. (1941-1942, NBC Blue)

French Mignon Trio. This is one of the less-memorable ensembles that performed in the early era. (c1937)

LaGaiete Parisienne. One of numerous Hummert musicals with French twists; no specific data appears to have survived. (c1937–1938)

Gems of Melody. Featured artists on this early song series (running for several months on dual chains, differentiated by times, days and stars) included John Herrick, Fred Hufsmith, Muriel Wilson and Harold Sanford's Orchestra. (1933-1934, NBC; 1933–1935, NBC Blue)

Hammerstein Music Hall. Ted Hammerstein and Lucy Laughlin were featured personalities on a half-hour music-variety series. (1934-1935, CBS; 1935-1936, NBC; 1936–1938, CBS)

Hollywood Nights. Singer Frank Luther starred in one of numerous revues bearing the film capital's name in the title. (1931-1932, NBC Blue)

The Imperial Hollywood Band. This is one of many instrumental groups that headlined their own shows during this early period. (c1935-1936)

Lavender and Old Lace. "Songs of other days" featured tenor Frank Munn, Fritzi Scheff and soprano Muriel Wilson (later replaced by soprano Lucy Monroe), the Gus Haenschen and Abe Lyman orchestras, a male trio and organist William Meeder. Ballads and waltzes were prominently featured. (1934–1936, CBS; 1936, NBC Blue)

Lazy Dan, the Minstrel Man. Versatile comic and tenor Irving Kaufman supplied all the speaking and singing roles. It was blackface humor with light music set in a hardware store with the proprietor playing a straight man. When it was time for a tune, the radio was turned on. (1933–1936, CBS)

London Merry-Go-Round. Aired in Great Britain, this was an English version of the Hummerts' well-liked *Manhattan Merry-Go-Round* in America. (c1939)

Matinee Melodies. One of numerous tune-filled features whose details haven't been preserved. (c1942)

Melodiana. Abe Lyman's Orchestra was featured along with guest artists. (1934–1936, CBS; 1936, NBC Blue)

MGM Radio Movie Club. A musical-variety showcase that plugged songs controlled by Metro-Goldwyn-Mayer's music publishing companies. The realistic setting of this miniscule movierama included a grinding camera, cameraman, shouting director and actors performing with the music. (1927–1936, New York City's WHN Radio)

Mr. Gallagher and Mr. Shean. A comedy-singing duo, the pair had already achieved fame for their early phonograph records. (c1933)

Monday Merry-Go-Round. A celebrated long-running Sunday night standard, *Manhattan Merry-Go-Round*, was spun off for a Monday-night insertion in the schedule. Singers Phil Duey and Bea Wain, backed by Victor Arden's Orchestra, were featured. (1941-1942, NBC Blue)

The Musical Revue. This was one of numerous poorly remembered series, all bearing similar appellations, that featured songs and artists of the day. (c1933–1935)

Night Club of the Air. Bands and crooners of the day were included in one of many such radio cabaret-style venues. (c1936-1937)

Paris Night Life. This was one of a handful of Hummert musical creations bearing French themes and settings. It presented the instruments of Bertram Hirsch's Orchestra. (1931-1932, 1933, 1936, NBC Blue)

Roxy Symphony Theater of the Stars. One of many similarly titled musical revues emanating from New York City's famous Roxy Theater during the early 1930s. (c1932-1933)

Showland Memories. This was one of several musical productions for which no further information has surfaced. (c1934–1939)

Sweetest Love Songs Ever Sung. Frank Munn starred, along with Metropolitan Opera soprano Natalie Bodanya. (1936-1937, NBC Blue)

Waves of Melody. Tenor Tom Brown was featured in a tune-filled fest accompanied by Vic Arden's Orchestra. (1931-1932, NBC Blue)

Your Song and Mine. Baritone Thomas

L. Thomas, a Hummert favorite, starred in a midweek musical outing. (1948, CBS)

It also seems appropriate to include a mention of the theme songs that introduced the many dramatic programs in the vast Hummert inventory. Unlike many other producers, they didn't rely on original compositions for most of their narratives. Instead, the twosome selected pieces of standard, easily identifiable works. Without commissioning someone to pen a tune for a given show, they saved money. They saved even more by selecting scores that, for the most part, were in the public domain. Translation: no copyright fees were paid to anyone for their usage. Could there be any doubt that their choices were heavily influenced by cost?

By relying on tunes that were already known and loved by listeners, their theme songs bred instant recognition and helped to draw audiences. Thus Hummert melodramas featured listener favorites like *Juanita* (*The Romance of Helen Trent*), *Red River Valley* (*Our Gal Sunday*), *In the Gloaming* and *Wonderful One* (*Young Widder Brown*), *Beyond the Blue Horizon* and *Finiculi Finicula* (*Lorenzo Jones*), *Darling Nellie Gray* and *Polly Wolly Doodle* (*Just Plain Bill*) and *You and I Know* (*Front Page Farrell*).

Frank and Anne Hummert possessed an uncanny ability to choose tunes that closely paralleled the themes of some of their individual series. This indicated that considerable care was given to matching the music with a program's premise. A few examples will illustrate.

As the studio organ poured forth with *How Can I Leave Thee?* weekday afternoons, the saga of *Stella Dallas* unfolded. While the melody played underneath, the announcer implored listeners to follow the tale of "mother love and sacrifice in which Stella Dallas saw her beloved daughter Laurel marry into wealth and society and—realizing the difference in their tastes and worlds—went out of Laurel's life." Think about it in the context of the theme song's title.

Immediately preceding that little gem, "The story of Mary Noble and what it means to be the wife of a famous star" wafted onto the airwaves. *Backstage Wife* was accompanied by *The Rose of Tralee*, a fair maiden from the little Irish burg of Tralee whose name, not surprisingly, was Mary.

Then there was the crime detective thriller *Mr. Keen, Tracer of Lost Persons*. *Someday I'll Find You* seemed utterly apropos, given that drama's title and premise in its earliest years. The familiar tune was unequivocally linked with the mystery in fans' intellects for nearly two decades.

Frank and Anne Hummert infused their entrepreneurial quests with a large helping of music and variety programming. While there is small doubt that they favored fictional melodrama since they produced so much of it, it's plain to see they recognized the implications in diversifying their offerings into a myriad of aural entertainment forms. Their musicales were festive expressions of an age in which vast numbers that tuned in every week were treated to popular and semiclassical melodies. In their case, however, unlike most of their contemporaries, the Hummerts consistently gave listeners something to enjoy multiple times a week.

The Kate Smith Show

Under a myriad of broadcast titles and formats, Kate Smith became an American icon, a pop diva who not only enthralled audiences with her vocal range but attracted a loyal following for deeply held values that she communicated through chatty dialogues. She became a symbol of American patriotism, raising buckets of money for wartime humanitarian efforts while proliferating in multiple entertainment venues—radio, television, stage, screen, recording and writing. Smith is best remembered for an enduring association with Irving Berlin's *God Bless America* which she introduced to listeners in 1938. Radio made her name a household word. In a career that extended across five decades, Smith captured the hearts of incalculable numbers of her fellow countrymen. In her epoch on the ether she was one of its most respected and prestigious figures.

Producer: Ted Collins

Directors: Bunny Coughlin, Bob Lee

Writers: Jay Bennett, Al Garry, Doris Gilbert, Mark Goodson, Art S. Henley, Jean Holloway, Edward Jurist

Host-Master of Ceremonies: Ted Collins

Announcers: Andre Baruch (most enduring), Tom Shirley, Robert Trout

Orchestra Conductor: Jack Miller, accompanying at the piano in an early series (*Kate Smith and Her Swanee Music*), later leading a 27-piece band

Musical Arranger: Tony Gale (Smith's personal arrangements)

Vocal Artists: La Brun Sisters, Ted Straeter Chorus, Three Ambassadors, Bea Wain

Other Features: Bud Abbott and Lou Costello (comedy duo), *The Aldrich Family* sketches with Ezra Stone (domestic sitcom), Cecil Brown (newscaster), Charlie Cantor and Minerva Pious (comedy duo), Jim Crowley (sports commentator), Elmer Davis (newscaster), *Ethel and Albert* sketches with Alan Bunce and Peg Lynch (domestic sitcom), Clyde Hager (comic), Bill Henry (newscaster), *It Pays to Be Ignorant* (comedy quiz), Nan Rae and Maude Davis (comedy duo), Bert Parks (quizmaster, vocalist, Miss America Pageant host), *Snow Village Sketches* narratives (drama), Henny Youngman (comic)

Theme Song: *When the Moon Comes Over the Mountain* (Harry Woods, Howard Johnson, Kate Smith); early series themes

Marching Along Together and *Time to Dream.*

Sponsors: Congress Cigar Company for La Palina cigars (September 14, 1931–October 31, 1933); Hudson-Terraplane Motor Car Company for Hudson automobiles (December 1934–May 22, 1935); The Great Atlantic & Pacific Tea Company for Bokar, Eight O'Clock and Red Circle coffees (October 1, 1935–1937); General Foods Corporation for Cain's mayonnaise, Calumet baking soda, Diamond Crystal shaker salt, Grape-Nuts Flakes cereal, Jell-O desserts, Postum and Sanka coffees, Sur-Jel canning aid, Swans Down cake flour (September 30, 1937–June 20, 1947, all series inclusive except *Kate Smith's Column*); multiple underwriters (June 23, 1947–June 15, 1951); Flagstaff jellies, Philip Morris Company for Philip Morris cigarettes, and other participants (September 20, 1948–April 22, 1949); Reader's Digest Association for *Reader's Digest* condensed books and Scranton Lace Company (January 6, 1958–January 2, 1959); at other times, sustaining or joint participation

Ratings: Prime time High — 19.6 (1939-1940 season); low — 8.5 (1944-1945); median — 14.3 (an extremely respectable ranking). Figures provided for 1931-1932 through 1946-1947 radio seasons. Daytime High — 8.9 (1940-1941); low — 3.3 (1938-1939); median — 7.1 (matching other daytime fare). Figures available for nine seasons only, 1938-1939 through 1946-1947.

On the Air: *Freddy Rich's Rhythm Kings*, 1930-1931 (specific dates unsubstantiated), CBS, Monday, 5:45–6:00 P.M. (all times Eastern); *Kate Smith Sings*, March 17–April 23, 1931, NBC, Tuesday, Thursday, 11:30–11:45 P.M.; *Kate Smith Sings*, April 27–May 23, 1931, CBS, Monday, Wednesday, Thursday, Saturday (inaugural Sunday, April 26), 7:45–8:00 P.M.; *Kate Smith Sings*, May 25–September 12, 1931, CBS, Monday–Saturday, 7:00–7:15 P.M.; *Kate Smith and Her Swanee Music*, September 14–November 28, 1931, CBS, 8:30–8:45 P.M., Monday, Wednesday, Thursday, Saturday; *Kate Smith and Her Swanee Music*, November 30, 1931–June 2, 1932, CBS, Monday, Tuesday Wednesday, Thursday, 8:30–8:45 P.M.; *Kate Smith and Her Swanee Music*, June 6–December 28, 1932, CBS, Monday, Tuesday, Wednesday, 8:30–8:45 P.M.; *Kate Smith and Her Swanee Music*, January 3–June 1, 1933, CBS, Tuesday, Wednesday, Thursday, 8:30–8:45 P.M.; *Kate Smith and Her Swanee Music*, June 5–September 13, 1933, CBS, Monday, Tuesday, Wednesday, 8:30–8:45 P.M.; *Kate Smith and Her Swanee Music*, September 18–October 31, 1933, CBS Monday, Tuesday, 8:30–8:45 P.M.; *Kate Smith and Her Swanee Music*, July 16–November 26, 1934, CBS, Monday, Thursday, Friday, 8:00–8:15 P.M.; *Kate Smith's Matinee Hour*, September 26–December 26, 1934, CBS, Wednesday, 3:00–4:00 P.M.; *Kate Smith's New Star Revue*, December 24, 1934–May 27, 1935, CBS, Monday, 8:30–9:00 P.M.; *Kate Smith's Hour*, May 30–September 5, 1935, CBS, Thursday, 8:00–9:00 P.M.; *Kate Smith's Coffee Time*, October 1, 1935–June 25, 1936, CBS, Tuesday, Wednesday, Thursday, 7:30–7:45 P.M.; *Kate Smith's Coffee Time*, June 30–September 10, 1936, CBS, Tuesday, Thursday, 7:30–7:45 P.M.; *Kate Smith's A&P Bandwagon*, September 17, 1936–June 24, 1937, CBS, Thursday, 8:00–9:00 P.M.; *Kate Smith Hour*, September 30, 1937–June 23, 1938, CBS, Thursday, 8:00–9:00 P.M.; *Kate Smith Hour*, September 29, 1938–June 29, 1939, CBS, Thursday, 8:00–9:00 P.M.; *Kate Smith Hour*, October 6, 1939–June 28, 1940, CBS, Friday, 8:00–8:55 P.M.; *Kate Smith Hour*, September 20, 1940–June 27, 1941, CBS, Friday, 8:00–8:55 P.M.; *Kate Smith Hour*, October 3, 1941–June 26, 1942, CBS, Friday, 8:00–8:55 P.M.; *Kate Smith Hour*, September 18, 1942–January 1, 1943, CBS, Friday, 8:00–8:55 P.M.; *Kate Smith Hour*, January 8–June 25, 1943, CBS, Friday, 8:30–8:55 P.M.; *Kate Smith Hour*, October 1,

1943–June 9, 1944, CBS, Friday, 8:00– 8:55 P.M.; *Kate Smith Hour*, September 17, 1944–June 10, 1945, CBS, Sunday, 7:00–8:00 P.M.; *Kate Smith's Column*, April 4–June 17, 1938, CBS, Monday, Wednesday, Friday, 3:30–3:45 P.M.; *Kate Smith Speaking Her Mind*, October 4, 1938–May 27, 1939, CBS, Tuesday, Thursday, Saturday, noon–12:15 P.M.; *Kate Smith Speaks*, October 2, 1939–June 20, 1947, CBS, Monday–Friday, noon–12:15 P.M.; *Kate Smith Speaks*, June 23, 1947–June 15, 1951, MBS, Monday–Friday, noon–12:15 P.M.; *Kate Smith Sings*, September 14, 1945–June 28, 1946, CBS, Friday, 8:30–8:55 P.M.; *Kate Smith Sings*, October 6, 1946–June 29, 1947, CBS, Sunday, 6:30–7:00 P.M.; *Kate Smith's Serenade*, March 22–June 7, 1947, MBS, Saturday, 10:15–10:30 A.M.; *Kate Smith's Serenade*, June 14–July 26, 1947, MBS, Saturday, noon–12:15 P.M.; *Kate Smith Sings*, September 20, 1948–April 22, 1949, MBS, Monday–Friday, 12:15–12:30 P.M.; *Kate Smith Calling*, August 8, 1949–January 30, 1950, ABC, Monday, 9:00–11:00 P.M.; *Kate Smith Show*, September 17, 1951–September 12, 1952, NBC, Monday–Friday, 12:05–12:45 P.M.; *Kate Smith Show*, January 6, 1958–January 2, 1959, MBS, Monday–Friday, 10:05–10:30 A.M.

* * *

During radio's golden age it was not uncommon for top stars to be billed with epithets that characterized their talents and auxiliary capacities. Early in his professional career, host-entertainer Arthur Godfrey was dubbed "Red Godfrey, the Warbling Banjoist." Other sobriquets abounded: Jan Garber was "The Idol of the Airwaves"; Wayne King was "The Waltz King"; Arthur Tracy, "The Street Singer"; Rudy Vallee, "The Vagabond Lover." There were similar labels for numerous performers.

Singer Kate Smith, who appeared on more than 15,000 broadcasts, collected in excess of 25 million fan letters, recorded an astounding 3,000 melodies over her lifetime—considered "the most listened to person on the airwaves" by 1933 — was instantly recognized by her legions of admirers as "The Songbird of the South." Yet an infinite litany of appellations applied to an enhanced "larger than life" image of the 235-pound contralto. Some observers christened her "a radio giant" while one hailed her as "the most influential woman in the history of radio." Her stage presence was embodied in such nicknames as the "first lady of radio," apparently originally conferred by *Time* magazine. An author labeled her the "Queen of the Air." A poll of Associated Press editors, meanwhile, tagged her as "radio's best entertainer."

In December 1934, the popular consumer fanzine *Radio Stars* listed Kate Smith among the "Nine Greatest Women in Radio" alongside Gracie Allen, Gertrude Berg, Jessica Dragonette, Eleanor Roosevelt and a few more. By 1942, she outstripped even that eminent coup when yet another poll placed her among the nation's three most popular females, including Helen Hayes and Eleanor Roosevelt. Uncompromisingly, Smith was a foremost presence on the aural airwaves throughout the 1930s and 1940s, a dominant figure who embodied many of the qualities that her countrymen prized most during the epoch in which she lived. An association that perpetuates her memory today labels her "an American original." It shouldn't take long to discover why.

Kathryn Elizabeth Smith was born May 1, 1907, in her family's home at 211 First Street, Washington, D.C., in the city's northwest sector, some recorded dates and places to the contrary notwithstanding. Kate herself gave rise to an oft-repeated myth that her delivery occurred in 1909 in Greenville, Virginia, a few miles distant. It's a premise that her very own birth certificate, Washington health department records and census files refute. Her father was proprietor of the Capitol News Company and dispensed out-of-town newspapers, national journals and slick-cover magazines. Three daughters were born to the Smith family—Helena, two and a half years Kate's senior; Kate; and Martha, between the two sisters, who died in infancy.

Kathryn took a concerted interest in music at a tender age, demonstrating a singing voice that was so good so early that others began to take notice. She put on outdoor vaudeville performances at her home and conquered high Cs in a church choir. By 1917, as American infantrymen departed to faraway places to engage in World War I combat, a nine-year-old Kathryn Smith sang patriotic tunes at military camps near her home. By age 12 she won a local amateur talent competition. Her successes enhanced a growing ambition within her to entertain.

Preferring to be called Kate, after high school she acquiesced to her family's request that she pursue nurse's training. Enrolling at George Washington School of Nursing, Kate spent nine months as a square peg in a round hole. A career in that field simply wasn't to be. She was convinced she was totally wasting her gifts. Kate returned to her first love, music, and from then on sought to fulfill what she was convinced was a promising destiny.

Initially performing at Washington area theaters, by 1926—still a teenager—Kate left the confines of the nation's capital to go on the road in a show called *Honeymoon Lane*. That led to Broadway, the vaudeville circuit and occasional recordings. Although already overweight, she could not only sing, she was still light on her feet—dancing remarkably well—offering an especially heralded version of the Charleston when requested.

She was habitually cast in the role of a stooge in several stage productions, becoming the target of incessant, nonstop fat-girl jokes. Not only were the audiences rollicking in aisles at her expense, the pundits poked fun at her, too. "In order to make [comedian Bert] Lahr's life richly comic they have mated him with Kate Smith, whose proportions are mountainous," said a *New York Times* review of the musical comedy *Flying High*. Writing about the same show, a *World Telegram* columnist cited "a fat girl named Kate Smith" in assessing it. "She weighs as much as four chorus girls," he observed. She was "a find of huge proportions," declared others. Later—having gained confidence and incredible status—she would tell *Newsweek* exuberantly, "I'm big and I'm fat, but I have a voice, and when I sing, boy, I sing all over!" But that time wasn't yet.

Especially were Kate's early days as an entertainer fraught with sadness of another origin. Her personal convictions, including a strong adherence to high moral ground, often resulted in inner pain that at times simply overwhelmed the young entertainer. Biographer Richard Hayes recalls what transpired[1]:

> Life offstage was not pleasant for Smith. She was shunned socially by her peers in the cast, so she spent many lonely hours crying herself to sleep in her small hotel room. Since she neither smoked nor drank, was offended by risqué jokes, and had a weight problem, she just did not fit in. In all these ways she would change very little during her long career. The "fat jokes" always smarted deep down inside, even as she would watch a late evening talk show many years later. She would ask, "Now why did they have to say that?" She never learned to live with it.... As grateful as she was [to participate in early stage productions]..., it is clear that she was exploited. There was even a clause in her contract stating that she must maintain a weight of over 200 pounds during the run.

That all began to change for Kate Smith in August 1930 after a Columbia Phonograph Company executive caught her show one night at the Apollo Theater. So enamored with Smith was Joseph Martin Collins—who was nicknamed Ted by a father who revered Theodore Roosevelt—that he quickly gained her trust. He was, in fact, the first to see the budding possibilities in Kate Smith's talent while visualizing elevated opportunities for himself. Then only 30, Collins was Smith's senior by nearly eight years. He was born in New York City on October 12, 1899.

Initially he asked Smith to record some vocals for the label for which he was a manager. At the same time he was astute enough to realize that problems lay directly ahead for the recording trade for which he earned his livelihood. Wary consumers were seeking merely to survive a Depression-epoch collapse of the national economy that offered them little in the way of discretionary spending for the foreseeable future. Meanwhile, just at that fortuitous juncture radio was experiencing a wildly enthusiastic reception. Once listeners purchased a receiver, its costs for providing home entertainment were generally negligible. The possibilities that radio—and Kate Smith—presented did not escape an enterprising, entrepreneurial Collins. He offered to become her personal manager, arranging bookings, overseeing finances, handling the promotion, legal aspects and logistics of appearances. "You do the singing and I'll fight the battles," he told her. "We'll split the profits equally."

It would be a good deal for her, as she was then still undiscovered by all but limited audiences, and profitable for him. Most managers received less than a fifth of their clients' incomes as a fee, some considerably less. Collins would take half. Smith was impressed by Collins' sincerity and believability. The two shook hands. Their alliance turned out to be a good supposition for both, one never put into writing but which extended to Collins' death nearly 34 years later. In that time Collins would persist in keeping Smith "at arm's length from the public, securely wrapped in patriotic bunting," assiduously reflected one wag.

Collins would also demonstrate "a full measure of both Irish wit and Irish temper." While he could spellbind an audience with all sorts of escapades, "when things did not go his way—or Kate Smith's way—he could come down with an iron fist."[2] One critic surmised: "Collins was a tough uncle, very sharp and totally ruthless."[3] A caretaker at Smith's home portrayed him as "immoral, miserable to get along with," and once wrote to him: "There aren't six men in town who have any use for you."[4] Despite those characterizations, Collins would be highly protective of his young protégé, no matter what anyone thought. His efforts would soon pay off in making her an entertainer of national acclaim.

Kate Smith began making records for the Columbia label. For a while Collins would continue as an emissary of that firm, but he would soon leave it to become Smith's full time manager and eventually her airtime producer and programming host, too. While Ted Collins was "a name that sounded something like a cocktail," according to a radio historiographer, "People who thought of Ted Collins as just another announcer hadn't done much probing into the life of Kathryn Elizabeth Smith. Even a superficial look reveals that Ted Collins was truly the man behind the woman that he molded and guided and influenced Kate Smith's career from beginning to end. Kate herself was always first to admit it." The Kated Corporation they formed became a multimillion-dollar business enterprise in due course.

It should be pointed out that Collins was married and the father of a daughter. During those early years, Ted and Jeanette Collins and their daughter, Adelaide, resided in Neponset near Rockaway Beach on Long Island. Smith often visited them during the summers. Two of her pet activities were readily accessible there, swimming and speedboating. When she stayed over for extended periods it "sometimes put Collins in an awkward position," said an informant, for he was "torn between the demands of his wife and his principal artiste." Smith "doubtless intimidated Jeanette Collins in the early years. Jeanette was her chief competitor for Ted's attention."

Their lives would become increasingly intermingled as a result of future vacation travel and business opportunities. Collins and Smith were seen together so frequently, in fact, that a segment of the public believed they were truly husband and wife. To correct that assumption the pair issued a form letter to those who inquired. They stated that while Smith *wasn't* married, Collins *was*, noting that he had a daughter and two grandchildren.

Parenthetically, insiders confirmed that Collins carried on affairs with several other women. At least one of his dalliances continued for years (and was brought to the nation's attention by broadcast journalist Walter Winchell). Nor was it any secret that Collins didn't hold his liquor well. He frequently returned home at night totally inebriated. On rare occasions a tinge of those effects lingered through his noontime arrival on the show the next day. Let it be understood that, while there is no evidence that he and Smith ever pursued a romantic tryst together — she emphatically denied the very hint of it when given an opportunity to respond to scandalous questions — in 1955 Collins separated from Jeanette. She permanently refused to divorce him, however.

More influential than the recordings in gaining widespread recognition for Smith, Collins booked her as a featured artist on a quarter-hour weekly broadcast over the fledgling Columbia network (now known as CBS) during the 1930-1931 season called *Freddy Rich's Rhythm Kings*. While this wasn't Smith's first appearance on radio — she was heard between 1923 and 1926 on various local outlets in Washington, D.C., and debuted nationally over NBC on April 4, 1929, for a single special with Sophie Tucker, Ted Lewis and Nick Lucas — this was her first *continuing* series before a coast-to-coast audience.

Even more important to her career than that program, as it turned out, was some added spotlight appearances she made on other aural features, in particular a trio of guest shots on a series headlined by a legendary entertainer, *The Rudy Vallee Fleischmann Sunshine Hour*. As a result of those exhibitions, she was boosted into her own show, albeit at an advanced hour for East Coast listeners. *Kate Smith Sings* premiered over NBC in the middle of the late-night dance band phenomenon for a quarter-hour at 11:30 P.M. Tuesdays and Thursdays starting March 17, 1931. She opened that show with what became one of her dual signature tunes, and the theme of almost every future feature in which she would star, *When the Moon Comes Over the Mountain*. She had written a portion of the lyrics in girlhood, later completed by Howard Johnson and set to music by Harry Woods. The song would come to be instantly identified with her by audiences whom she would entertain over several decades.

Meanwhile, Smith continued making personal appearances between radio broadcasts. Ted Collins brought the gifted young contralto before the discerning ear of highly competitive Columbia network owner William S. Paley during a Capitol Theatre performance. The radio mogul was likewise eager to find her a spot on his chain's schedule. She left NBC after six weeks, moving to Columbia under the same series title, *Kate Smith Sings*, but then at 7:45 P.M. Monday, Wednesday, Thursday and Saturday evenings. She debuted in a one-time Sunday showcase on April 16, 1931.

A month later, Paley—frustrated that his network hadn't fielded a serious contender to stem a raging tide against NBC's near-universal dominance of the 7 o'clock quarter-hour *Amos 'n' Andy* show—flung Smith into the fray six nights weekly in that period. Unfortunately for him, of several artists dispersed to that pivotal spot, including Morton Downey, the Mills Brothers and Bing Crosby, only Crosby struck even a tiny notch in the comedians' seemingly insuperable ratings. While Smith's brief tenure there failed to unseat the competition, it did wonders for *her* career: it provided exposure she had never previously enjoyed, and signified a perceptively quick ascendancy by audiences and network brass alike. There could be no turning back.

In rapid-fire succession over several years, Smith signed for a myriad of additional Columbia features, each one likely increasing her public esteem over previous outings. Her series included monikers like *Kate Smith and Her Swanee Music, Kate Smith's Matinee Hour, Kate Smith's New Star Revue, Kate Smith's Hour, Kate Smith's Coffee Time, Kate Smith's A&P Bandwagon* and the *Kate Smith Hour*. While in many of these her singing predominated and she often featured guests in a variety format, Smith also developed an interesting conversational style that instantly resonated with audiences. Soon the fans were following her commentary just as avidly as they were her music.

Smith offered little pretense in how she felt about the common man. In a folksy, down-to-earth style, she confessed that she "genuinely liked people." She once wrote: "I make it my business (with me it's a pleasure, since I like people and love to mingle with them) to keep in close personal touch with the kind of typical, average American folks who make up my audiences. I listen to housewives and business girls, to all types of people: hear how they talk and react to each other, at soda fountains, in stores, wherever I happen to be. I read a great deal, see as many movies and plays as I can. This familiarity with what's going on helps in planning my shows."

It was an easy stretch from that prevailing attitude to understand why she consistently opened her shows with the simple greeting "Hello everybody" and closed with "Thanks for list'nin'!" The twin taglines became a trademark, almost as much as her longstanding theme. (Yet on the flip side of that, years later comic Henny Youngman, who gained his start on Smith's early radio shows, classified both her and Collins as "cold and rather distant," noting he was never invited to their homes. They had a "little clique" and Youngman viewed himself outside it.[5] But another informant contradicted: "She's not high hat, nor stuck up. She mingles with everyone."[6]) As a throwback to Smith's "Hello everybody" the irascible radio humorist Henry Morgan opened his shows with a ho-hum greeting, "Good evening anybody," perceived as a "kick in the pants" to Smith's bouncy welcome.

She engaged in a mission to solicit certain types of fans and insisted that it could be accomplished by a couple of fervent thrusts:[7]

1. Find out all you can about the particular group of listeners you want to reach: their philosophy, their psychology, what they like or dislike, and their current interests in response to changing events.

2. Use all your skill and judgment as an entertainer to please that particular segment of the audience, keeping in mind all you know about their listening preferences: both their basic likes and their preferences of the moment.

Evolving out of the bent toward talk may have been Smith's single best-remembered broadcast series, *Kate Smith Speaks*, which for a dozen years captivated a fervent midday crowd reaching as many as 10 million listeners. It originated from a sustaining afternoon quarter-hour titled *Kate Smith's Column* that debuted over CBS on April 4, 1938. The more established *Speaks* series boasted a sponsor from its start, General Foods Corporation, premiering over CBS on October 2, 1939. Over the years she would pitch such familiar culinary brands as Calumet, Grape-Nuts, Jell-O, Sanka and Swans Down. In connection with her sponsorships—after Smith's multiple series had been running for a while—a wag acknowledged: "The network reportedly was ... upset with [Ted] Collins's refusal to have Smith make personal identifications for products of the show's sponsors, a policy that did nothing to win or hold advertisers."[8]

The weekday show normally included some laid-back exchanges between Smith and Collins (who by then had joined her as air host of her programs) on varied topics of interest to women—homemakers were the prevailing listeners. Such stuff as books, cooking, fashions, gardening and movies were prime bait for their folksy tête-à-têtes. A staff of eight prepared the human-interest segments and a script was provided.

Sometime during their quarter-hour Collins read a few news bulletins supplied by United Press International. He'd introduce the show with "It's high noon in New York and time for Kate Smith" followed by her traditional effervescent salutation, "Hello everybody." A pundit mistakenly dismissed the feature as little more than a "series of chatty fifteen-minute uplift sermonettes." While Smith unmistakably placed her stamp of approval on some high moral tenets—values, incidentally, that could be ascribed to the vast majority of those tuning in—there was more transpiring there than merely communicating lofty plateaus.

She used her forum as a platform to promote charitable and patriotic fronts, for sure, some of which will be highlighted in due time. First of all, "The format ... characterizes her [Smith] as a God-fearing, country-loving, humanity-sympathizing woman who still manages to keep a sense of humor" an observer noted. Beyond the homilies, Smith offered recipes for homemade delicacies like baked squash, fried chicken, butter cake with chocolate icing (her personal favorite) and peppermint ice cream that were highly receptive to milady. They were sometimes printed and distributed extensively by the sponsor. In an effort to be helpful and tuned in, at the same time she discussed listeners' personal problems, raised civic questions and offered a slant on current events.

As an aside, it also should be noted that this program emanated from Smith's Park Avenue apartment during most of the year. Yet in the warm months it was broadcast from her summertime retreat, "Camp Sunshine," on Buck Island near Lake Placid, New York. A wardrobe closet in her guesthouse was remodeled to accommodate the radio show transmissions, officially cited by Ripley's *Believe It or Not* as "the world's smallest broadcast studio." The quarters were so infinitesimal, in fact, that broadcasting was soon transferred to larger space in a boathouse.

Actually, Smith and Collins had for several years refused to surrender the 13-week summer hiatus they, and Collins' family, had enjoyed for several summers while vacationing in the Adirondacks. (The Collinses rented a place there each summer.) Sponsors implored Smith and Collins to continue broadcasting year-round, nonetheless, and CBS at last handed down an ultimatum that they provide 52 weeks or vacate their quarter-hour. They agreed when a cable line was installed connecting Smith's property on a small island in the middle of a lake, allowing uninterrupted transmission of their popular midday feature year-round.

Smith had accidentally discovered the bucolic site of Lake Placid, 250 miles north of New York City, in 1932. A physician advised her to take a break and get away from singing to counter a nagging bronchitis condition that could ultimately lapse into pneumonia. She found that tranquil village hypnotic and returned to vacation there the following year. In 1934, she purchased a rustic abandoned farmhouse on a decent-sized island at Lake Placid, dubbing it "Camp Sunshine." It would become a serene haven to her for the rest of her professional life. She used the place not only to entertain guests, which she professed she loved to do, but to satisfy a lifelong passion for collecting and displaying authentic early American antiques. (Her major "indulgence," she admitted, was a 2,000-piece collection.) Among her particular favorites was a set of glassware from the period, including some pitchers she unequivocally prized. She often took visitors on jaunts in which she poked into quaint nearby art shops and antique emporiums searching for newfound treasures. She savored such respites over the four decades that she called Lake Placid her summer home.

Returning to her midday CBS broadcast, of course all good things eventually come to an end. In the spring of 1947, General Foods decided to switch its allegiance from *Kate Smith Speaks* to something else. While she continued to boast enormous popularity, her midday ratings had begun to slide, from 8.9 a few years before to 6.2 by early 1947. Meanwhile, having broadcast her multiple series exclusively over Bill Paley's CBS chain for 16 years, Smith simultaneously astonished a Chicago press conference: she expressed strong disaffection for that network, announcing she was severing her longstanding relationship and moving to the Mutual Broadcasting System. She would air there at the same hour (noon) in the same format under the same title and be underwritten by multiple sponsors. She told the media: "You don't have freedom of speech on CBS. Every day I get orders that I must take this or that out of my script.... I don't see why I should let anybody tell me how to run my program." It was obvious that something had changed dramatically in the years since Paley hoisted her away from NBC.

Her replacement in the time period at CBS, by the way, showed some enduring characteristics of the Smith legacy. Let us digress momentarily to explore it. The network decided to complete its noon-hour grid of daytime quarter-hour serials with a fourth drainboard drama. Mindful that Ted Collins' news headlines had been a popular feature with audiences for years, CBS advanced an atypical motif: it created a soap opera that integrated a brief news segment within its fictionalized story line.

Focusing on a mythical news journalist who combined her career in print and electronic media, the chain premiered *Wendy Warren and the News* on June 23, 1947. General Foods picked up the tab, desiring to retain that significant time period. The program relied upon the authoritative voice of CBS newsman Douglas Edwards to deliver the news dispatches. The sound of telegraph keys clicking as the narrative came on the air each day was reminiscent of Ted Collins' "It's high noon in New York" and gave it a sense of urgency.

Unlike peer soap operas where story lines lingered for interminable periods, each day was a new one on *Wendy Warren* due to the reportorial feature, branding it with respectability and reality. The news aspect coupled with its immediacy, the lunchtime broadcast hour in the East when many people could tune in and the fact the plots often revolved around mystery and intrigue as the heroine and her cohorts exposed subversive government agents expanded the audience, consistently attracting many men, too. The hybrid serial was earning a very respectable rating of 10.2 by

January 1950, ranking it the third most-listened-to show in daytime radio, just behind CBS's *The Romance of Helen Trent* (11.0) and *Arthur Godfrey Time* (10.5). From a practical standpoint, for both CBS and General Foods, it would appear on the surface, at least, that their joint decision to drop Kate Smith when they did was a prudent one.

As an interesting side note to this, soap opera programmers sometimes cited Smith's daytime show in arguing what modest sums were necessary to produce a successful serial in comparison to the substantial budget Smith's program required. In 1943, for example, *Kate Smith Speaks* was the highest-rated weekday program on the air. Its all-important production costs per ratings point were $609.76. Daytime radio's second-rated *When a Girl Marries*, on the other hand, cost only $287.50 per ratings point. And the well-respected *Ma Perkins*, boasting an overall rating very near Smith's, entailed a mere $164.56 per point. General Foods was paying $5,000 weekly to produce *Kate Smith Speaks* while Procter & Gamble put *Ma Perkins* on for $1,300 a week. Expenses were an impressive factor that the critics of the drainboard dramas—and there were legions seemingly looking for ways to assail that successful phenomena—could never substantially repudiate.

Smith, meanwhile, moved on to MBS without missing a broadcast day. She carried millions of loyal fans with her to the smallest of the four major national hookups, a broadcast service that had everything to gain and little to lose by acquiring her. It was definitely a feather in the cap of the chain billing itself "the network for all America" to acquire Smith and the prestige she brought. She and Ted Collins continued to thrive for 15 minutes daily at high noon for yet another four years, through June 15, 1951, as they bantered back and forth around the microphone on the issues of the day of special interest to the homemakers.

Perhaps this is a good time to introduce some of the topics Smith discussed during her commentaries. Then we'll examine her hallmark contributions that endured for decades and hailed her as one of the nation's great stateswomen.

First, living well ahead of her time, she wasn't afraid to tackle themes like the need to avoid published illustrations and subject matter of an offensive (yea, sexual) nature that could be witnessed by children. She deplored child labor, age discrimination in the workplace, racial prejudice and combat between nations while citing the saintliness of motherhood. She spoke of positive things and took pains to suggest better ways of improving the quality of life for humanity. Sometimes her moralized messages weren't universally understood and possibly went unappreciated by some of her listeners. She made no apology. The bulk of her fans obviously got it and bought into the program.

Periodically she visited other radio series and delivered missives that resonated with the public. A typical discourse was imparted on a visit to a May 1945 broadcast of *We, the People*. It so struck a nerve with the audience that the sponsors were flooded with more than 20,000 requests for printed copies of her treatise. It sounded very much like the Kate Smith daytime listeners had come to love years before.

> It seems to me that faith in the decency of human beings is what we *must* have *more* of, if there is to be a future for all of us in this world. We read in the papers every day about conferences on the best way to keep the peace. Well, I'm not an expert on foreign affairs—and I don't pretend to know all the complex things that will have to be done for a lasting peace. But I am a human being—and I do know something about people. I know that our statesmen—our armies of occupation—

our military strategists—may all fail if the peoples of the world don't learn to *understand* and *tolerate* each other. Race hatreds—social prejudices—religious bigotry—they are all the diseases that eat away the fibres [*sic*] of peace. Unless they are exterminated it's inevitable that we will have another war. And where are they going to be exterminated? ... In your own city—your church—your children's school—perhaps in your own home. You and I must do it—every father and mother in the world, every teacher, everyone who can rightfully call himself a human being. Yes, it seems to me that the one thing the peoples of the world have got to learn if we are ever to have a lasting peace, is—tolerance. Of what use will it be if the lights go on again all over the world—if they don't go on ... in our hearts?

Not only was Smith's righteous indignation delivered over the airwaves, there were legions of added chances to communicate her brand of noble precepts. Magazine writers, for example, prepared articles under her byline to capitalize on her popular reflection as a purveyor of principled precepts, publishing them as if she had authorized them herself. Upon reflection, at least one such editorial seems inconsistent with those deeply rooted values the chatty diva espoused. (Keep in mind that she may not have approved of all that went out under her name.) In a piece surfacing during the war years she encouraged the women of America (primarily targeting the nation's homemakers) to can and preserve food grown in home gardens, urged them to work in war plants while their men were away and asked them to make bandages, donate blood and bake cookies and crullers for big jars in USO clubrooms. Then, somewhat incongruously, Smith added: "We must dance with the boys stationed in our city or our town, because dancing to a good hot band is one of the things they love most. We must be up early with hot coffee and cigarettes any time the troops come through." If the advice to the housewives to boogie with the boys to hot bands didn't raise any eyebrows in that day, something was probably amiss. And from the perspective of six decades later, feeding those boys cigarettes appears likely to have written them tickets for early tombstones another way.

Kate Smith was one of America's greatest humanitarians in the epoch in which she lived. Beyond that she was acclaimed as one of the homeland's strongest advocates. At times she was unequalled in an ability to raise cash for charitable causes and patriotic themes, and used her radio base to do so willingly and enthusiastically wherever she knew of a need. Furthermore, Smith maintained an ability to motivate other people to support great caring efforts that sometimes resulted in personal sacrifices of time, energy and other intangible resources. Stories of her successes are legion and virtually unmatched in both achievement and method. A few examples will suffice.

In radio, live remote broadcasts were commonplace throughout the 1940s. During World War II, Kate Smith took her ethereal entourage on the road for weeks at a time, becoming one of the top benefit performers of the air. She appeared before military camps across this nation and Canada performing in lady-like Bob Hope style. She raised enormous sums on behalf of orphanages and sold war bonds like they were going out of style. These bonds, issued by the U.S. government, markedly contributed to financing and ultimately winning the global confrontation.

As the battle raged, Smith stumped from coast to coast asking U.S. citizens to purchase bonds. They responded with wild abandon, buying $600 million of them to aid America's crucial military effort.

Between 8 A.M. on September 21, 1943, and 2 A.M. the following morning she raised $39 million through 65 petitions to radio listeners to procure war bonds.

On one occasion, during an hour-long stint over the CBS Radio network, she reportedly sold $107 million in war bonds.

During a 24-hour marathon that was broadcast February 1, 1944, she made 57 appeals on the air and netted an unprecedented $112 million in bonds.

Psychologists and sociologists, probing into Smith's phenomenal ability to raise dough, conjectured from scores of interviewees that she exuded an "aura almost of saintliness." Here was, they reported, "a public figure who is thought to incarnate the virtues of sincerity, integrity, good fellowship and altruism.... For her adherents, Smith has become the object of their faith. She is seen as genuine by those who seek redemption from the spurious." This, they felt, aided her greatly in motivating followers to give generously. The fact that audiences were told Smith was donating her time for charitable and humanitarian causes rather than being compensated for it apparently went a long way in confirming their faith in her.

Smith certainly didn't need the money, by the way. As early as 1932 she was taking at least $9,000 weekly out of radio and personal appearances, a small fortune that would rise dramatically with increasing radio work, recordings and — eventually — television shows. Yet when measured against some peer entertainers, she lived modestly although she certainly could have afforded a more resplendent lifestyle. Smith rented several New York apartments, owned a home primarily for her mother in Arlington, Virginia, and maintained her Lake Placid island summer place. She also kept a small personal staff of caretakers and cooks. Over her professional career she reportedly accumulated $35 million, no small potatoes in that epoch.

Easily the preeminent reference that American generations living in Kate Smith's lifetime, and those remembering it today, tell of is her performing Irving Berlin's imposing patriotic refrain *God Bless America*. Some say it was Berlin's masterpiece. He penned it for an Army show (*Yip, Yip, Yaphank*) during World War I while stationed at Camp Yaphank on Long Island. When it was deleted from that production, Berlin added it to a stack of rejected compositions and apparently forgot about it until two decades later. It was then that Ted Collins requested he supply something patriotic for Kate Smith to sing that would commemorate the 20th anniversary of the signing of the peace accord signifying the end of World War I, known as Armistice Day.

That evening, November 10, 1938, Smith premiered *God Bless America* on her 60-minute *Kate Smith Hour* over CBS, a performance critic Leonard Maltin asserted "made the song an anthem overnight." The new piece "electrified the nation" claimed another source. Earlier that same afternoon she had advised noontime listeners that the Berlin work she was to introduce that night "will be timeless — it will never die — others will thrill to its beauty long after we are gone." As she often was, Kate Smith would prove to be right. (Can any who lived through the Smith era dispassionately dismiss her rendition of that tune in a contemporary celebration of Independence Day? It would likely be difficult for millions to disassociate the two.)

Certainly her authoritative delivery of the epic melody established it as the national anthem in a large segment of the populace's psyches. There was even a movement to replace *The Star-Spangled Banner* in that venerated province. Despite a groundswell of enthusiasm for it, Smith herself lobbied the Congress against it, arguing that Francis Scott Key's *Banner* was composed during an actual battle (the War of 1812) and should continue to be so revered. As in most of her zealous endeavors, she would win that challenge, too.

That didn't prevent her from performing Berlin's harmony into immortality. He granted her exclusive permission to sing and record it for about two years before granting others similar privileges. Gene Autry, Bing Crosby, Horace Heidt's orchestra, Barry Wood and others would try to emulate Smith's success. To no avail. Nobody even got close to chipping away the precedent she had already established. The public would always link *God Bless America* and Kate Smith.

Smith recorded the anthem for RCA Victor on March 21, 1939. It became a classic standard that has been reissued many times. The piece soon ranked third among sheet music sales. She would also sing it the 1943 Warner Brothers feature-length Berlin film *This Is the Army* in which she had a cameo role. (In 1932, she appeared in a similar capacity in Paramount's major film release featuring Bing Crosby and Stuart Erwin, *The Big Broadcast*.) Both Berlin and Smith assigned their royalties for the number to the God Bless America Foundation, supporting the Boy Scouts and Girl Scouts of America, a pact that still exists, although she continued receiving performance fees. Berlin said he wanted to give something back to his adopted country. He had emigrated from Russia at age five in 1893.

For three weeks following Armistice Day, Smith sang her heart out as she performed the number weekly. Omitting it the following week she was deluged with protests calling for it to be reinstated at once. She included it on nearly every program through the end of World War II and her listeners never seemed to grow tired of it.

As a result of Smith's highly visible bent toward patriotism — a fervid expression of love and concern for her homeland — the critics quickly took notice. Reviewer John Crosby observed that she was "presented as a sort of American institution like Thanksgiving." Once, on television, the camera panned rolling waves on rocky shores followed by a cut to the U.S. flag. "I half expected her to sing the Constitution in C-sharp minor," wrote Crosby. Said another: "*God Bless America* turned her into a sort of singing Statue of Liberty." As a result, yet another analyst claimed Smith was "considered a national institution." One source observed: "Singer and song joined together to create an imperishable emblem of America."

The pinnacle in her upward mobility as an unpaid, flag-waving American ambassador probably occurred when President Franklin D. Roosevelt invited her to the White House in 1939 during a state visit by the king and queen of England. Presenting her to them, he remarked: "Your majesties, this is Kate Smith. This is America!" ("This is Kate Smith — This is America" was inscribed on her pink granite mausoleum nearly five decades hence.)

On October 26, 1982, Ronald Reagan, then president, went to Raleigh, North Carolina, where Kate Smith spent her final years, to present her the Presidential Medal of Freedom. In formal remarks, he allowed:

> The voice of Kate Smith is known and loved by millions of Americans, young and old. In war and peace, it has been an inspiration. Those simple but deeply moving words, "God bless America," have taken on added meaning for all of us because of the way Kate Smith sang them. Thanks to her they have become a cherished part of all our lives, an undying reminder of the beauty, the courage and the heart of this great land of ours. In giving us a magnificent, selfless talent like Kate Smith, God has truly blessed America.

Late in her career Smith would inspire a revival of that signature song. While she would be asked to perform it on the occasion of the nation's bicentennial during a special "Stars and Stripes Show" televised from Oklahoma City on June 30, 1976 — one of her last public appearances —

Pianist Jack Miller became Kate Smith's permanent orchestra conductor in 1933. He looks over a piece of music with the singing star. The band eventually included 27 members and the show required five composer-arrangers while including a 12-piece vocal ensemble all preparing unremittingly for their daily and weekly performances.

1973 to 1975 she turned up to sing *God Bless America* prior to their games. Most of the time the team won when Smith was present. Officials noted that, even if she didn't attend, when they played a recording of her singing the anthem the Flyers usually won. It was an unusual capstone to a career that supported many enterprises, then reaching professional sports.

Aside from Smith's highly successful midday radio venture, her fame proliferated as a vocalist of universal appeal on broadcast series she hosted as well as those hosted by others. For the record, on radio—in addition to those features already named—she presided over *Kate Smith Sings*. Initially a nighttime outing over CBS in 1945, it soon segued into a variety program commanding a live audience. Under that title the program shifted to MBS in 1948 with a change in format: as disc jockeys, Smith and Collins spun her recordings. She joined a fourth chain, ABC, in 1949 for a mixed bag labeled *Kate Smith Calling* in which she

she gained the unusual oddity of becoming, of all things, a good luck charm for the Philadelphia Flyers ice hockey team. "It was the ... most unexplainable, and the most wonderful and memorable partnership imaginable, unmatched anywhere in the history of sports—the partnership of a sixty-six-year-old pop singer of thirty years before with a rough and crazy bunch of mostly Canadians called the Broad Street Bullies, all bound together by the singing of a patriotic song about America," acknowledges a contemporary Web site. On several occasions by special request from sang, talked and telephoned listeners at home. *The Kate Smith Show*, combining records, talks and guests, premiered over NBC in 1951. Her final aural network series as a host, also titled *The Kate Smith Show*, ran weekday mornings for a year over MBS in 1958. In the meantime, she appeared as a guest on other entertainers' programs, including some headlined by Jack Benny, Benny Goodman, Bob Hope and Walter Winchell.

By September 1933, Jack Miller, who had accompanied her on piano in earlier radio days, was selected as Smith's permanent musical director for radio and then television. In time he would conduct a 27-piece orchestra for Smith's shows and together they would generate work for five composers and arrangers, plus a dozen-voiced chorus directed by Ted Straeter. Andre Baruch was her most durable announcer, although Tom Shirley and Robert Trout each filled that spot briefly.

Incidentally, Smith was among a handful making television history at 10:15 P.M. on July 21, 1931, when CBS launched its video offensive with a 45-minute live gala. The variety broadcast aired over CBS's experimental W2XAB station in New York City featuring sportscaster Ted Husing as host and an introduction by New York mayor Jimmy Walker. Smith performed her signature *When the Moon Comes Over the Mountain* and the Boswell Sisters (then popular radio stars) and composer-conductor George Gershwin contributed to the celebratory inaugural. CBS' chief engineer speculated on "What to Expect of Television." The occasion followed NBC's foray into the small screen by a year.

While noting superlatives, radio historiographers have documented that — over her impressively lengthy career — only Kate Smith and one other individual, comedian Jack Benny, signed radio contracts that prevented them from being canceled from the air, with the singular exception of wartime emergencies. This was surely a testimony to the powerful influence wielded by the eminent entertainers and spoke volumes about their acceptance not only by the public but by the industry they represented. (Parenthetically, when Smith's CBS show was thrown against Benny's NBC Sunday night stronghold in 1946, she didn't fare nearly as well.)

By September 25, 1950, Smith was also hosting *The Kate Smith Hour*, a live daytime variety series, over NBC-TV, five afternoons weekly. It ran through June 18, 1954. Once again Collins took an active on-camera role just as he did behind it. Smith headlined a couple of other TV series: *The Kate Smith Evening Hour*, September 19, 1951–June 11, 1952, a Wednesday night variety hour over NBC; and *The Kate Smith Hour*, January 25–July 18, 1960, a Monday night musical performance over CBS. A plethora of star-studded entertainers showed up on her various series as guests, among them John Barrymore, Mary Boland, Greta Garbo, Grace George, Bert Lahr, Bert Lytell, Helen Menken, Edward G. Robinson, Margaret Sullivan and Henny Youngman. The singing McGuire Sisters made their network tube premier on Smith's TV series as did vocalist Josephine Baker and the Tommy Dorsey Orchestra, while U.S. Senator Robert Taft informed Smith's viewers in 1952 that he was running for president.

Significantly, by late 1950 the daytime TV series, while boasting an impressive 18.5 rating — and the first network show to measure in double digits in the sunshine hours — was also one of the priciest. The series required $13,000 a day to produce and involved a 91-member staff. NBC didn't come unglued over the gargantuan budget, however — a year later *Variety* observed that Smith was running neck-and-neck with CBS's Arthur Godfrey as the top commercial broadcasting personality, grossing $12 million annually with her radio and TV shows. No price could be placed on the resulting publicity and image for the chain. But Smith didn't fare well when NBC-TV flung her against Godfrey in prime time in the 1951-1952 season and her series soon folded. She was a nationally known broadcasting icon in the decade before Godfrey reached a similar pinnacle, a historiographer suggested.

Smith made at least 100 guest appearances on other video series including the programs of Pearl Bailey, Milton Berle, Johnny Carson, Perry Como, Mike Douglas, Jimmy Durante, Eddie Fisher, Tennessee

Ernie Ford, Jackie Gleason, Dean Martin, Garry Moore, Jim Nabors, Tony Orlando and Dawn, Donny and Marie Osmond, Jack Paar, Rowan and Martin, The Smothers Brothers, Sonny and Cher, Ed Sullivan, Lawrence Welk and Andy Williams. She turned up as a mystery guest on *What's My Line?* in 1963 and offered a hearty chortle for a week's worth of *Hollywood Squares* in 1976.

Kate Smith would also be responsible for perpetuating the careers of several well-known entertainers. Particularly was this true of her various radio series. Among them: (Bud) Abbott and (Lou) Costello (comedians), *The Aldrich Family* (sitcom with Ezra Stone), *Ethel and Albert* (domestic sitcom), Parker Fennelly (comic actor), Mark Goodson (radio director and most prolific radio–TV game show producer), Clyde Hager (comedian), *It Pays to Be Ignorant* (the comedy-quiz series), Bert Parks (vocalist, quiz show and Miss America Pageant host), Bea Wain (*Your Hit Parade* vocalist) and Henny Youngman (stand-up comedian).

She made records (at least 3,000 by one count), released volumes of sheet music, appeared in nine films (although she starred in only one, Paramount's *Hello Everybody!* in 1933), performed in a myriad of stage productions, wrote extensively for magazines and other periodicals and authored four books—*Living in a Great Big Way*, a 1938 autobiography; *Stories of Annabelle*, a children's volume issued in 1951 based on a segment of her TV series; *Kate Smith's "Company's Coming" Cookbook* in 1958; and *Upon My Life a Song*, a second autobiography published in 1960.

As she advanced in age with increasingly debilitating health problems, Smith would find herself without many close friends in either gender, possibly as a result of Ted Collins' years of discouraging her from forming those bonds. "She shunned other celebrities, preferring to associate with ordinary folks and she was suspicious of the motives of those who tried to get close to her. Could they be trusted or were they using her because of who she was?" an introspective examiner inquired.[9] It appears that the man who wrote her life story—who was also Smith's longtime friend—attempted to portray her life as objectively as he could. Thus his readers see the warts as well as the achievements in the life of the pop diva, a sort of behind-the-scenes "tell-all" exposé, written without malice.

Kate Smith's physical condition continued to decline. She died in Raleigh on June 17, 1986, at age 79. Her body was carried to Lake Placid. She left a magnanimous mark on several media—and in particular, radio. Most of all, she left a legacy to a nation that forever identified her as one of its most ardent patriots. The ether had provided her access to virtually every citizen in the land. She capitalized on the opportunities that she was given to instill deeply compelling ideologies that were not soon forgotten by the masses she had entertained for so long.

The Railroad Hour

Two of America's great industries met similar fates in the middle of the twentieth century. Innovative new performers overtook network radio and passenger trains. Television superseded the one while air travel replaced the other. The freight-moving rails simultaneously saw truckers gain mightily. Yet, in radio's fading days there was one aural feature that brought trains to the airwaves, albeit merely as an underwriter. *The Railroad Hour*, a high-budget affair focusing mainly on musical dramas, presented some of the greatest names of recording, stage, screen, radio and operatic concert halls. Along with singing host Gordon MacRae, it offered one of the zestiest packages of tuneful fare on the air. While the show never drew large audiences, those who found their way to it were treated with some of the most gratifying musical delicacies around. In what it attempted, there may have been none better. Had it appeared earlier in radio's halcyon era, it would surely have persisted longer.

Directors: Murray Bolen, Ken Burton, Fran Van Hartesveldt.

Host — Male Vocal Lead: Gordon MacRae.

Costars: Ann Ayars (soprano), Kenny Baker (actor/tenor), Marion Bell (actress/soprano), William Bendix (actor), Mimi Benzell (coloratura soprano), Eddie Bracken (actor), Francis X. Bushman (actor), Eddie Cantor (actor/pop vocalist), Leo Carillo (actor), Evelyn Case, Jeff Chandler (actor), Michael Checkov, Jan Clayton (actress), Nadine Conner (lyric soprano), Douglas Coulter (media executive), Doris Day (pop vocalist), Vivian Della Chiesa (soprano), Annamary Dickey (soprano), Joan Edwards (mezzo soprano), Leon Errol (actor), Virginia Haskins (soprano), Sterling Holloway (actor), Marian Hutton (pop vocalist), Gene Kelly (actor/dancer/pop vocalist), Dorothy Kirsten (soprano), Frances Langford (pop singer), Jeanette MacDonald (actress/soprano), Elaine Malbin (soprano), Irene Manning (soprano), Groucho Marx (comedian), Louise Massey (pianist/country vocalist), Adolphe Menjou (actor), Victor Moore (comedian), Patricia Morison (actress), Patrice Munsel (soprano), George Murphy (actor), Lloyd Norman, Lucille Norman (soprano), Jarmila Novotna (soprano), Irra Petina (mezzo-soprano), Jane Powell (soprano), Dorothy Sarnoff (soprano), Dinah Shore (pop vocalist), Ginny Simms (soprano), J. S. Smith, Jo Stafford (pop vocalist), Risë Stevens (mezzo-soprano), Gladys Swarthout (mezzo-soprano), Nell Tageman (mezzo-soprano), Blanche Thebom (mezzo-soprano), Martha Tilton (pop vocalist), Margaret Truman (pianist), Rudy Vallee (saxophonist/pop vocalist), Dorothy Warenskjold (lyric soprano), Margaret Whiting (pop vocalist), Eileen Wilson (pop vocalist), Ilene Woods (soprano), Frances Yeend (soprano).

Orchestra Conductors: Carmen Dragon (NBC), John Rarig (ABC).

Choral Director: Norman Luboff.

Choral Ensembles: Norman Luboff Choir, The Sportsmen.

Story Adaptations: Jerry Lawrence and Robert Lee.

Announcer: Marvin Miller.

Writers: Jean Holloway, Jerome Lawrence, Robert Lee.

Theme Song: *I've Been Working on the Railroad.*

Sponsor: Association of American Railroads.

Ratings: High—10.9 (1949-1950 season); low—4.1 (1953-1954); median—7.9. While the series presented many excellent performances, it seldom achieved the potential commensurate with its effort.

On the Air: October 4, 1948–April 25, 1949, ABC, Monday, 8:00–8:45 P.M. Eastern Time; May 2–September 26, 1949, ABC, 8:00–8:30 P.M.; October 3, 1949–June 21, 1954, NBC, 8:00–8:30 P.M.

* * *

The Railroad Hour wasn't the first radio series to generate thrills growing out of a railway connotation. *Empire Builders*, sponsored by Great Northern Railroad, which appeared over NBC Blue from 1928 to 1931, is cited as the ether's first action-packed thriller adventure. Its tales of the rails spotlighted the recurring talents of actors Don Ameche and Harvey Hayes. The series offered an early precedent for the tradition that *The Railroad Hour* rode to a conclusion in the sunset of radio's glory days.

The latter feature started out like this:

ANNOUNCER: Ladies and gentlemen, *The Railroad Hour!*
SFX: Train whistle blast, hiss of escaping steam, chugging locomotive and cars.
ANNOUNCER: And here comes our star-studded show train!
CHORUS (*over music, sounding like "Choo Choo"*): Oooo Oooo!
ANNOUNCER: Tonight the Association of American Railroads presents the great Irving Berlin musical *Miss Liberty* starring Gordon MacRae and his bright young guest Virginia Haskins. Our choir is under the direction of Norman Luboff and our music is prepared and conducted by Carmen Dragon. Yes, tonight another memorable musical play is brought to you by the American Railroads, the same railroads that bring you most of the food you eat, the clothes you wear, the fuel you burn, and all the other things you use in your daily life. And now, here is our star, Gordon MacRae!
CHORUS (*over music, humming a single line*): *I've Been Working on the Railroad.*
STUDIO AUDIENCE APPLAUSE

The opening of *The Railroad Hour* must have made railfans utterly giddy even though the show was never about trains, unless by coincidence. Rather, its greater appeal was to popular and semiclassical music lovers who enjoyed operettas, Broadway and film musicals, the lives of legendary composers and writers like Robert Schumann, waltz king Johann Strauss and Mark Twain, plus further cabaret venues for talented artists. "It was," observed one critic, "the best show of its kind since Jessica Dragonette had starred in the short-lived *Palmolive Beauty Box Theatre* during the spring of 1937."[1] While a handful of its 299 performances were penned exclusively for *The Railroad Hour*, the compositions of George Gershwin, Gilbert and Sullivan,

Victor Herbert, Jerome Kern, Franz Lehar, Richard Rodgers and Oscar Hammerstein II, and Sigmund Romberg predominated.

Gordon MacRae rose to the occasion weekly, lending a commanding quality to whatever musical potpourri had been selected. Invariably he appeared in perfect form, able to fulfill whatever an outing demanded, seemingly with ease. He was one of the most gifted singers of his day and possibly the preeminent baritone of the 1950s. *Life* magazine christened him "radio's most versatile singer." While his radio career would be but a launching pad for still more expressive achievements, had it not been for the aural medium, and especially *The Railroad Hour*, he might never have gained the spotlight among America's leading male vocalists. Did destiny project him?

Born in East Orange, New Jersey, on March 12, 1921, young Gordon MacRae was attracted to music from the start. He was influenced both by his dad, "Wee Willie" MacRae, an early local radio personality, and his mom, a renowned concert pianist. The boy the couple doted on mastered the clarinet, piano and saxophone. He joined the high school drama club and won several acting roles. Those that called for singing were particularly alluring. Later, he attended Deerfield (Massachusetts) Academy, a prep school where he performed in amateur theatricals. In 1940, at age 19, he won a vocal competition and with it a two-week singing engagement at the New York World's Fair accompanied by bands fronted by Les Brown and Harry James.

Horace Heidt hired him that year as a singer with his entourage. (Heidt had a penchant for turning up future stars. Frankie Carle, Art Carney, Larry Cotton, Al Hirt, Ronnie Kemper, The King Sisters and Fred Lowrey were his alumni.) MacRae's identification with Heidt ended when the singer joined the Air Force as a navigator, serving his country from 1942 to 1944.

On his return, MacRae debuted on Broadway in *Junior Miss*. In 1946, he reappeared there in Ray Bolger's revue *Three to Make Ready*. Capitol Records agents spotted him in the show and, in 1947, signed him to a recording contract that prevailed for more than two decades. In the meantime, he was already getting his feet wet in radio.

His first attempt, *The Gordon MacRae Show*, though brief, gave him a "feel" for the ether while exposing him to a wider audience. The five-day-a-week sustaining musical variety feature over CBS premiered on December 3, 1945, and lasted through March 21, 1946. The newcomer was picked up by NBC and carried for another season (1946-1947). Vocalists appearing with MacRae in those days were little-known Marian Bell and Sheila Stevens backed by Archie Bleyer's (at CBS) and Johnny Guarnieri's (at NBC) orchestras. MacRae's announcer was Dan Seymour of *Aunt Jenny's Real Life Stories* and later, *We, the People* fame.

Simultaneously, MacRae headlined a brief 1946 variety series for CBS titled *Skyline Roof*. Archie Bleyer, then just launching his career as Arthur Godfrey's multiple-series bandleader, accompanied him again in a program of vocals and instrumentals. Harry Clark announced on that one. In the same time frame (1947) MacRae was also singing for a quarter-hour Tuesdays and Thursdays over NBC for Gulf Oil Corporation for its Gulfspray insect repellent.

A subsequent series under the long-running title *The Texaco Star Theater* (with several permutations since 1938) added MacRae as host from January 11–September 15, 1948, on CBS. It ran through March 21 on Sunday nights and from March 24 on Wednesday nights, always for the Texas Company's Texaco gasoline and oil products and services. Vocalist Evelyn Knight and comedian Alan Young flanked MacRae. Jeff Alexander, perpetually identified as bandmaster of *The Amos 'n' Andy Show*, was choral director. Victor Young's orchestra accompanied and John Reed King, emcee of his own CBS quiz program, *Give and Take*, announced.

All of the preliminaries prepared Gordon MacRae for his biggest series in radio, *The Railroad Hour*, which bowed on October 4, 1948, over ABC. It would expose him to still more music lovers. The show premiered as an expensive 45-minute extravaganza on Monday nights underwritten by the Association of American Railroads. It continued on NBC in its second season as a half-hour showcase featuring some of the very biggest names as MacRae's costars. It remained there through June 21, 1954.

MacRae's career spiraled upward in other directions simultaneously. In addition to his long-term recording contract, the year he launched *The Railroad Hour* he signed a seven-year pact with Warner Brothers to appear in major motion picture productions. His first, *The Big Punch*, released in 1948, was a nonmusical. But that would soon change.

The following year he starred in the first of a string of musicals, *Look for the Silver Lining* (1949). His other tune-filled silver screen triumphs included *The Daughter of Rosie O'Grady* (1950), *Tea for Two* (1950), *West Point Story* (1950), *On Moonlight Bay* (1951), *The Desert Song* (1953), *Three Sailors and a Girl* (1953), *By the Light of the Silvery Moon* (1953), *Oklahoma!* (1955), *Carousel* (1956) and *The Best Things in Life Are Free* (1956). But in filmgoers' minds, MacRae was always remembered for two incomparable parts, as Curly in *Oklahoma!* and Billy Bigelow in *Carousel*. Nothing quite surpassed those performances. Both were Richard Rogers and Oscar Hammerstein II collaborations and in both films MacRae played opposite movie newcomer Shirley Jones. Across his extensive career he appeared in 18 celluloid productions and sang the title song for *The Last Command* (1955). His final film, *The Pilot*, was released in 1979.

On CBS's *Lux Radio Theater*, MacRae reprised his starring role in *On Moonlight Bay* opposite actress Jane Wyman on the broadcast of May 5, 1952. A few weeks earlier, on March 20, 1952, he played opposite Phyllis Thaxter in a recreation of the movie *Christmas in Connecticut* for CBS's *Stars in the Air*.

Network radio would continue to provide an opportunity for MacRae's services to its uttermost days. He may have been the final guest host substituting for a vacationing Don McNeill on *The Breakfast Club* over ABC for multiple weeks in August 1968. After nearly 36 years on the air that durable series was cancelled on December 27, 1968.

In the late 1950s, MacRae began suffering from alcohol addiction. By his own admission he was "picked up for drunk driving" during the filming of *Carousel*. Although it troubled him for many years, he conquered alcohol's hold in the 1970s and was able to counsel others with the dependence.

While *The Railroad Hour* was still running on radio, in 1953 MacRae branched out into video, initially substituting for host Eddie Fisher when he was absent from his *Coke Time* series on NBC-TV. MacRae was soon substituting for other major stars on the small screen including Perry Como, Jackie Gleason and Ed Sullivan. Between November 1954 and November 1955 he appeared on NBC-TV's *Colgate Comedy Hour* a total of 14 times, 11 of those as host. He was a frequent guest on others' shows, too, sometimes several times, including headliners Polly Bergen, Joey Bishop, Pat Boone, Dick Clark, Perry Como, Sammy Davis Jr., Mike Douglas, Jimmy Durante, Tennessee Ernie Ford, David Frost, Jackie Gleason, Merv Griffin, Art Linkletter, Dean Martin, Garry Moore, Jack Paar, Martha Raye, Dinah Shore, Red Skelton and Ed Sullivan.

From March 5 through August 27, 1956, he presided over his own weekly quarter-hour *Gordon MacRae Show* on NBC-TV. It included a choral group, The Cheerleaders, and Van Alexander's Orchestra. The set for the live production was a replica of MacRae's living room with a large picture window peering onto a scene appropriate for the melodies performed on each individual show.

MacRae continued turning up all over the television channels, often in the company of his wife, actress Sheila MacRae, whom he met while performing in summer stock in the 1940s at Millpond Playhouse in Roslyn, Long Island. She later played Alice Kramden in Jackie Gleason's *The Honeymooners* on CBS-TV. MacRae made nine appearances on CBS's *What's My Line?*, sometimes as a panelist but most often as a mystery guest, frequently accompanied by Sheila. He turned up on lots of other game shows including *Beat the Clock, The Celebrity Game, Masquerade Party, Match Game, Musical Chairs, Password, Snap Judgment, Stump the Stars* and others. He was a singing favorite on *The Bell Telephone Hour*, appearing there four times. He also played in an occasional dramatic role on the tube, as a sheriff in *McCloud* in 1974, for example. He appeared in several Rogers and Hammerstein tributes, including his last televised appearance on March 9, 1985.

MacRae was the father of actress Meredith MacRae whose most memorable role was from 1966 to 1970 as Billie Jo Bradley in the CBS-TV country comedy *Petticoat Junction*. Earlier, she played Mike Douglas's girlfriend, Sally Ann, on *My Three Sons* (1963–1965, ABC-TV). She made her film debut with her father and Doris Day in *By the Light of the Silvery Moon*. Meredith MacRae devoted much of her life to charity work and died at 56 in 2000.

Gordon MacRae died on January 24, 1986, at his home in Lincoln, Nebraska, a victim of pneumonia, the result of complications of mouth and jaw cancer.

In addition to *The Railroad Hour's* MacRae, a star of a number of mediums, about three score guest performers—who most often played the feminine leads opposite MacRae's masculine role—included some of the legendary names of the Broadway stage, radio, movies, recordings and operatic and semiclassical concert halls. A half-dozen of that number were on hand for the radio series so often they might have been mistaken for resident status.

Lucille Norman was first in number of appearances with 73 in all, including a string of 23 consecutive performances between May and October 1949 and another 19 in a row between May and September 1950. Dorothy Warenskjold followed with 61 appearances that included 13 between July and September 1951 and another 21 from May to October 1953. Third in durability was Dorothy Kirsten, whose aggregate totaled 39 performances; Nadine Conner, with 27, was fourth; Mimi Benzell, with 11, was fifth; and Jane Powell, with nine, sixth. Their careers included numerous opportunities performing in other venues. [For a complete directory of *Railroad Hour* guest artists and presentations, the reader is referred to the compilation of radio logs titled *Radio Drama: American Programs, 1932–1962* (McFarland, 2000) by Martin Grams Jr. See pages 403–409.]

Lucille Norman was born June 15, 1926, in Lincoln, Nebraska. By odd coincidence, this was the same town in which her *Railroad Hour* costar, Gordon MacRae, was living when he died. A biographer noted, "MacRae hoped to sing on screen with the photogenic soprano but her few movie parts were with others and generally undistinguished."

After singing with the Columbus (Ohio) Symphony at a tender age, at 12 she was chosen to try out on *The Metropolitan Opera Auditions on the Air*. Her scheduled performance, on December 7, 1941, was broken up by news coverage of the Japanese attack on Pearl Harbor. She pursued musical interests by studying voice at the Cincinnati Conservatory of Music, the same institute that graduated vocalist Jane Froman and dramatist Virginia Payne (*Ma Perkins*).

At 16, Norman was performing on a regional show, *Names of Tomorrow*, in southern California over Los Angeles' KNX. At 17, she appeared on NBC's *The Time, the Place and the Tune* for a brief run. By the early 1950s, she was on *Al Goodman's Musical Album* on NBC and was singing light opera in concert halls. She died April 1, 1998, at Glendale, California. While her name isn't well recognized beyond *The Railroad Hour*, Lucille Norman made an enduring impression there with appearances second only to Gordon MacRae.

Dorothy Warenskjold was born in 1921 in San Leandro, California. Her mother was a concert pianist and at age three, little Dorothy was taking piano lessons. At nine, at her dad's bidding, she also took up violin. In 1940, she received a bachelor's degree from the University of California, Berkeley. Between 1948 and 1964, she sang with several symphonies, including a long run with the San Francisco Opera. When her father, who had come to see her perform with that group, died shortly before the show was to begin, she sang anyway in a "deeply touching performance." She appeared on numerous radio and television series. In addition to *The Railroad Hour*, Warenskjold often crossed the station break on Monday nights to perform on *The Voice of Firestone* on NBC, later on ABC, in dual mediums.

By mid-twentieth century she was leader of the True Name Society, an outfit whose members pledged to retain their legal monikers in professional life. They included notables like Leonard Bernstein, Rosemary Clooney and Marguerite Piazza.

"Once people learn my name, they never forget it," Warenskjold told a reporter. She once turned down an attractive movie role because the production house insisted that her name be shortened. The lyric soprano was producer-director-vocalist of the Dorothy Warenskjold Musical Theater between 1969 and 1971. Starting in 1984 she was a visiting professor in music at the University of California at Los Angeles.

Dorothy Kirsten was born July 6, 1910, in Montclair, New Jersey, and died November 18, 1992, in Los Angeles. In between, the talented and stunning lyric soprano was a popular figure on such broadcast features as *Keepsakes*, a musical variety series that she co-hosted with Mack Harrell over NBC Blue from September 5, 1943, to September 24, 1944; *Highways in Melody* (her appearances sporadic between 1940 and 1948, on NBC), *Kraft Music Hall* (1949, NBC), where she sang with Nelson Eddy; *Light Up Time* (1949-1950, NBC), a regular on a show hosted by Frank Sinatra; and *The Voice of Firestone* (1950s, NBC and ABC radio and television), as an intermittent guest vocalist. She also experienced some success in movies, appearing in *The Great Caruso* with Mario Lanza and *Mr. Music* with Bing Crosby.

Kirsten underwrote her vocal lessons and studies at Julliard School of Music by singing with dance orchestras in choral groups performing with vocalist Kate Smith. In 1942, she appeared as Mimi in *La Boheme* with the San Carlo Opera Company in a New York premiere. Three years later, Kirsten went on stage at the Metropolitan Opera in the same role. Kirsten would always maintain that she was a singing actress as opposed to an opera singer. Despite the assertion, she gained an unprecedented three-decade run with the Met before retiring. A *New York Times* music critic claimed her final appearance demonstrated "the vocal control and dramatic acuity of a prima donna in mid-career."

Nadine Conner was born February 20, 1907, at Los Angeles, California. (Her maiden name was Evelyn Nadine Henderson, although she married at 18, establishing a new surname before she became famous.) After appearing on radio with some classmates at age 19 while a student at the University of Southern California, she was engaged by Los Angeles' station KHL as staff vocalist. That catapulted her into a singing stint over CBS's *California Melodies* and vocals on bills with Bing Crosby and Al Jolson. At 34, she debuted at the Metropolitan Opera as Pamina in *The Magic Flute*. She remained with the Met for two decades, returning to California in 1960 to devote full time to her family, having remarried and adopted children a few years earlier. She died in Los Alamitos, California, on March 1, 2003.

In the years preceding retirement, Conner, a lyric soprano "of even scale and purity of tone," turned up all over the radio dial. Besides *The Railroad Hour*, she performed regularly on *Show Boat* with Lanny Ross (1937, NBC), *The Song Shop* which she hosted (1938, CBS), *The Nelson Eddy Show* (1942-1943, CBS), *Salute to Youth* (1943-1944, NBC), *Kraft Music Hall* with Nelson Eddy (1947, NBC) and *The Voice of Firestone* where she was a recurring guest artist (1950s, NBC and ABC radio and television).

Mimi Benzell was born April 6, 1924, in Bridgeport, Connecticut. She became one of those budding talents "discovered" by Major Edward Bowes on his *Original Amateur Hour* (along with Teresa Brewer, Jack Carter, Robert Merrill, Beverly Sills and Frank Sinatra) at CBS. The lyric coloratura had a colorful professional career extending from Broadway to opera to personal engagements to radio back to Broadway and winding up with radio where it all began. The theater was next, where she was cast as a teenager in the starring role of *Rosalinda* on the Great White Way. Not long afterward, at age 21, she debuted at the Metropolitan Opera as Queen of the Night in *The Magic Flute*. But her career lasted only four seasons there.

In 1949, Benzell refused to sign a contract extension when the Met declined to allow her to take a two-week supper club engagement in New York City. It took her a dozen years to regain the level of accomplishment she had realized previously with the Met. In the intervening years she turned to radio and shows like *The Railroad Hour, The Jack Pearl and Mimi Benzell Show* (1951, NBC) and popular standby *The Voice of Firestone*. She reached the pinnacle of success a second time in 1961 when cast opposite Robert Weede as a star of the long-running Broadway musical *Milk and Honey*. Benzell's career ended on a high note as she hosted a daily two-hour talk show, *Lunch with Mimi*, over the NBC flagship station in New York, WNBC. A critic characterized that venture as "diffuse, freewheeling and sporadically interesting." Benzell died at Manhasset, New York, on December 23, 1970.

Jane Powell was born under the name Suzanne Burce on April 1, 1929, in Portland, Oregon. A pundit described her as a "perennial teenage soprano who looked like the girl next door in some 20 films." (At 59 she wrote her memoir, *The Girl Next Door—and How She Grew*.) Indeed, she seemed to qualify as a forever teen. By age 15, she signed a film contract with Metro-Goldwyn-Mayer after singing pop and classical standards on Portland's KOIN radio and winning top honors with an aria from *Carmen* on CBS's *Hollywood Showcase* in Los Angeles. Her movies included *A Date with Judy* (1948), *The Girl Most Likely* (1957), *Hit the Deck* (1955), *Royal Wedding* (1951), *Seven Brides for Seven Brothers* (1954), *Small Town Girl* (1953), *Three Sailors and a Girl* (1953), *Two Weeks with Love* (1948) and several more. In her film debut in 1944, *Song of the Open Road* with W. C. Fields, she played a girl named Jane Powell. The name stuck.

Before signing with MGM, the young vocalist was tapped by NBC in the 1943-1944 season as Charlie McCarthy's girlfriend on *The Chase and Sanborn Hour.* MGM, however, vetoed any weekly radio series. Powell became a guest on several NBC shows in the 1940s including *Carnation Contented Hour, Harvest of Stars* and *The Railroad Hour* (beginning on ABC). When the movie musicals faded, Powell concentrated on nightclubs and provincial theater, appeared in TV dramas (1970s) and succeeded Debbie Reynolds in a 1973 Broadway reprisal of *Irene.* In the 1980s and 1990s, she appeared at Carnegie Hall and turned up on several television specials.

All the other leading ladies on *The Railroad Hour* appeared in two or three shows at most. That coterie, nonetheless, was comprised of some pretty impressive names, among them Doris Day, Jeanette MacDonald, Patrice Munsel, Dinah Shore, Ginny Simms, Jo Stafford, Risë Stevens, Gladys Swarthout, Blanche Thebom, Margaret Whiting and Eileen Wilson. On one very special occasion, an immediate past president's daughter sang with MacRae — Margaret Truman, on March 17, 1953.

During *The Railroad Hour's* initial season, several of Hollywood's leading men performed in those dramatic musicals, too, although they appeared only once. William Bendix, Eddie Cantor, Jeff Chandler, Gene Kelly, Groucho Marx, Adolphe Menjou, George Murphy and Rudy Vallee were among their number. A large dramatic company was available for those shows and adaptable announcer Marvin Miller frequently doubled in acting roles, even singing when an occasion demanded. Miller was considered one of radio's most versatile announcer-actors, by the way, turning up in no fewer than 15 daytime serials and one of the most prolific voices on the air elsewhere for many years. From 1955 to 1960 he played the dramatic role of *The Millionaire's* personal envoy, Michael Anthony, on CBS-TV.

The Railroad Hour productions were adapted — in a phrase repetitiously uttered on the air — by "Lawrence and Lee," although their first names seemed overlooked in a rush to list the credits. They *did* have first names, however — Jerry Lawrence and Robert Lee. And the shows they adapted led to many grand nights of singing. Here, alphabetically, are a few:

Anything Goes
Around the World in Eighty Days
Babes in Toyland
Carousel (twice)
The Desert Song (thrice)
HMS Pinafore
Holiday Inn (thrice)
Kiss Me Kate (twice)
The Merry Widow (four times)
The Mikado
Naughty Marietta (twice)
No, No Nanette
Oklahoma!
The Pirates of Penzance
Porgy and Bess
Showboat (five times)
The Song of Norway (thrice)
State Fair (thrice)
The Student Prince (thrice)
Swan Lake
The Vagabond King (thrice)
The Wizard of Oz

The fact that there was an earlier radio series that incontrovertibly inspired the formula adopted by *The Railroad Hour* must not be slighted. On October 5, 1940, *The Chicago Theater of the Air* premiered over the MBS chain, having already debuted on May 9, 1940, over the Windy City's WGN. Its overriding focus — at least at its start — was the operetta, one of the provinces in which *The Railroad Hour* was to concentrate a few years later. A survey taken by WGN found that a significant portion of its audience favored the music of opera and the escapism of drama. Operettas seemed a rewarding solution.

The Chicago Theater of the Air prevailed through May 7, 1955, being a Saturday midday feature sustained (never sponsored) for an hour. Its 449 program bills offered many of the shows that *The Railroad Hour* listeners became accustomed to on Monday night, to wit: *Babes in Toyland, The Desert Song, Finian's Rainbow, Hansel and Gretel, HMS Pinafore, Madame Butterfly, The Merry Widow, The Mikado, Naughty Marietta, No No Nannette, The Student Prince, The Vagabond King* and more. Many of the most favorably received were repeated frequently. In addition, there were condensed renderings of operas like *Carmen, Faust, La Traviata* and *Rigoletto*, all reminiscent of the live Metropolitan Opera concerts that aired a short time later on Saturday afternoons.

The guests on this classy Chicago recital had many familiar names. Artists like Igor Gorin, Virginia Haskins, Lauritz Melchior, James Melton, Conrad Thibault and Thomas L. Thomas were regulars. They, and others, were prominent on one or more of NBC's Monday night songfests.

Staging for the Chicago performances was engaging. An orchestra, composed largely of members of the Chicago Symphony, was down front under the baton of maestro Henry Weber. On the stage to the audience's right was a 30-voice ensemble led by choral director Robert Trendler. Opposite them, at the left of the stage, were

Musical movie starlet Jane Powell turned up regularly as one of host Gordon MacRae's singing costars for weekly performances of *The Railroad Hour*. The charming lady was one of several MacRae was routinely paired with for re-creations of operettas, Broadway and film musicals, and the lives of legendary composers and writers, tailored in lavish productions.

the dramatic actors. Soloists occupied center stage. Col. Robert R. McCormick, *Chicago Tribune* publisher and WGN's owner, offered what one critic termed "a dry history lesson, usually of five-to-ten-minute duration" during intermission — similar to some of the Met broadcasts.

The Chicago Theater of the Air undoubtedly set a broadcasting precedent. But even as it did so, it never enjoyed the notoriety and loyalty that an NBC show that emulated its pioneering techniques obviously perfected.

The Railroad Hour deviated from its standard practice of presenting stage, screen and operetta productions now and then to offer tributes to the lives of musicians Hoagy Carmichael, Stephen Foster, Richard Rodgers and Oscar Hammerstein II and others of that ilk. The producers found other topics to capitalize on like a salute to the Chicago World's Fair in 1949, Christmas perennially and other themes occasionally. A major departure was a review, year by year, of the music of a given era. A few times those features concentrated on multiyear periods but mostly they highlighted songs made famous in, for instance, 1937 or 1926 or whenever. Invariably, the music selected was stirring and left those tuning in jubilant.

The commercials, concentrated at each week's midpoint, didn't simply enumerate the merits of rail travel but were often a political platform for the railroads. Announcer Marvin Miller pressed the group's legislative strategy as a threatened industry steadily lost ground to its menacing rivals, the trucking and airline behemoths.

As each week's performance drew to a close, *The Railroad Hour* mined a scenario that had long been part of the landscape at the infinitely more popular *Lux Radio Theater* on CBS, also on Monday nights. Following the show, MacRae and his leading ladies (and gentlemen of celebrity status) exchanged humorous jibes in a brief tête-à-tête before revealing to the audience—a group that always appeared primed to audibly "ooohhh" and "aaahhh" at a precise moment—the name of the play and costar for the following week's show. It was exactly the same reaction elicited from *Lux's* live studio audience.

Next there was a blast from a train whistle. Just then Marvin Miller cried "All aboard!" MacRae deftly reminded listeners of the obvious fact: "Well, it looks as though we're ready to pull out and so, until next week, goodbye." The locomotive's bell clanged as the old steamer slowly headed from the station.

The series moved from ABC to NBC in its second year and remained there until the end of the run. In switching chains, it gained—at least, from NBC's perspective, if not from the listeners'—a clear benefit by being clustered with a trio of other important weekly half-hour musical showcases also aired on Monday night: *The Voice of Firestone* (at 8:30), *The Bell Telephone Hour* (at 9:00) and *The Cities Service Band of America* (at 9:30). Long before that day, the networks had witnessed the advantage of grouping several comedy programs back-to-back just as they had mysteries, soap operas and juvenile adventure serials. It certainly made sense that—if a listener was attracted by a particular strain—he might stay tuned for more of the same if it surrounded a favorite show. The same practice is still followed by today's TV sitcoms and drama hours.

The Railroad Hour should have been in an advantageous spot for audience building on NBC, thanks to the astute schedule planning. Alas, for not altogether clear reasons, that still didn't translate into superior ratings for much of the show's run, and certainly not when compared against a portion of the remainder of NBC's Monday night lineup. A contributing factor probably was that the other musical gems programmed there had aired so many more years than *Railroad* and, therefore, had a greater opportunity to establish a well-entrenched following. Beyond that, of course, was the fact that *Railroad* appeared just as television was gaining a foothold in American living rooms, leading to increased competition for people's time and leisure focus.

The productions themselves were top-notch and little expense was spared in producing a quality product. *The Railroad Hour* was a class act by every gauge. And as the final train pulled out of the radio station, the listeners knew it was splendid to have been aboard.

The Sacred Singers

Church music was all over the dial from the 1920s to the 1950s. You could start your day with it each morning with "Hymn Time" on Don McNeill's *Breakfast Club*. Large segments of Sunday's agendas were driven by it. It poured forth from broadcast outlets large and small. While some of it was recorded, most local stations of any size maintained one or more paid or volunteer soloists along with vocal and instrumental ensembles, organists and pianists. There seldom appeared to be a dearth of individuals willing to sing praises to the Lord, possibly because that was music infinite numbers of listeners could identify with out of their own experience. It was natural that several hymn-singing features sprang up to offer comfort and assurance, particularly in times of duress. A handful of those programs persisted for years. Radio readily incorporated church music into multiple formats, too, including major productions like *The Big Show* (*May the Good Lord Bless and Keep You*).

* * *

The fact that precious little in the annals of a few documentaries on golden age radio devote mention to religious broadcasting—and its music, as an explicit concentration—hints that such programming really wasn't very prevalent. But those absences belie the fact that a great deal of radio's origins were bathed in messages of redemption, sometimes celebrated by fiery sermons but more often by appealing to the ears through musical forms that resonated with listeners out of their individual backgrounds.

As early as 1923—three years before the birth of the National Broadcasting Company—the organization's future flagship station, New York's WEAF, presented the singing of baritone Arthur Billings Hunt. A musicologist, Hunt was an authority on American hymns and folk songs. By the time NBC was launched his reputation had earned him the chance to anchor the chain's *Midweek Hymn Sing* (1926–1936) while also hosting the *Shut-In Hour* locally over New York's WNEW.

On the network series, Hunt was accompanied the first year by a mixed quartet consisting of tenors Clyde and Hunt Dengler, contralto Helen Janke and soprano Muriel Wilson, along with George Vause, pianist. By 1927, the quartet was comprised of Hunt, tenor Richard Maxwell, Janke, and Muriel Savage, contralto, soon settling into a weekly quarter-hour on Tuesday nights. George Vause remained at the keyboard. The program reportedly received more than 100,000 requests for specific hymns within one six-year segment.

It was a primitive time in which all sorts of program formats were tested. The fact that Hunt aired for 13 consecutive years during that pioneering epoch suggests that millions of Americans were receptive to gospel singing, which had often stemmed from lifelong traditions. Local radio stations regularly picked up church services and programmed hymn singing everywhere. Pittsburgh's KDKA was reportedly the first to do so, broadcasting a series titled *Sacred Song Concert* in the early 1920s. "Almost daily," noted one reviewer, "stations—large and small, urban and rural—paused for hymns and gospel songs."

Before Arthur Billings Hunt was network history, the national chains extended their grasp of hymn-singing to foster a weekday series titled *Hymns of All Churches* which was carried on one hookup or another for a dozen years (1935–1947), frequently in the midst of soap opera's dilemmas. (The program began on MBS, shifted to CBS in 1936, then NBC in 1938 while also running concurrently over CBS in 1941-1942, and left NBC for ABC in 1945. General Mills underwrote all but the Mutual year.) It featured baritone Joe Emerson and the Joe Emerson Choir. Emerson emanated from Cincinnati's WLW where he appeared as "The Bachelor of Song," warbling secular tunes.

The vocalist-choirmaster followed the network series with another on the web, *Joe Emerson's Hymn Time*, a quarter-hour weekdays at 3 o'clock over ABC between 1951 and 1954, also sponsored by General Mills. This alone suggests that there was an aural audience for hymn singing until virtually the close of radio's halcyon days, a pattern that had been implemented more than three decades before.

And prior to that, Edward McHugh, who launched his career in 1925 at Boston's WBZ, appeared as *The Gospel Singer* on network radio for a decade: 1933–1939, NBC Blue; 1938–1942, NBC; 1938, CBS; 1942-1943, NBC Blue. During part of this time he sang on three networks simultaneously, indicating the popularity of Christian hymnody. Most of his shows were scheduled five or six days a week. McHugh claimed to have performed over 3,000 hymns on his series, his most frequently requested number being *The Old Rugged Cross* according to *Radio Guide*.

There were many regional gospel music series that eventually saw their way to network status. Luther Sies offers background on one atypical feature growing out of Appalachia's culture.[1]

> The *Renfro Valley Barn Dance*, created by John Lair in 1937, was located in a replica of a nineteenth century Kentucky town. Lair, who had been born in Renfro Valley, Kentucky, went north in 1927 to become program director and music librarian at station WLS, Chicago. He was one of those who encouraged folk musicians to appear on the *National Barn Dance* and other WLS shows. Lair joined with country comedian [Benjamin "Whitey"] Ford and country-western singer Red Foley to buy some Kentucky land in 1937 with the intention of building a music barn.

By 1940, Lair's Saturday night barn dance was drawing a huge crowd, at times topping 10,000 paid patrons. So successful was it that the program appeared at one time or other on all four networks between 1938 and 1951, and it continued in syndication later. In the 1940s Lair, ever the entrepreneur, saw an opportunity to extend his fortune by instituting an exclusive religious-oriented country-folk music series to be established on the popularity of his Saturday night *Renfro Valley Barn Dance*. He added the *Renfro Valley Sunday Mornin' Gatherin'* and CBS carried a 45-minute segment at 8:30 A.M. weekly for several years in the 1940s and 1950s, sponsored by General Foods.

Lair penned an original theme song, *Take Me Back to Renfro Valley*, that was associated with the program throughout its life. The series consisted largely of hymns accompanied by an organ and sung by members of the audience (most of whom had attended the *Barn Dance* the night before) — gospel numbers familiar to singers and listeners alike. The enterprising Lair thus netted two nationwide audiences every weekend.

Popular radio organist Rosa Rio, whose chords could be heard daily for decades on soap operas and other dramatic series, offered an interesting slice of commentary on the instrument she played: "The organ has been associated with church music for hundreds of years. Its literature actually dates back to ancient times. Since most sacred music had been written for this instrument, radio also adopted it for programs of a religious nature. Sacred music played on a pipe or electric organ generated a warm, soothing feeling and gave spiritual comfort to listeners, especially shut-ins."[2]

Undoubtedly the most audible exponent of the organ, who often incorporated church music into his long run of weekly CBS recitals (1942–1958), was E. Power Biggs. Those brief interludes aired from the Germanic Museum at Harvard University on an Aeolian-Skinner classic-style organ put him in a class by himself.

Born in Westcliff, Exxex, on March 29, 1906, Biggs studied at the Royal Academy of Music in London. After touring America in 1929 as an ensemble soloist, he moved here the following year, becoming a citizen in 1937. Initially he held church and teaching positions before embracing a career as a recitalist, broadcaster and recording artist. His rise to prominence popularized the concert organ and organ music in general. He played with most major American orchestras.

On Biggs' weekly concert broadcasts given to music from many genres — while there was no singing on the air — multitudes of Americans tuning in who recognized the refrains of his memorable gospel melodies were quite likely humming right along with him. Biggs died March 10, 1977, in Boston.

All of the major churches or denominations maintained their own presences on radio via paid network features. Music was a vital part of these efforts. Baptists, Catholics, Christian Reformed, Lutheran, Seventh-Day Adventists and other churches and denominations produced weekly series. In addition, the networks themselves offered several productions that became permanent fixtures in their weekend agendas, all providing sacred music. Among the most durable: *The Church of the Air, The National Radio Pulpit, National Vespers, The Old-Fashioned Revival Hour* and *Radio Bible Class*.

Clearly the most memorable and resilient of the religious music programs, however, was one that went by several monikers. To some it was the *Salt Lake City Tabernacle Choir*. To others, the *Mormon Tabernacle Choir*. Purists, however, insisted that its proper designation was (and is) *Music and the Spoken Word from the Crossroads of the West* (*MSWCW*). The broadcasts of the 350-voice choir of the Church of Latter-Day Saints (the Mormons) have emanated from Temple Square, the church's headquarters, in Salt Lake City since 1924, according to one source, when it began locally over KEPT.[3] (If that is the case, it makes the series the longest running radio program in the world, exceeding the *Grand Ole Opry*'s longevity record dating to October 1925. Since that hasn't been challenged, the 1924 start date appears dubious. Even church literature advocates a launch of the Mormon broadcasts in 1929.)

The choir is still going strong today, heard weekly over a hookup of stations nationwide. Meanwhile, a Sunday daytime half-hour was still carried by CBS in the late 1970s.

On July 15, 1929, KSL, then a NBC Blue affiliate, began piping the broadcasts across the nation. When the station realigned with CBS in 1932, *MSWCW* moved with it. Professor Anthony C. Lund of Brigham Young University was the group's first choirmaster. Earl J. Glade produced and announced from the beginning. Upon Lund's death in 1935, J. Spencer Cornwall presided over the mass choir (1935–1957). Richard L. Evans assumed responsibilities as producer, director and announcer in 1930 and remained at the helm until his death in 1971. He was followed by Spencer Kinard, who was succeeded in 1990 by a one-time anchor of CNN Headline News in Atlanta, Lloyd Newell. The announcers' brief editorial vignettes ("The Spoken Word") in the midst of the half-hour musicale are still recalled by millions for their inspirational tone. Other famous organists to play the grand instrument have included Frank Asper, Clay Christiansen, Richard P. Condie, Richard Elliott, John Longhurst, Jerrold Ottley and Alexander Schreiner. The nonpaid choir, all church members representing many occupations, is purportedly the largest permanent singing group in the world. There is a long waiting list to audition for the choir and most aspirants have extensive singing and choral backgrounds. Members must be at least 25 years of age; they can participate until age 60 or 20 years' tenure, whichever comes first.

The organ itself is one of the best-known, most widely heard instruments in the nation. Australian convert Joseph Ridges built it out of straight-grained soft pine taken from southern Utah. He spent a dozen years shaping the seasoned logs into 2,000 pipes. The task was completed in 1858. The organ has subsequently been increased to 11,623 pipes in 206 rows, with the console featuring five 61-note keyboards and a 32-note keyboard.

Author Tom DeLong provides some helpful research on the matter of acoustics surrounding the vast domed performance venue seating 6,000 worshipers, indicating that the program's producers were working well ahead of their time.[4]

> The placement of microphones contributes significantly to the success of the weekly broadcasts. Initially, a single microphone picked up the Mormon Tabernacle Choir. However, because the large ensemble occupied considerable floor space, engineers began to notice a "sound lag" from mike to control room. To correct this, they installed nine microphones. The engineer for each broadcast — which had no full rehearsal due to the long-distance travel necessitated by some choir members — literally "played" his control board in the manner of an instrumentalist. Sopranos, altos, baritones, tenors, and bassos each utilized a mike. Their voices were "Mixed" with the pickup from a trio of microphones flanking the organ and from an all-directional one suspended from the 100-foot-high ceiling. The result was a rich stereolike sound, years before even hi-fi had come into the audio vocabulary.

(Parenthetically, a new auditorium was opened in 2000 to accommodate growing space requirements, but the tabernacle continues to house the choir and its radio, television and recording activities.)

The program has been simultaneously carried by hundreds of television stations for decades. By 2003 it was estimated that 2,000 radio and TV stations worldwide were airing the broadcasts.

Music and the Spoken Word arrives weekly with this epigraph: "Once more, we welcome you within these walls with music and the spoken word from the Crossroads of the West." Half an hour later, the organ tolling softly in the background, the announcer concludes with these words: "Again we leave you from within the shadows of the everlasting hills. May peace be with you this day and always."

In 2003, old-time radio researcher-writer Jim Snyder reported his impressions of multiple journeys to Temple Square to witness the Mormon broadcasts himself. A portion of his summary follows.[5]

> Visitors to Salt Lake City have the opportunity to hear the Mormon Tabernacle Choir two times each week. Each Thursday, from 8:00 to 9:30 P.M., a rehearsal for the Sunday broadcast is held. Visitors are free to wander in and out at their pleasure during the rehearsal. Each Sunday the *Music and the Spoken Word* broadcast begins at 9:30 A.M. although the doors are closed and visitors must be seated by 9:15 to avoid interruptions during the broadcast. There is no charge for attending these programs but visitors are asked to fill out a card before entering giving their name, address, and answering a yes or no question whether they wish to receive a complimentary copy of the *Book of Mormon*. Be warned, however, that based on my three visits, a couple months after your visit two missionaries will show up at your door with "your" *Book of Mormon* even if you checked 'no' on that entrance card.

The Mormons, and a significant contingent of their peers, discovered early that radio was a priceless means of communicating their messages of hope to the masses. Sacred music was most frequently the vehicle of choice in doing so. Their good intentions translated into reassurance and inspiration for vast numbers tuning in.

The Vocalists

Vocalists during the golden days of radio were utterly legion in number. Every music series and every variety show featured one or more soloists, duos, trios or vocal ensembles. Singers were endemic on many comedy and dramatic features. Traditionally, vocalists were about as ubiquitous as organists, pianists and other instrumentalists, appearing on a diversified assortment of recurring aural series.

Many of these virtuosos were stars in their own right. Some — whose primary achievements were habitually expressed in film, stage, opera, recordings, pop concerts, nightclubs, ballrooms, vaudeville, summer stock and touring circuits—frequented radio shows as guest performers. Others were there as a result of their links to specific bands and orchestras, often emanating from remote venues. Still more were radio entertainers first and foremost.

Some of these were confined to small studios, often accompanying themselves or maybe backed by a pianist or a small instrumental ensemble. Many others routinely performed in front of large studio audiences, being supported by grand orchestras comprising scores of skilled artists under the direction of well-recognized conductors.

Radio not only featured stars from other genres, it established the careers of numerous budding aspirants by providing them with instant, far-reaching adulation. Simultaneously, many lesser-known talents achieved discernible popularity from their exposure on the ether. Together it sustained a win-win climate for the artists, audiences, advertisers and airwaves.

Some of the premier vocalists — including singles, duos, trios and ensembles — that dominated the dial during radio's golden age are included in the two dozen biographical vignettes that follow. Most of the true "stars" are among them — *but not all*. Some are more properly represented in other chapters of this book for they were the magnets around which entire series were developed. Appearing elsewhere, for instance, are singing celebrities like Gene Autry, Bing Crosby, Vivian Della Chiesa, Jessica Dragonette, Evelyn MacGregor, Gordon MacRae, Frank Munn, Dinah Shore, Frank Sinatra, Kate Smith, Thomas L. Thomas and a nearly infinite register of operatic virtuosos. All of them emerge at more appropriate places in the text where their careers are duly honored along with the shows they signified. (Turn to the index for specific references.)

The author can pledge with integrity that he labored long and anxiously about whom to include and omit in the following summaries. The choices were never randomly made without weighing an individual's collective contributions to the medium and each artist's substantial impact on millions of listeners, which normally included multitudes of adoring and sometimes rabid fans. The reader can be reassured that each one profoundly enhanced the airwaves while maintaining a following that characterized the ether in the epoch in which he or she performed.

These facts, incidentally, were gathered from the works of radio historiographers and a wide range of biographies and other texts dealing with the era, plus incorporating voluminous data appearing on multiple Web sites that pertain to most of the artists. Painstaking effort was made to verify material found to be in conflict in duplicate sources. The author is convinced that the details presented here are as accurate as humanly possible at the time of its preparation.

Performers

THE ANDREWS SISTERS

Born: LaVerne (contralto) — July 6, 1911, Mound, Minnesota; Maxene (second soprano) — January 3, 1916, Mound, Minnesota; Patty (lead soprano) — February 16, 1918, Mound, Minnesota.
Died: LaVerne — May 8, 1967, Brentwood, California; Maxene — October 21, 1995, Hyannis, Massachusetts.
Signature Song: *(I'll Be with You in) Apple Blossom Time.*
Legendary Tunes: *Ac-Cent-Tchu-Ate the Positive, Along the Navajo Trail, Beat Me Daddy Eight to the Bar, Bei Mir Bist du Schoen, The Big Brass Band from Brazil, Boogie Woogie Bugle Boy, Chattanooga Choo-Choo, Christmas Island, Cuanto La Gusta, Don't Fence Me In, Don't Sit Under the Apple Tree, Ferryboat Serenade, Hold Tight — Hold Tight, I Can Dream Can't I?, I Wanna Be Loved, I Yi Yi Yi Yi, I'm Biting My Fingernails and Thinking of You, Is You Is or Is You Ain't My Baby?, Jingle Bells, Pistol Packin' Mama, Rhumboogie, Roll Out the Barrel, Rum and Coca-Cola, Say Si Si, Shoo-Shoo Baby, Sparrow in the Tree Top, Victory Polka, You Call Everybody Darling.*
Highlights: Veterans of the Midwestern vaudeville circuit, toured in teen years with Larry Rich's orchestra, influenced by Dixieland style of the predecessor Boswell Sisters; landed steady jobs with Leon Belasco's society orchestra (1936); enlarged focus, including swing era ballads, South American dance tunes, boogie-woogie numbers, novelties; big break an instant hit Decca recording of Yiddish *Bei Mir Bist du Schoen* (1938); often turned up in war years as guests on *Command Performance, Radio Hall of Fame* and later, *Stars on Parade*; entertained U. S. battle forces while recording 1,800-plus songs, selling 90 million-plus records, singular most popular feminine vocal ensemble of pre-rock era; "America's Wartime Sweethearts" who "gave hope to an entire country trying to survive the hardships of war" said a pundit; appeared in 17 films (1940–1948), often playing themselves (*Always a Bridesmaid, Buck Privates, Follow the Boys, Hollywood Canteen, In the Navy, Road to Rio,* et al.); act broke up in 1953 as Patty pursued full time solo career with little success, trio resuming in 1956; after LaVerne's death from cancer, Maxene and Patty starred in *The Andrew Sisters in Over Here,* Broadway musical that played 341 performances (1974-1975) from World War II homefront narra-

tive; surviving siblings continued as separate solo acts for a while.

Radio Shows:

Double Everything. 1938, CBS, William J. Wrigley Company (Wrigley's Doublemint chewing gum).

Just Entertainment. 1938, CBS, William J. Wrigley Company (Wrigley's Doublemint, Juicy Fruit and Spearmint chewing gums).

Honolulu Bound (aka *The Phil Baker Show*). 1939, CBS, Hawaiian Pineapple Company (Dole pineapple fruit and juice and other foodstuffs).

Glenn Miller Orchestra. 1939, CBS, sustaining; 1940–1942, CBS, Liggett & Myers Tobacco Company (Chesterfield cigarettes).

The Andrews Sisters Eight-to-the-Bar Ranch (aka *N-K Musical Showroom*). 1944–1946, ABC, Nash-Kelvinator Corporation (Kelvinator and Norge home appliances).

Bob Crosby's Club 15 (aka *Club 15*). 1947–1953, CBS, Campbell Soup Company (Campbell's juices and soups, Franco-American spaghetti and macaroni and other foodstuffs).

Jack Berch

Born: August 26, 1907, Sigel, Illinois.

Died: December 10, 1992, Jamaica, New York.

Signature Song: *I'm a-Whistlin'.*

Highlights: Baritone who incorporated whistling into daily performances, a provocative facet labeled "flirtatious" by a pundit; door-to-door tea-coffee salesman whose lively shrill arrested an official's spouse at Youngstown's WKBN and led to an audition; more air exposure at Cincinnati's WLW (1935) and Newark's WOR (1936) as *The Jack Berch Orchestra*; by 1938, appearing on CBS in primetime with a coterie of instrumentalists and vocalists; most memorable features daytime quarter-hours backed by Mark Warnow's orchestra or Charles Magnante's instrumental trio combining the door-to-door techniques— whistling, chatting, singing, poetry reading; self-ascribed as "the friendliest show in radio"; a unique component, "Heart-to-Heart Hookup," related incidents of less-fortunate listeners, dedicating tunes to same.

Radio Shows:

The Jack Berch Show. 1936-1937, MBS, Wasey Products.

The Jack Berch Show. 1937 (two series), CBS, Fels Naphtha laundry products.

The Jack Berch Show. 1938-1939, CBS, sustaining.

Sweetheart Serenade (aka *The Jack Berch Show*). 1939-1940, NBC, Manhattan Soap Company (Sweetheart soap); 1939-1940, NBC Blue, sustaining; 1939-1940, MBS, sustaining.

The Jack Berch Show. 1941, MBS, sustaining.

The Jack Berch Show. 1942, network unsubstantiated, Gulf Oil Corporation (Gulf spray insect repellent).

The Jack Berch Show. 1943-1944, MBS, W. K. Kellogg Company (Kellogg cereals).

The Jack Berch Show. 1944, ABC, W. K. Kellogg Company (Kellogg cereals).

Jack Berch and His Boys. 1945-1946, ABC, Prudential Insurance Company (Prudential insurance).

Jack Berch and His Boys. 1946–1951, NBC, Prudential Insurance Company (Prudential insurance).

Jack Berch and His Boys. 1951–1954, ABC, Prudential Insurance Company (Prudential insurance).

Jack Berch Show. Syndicated transcriptions, 50 five-minute programs, Canada Dry Bottling Company (Canada Dry ginger ale).

CONNEE BOSWELL

Born: December 3, 1907, New Orleans, Louisiana.

Died: October 11, 1976, New York, New York.

Highlights: Crippled by accident at age 4 that left paralysis, in wheelchair; harmonized with siblings Martha and Vet (Helvetia) as the Boswell Sisters in New Orleans vaudeville and over WSMB (1922) before touring the Midwest; appearing on Los Angeles' KFBW, aired a spot on CBS from the West Coast; set standards for successive sister singing acts and capable of providing own accompaniment on cello, guitar, piano, saxophone, trombone, violin; appeared with Bing Crosby, Kate Smith, Arthur Tracy in Paramount's *The Big Broadcast* in 1932, crafting a link to Crosby enduring for years; more movies followed; considered the "hottest vocal group in the country" (1930–1936), disbanding as Vet and Martha both wed; Connee persisted solo on shows like *Command Performance* and *Radio Hall of Fame* while gaining own durable series; physical infirmity helped relate to disabled in military hospitals during World War II; only regular foray into TV as singer in *Pete Kelly's Blues* (NBC, 1959).

Radio Shows:

The Goodrich Silvertown Orchestra. c1927–c1928, NBC, B. F. Goodrich Tire Company (Silvertown tires).

The Baker Chocolate Program. 1931-1932, CBS, General Foods Corporation (Baker's chocolate).

The Chesterfield Quarter-Hour. 1931-1932, CBS, Liggett & Myers Tobacco Company (Chesterfield cigarettes).

Pompeian Makeup Box. 1932, CBS, Pompeian Cosmetics Company (Pompeian face creams).

The Pleasure Hour. 1932, NBC, sponsorship unsubstantiated.

California Melodies. 1932–c1936, CBS, sponsorship unsubstantiated.

Music That Satisfies. 1932, CBS, Liggett & Myers Tobacco Company (Chesterfield cigarettes).

The Bing Crosby Show (aka *The Woodbury Show*). 1933–1935, CBS, Andrew Jergens Company (Woodbury soap).

Camel Caravan. 1934, CBS, R. J. Reynolds Tobacco Company (Camel cigarettes).

The Magic Hour. 1935, Chicago's WLS, sponsorship unsubstantiated.

Refreshment Time. 1935-1936, CBS, Coca-Cola Bottling Company (Coca-Cola soft drink).

You Said It (aka *The Monday Night Show*). 1938, CBS, National Brewer's Association (beverage alcohol).

Hollywood Rendezvous. 1938, CBS, sponsorship unsubstantiated.

Kraft Music Hall. 1940–1942, NBC, Kraft Foods Company (Kraft cheese and other foodstuffs).

Stage Door Canteen. 1942–1945, CBS, Corn Products Refining Company (Linit bath commodities).

Camel Caravan. 1942-1943, CBS, R. J. Reynolds Tobacco Company (Camel cigarettes).

Connee Boswell Presents. 1944, NBC Blue, sponsorship unsubstantiated.

Music That Satisfies. 1944-1945, CBS, Liggett & Myers Tobacco Company (Chesterfield cigarettes).

Tonight on Broadway (aka The *Variety Show*). 1946, CBS, Eversharp Company (Schick razors and blades).

EDDIE CANTOR

Born: January 31, 1892, New York, New York (born Isadore Itzkowitz).

Died: October 10, 1964, Beverly Hills, California.

Signature Song: *One Hour with You.*

Legendary Tunes: *Alabamy Bound, Dinah,*

Everybody's Doin' It, How Ya Gonna Keep 'Em Down on the Farm?, Ida (Sweet as Apple Cider), If You Knew Susie, Keep Young and Beautiful, Laugh Your Way Through Life, Ma — He's Makin' Eyes at Me, Makin' Whoopee, Margie, Merrily We Roll Along, My Baby Just Cares for Me, Now's the Time to Fall in Love, Oh You Beautiful Doll, There's Nothing too Good for My Baby, We're Having a Baby, Yes Sir That's My Baby, You Must Have Been a Beautiful Baby, You'd be Surprised.

Highlights: Vaudeville-burlesque comic vocalist tabbed "Banjo Eyes"; launched as a Bowery performer and Coney Island singing waiter; popular singing-dancing-clowning act on *Ziegfeld Follies* bills with W.C. Fields and Will Rogers (1917–1919) and a string of Broadway shows following; first heard on the air over Roselle Park, New Jersey's WDY (December 14, 1921), guesting on WEAF's *The Eveready Hour* in 1925; acted or sang in 23 motion pictures, from silents to talkies, beginning 1924, including 1944's *Hollywood Canteen*, 1952's *The Story of Will Rogers*, 1953's *The Eddie Cantor Story*; early proponent of studio audiences, convincing NBC to let spectators in and add impulsive applause at his shows; talent scout who introduced Eddie Fisher, Dinah Shore and others to vast throngs; recurring guest on programs headlined by Jack Benny, George Burns and Gracie Allen, Hildegarde, Dinah Shore, Bill Stern, more as well as NBC's *The Big Show* (1950–1952) and NBC-TV's *The Colgate Comedy Hour* (1950–1955); hosted *The Eddie Cantor Comedy Theater* syndicated TV humor-variety series (1955); combined platters and chatter as DJ (1951–1954); held presidencies of American Federation of Radio Artists and Screen Actors Guild; authored dual autobiographies, *My Life Is in Your Hands* (1928), *Take My Life* (1959) and a treatise on 1929 stock market crash, *Caught Short*, when he briefly lost millionaire status; assisted Franklin D. Roosevelt in starting March of Dimes, supported Jewish refugees in World War II, gave freely to out-of-work actors, participating generously in myriad of other philanthropic endeavors.

Radio Shows:

The Chase & Sanborn Hour. 1931–1934, NBC, Standard Brands, Inc. (Chase & Sanborn coffee).

The Eddie Cantor Show. 1935-1936, CBS, Pebeco toothpaste.

Texaco Town. 1936–1938, CBS, Texas Company (Texaco gasoline, oil and other vehicle products and services).

Camel Caravan. 1938-1939, CBS, R. J. Reynolds Tobacco Company (Camel cigarettes).

Time to Smile. 1940–1946, NBC, Bristol-Myers, Inc. (Ipana toothpaste and Sal Hepatica distress reliever).

The Eddie Cantor Show. 1946–1949, NBC, Pabst Brewing Company (Pabst Blue Ribbon beer).

Take It or Leave It. 1949-1950, NBC, Eversharp Company (Schick razors and blades).

Show Business Old and New. 1951-1952, NBC, Philip Morris Company (Philip Morris cigarettes); 1952–1954, NBC, multiple sponsorship including Coleman Company (fall 1953).

The Eddie Cantor Show. 1956, ZIV transcribed syndicated series (258 broadcasts).

Ask Eddie Cantor. 1961–1963, network unsubstantiated, Copper-Glo and Aluminum-Glo cleaning agents.

ROSEMARY CLOONEY

Born: May 23, 1928, Maysville, Kentucky.
Died: June 29, 2002, Beverly Hills, California.

Signature Song: *Come on-a My House.*
Legendary Tunes: *Half as Much, Hey There, Kentucky Waltz, Mambo Italiano, Sentimental Journey, Tenderly, This Ole House, You're Just in Love.*
Highlights: Launched career in 1945 with younger sister Betty as vocal duo over Cincinnati's WLW on *Moon River* series; toured with Tony Pastor's orchestra (1945–1949) singing Ralph Flanagan arrangements; recurring artist on *The Bing Crosby Show* and *Songs for Sale* (1950-1951); achieved overnight fame when Mitch Miller offered *Come on-a My House*, smash hit recorded for Columbia (1951); record contracts followed and quartet of Paramount musicals (most memorable, 1954's *White Christmas*, with Crosby and Danny Kaye), own radio shows and inclusion in others (*Guest Star, Stars on Parade, Your Rhythm Revue*); moved into TV with trio of series—*The Johnny Johnston Show* (1951, CBS), *The Rosemary Clooney Show* (1956-1957, syndicated), *The Lux Show Starring Rosemary Clooney* (1957-1958, NBC); toured with Crosby (1976); overcame alcohol and drugs, rejuvenating flagging career as winning recording and personal appearance artist.
Radio Shows:
Stepping Out. 1950, CBS, sustaining.
The Rosemary Clooney Show. 1953, NBC, sustaining.
The Rosemary Clooney Show. 1954-1955, CBS, sustaining.
The Rosemary Clooney Show. 1955, CBS, sustaining.
The Bing Crosby–Rosemary Clooney Show. 1957-1958, CBS; 1960–1962, CBS, multiple participation.

PERRY COMO

Born: May 18, 1912, Canonsburg, Pennsylvania.
Died: May 12, 2001, Jupiter Inlet Beach Colony, Florida.
Signature Song: *Dream Along with Me.*
Legendary Tunes: *A — You're Adorable, And I Love You So, Because, Catch a Falling Star, Don't Let the Stars Get in Your Eyes, Far Away Places, For the Good Times, Hoop-Dee-Doo, Hot Diggity, If, It's Impossible, Ko Ko Mo, Long Ago and Far Away, Magic Moments, More, No Other Love, Papa Loves Mambo, Prisoner of Love, Round and Round, Some Enchanted Evening, Temptation, Till the End of Time, Wild Horses.*
Highlights: Industrious lad employed in barber shop at 10, owning own shop at 14 while performing weekends with groups like Sons of Italy; played baritone horn, organ and sang; joined Freddie, Tony and Frank Carlone's band as baritone vocalist (1932–1937) and Ted Weems' outfit (1937–1943); launched radio and recording career while playing Atlantic City's Steel Pier and New York's Paramount Theater, plus less-than-successful seven-year deal with Twentieth Century Fox ("I was wasting their time and they were wasting mine," he recalled); *Billboard* ranked him second only to his idol Bing Crosby among top 1946 vocalists; adored by TV audiences (*The Chesterfield Supper Club*, 1948–1950, NBC, and 1950–1955, CBS; *The Perry Como Show*, 1955–1959, NBC; *Kraft Music Hall*, 1959–1963, NBC) and backed by Mitchell Ayers' orchestra; appeared on ABC-TV Christmas specials (1948–1987); dubbed "Mr. Nice Guy" and "Mr. Class" by legions of fans who recall cardigan sweaters as trademark; sold 100 million-plus records with 14 tunes ranked first place; received Grammy as 1958's best male vocalist for *Catch a Falling Star*.
Radio Shows:
Fibber McGee & Molly. 1936-1937, NBC,

S. C. Johnson & Sons (Johnson's wax and other home and automotive cleansers).
Beat the Band. 1940-1941, NBC, W. K. Kellogg Company (Kix cereal).
The Perry Como Show. 1943, CBS, sustaining.
Columbia Presents Perry Como. 1944, CBS, sustaining.
The Chesterfield Supper Club. 1944–1949, NBC, Liggett & Myers Tobacco Company (Chesterfield cigarettes).
The Perry Como Show. 1950s, AFRS transcribed quarter-hour.
The Perry Como Show. 1953-1954, MBS, Liggett & Myers Tobacco Company (Chesterfield cigarettes).
The Perry Como Show. 1954, MBS, sustaining.
The Chesterfield Supper Club. 1954-1955, CBS, Liggett & Myers Tobacco Company (Chesterfield cigarettes). [Simulcast over CBS-TV.]
Weekend with Perry. c1970s–c1990s, transcribed syndicated weekly feature.

BOB CROSBY

Born: August 23, 1913, Spokane, Washington.
Died: March 9, 1993, La Jolla, California.
Signature Song: *Summertime.*
Legendary Tunes: *Big Noise from Winnetka, Rampart Street Parade, You and the Night and the Music.*
Highlights: At times in shadow of more famous elder brother Bing (senior by nine years); took vocal job with Anson Weeks' band (1931), then Dorsey Brothers aggregate; by 1935 front man for group led by Gil Rodin from Ben Pollack's outfit — Rodin ran it from the side as Crosby put his name on popular Dixieland sound; by 1937 Bob Cats emerged, "band within a band" ensemble featuring swing tunes and danceable ballads; Crosby's stock rose with radio exposure; drafted by Marines, led Pacific bands; postwar, fronted new orchestra favoring mellow music; often on the aural dial, grabbed daily daytime telecast (*The Bob Crosby Show*, 1953–1957, CBS) and supplied for Perry Como over NBC-TV (1958); reunited Bob Cats in early 1970s, touring again; several artists working by him in later years played jazz festivals and other concerts as Bob Cats (1996 on), led by pianist-arranger-conductor Ed Metz, Crosby standby in fading days.

Radio Shows:
The Bob Crosby Show. 1935-1936, NBC, Roger and Gallet perfume.
Ford V8 Revue. 1936, CBS, Ford Motor Company (Ford automobiles and trucks).
The Dixieland Song Shop. 1939, CBS, R. J. Reynolds Tobacco Company (Camel cigarettes).
Camel Caravan. 1939, CBS, R. J. Reynolds Tobacco Company (Camel cigarettes).
The Dixieland Music Shop. 1940, NBC, R. J. Reynolds Tobacco Company (Camel cigarettes).
The Bob Crosby Show. 1940, MBS, sustaining; 1940, NBC, sustaining.
Camel Caravan. 1940, NBC Blue; 1940-1941, NBC, R. J. Reynolds Tobacco Company (Camel cigarettes).
Three Ring Time. 1941-1942, NBC Blue, P. Ballantine & Company (Ballantine ale and beer).
Kraft Music Hall. 1942, NBC, Kraft Foods Company (Kraft cheese and other foodstuffs).
The Bob Crosby Show. 1943-1944, NBC, P. Lorillard, Inc. (Old Gold cigarettes).
The Bob Crosby Show. 1944-1945, NBC, sustaining.
The Bob Crosby Show. 1946, CBS, Ford Motor Company (Ford automobiles and trucks).

Bob Crosby's Club 15. 1947–1949, 1950–1953, CBS, Campbell Soup Company (Campbell's juices and soups, Franco-American spaghetti and macaroni and other foodstuffs).

The Pet Milk Show. 1949-1950, NBC, Pet Milk Company (Pet evaporated milk).

The Lucky Strike Program (aka *The Jack Benny Program*). 1952–1955, CBS, American Tobacco Company (Lucky Strike cigarettes).

MORTON DOWNEY

Born: November 14, 1901, Wallingford, Connecticut.

Died: October 25, 1985, Palm Beach, Florida.

Signature Song: *Wabash Moon.*

Legendary Tunes: *At the Café Continental, Auf Wiederseh'n My Dear, Carolina Moon, Danny Boy, I'll Always Be in Love with You, I'll Always Be Mother's Boy, In the Middle of a Kiss, Lovely Lady, More Than You Know, My Inspiration Is You, My Romance, Remember Me, Say a Little Prayer for Me, Say It Isn't So, Snuggled on Your Shoulder (Cuddled in Your Arms), Spring Will Be a Little Late This Year, Stormy Weather, The Touch of Your Lips, Two Cigarettes in the Dark, Until Tomorrow, When They Sing "The Wearin' o' the Green."*

Highlights: In adolescence, sang Irish ballads at amusement parks, annual gatherings of hometown firemen, Elks Club affairs and church socials; beyond high school performed in New York bistros, clubs, theaters and political rallies; in 1920s sang way across Atlantic on cruise ships more than a score of times backed by Paul Whiteman's orchestra, presumably first vocalist to obtain comparable billing with a band; introduced to radio audiences over New York's WEAF (1927), following year by British Broadcasting Corporation, London; assigned several appellations stressing heritage, light tenor style — "The Irish Thrust," "The Irish Nightingale," "The Irish Troubadour"; left Whiteman's entourage to perform for Palm Beach *Ziegfeld Follies* revue; broadcast quarter-hour four times weekly from New York's Delmonico Club on CBS (1930), soon drawing 10,000 fan letters per week; selected Radio Singer of the Year (1932); possibly only artist to host series on four major chains within brief span for one sponsor (Coca-Cola), for which he was paid $4,500 weekly and held a directorship in the firm; shrewd businessman who dabbled lucratively in real estate, perfume production, chemical patents; credited with more than 1,000 recordings, three early Hollywood talkies; hosted two television series, *The Mohawk Showroom* (1949, NBC), *Star of the Family* (1950-1951, CBS); father of infamous divisive DJ-talk show host Morton Downey Jr. (1933–2001).

Radio Shows:

The Morton Downey Show. 1930-1931, CBS, sponsorship unsubstantiated.

The Camel Quarter-Hour. 1931-1932, CBS, R. J. Reynolds Tobacco Company (Camel cigarettes).

The Woodbury Show. 1932-1933, NBC Blue, Andrew Jergens Company (Woodbury soap).

The Morton Downey Show. 1933, NBC Blue, sustaining.

The Morton Downey Show. 1933-1934, CBS, sustaining.

Morton Downey's Studio Party. 1934, CBS, Andrew Jergens Company (Woodbury soap).

The Morton Downey Show. 1934-1935, NBC Blue, Carlsbad; 1934-1935, NBC Blue (separate series), Sprudel Salt Company (Sprudel salt).

The Morton Downey Show. 1935, NBC Blue, sustaining.

Presenting Mark Warnow (aka *Evening in Paris*). 1935-1936, CBS, Bourjois Company (Evening in Paris fragrances).
Paul Whiteman's Musical Varieties. 1936, NBC Blue, Andrew Jergens Company (Woodbury soap).
The Eddy Duchin Show. 1938-1939, NBC, Brown & Williamson Tobacco Company (Pall Mall cigarettes).
The Coke Club (aka *Songs by Morton Downey*). 1943-1944, NBC Blue/ABC; 1945–1947, MBS; 1948–1950, NBC; 1950-1951, CBS, Coca-Cola Bottling Company (Coca-Cola soft drink).

EDDIE FISHER

Born: August 10, 1928, Philadelphia, Pennsylvania.
Signature Song: *Any Time.*
Legendary Tunes: *Cindy Oh Cindy, Count Your Blessings, Dungaree Doll, Heart, I Need You Now, I'm Walking Behind You, I'm Yours, Lady of Spain, Oh My Papa, Tell Me Why, Turn Back the Hands of Time, Wish You Were Here.*
Highlights: Radio at 13; vocalist for bands headlined by Buddy Morrow and Charlie Ventura at 18; "discovered" at 20 by Eddie Cantor (1949); joined Cantor's show, performing on air and across country; bobbysoxer labeled "America's Most Promising Male Vocalist" by nation's DJs, recording string of 22 hits; served in Korea (1952-1953); classic *Coke Time* radio series easily shifted to TV (1953–1957, NBC) followed by *The Eddie Fisher Show* (1957–1959, NBC); bad press and public disfavor resulted on divorcing singer-actress Debbie Reynolds (with whom he starred in 1956 film *Bundle of Joy*) to marry Hollywood icon Elizabeth Taylor in 1959 (with whom he appeared in 1960's *Butterfield 8*); later married, divorced actress Connie Stevens; attempted unsuccessful comeback (1970s); subsequently treated for gambling and alcohol addiction.
Radio Shows:
The Horn and Hardart Children's Hour. c1941, New York's WEAF, Horn and Hardart Automat restaurants.
The Eddie Cantor Show. 1949, NBC, Pabst Brewing Company (Pabst Blue Ribbon beer).
Songs by Eddie Fisher. 1950, NBC, sustaining.
The Eddie Fisher Show. 1951–1953, ABC, sustaining.
Stars in Khaki 'n' Blue. 1952, NBC, sustaining.
The Eddie Fisher Show. 1952-1953, CBS, sustaining.
The Eddie Fisher Show. 1953, NBC, Coca-Cola Bottling Company (Coca-Cola soft drink). [Simulcast over NBC-TV.]
The Eddie Fisher Show (aka *Coke Time*). 1953, MBS, Coca-Cola Bottling Co. (Coca-Cola soft drink). [Simulcast over NBC-TV.]
Coke Time. 1954-1955, MBS, Coca-Cola Bottling Company (Coca-Cola soft drink). [Simulcast over NBC-TV.]
Coke Time with Eddie Fisher. 1954–1956, ABC, Coca-Cola Bottling Company (Coca-Cola soft drink).

JANE FROMAN

Born: November 10, 1907, St. Louis, Missouri.
Died: April 22, 1980, Columbia, Missouri.
Signature Song: *With a Song in My Heart.*
Legendary Tunes: *I Believe, I Only Have Eyes for You, I'll Walk Alone, Robe of Calvary, Wish You Were Here.*
Highlights: Pursued voice at Cincinnati Conservatory of Music (on *Honey Adams*, one of 22 commercial series singing on weekly over WLW, she supplied vocals for novice actress Virginia Payne, soon dubbed *Ma Perkins*); toured with Paul Whiteman's orchestra;

debuted on Broadway in *Ziegfeld Follies of 1934*; popular supper club act and radio; sang often for Franklin D. Roosevelt; critically injured in February 1943 USO plane crash in Lisbon harbor en route to entertain servicemen in Europe; recuperated, resumed touring, recording bigger hits, plus soundtrack of Twentieth Century Fox memoir picture (1952's *With a Song in My Heart*) starring Susan Hayward; christened "Sweetheart of the Armed Forces," later Missouri's "First Lady of Song"; presided over *Jane Froman's U.S.A. Canteen* (aka *The Jane Froman Show*) on CBS-TV, 1952–1955; retired in 1961.

Radio Shows:

Florsheim Frolics. 1931-1932, NBC, Florsheim Company (Florsheim shoes).

The Pontiac Hour (aka *The Paul Whiteman Show*). 1932, NBC Blue, later NBC, Pontiac Motor Car Company (Pontiac automobiles).

The Jane Froman Show. 1932-1933, NBC, sustaining.

The Iodent Program. 1932-1933, NBC, Iodent toothpaste.

Music That Satisfies. 1933, CBS, Liggett & Myers Tobacco Company (Chesterfield cigarettes).

The Jane Froman Show. 1933, CBS, sponsorship unsubstantiated.

The Linit Show. 1933, CBS, Corn Products Company (Linit bath commodities).

The Pontiac Parade. 1934-1935, NBC, Pontiac Motor Car Company (Pontiac automobiles).

Palmolive Beauty Box Theater. 1934-1935, NBC; 1935, NBC Blue; 1936, CBS, Colgate-Palmolive-Peet Company (Palmolive soap).

Tune Twisters. 1935, NBC Blue, sustaining.

The Intimate Hour (aka *The Bob Hope Show*). 1935, NBC Blue, Emerson Drug Company (Bromo-Seltzer distress reliever).

California's Hour. San Francisco's KFRC, 1936, Chain Stores of California.

The Jane Froman and Don Ross Show (aka *The Jell-O Summer Show*). 1937, NBC, General Foods Corporation (Jell-O desserts).

The Jane Froman Show. 1938, CBS, sustaining.

The Texaco Star Theater. 1938, CBS, Texas Company (Texaco gasoline, oil and other vehicle products and services).

The Gulf Musical Playhouse (aka *The Jane Froman and Jan Peerce Show*). 1939, CBS, Gulf Oil Corporation (Gulf gasoline, oil and other vehicle products and services).

The Jane Froman Show. 1942, CBS, Texas Company (Texaco gasoline, oil and other vehicle products and services).

Stage Door Canteen. 1942–1945, CBS, Corn Products Company (Linit bath commodities).

The Andrews Sisters Eight-to-the-Bar Ranch (aka *The N–K Musical Showroom*). 1944-1945, ABC, Nash-Kelvinator Corporation (Norge and Kelvinator home appliances).

The Pause That Refreshes on the Air (aka *The Coca-Cola Hour*). 1948-1949, CBS, Coca-Cola Bottling Company (Coca-Cola soft drink).

Yours for a Song (aka *The Conti Castille Show*). 1948-1949, MBS, Conti Castille shampoo.

THE HAPPINESS BOYS

Born: Ernie Hare (bass-baritone)—March 15, 1883, Norfolk, Virginia; Billy Jones (tenor)—March 15, 1887, New York, New York.

Died: Ernie Hare—March 9, 1939, Jamaica, New York; Billy Jones—November 23, 1940, New York, New York.

Signature Song: *How Do Ya Do?* (*Everybody, How Do Ya Do?*)

Legendary Tunes: *Down at the Old Swimming Hole, Down Where the South Begins, Down Yonder, Ha Boiled Rose, Hinky Dinky Parlay Voo, I Like It, I Miss My Swiss, Nestle in Your Daddy's Arms, Oh! Eva, When Lindy Comes Home to His Mother.*

Highlights: Radio comic harmony duo formed in early 1920s with 2,000-plus broadcasts on which they may have sung 10,000 tunes; at least one Blue Amberol recording (*Down at the Old Swimming Hole*) made June 25, 1921, at Edison studios predated exposure to radio audiences; other songs may have been put on discs earlier at Brunswick studios—eventually recorded for 16 labels, never exclusive property of one company; initially aired over Newark's WJZ (October 18, 1921), later signing five-year pact with Happiness Candy Stores to sing over Manhattan's WEAF (effective August 22, 1923); three-man act at one point included Larry Briers, each of trio receiving $300 per appearance for WEAF work by 1925; Briers departed in 1926 and duo retitled selves and show with successive sponsors' names for sox, bug spray, bread, mayonnaise, razors; even accompanists got into act, touting themselves "Dave Kaplan with His Happiness Orchestra" (1927), later the "Taystee Breadwinners" led by Ben Selvin; in mid-1920s Jones sang on NBC's *The Ipana Troubadors* while he and Hare recorded solos separately, performing with other artists; by mid-1930s pair "worked in relative obscurity," a newsman noted; Hare's final broadcast was January 29, 1939, and he died a few weeks later, his daughter Marilyn, 16, succeeding him to March 1940; Jones persisted alone to own demise eight months hence.

Radio Shows:

The Happiness Boys. 1926–1929, NBC Blue, Happiness Candy Stores (Happiness confections).

The Interwoven Pair. 1929–1931, NBC Blue, Interwoven Sock Company (Interwoven sox).

The Flit Soldiers. 1929-1930, NBC, Standard Oil of New Jersey (Flit insect repellent).

The Tastyeast Jesters (aka *The Taystee Loafers*). 1931–1938, NBC Blue, Tastyeast Bakers (Taystee bread).

The Best Food Boys. 1932, NBC Blue; 1932, NBC, Richard Hellman, Inc. (Hellman's mayonnaise).

Community Sing (aka *Summer Hotel*). 1936-1937, CBS, Gillette Safety Razor Company (Gillette razors and blades).

The Sachs Program. New York's WMCA, 1939-1940, Sachs Furniture Company (Sachs retail store).

DICK HAYMES

Born: September 13, 1916, Buenos Aires, Argentina.

Died: March 28, 1980, Los Angeles, California.

Signature Song: *The More I See You.*

Legendary Tunes: *Count Every Star, How Are Things in Glocca Morra?, I Wish I Didn't Love You So, I Wish I Knew, I'm Always Chasing Rainbows, It Can't Be Wrong, It Had to Be You, It Might As Well Be Spring, It's a Grand Night for Singing, It's Magic, Laura, Little White Lies, Long Ago and Far Away, Love Letters, Mamselle, Maybe It's Because, The Old Master Painter, Put Your Arms Around Me Honey, Room Full of Roses, Some Sunday Morning, There's No Business Like Show Business, Till the End of Time, Together, You Can't Be True Dear, You'll Never Know, You're Just in Love.*

Highlights: Baritone crooner with international history, born in Argentina, educated in France and Switzerland, settled in U. S., moved to Ireland (1961), returned to U. S. (1971); early jobs as radio announcer (Los Angeles' KHJ), MGM film extra and stuntman, small parts in vaudeville; trained by concert singer-vocal coach mom, debuted at New York's La Martinique nightclub with Johnny Johnson's orchestra (1931); sang with outfits successively headlined by Harry James (1939–1942), Benny Goodman, Tommy Dorsey, Ray Bloch, Gordon Jenkins; "his Decca discs and [Twentieth Century] Fox films rivaled [Frank] Sinatra's" noted an entertainment writer as another allowed "For a time Dick Haymes was considered a serious rival to Bing Crosby and Frank Sinatra"; movie musicals encompassed 1944's *Irish Eyes Are Smiling*, 1945's *State Fair*, 1948's *One Touch of Venus*, 1953's *Cruisin' Down the River* and nearly dozen more; at end of radio career, turned up acting as freelance pilot Dockery Crane in *I Fly Anything* adventure series; occasional TV dramatic parts; returning to America later, comeback launched with show dates and recordings; beset by personal troubles — alcohol addiction, seven wives, alimony payments, back taxes owed and a concerted but failed federal effort to deport him to Argentina for draft-dodging in World War II (registered as "resident alien," waiving citizenship rights); spouses included Joanne Dru, Rita Hayworth, Fran Jeffries; name perpetuated by Dick Haymes Society.

Radio Shows:

The Tommy Dorsey Show. 1942-1943, NBC, Brown & Williamson Tobacco Company (Raleigh cigarettes and Sir Walter Raleigh pipe tobacco).

Here's to Romance. 1943, NBC Blue, 1943-1944, CBS, Bourjois Company (Evening in Paris fragrances).

Everything for the Boys (aka *The Dick Haymes Show*). 1944-1945, NBC; 1945–1948, CBS, Electric Autolite Company (Autolite batteries, headlights, spark plugs and other vehicle power supplies).

Romance, Rhythm and Ripley. 1945, CBS, Bourjois Company (Evening in Paris fragrances).

Your Hit Parade. 1947, NBC, American Tobacco Company (Lucky Strike cigarettes).

Club 15. 1949-1950, CBS, Campbell Soup Company (Campbell's juices and soups, Franco-American spaghetti and macaroni and other foodstuffs).

The Carnation Contented Hour. 1949–1951, CBS, Carnation Company (Carnation evaporated milk).

The Dick Haymes Show. 1951, ABC, Procter & Gamble Company (household cleaning and personal care products).

I Fly Anything. 1950-1951, ABC, sustaining.

AL JOLSON

Born: May 26, 1886, Srednick, Lithuania (born Asa Yoelson).

Died: October 23, 1950, San Francisco, California.

Signature Song: *Swanee*.

Legendary Tunes: *April Showers, Avalon, California Here I Come, For Me and My Gal, Mammy, Rockabye Your Baby with a Dixie Melody, Sonny Boy, Toot Toot Tootsie Goodbye, You Made Me Love You.*

Highlights: Sang as lad in New York Bowery saloon and for military bands during Spanish-American War; by 1908, in minstrel blackface vaudeville skits, delivering down-on-one-knee southern tunes; migrated to Broadway for part in *La Belle Paree* (1911); billed to theater crowds as "America's Greatest Entertainer" by 1915; first radio appearance over Chicago's KYW (1921); the lead in first talkie movie, 1927's *The Jazz Singer*; appeared in 17 films, mostly in 1920s and 1930s; radio guest star (1928); "buckets of charisma" and could easily "project his dynamic, forceful nature over the air" noted a critic; worked erratically in early radio, disappearing midseason from series sponsored by Kraft, Lever, Shell; semiretired by 1942; entertained U.S. troops in World War II, Korea; recorded soundtrack of 1946 motion picture *The Jolson Story* starring Larry Parks, resurrecting broadcasting, recording careers; turned up on every major headliner's show at $10,000 a pop (Fred Allen, Jack Benny, Edgar Bergen, Eddie Cantor, Bing Crosby, Bob Hope, et al.); so often on Crosby's *Philco Radio Time* (1946–1949, ABC) considered a cast member; second film on himself, 1949's *Jolson Sings Again*; versions of *Jolson, the Musical* stage show debuting London (1995) toured Canada, America, Australia; global fraternity perpetuates his memory.

Radio Shows:

Presenting Al Jolson. 1932-1933, NBC, General Motors Corporation (Chevrolet automobiles and trucks).

The Kraft Program. 1933-1934, NBC, Kraft Foods Company (Kraft cheese and other foodstuffs).

Shell Chateau. 1935-1936, NBC, Shell Oil Company (Shell gasoline, oil and other vehicle products and services).

The Lifebuoy Program (aka *The Rinso Program, The Tuesday Night Party*). 1936–1939, CBS, Lever Brothers Company (Lifebuoy soap and Rinso detergent).

The Colgate Program. 1942-1943, CBS, Colgate-Palmolive-Peet Company (Colgate toothpaste and other personal care products).

Kraft Music Hall. 1947–1949, NBC, Kraft Foods Company (Kraft cheese and other foodstuffs).

PEGGY LEE

Born: May 26, 1920, Jamestown, North Dakota (born Norma Dolores Egstrom).

Died: January 21, 2002, Bel Air, California.

Signature Song: *Is That All There Is?*

Legendary Tunes: *Alright — Okay — You Win, Bali Ha'i, Big Spender, Blues in the Night, Fever, Golden Earrings, I Don't Know Enough About You, I Got It Bad and That Ain't Good, I'm a Woman, It's a Good Day, Lover, Manana, Mr. Wonderful, The Old Master Painter, Pass Me By, Somebody Else Is Taking My Place, Waitin' for the Train to Come In, The Way You Look Tonight, What More Can a Woman Do?, Where or When, Why Don't You Do Right?, You Was Right Baby.*

Highlights: Sultry-voiced singer-turned-actress who seemed mired as substitute for Perry Como and Jo Stafford until Jimmy Durante chose her as his vocal star; sang in church choir, high school glee club and with college bands; tried launching career in Hollywood to no avail (1938) and returned home, airing over Fargo's WDAY (management nicknamed her Peggy Lee) while supplementing income by slicing bread in a bakery; Minneapolis Standard Oil radio show next with live vocals from Radisson Hotel café; sang with Will Osborne's band and on tour dates with Benny Goodman's outfit at peak of his success (1941–1943); several radio series; on CBS-TV, co-host of *TV's Top Tunes* (1951) with Mel Torme, singer on *Songs for Sale* (1951-1952), *The Steve Allen Show* (1952) and a single-shot video drama on *The General Electric Theater* (March 13, 1960); earned film credits for *The Jazz Singer, Mr. Music, Pete Kelly's Blues* (1956 Oscar nomination), *The Powers Girl, Stage Door Canteen* and more; collaborated with spouse Dave Barbour to pen hits *It's a Good Day* and *Manana*; lyricist on tunes for Disney's *Lady and the Tramp* (1955), speaking lines for some animal characters, winning $2.3 million lawsuit in 1991 for video sales of the movie, a benchmark verdict in artists' rights; recorded more than 650 tunes, over 60 albums; cited by Cancer Society, Heart Fund, National Brotherhood of Christians and Jews for philanthropic munificence; poet, screenwriter, author, fabric-greeting card designer, painter, concert artist.

Radio Shows:

Meet Me at Parky's. 1945–1947, NBC, P. Lorillard, Inc. (Old Gold cigarettes); 1947-1948, MBS, sustaining.

Kraft Music Hall. c1945-1946, NBC, Kraft Foods Company (Kraft cheese and other foodstuffs).

King Cole Trio Time (aka *King and His Court*). 1946–1948, NBC, Wildroot. (Wildroot men's hair preparations).

Rhapsody in Rhythm. 1947, CBS, P. Lorillard, Inc. (Old Gold cigarettes).

The Electric Hour Summer Series. 1947, CBS, Electric Cooperative (170 local electric companies).

The Jimmy Durante Show (aka *The Rexall Drug Program*). 1947-1948, NBC, Rexall Drug Company (Rexall drug stores).

The Chesterfield Supper Club. 1949-1950, NBC, Liggett & Myers Tobacco Company (Chesterfield cigarettes).

The Peggy Lee Show. 1951, CBS, Rexall Drug Company (Rexall drug stores).

The Frankie Laine Show. 1951, CBS, U.S. Army (Army recruiting).

CURT MASSEY

Born: May 3, 1910, Midland, Texas.
Died: October 21, 1991, Rancho Mirage, California.
Signature Song: *We Sing the Old Songs* (with vocalist Martha Tilton).
Highlights: One of five members of popular southwestern family band performing in U.S. and Canada at church socials and on stages; radio debut over Kansas City's KMBC (1930) as hillbilly crooner, leading to Chicago and *National Barn Dance* three years later; by mid decade fiddler in The Westerners family entourage on *Showboat* from New York; landing couple of series, they appeared intermittently on shows like *Al Pearce and His Gang* and *The Magic Key*; later, Curt played trumpet, piano, joining The Westerners in a Tex Ritter film, 1938's *Where the Buffalo Roam*; replaced singer Red Foley on *Avalon Time*, establishing on-air baritone vocal act lasting two decades; teamed with KMBC colleague Paul Henning, creator of prime-time comedy *Petticoat Junction* (1963–1970, CBS-TV), composing, singing show's theme; musical director for the show and even more winning *Beverly Hillbillies* (1962–1970, CBS-TV), also credited with penning its memorable theme vocalized by Nashville pickers Lester Flatt, Earl Scruggs.

Radio Shows:

National Barn Dance. 1933–date unsubstantiated, NBC Blue, Miles Laboratories, Inc. (Alka-Seltzer stomach distress remedy).

The Maxwell House Showboat. 1935-1936, NBC, General Foods Corporation (Maxwell House coffee).

Louise Massey and the Westerners. 1936, NBC Blue, sustaining.

The Log Cabin Dude Ranch (aka *The Log Cabin Bar Z Ranch*). 1936-1937, NBC Blue, General Foods Corporation (Log Cabin syrup).

Plantation Party (aka *Paducah Plantation*). c1938, MBS; 1938–1940, NBC Blue; 1940–1942, NBC, Bugle Tobacco Company (Bugle chewing tobacco); 1942-1943, NBC, sustaining.

Avalon Variety Time. 1939, NBC, Brown & Williamson Tobacco Company (Avalon cigarettes).

Reveille Round-Up. 1941–1947, NBC, Grove

Laboratories, Inc. (Bromo-Quinine distress reliever and Murine eye drops).
Curt Massey Time. 1943, CBS, Miles Laboratories, Inc. (Alka-Seltzer stomach distress remedy).
Curt Massey Time. 1943, CBS; 1944-1945, NBC, Schutter Candy Company (Schutter candy).
The Andrews Sisters Eight-to-the-Bar Ranch (aka *The N–K Musical Showroom*). 1944-1945, ABC, Nash-Kelvinator Corporation (Norge and Kelvinator home appliances).
Curt Massey Time. 1945, MBS, sustaining.
Sunday at the N–K Ranch. 1945, ABC, Nash-Kelvinator Corporation (Norge and Kelvinator home appliances).
Holiday for Music. 1946, CBS, Nash-Kelvinator Corporation (Norge and Kelvinator home appliances).
Curt Massey Time. 1948, ABC, sustaining.
Plantation Jubilee. 1949, MBS, sustaining.
Curt Massey Time. 1949, ABC, sustaining.
The Curt Massey-Martha Tilton Show. 1949–1954, CBS, Miles Laboratories, Inc. (Alka-Seltzer stomach distress remedy).
The Curt Massey-Martha Tilton Show. 1952–1954, MBS, sustaining.
Curt Massey Time. 1956, CBS, sustaining.

VAUGHN MONROE

Born: October 7, 1911, Akron, Ohio.
Died: May 21, 1973, Stuart, Florida.
Signature Song: *Racing with the Moon.*
Legendary Tunes: *Ballerina, Black Denim and Motorcycle Boots, Cry Cry Cry, Ghost Riders in the Sky, How Soon, Let's Have a Cigarette Together, A Man's Best Friend Is His Horse, The Pleasure's All Mine, Rasputin's Tootin', Red Roses for a Blue Lady, Seems Like Old Times, Singin' My Way Back Home, Something Sentimental, Sound Off, There! I've Said It Again, The Trolley Song.*
Highlights: Hoping to be opera star; trumpeter, trombonist in Depression-era bands led by Gibby Lockhard, Austin Wylie, Larry Funk, Jack Marsha before forming own orchestra (1940); in mid-1940s, teen girls, older sisters, mothers, grannies swooned to his devilishly striking looks, nasal baritone; a pundit called him his generation's Rudy Vallee, claiming "he was the Robert Goulet of his day" while his band was "dull" and "never brilliant"; appeared in quartet of flicks—*Meet the People* (1944), *Carnegie Hall* (1947), *Singing Guns* (1950), *Toughest Man in Arizona* (1952); recorded heavily for Victor, becoming parent firm's corporate icon in televised commercials; hosted trio of musical variety TV series: *Camel Caravan* (1950-1951, CBS), *The Vaughn Monroe Show* (1954, 1955, NBC), *Air Time '57* (1956-1957, ABC); operated Boston bistro later; legacy touted by a preservation society.

Radio Shows:
Penthouse Party. 1941, CBS, then NBC Blue, R. J. Reynolds Tobacco Company (Camel cigarettes).
How'm I Doin'? 1942, CBS, R. J. Reynolds Tobacco Company (Camel cigarettes).
The Vaughn Monroe Show (aka *Camel Caravan*). 1946–1954, CBS; 1952, NBC (simultaneous series), R. J. Reynolds Tobacco Company (Camel cigarettes).

JANE PICKENS

Born: August 10, 1908, Macon, Georgia.
Died: February 21, 1992, Newport, Rhode Island.
Signature Song: *Alone Since We've Parted.*
Legendary Tunes: *Autumn in New York* (with sisters), *Just You and I* (with sisters).
Highlights: From musically oriented home, after she won Curtis Institute and Julliard music scholarships Jane's family packed duds, left Atlanta digs

for Manhattan (1932); Jane, sisters Patti, Helen originally known as Three Little Maids from Pixie, accompanied by pianist-dad; Victor audition record prompted such a stir at NBC trio hired sight unseen to compete with CBS's Boswell Sisters; Jane picked tunes, prepared arrangements, orchestration; trio visited *Hollywood on the Air, The Magic Key, Musical Headliners, The Paul Whiteman Buick Program* regularly while doing own shows; ambitious soprano Jane then chose solo career, appearing in *Ziegfeld Follies of 1936* as sisters married, ending the act; Jane sang to accompaniment of Eddy Duchin's piano, appeared at New York's Plaza Hotel, onstage in *Boys and Girls Together* (1940-1941), *Regina* (1949), *Echoes of New York* WJZ local show (1946), with New York Philharmonic and Philadelphia Opera Company, aired her own aural series; hostess of ABC-TV's *The Jane Pickens Show* (1954); civic leader, philanthropist and Newport, Rhode Island socialite (1960s forward); received Distinguished Volunteer Service Award from Lady Bird Johnson (1968); unsuccessful Manhattan GOP candidate for U. S. Congress (1972); first president classical Newport Musical Festival; Newport's Strand Theatre renamed Jane Pickens Theatre (1974) with Jane, Patti reprising vocal act of four decades earlier.

Radio Shows:

The Pickens Sisters. 1932-1933, NBC, sustaining.

The Pickens Sisters. 1932-1933, NBC Blue, sustaining.

The Pickens Sisters. 1933-1934, NBC Blue, sustaining.

The Pickens Sisters. 1934-1935, NBC Blue, sustaining.

The Adventures of Gracie. 1934-1935, CBS, White Owl Cigar Company (White Owl cigars).

Gulf Headliners. 1935, CBS, Gulf Oil Corporation (Gulf gasoline, oil and other vehicle products and services).

Evening in Paris. 1935-1936, NBC Blue, Bourjois Company (Evening in Paris fragrances).

The Ford Summer Hour. c1935–1941, CBS, Ford Motor Company (Ford automobiles and trucks).

Saturday Night Party. 1936-1937, NBC, Sealtest Dairies (Sealtest dairy products).

Ben Bernie, the Old Maestro. 1938, CBS, U. S. Tire and Rubber Company.

The Jane Pickens Show. 1948-1949, NBC, Tums stomach distress remedy (summer 1948), sustaining or multiple participation (other); 1951–1955, NBC, multiple participation.

The Chamber Music Society of Lower Basin Street. 1950, NBC, sustaining.

Pickens Party. 1951, transcribed, local sponsorship.

Through the Years. 1952, NBC, sustaining.

Pickens Party. 1955–1957, NBC, multiple participation.

LANNY ROSS

Born: January 19, 1906, Seattle, Washington.

Died: April 25, 1988, New York, New York.

Signature Song: *Moonlight and Roses*.

Legendary Tune: *Ah, Sweet Mystery of Life*.

Highlights: Well educated, studied at Yale, Columbia Law School and Julliard School of Music; Yale athletic superstar with 300-yard national track championship, forsaking try for 1928 Olympic team to tour with glee club; weekly on New York radio with The Whiffenpoofs octet (late 1920s); lyric tenor deserting ambitions to be lawyer to initiate NBC Radio career paying five times law firm's salary; major network radio presence three decades; acted in five 1930s film musicals (*Yours Sincerely, College Rhythm, Melody in Spring, The Lady Objects, Gulliver's Travels*), on Broadway (*Petticoat Fever*); hosted *The Lanny Ross Show* (aka *The Swift Show*) on NBC-TV in 1948–1949.

Radio Shows:

National Broadcasting Company Concert Bureau Hour. 1929, NBC, sustaining.

The Lanny Ross Show. 1929–1931, NBC, sustaining.

The Troubador of the Moon. 1930-1931, CBS, sustaining.

The Hellman Mayonnaise Troubador. 1931, NBC, Richard Hellman, Inc. (Hellman's mayonnaise).

The Maxwell House Showboat (aka *The Maxwell House Ensemble, The Lanny Ross Show*). 1931–1937, NBC, General Foods Corporation (Maxwell House coffee).

The Lanny Ross Show. 1932-1933, NBC, Campbell Soup Company (Campbell's juices and soups, Franco-American spaghetti and macaroni and other foodstuffs).

Maria Certo's Matinee. 1934, NBC, sustaining.

The Log Cabin Inn (aka *Lanny's Log Cabin Inn*). 1934-1935, General Foods Corporation (Log Cabin syrup).

Lanny Ross and His State Fair Concert. 1935, NBC Blue, General Foods Corporation (Jell-O desserts).

Hollywood Mardi Gras (aka *The Packard Hour*). 1937-1938, NBC, Packard Motor Car Company (Packard automobiles).

Your Hit Parade. 1938-1939, NBC, American Tobacco Company (Lucky Strike cigarettes).

Presenting Mark Warnow. 1939, CBS, American Tobacco Company (Lucky Strike cigarettes).

The Lanny Ross Show. 1939-1940, 1940 (two series that year), 1940–1942, CBS, Campbell Soup Company (Franco-American spaghetti, macaroni and other foodstuffs).

Steamboat Jamboree. 1940s, half-hour syndicated transcribed series, local sponsorship.

Camel Caravan. 1942-1943, CBS, R. J. Reynolds Tobacco Company (Camel cigarettes).

The Lanny Ross Show. 1946, CBS, Procter & Gamble Company (Ivory soap).

The Lanny Ross Show. 1948–1950, MBS, Gulf Oil Corporation (Gulf gasoline and oil and other vehicle products and services).

The Lanny Ross Show. 1951, MBS, Dictograph Corporation (Dictograph office machines).

The Lanny Ross Show. 1951-1952, MBS, participating sponsorship.

The Lanny Ross Show. 1954–1957, CBS, participating sponsorship. (DJ series continuing locally in New York over WCBS into the 1960s.)

Ginny Simms

Born: May 25, 1914, San Antonio, Texas.

Died: April 4, 1994, Palm Springs, California.

Highlights: Studied piano early intending to teach but joined vocal trio at Fresno State Teachers College, singing with several small outfits; won solo spot with Tommy Gerun's band, signing with Kay Kyser (1934); accompanied Kyser on band tours and on his radio show leading to recording contracts and pact with RKO films (*That's Right—You're Wrong, You'll Find Out, Playmates, Here We Go Again, Seven Days Leave, Hit the Ice, Broadway Rhythm, Shady Lady, Night and Day*); left road in 1941, gaining own popular radio series singing and interviewing GIs, delivering love notes on-air to folks back home; unlike most peers, abhorred radio applause, preferring to work sans audience; operated real estate concern Montana Corporation as sideline; fleeting marriages to two incredibly wealthy men — industrial engineer Hyatt Robert Von Dehn (then launching hotel chain which she suggested he call "Hyatt") and oilman Bob Calhoun; third nuptials (1962) to Washington state attorney general Donald W. Eastvold Sr. lasted but cloaked in secrecy; after Eastvolds' multimillion-dollar California and Minnesota real estate developments collapsed, unhappy parties lingered and the couple vanished, allegedly to avoid lawsuits and potential prosecution, resurfacing years later in Hawaii, ultimately returning to California.

Radio Shows:

Surprise Party (aka *Kay Kyser's Orchestra*). 1937, MBS, Willys Overland Motor Car Company (Willys Jeep vehicles).

Kay Kyser's Kollege of Musical Knowledge. 1938–1941, NBC, American Tobacco Company (Lucky Strike cigarettes).

The Arkansas Traveler (aka *The Bob Burns Show*). 1941-1942, CBS, Campbell Soup Company (Campbell's juices and soups, Franco-American spaghetti and macaroni and other foodstuffs); 1942, CBS, 1943–c1944, Lever Brothers Company (household detergents and soaps).

The Ginny Simms Show. 1941-1942, CBS, Kimberly-Clark Corporation (Kleenex tissues).

Johnny Presents Ginny Simms (aka *The Purple Heart*). 1942–1945, NBC, Philip Morris Company (Philip Morris cigarettes).

The Camel Comedy Caravan. 1943–1945, CBS, R. J. Reynolds Tobacco Company (Camel cigarettes).

Talent Theater. 1945, NBC, Philip Morris Company (Philip Morris cigarettes).

The Ginny Simms Show. 1945–1947, CBS, Borden Company (Borden's milk and other dairy products).

The Jack Smith Show (aka *The Oxydol Show*). Mid to late 1940s, CBS, Procter & Gamble Company (Oxydol detergent).

Your Hit Parade. 1947, NBC, American Tobacco Company (Lucky Strike cigarettes).

The Pause That Refreshes on the Air (aka *The Coca-Cola Hour*). 1947-1948, CBS, Coca-Cola Bottling Company (Coca-Cola soft drink).

The Botany Song Shop (aka *Ginny Simms Song Book*). 1950-1951, ABC, Botany Mills (Botany clothing fabrics).

Jack Smith

Born: November 16, 1913, Bainbridge Island, Seattle, Washington.

Legendary Tunes: *Baby Face, Big Brass Band from Brazil, Civilization (Bongo, Bongo, Bongo), Cruising Down the River, Cuanto La Gusta, I'll Be with You in Apple Blossom Time, Jack! Jack! Jack! (Cutu-Gu-Ru), Lavender Blue (Dilly Dilly), Shaunty O'Shea, Sunflower, Takin' Miss Mary to the Ball, On Moonlight Bay, You Call Everybody Darling.*

Highlights: Not to be confused with 1920s–1930s radio performer "Whispering" Jack Smith nor Spanish guitarist-singer "Smiling" Jack Smith, this "Smiling" Jack Smith boasted smooth tenor voice making him weeknight favorite of American radio audiences in 1940s–1950s (opera critic Deems Taylor dubbed him "The Man with the Smile in His Voice"); at 15, with two high school buddies, formed the Three Ambassadors vocal trio, performing with Gus Arnheim's dance band at Cocoanut Grove in Los Angeles' Ambassador Hotel (1931); took subsequent engagements with aggregates headlined by Jimmie Grier, Anson Weeks, Phil Harris; Capitol records artist with several hits; appeared onstage in *One*

Touch of Venus with Mary Martin (1943) and in two movie musicals (1949's *Make Believe Ballroom* and 1951's *On Moonlight Bay*); weeknight radio series aired live for seven years on East Coast at 7:15, repeated live at 11:15 for West Coast; performed prolifically on TV sans singing: emceed NBC-CBS quiz *Place the Face* (1953), cohosted dual CBS game shows *Welcome Travelers* (1955), successor *Love Story* (1955-1956), occasionally supplanted Jack Bailey hosting 1956–1964 NBC-ABC audience participation series *Queen for a Day*, persistent host of human interest show *You Asked for It* (1958-1959, ABC-TV, 1972 in syndication—continuing with other syndicated versions to 1991), host of 1966–1971 syndicated travelogue, *The American West*.

Radio Shows:

Nine to Five. 1935-1936, NBC Blue, L. C. Smith Corona Typewriter Company (L. C. Smith Corona business machines).

Kate Smith's Coffee Time (aka *Kate Smith's A&P Bandwagon*). c1936-1937, CBS, The Great Atlantic & Pacific Tea Company (Bokar, Eight O'Clock and Red Circle coffees).

The 1937 Radio Show. 1937, MBS, Aspergum laxative.

The Kate Smith Hour. 1937–1939, CBS, General Foods Corporation (Cain's mayonnaise, Calumet baking soda, Diamond Crystal shaker salt, Grape-Nuts Flakes cereal, Jell-O desserts, Postum and Sanka coffees, Sur-Jel canning aid, Swans Down cake flour).

Johnny Presents (aka *The Philip Morris Show*). c1937–c1941, CBS, Philip Morris Company (Philip Morris cigarettes).

Town Hall Tonight (aka *The Fred Allen Show*, *The Texaco Star Theater*). cLate 1930s–early 1940s, NBC, Bristol-Myers, Inc. (Ipana toothpaste and Sal Hepatica stomach distress remedy) and Texas Company (Texaco gasoline, oil and other vehicle products and services).

Breezing Along (aka *Singo, Rhymo, Jingo*). 1939-1940, network unsubstantiated, Philip Morris Company (Philip Morris cigarettes); 1939, MBS, sustaining; 1939-1940, NBC Blue, sustaining; 1940, CBS, sustaining.

Raymond Scott Orchestra. c1940, 1942, 1943 (two series), 1943-1944, 1944, CBS, sustaining.

Your Hit Parade. Early 1940s (vocal group), NBC, American Tobacco Company (Lucky Strike cigarettes).

The Prudential Family Hour. 1941–1948, CBS, Prudential Insurance Company (Prudential insurance).

The Jack Smith Show. 1943-1944, CBS, sustaining.

Glamour Manor. 1944–1946, ABC, Procter & Gamble Company (Ivory soap).

Gaslight Gaieties. 1944-1945, NBC, Procter & Gamble Company (household detergents and soaps).

The Jack Smith Show (aka *The Oxydol Show, The Tide Show*). 1945–1952, CBS, Procter & Gamble Company (Oxydol and Tide detergents).

The Doris Day Show. 1952-1953, CBS, sustaining.

JO STAFFORD

Born: November 12, 1917, Coalinga, California.

Signature Song: *You Belong to Me*.

Legendary Tunes: *Candy, For You, I'll Never Smile Again, Jambalaya, Keep It a Secret, Make Love to Me, Manhattan Serenade, Serenade of the Bells, Shrimp Boats, Some Enchanted Evening, Tennessee Waltz, That's for Me, Timtayshun, Whispering Hope*.

Highlights: Serious music pupil in high school intending to be classical soprano but joined two siblings in country music act, The Stafford Sisters, on local dates and over Los Angeles' KHJ; freelanced on radio with Pied Pipers vocal ensemble, joining Tommy Dorsey's outfit in late 1930s; recorded for Capitol (1943–1950) with string of solo pop hits followed by more with Columbia; taped weekly quarter-hour for overseas broadcast by Voice of Democracy (1950) followed by half-hour series weekly over 200,000-watt Radio Luxembourg heard by millions of continentals ("In her own quiet way Stafford is selling America to Europe," allowed station's Brit director); married ex-Dorsey arranger Paul Weston (1952) whose orchestra often backed her on air, personal appearances, discs; turned up spasmodically on *The Voice of Firestone* simulcasts (early 1950s); *The Jo Stafford Show* continued on CBS-TV (1954-1955); 1961 British TV series shown in U.S., Australia, Canada, New Zealand; past president SHARE, aiding mentally challenged kids.

Radio Shows:

The Raleigh-Kool Program. 1938-1939, 1940, NBC, Brown & Williamson Tobacco Company (Raleigh and Kool cigarettes).

Summer Pastime. 1940, NBC, The Pepsodent Company (Pepsodent toothpaste).

Fame and Fortune. 1940-1941, NBC Blue, Nature's Remedy health products.

Tommy Dorsey's Variety Show. 1942, NBC Blue, sustaining; 1942, NBC, Brown & Williamson Tobacco Company (Raleigh cigarettes and Sir Walter Raleigh pipe tobacco).

Tommy Dorsey Orchestra. 1942-1943, NBC, Brown & Williamson Tobacco Company (Raleigh cigarettes and Sir Walter Raleigh pipe tobacco).

The Colgate Program (aka *The Al Jolson Show*). 1942-1943, CBS, Colgate-Palmolive-Peet Company (Colgate dental cream).

The Johnny Mercer Music Shop (aka *The Chesterfield Music Shop*). 1943, NBC, The Pepsodent Company (Pepsodent toothpaste); 1944, NBC, Liggett & Myers Tobacco Company (Chesterfield cigarettes).

The Bob Crosby Show. 1943-1944, NBC, P. Lorillard, Inc. (Old Gold cigarettes).

The Chesterfield Supper Club. 1944–1949, NBC, Liggett & Myers Tobacco Company (Chesterfield cigarettes).

The Jo Stafford Show. 1945, CBS, sustaining.

The Bob Crosby Show. 1946, CBS, Ford Motor Company (Ford automobiles and trucks).

The Jo Stafford Show. 1948-1949, ABC, Revere Camera Company (Revere cameras and photographic supplies).

The Carnation Contented Hour (aka *The Contented Hour*). 1949–1951, CBS, Carnation Milk Company (Carnation evaporated milk).

Bob Crosby's Club 15. 1950–1953, CBS, Campbell Soup Company (Campbell's juices and soups, Franco-American spaghetti and macaroni and other foodstuffs).

Paul Weston Orchestra. 1951-1952, network unsubstantiated, sustaining.

The Jo Stafford Show. 1953, CBS, sustaining.

The Chesterfield Supper Club. 1954-1955, NBC, Liggett & Myers Tobacco Company (Chesterfield cigarettes).

MEL TORME

Born: September 13, 1925, Chicago, Illinois.

Died: June 5, 1999, Los Angeles, California.

Signature Song: *The Christmas Song* (aka *Chestnuts Roasting on an Open Fire*).

Legendary Tunes: *Again, Blue Moon, California Suite, Careless Love, Careless Hands, Comin' Home Baby, Homeward*

Bound, It Might as Well Be Spring, Lament for Love, Lulu's Back in Town, Mountain Greenery, Oh You Beautiful Doll, Raindrops Are Falling on My Head, Red Rubber Ball, Secret Agent Man, Sunny Side of the Street, Sunshine Superman, What Is This Thing Called Love?, You're Driving Me Crazy.

Highlights: Began singing professionally at age 4 with Coon-Sanders band; singer whose career embraced acting, including ongoing role of Joe Corntassel, heroine's pal on juvenile adventure serial *Little Orphan Annie*, several other dramatic roles as adolescent thespian, and — in final aural variety series— as college student in comedy sketch, plus intermittent visits to a 1980s-1990s TV sitcom; left early dramatic radio roles when voice changed, becoming rhythm vocalist with Chico Marx band (1942); formed Mel-Tones ensemble in 1944 backing Torme on radio, recordings; excelled as drummer, pianist, arranger, composer, penning more than 300 tunes, best recalled for *The Christmas Song* (1947); appeared in several movies, authored four books including 1988 autobiography, *It Wasn't All Velvet*; labeled "the Velvet Fog" by publicist for husky-voiced sensual lyrical style; appeared on plethora of TV series including emcee of CBS daytime variety series *The Mel Torme Show* (1951-1952), co-host with Peggy Lee of TV's *Top Tunes* on CBS (1951), co-host with Teresa Brewer of CBS musical escape *Summertime U.S.A.* (1953), random visits to CBS's *Judy Garland Show* (1963-1964), host of ABC anthology *It Was a Very Good Year* (1971), sporadically acted as self on NBC's *Night Court* sitcom (1984–1992); nominated for best supporting actor in "The Comedian" on CBS-TV's *Playhouse 90* (1956); earned Grammy as best male jazz vocalist (1982 and 1983) and Grammy Lifetime Achievement Award shortly before death in 1999.

Radio Shows:

Little Orphan Annie. 1930, Chicago's WGN, sustaining; 1931–1936, NBC Blue, and 1936–1940, NBC, Wander Company (Ovaltine flavored milk beverage); 1940–1942, MBS, Quaker Oats Company (Quaker Oats cereal). [Torme did not appear on the programs throughout the series' life.]

Jack Armstrong, the All American Boy. 1933–1936, CBS; 1936–1939, NBC; 1941–c1942, MBS, General Mills, Inc. (Wheaties cereal). [Torme did not appear on the programs throughout the series' life.]

The Romance of Helen Trent. 1933–c1942, CBS, Edna W. Hopper (Hopper's White Clay Pack facial mask) in the early years, from late 1930s by American Home Products Corporation (Black Flag and Fly-Ded insect repellents, Aerowax and Olde English floor cleaners, Wizard Wick room deodorizer, Sani-Flush toilet bowl cleanser, Easy-Off oven cleaner, Kolynos toothpaste and tooth powder, Anacin pain reliever, Kriptin antihistamine, Bi-So-Dol analgesic, Freezone corn remover, Heet liniment, Dristan and Primatene cold remedies, Preparation H hemorrhoid medication, Neet hair remover, Infrarub sore muscle balm, Sleep-Eze calmative and similar commodities).

Lights Out. 1934-1935, Chicago's WENR; 1935–c1939, NBC, sponsorship unsubstantiated. [Torme did not appear on the programs throughout the series' life.]

Song of the City (aka *Rainbow Court*). 1934-1935, NBC Midwest, Procter & Gamble Company (Dreft dishwashing detergent).

The Fitch Bandwagon. 1944-1945, NBC, F. W. Fitch Company (Fitch shampoo).

Ice Box Follies (aka *Niles and Prindle*).

1945, ABC, Hires Company (Hires Root Beer soft drink).
Torme Time. 1947, NBC, Gillette Company (Toni home permanents and other women's hair care commodities).
The New Mel Torme Show. 1948, NBC, Philip Morris Company (Philip Morris cigarettes).

ARTHUR TRACY

Born: June 25, 1899, Kamenetz-Podolsk, Moldavia (born Abba Tracovutsky).
Died: October 5, 1997, Manhattan, New York.
Signature Song: *Marta (Rambling Rose of the Wildwood).*
Legendary Tunes: *Because, The Breeze and I, Danny Boy, I'll Have the Last Waltz with Mother, I'll See You Again, Kiss Me Goodnight, The Last Roundup, Little Old Lady, My First Love My Last Love for Always, Old Pal of Mine, Pennies from Heaven, Play to Me Gypsy, Red Sails in the Sunset, Reflections in the Water, San Antonio Rose, Say It, There's a Gold Mine in the Sky, Was it Rain?, When I Grow Too Old to Dream.*
Highlights: Arriving in the U.S. at age 6, raised in Philadelphia, self-taught singer imitating Caruso's recordings; learned (and sang) half-dozen dialects, first concert in daddy's grape arbor; studied at Philly's Curtis Institute for Voice Development and assistant cantor at synagogue; on local airwaves by 1924 and New York's WMCA in 1930; sang at Philadelphia vaudeville venues, lobbies of fashionable Atlantic City hotels, New York theater amateur nights and toured with hit Broadway musical *Blossom Time*; given a quarter-hour slot on CBS by network president William Paley, added dimension of mystique to performances by hiding identity, appearing as "The Street Singer" on radio, records, club and show bills; evening songfests on ether introduced by David Ross with "Round the corner and down your way comes *The Street Singer* to sing to you his romantic ballads of yesterday and yore," viewed as throwback by current pundits to "the way radio used to be"; publicity stills depicted young man in felt hat with accordion; radio contract netted him $3,000 weekly; movie debut in *The Big Broadcast* (1932) with Bing Crosby, Kate Smith, The Boswell Sisters; after identity revealed and popularity waned, sailed for England and entertained (1935–1939) at personal appearances and in several British films (*Limelight, The Street Singer, Command Performance, Follow Your Star*), returning for U.K. performances in 1948 and tributes from veteran entertainers in 1995; guest appearances on U. S. television (1960s) and at age 82 comeback singing at The Cookery's cabaret, Greenwich Village; toured with Broadway play *Social Security* and appeared in final film, *Crossing Delancey* (1980s); received Ellis Island Medal of Honor (1996); biography, *The Street Singer*, released shortly after death.
Radio Shows:
Pillsbury Pageant. 1931-1932, CBS, Pillsbury Mills (Pillsbury baking goods).
Music That Satisfies. 1932, CBS, Liggett & Myers Tobacco Company (Chesterfield cigarettes).
The Street Singer. 1932, 1932-1933, 1933 (two series), CBS, sponsorship unsubstantiated except for final 1933 series by Non-Spi Company.
The Street Singer. 1935, 1940, MBS, sponsorship unsubstantiated.
The Street Singer. 1942, NBC Blue, Ex-lax laxative.

RUDY VALLEE

Born: July 28, 1901, Island Pond, Vermont (born Hubert Prior Vallee).

Died: July 3, 1986, North Hollywood, California.

Signature Song: *My Time Is Your Time.*

Legendary Tunes: *As Time Goes By, Betty Co-ed, Brother Can You Spare a Dime?, Casablanca, Deep Night, Don't Play with Fire, Heigh-ho Everybody — Heigh-ho, Honey, I'd Rather Lead a Band, If I Had a Girl Like You, If You Haven't Got a Girl, I'm Just a Vagabond Lover, I'm Putting All My Eggs in One Basket, I'm Still Caring, Just an Echo in the Valley, Let's Put Out the Lights, A Little Kiss Each Morning (A Little Kiss Each Night), Lonely Troubadour, Marie, Nola, Oh Ma-Ma, Two Little Blue Eyes, Vieni Vieni, When Yuba Plays the Rumba on the Tuba, Would You Like to Take a Walk?, You're Driving Me Crazy.*

Highlights: "The original crooner" (even predating Crosby), one of radio's most durable stars; initially appeared on ether in London (1924), later performing over New York's WABC (*Heigh Ho Club*, 1928) with Rudy Vallee and His Connecticut Yankees band, having been saxophonist with Vincent Lopez's outfit earlier; celebrated aural entertainer who frequented guest lists of other NBC luminaries (Fred Allen, George Burns and Gracie Allen, Edgar Bergen, Judy Canova, Eddie Cantor, Phil Harris and Alice Faye, Frank Sinatra, Red Skelton, ad infinitum); talent scout introducing unknowns who later became headliners; termed "the most difficult taskmaster of all" by industry cohorts; acted in 35 films, 1929's *The Vagabond Lover* among more prominent; during radio's twilight, one of surfeit of celebrities succumbing to trend toward spinning records, mixing chatter and turntables, over New York's WOR (1950-1951), CBS (1955); recurring appearances on NBC's *The Big Show* (1950–1952); turned up on television hosting variety series *On Broadway Tonight* (1964, 1945, CBS), occasional guest shots elsewhere; starred in four-year smash Broadway hit, *How to Succeed in Business without Even Trying* (1961–1965) and later movie version (1967).

Radio Shows:

The Fleischmann Hour (aka *The Sunshine Hour*). 1929–1936, NBC, Standard Brands, Inc. (Fleischmann's yeast).

Rudy Vallee Orchestra. 1934–1936, NBC Blue, sponsorship unsubstantiated.

The Royal Gelatin Hour. 1936–1939, Standard Brands, Inc. (Royal gelatin desserts).

Vallee Varieties (aka *The Sealtest Show*). 1940–1943, NBC, Sealtest Dairies (Sealtest dairy products).

The Drene Show. 1944–1946, NBC, Drene shampoo.

The Rudy Vallee Show. 1946-1947, NBC, Philip Morris Company (Philip Morris cigarettes).

The Rudy Vallee Show. 1955, CBS, Kraft Foods Company (Kraft cheese and other foodstuffs).

The Voice of Firestone

Here was a big production that cut across the boundaries of musical tastes, offering classics and spirited marches, show tunes and pop standards. Confirmed a critic: "*The Voice of Firestone* was popular because its music was beautiful and familiar." The broadcast strongly influenced the listening habits of Americans for at least two generations. It was the keystone of NBC's "Monday Night of Music" in the 1940s and early 1950s, a dominant force for bringing music of its type to radio and eventually to television. Over the years it presented some of the most gifted artists of the Metropolitan Opera and other important venues. Because the music varied, listeners could hear identifiable names singing melodies from Broadway and movies and opera. The program set a record of longevity for its mixed blend, continuing from 1928 to 1959, adding a final season in 1962-1963. It offered quality programming every time out. When it was gone, fans grieved its passing.

Director/Writer: Edwin L. Dunham.

Orchestra Conductors: Hugo Mariani (1928–1930), William Daly (1931–936), Alfred Wallenstein (1936–1943), Howard Barlow (1943–1957), Wilfred Pelletier (part of 1955).

Guest Artists: Franklyn Baur (tenor), Mimi Benzell (coloratura soprano), Jussi Bjoerling (tenor), Frank Chapman (baritone), Eugene Conley (tenor), Nadine Conner (lyric soprano), Richard Crooks (tenor), Vaughn DeLeath (soprano), Nelson Eddy (baritone), Eileen Farrell (soprano), Igor Gorin (baritone), Jerome Hines (bass), Lois Hunt (lyric soprano), Dorothy Kirsten (soprano), George London (bass-baritone), Christopher Lynch (tenor), Elaine Malbin (soprano), Lauritz Melchior (tenor), James Melton (tenor), Robert Merrill (baritone), Patrice Munsel (soprano), Roberta Peters (soprano), Ezio Pinza (bass), Gladys Rice (soprano), Robert Rounseville (tenor), Cesare Siepi (bass), Beverly Sills (soprano), Margaret Speaks (soprano), Eleanor Steber (soprano), Risë Stevens (mezzo-soprano), Brian Sullivan (tenor), Gladys Swarthout (mezzo-soprano), Thomas L. Thomas (baritone), Lawrence Tibbett (baritone), Helen Traubel (soprano), Dorothy Warenskjold (lyric soprano).

Announcer: Hugh James.

Theme Songs: *In My Garden, If I Could Tell You* (both by Mrs. Harvey S. [Idabelle] Firestone Sr.).

Sponsor: Firestone Tire and Rubber Company.

Ratings: High — 17.3 (1933-1934 season); low — 5.7 (1948-1949); median — 10.3. Figures include 18 seasons (1933–1951). In its heyday era, for a concert program this one performed exceptionally well.

On the Air: December 3, 1928–May 26, 1930, NBC, Monday, 8:00–8:30 P.M. Eastern Time; September 7, 1931–June 7, 1954, NBC, Monday, 8:30–9:00 P.M.; June 14, 1954–June 10, 1957, ABC, Monday, 8:30–9:00 P.M. Simulcast on NBC-TV from September 5, 1949–June 7, 1954; simulcast on ABC-TV from June 14, 1954–June 10, 1957, with series continuing on ABC-TV through 1958-59 season and again in 1962-63 season.

* * *

The Voice of Firestone was one of radio's most prestigious and durable contributions to listeners, substantially lifting the stature of understanding and appreciation of the fine arts in millions of American households. Across 32 years (counting its radio inception and television extension) the legendary feature became a hallmark of outstanding musical accomplishment, fostering an impervious quality of blended instruments and voices that its audience grew to anticipate with savor every week. Its stars — and there were many — were commonly recognized in homes across the land. Offering an entertaining format, it exuded culture without being overbearing. The program's upbeat style and choice selections of classical, semiclassical and standard musical favorites resonated with listeners, lifting the hearts of legions of admirers, some of whom worshiped faithfully at the temple of Firestone for many years.

More than two decades into its long run *The Voice of Firestone* surfaced on tiny black-and-white television screens, just then being widely introduced into the nation's living rooms. For the first time millions could see what they had been hearing for so many years. It included guest artists in tuxes or evening gowns, well-groomed instrumentalists and a sprightly choral ensemble, along with a coterie of dancers that was added for the home viewing audience. But the music itself remained as inspiring visually as it was tonally. Although TV removed the element of imagination — developing one's own image of what that hallowed stage looked like — the camera made it possible to experience it as it really was, and to do so while it was actually taking place.

For eight years those concerts were among a small handful of simulcast features — a fresh, never-repeated live broadcast on radio and on television at the same time for a half-hour in prime time every Monday night. Those who had access to a TV and missed a telecast might pick it up on their portable or vehicle radios. Millions more who hadn't yet shelled out big bucks for a television set could still hear their show every week in audio only. In that epoch, they undoubtedly had the best of both worlds.

Over its lifetime the show won many impressive awards. In 1948, *Musical America* named it the most outstanding musical program with featured artists. There were numerous others.

The Voice of Firestone began on December 3, 1928, as *The Firestone Hour*, altering its name in time to the more familiar, long-remembered moniker. The sponsoring Firestone Tire and Rubber Company of Akron, Ohio, was a major American family enterprise. The Firestone organization maintained a strong identification with the program for as long as it aired, much more so than average bankrolled series relationships. On its very first broadcast, Harvey S. Firestone Sr., the concern's founder, appeared at the show's conclusion.

"I hope this program has been a wholesome feature in your household," said he, offering a hint about where the new venture was headed. *The Firestone Hour* would remain under constant scrutiny of the watchful eyes of Harvey Sr. and his wife, Idabelle, for the rest of their lives, and occupy a prominent role in the future of their heirs. Speaking of the senior Firestone, a critic confirmed: "He and his family took a personal, almost paternalistic, interest in the proceedings."

The Firestone Hour embraced the popular music of its day and included show tunes and numbers echoing a strong allegiance to God and country. It was, in the purest sense, a weekly family values-oriented production. During its first couple of years, much of the actual performing was vested in tenor Franklyn Baur and soprano Vaughn DeLeath accompanied by an orchestral aggregate of 17 pieces that was rapidly enlarged to 35 members, under the baton of maestro Hugo Mariani. (After Mariani's departure in 1930 that number eventually swelled to 90 musicians and become popularly known as the Firestone Symphony Orchestra.) A pundit observed: "Neither [Baur nor DeLeath] had an extensive serious music background, but in 1928 and 1929, listeners had leaned toward lighter melodies, especially Broadway tunes, Irish ballads, and Stephen Foster songs."

Baur, a Brooklynite and only 25 at the program's inception, had been a church soloist before joining the Shannon Four, predecessor of The Revelers, an eminent New York quartet of that period. His involvement there thrust him into *Ziegfeld Follies of 1927* as well as recordings and personal appearances. That resulted in a stint on the debuting *Palmolive Hour* in 1928, a weekly musical showcase over NBC. The show undoubtedly influenced Firestone officials to pick him as the male vocalist for their premiering feature later that same year.

In December 1919, DeLeath earned a distinction as "The Original Radio Girl." At New York's World Building she purportedly was the first female to speak into a microphone, talking and singing *Swanee River* sans accompaniment. No more than three dozen people heard her that day on a "show" engineered by radio pioneer Lee De Forest. Yet it was a start. In a progression to several New York radio outlets she learned to speak, sing, announce and direct programs as well as to manage a station. She was well known locally when Firestone approached her to be its feminine vocalist for the national series in 1928. She continued singing beyond that outing, winding down her career at stations in Oklahoma City, Bridgeport and Buffalo.

From its inception, the *Firestone* series contributed heavily to turning Monday evening's radio programming agenda to one where quality music was commemorated. A new tradition had been launched that would survive on the originating network for more than a quarter of a century. Debuting at 8 o'clock in the evening from New York, a second live show was broadcast at 11 o'clock for listeners living in the Pacific Time zone. *Firestone* was responsible for so many firsts in broadcasting — at that juncture it staged the first transcontinental repeat, setting a pattern that scores of live shows that emanated from the East Coast would practice.

Everything was running smoothly in the first few months of the *Firestone* show. In addition to the two principal vocalists backed by the orchestra, a male quartet was occasionally inserted into the schedule. Audiences were discovering that the semiclassics and other favorite melodies were being broadcast on the airwaves. They were drawn to it in increasing numbers. Sponsor and network officials were satisfied and settled into what was to become a longstanding tradition that was mutually rewarding to both parties. Had it not been for an unexpected turn of events precipitated by an ungrateful artist, the series might have continued at its current pace with little fanfare or notoriety, gaining most of its new listeners from people who stumbled across it on their dials or simply by word of mouth. What occurred in 1929, however, netted some unsolicited and unwelcome publicity.

The sponsor asked Franklyn Baur to sing at a celebratory affair scheduled in Dearborn, Michigan, headquarters of the Ford Motor Company. The occasion was the 1929 Golden Jubilee of the electric light bulb. Among scheduled participants for the event were President Herbert Hoover and inventor Thomas A. Edison, the latter one of carmaker Henry Ford's chums. (Harvey Firestone Sr. and Ford had been pals for years, too, a connection that spilled over beyond personal interests into business relationships. The association of their respective organizations persisted for nearly a century.)

Instead of honoring the request made of him to perform, however, Baur demurred, holding out for a $1,000 talent fee on top of his presumably generous compensation for his *Firestone* appearances. The sponsor was discomfited and incensed. When Baur's contract expired a short time later he was swiftly terminated. His refusal apparently cost him more than the loss of his role on that prestigious show. NBC refused to book him on any of its programs in the future. Potential sponsors, learning of his exploit, spurned him. Ironically, he did put in an appearance at *Firestone's* 10th anniversary broadcast in late 1938. (Harvey S. Firestone Sr. had died that year and that may have allowed it. Harvey's widow, Idabelle, and son, Harvey Jr., took a hand in shaping the broadcasts following the passing of Harvey Sr., incidentally.)

Baur, meanwhile, had abandoned radio to study voice in France. He returned to debut in a recital at New York's Town Hall in 1933. "It did little for a fast-fading career," an observer informed. Falling into obscurity, Baur became "a victim of his own blatant avarice" claimed another. Baur died in his native Brooklyn in 1950. He was just 46. (Ironically, his singing partner, Vaughn DeLeath, was also only 46 when she died in 1943.)

The talent and direction on the *Firestone* show was overhauled. The Jazz Age of the 1920s concluded and the Firestones began to favor more serious music, infrequently including operatic artists. Tenor James Melton and soprano Gladys Rice replaced Bauer and DeLeath about 1930. The following year, the star system transitioned to a single soloist with tenor Richard Crooks and baritone Lawrence Tibbett, the first Metropolitan Opera star, assuming alternate weeks as vocalists. By 1934, Tibbett was elsewhere and a trio of singing celebs appeared at sundry times including Crooks, baritone Frank Chapman and mezzo-soprano Gladys Swarthout (Chapman and Swarthout were married to each other). The composition changed again a couple of years hence with Crooks remaining and soprano Margaret Speaks joining him for what was lauded as "many memorable duets." That pattern prevailed into the 1940s, although the duo normally alternated weeks.

Speaks made her final appearance on May 31, 1943. For a year, Crooks carried on virtually alone. In the summer of 1944, *The Voice of Firestone* began to open up its guest roster to other voices, a format that proliferated and became standard practice for the rest of the program's history. While Richard Crooks was the only soloist many times through March 26, 1945, and had a few more appearances before quitting altogether, the near "exclusivity" that he and the others enjoyed finally came to an end. From mid-1944 onward there were many recurring *Firestone* voices, several repeated frequently, but no artists that turned up literally every week.

While Eleanor Steber, Christopher Lynch, Risë Stevens and Thomas L. Thomas would appear scores of times in the years ahead, there would be many more just as skilled who would appear less often but be able to carry the legendary performing traditions of the *Firestone* fame. The fact that they aired fewer times from the Firestone dais in no way diminishes the abilities of those talented musical artists. Included in this rotating coterie were notables like Mimi Benzell, Jussi Bjoerling, Nadine Conner, George London, Elaine Malbin, James Melton, Robert Merrill, Mildred Miller, Patrice Munsel, Roberta Peters, Robert Rounseville, Cesare Siepi, Brian Sullivan, Dorothy Warenskjold and Leonard Warren, all of whom appeared several times. There were many more who turned up for only one or two performances.

The orchestra leaders were also changing. When Hugo Mariani, who had been there at the start, departed in 1930, William Daly ascended the podium in 1931 as permanent successor. But before Daly's arrival there was a succession of impresarios who briefly occupied that venue. They included Rosario Bourdon, Gustave Haenschen, Nathaniel Shilkret and Wilfred Pelletier. Upon Daley's death five years hence, Alfred Wallenstein accepted the *Firestone* baton, relinquishing it seven years later to direct the Los Angeles Symphony. The fourth, most durable and best remembered of *Firestone's* maestros was Howard Barlow, who took over in 1943. He persisted through the radio reign and most of the television epoch. His arrival signaled a shift toward more traditional music, one critic describing it as "somewhat old-fashioned yet comfortable as an old shoe." Barlow embodied the musical series in the minds of millions of Americans that were entertained by the program weekly. He left significant handprints on all of those productions over the next decade and a half.

Howard Barlow was born May 1, 1892, in Plain City, Ohio. Having begun his career as a boy soprano, he later attended Reed College and Columbia University (the latter on scholarship) while conducting choral groups and arranging choral works for music publishers during the pre–World War I era. When the war intervened he became an infantry sergeant. Returning to New York, he developed as an orchestral conductor, practicing his skills at a 1919 festival sponsored by the Federation of American Music Clubs. In 1923, he formed the American National Orchestra, employing only native-born Americans. When the Columbia network was established eight years later, Barlow was one of its first staff conductors. A biographer noted that he was responsible for much of the chain's "serious music presence." He was also maestro of the Columbia Symphony Orchestra, a widely esteemed outfit.

The first classical musical piece CBS aired, *Ballet Egyptienne*, featured Barlow and his newly fashioned group. Remembering those initial weeks on the air, Barlow recounted: "The matter of getting off the air on time was not very important then. The Telephone Company allowed us up to three minutes overtime."

From March 3, 1931, through July 1, 1943, Barlow conducted music for the celebrated *March of Time* documentary. It began on CBS, drifted to NBC Blue in 1937 and wound up at NBC in his final season. Simultaneously he was impresario with the Baltimore Symphony in 1939 and guest conductor of the New York Philharmonic Orchestra in 1942 and 1943. The latter body aired weekly over CBS. In 1940, he received a certificate of merit given by the National Association of American Composers and Conductors as "the outstanding native interpreter of American music."

Barlow relinquished his duties with *The March of Time* when he was tapped for *The Voice of Firestone*, which was to be the crowning achievement of an extensive career, continuing throughout the 1950s. There he not only conducted an orchestra but also coordinated a large choral group and a cluster of dancers. He was "fastidiously attired," according to one pundit, in white tie and tails, having often worn a sweatshirt and blue jeans when he started in radio. In 1954, he also directed music for the CBS Sunday afternoon series *Twentieth Century Concert Hall*. Barlow died January 31, 1972, in Bethel, Connecticut.

The program lineups for *The Voice of Firestone* have been partially maintained from September 1, 1941, and close to fully preserved since January 1, 1945. They depict a flexible range of music that veered between classics, semiclassics, pop numbers and old standards. Almost all of the bills featured one or two "name" artists (nearly always vocalists, seldom instrumentalists, a prime distinction separating *Firestone* from *The Bell Telephone Hour*). Only on very rare occasions did three or more performers turn up as guests on a single broadcast; usually that was prompted by an extra special celebration marking a noteworthy event. Duets, however, were not uncommon and on average may have occurred every fourth or fifth week.

In addition to three or four numbers sung by a guest artist, usually there would be a couple of orchestra instrumentals and possibly a choral number or two comprising each weekly lineup. During the simulcast (radio–TV) era beginning in 1949, the show often opened with a stirring choral classic in the vein of *Strike Up the Band, Washington Post March, King Cotton March, June is Busting Out All Over, Blue Skies* and *Stars and Stripes Forever* before launching into a more subdued aria or other slower-paced selection sung by the evening's featured vocalist. Chosen at random, here are a half-dozen program offerings and their celebrity performers from the series' final dozen years appearing to be representative of the period.

Air Date: March 5, 1945
Guest Artist: Richard Crooks
Pomp and Circumstance March (Elgar)
Then You'll Remember Me (Balfe)
Hungarian Dance No. 6 (Brahms)
Come Where My Love Lies Dreaming (Foster)
Smilin' Thru (Penn)
Stradella Overture (Liadov)
Melody of Love (Firestone)

Air Date: July 28, 1947
Guest Artist: Igor Gorin
1904 Medley (Arrangement)
Through the Years (Youmans)
Minuet (Paderewski)
Pale Moon (Logan)
Thine Alone (Herbert)
March ["Aida"] (Verdi)
Stouthearted Men (Romberg)

Air Date: January 30, 1950
Guest Artist: Risë Stevens
Marching Along Together (Steininger)
They Say It's Wonderful (Berlin)
Melodie in E Flat (Tchaikovsky)
A Dream (Bartlett)
Skater's Waltz (Waldteufel)
March ["Tannhauser"] (Wagner)
Seguidilla ["Carmen"] (Bizet)

Air Date: August 25, 1952
Guest Artist: Jerome Hines
Semper Fidelis (Sousa)
A Pretty Girl Is Like a Melody (Berlin)
Blue Danube Waltz (Strauss)
Air du Tambour ["Le Cid"] (Thomas)
Home on the Range (Guion)
Espana (Chabrier)
Song of the Open Road (Malotte)

Air Date: November 29, 1954
Guest Artists: Eugene Conley and Nadine Conner
Farandole ["L'Arlesiane"] (Bizet)
Ohe Gelida Marina (Puccini)
Si Mi Chiamano Mimi (Puccini)
O Soave Fanciuilla ["La Boheme"] (Puccini)

Dance of the Comedians (Smetena)
Give Me One Hour (Friml)

Air Date: May 20, 1957
Guest Artist: Robert Merrill
King Cotton March (Sousa)
Because (D'Hardalot)
Medley (Foster)
On the Street Where You Live (Lerner-Lowe)
Il Balen ["Trovatore"] (Verdi)
Night on a Bald Mountain (Mussorgsky)
Every Day Is Lassies Day (Herbert)

The Voice of Firestone presented scores of guest artists during its long run. While there is no known documentation for the years 1928–1941 (although we know the names of talent appearing most frequently in that period, previously noted), a complete list is available from September 1, 1941, through the end of the series, including television, on June 16, 1963. Focusing on those years, it's a matter of simple arithmetic to learn whom the Firestones (who controlled many decisions surrounding the program) favored by the number of times an individual performed. While many paid recurring visits to that stage, a few were summoned scores of times. Between 1941 and 1963, the 10 most active *Firestone* vocalists were, in descending order:

Richard Crooks (115 appearances), Eleanor Steber (107), Christopher Lynch (69), Risë Stevens (58), Thomas L. Thomas (43), Margaret Speaks (40), Jerome Hines (37), Gladys Swarthout (34), Igor Gorin (33), Eugene Conley (28). Of course, if the hundreds of performances by Richard Crooks between 1932 and 1941, for which no permanent record is available, were included in the tally, the figures for him alone would exceed the remainder of the most active 10 combined.

Because their names are the most familiar to listeners of the popular series, capsule introductions of the top 10 artists in number of appearances follow.

Richard Crooks was born June 26, 1900, in Trenton, New Jersey. He began his career as a boy soprano in a church choir. He later studied with Sidney H. Bourne and Frank LaForge in New York City. Following several hectic concert seasons as an oratorio and song recital specialist, he went to Germany, making his operatic debut in Hamburg as Cavaradossi in 1927. His American introduction three years later in the same role was with the Philadelphia Symphony. Three years after that (February 25, 1933) he premiered on the stage of the Metropolitan Opera House as Massenet's Des Grieux. He remained with the Met to 1943, leaving it on the advice of a physician. Crooks also appeared with the New York Philharmonic Orchestra and in recitals across the U.S.

His "sweet, yet virile" tenor voice allowed him "to sing any kind of music with exquisite taste," according to a music historian. "He sang with ease a broad range of material, from art songs to popular numbers, from French operatic arias to old English ballads." Music critic Harold Schonberg cited Crooks' "impeccable phrasing and musical dignity" as prime attributes. Wrote Peter Davis in *The American Opera Singer*: "From his photographs at least, Crooks always gave the impression of a friendly insurance salesman. But the voice was by far the most attractive among the American tenors of his generation."

He joined *The Voice of Firestone* staff in early 1932 and from then through March 26, 1945, was its most visible personality. He was obviously pleasing to the Firestone family, too, in whose home he visited. On one occasion he listened as Idabelle Firestone (Mrs. Harvey S. Sr.) played a piece for him titled *In My Garden* that she had recently composed. Crooks was genuinely impressed by both the melody and lyrics. Upon the song's publication, he got her permission to sing it on the program of July 25, 1932. In the next few years Crooks and Lawrence Tibbett performed the ballad many times. A quadrennial after its debut the song was adopted as the show's permanent theme.

When the American Society of Composers, Authors and Publishers (ASCAP) mounted a legal challenge a few years later to radio's access to its compositions without the medium paying usage fees, then banning all of its existing tunes from the air, Mrs. Firestone composed a new theme, *If I Could Tell You*. It was substituted for the original work and received favorable acclaim. When radio and the ASCAP at last made peace, *If I Could Tell You* opened the weekly program and *In My Garden* concluded it. The dual numbers continued for the rest of the program's life, becoming familiar to millions of listeners and viewers. Richard Crooks had been pivotal in introducing both melodies to the airwaves.

Crooks once testified that singing on the radio gave him "the loneliest feeling in the world, to have no audience to sing to," thus he pursued a heavy concert and operatic agenda between *Firestone* broadcasts. He promised himself that he would relinquish his stage and radio appearances when he could no longer project a worthy singing voice. On his final 1945 *Firestone* outing he lost a top note. Possessing a degenerative throat condition, Crooks found it increasingly difficult to gain muscular support following a string of operations for peritonitis. He retired on the spot, canceled his Victor recording contract and — within five years—ceased all professional work. He moved to California to be nearer his children and was often called upon to sing solos in churches. It was reminiscent of his vocal start years earlier. Crooks died on October 1, 1972, in San Mateo, California.

Eleanor Steber was born July 17, 1914, in Wheeling, West Virginia. Her mother, an amateur vocalist and voice and piano teacher, pushed her toward a music career. The girl sang in school and community shows before pursuing a bachelor's degree in voice at Boston's New England Conservatory of Music, earned in 1938. Two years earlier, she made her operatic debut with the Commonwealth Opera as Senta in *The Flying Dutchman*. She went to New York in 1939 to study with Paul Althouse. The following year she won first prize on *The Metropolitan Opera Auditions of the Air*, complete with accompanying Met contract. She also sang in churches and oratorio concerts and signed an exclusive Columbia recording contract.

The New York press classified her as "a star that sings like an angel." Another source evaluating her career surmised: "Steber was one of the most important sopranos in the USA during the 1940s and 1950s, with a sweet and yet full voice, and outstanding versatility." Soon appearing with the NBC Symphony Orchestra on radio, she debuted on *The Voice of Firestone* on September 18, 1944. So well was she received by that audience — and perhaps more importantly, by the Firestones themselves— that she was asked to return 106 more times. It soon became obvious to bystanders that someone was looking out for her interests for she gained several plum assignments there. For 13 years (1945–1957) Steber was the sole vocalist for the show's annual Christmas concert. When the series staged a one-time simulcast tryout on NBC Radio and TV on March 22, 1948, Steber was featured on that Easter outing. She was also one of six artists (two women) invited to perform at the celebration of the program's 25th anniversary in 1953.

In the meantime, both her professional career and personal life were experiencing ups and downs. Steber debuted in more premiers at the Met than any other artist, appearing in 50 different leading operatic roles altogether. She performed on stage 404 times, 118 while on tour and 286 in New York. When Rudolph Bing was appointed as the Met's new executive leader, however, Steber felt frozen out, passed over for roles she had handily won in the past. When offered a contract in 1961 stipulating only "covering" roles, she quit, choosing concerts and recitals instead. She wasn't happy in her private life either. Two marriages dissolved, she suffered asthma and was addicted to alcohol.

Things turned around for her down the road. From 1963 to 1972, Steber was head of the voice department at the Cleveland Institute of Music. Beginning in 1971, she also taught at Julliard School of Music in New York and the New England Conservatory of Music in Boston (her alma mater). From 1978 to 1980 and again in 1988, she taught at the American Institute of Music Studies in Graz. In 1975, the concert diva established the Eleanor Steber Music Foundation with the purpose of aiding aspiring young singers. Her autobiography was published posthumously; she died October 3, 1990, in Langhorne, Pennsylvania.

Christopher Lynch was born in 1920 in County Limerick, Ireland. He died April 15, 1994, in Worcestershire, England. In a sense, he never got away from his roots, normally spending summers in Ireland, despite a brief working career in the United States. He signed recording contracts with Columbia and Victor labels yet remained one of only a handful of *Firestone* artists without direct ties to the Metropolitan Opera during the show's halcyon days.

John McCormack picked him as his vocal "heir" after Lynch was a pupil of the unrivaled Irish tenor in Ireland. The first of Lynch's 69 appearances on *The Voice of Firestone* occurred on September 30, 1946. Harvey S. Firestone Sr. personally selected the young Irish tenor as a replacement for Richard Crooks, who had departed as lead singer 18 months before. Firestone booked Carnegie Hall for the gala affair—concurrently it was also Lynch's American premiere. For a season, Lynch, 26, and Eleanor Steber, 32, carried much of the vocalizing on the radio feature. By 1947, columnist John Crosby was telling *New York Times* readers that Lynch "sings *Beautiful Isle of Somewhere* so you can smell the shamrocks in it ... he has a lovely full tenor, which is enough to be thankful for in this era of thin barytones [*sic*]."

Lynch took two months off in 1949 for a singing tour to the West Coast. Coupled with the annual vacation to his homeland, it was obvious that his heart was elsewhere. While he made an occasional appearance on *Firestone* in the early 1950s, his day was effectively over. With his departure—and possibly with only the exception of Eleanor Steber, Risë Stevens and Thomas L. Thomas—*The Voice of Firestone* would present no more dominant "stars" once or twice a month or even more often as in the past. Lynch's exodus seemed to hint at a philosophical change in the program's direction for—from then on—a much wider range of guest artists would be in evidence. A music critic summarized Lynch's brief American career by stating that he "never achieved the star status of his mentor McCormack or predecessor Crooks in the United States."

Risë Stevens was born Risë Steenberg on June 11, 1913, in New York City. She not only was an eyewitness to the growth of radio broadcasting but was also a part of it, performing in the medium's infancy on juvenile features and in singing ensembles. In the mid-1930s, she appeared on *The Palmolive Beauty Box Theater*, an NBC anthology. She made it to the semifinals of *The Metropolitan Opera Auditions of the Air* in 1936. Vocal studies at Julliard School of Music and with private tutors in Manhattan and abroad netted invitations for her to sing opera in Prague, Vienna and Buenos Aires.

She was invited to join the Met in 1938 (her debut was on December 17 of that year) and signed an exclusive contract with

Columbia Records. In her lifetime she sang more than a dozen mezzo-soprano roles there to great acclaim, her most celebrated as *Carmen* (she performed it 11 times on Met broadcasts), but also as *Delilah, Octavian* and *Orfeo*. One source termed her "the best Carmen after Conchita Supervia." "No mezzo-soprano of her generation exceeded her star-power or glamour," another review insisted. She made 58 appearances on *The Voice of Firestone* while also singing intermittently on CBS's *Prudential Family Hour* on Sunday afternoons in the 1940s. She hosted a musical variety feature, *The Risë Stevens Show*, Mondays at 9:30 P.M. on NBC between July 2 and September 3, 1945, and was an infrequent guest on a couple of other Monday night musical features on NBC, *The Bell Telephone Hour* and *The Railroad Hour*.

Early in her career she reached even wider audiences by appearing in a couple of major motion pictures. She starred with Nelson Eddy in *The Chocolate Soldier* (1941) and with Bing Crosby and Barry Fitzgerald in *Going My Way* (1944). Reflecting on the experience years later, she spoke with candor: "I thought making movies a bore, a total bore! All that standing around, waiting. And so much time wasted. I mean, I enjoyed making movies, but I wasn't willing to give up my opera career. And in films, there's no audience, so there's no reaction. I really missed that because I love people and having them around me."

She retired from the Met in 1961. "I had physical problems," she confirmed a few years ago. "My shoulders go out of joint very easily and they started doing that on stage and a good many of my roles were very physical. Especially Carmen. I got handled roughly many times by the tenors.... I finally decided I would continue to sing concerts.... But physically, I couldn't do the roles." She added a second reason for quitting: "When you've been singing as long as I had been since age 10 (on *The Children's Hour*), and when you sing year after year, you get tired! I started looking for other things to do."

She turned up in a successful revival of Rodgers and Hammerstein's *The King and I* at Lincoln Center, recorded by RCA Victor. She recorded Kurt Weill and Ira Gershwin's *Lady in the Dark*. There were many television appearances. She became president of Mannes College of Music in New York. And even in advanced years she remained active in Metropolitan Opera affairs, serving as chairman of its Encore Society, a planned giving effort. In that capacity she met with potential givers visiting New York, attempting to persuade them to bequeath some of their assets to the world famous musical organization. Her autobiography, *Subway to the Met*, details her varied experiences before, during and after her sterling professional achievements. At this writing (early 2004) she still lives in New York.

Thomas L. Thomas was born February 23, 1912, in Maesteg, South Wales. The "L" stood for "Llyfwny," a common moniker in the singer's native land. "The Welch-born baritone had little in the way of formal training but learned quickly by on-the-job observation and coaching," wrote an observer. Having moved to Scranton, Pennsylvania, and worked as a machinist, Thomas won the *National Radio Auditions* sponsored by Atwater-Kent in 1932. That led to singing in choruses with an occasional solo. He gained featured roles with Jessica Dragonette on NBC's *Palmolive Beauty Box Theater* in the mid-1930s. In 1937, he won *The Metropolitan Opera Auditions of the Air* and debuted in *Pagliacci* before a crowd of locals in Scranton.

In addition to his appearances at the Met, Thomas came to prominence in American homes as the "beloved singer of stage and radio" starring on a couple of Frank and Anne Hummert musical showcases,

Manhattan Merry-Go-Round (1943–1949, NBC) and *Your Song and Mine* (1948, CBS). On the former, he headlined a Sunday night outing where tunes were decided by current sales of sheet music and recordings, following *Your Hit Parade's* lead. Surrounding him there were several singers including Glenn Cross, Rodney McClennan, Marian McManus, Lucy Monroe, Dick O'Connor, Barry Roberts and Dennis Ryan. On the 1948 show, flanking Thomas were Mary Martha Briney, Felix Knight and Charles Meynante. (See The Hummert Musicales chapter for more on these series.) At the same time Thomas was performing on NBC's *Highways in Melody* on Friday nights into 1948. (See Cities Service Concerts chapter.) He appeared on *The Voice of Firestone* 43 times between the late 1940s and mid 1950s.

Thomas devoted the final years of his career to coaching voice students in the Southwest. He died April 17, 1983, in Scottsdale, Arizona.

Margaret Speaks was born October 23, 1904, in Columbus, Ohio. She hailed from a musical family (her uncle, composer Oley Speaks, penned *On the Road to Mandalay* and *Sylvia*). As an undergrad at Ohio State University, she sang over a small radio station that aired Sunday night concerts from a local hotel. In 1927, she won a singing audition at New York's WOR Radio. Speaks also performed in a trio known as the Humming Birds over WJZ with *Whispering Jack Smith* during his prenetwork era.

On *The Voice of Firestone* she became a mainstay, appearing often between the mid-1930s and mid-1940s for a total of 40 performances. When she left, she had no other major singing roles in radio but she debuted with the San Francisco Opera in 1941. Margaret Speaks died July 16, 1977, in Blue Hill, Maine.

Jerome Hines was born Jerome Albert Link Heinz on November 8, 1921, in Hollywood, California. He altered his surname during the Second World War to curtail anti–German sentiment. He was not dissuaded when his junior high school glee club rejected him "because his voice didn't blend"; instead, he was to become one of the most important singers in Metropolitan Opera history, prevailing for an incomparable run of 41 years. He studied math and chemistry at the University of Southern California while taking singing lessons as a sideline. But at 19 he debuted professionally in the singing role of Borsa in *Rigoletto* at the San Francisco Opera.

By the time he was 25, Hines had graduated from UCLA, taught chemistry there for a year and labored as a chemist for an oil company. He had also been a soloist with the Los Angeles Philharmonic Orchestra. Favorably auditioning for the Met on March 18, 1946, Hines sang selections from *Aida, Boris Godunov* and *Faust*; his debut on that stage was in an all–Italian language performance with Ezio Pinza who sang Boris Godunov, a part that would frequently go to Hines within a few years. His debut occurred on November 21, 1946. Hines would capture 45 roles in 39 works with 868 Met performances before his retirement on January 24, 1987, after appearing in all of the great roles for bass voices— Don Giovanni (Wolfgang Mozart's *Don Giovanni*), Jacopo Fiesco (Giuseppe Verdi's *Simon Boccanegra*), Gurnemanz (Richard Wagner's *Parsifal*), King Marke (Wagner's *Tristan and Isolde*), Padre Guardiano (Verdi's *La Froza del Destino*), Wotan (Wagner's *Der Ring des Nibelungen*) and Zaccaria (Verdi's *Nabucco*). He was adaptable in so many ways because he sang German and Russian repertory in addition to Italian and French. "His innate musicianship stood him in great stead," claimed one review. Said another: "Hines was known for his rich timbre, as well as the research he conducted into the historical and psychological background of the roles he portrayed."

Hines was deeply religious and a superb writer, too. He combined those attributes in his own opera, *I Am the Way*, a work about Jesus Christ. Hines appeared as the protagonist in it at a Philadelphia performance in 1969. A year earlier his autobiography, *This Is My Story, This Is My Song*, was released. But the book for which he became renowned, however, was *Great Singers on Great Singing*. Published in 1982, it provided the author's discriminating annotations concerning the talents of a number of his contemporaries. He played several roles in keeping with his advancing years later in life. His final stage appearance was as Sarastro in New Orleans in 1998 when he was 77. He also taught future professional singers in the late years of his life.

Jerome Hines made infrequent appearances on *The Bell Telephone Hour* on NBC's "Monday night of music" lineup, in addition to performing 37 times on *The Voice of Firestone*. On a couple of occasions before the final curtain fell on *Firestone's* long radio run, Hines and his wife, soprano Lucia Evangelista, were paired as guest soloists, May 23, 1955, and again on June 10, 1957, the show's last radio performance. By an odd coincidence, Hines was also one of three artists appearing on the final *Firestone* telecast June 16, 1963. He died February 4, 2003, in New York City.

Gladys Swarthout was born December 25, 1900, in Deepwater, Missouri. That Ozark mining community esteemed her eventual successes highly, claiming her as its most celebrated daughter, even considering a name change for the hamlet to Swarthout, although that never met fruition. The family developed a musical legacy, however; her sibling became a music teacher in New York while a couple of cousins were deans of music at the universities of California and Kansas. In a short while the family moved to Kansas City where the child's promising voice led her to take vocal lessons. At 13, she was so frustrated with the church choir's lead singer that she asked for and received that paid job!

Following high school, she enrolled in nearby Metropolitan Junior College. At 18, she sang with the Detroit Symphony. When her voice training advanced beyond the capabilities of local tutors, one recommended her to Chicago's Clark Conservatory of Music for more study. An audition with the Chicago Civic Opera Company landed her a contract, although she didn't know a single operatic role. By the time she debuted a few months hence she had memorized 23 parts, participating in more than half of the season's operas. Completing a four-year music course, she performed with the Vienna Opera Company at Highland Park in suburban Chicago. For three seasons she sang with Chicago's Ravinia Opera Company. The mezzo-soprano's Met debut as La Cieca in *La Gioconda* came on November 15, 1929, and she remained there until 1945. "Never content with her abilities," said a reviewer, "when not performing, she regularly worked eight hours a day with vocal coaches, and would spend an hour or more singing duets with her husband."

Swarthout starred in several films for Paramount Pictures including *Champagne Waltz*, *Romance in the Dark* and *Rose of the Rancho*. On radio she made recurring visits to *The Bell Telephone Hour*, *The Camel Caravan*, *The Ford Sunday Evening Hour*, *General Motors Concerts*, *The Magic Key*, *The NBC Symphony Orchestra*, *The Palmolive Beauty Box Theater*, *The Prudential Family Hour*, *The Railroad Hour* and 34 times to *The Voice of Firestone*. She hosted her own *Gladys Swarthout* music series between February 10 and May 9, 1937, on NBC. She testified that broadcasting was "the most demanding and most frightening of all my various performances. In Hollywood, with light and camera they can bring out most of your beauty, hide all of your flaws. In opera you play your part, warmed by a friendly audience. But one mistake over the air goes into the ears of millions of people and can never be taken back."

Swarthout retired from public life in 1954 following heart surgery. She and her husband moved to an Italian villa where she died in Florence on July 7, 1969, of a lifelong heart condition.

Igor Gorin was born October 26, 1908, in Grodek, Ukraine. Following the Russian Revolution, the Gorin clan relocated in Vienna, Austria. There the youth studied music as well as medicine. Entering the Vienna Conservatory of Music on scholarship, he graduated in 1930, debuting that same year with the Czech State Opera. Later, in 1930, he moved to the United States, becoming a naturalized citizen nine years later. His American singing premier occurred in 1939 at the Hollywood Bowl.

The baritone went on several radio series beyond his 33 appearances on *The Voice of Firestone*, turning up intermittently on *The Bell Telephone Hour*. He appeared in several movies and became a high-profile operatic stage singer. In 1941, he joined the American Society of Composers, Authors and Publishers, penning several pop compositions—*Caucasian Song, Lament, Lullaby, Safe by de Lawd, Within My Dreams.*

Gorin joined the Met late in his career, debuting there as Germont Pere in *La Traviata* on February 10, 1964. Following that, he taught voice at the University of Arizona. He died March 24, 1982, in Tucson.

Eugene Conley was born March 12, 1908, in Lynn, Massachusetts. According to one source he "had the misfortune of competing with other more famous tenors of his time—fellow Americans Richard Tucker and Jan Peerce—as well as European stars Jussi Bjoerling, Giuseppe di Stefano and Ferruccio Tagliavini." He studied in Boston and New York, debuting in *Rigoletto* with the Slamaggi Opera Company at the Brooklyn Academy of Music. The San Carlo Opera Company of Tampa, Florida, hired him a year later, followed by stints with the Cincinnati Summer Opera and the New York City Opera.

Conley premiered at the Met on January 25, 1950, remaining there six years. During the 1950s, the tenor sang on *The Voice of Firestone* 28 times, frequently in duets with lyric soprano Nadine Conner. In 1960, he joined the faculty of Texas State University in Denton as professor of voice. He retired in 1978 and died in Denton, Texas, on December 18, 1981.

There was one more recurring personality on the Firestone broadcasts who, in the 1940s and 1950s, was present virtually every week. Announcer Hugh James was born October 13, 1915, in the Bronx, New York. For all intents and purposes, the busy radio narrator literally *was* the *voice* of Firestone. He determined to make radio his career while a high school student. From an NBC page in his teen years he advanced to tour guide and then delivered on-air station breaks. At 20, he was an NBC staff announcer at Philadelphia, moving on to Washington, D. C., soon after. He aired the second-term inauguration of President Franklin D. Roosevelt in 1937 and returned to New York later that year to announce nightly commentaries of *Lowell Thomas and the News*.

For 15 years James presided over four daily network shows. His assignments across his career included *Big Town, Famous Jury Trials, House in the Country, The Parker Family, The Right to Happiness, The Second Mrs. Burton, Star for a Night, Three Star Final, True Detective Mysteries, Wendy Warren and the News* (where he applied the pseudonym Bill Flood), *When a Girl Marries* and *The Voice of Firestone* (the latter on radio and TV). His deep bass voice worked well in commercials and in introducing the musical selections there. He once professed, "Sincerity is the most important quality an announcer can possess." James, attired in tux, tails, white shirt and bow tie, was the epitome of the traditions espoused by the Firestones. He died on June 17, 2001, in Madison, Connecticut.

When the program left radio, the panel moderator of CBS's *What's My Line?* and ABC-TV's evening news anchor, an erudite John Daly, replaced James. He, too, looked the part.

A funny thing happened — though some might label it perplexing — on the way to the forum as *The Voice of Firestone* edged closer to extinction (translation: cancellation) in its latter days, then in television-only mode. The powers that be, clamoring for profit, ordered a decided revamping of its guest artist list. While viewers could still catch glimpses of Robert Merrill, Roberta Peters, Risë Stevens, Brian Sullivan and a few of their contemporaries, TV by then was attempting to hold the audience by offering all things to all people.

As a result, by 1958 (the year after the radio–TV simulcast ended and the show was exclusively on the tube) viewers saw the likes of more mainstream and pop artists like the Boston Pops Orchestra, Rosemary Clooney, Xavier Cugat and Abbe Lane, Dennis Day, Mahalia Jackson, Spike Jones, Howard Keel, Eartha Kitt, Paul Lavalle and the Band of America, Julie London, Tony Martin, Jo Stafford, Fred Waring and His Pennsylvanians and Margaret Whiting. It would have been unfathomable to imagine any of these and others of their ilk appearing on *Firestone* in the 1920s, 1930s, 1940s and early 1950s. Yet, here they were, singing and playing their hearts out, incontrovertibly turning the program into something it had never been.

Old-time radio buff Ted Meland, who maintains an abiding interest in many genres of music, offered an opinion on what might have transpired in that epoch: "While this is nothing I can prove, I think that postwar America was not as highbrow. While parents of the 1930s and 1940s could spend an evening listening to the symphony or an opera on the radio, their offspring came back from the war with different tastes. The war vets became more influential in society in the early 1950s, so changed entertainment. In that one decade we went from the likes of Rosemary Clooney, Teresa Brewer, Bing Crosby, Frank Sinatra and many more to Elvis, Jerry Lee Lewis and rock 'n' roll. Did TV feed this change, or just react to it? I don't know. But whichever way it was, the public sure loved it and demanded more."

Hence you had striking differences in *The Voice of Firestone* of the 1930s and the 1960s. Added Meland: "The 1950s saw the start of the biggest social changes the country had ever seen. And that was bound to be echoed in the most pervasive entertainment medium ever created — television."

These weren't the first singers to perform on *Firestone's* stage without being card-carrying, operatic-ensconced performers to the near exclusion of every other musical form. Singer Jane Froman appeared in both 1950 and 1951 while Jeanette MacDonald sang in 1950. But those occasions were isolated. Twice — in 1955 and 1956 — there were no guest artists at all. Instead, soloists from the Firestone Chorus, normally the background singers, were brought to the front of the stage to display their wares. Metropolitan Opera audition winners performed on July 23, 1956. Accomplished concert pianist Elizabeth Firestone, daughter of the sponsor, accompanied Eleanor Steber on the program of January 10, 1949. Upon the death of Idabel Firestone, a memorial concert featuring works composed entirely by Mrs. Firestone was held on July 12, 1954. Risë Stevens was guest artist. The melodies included *If I Could Tell You, Bluebirds, You Are the Song in My Heart, In My Garden* and *Do You Recall?*

In 1949, piano virtuoso Elizabeth Firestone (seated), daughter of Harvey S. Firestone Sr., Firestone Company chairman and sponsor of *The Voice of Firestone*, was flanked by soprano Eleanor Steber and impresario Howard Barlow, who conducted the Firestone Orchestra for many years. The owners took great pride as well as a personal hand in managing their durable series.

The Firestones liked to celebrate the milestones of their program's life. They did so on the occasion of its 10th birthday in 1938 when Richard Crooks and Margaret Speaks were program regulars. They signified the program's 30th anniversary on November 24, 1958, in a tribute titled "The Best of Opera." Guests included contralto Rosalin Elias, soprano Anna Moffo, bass Cesare Siepi, and tenor Cesare Valetti. By then it should have been obvious to everybody who followed the program closely that change was in the air. Of the four, only Siepi had any history with the show.

But the biggest of these celebrations occurred on the program's 25th anniversary, marked by an hour-long broadcast in dual media on November 30, 1953. Impresario Howard Barlow held the baton, conducting orchestra, chorus and dancers. Six popular semiregulars appeared, singing the familiar tunes that had altered the perceptions of highbrow music of many in its vast audience, including bass Jerome Hines, tenor Robert Rounseville, soprano Eleanor Steber, mezzo-soprano Risë Stevens, tenor Brian Sullivan and baritone Thomas L. Thomas. The distinguished bass modulation of announcer Hugh James, who for so many years literally *was* the "voice" of Firestone, introduced the artists and their selections. The themes, *If I Could Tell You* and *In My Garden*, preceded and concluded the gala occasion.

On that auspicious evening, Hugh James acknowledged that the venerable series was the oldest coast-to-coast network program on the air. He added that it was the first commercially sponsored musical program to be televised and the first of its genre to be broadcast simultaneously on radio and TV. During a commercial break he introduced Gen. David Sarnoff, the chairman of the Radio Corporation of America, NBC's parent company. Sarnoff paid tribute to the late Harvey S. Firestone Sr. who stated at the close of the initial broadcast 25 years earlier: "I hope this program has been a wholesome feature in your household." Sarnoff affirmed that that hope had been "fully realized" for a quarter of a century. Concluding, he praised "a fine American family and a great American business organization, the Firestones," and expressed "our appreciation to their significant contributions to the prosperity and culture of America."

It was only a short time following that celebration that the sponsor and network were at loggerheads over a matter of paramount importance to NBC—the show's declining ratings. CBS was simulcasting a successful series of its own at that same hour (8:30) on Monday night, *Arthur Godfrey's Talent Scouts*. The show fed TV viewers to its incredibly popular sitcom *I Love Lucy* at 9:00. In the 1952-1953 season *Lucy* was first in the numbers, immediately followed by *Talent Scouts*. The next year *Lucy* was still first and *Talent Scouts* was third. To put it mildly, the combined CBS features were blowing away the competition. On radio, CBS was still programming its venerable *Lux Radio Theater* at 9:00, one of its most durable and esteemed offerings. While *The Voice of Firestone* had long been considered "one of radio's few untouchables," officials at NBC complained to the sponsor that airing *Firestone* at 8:30 was doing irreparable harm to its Monday night agenda, especially citing features that succeeded the concert series on the air. One report claimed that the chain simply had no luck in selling the time following the *Firestone* performances. Thus, while NBC was willing to continue those simulcasts at another time, it demanded an adjustment in the scheduling.

That's when the dirt hit the fan. Firestone officials would have none of it, claiming if the program were moved from 8:30 on Monday nights—an hour it had occupied since September 7, 1931—"many of the program's faithful viewers [and presumably listeners] would not be able to watch [hear] in a less desirable time period." At first blush, for a brief while it literally appeared that the show was going off the air forever at the end of the season. NBC and Firestone didn't see eye to eye at all; apparently, after 25 years of wedded bliss, those two were no longer capable of civil conversation.

Just at that instant, however, a hungry network emerged that believed programming a prestigious series like *The Voice of Firestone* would be the saving grace of a weak Monday night schedule. ABC and Firestone forged a pact that would keep the program on the air at its accustomed 8:30 P.M., continuing on both radio and television. Long-term advocates breathed an audible sigh of relief and fans broke into hearty applause.

The program ended on NBC Radio and Television on June 7, 1953. The following Monday, June 14, it continued on ABC Radio and Television as if it had always been there—same setting, same cast, same everything, airing live just as it had always done. The radio audience dwindled to such minuscule proportions during the ABC years as more people purchased TV sets, however, that the sponsor finally decided to end a 29-year tradition in that medium. The final simulcast was scheduled for June 10, 1957. Fortunately, the long-standing feature was to live on in television, for a while, at least. A couple of years later, nonetheless, ABC-TV began to experience the same circumstances that had driven the program from NBC. A sales-oriented staff offered *Firestone* the 10 P.M. timeslot "so as not to hurt the shows that followed." The Firestone family was not happy and said so. This time, there was no meeting of the minds; the two parties came to an impasse and the venerable series left the air, presumably forever, on June 1, 1959.

As could be anticipated, faithful followers of the series—some of whom had been engrossed by it for decades—raised a ruckus, their protests pointed and loud, but falling on deaf ears just the same. *The Voice of Firestone* didn't return that fall (it had taken the summer "off" for the first time in 1957 and 1958 after the radio version ended) and it seemed it wasn't coming back. Even when all three networks offered less-than-favorable time periods to pacify the frustrated viewers, the Firestones still turned thumbs down. They felt their $1 million-plus annual investment entitled them to better treatment.

Over the next three years, a couple of factors transpired that *did* allow the program to return, however. For one thing, there was a management change at ABC-TV that was more receptive (as opposed to hostile) to the Firestones. Once again it offered a 10:00 spot, this time on Sunday night—take it or leave it. Apparently, the heart of Harvey S. Firestone Jr.—possibly convinced by never-ceasing dissention by viewers disheartened by the cancellation—softened. He agreed to ABC-TV's terms. "Although the audience was relatively small by TV standards, the appreciation of those who did watch, and the considerable prestige, made Firestone quite content to continue funding the show," a pundit advised. "You're bringing back Voice of Firestone," declared Connecticut Senator Thomas E. Dodd. "I find that commendable."

By then Howard Barlow was history, replaced by visiting conductors like Harry John Brown, Xavier Cugat, Percy Faith, Arthur Fiedler, Spike Jones, Andre Kostelanetz, Paul Lavalle, Eugene Ormandy, Wilfred Pelletier, Fred Waring, Paul Whiteman and a few more. The series returned on Sunday, September 30, 1962. But it was not enough, perhaps a case of too little, too late—too little audience, too late an hour, too much time having elapsed since a viewer segment was so addicted. Typically only 2.5 million viewers were in the audience. In ABC's mind it was time to pull the plug. June 16, 1963, was announced as the execution date. Nobody would come to the rescue that time.

Public broadcasting discovered the value of classical music programming after a while. But with the passing of *Firestone*, ongoing network provisions for the genre were a thing of the past.

In connection with those TV performances, a couple of critics termed the "tuxedos and starched shirts" era "a bit stiff—pleasing to hear, but sometimes boring to watch." During TV's incubation period, music historian Tom DeLong insisted: "A significant factor in the *Voice's* durability undeniably rested before the lens of a TV camera." He offered an opinion on what transpired when cameras were trained on *The Voice of Firestone* and others of its breed in those early days of cathode-ray tubes.[1]

> Sight ... seemed to hinder rather than to enhance the full appreciation of its music.... Singers stood at fixed places before an upright floor microphone. Scripts were hand-held by the announcer. Guest soloists were always shown from the same camera angle. Although radio listeners heard no difference, viewers were disturbed. Critics fretted, calling the telecasts singularly static and stilted to the eye.
>
> Video coverage, of course, improved when TV audiences outnumbered radio listeners. But the venerable musical pro-

grams that had helped build Radio City suffered most.

The open mouths of singers, the hand-waving of conductors, and the bowing arms of violinists did not represent the maximum visual entertainment. Audiences wanted something more dramatic and theatrical above and beyond the gestures involved in singing and playing. TV cameras sometimes became a distraction, taking away from the impact of the sound.

When background effects and visual devices were incorporated, the musical purists took objection.

"When one listens to music, one's own imagination should be able to roam freely," [NBC conductor] Frank Black observed. "Radio allows this freedom; television, with all good intent, too often suggests the meaning. No one likes to have thrust on him what someone else thinks the music suggests. His own conception of the music is what brings sparkle to the eye, pleasure to the ear."

A plethora of worthy causes was espoused on the show such as highway safety, 4-H clubs and the United Nations. In 1954, there was an essay competition on the theme "I Speak for Democracy." A 16-year-old schoolgirl from Akron, Ohio, who won the contest, read her essay on the program.

Several years after *The Voice of Firestone* departed from both radio (June 10, 1957) and television (June 16, 1963), a Japanese conglomerate purchased the enterprise that had borne the Firestone name for decades. In 2000, the latter fell on hard times as millions of its flagship products were recalled, creating a financial and public relations nightmare. In late summer that year, *The New York Times* speculated that the grand old tiremaker, and its revered moniker, could ultimately fade into oblivion as a final consequence. It seemed, for all who had experienced *The Voice of Firestone* and made it a welcome guest in their homes for so long, an unthinkable incongruity.

A summary news report, originally published in *The Detroit News* in April 2003, indicated just how strained matters had become:

> The century-old business relationship that began with a handshake between Henry Ford and Harvey Firestone and erupted into one of the ugliest corporate feuds in history ended quietly last week.
>
> Earlier this month, a batch of spare tires left Bridgestone-Firestone's Oklahoma City plant en route to Ford Motor Co.'s Kansas City assembly plant.
>
> The next day, Bridgestone-Firestone sales executive John Behr sent a note to Ford's purchasing department, briefly noting the end of the historic partnership.
>
> "That shipment (represents) the end of the business relationship between Ford and Bridgestone-Firestone in the U.S. and Canada," Behr wrote.

It was a sad commentary on an association that had prevailed for 97 years between two great American enterprises. In some ways, ironically it seemed like a final epitaph to the Firestones' great entertainment tradition that had brought so much pleasure to so many households for so long. Those who witnessed that forum still possess resplendent memories referencing a time when Americans contented themselves on Monday nights with one of the most prestigious programming efforts broadcasting ever developed. For many, there was little of comparable quality.

Your Hit Parade

Your Hit Parade—launched on radio and later shifted to television—could certainly lay claim to virgin territory on the ether. It instituted the notion of tracking popular music according to widespread public preferences. Until it arrived, not much thought had been given to classifying the songs Americans were humming. The radio series contrived a ranking system that ultimately was copied, modified and expanded by others. For the very first time, people may have realized they were whistling the same tunes at the same time coast-to-coast. *Your Hit Parade* made further contributions in unexpected ways, expanding a recovering Depression-era economy by developing related industries (recordings, phonographs, radios, jukeboxes, sheet music, dance halls, ballrooms and other venues, instrument sales, etc.). Few aural entertainment series may have manifest equal impact in that dominion.

Producers: George Washington Hill, Vincent Riggio.
Director: Lee Strahorn.
Writers: Bunny Coughlin, Richard Dana, Paul Dudley, Jacques Finke, John Henderson Hines, Gail Ingram, Tom Langan, Alan Jay Lerner.
Announcers: Andre Baruch, Martin Block, Kenny Delmar, Ben Grauer, Warren Hull, Basil Ruysdael, Del Sharbutt.
Commercial Pitchers: F. E. Boone, L. A. "Speed" Riggs.
Orchestra Conductors: Lennie Hayton (April 1935–? 1935), Al Goodman (November 1935–? 1938), Carl Hoff (January 1936–? 1938), Ray Sinatra (February 1936–? 1936), Freddie Rich (May 1936–? 1936), Harry Salter (August 1936–? 1937), Harry Sosnik (September 1936–? 1936, October 10, 1958–April 24, 1959), Abe Lyman (March 1937–? 1937), Mark Warnow (March 1937–? 1939, April 1939–August 1947, June 1949–October 1949), Richard Himber (June 1937–? 1937), Peter Van Steeden (July 1937–? 1938), Leo Reisman (October 1937–? 1939), Axel Stordahl (September 1947–May 1949), Scott Quintet (November 1938–July 1939), Raymond Scott (October 1949–June 8, 1957), Don Walker (September 7, 1957–December 7, 1957), Dick Jacobs (December 14, 1957–June 7, 1958), Johnny Green and Orrin Tucker (dates unsubstantiated).
Organist: Ethel Smith.
Harpists: Lucile Lawrence, Verlye Mills.

Vocalists: Charles Carlisle (April 1935–November 1935), Gogo Delys (April 1935–August 1935), Johnny Hauser (April 1935–September 1935), Kay Thompson (April 1935–November 1935), Stuart Allen (November 1935–January 1936, June 1937–October 1937), Loretta Lee (November 1935–January 1936), Willie Morris (November 1935–January 1936), Edith Dick (January 1936–January 1937), Bob Simmons (January 1936–June 1936), Len Stokes (February 1936–June 1936), Buddy Clark (May 1936–June 1937, October 1937–November 1938), Margaret McCrae (May 1936–July 1936), Patricia Norman (April 1937–May 1937), Fredda Gibson, aka Georgia Gibbs (May 1937–December 1938), Lanny Ross (November 1938–October 1939), Kay Lorraine (January 1939–August 1939), Bea Wain (August 1939–May 1941, July 1943–August 1944), Barry Wood (October 1939–November 1939), "Wee" Bonnie Baker (January 1940–September 1940), Louise King (May 1941–October 1941), Joan Edwards (November 1941–July 1943, November 1943–January 1947), Frank Sinatra (February 1943–December 1944, September 1947–May 1949), Ethel Smith (October 1942–August 1943), Lawrence Tibbett (January 1945–July 1945), Dick Todd (July 1945–January 1946), Joe Dosh (February 1946–May 1946), Johnny Mercer (February 1946–May 1946), Andy Russell (June 1946–May 1947, August 1947), Peggy Mann (August 1946–October 1946), Dinah Shore (January 1947–February 1947), Ginny Simms (February 1947–May 1947), Martha Tilton (May 1947–July 1947), Dick Haymes (July 1947–August 1947), Doris Day (September 1947–November 1947), Beryl Davis (December 1947–November 1948), Eileen Wilson (November 1948–November 1951), Bill Harrington (June 1949–October 1949), Jeff Clark (October 1949–June 1950), Snooky Lanson (June 1950–August 1957), Dorothy Collins (October 1950–August 1957, October 10, 1958–April 24, 1959), Russell Arms (February 1951–August 1957), Sue Bennett (July 1951–June 1953), June Valli (1952–1953), Gisele MacKenzie (September 1953–August 1957), Alan Copeland (July 1957–July 1958), Jill Corey (July 1957–July 1958), Virginia Gibson (July 1957–July 1958), Tommy Leonetti (July 1957–July 1958), Johnny Desmond (October 10, 1958–April 24, 1959); specific dates unsubstantiated for Marie Green (early 1940s), Loretta Lee (1930s), Jerry Wayne (early 1940s), Margaret Whiting (c1939), Bonnie Lou Williams.

Vocal Groups: The Songsmiths, with tenor Scrappy Lambert, bass Robert Moody, baritone Leonard Stokes and tenor Randolph Weyant (mid-1930s); the Lyn Murray Chorus (1940s); the Merry Macs, including Cheri McKay and Joe, Judd and Ted McMichael (August 1939–October 1939); the Pied Pipers (June 1947–July 1947); the Ken Lane Chorus (September 1947–May 1949); the Hit Paraders (a designation used throughout the run but particularly in the 1950s).

Other Regulars: Comics Elvia Allman, W.C. Fields, Hanley Stafford and Walter Tetley (1938).

Sound Technician: Donald Bain.

Theme Songs: *Happy Days Are Here Again* (1930s, by Jack Yellen and Milton Ager), *Lucky Day* (DeSylva, Brown and Henderson), *So Long for Awhile* (Alex Kramer).

Sponsor: American Tobacco Company for Lucky Strike cigarettes (entire run).

Ratings: High — 19.1 (1943-1944 season); low — 3.9 (1952-1953 season); median — 13.5. Remained in double digits for all radio-only seasons, falling to single digits after the series was simulcast with television starting in 1950-1951.

On the Air: April 20, 1935–April 25, 1936, NBC, Saturday, 8 P.M. Eastern Time; March 11, 1936–December 1, 1937, NBC, Wednesday, 10 P.M.; May 2, 1936–July 1,

1939, CBS, Saturday, 10 P.M.; July 8, 1939–April 19, 1947, CBS, Saturday, 9 P.M.; April 26, 1947–July 7, 1951, NBC, Saturday, 9 P.M.; September 6, 1951–June 26, 1952, NBC, Thursday, 10 P.M.; August 29, 1952–January 16, 1953, NBC, Friday, 8 P.M. 60 minutes on NBC through November 18, 1936 and on CBS between February 13, 1937– 1938; 45 minutes 1938–1944; 30 minutes in other time periods.

* * *

As dominant as music was in engulfing the ether, the bulk of pop music shows accentuated the variety format, including a combination of features—comedy, light drama, contests, monologues and banter between two or more participants and so forth, which would be added to the music on most of those programs. Only a single show that consistently appeared among the Top 10 in ratings, in fact, offered music to the exclusion of almost everything else: *Your Hit Parade*, which easily was the long-haul exception to the norm.

It was a "big, brassy, breathless show" (at its debut *Variety* called it "the noisiest show on the air") and it was indeed unique by every conceivable measure.

It would have been distinguished by the fact alone that — in an era when early methods of mass communications were still in developmental phases—*Your Hit Parade* was *the* recognized, trusted authority on popular music in this nation. Alleged one scribe: "To anyone whose musical consciousness began in 1935, the *Hit Parade* seemed as permanent, authoritative, and civilizing a force as the presidency itself."[1]

Until the 1950s, in fact, when a pervading dominance of the disc jockey— complete with play-lists of top-40 tunes (irrefutable factors that drove a final nail in the coffin of radio's *Your Hit Parade*)— was ushered in, people looked to this show as their only established source for America's tastes in popular music. And as the nation's exclusive oracle of pop music fads, the radio feature reigned absolute as a form of Grammy Awards every week. Its insuperable influence continues to be felt: "Practically all of the music programming on radio today, particularly 'hits' radio, owes a debt to this concept."[2]

As if this didn't relegate the program to a class by itself, there was likely no other series on the air equally durable which experienced as many total changes of format, character and personnel as did *Your Hit Parade*.

At its start, with 60 minutes to fill, the show offered 15 listener favorites every week — the tunes that an unscientific survey projected as the most popular songs of the week. As the program decreased to 45- and then 30-minute versions, the top 15 songs shrank to the top 10, then they diminished to the top nine, and the top seven and, finally — toward the end of the run during the television-only era — by February 1958 it proffered only the top five.

The emphasis in the early days was clearly on the music itself. In that epoch the performers were seldom highlighted. That all gradually changed in time as the fans began to identify with favorite singers. Within a few years an entourage of teenyboppers and servicemen became so enthralled by specific "stars" that some individual artists superseded the melodies as a drawing card for those effusive listeners.

Then there were the cast changes. In less than a quarter of a century in dual media, *Your Hit Parade* witnessed a score of bandleaders holding its baton. Vocalists— more than 50 in number, some with names that were rapidly becoming well known in American households— also swung through the show's revolving doors.

Simultaneously, *Your Hit Parade* was

also a series that introduced some innovative marketing applications on behalf of its sole commercial underwriter. Not only did those successful experiments affect that sponsor's other broadcast series but also countless supplementary programs on the air. As other promoters witnessed the advertising acumen practiced here, they jumped on the bandwagon, employing some of the same creative dynamics elsewhere, ultimately initiating some new trends in radio commercials.

For many reasons, therefore, *Your Hit Parade* was unlike any other aural feature that arrived before it or even after its inception. It was a one-of-a-kind program. Legions of American listeners— spellbound by the secrecy surrounding the show's last-minute revelation of the week's top tune — were humming, whistling and crooning from coast to coast. The series had *winner* written all over it, just as did many of the 1,278 different songs that it brought into the nation's homes over an enduring run.

Although it arrived in 1935, *Your Hit Parade* had been preceded on the ether by an earlier music series from the same source that may have intimated there were still better things to come. Capitalizing on America's dance craze of the roaring '20s, between 1928 and 1931 a fledgling NBC radio network (which itself had been launched only in late 1926) offered its listeners a congenial 60-minute Saturday night dance marathon. The *Lucky Strike Dance Orchestra* arrived under the direction of impresario B.A. Rolfe. One of the truly noteworthy characteristics of the show was that — while operating well out of the range of public visibility, yet unmistakably in total control— sat a gifted, tireless, determined advertising strategist who stubbornly affixed his personal stamp on every facet of the production.

George Washington Hill, son of the former president of the American Tobacco Company, the series' sponsor, launched his own professional career as a $5-a-week trainee for that firm. Given time he would be a widely respected industry logician, in due course becoming one of the nation's more brilliant sales and marketing trendsetters during the first half of the twentieth century. Hill was awarded more extensive assignments. He introduced many novel concepts in packaging, promoting and distributing his firm's cigarette brands (including Lucky Strike, Pall Mall, Herbert Tareyton, Sovereign, Hit Parade and others). More of his achievements will be examined presently. Yet, as if by some measure of affirmation, his innovative approaches were widely adopted by enterprising peer promotional gurus operating elsewhere who copied them and used them to personal excess. In significant ways, Hill permanently altered the application of commercial advertising.

By 1926, Hill followed in his father's footsteps, ascending to the presidency of American Tobacco. In that capacity he not only had greater opportunity to influence the firm's future but also espoused a free hand for himself to intrude into whatever aspect of the organization's existence he desired — no matter how ostensibly trivial it might appear on the surface.

Quite early he caught a glimpse of the possibilities offered by the new medium of radio as a key marketing tool. So enamored was he with its prospect that he became one of its most zealous exponents. He temporarily canceled his company's print advertising contracts to channel the business' promotional resources into aural series, specifically the *Lucky Strike Dance Orchestra*. That by itself could explain his overbearing interest in the radio program's success. But he wasn't content to leave the show alone when — just two months into the trial test period — Lucky Strike reflected a 47-percent increase in sales. Hill's heavy-handed tactics would become pervasive and all-consuming, reflected in practically everything he touched.

For that groundbreaking radio series Hill would personally approve not only the selection of every number beamed over the airwaves but also the tempo at which it was played, plus the individuals who performed it (including instrumentalists and vocalists). He preferred, for instance, a simple upbeat tempo (insiders tagged it "the businessman's bounce") in deference to fancy arrangements that were synonymous with other music shows.

Stories proliferated about how he approached such matters with great abandon. One account implied that, during practice sessions, he enlisted American Tobacco Company secretaries to dance with one another so he could ascertain how "danceable" the tunes were. Another had it that Hill and his secretary (singular) rehearsed the melodies together. Yet a third version indicated that he required NBC personnel to swing and sway to the orchestral arrangements, with secretaries and script girls obliged to try out the tunes on an improvised dance floor. Whatever the circumstances, one thing was clearly understood by those working on the production: "No one said *no* to Mr. Hill! His word was *the* authority on the show."

Once classified as a "larger-than-life character," Hill's "sole reason for living seemed to be to sell his tobacco products," one authority acknowledged. Another, Albert Lasker, a powerful tycoon then running Lord and Thomas, American Tobacco's ad agency, surmised: "The only purpose in life to him [Hill] was to wake up, to eat, and to sleep so he'd have strength to sell more Lucky Strikes." Meanwhile, a radio historiographer who cataloged some of Hill's predilections took note of his organization's contributions to the ether: "The American Tobacco Company," said he, "did more than any other commercial enterprise to bring dance band music to radio."[3] His contention was probably correct.

Hill definitely could be considered an eccentric. He customarily wore outlandish hats and was chauffeured to his office in a limousine bearing photos of Lucky Strike cigarette packages. During the depths of the Depression, Hill typically took home an annual salary and bonuses amounting to more than $400,000 while he "stopped at nothing to get what he wanted." He required his employees to sign loyalty oaths and was never hesitant to telephone someone when he was displeased with what he heard on his radio shows. (Singer Margaret Whiting lasted on *Your Hit Parade* just four weeks—rejected by Hill for a style "too hip" for his taste.) Although he had a reputation for paying his people well, his abrasive, controlling technique was repugnant to many in his employ.

Contemporary pundits haven't been altogether kind to the tobacco baron. One characterized him as "a ruthless and eccentric nabob"[4] while another labeled him "a notorious despot."[5] All the while he still infused electronic communications—and especially radio—with forms of leisure pastimes that were widely appreciated by multitudes of listeners. To overlook that important conclusion is to miss one of the man's significant contributions to America's newest home entertainment medium. While he would take a somewhat diminished role in the day-to-day operations of some broadcast series underwritten by his firm, there would never be any doubt about who was the ultimate authority.

Even the redoubtable Jack Benny, perhaps radio's most celebrated comedian, who was also sponsored by Lucky Strike for several years, harbored some apprehension of recriminations over the possibility of getting out of line. Benny once told a peeved Walter Winchell that he would be unable to promote the Damon Runyon Cancer Fund, one of Winchell's pet charities, on his show. "Because I am sponsored by a cigarette company we are not permitted at any time to mention the word *cancer*," Benny explained. Then he pleaded with Winchell: "Please keep this confidential for my sake."

At its inception, the *Lucky Strike Dance Orchestra* was extremely chic with radio listeners. Was it the program itself that drew a crowd of faithful followers or possibly the fact that they didn't have a lot else to choose from on the airwaves in 1928? Perhaps it was some of both. Either way, after a while the series' popularity began to slide. Gradually public preferences for softer ballads evolved and the show's strong emphasis on a brassy, nearly martial-sounding style of music fell out of favor with many tuning in. The audience started to spiral downward.

With that experience under his belt, a resourceful George Washington Hill was hardly dissuaded by radio's potential. *Hardly.* The enterprising fellow with an abundance of creative ingenuity sought instead a new audio vehicle that could draw still greater audiences—including still more prospective smokers—to his programming. The next brainstorm didn't come about overnight. But when it arrived, it struck like a bolt of lightning: how about a radio series that would offer an authentic-sounding "scientific" means of certifying the nation's current preferences in popular music every week? No such data was available. But Hill, ever the strategist, conceived a fail-proof plan to get it.

For the new show, to be called *Your Hit Parade*, he would enlist hundreds of "song scouts" nationwide. These individuals would be dispatched each week, calling on America's disc jockeys, bandleaders and record and sheet music sales clerks. From those "authoritative sources" they would gather critical data on what songs were being most requested and what recorded tunes were being purchased throughout the country.

The music industry itself would also feed off the frenzy, it was later determined; the recognized favorites aired by the radio show became self-perpetuating, improving jukebox and phonograph record sales. More than 33 million discs were purchased in 1938, an increase of 27 million over 1932 sales. A third of those discs were relegated to jukeboxes. Record-player sales skyrocketed, too. None of that was Hill's concern, of course, and it remained inconsequential to his scheme.

The data that his people gathered in the field ultimately would wind up in the hands of the advertising agency responsible for production of *Your Hit Parade* (originally Lord and Thomas, later Batten, Barton, Durstine & Osborne). And it would be held tightly under lock and key until the moment it was revealed to the world during the live broadcasts. It was possibly easier in those days to bust into Fort Knox than to acquire the results of those closely guarded melody secrets. The system was "infallible," the agency intimated. One correspondent maintained that—in a display apparently designed to impress eyewitnesses (and those who heard about it from them) surrounding the enormous precautions to dissuade any subterfuge with such critical data—the information was transported to the ad bureau by armored truck.

If indeed that was the case, one wonders where it originated on its ramble through the streets of downtown Gotham. Did those reports from the footmen in the field initially pass under the discerning eyes of George Washington Hill perhaps? Given his history of interference in the *Lucky Strike Dance Orchestra*, it certainly wouldn't be out of character. At least one source hints at that possibility although that isn't corroborated elsewhere. If the story of the armored truck is true, the journey had to begin at a collection point *somewhere*. At this distant juncture, the offices of the

American Tobacco Company seem a logical conclusion.

Radio Guide, incidentally, insisted that all of this made *Your Hit Parade* "the most complex broadcast on the air" as it resulted in "an endless popularity poll on a nationwide scale."

With the weekly list in hand, the advertising agency prepared a script mainly consisting of commercial and continuity text. Alan Jay Lerner wrote the latter copy for a while. There was a brief comedy sketch of a few weeks' duration in the fall of 1938 featuring Elvia Allman, W.C. Fields, Hanley Stafford and Walter Tetley. In that era, the music was interrupted on occasion for tributes ("salutes," in contemporary parlance) to eminent Americans— Will Hays, Helen Keller and Gen. John J. Pershing were among the qualified. There was little attempt to offer anything more than introductions between songs. One wag referred to the diversionary attempts as "window dressing."

"The program had a rigorously spare approach" claimed a witness. TV would later offer it much more opportunity to develop a personality that connected with audiences. A permanent cast of singers was surrounded by stylish sets framing the various numbers, often with dramatic, comic or gimmicky distractions. In addition, some of the most imaginative choreographers available (Tony Charmoli, Ernie Flatt, Peter Gennaro) were hired to plan sequences involving an ongoing troupe of talented dancers. Considerable ingenuity was employed in creating an elaborate production for a visual audience. Even then, however, the stars never spoke, except in commercials. Dorothy Collins regularly pitched Luckies at the opening of the video shows, providing tacit approval to the product from a celebrity.

On seeing each week's script the bandleader added one, two or three "Lucky Strike extras" (songs not included in the current pop selections, which filled out the show's allotted time). These "extras," at least in the 1950s, often showcased new tunes for which a quick ascendancy was expected. Orchestra rehearsals on Friday before Saturday night performances usually required all day, normally running about eight hours for an average 45-minute broadcast.

Meanwhile, great care was taken to amplify the reputation of the authentic-sounding survey *Your Hit Parade* offered its fans every week. After all, that was the premise of the entire show, the foundational bedrock upon which it all rested. Nothing less than something the audience could take to the bank as absolute and unchallengeable would be acceptable. The announcer's words were deliberately measured to underscore the impeccable trust that audiences placed in the survey. Data had been tediously collected, deciphered and chronicled to offer an accurate register of current pop music partiality among the populace.

In the early days that announcement sounded like this:

> *Once again, the voice of the people has spoken. New Yorkers and Californians, northerners and southerners, Republicans, Democrats, men, women and children — 120 million of you have told us what songs you want to hear this Saturday night. You've told us by your purchase of sheet music and records, by your requests to orchestra leaders in the places you've danced, by the tunes you listen to on your favorite radio programs. That's why the Hit Parade is your own program.*

As the seasons passed the statement was refined, pared down and at last sounded like this:

> *Your Hit Parade checks the best sellers on sheet music and phonograph records, the songs most heard on the air and most played in automatic coin machines — an accurate, authentic tabulation of America's taste in popular music.*

It really didn't matter that the patronizing embellishment of that affirmation professed no scientific validity. Listeners believed it anyhow. They didn't need to know expressly how those surveys were taken. Perhaps that simply contributed to the mystique of the series and its deliberate bent toward secrecy. It was just enough that the claims came across as bona fide. Besides, how would anyone refute them if he wished to challenge their validity? It was a model that really couldn't fail.

The program took to the air for its inaugural on April 20, 1935, at 8 o'clock in the evening. Lennie Hayton (who would later marry singer Lena Horne and become her arranger-accompanist) was the first in a long line of impresarios to emerge through the revolving door, holding the baton over the Lucky Strike Orchestra. The Hit Paraders, nameless singers who went uncredited for their efforts, pitched in on the refrains. (It was George Washington Hill's decision to emphasize *songs*, not *singers*.) Appearing at the program's inception, however, were vocalists Charles Carlisle, Gogo Delys, Johnny Hauser and Kay Thompson—none of those instantly recognized monikers in average households.

Introduced by announcer Warren Hull—the very same Hull who years later tended the tear-jerking reality show *Strike It Rich*—*Your Hit Parade*'s first tune across the ether was a Rodgers and Hart ballad called *Soon*. Was the song title prophetic? Within a brief spell, Al Goodman was replacing Maestro Hayton as the orchestra's second conductor. And can anyone name the number-one melody on the very first show? It was *Lovely to Look At*, drawn from a stage play that later was the handle of a movie musical.

Your Hit Parade rolled along on Saturday nights over NBC as an hour-long feature. But by the start of its second year, in spring 1936, that format had been modified. The series was split into dual weekly performances—an hour over NBC on Wednesday nights through late 1937, later reduced to 30 minutes; and its Saturday night stand continued, then over CBS in spasmodic 45- and 30-minute patterns during the next 11 years. The show returned to NBC as an exclusive property in the spring of 1947. There it made a final dash in its original medium—six years spread intermittently over Saturday, Thursday and Friday nights, finally biting the dust as an audio feature on January 16, 1953. In some of those latter years, it was offered as a simulcast with an NBC-TV series that experienced its first live outing on July 10, 1950. Even at the close of the radio run the concept wasn't finished, however; *Your Hit Parade* continued through April 24, 1959, virtually without interruption over NBC-TV and finally CBS-TV. A one-month reprise of its title, but not its accepted format, surfaced in August 1974 over CBS-TV.

When the program premiered in the mid-1930s, what would become its most memorable, distinguishing and qualifying feature didn't exist. It was a few years into the run, in fact, before someone (George Washington Hill perhaps?) stumbled upon a clever notion: rearrange the musical selections to add a dramatic build-up to the announcement of the top three tunes (and eventually, to number one) for the week. Before that, those 15 hottest songs were merely offered in random order, minus any regard for suspense in their staging. But once that was instituted those last-minute current favorite revelations absolutely electrified audiences, causing them to squirm as they anxiously stuck like glue to their radios, laboring through intoxicating countdowns to a final verdict. The number-one tune incessantly arrived to a drumroll and trumpet blast followed by an interlocutor's vocal flourish (most often the familiar timbre of the durable Andre Baruch).

One could make no mistake: it was

the attention-grabbing device on this show and promptly and forever became the series' dynamic trademark. Millions would gather around their radios on Saturday nights in the World War II epoch, probably the program's zenith, and cheer for their choices to win, place or show. In 1943, *Radio Life* wrote: "It's not unusual to see devotees of certain songs become joyous, vindictive, or disappointed." (A source dubbed it "America's chief Saturday-night mania" while millions tuning in to the zany antics of Ralph Edwards' Saturday night audience participation melee, *Truth or Consequences*, might view the latter show as the evening's *real* mania.)

Gerald Nachman recalls it this way: "You felt a little tingle as the top song on the charts was named, followed by a groan if it turned out to be the same song as the previous fourteen weeks. Every song on the week's *Hit Parade* was given a triumphal send-off with rippling harp strings as Baruch cried, 'And now! In the number seven spot! Peggy Lee sings 'Sentimental Journey'!" Baruch's steady, charismatic delivery, even for those lesser-rated melodies, had an effect of energizing every performance from start to finish.

Gamblers—especially the penny-ante kind—placed bets on the chart-toppers. It became a casual but consistent activity in many places. One pundit wrote: "It's the one burning question that every American who can carry a tune wants answered: What's Number One on the *Hit Parade*?"

The swinging door through which the assorted *Hit Parade* cast members entered and exited their chambers would witness literally scores of individuals traversing its portals across two dozen years. Included were 20 bandleaders. One (Harry Sosnik) made a second appearance there 22 years after his first one! Another (Harry Warnow) turned up *three times* within a dozen years and became the show's most enduring maestro. "During his [Warnow's] eight-year stewardship, the Hit Parade developed into one of radio's best pop music shows," noted an observer.

Parenthetically, when Warnow died unexpectedly in October 1949, his brother, Raymond Scott, a CBS staff conductor, was named to pick up the baton as successor-director. He continued the family tradition through June 1957.

A preponderance of the instrumentalists remained in place as the ground around them shifted. At times it almost seemed like there was a "guest conductor" holding the baton because some of those leadership stints lasted only a few weeks or, at best, months. Calling the band the Lucky Strike Orchestra simplified (and diminished) recurring leadership changes. To label the musicians "Harry Sosnick's Orchestra" or by the name of any other conductor would have almost surely prompted questions as to whether there was trouble in paradise. Besides, every time Andre Baruch acknowledged, "So and so now sings a number backed by the Lucky Strike Orchestra," it was another overt plug for the sponsor, something G.W. Hill certainly wouldn't have missed.

In addition to Sosnick and Warnow, there were several more impresarios who gained well-placed notoriety before, during or after their experiences with *Your Hit Parade*. Among them: Abe Lyman, Freddie Rich, Harry Salter, Raymond Scott, Alex Stordahl and Peter Van Steeden. For details on their achievements, turn to the chapter on Big Bands.

If there was a glut of bandleaders on *Your Hit Parade*, as might be expected, the number of vocalists was legion. No fewer than 53 individuals were designated as recurring vocalists on the show between 1935 and 1959, plus three others in a 1974 reprise. At least 47 performed regularly on the radio version ending in 1953. As with the maestros, several paid return visits to the cast: Stuart Allen, Buddy Clark, Dorothy Collins,

Joan Edwards, Andy Russell, Frank Sinatra and Bea Wain.

A half-dozen choral groups also steadily appeared on *Your Hit Parade*: the Songsmiths (mid-1930s); the Merry Macs (1939); the Lyn Murray Chorus (Murray frequently doubled as the show's musical director in the 1940s); the Ken Lane Chorus (1947–1949); the Pied Pipers (1947); and the Hit Paraders (an unnamed group of talented professionals who both sang and danced during the radio–TV era, 1950–1958).

A few respected sources imply that the Andrews Sisters took up permanent residence on *Your Hit Parade*. A biographer who appears to have researched every shred of data available to him about the show turned up no evidence to support such a claim. While photographs have appeared indicating the possibility that the trio of famous siblings did sing there, if so it could have been an infrequent guest shot as was the case with opera singer Mario Chamlee. On rare occasions, *Your Hit Parade* trotted out the actual recording artists and asked them to perform their chart-toppers on the air.

While there were plenty of unknowns in their midst, there were several among the 47 radio singers who were rising or already celebrated artists in that era. Several are remembered today: Russell Arms, Bonnie Baker (who was patched in live from across the nation during a road production of *Oh, Johnny, Oh*), Dorothy Collins, Doris Day, Joan Edwards, Georgia Gibbs, Dick Haymes, Snooky Lanson, Johnny Mercer, Lanny Ross, Dinah Shore, Frank Sinatra, Lawrence Tibbett, Martha Tilton, Bea Wain, Margaret Whiting and Eileen Wilson. The TV extension added Jill Corey, Johnny Desmond, Gisele MacKenzie and June Valli. While some of their stints were all too brief, they all made a contribution to pop music. *Your Hit Parade*, for most of those talents, became a steppingstone to still greater career feats. Several are cited in the separate chapter on Vocalists.

The luminary who was invariably linked with *Your Hit Parade* in the public's collective mind was Frank Sinatra, "the most popular singer since Crosby." One authority allowed: "Radio, and mainly *Your Hit Parade*, took Sinatra from big-band star to superstar." Although he didn't appear on the video version that occurred later, he was a teenage idol of the 1940s, vigilantly pursued wherever he went by hordes of shrieking bobbysoxers. Columnist Earl Wilson christened the phenomena "Swoonatra" as hysterical screams and fainting spells swept through his feminine following. Frenzied fanatics dubbed him "The Voice."

Tickets were reportedly scalped to teenage girls outside the *Your Hit Parade* studios during Sinatra's time on the program. The squeals accompanying his appearances were so deafening to so many listeners—and especially to George Washington Hill—that a revised studio admittance policy was swiftly adopted: ticketholders were required to be at least 21 years of age to see the show. In addition to the audio disturbance, the out-of-control mania eclipsed the program's very purpose for existing, a further reason to qualify its patrons.

From late 1941 to early 1947, minus a four-month interlude in 1943, distaff singer Joan Edwards meted out a little comeuppance to the bobbysoxers, summarily becoming the darling of GIs everywhere. She was their response, in fact, to the teenyboppers' allure with Sinatra. Landing in Naples, servicemen named a jeep for her. Wounded soldiers confined in San Francisco's Letterman General Hospital launched a "Moan and Groan for Joan" fan club which became widespread. Edwards collected hundreds of requests for pin-up photos from ardent admirers. Many sent her V-discs on which they warbled lullabies for her infant daughter. In this instance, *Your Hit Parade's* producers learned that what worked for the gander could work just as well for the goose. Edwards left the show when it transferred from New York to Hollywood in 1947.

Sinatra, resembling "an undernourished schoolboy," arrived in February 1943 and left the show in December 1944. But less than three years later, in September 1947 (and a mere year following the death of George Washington Hill), he returned, taking control over his own arrangements and replacing Mark Warnow as the Lucky Strike Orchestra's maestro. Sinatra's personal recording conductor, Alex Stordahl, accepted the baton. The duo remained with the show through May 1949 when both left forever.

Sinatra once faced a crestfallen President Franklin D. Roosevelt during a White House reception when the teen idol was unable to tell the nation's chief what song would be number one the following Saturday night. Even the "stars" were prevented from knowing such details, thus inadvertently divulging those closely guarded secrets.

Songstress Bea Wain would later claim that there was no opportunity for input from the vocalists in the show's design, claiming a "committee" put it together. Individuals were assigned specific tunes on their arrival at the studio and rendered them backed by a 45-piece orchestra. "Not even we on the show ever knew what numbers one, two, and three would be," she acknowledged. "They were legit surveys. We weren't told until the dress rehearsal that day."

But at least one skeptic had other thoughts about the show's credibility. Writing in the early 1970s, he allowed: "*Your Hit Parade* was not always the most reliable index of popularity. In 1935 we used to make frantic efforts to guess all fifteen songs in advance of the broadcast. We were naïve enough to believe with the fierceness of fundamentalist Bible-belt preachers in the absolute authenticity of the survey. But by 1945, when *Billboard* began to run its 'Honor Roll of Hits,' with a dozen accompanying pages of charts and calculations, our faith in the radio survey was shaken. *Billboard* was surely 'an accurate and authentic survey,' if ever there was one." The show had other detractors. *Variety*, which provided its own record charts, in a reference to *Your Hit Parade*, insisted: "The sponsor's mother-in-law sends over a list of her favorite songs, and they play those."

In the mid-1940s, menacing inquiries began arriving from disgruntled music publishers wondering why their songs weren't featured on the air since they turned up in surveys elsewhere. It was a classic example of "everybody wants to get in on the act" as a surplus of sampling systems proliferated. One publisher (of *Don't Sweetheart Me*, a song best forgotten) carried its umbrage all the way to the New York Supreme Court.

Wain, referred to as a "hot canary" by one critic and whose time with the show partially overlapped Frank Sinatra's, recalls: "I never felt any sense of competition. Sinatra did his own thing, and of course he was wonderful, but he had an entourage. I was too busy thinking what I had to do to worry about anything else. You minded your own business because you had to produce. There was no time for coyness." She did notice that the other male vocalists on the show were envious of Sinatra's adolescent feminine cult, however.

Wain also remembers: "Frank Sinatra got bored with singing 'Now Is the Hour' on *Your Hit Parade*. There's a soprano in the background doodling while he's singing 'Now Is the Hour,' and he said, 'Thank you, Marjorie Main' in the middle of it. Which is fun for all of us, but the next morning, there was a call from Vincent Riggio, who was then the head of Lucky

Strike, and that was the start of the decline with Frank on *Hit Parade*."

When Sinatra's contract ran out in late 1944, George Washington Hill sought "a new twist, packed with tremendous publicity potential." He found his answer in—of all people—Metropolitan Opera baritone Lawrence Tibbett. Tibbett eased into an unaccustomed role as Sinatra instructed his loyal fans: "Now listen, this man is a friend of mine. You be very sweet and nice to him." The pandemonium in the 1,200-seat theater at 1697 Broadway between Fifty-Third and Fifty-Fourth streets (which was later named for Ed Sullivan)—from which *Your Hit Parade* emanated during its CBS tenancy—ended abruptly. Although some didn't approve of the replacement, the majority accepted Tibbett. Almost overnight the show's ratings ascended seven points. Within a month, the Amalgamated Frank Sinatra Clubs of Brooklyn, representing 36 organizations and thousands of pubescent adherents, proclaimed they were transferring loyalties from Sinatra to Tibbett.

The Met's esteemed "Rigoletto" remained with the show only six months, to July 1945. Tibbett was replaced by "Canada's answer to Bing Crosby," Dick Todd, who lasted another six months. When Andy Russell arrived in June 1946, the teener-screamers returned. Someone aptly nicknamed his idolizing entourage "Russell's Sprouts."

Of *Your Hit Parade's* stars, two—Dorothy Collins and Snooky Lanson ("two rookies" by one estimate)—held the show's endurance records. Both were featured performers from 1950 to 1957, including the last three years of the radio series and most of the overlapping television era. Furthermore, four additional female singers appeared for three or more years: Joan Edwards, Gisele MacKenzie (TV only), Bea Wain and Eileen Wilson. MacKenzie, incidentally, had the distinction of being *Your Hit Parade's* only performer to sing one of her own recorded numbers from the charts, *Hard to Get*, initially on July 30, 1955. Her tune made eight appearances before it vanished, ranking as high as second spot.

The remuneration for those appearing on *Your Hit Parade* may have been commensurate with what artists were receiving on other shows at the time. In the early days, Hill paid unidentified vocalists a top fee of $100 per performance while musicians could expect $75 (including rehearsal time) and announcers began at $35. At *Your Hit Parade's* inception, Hill shelled out $12,000 weekly compared to $26,000 five years later. Performers' income continued to improve steadily as time elapsed, incidentally. Lawrence Tibbett, who already had name recognition when he replaced Frank Sinatra, earned $4,500 per show for his vocalizing.

And what types of songs made the charts in those days? They ran the gamut, from ballad to blues and everything between—country, jazz, novelty, seasonal—instrumentals, vocals, groups, whatever. Actually, the only binding rule was that the songs must be popular. George Washington Hill insisted upon it, believing listeners would be receptive to familiar tunes, thereby open to the program's commercial missives, too.

There were lots of songs that placed high on the charts and thus on *Your Hit Parade*. *Too Young* held first place 12 times, more than any other melody, in 22 appearances on the show beginning May 19, 1951. Close on its heels was *Because of You*, in first place 11 times in 23 appearances starting July 21, 1951. A dozen tunes climbed into the coveted first spot 10 times each: *Buttons and Bows, Hey There, I Hear a Rhapsody, If, I'll Be Seeing You, Love Letters in the Sand, Now is the Hour, Peg o' My Heart, Some Enchanted Evening, Tammy, A Tree in the Meadow* and *White Christmas*. Several were ranked 20 or more times—none fewer than 14. The show's most frequently recurring hit, Irving Berlin's *White Christmas*, premiering October 17, 1942, was performed 38 times, often running for several weeks at that season (15 times during 1942-1943 alone).

"But for sustained popularity no song can equal the [Richard] Rodgers–[Oscar] Hammerstein *People Will Say We're in Love* [from their Broadway stage play and the later movie musical *Oklahoma!*]," wrote one reviewer. "Its appeal was immediate, and its fresh and inventive words and music never palled through a full thirty weeks in 1943-44." Ballads with overt appeal to wartime sentiment were that immortal song's two nearest contenders, each with 24 appearances—*I'll Be Seeing You* by Irving Kahal and Sammy Fain (1944-1945) and *You'll Never Know* by Mack Gordon and Harry Warren (1943). All three songs landed in first place only once each, by the way, but obviously sustained remarkable popularity.

The briefest life of the luminous tunes was *I Saw Mommy Kissing Santa Claus*, appearing only once, on January 3, 1953, yet in *first place*! Another song similarly ranked was *Peter Cottontail* which hit second place in its single appearance April 15, 1950.

The *Hit Parade* tunes at times traveled from the sublime to the ridiculous, reflecting dramatic shifts in the nation's musical tastes. Among selections making the charts in the 1950s, for example, were such numbers as *Get a Job*, *Little Darlin'*, *Purple People Eater*, *Short Shorts* and *Witch Doctor*. Those could be tempered with moderating melodies like *April Love*, *Blue Tango*, *I'm Yours*, *The Song from Moulin Rouge* and *You Belong to Me*.

Lyricist Mack Gordon and composer Harry Warren are most frequently represented among the tunesmiths featured on *Your Hit Parade*. While each also worked with others, their paramount achievements were probably the movie refrains the pair collaborated on like *Chattanooga Choo Choo* and *The More I See You*. Together they penned *At Last*, *Kalamazoo*, *Serenade in Blue*, *There Will Never Be Another You* and many, many more *Hit Parade* favorites.

Thirty-nine of Gordon's lyrics turned up on *Your Hit Parade's* top 10 while 42 Warren-inspired melodies were there. Runner-up lyricists included Irving Berlin (33), Johnny Mercer (32), Johnny Burke (28), Leo Robin (26), Sammy Cahn (23), Al Dubin (23) and Frank Loesser (23). Runner-up composers included Irving Berlin (33), Jimmy Van Heusen (25), Jimmy McHugh (20), Harry Revel (20), Richard Rodgers (19), Ralph Rainger (17), Jule Styne (17) and Cole Porter (16). A researcher who painstakingly poured over their work noted that the lyricists wrote primarily about slumming on Fifth Avenue, dreams, pennies from heaven, moonlight and shadows, lonely Saturday nights, Indian summers and strange enchantments; the composers, meanwhile, focused on top hats, swinging on stars, the mood for love, a date with a dream, a small hotel by a wishing well, blossoms on Broadway, walking alone and getting out of town.[6]

Seeking to relate *Your Hit Parade* to modern entertainment, the same researcher allowed:[7]

> The horizon was limited in the radio days of the *Hit Parade*. There were no songs of social protest, no ecstasies of gospel and soul, no explorations of non–Western musical traditions, no affirmations of the essential humanity of all races. But neither were there the bathos, the crassness, the sensation-seeking one hears at such ear-splitting intensity today. Silliness, yes. Sentimentality in abundance. But often too a subtlety, a genial understatement, a formal discipline, and above all a melodiousness that pop music since 1950 never attained.

Author John R. Williams also possessed an abiding appreciation for *Your Hit Parade* (including radio and television versions). He scrupulously provided complete show-by-show lists of all survey songs performed on the series in his trivia-packed chronicle, *This Was Your Hit Parade*, released in 1973, which may be of added interest to some readers.

The significant marketing impact of George Washington Hill, president of the American Tobacco Company from 1926 to 1946, hasn't been properly calculated, nor the enormous effect it had on *Your Hit Parade* and other broadcast series. Closer scrutiny of a few models of his profound contributions to the advertising and promotional industry of his day is in order. Beginning in 1917, he developed his product "from scratch," skillfully touting it to the public by capitalizing on an excess of attention-grabbing devices and highlighting several inspired mottos far beyond any previous attempts to manipulate similar persuasive tactics. "Hill certainly had a way with words," observed one biographer. "He had the ability to transform sophisticated or technical terms into language everyone could relate to.... His slogans and sound gimmicks became part of American folklore."[8]

When he pondered, for example, that the tobacco was warmed during cigarette manufacturing to stimulate an inimitable aroma, he impulsively considered how to exploit that function for promotional advantage. To state that the tobacco was cooked seemed overdoing it and wouldn't be effective, he mused, although that's precisely what was happening. Better, he deduced, to play up the heating angle, a softer processing concept. Soon the words he was seeking came to him: *It's toasted!* Toasting communicated a genial, flavorful, engaging aura. The axiom was added to Lucky Strike's packages and soon burst forth in the brand's print and broadcast advertising.

Earlier, as Hill was managing the *Lucky Strike Dance Orchestra* radio series (literally!), he found himself in something of a contentious quagmire over one of his catchphrases. Noting that an increasing portion of the female market had become smokers, he fully intended to use whatever resources were available to broaden the category. Hill pursued the idea both resolutely and tangentially. He was also conscious of the fact that many women were concerned about their figures. He hit upon and imaginative solution: he would project a weight-loss program calling for replacing sugar with smoke! Hence, "Reach for a Lucky instead of a sweet!" was integrated into commercials on the radio show and in print media. The confectionary trade wasn't all that impressed and protested vehemently, doing its best to torpedo Hill's novel advertising campaign.

Strictly as a result of circumstances, Hill was engaged in yet another crusade that also attracted still more women to his favorite brand. It came about during the war years. Until 1942, Lucky Strike was sold in green packages, reportedly never a particular favorite of Hill. His purchasing agent notified him that the government was requiring that commercial use of chromium be suspended to channel the commodity's use into the supply of tanks available for military operations. Chromium was a prime ingredient from which the jade ink on the Lucky Strike wrappers was derived. "Green ink has gone to war just like the soldiers," said the firm's buyer.

Hill ruminated over the matter. He had previously harbored fleeting thoughts about altering the packaging, thinking that a white container with a color other than emerald might draw more female smokers. After all, Luckies' strongest competitor, Chesterfield (manufactured by Liggett & Myers Tobacco Company) appeared in white. (Let us digress: *Your Hit Parade's* classy uptown challenger from 1944 to 1950 was *The Chesterfield Supper Club* featuring pop singers Perry Como, Peggy Lee and Jo

Stafford. With its *Smoke Dreams* theme ("Smoke dreams from smoke rings, while a Chesterfield burns"), the brand touted its own famed adage: "*They satisfy!*")

Hill, meanwhile, favored a white pack for his Luckies bearing a bright red circle. Furthermore, he was unable to let go of something else the purchasing official had told him. "Green ink has gone to war just like the soldiers." Hill had another brainstorm and as a result Luckies' famous wartime cliché "Lucky Strike green has gone to war" was born. It was a textbook example of taking a lemon and making lemonade.

The new catchphrase, which was as well recognized by the public as "Remember Pearl Harbor," so a reporter allowed, became an obsession with Hill. Soon the term was inserted into every available spot on Lucky-sponsored radio programs. On *Your Hit Parade* it was repeated multiple times during every commercial. By 1943, it was inserted throughout the show wherever a few seconds' pause occurred. Listeners chanted "Lucky Strike green has gone to war" while on some Lucky Strike programs even studio audiences got in on the act in a kind of patriotic indulgence. Who could fault a series for that? Hill got the new package he desired, more women were cuddling up to tobacco, Lucky Strike was doing its part (if not immodestly) to assist the country and everybody felt good about the shared momentum. And Luckies didn't do so bad either. Their sales jumped an astounding 38 percent.

The campaign seemed to work in every place but one. That was on the illustrious *Information Please* radio series on which erudite celebrities attempted to answer perplexing queries posed by an audience of commoners. Between 1938 and 1951, the feature eventually touched all four national chains. From late 1940 until early 1943, the American Tobacco Company underwrote the program for Lucky Strike. This created a scenario that permitted two powerful juggernaut personalities to collide, an almost inevitable conclusion.

Dan Golenpaul, the show's creator, owner, producer and director, could be, on occasion, a highly belligerent, antagonistic man. He, too, seldom let anything prevent him from getting his way. The reader knows already that George Washington Hill often carried the same chips on his shoulder. In late 1942, on *Information Please*, "Lucky Strike green has gone to war" interrupted the show and virtually took control of it. The slogan was perpetually bellowed by announcers between questions, in fact any time dead air occurred, totally neglectful of established commercial slots.

Golenpaul went off the deep end. "You're lousing up my program and I won't stand for it," he told Hill. The two had butted heads several times before so this was nothing new. This time Hill pointed out that as he was paying the bills it was *his* show and Golenpaul couldn't do a thing about it. But an equally possessive Golenpaul didn't take it lying down. He filed a lawsuit to force the issue while the news media had a field day with it. In the end, the petition was dismissed at the hall of justice while Golenpaul won an enormous triumph in the court of public opinion. Hill and his company were perceived as surly and stingy while Golenpaul was seen as championing integrity and quality. The backlash led Hill to dissolve his contract with the program and he bowed out in a spate of extremely bad publicity. It was certainly the most public disparagement and likely humiliation of his career.

George Washington Hill wasn't finished as an advertiser of substantial repute, however. His ultimate ploy — some think it his crowning achievement — was a device that has been commonly referred to as the "triphammer commercial." When he withdrew it from his arsenal of promotional gimmickry and unleashed it on a receptive public, he proved his ability as an unassailable marketing genius. It became the capstone of his professional offerings to marketing, affecting not only sales of Lucky Strike but the methods by which commodities would be advertised and sold in many industries. And it began with Hill's simple observations at several tobacco warehouses across the South.

On those visits he was fascinated by the rapid-fire delivery of the auctioneers and with the prospect of some way capturing that experience and pressing it into an effective merchandising tool. An idea was born. Hill began making inquiries, soliciting the names of individual auctioneers who were quick on the trigger. He was referred to a couple of gentlemen — L.A. "Speed" Riggs of Goldsboro, North Carolina, and F.E. Boone of Lexington, Kentucky. He offered to pay them $25,000 a year, about twice what they were then making, to chant during a couple of 90-second commercials on *Your Hit Parade* and his other Lucky Strike programs. They accepted and some of the most memorable sales pitches in broadcast history ensued.

Capitalizing on repetition, a Hill trademark, Riggs (in singsong fashion) or Boone (employing a monotone style) rolled out this exceedingly rapid blockbuster:

> Hey TWENTY NINE nine nine nine nine nine nine, roundem roundem roundem roundem roundem, am I right at thirty thirty thirty thirty thirty thirty thirty thirty thirty thirty thirty thirty THIRTY ONE thirty one thirty one one one one one one one one one one one one TWO thirty two two two two two two two two two two two two two THREE thirty three three three three three three three FOUR thirty four four four four four come along come along long long long four four thirty four four four FIVE thirty five five five five grab it grab it grab it five thirty five thirty five thirty five five five am I right am I right am I right at thirty five five five SIX six thirty six six six six six six six six six SEVEN seven seven seven seven thirty seven seven seven seven seven seven seven EIGHT eight eight eight thirty eight eight eight eight — sol-l-l-d A-merican!

At that announcer Andre Baruch or Basil Ruysdael delivered a distinctive message following the sound of a clicking telegraph, claiming: "From men who know tobacco best, it's Luckies, two to one!" Then an authoritative-sounding voice enunciated: "LS/MFT ... LS/MFT ... Lucky Strike Means Fine Tobacco!"

Years later Baruch recalled that Hill had required him to tour tobacco factories and attend some auctions to increase his familiarity with the product. "Hill's dictum [was that] you've got to learn the business so when you get up before the microphone, you're not just reading words," Baruch remembered.

LS/MFT was added to the bottom of every Lucky Strike pack and quickly became a part of the American vernacular. The trick was that it wasn't soon discarded. It fell from the lips of just about everybody at one time or other. Some turned it into humor. A common expression that this author recalls being exchanged among school chums: "LS/MFT ... LS/MFT ... Lord, save me from Truman!" The 1940s advertising jingle was so widely recognized by millions, so unforgettable and so compelling that *Your Hit Parade*, *The Jack Benny Program* and other Lucky Strike radio features carried it over to their television extensions in the 1950s.

The commercial's effective use of sound other than the human voice (the clicking telegraph) and the repetitive, rapid-fire delivery of the auctioneers infused something fresh and exciting into broadcast marketing. It went well beyond the triteness of a mere voice reading staid commercial copy. This was a new day for advertisers and for those who conveyed their products and services on the ether. George Washington Hill raised the bar in aural pitching. Many of his peers would never again be content with the traditional methods of communicating their wares.

Ultimately, Hill became an icon in several fields. He significantly increased the sales of his company's cigarettes. He filled the air with popular entertainment programming. And he is among a handful of innovative thinkers who infused marketing with some dramatic, untried patterns. While he may have been a tough cookie in his day-to-day dealings, he left an indelible mark upon the terrain that he touched.

Although several announcers appeared on *Your Hit Parade* over its long run, the best remembered is Andre Baruch, a debonair Frenchman whose commanding introductions to the various tunes were familiar to audiences in both the radio and television eras. While flanked by other well-known cohorts like Ben Grauer, Warren Hull and Del Sharbutt, it was Baruch who was there for the long haul and who is identified by most people today.

Born in Paris on August 20, 1906, Baruch arrived in the United States 13 years later, applying for and gaining permanent citizenship. During World War II, as a major in the U.S. Army Signal Corps stationed in North Africa, he was assigned to the Armed Forces Radio Service. By that time, of course, he had already established himself in civilian life as a major network interlocutor.

Baruch was a pianist; yet when he went to audition at CBS in New York in 1932 he inadvertently fell into the wrong line, being given the printed names of composers from abroad to read aloud. That launched his career as a radio announcer. In some of his early duties he covered baseball games and band remotes. He may be recalled as the advertising voice of U.S. Steel. For 22 years he was a commercial spokesman for the American Tobacco Company, appearing not only on *Your Hit Parade* but also on several other Lucky Strike series.

His radio announcing credits were massive, including *The American Album of Familiar Music, The Andrews Sisters Eight-to-the-Bar Ranch, Bobby Benson and the B-Bar-B Riders, Dr. Christian, Exploring the Unknown, The FBI in Peace and War, Guy Lombardo Time, The Jack Benny Program, Just Plain Bill, The Kate Smith Show, Leave It to the Girls, Linda's First Love, Little Orphan Annie, Marie the Little French Princess, The Mark Warnow Show, Myrt and Marge, My Son and I, Second Husband, The Shadow, Stoopnagle and Budd, Your Hit Parade* and *Your Song and Mine*. On television, Baruch hosted *Masters of Magic* (1949), appeared in the cast of *Shoppers Matinee* (1950) and announced *Your Hit Parade* (1950–1957). He also recorded newsreel voice-overs that played in movie theaters.

Death came in Beverly Hills, California, on September 15, 1991.

Baruch was married to *Your Hit Parade* songstress Bea Wain, who at the time of this writing not only survives him but also frequently appears on the agendas of old-time radio and nostalgia conventions on both coasts. The singer, born April 30, 1917, who was Baruch's business partner, welcomes those opportunities to perpetuate her legendary late spouse's name. In retirement, they conducted a 1970s talk show over station WPBR in Palm Beach, Florida.

In 1955, Baruch and Wain, appearing as *Mr. & Mrs. Music*, attempted to revive the aura of *Your Hit Parade* over WMCA radio in New York by playing records of the day's top tunes. Their effort was only modestly successful — by then almost every local station had its own survey and its own stack of records. As time intervened, however, and people nostalgically reflected on past experiences, Baruch and Wain met with favor as they tried a new approach to the same inspiration in the 1970s and 1980s.

The pair cohosted an extensive run of transcribed syndicated features for which they summoned the *Your Hit Parade* tunes that actually appeared on the air featuring the original vocalists and instrumentalists. Each segment echoed the song charts for a specific week and year from decades earlier. The countdown was included, holding listeners of a contemporary era at rapt attention until the number-one song was revealed at the conclusion, just as in the old days. While the live series played on the air for 24 seasons, by transcription it continued for many more years, disseminating a program that had entertained millions, introducing it to multitudes in successive generations.

Beyond the fact the concept of featuring current top songs from the charts on the air originated with *Your Hit Parade*, there were a couple of spin-off series also spawned here. From February 12, 1943, to September 24, 1944, NBC aired *Your All-Time Hit Parade* live from Carnegie Hall, also sponsored by Lucky Strike. (The Friday night series was a Sunday night summer replacement for *The Jack Benny Program* in 1944.) The show mixed current hits (like *I'll Be Seeing You*) with those of an earlier era (like *Wagon Wheels*). Said one reviewer: "This no doubt would have been just another music show but for one factor—American Tobacco and its feisty president, George Washington Hill." He promoted it surreptitiously on his other radio series with a relentless rhyme: *The best tunes of all have moved to Carnegie Hall!* Mark Warnow directed the orchestra. Vocalists Marie Green, Ethel Smith, Martha Stewart, Bea Wain, Jerry Wayne and the Lyn Murray Chorus were regulars.

A somewhat similar series, *Your Hit Parade on Parade*, replaced *Benny* between June 5 and September 4, 1949, over CBS, also for Lucky Strike. Soloists Stuart Foster and Marjorie Hughes, backed by Russ Case's orchestra, offered the top 10 tunes of the previous 14 years (since *Your Hit Parade's* inception).

Although the national radio series ended in 1953, television kept *Your Hit Parade* before large audiences weekly through 1959. But musical styles began to change drastically by mid decade and it soon became obvious that the show's fate was sealed as Snooky Lanson dawdled *You Ain't Nothin' But a Hound Dog.* Rock 'n' roll suddenly permeated the charts. Not only were the show's regulars poorly suited to perform such raucous music (it appeared ludicrous), the adolescents who purchased the phonograph records preferred the original artists. *Your Hit Parade* had encountered a roadblock it wasn't prepared by training to deal with.

The show experienced a metamorphosis at the start of its final season on NBC-TV in autumn 1957. (Viewers may not have realized they were seeing video history unfold at the start of *Your Hit Parade* on September 7, 1957, when an animated peacock proudly opened its feathers and announcer Ben Grauer revealed for the first time: "The following program is brought to you in living color on NBC.") To project a more youthful image, *Your Hit Parade's* aging quartet of stars—Russell Arms, Dorothy Collins, Snooky Lanson and Gisele MacKenzie—was dismissed in favor of a younger set including Alan Copeland, Jill Corey, Virginia Gibson and Tommy Leonetti (although none of them were rock stars). Within five months the show was revamped again. This time, the hit parade was reduced to five numbers with five "extras" that hadn't made the charts. Added was a $200,000 mystery tune contest in an era in which *The $64,000 Question, The $64,000 Challenge, The Big Surprise, Twenty-One, Dotto* and a handful of other big-moneyed games fed a frenetic craze sweeping the nation. All would be gone shortly following a collapse in the infamous TV quiz show scandals.

None of that worked for *Your Hit Parade*, either. When the show transferred to

CBS-TV that fall (1958), the new cast was replaced by part of the old as Dorothy Collins returned, teaming with singer Johnny Desmond. But by then the bloom was off the rose. American Tobacco's Hit Parade cigarettes underwrote the series during alternate weeks yet a second sponsor couldn't be found. And in search of a loyal audience the program shifted from Saturdays to Tuesdays to Fridays. It didn't matter. *Billboard*'s charts, the frequently shifting musical patterns, the public's unstable preferences and those unforgivable DJs with their own top-tune lists on so many stations bit the hand that set it all in motion — and ultimately had a final laugh. It ended mercifully on April 24, 1959.

In August 1974, *Your Hit Parade* was revived for five weeks over CBS-TV but again failed to connect with a following. That brief series' regulars included Kelly Garrett, Sheralee, and Chuck Woolery (the latter to become a TV game show host in 1975 with *Wheel of Fortune* followed by *Love Connection* and more). Milton Delugg's orchestra was featured.

The question of what finally eliminated the hit parade is many-faceted. In addition to the reasons credited, the advent of television played a role just as much as improved technology paved the way for the disc jockey with palms greased by payola that soon dominated much of pop music's domain. There may have been at least one other culprit. The show's biographer cites the electric guitar as a culpable party. That instrument's inception "signaled a change in popular music from orchestrated arrangements to small guitar-led groups with their amplifiers turned way up." There were, to be sure, a number of reasons why *Your Hit Parade* didn't survive.

The difference between a contemporary age with its youth-oriented, hard-rock, country, beautiful music and gospel-singing radio outlets and the medium's golden age was just this: "In 1942 everyone in the country was singing, listening, and dancing to the *same* tunes, which were played on *all* radio stations *and* on juke boxes, and selling both sheet music and single records." Diversification killed all of it.

Somewhere in the subconscious minds of millions of Americans who were caught up in the heart-stopping chart topping of the resonance of a few decades ago, one still hears the dreamy melody of the Hit Paraders as they harmonize on Alex Kramer's familiar refrain that climaxed every show:

> *So long, for a while*
> *That's all the songs, for a while*
> *So long to Your Hit Parade,*
> *And the tunes that you picked to be played…*
> *So lon-g-g-g-g!*

Chapter Notes

The Bell Telephone Hour

1. Tim Brooks, and Earle Marsh, *The Complete Directory to Prime Time Network TV Shows, 1946–Present*. Fourth Edition (New York: Ballantine Books, 1988), p. 71.

The Big Bands

1. George T. Simon, *The Big Bands* (Toronto: Macmillan, 1969), p. 28.
2. Gerald Nachman, *Raised on Radio: In Quest of The Lone Ranger, Jack Benny, Amos 'n' Andy, The Shadow, Mary Noble, The Great Gildersleeve, Fibber McGee and Molly, Bill Stern, Our Miss Brooks, Henry Aldrich, The Quiz Kids, Mr. First Nighter, Fred Allen, Vic and Sade, The Cisco Kid, Jack Armstrong, Arthur Godfrey, Bob and Ray, The Barbour Family, Henry Morgan, Joe Friday and Other Lost Heroes from Radio's Heyday* (New York: Pantheon Books, 1998), p. 163.
3. Leo Walker, *The Wonderful Era of the Great Dance Bands* (New York: De Capo Press, 1990), p. 168.
4. Christopher H. Sterling and John M. Kittross, *Stay Tuned: A Concise History of American Broadcasting*. Second Edition (Belmont, CA: Wadsworth Publishing, 1990), p. 72.
5. George Ansbro, *I Have a Lady in the Balcony: Memoirs of a Broadcaster* (Jefferson, NC: McFarland, 2000), pp. 80–81.
6. Simon, p. 25.
7. Francis Chase, Jr., *Sound and Fury: An Informal History of Broadcasting* (New York: Harper & Brothers, 1942), pp. 252–253, 254.
8. Chase, p. 255.
9. Leonard Maltin, *The Great American Broadcast: A Celebration of Radio's Golden Age* (New York: Penguin Putnam, 1997), p. 264.
10. *Ibid.*

The Bing Crosby Show

1. Sally Bedell Smith, *In All His Glory: The Life of William S. Paley, The Legendary Tycoon and His Brilliant Circle* (New York: Simon and Schuster, 1990), p. 91.
2. Thomas A. DeLong, *The Mighty Music Box: The Golden Age of Musical Radio* (Los Angeles: Amber Crest, 1980), p. 79.
3. A few scholars suggest that Crosby's premier with CBS paid him only $600 weekly. This appears doubtful, since several others allow the higher figure of $1,500. Due to his previously demonstrated prudence, it would hardly seem likely that he would demand $2,000 from NBC and settle for a rate that was $1,400 lower from CBS.
4. Charles Hull Wolfe, *Modern Radio Advertising* (New York: Funk & Wagnalls and Printers' Ink Publishing Co., 1949), p. 169.
5. Donald Shepherd and Robert F. Slatzer, *Bing Crosby: The Hollow Man* (New York: St. Martin's Press, 1981), p. 159.
6. Shepherd and Slatzer, p. 161.

7. Michael Freedland, *Bing Crosby: The Illustrated Biography* (London: Chameleon Books, 1998), p. 11.
8. Smith, p. 92.
9. Freedland, p. 72.
10. John Dunning, *On the Air: The Encyclopedia of Old-Time Radio* (New York: Oxford University Press, 1998), p. 92.
11. Frank Buxton and Bill Owen, *The Big Broadcast, 1920–1950* Second Edition (Lanham, MD: Scarecrow Press, 1997), p. 126.
12. Hal Kanter, quoted in Leonard Maltin, *The Great American Broadcast: A Celebration of Radio's Golden Age* (New York: Penguin Putnam, 1997), p. 200.
13. Freedland, pp. 56–57.
14. Maltin, pp. 280–281.
15. Nachman, p. 166.
16. Nachman, pp. 165–166.
17. Christopher H. Sterling and John M. Kittross, *Stay Tuned: A Concise History of American Broadcasting*, Second Edition (Belmont, CA: Wadsworth Publishing, 1990), p. 251.
18. Dunning, 1998, pp. 92–93.
19. Shepherd and Slatzer, p. 181.
20. Maltin, pp. 177, 199.
21. Robert L. Mott, *Radio Sound Effects: Who Did It, and How, in the Era of Live Broadcasting* (Jefferson, NC: McFarland, 1993), pp. 204–206.
22. Charles Thompson, *Bing: The Authorized Biography* (New York: David McKay, 1975), p. 138.
23. DeLong, 1980, p. 271.
24. Maltin, p. 284.
25. Freedland, p. 84.
26. Ken Barnes, *The Crosby Years* (New York: St. Martin's Press, 1980), p. 10.
27. Shepherd and Slatzer, dust jacket liner notes.
28. Freedland, pp. 50, 52.
29. *Ibid.*, pp. 82–83.
30. Kathryn Crosby, *My Life with Bing* (Wheeling, IL: Collage, 1983), p. ix.

The Chamber Music Society of Lower Basin Street

1. Marc Robinson, *Brought to You in Living Color: 75 Years of Great Moments in Television & Radio from NBC* (New York: John Wiley & Sons, 2002), p. 80.

Cities Service Concerts

1. Thomas A. DeLong, *Radio Stars: An Illustrated Biographical Dictionary of 953 Performers, 1920 through 1960* (Jefferson, NC: McFarland, 1996), p. 82.
2. There is a slight discrepancy in the date that Jessica Dragonette joined the *Cities Service Concert* show. In his 1976 volume, John Dunning claims it was December 27, 1929, while he updates that to January 3, 1930, in his 1998 text. Some sources state her tenure with the series extended from 1929 to 1937 while others maintain it was 1930–1937. Assuming Dunning became privy to more authentic data in the 22 years that elapsed between his radio encyclopedias, the 1930 date probably carries a greater likelihood of accuracy.
3. John Dunning, *On the Air: The Encyclopedia of Old-Time Radio* (New York: Oxford University Press, 1998), p. 157.

The Classics

1. Sally Bedell Smith, *In All His Glory: The Life of William S. Paley, the Legendary Tycoon and His Brilliant Circle* (New York: Simon and Schuster, 1990), pp. 145–146.
2. Taylor was mistaken about the year — the Philharmonic was formed late in 1842.
3. Thomas A. DeLong, *The Mighty Music Box: The Golden Age of Musical Radio* (Los Angeles: Amber Crest, 1980), pp. 95–96.
4. Eugene Lyons, *David Sarnoff: A Biography* (New York: Harper and Row, 1966), p. 199.
5. Lyons, p. 200.
6. DeLong, 1980, pp. 245–246.

The Contests

1. Albert McCarthy, *The Dance Band Era: The Dancing Decades from Ragtime to Swing, 1910–1950* (Radnor, PA: Chilton, 1982), p. 155.
2. George T. Simon, *The Big Bands* (Toronto: Macmillan, 1969), p. 239.
3. Nachman, pp. 360–361.
4. Leo Walker, *The Wonderful Era of the Great Dance Bands* (New York: De Capo Press, 1990), p. 253.

The Disc Jockeys

1. Nachman, p. 179.
2. Walker, p. 155.
3. *Ibid.*, p. 157.
4. DeLong, p. 273.
5. Personal communication with the author from Elizabeth McLeod, December 13, 2003. Used by permission.
6. Wes Smith, *The Pied Pipers of Rock 'n' Roll: Radio Deejays of the 50s and 60s* (Marietta, Ga.: Longstreet Press, 1989), pp. 81–82, 58.
7. Dennis Hart, *Monitor: The Last Great Radio Show* (San Jose, CA: Writers Club Press, 2002), p. 89.
8. Smith, Wes, p. 9.
9. Nachman, p. 180.

The Fred Waring Show

1. Personal communication to the author from Peter T. Kiefer, November 28, 2003. Used by permission.
2. DeLong, p. 208.
3. *Ibid.*
4. George T. Simon, *The Big Bands* (Toronto: Macmillan, 1969), p. 285.
5. Personal communication to the author from Peter T. Kiefer, November 28, 2003. Used by permission.
6. Leo Walker, *The Wonderful Era of the Great Dance Bands* (New York: De Capo Press, 1990), pp. 144–145.

Grand Ole Opry

1. *Official WSM Grand Ole Opry History-Picture Book* (Nashville: WSM, Inc., 1961), p. 1.
2. Jack Hurst, *Nashville's Grand Ole Opry: The First Fifty Years, 1925–1975* (New York: Harry N. Abrams, 1989), p. 74.
3. Hurst, p. 142.
4. Personal communication with the author from Bill Knowlton, January 31, 2004. Used by permission.

The Horse Operas

1. David Rothel, *Who Was That Masked Man?: The Story of the Lone Ranger* (Cranbury, NJ: A.S. Barnes & Co., 1976), p. 25.

2. Kenneth M. Johnson, *The Johnson Family Singers: We Sang for Our Supper* (Jackson, MS: University Press of Mississippi, 1997), pp. 64–65.
3. DeLong, p. 169.
4. *Ibid.*, pp. 169–170.

The House Bands

1. George T. Simon, *The Big Bands* (London: Macmillan, 1967), p. 58.
2. Arthur Anderson, *Let's Pretend: A History of Radio's Best Loved Children's Show by a Longtime Cast Member* (Jefferson, NC: McFarland, 1994), p. 45.
3. *Ibid.*, p. 58.
4. Personal communication with the author from Ted Meland, September 29, 2003. Used by permission.
5. Personal communications with the author from Martin Grams Jr., October 19, 2003, and April 12, 2004. Used by permission.

The Hummert Musicales

1. Robert J. Landry, "Pioneer Soaper Frank Hummert, Ever the Hermit, Almost 'Sneaks' His Obit," *Variety*, April 27, 1966.
2. Frank Buxton and Bill Owen, *The Big Broadcast, 1920–1950*, Second Edition (Lanham, MD: Scarecrow Press, 1997), p. 145.

The Kate Smith Show

1. Richard K. Hayes, *Kate Smith: A Biography, with a Discography, Filmography and List of Stage Appearances* (Jefferson, NC: McFarland, 1995), p. 10.
2. *Ibid.*, p. 16.
3. Nachman, p. 163
4. Hayes, p. 146.
5. *Ibid.*, p. 145.
6. Charles A. Siepmann, *Radio, Television and Society* (New York: Oxford University Press, 1950), p. 91.
7. Wolfe, pp. 167–168.
8. Wesley Hyatt, *The Encyclopedia of Daytime Television: Everything You Ever Wanted to*

Know about Daytime TV but Didn't Know Where to Look! (New York: Billboard Books, 1997), pp. 246–247.
9. Hayes, p. 221.

The Railroad Hour

1. John Dunning, *Tune in Yesterday: The Ultimate Encyclopedia of Old-Time Radio, 1925–1976* (Englewood Cliffs, NJ: Prentice-Hall, 1976), p. 504.

The Sacred Singers

1. Luther F. Sies, *Encyclopedia of American Radio, 1920–1960* (Jefferson, NC: McFarland, 2000), p. 470.
2. DeLong, p. 120.
3. *Ibid.*, p. 122.
4. *Ibid.*
5. Jim Snyder, "The Longest Running Program in Radio," *Radio Recall*, June 2003, p. 7.

The Voice of Firestone

1. DeLong, pp. 289–290.

Your Hit Parade

1. Owen Lee, "America's Changing Tastes in Popular Music," *High Fidelity Magazine*, October 1972, p. 63.
2. Marc Robinson, *Brought to You in Living Color: 75 Years of Great Moments in Television & Radio from NBC* (New York: John Wiley & Sons, 2002), p. 17.
3. Thomas A. DeLong, *Quiz Craze: America's Infatuation with Game Shows* (New York: Praeger, 1991), p. 66.
4. *Ibid.*
5. Maltin, p. 158.
6. Lee, p. 70.
7. *Ibid.*
8. Norman H. Finkelstein, *Sounds in the Air: The Golden Age of Radio* (New York: Charles Scribner's Sons, 1993), p. 72.

Bibliography

Anderson, Arthur. *Let's Pretend: A History of Radio's Best Loved Children's Show by a Longtime Cast Member.* Jefferson, NC: McFarland & Co., 1994.

Ansbro, George. *I Have a Lady in the Balcony: Memoirs of a Broadcaster.* Jefferson, NC: McFarland & Co., 2000.

Barnes, Ken. *The Crosby Years.* New York: St. Martin's Press, 1980.

Blum, Ronald. "Met Radio Broadcast Loses Sponsor." *The Courier-Journal*, Louisville, KY, May 25, 2003.

Brooks, Tim, and Earle Marsh. *The Complete Directory to Prime Time Network TV Shows, 1946–Present.* 4th ed. New York: Ballantine Books, 1988.

Buxton, Frank, and Bill Owen. *The Big Broadcast, 1920–1950.* 2nd ed. Lanham, MD: Scarecrow Press, 1997.

Chase, Francis, Jr. *Sound and Fury: An Informal History of Broadcasting.* New York: Harper & Brothers, 1942.

The Courier-Journal, Louisville, KY, April 10, 2003.

"The Cover Girl." *Radio Mirror*, February 1944.

Cox, Jim. *Frank and Anne Hummert's Radio Factory: The Programs and Personalities of Broadcasting's Most Prolific Producers.* Jefferson, NC: McFarland & Co., 2003.

_____. *The Great Radio Audience Participation Shows: Seventeen Programs from the 1940s and 1950s.* Jefferson, NC: McFarland & Co., 2001.

_____. *The Great Radio Soap Operas.* Jefferson, NC: McFarland & Co., 1999.

_____. *Mr. Keen, Tracer of Lost Persons.* Jefferson, NC: McFarland & Co., 2004.

_____. *Radio Crime Fighters: Over 300 Programs from the Golden Age.* Jefferson, NC: McFarland & Co., 2002.

_____. "Robert Q. Lewis: The Quintessential Substitute Host." *Nostalgia Digest*, Autumn 2003.

_____. *Say Goodnight, Gracie: The Last Years of Network Radio.* Jefferson, NC: McFarland & Co., 2002.

Crosby, Kathryn. *My Life with Bing.* Wheeling, IL: Collage, 1983.

DeLong, Thomas A. *The Mighty Music Box: The Golden Age of Musical Radio.* Los Angeles: Amber Crest, 1980.

_____. *Quiz Craze: America's Infatuation with Game Shows.* New York: Praeger, 1991.

_____. *Radio Stars: An Illustrated Biographical Dictionary of 953 Performers, 1920 through 1960.* Jefferson, NC: McFarland & Co., 1996.

Doolittle, John. *Don McNeill and His Breakfast Club.* Notre Dame, IN: University of Notre Dame Press, 2001, p. 9.

Douglas, Doug. Personal communication with the author, December 15, 2003. Used by permission.

Duncan, Jacci, ed. *Making Waves: The 50 Greatest Women in Radio and Television as Selected by American Women in Radio and Television, Inc.* Kansas City: Andrews McMeel, 2001.

Dunning, John. *On the Air: The Encyclopedia of Old-Time Radio.* New York: Oxford University Press, 1998.

_____. *Tune in Yesterday: The Ultimate Ency-*

clopedia of Old-Time Radio, 1925–1976. Engelwood Cliffs, NJ: Prentice-Hall, Inc., 1976.

Edmondson, Madeleine, and David Rounds. *The Soaps: Daytime Serials of Radio and TV*. New York: Stein and Day, 1973.

"Famous New York Orchestra, Longines Symphonette, Coming Here." *The Chronicle-Express*, Penn Yan, NY, March 12, 1953.

Fiedler, Johanna. *Molto Agitato: The Mayhem Behind the Music at the Metropolitan Opera*. New York: Doubleday, 2001.

Finkelstein, Norman H. *Sounds in the Air: The Golden Age of Radio*. New York: Charles Scribner's Sons, 1993.

Frank, Mortimer H. *Arturo Toscanini: The NBC Years*. Portland, OR: Amadeus Press, 2002.

Freedland, Michael. *Bing Crosby: The Illustrated Biography*. London: Chameleon Books, 1998.

Gentry, Linnell. *A History and Encyclopedia of Country, Western, and Gospel Music*. Nashville: McQuiddy Press, 1961.

Giddins, Gary. *Bing Crosby: A Pocketful of Dreams—The Early Years, 1903–1940*. Volume One. Boston: Little, Brown, 2001.

Grams, Martin, Jr. Personal communication with the author on October 19, 2003, April 12, 2004, and other dates. Used by permission.

_____. *Radio Drama: American Programs, 1932–1962*. Jefferson, NC: McFarland & Co., 2000.

Granger, William W. *We Proudly Sang at the Met—'83–'83*. Los Angeles: Westland Printing, 1984.

Griffiths, Lawn. "'Music and the Spoken Word' is on the Air with Spirit." *East Valley Tribune*, Mesa, AZ, August 9, 2003.

Harmon, Jim. *Radio Mystery and Adventure and Its Appearances in Film, Television and Other Media*. Jefferson, NC: McFarland & Co., 1992.

Hart, Dennis. *Monitor: The Last Great Radio Show*. San Jose, CA: Writers Club Press, 2002.

Harvey, Rita Morley. *Those Wonderful, Terrible Years: George Heller and the American Federation of Television and Radio Artists*. Carbondale, IL: Southern Illinois University Press, 1996.

Havig, Alan. *Fred Allen's Radio Comedy*. Philadelphia: Temple University Press, 1990.

Hayes, Richard K. *Kate Smith: A Biography, with a Discography, Filmography and List of Stage Appearances*. Jefferson, NC: McFarland & Co., 1995.

Hickerson, Jay. *The Second Revised Ultimate History of Network Radio Programming and Guide to All Circulating Shows*. Hamden, CT: Presto Print, 2001.

Hurst, Jack. *Nashville's Grand Ole Opry: The First Fifty Years, 1925–1975*. New York: Harry N. Abrams, 1989.

Hyatt, Wesley. *The Encyclopedia of Daytime Television*. New York: Billboard Books, 1997.

Jackson, Paul. *Saturday Afternoons at the Old Met: The Metropolitan Opera Broadcasts, 1931–1950*. Portland, OR: Amadeus Press, 1992.

Johnson, Kenneth M. *The Johnson Family Singers: We Sang for Our Supper*. Jackson, MS: University Press of Mississippi, 1997

"Kate Smith Speaks." *Radio Mirror*, March 1943.

"Kate Smith's Summer." *Radio and Television Mirror*, August 1949.

Kiefer, Peter T. Personal communication with the author, November 28, 2003. Used by permission.

Knowlton, Bill. Personal communication with the author, January 29, 2004, and January 31, 2004. Used by permission.

Kolodin, Irving. *The Metropolitan Opera, from 1883 to 1966*. New York: Alfred Knopf, 1996.

Lackmann, Ron. *Remember Radio*. New York: G.P. Putnam's Sons, 1970.

_____. *Same Time ... Same Station: An A–Z Guide to Radio from Jack Benny to Howard Stern*. New York: Facts On File, 1996.

LaGuardia, Robert. *From Ma Perkins to Mary Hartman: The Illustrated History of Soap Opera*. New York: Ballantine Books, 1977.

Landry, Robert J. "Pioneer Soaper Frank Hummert, Ever the Hermit, Almost 'Sneaks' His Obit." *Variety*, April 27, 1966.

Lee, Owen. "America's Changing Tastes in Popular Music." *High Fidelity Magazine*, October 1972.

Lee, M. Owen. *First Intermissions: Twenty-One Great Operas Explored, Explained and Brought to Life from the Met*. New York: Oxford University Press, 1995.

Lyons, Eugene. *David Sarnoff: A Biography*. New York: Harper and Row, 1966.

MacDonald, J. Fred. *Don't Touch That Dial!: Radio Programming in American Life from 1920 to 1960*. Chicago: Nelson-Hall, 1991.

Maltin, Leonard. *The Great American Broadcast: A Celebration of Radio's Golden Age*. New York: Penguin Putnam, 1997.

The Marion Star, Marion, Ohio, March 31, 1952.

McCarthy, Albert. *The Dance Band Era: The Dancing Decades from Ragtime to Swing, 1910–1950*. Radnor, PA: Chilton, 1982.

McKean, Gil. Liner notes for "NBC's Chamber Music Society of Lower Basin Street" album CAL-802 released by RCA Camden records, 1964.

McLeod, Elizabeth. Personal communication with the author, December 13, 2003. Used by permission.

McNeil, Alex. *Total Television: The Comprehensive Guide to Programming from 1948 to the Present.* 4th ed. New York: Penguin Books, 1996.

Meland, Ted. Personal communication with the author, September 29, 2003, and numerous other dates. Used by permission.

Mercer, Gary L. Personal communication with the author, December 11, 2003. Used by permission.

Merton, Robert. *Mass Persuasion.* New York: Harper & Brothers, 1946.

Mili, Gjon, and Mary Ellis Peltz. *The Magic of the Opera: A Picture Memoir of the Metropolitan.* New York: Praeger, 1960.

Miller, Sarah Bryan. "Helen Traubel." *The St. Louis Post-Dispatch,* January 13, 2004.

Millis, E. C. *The New York Times,* February 3, 1924.

Mott, Robert L. *Radio Sound Effects: Who Did It, and How, in the Era of Live Broadcasting.* Jefferson, NC: McFarland & Co., 1993.

Nachman, Gerald. *Raised on Radio: In Quest of The Lone Ranger, Jack Benny, Amos 'n' Andy, The Shadow, Mary Noble, The Great Gildersleeve, Fibber McGee and Molly, Bill Stern, Our Miss Brooks, Henry Aldrich, The Quiz Kids, Mr. First Nighter, Fred Allen, Vic and Sade, The Cisco Kid, Jack Armstrong, Arthur Godfrey, Bob and Ray, The Barbour Family, Henry Morgan, Joe Friday and Other Lost Heroes from Radio's Heyday.* New York: Pantheon Books, 1998.

The New Grove Dictionary of Music and Musicians, Vol. 3. 2nd ed. London: Macmillan, 2001.

The New York Times, February 26, 1961.

Official WSM Grand Ole Opry History-Picture Book. Nashville: WSM, Inc., 1961.

The Oxnard Press-Courier, Oxnard, CA, December 10, 1951.

Robinson, Marc. *Brought to You in Living Color: 75 Years of Great Moments in Television & Radio from NBC.* New York: John Wiley & Sons, 2002.

Rothel, David. *Who Was That Masked Man?: The Story of the Lone Ranger.* Cranbury, NJ: A.S. Barnes, 1976.

Ryan, Nick. Personal communication with the author, January 11, 2002. Used by permission.

Sanger, Elliott M. *Rebel in Radio: The Story of WQXR.* New York: Hastings House, 1973.

Schaden, Chuck. *Speaking of Radio: Chuck Schaden's Conversations with the Stars of the Golden Age of Radio.* Morton Grove, IL: Nostalgia Digest Press, 2003.

Seligman, Paul. *Debuts & Farewells: A Two-Decade Photographic Chronicle of the Metropolitan Opera.* New York: Alfred A. Knopf, 1972.

Settel, Irving. *A Pictorial History of Radio.* New York: Grosset & Dunlap, 1967.

Shepherd, Donald, and Robert T. Slatzer. *Bing Crosby: The Hollow Man.* New York: St. Martin's Press, 1981.

Siepmann, Charles A. *Radio, Television and Society.* New York: Oxford University Press, 1950.

Sies, Luther F. *Encyclopedia of American Radio, 1920–1960.* Jefferson, NC: McFarland & Co., 2000.

Simon, George T. *The Big Bands.* Toronto: Macmillan, 1969.

Singer, Arthur J. *Arthur Godfrey: The Adventures of an American Broadcaster.* Jefferson, NC: McFarland & Co., 2000.

Slide, Anthony. *Great Radio Personalities in Historic Photographs.* Vestal, NY: Vestal Press, 1982.

Smith, Sally Bedell. *In All His Glory: The Life of William S. Paley, the Legendary Tycoon and His Brilliant Circle.* New York: Simon and Schuster, 1990.

Smith, Wes. *The Pied Pipers of Rock 'n' Roll: Radio Deejays of the 50s and 60s.* Marietta, GA: Longstreet Press, 1989.

Snyder, Jim. "The Longest Running Program in Radio." *Radio Recall,* June 2003.

The Sound of Your Life: A Record of Radio's First Generation. New York: Columbia Broadcasting System, Inc., 1950.

Sports Illustrated, November 3, 2003.

Stedman, Raymond William. *The Serials: Suspense and Drama by Installment.* Norman, OK: University of Oklahoma Press, 1971.

Sterling, Christopher H., ed. *Telecommunications: Special Reports on American Broadcasting, 1932–1947.* New York: Arno Press, 1974.

Sterling, Christopher H., and John M. Kittross. *Stay Tuned: A Concise History of American Broadcasting.* 2nd ed. Belmont, CA: Wadsworth Publishing, 1990.

Studwell, William E., and Mark Baldin. *The Big*

Band Reader: Songs Favored by Swing Era Orchestras and Other Popular Ensembles. New York: Haworth Press, 2000.

Sultanof, Jeff. *The Big Bands: Theme Songs and Top Hits.* Milwaukee, WI: Hal Leonard, 1996.

Summers, Harrison B., ed. *A Thirty-Year History of Programs Carried on National Radio Networks in the United States, 1926–1956.* New York: *The New York Times*, 1971.

Swartz, Jon D., and Robert C. Reinehr. *Handbook of Old-Time Radio: A Comprehensive Guide to Golden Age Radio Listening and Collecting.* Metuchen, NJ: Scarecrow Press, 1993.

Terrace, Vincent. *Radio Programs, 1924–1984: A Catalog of Over 1800 Shows.* Jefferson, NC: McFarland & Co., 1999.

Thomas, Robert M., Jr. "Anne Hummert, 91 Dies; Creator of Soap Operas." *The New York Times*, July 21, 1996.

Thompson, Charles. *Bing: The Authorized Biography.* New York: David McKay, 1975.

Tracy, Sheila. *Bands, Booze and Broads.* Edinburgh: Mainstream Publishing, 1997.

Walker, Leo. *The Wonderful Era of the Great Dance Bands.* New York: De Capo Press, 1990.

Whiteside, Thomas. "Life Can Be Terrible." *New Republic*, July 14, 1947.

Who's Who in TV and Radio, 1951.

Williams, John R. "This Was Your Hit Parade." *Courier-Gazette*, Rockland, ME, 1973.

WNEW: Where the Melody Lingers On, 1934–1984. A hardcover celebration of the station's fiftieth anniversary.

Wolfe, Charles Hull. *Modern Radio Advertising.* New York: Printers' Ink, 1949.

Woods, Bernie. *When the Music Stopped: The Big Band Era Remembered.* New York: Barricade Books, 1994.

Wylie, Max, editor. *Best Broadcasts of 1939–40.* New York: Whittlesey House, 1940.

Index

Page numbers in *italics* indicate photographs.

A&P Gypsies 93, 97, 115
Aaronson, Irving 21
Abbott, Bud 57, 245
The Abbott and Costello Show 226
ABC Dancing Party 25
ABC Radio 70
Abe Lyman and Moveland's Favorite Band 235, 242
Abravanel, Maurice 113
AC Delco Corporation 213
Academy Award Theater 226
Ace, Jane 151
Acuff, Roy 177, 182, 185–186
Adams Gum Company 222
Adolescent talent contests 131–132
Adventures in Rhythm 215
The Adventures of Ellery Queen 142, 221, 226
The Adventures of Gracie 37, 291
The Adventures of Helen and Mary 208, 209
The Adventures of Mr. and Mrs. North 118
The Adventures of Sam Spade 213, 216
The Adventures of the Falcon 225
Advertising jingles 332
Advertising slogans 330–332
Ager, Milton 318
Agnew, Charlie 29
Air Features, Inc. 233
Akeman, David 178
Al Goodman's Musical Album 217, 266
The Al Jolson Show 61, 63, 216, 220, 295

Al Pearce and His Gang 224, 289
The Al Pearce Show 224
Alamo, Tony 41
Albanese, Licia 3
Album of Familiar Canadian Music 242
Alcock, Merle 12
The Aldrich Family 245
Alec Templeton Time 222
Alemite 127
The Alemite Half-Hour 127
Aless, Tony 40
Alexander, Jeff 263
Allen, Barclay 46
Allen, Bill "Hoss" 158
Allen, Fred 3, 7, 66, 85, 141–142, 210
Allen, Gene 35
Allen, Gracie 54, 67, 77, 247
Allen, Steve 161
Allen, Stuart 318, 325
Allied Paint Company 50
Allman, Elvia 318, 323
Allyson, June 48
Along the Boulevard 242
Alpert, Trigger 47
Althouse, Paul 306
Aluminum-Glo cleaning agents 280
Amalgamated Frank Sinatra Clubs of Brooklyn 328
Amanda of Honeymoon Hill 117
Amara, Lucine 3, 113
The Amateur Hour 129
Amateur performance music contests 131
The Amazing Mr. Smith 216

The Amazing Mr. Tutt 216
Ameche, Don 66, 262
America — Ceiling Unlimited 219
America Sings 227
America the Free 242
American Academy of Arts and Letters 115, 124
The American Album of Familiar Music 93, 117, 228–229, 231, 234–236
American Band, Army Air Force 48
American Broadcasting Company 70, 77, 115
American Cigar Company 53, 58
American Cruise 216
American Dairy 215
American Federation of Musicians (AFM) 147
American Federation of Radio Artists and Screen Actors Guild 280
American Guild of Radio Announcers and Producers (AGRAP) 124
American Hocking Glass Corporation 214
American Home Products Company 130, 219, 227, 296
American Institute of Music Studies 307
American Marconi Company 108
American Meat Packers Association 165
American Melody Hour 12, 117, 229–230, 236–238, 240–241

345

American National Orchestra 303
American Portraits 118
American Society of Composers, Authors and Publishers (ASCAP) 63, 148–149, 218, 239–240, 306
American Theatre Organ Society 221
American Tobacco Company 43, 104, 120–129, 138, 217–218, 221–226, 283, 287, 292–294, 318–323
The American Way 128
"America's Singing Sweethearts" 10
America's Town Meeting of the Air 115, 118
Ammons, Gene 40
Amos 'n' Andy 54, 98, 108, 152
The Amos 'n' Andy Music Hall 152–153
The Amos 'n' Andy Show 216, 217, 222
Ampex Company 75
The Amsterdam Chorus 229
Anahist 225
Anchor Hocking Glass Company 219
Anderson, Arthur 209
Anderson, Bill 177
Anderson, Cat 38
Anderson, George 192
Anderson, Ivy 38
Anderson, Marian 3, 8, 10
Andrew Jergens Company 50–59, 82, 225, 279, 283–284
Andrews Sisters 66, 154–155, 277–278, 326
The Andrews Sisters Eight-to-the-Bar Ranch 278, 285, 290
Anglin, Jack 178
Anniversary Night with Horace Heidt 127
Ann-Margret 134
Announcers, radio broadcast 28, 30, 61, 63
Ansbro, George 22, 229, 240
Answers by the Dancers 127, 130, 131
Anthony, Ray 29, 32, 47
Antonicelli, Giuseppe 113
Antonini, Alfredo 106, 157, 207
Anything Goes 268
Apollo Boys Choir 3, 8
Aragon Ballroom, Chicago 43
Aragon Ballroom, Ocean City, California 36
Archer, Jack 40
Archie Bleyer and His Commodore Hotel Orchestra 214

Archie Bleyer Orchestra 214
Arden, Victor 207, 212, 229, 239, 240, 242
Arden and Arden 228, 236
Arden Hour of Charm 37
The Arkansas Traveler 293
Armbruster, Robert 207, 212–213
Armed Forces Radio Service 13, 227
Armen, Kay 86, 130, 141
Armistice Day 256–257
Arms, Russell 318, 326
Armstrong, Louis 21, 29, 67
Arnaz, Desi 29, 33, 34
Arnheim, Gus 21, 29, 40, 55, 56, 293
Arnold, Eddy 177, 188, 203
Arnold, Murray 46
Around the World in Eighty Days 268
Arquette, Cliff 202
Arrau, Claudio 3
Arthur Godfrey and His Friends 93
Arthur Godfrey Digest 93, 214
Arthur Godfrey Roundtable 215
Arthur Godfrey Time 79, 93, 134, 172, 214
Arthur Godfrey's Talent Scouts 128, 134, 214, 314
Arthur Smith and His Dixie Liners 182
Artists Service Bureau 188
Arus, George 48
ASCAP *see* American Society of Composers, Authors and Publishers (ASCAP)
Ashenhurst, Anne S. 230–232
Ashenhurst, John W. 232
Ashkenazy, Irwin 192
Ask Eddie Cantor 280
Asper, Frank 274
Association of American Railroads 262, 264
Astaire, Fred 66, 67
Astor, Mary 140
Astring-O-Sol mouthwash 240
Athens Club, Oakland 132
Atkins, Chet 177, 186
Atkins, Jimmy 164
Atlantic Spotlight 118
The Atwater Kent Hour 5
Atwell, Roy 165
Audience participation contests 127–143
Auer, Leopold 8
Auld, George 48
Aunt Jemima 242
Austin, Gene 210
Austin, Johnny 47

Austin, Ray 46
Autry, Gene 186, 192, 195–199, 202
Avalon Time 203, 289
Avalon Variety Time 289
Avery Fisher Hall 110
Ayars, Ann 261
Ayers, Mitchell 207, 213–214, 281
Aylesworth, Merlin H. 112

Babasin, Harry 40
Babbitt, Harry 30, 129, 139–140, *140*
Babes in Toyland 268, 269
Babs and Her Brothers 164
Bacall, Lauren 66
Backstage Wife 118
Badger State Barn Dance 190
Baggy, Roy 49
Baguena, Teresa 12
Bailey, Mildred 49, 51, 151, 210
Bain, Donald 318
Baker, Bonnie 30, 318, 326
Baker, Harold 38
Baker, Kenny 261
The Baker Chocolate Program 279
The Baker's Broadcast 118
Baldwin, Richard 81, 84
Ball, Lucille 139
Ballantine, Eddie 207
Ballantine Brewing Company 44
Ballet Egyptienne 303
Ballew, Smith 29
Baltimore Symphony 303
Bampton, Rose 113, 121, 242
Band of America 312
The Band of America 91, 94, 101–102
Bandstand USA 25
Bandwagon Mysteries 226
Bankhead, Tallulah 66, 227
Banner, Bob 164
Banta, Frank 90, 96
Barbirolli, John 11, 109
Barbour, Dave 38, 288
Barlow, Howard 106–107, 207, 299, 303–304, 313, *313*
Barnet, Charlie 24, 29
Barnyard Frolics 190
Baron, Paul 207
Barris, Harry 49, 55
Barron, Blue 24
Barry, Gene 30
Barrymore, John 140
Barrymore, Lionel 66
Bartell, Harry 202
Bartlett, Ethel 109
Baruch, Andre 151, 228–230,

236–238, 240–245, 259, 317, 332–333
Basie, Count 24, 27, 29, 38
Bates, Ted 224
Batten, Barton, Durstine & Osborne agency 322
The Battle of the Sexes 118
Bauduc, Ray 34
Bauer, Billy 40
Bauer, Joe 35
Baur, Franklyn 92, 299, 301–302
Bayz, Gus 192
Beach, Frank 48
The Beachcombers 35
Beat the Band 131, 225, 281
Beecham, Sir Thomas 113
Behind the Mike 118
Beiderbecke, Bix 49
Belasco, Leon 277
Belcher, Elmer 49
Believe It or Not 118
Bell, Marion 261, 263
The Bell Symphony Orchestra 5
Bell Telephone Company 4
The Bell Telephone Hour 3–15, 102, 239
The Bell Telephone Hour Orchestra 3, 7
Bellezza, Vincenzo 113
Bellson, Louis 35, 38
Ben Bernie, the Old Maestro 291
Ben Bernie's Musical Quiz 131
Ben Pollack's Californians 21
Bence, Bob 140
Benchley, Robert 66
Bendix, William 261, 268
Beneke, Gordon "Tex" 47, 48
Bennett, Jay 245
Bennett, Lee 30
Bennett, Lois 229, 240
Bennett, Sue 318
Bennett, Tom 81, 164
Bennett, Tony 54, 134
Benny, Jack 54, 61, 66, 77, 125, 210, 259, 321–322
Benny Goodman Caravan 39
Benny Goodman Orchestra 39
Benny Goodman's Swing School 39
Benson, Red 143
Benton & Bowles advertising agency 90, 98
Benzell, Mimi 113, 137, 261, 265–267, 299, 303
Berch, Jack 278
Berg, George 38
Berg, Gertrude 247
Bergen, Edgar 11, 54, 61, 77, 82–86, 141
Bergen, Polly 264

Berger, Gordon 164
Bergman, Eddie 46
Bergman, Ingrid 67
Berigan, Bunny 25, 29, 35, 38
Berle, Milton 165, 170
Berlin, Irving 8, 174, 256, 329
Berman, Sonny 40
Berner, Sara 192
Bernhard, Milt 38
Bernie, Ben 21, 85, 86
Bernier, Daisy 164
Bernstein, Arty 38
Bernstein, Leonard 12, 98, 103, 109, 266
Berry, Bill 40
Berry, Chuck 158
Bert, Eddie 38
Bertram Hirsch's Orchestra 243
Best, Johnny 38, 47, 48
The Best Food Boys 286
Betty and Bob 115
B.F. Goodrich Tire Company 279
The Bickersons 66
Biegel, Les 47
The Big Bands 6–51
The Big Broadcast 58, 279
Big D Jamboree 190
The Big Preview 151
The Big Show 227, 271, 280
Big Town 226
Bigard, Barney 38
Biggs, E. Power 273
Bill Green's Casino, Pittsburgh 42
Billy Mills Orchestra 221
Billy Rose's Music Hall, New York 21
Biltmore Hotel, New York 132
Bing, Rudolph 12, 103, 306
Bing Crosby 54
The Bing Crosby Chesterfield Show 52, 54, 78
Bing Crosby Enterprises 74, 76, 80
The Bing Crosby — Rosemary Clooney Show 54, 281
The Bing Crosby Show 52–80, 212, 279, 281
Bing Crosby — The Cremo Singer 53
Bing Crosby's Club 15 278
Biography in Sound 226
The Birds Eye Open House 85
Bishop, Joe 40
Bishop, Joey 264
Bivens, Bill 164
Bjoerling, Jussi 3, 113, 299, 303
Black, Frank 90, 94, 207, 212, 229, 242
The Black Book 226

Blackett, Hill 232
Blackett and Sample ad agency 231–232
Blackett-Sample-Hummert, Inc. 231, 233
Blackhawk Restaurant, Chicago 19, 138–139
Blaine, Vivian 30
Blair, Jimmy 81
Blake, Jimmy 35, 38
Blanton, Jimmy 38
Bleyer, Archie 128, 207, 214–215, 263
Bloch, Ray 130, 141, 287
Block, Martin 85, 86, 153–155, 155, 317
Block, Sid 35
Blue, Ben 140
Blue Jay Corn Plasters 227
Blue Ribbon Music Time 223
Blue Ribbon Time 213
Blue Ribbon Town 213
Blue Room, Hotel Lincoln, New York 36
Blue Star razor blades 223
Bluebird phonograph label 27
The Bluegrass Ramble 190
BMI *see* Broadcast Music, Inc. (BMI)
Bob and Ray 82
Bob Burns Show 293
The Bob Burns Show 220
Bob Cats 282
The Bob Crosby Show 85, 282, 295
Bob Crosby's Club 15 283, 295
The Bob Hope Show 215, 217
Bobby Benson and the B-Bar-B Riders 203
Bodanya, Natalie 243
Bodanzky, Artur 113
Bodie, Louis "Satch," Jr. 83
Bogart, Humphrey 66
Boghetti, Giuseppe 10
Bogue, Merwyn A. 129
Bold Venture 223
Bolen, Murray 261
Boles, Jim 192
Bolger, Ray 263
Bologna Conservatory 9
Bolshoi Opera, Moscow 11
Bond, Ford 90, 95, 99, 229–230, 239–240
Bond, Johnny 192, 195
Bond Baking Company 44
Bone, Red 35
Boone, F.E. 317, 332
Boone, Pat 134, 264
Borden Company 215, 293
Borden Special Edition 118
Borge, Victor 53, 65

Borscher, Bill 167
Bose, Sterling 47
Boston Pops Orchestra 312
The Boston Pops Orchestra 118
Boswell, Connee 52, 65, 86, 279
Boswell Sisters 52, 59, 67, 259, 277
Botany Mills 293
The Botany Song Shop 293
Botkin, Perry 193
Boulevard Theater 55
Boult, Adrian 121
Bourdon, Rosario 90–92, 94, 96, 303
Bourjois Company 224, 284, 287, 291
Bourne, Sidney H. 305
Bowen, Claude 48
Bowes, Jean 40
Bowes, Major Edward 135–137, *136*, 267
Boy Scouts and Girl Scouts of America 257
Boyd, William 202
Boyer, Anita 30, 35, 48
The Boys and Girls of Manhattan 38, 229
Bracken, Eddie 261
Bradley, Curley 203–205
Bradley, Will 29
Brady, Pat 193, 202
Brandon, George 41
Brannum, Hugh "Lumpy" 164 165, 170
Brant, Henry 81, 84
Branzell, Karin 113
Brasfield, Rod Leon 177, 186, *187*
Break the Bank 130
The Breakfast Club 204, 209, 264, 271
Breezing Along 294
Breisach, Paul 113
Bresler, Jerry 128
Brewer, Teresa 137, 267, 296
Brewster, Ralph 47
Brice, Fanny 242
Bride and Groom 93
Briers, Larry 286
Briney, Mary Martha 238, 309
Bring, Lou 45
Brinkley Brothers and Their Clod Hoppers 182
Bristol-Myers, Inc. 34–39, 214, 220, 225, 280, 294
British Broadcasting Corporation 283
Broadcast Music, Inc. (BMI) 149
Broadway Is My Beat 219
Broadway Matinee 219

Broadway Melodies 242
Broadway Merry-Go-Round 236, 242
Broadway Varieties 242
Brooklyn Academy of Music 311
Brookman, Thomas 3
Brookmeyer, Bob 40
Brown, Cecil 245
Brown, Dick 130
Brown, Harry John 315
Brown, Hilman 212
Brown, James 158
Brown, Jimmy 41
Brown, Lawrence 38
Brown, Les 26, 29, 32, 207, 215
Brown, Russell 48
Brown, Ted 161
Brown, Tom 243
Brown, Vernon 38
Brown & Williamson Tobacco Company 35–36, 218, 223–225, 284–289, 295
Brown Derby 61
Brownell, Betty 30
Browning, Douglas 130
Bruce, Lenny 134
Brunswick New Hall of Fame 235
Brunswick Records 55
Brunswick studios 286
Brush Creek Follies 190
Bryan, George 128
Buck, Fred 164, 166
Buck, Louie 177
The Buckingham Choir 228, 236
Buckley, Emerson 225
Buckner, Ferne 164
Buckner, Milt 41
The Buddy Clark Show 218, 226
Buddy Clark's Musical Weekly 226
Buddy Clark's Summer Colony 226
Buddy Cole Trio 78
Budwig, Monty 40
Bughouse Rhythm 84, 115
Bugle Tobacco Company 289
Buick Hour 50
Bunce, Alan 245
Bundoc, Rolly 47
Burch, Bill 192
Burke, Johnny 329
Burke, Sonny 34
Burness, Les 48
Burnett, Carol 86
Burnette, Smiley 197
Burns, Bob 34, 53, 62–63, 65
Burns, George 54, 67, 77
Burns, Kenneth C. 178

Burns, Ralph 40
Burton, Ken 261
Busch, Fritz 113
Bushkin, Joe 35
Bushman, Francis X. 261
Busse, Henry 29, 49, 151
Butterfield, Billy 29, 38, 48
Butterfield, Herb 193
Buttram, Pat 192, 193, 195, 198
Byrne, Bill 40
Byrne, Bobby 29, 34
Byron, Ward 81

Caceres, Ernie 47
Cadillac Motor Car Company 37
Cahn, Sammy 329
Calhoun, Bob 293
California Melodies 58, 215, 222, 223, 267, 279
California Theatre of the Air 242
California's Hour 285
Call for Music 85
Calling All Cars 218
Calloway, Cab 25, 27, 67, 138
Calusio, Feruccio 113
Camarata, Tutti 34, 49
Camel Caravan 23, 39, 224, 279–282, 290, 292
Camel cigarettes 25
The Camel Comedy Caravan 33, 293
The Camel Quarter-Hour 283
The Camel Screen Guild Players 219
Campana cosmetics 216
Campana Serenade 216
Campbell, Clyde 203
Campbell Soup Company 37, 216–226, 278, 283, 287, 292–295
The Campbell's Tomato Juice Program 216
Campho-Phenique canker sore reliever 240
Can You Top This? 130
Canada Dry Bottling Company 227, 278
Cancer Society 289
Candoli, Conte 40
Candoli, Pete 35, 40
Cannon, Sarah Ophelia Colley 178
Cantor, Charlie 245
Cantor, Eddie 85–86, *87*, 142, 151, 261, 279–280
Capitol Family 135
Capitol Theater, New York 135
Capitol Theater Concert 129
Capitol Theater Musicale 129

Captain Dobbsie's Ship of Joy 127
Carefree Carnival 227
Carillo, Leo 261
Carlay, Rachel 229, 238
Carle, Frankie 29, 76, 132, 263
Carlisle, Charles 318, 324
Carlson, Frankie 40
Carmen 269
The Carmen Miranda Show 224
Carmichael, Hoagy 270
The Carnation Contented Hour 85, 239, 268, 287, 295
Carnation Milk Company 287, 295
Carnegie Hall 13, 41, 110, 120, 125
Carney, Art 30, 132, 263
Carney, Harry 38
Carney, Jack 128
The Carnival of Musical Contrasts 218
Carolina Hayride 190
Carpenter, Ken 52, 63–65, 71, 77–78
Carroll, Bob 34
Carroll, Carroll 52, 61–62, 65–66, 72, 192
Carroll, Christina 3
Carroll, Georgia 129, 139–140
Carson, Martha 177
Carson, Shorty 204
Carter, Benny 32, 35, 81
Carter, Jack 137, 267
Carter, June 177
Carter, Lou 34
Carter Company 219
Carter Products Company 225
Caruso, Enrico 106
Casadesus, Gaby 3
Casadesus, Robert 3, 7
Casals, Pablo 93
Case, Evelyn 261
Case, Russ 334
Casey, Crime Photographer 214
Casey, Press Photographer 214
Cash, Johnny 177
Cashman, Ed 129
Casino Gardens, Ocean City, California 36
Cass County Boys 192, 195
The Cass Daley Show 213
Cassado, Yasoar 109
Cassel, Walter 3
Castle, Lee 38, 48
The Castoria Program 5
Cathy and Elliott Lewis on Stage 217
Catlett, Sid 38
Caulfield, Joan 67
The Cavalcade of America 6, 213

The Cavaliers 90, 92–93, 98
Cavallaro, Carmen 37
The CBS Radio Mystery Theater 212
CBS Symphony Orchestra 227
Ceiling Unlimited 216
Central Park, New York 92
Chain Stores of California 285
Chaloff, Serge 40
The Chamber Music Society of Lower Basin Street 81–89, 115, 126, 291
Chamlee, Mario 326
Chandler, Jeff 261, 268
Chandu, the Magician 222
Chapman, Frank 299, 302
Chappell, Ernest 81
Charioteers 69
Charis Corset Company 222
Charles, Milton 193
The Charlie Ruggles Show 214
Charmoli, Tony 323
Charo 34
Chase, Francis, Jr. 24
The Chase and Sanborn Hour 11, 85, 213, 268, 280
Chavez, Carlos 121
Checkov, Michael 261
The Cheerleaders 265
Chelsea 44
Chesterfield 24, 25, 58–59
The Chesterfield Music Shop 295
Chesterfield Presents 50
The Chesterfield Quarter Hour 224, 279
Chesterfield Supper Club 41, 118, 214, 289, 295
Chesterfield Time 48, 165
Chevalier, Maurice 72
Chevron Incorporated 116
Chevron Texaco Corporation 116
Chicago Civic Opera 115
Chicago Civic Opera Company 310
Chicago Opera Company 93
Chicago Symphony 269
The Chicago Theater of the Air 268–269
Chicago World's Fair 224, 270
Chico Marx band 296
The Children's Hour 308
The Choraliers 126
The Chordettes 134
Chotzinoff, Samuel 8, 119–120
Christian, Charlie 38
Christiansen, Clay 274
Christie, Ken 4, 90, 94
Christy, June 30
Chrysler Corporation 35, 42, 128, 193, 217, 218

Church music 271–275
The Church of the Air 273
Churchill, Stuart 164
Cigarette advertising 320–335
Cimara, Pietro 113
Cincinnati Conservatory of Music 266, 284
Cincinnati Summer Opera 311
The Circle 61, 222
Circus Days 118
Cities Service Band of America 4, 84, 91, 94
Cities Service Concerts 90–102
The Cities Service Concerts 212
Cities Service Petroleum Company 90, 91, 95, 102
Cities Service Salon Orchestra 91
The Cities Service Singers 90, 94
The City 219
City College of New York 118
Civic Auditorium, Pasadena 26
Claire, Bernice 228, 229, 236, 240
Claire, Dorothy 47
Claney, Howard 117–118, 228, 230, 236
Clark, Buddy 30, 318, 325
Clark, Dick 161, 264
Clark, Harry 263
Clark, Jeff 318
Clark, Roy 134
Clark Conservatory of Music 310
Clayton, Jan 261
Cleary, John 129
Cleveland Institute of Music 307
Cleveland Symphony Orchestra 121
Cliburn, Van 134
Cline, Patsy 134, 177
Clinton, Larry 24, 34
Clooney, Rosemary 78–80, 134, 266, 280–281, 312
Clorets breath mints 221
Club Fifteen 61, 95, 278, 287
Club Matinee 204
Coast-to-Coast on a Bus 115
Cobb, David 177
Coca-Cola Bottling Company 25, 184, 279, 284, 293
"Coca-Cola girl" 7
The Coca-Cola Hour 293
Cocoanut Grove, Los Angeles 47, 55, 63, 69, 293
Coelho, Olga 3, 7
Cohn, Al 40
The Coke Club 284
Coke Time 284
Coke Time with Eddie Fisher 284

Cold War 52, 102
Cole, Buddy 52, 78
Cole, Nat King 66, *71*, 154
Colgate-Palmolive-Peet, Inc. 43–44, 129, 213–225, 285, 288, 295
The Colgate Program 220, 288, 295
Collier, Ralph 38
The Collier Hour 210
Collins, Dick 40
Collins, Dorothy 30, 318, 323, 325–328
Collins, Joseph Martin "Ted" 151 245, 249–252
Collyer, Clayton "Bud" 137
Colonna, Jerry 53, 65
Columbia Broadcasting System 77, 107
Columbia Phonograph Company 248
Columbia Presents Corwin 118, 216
Columbia Presents Perry Como 281
Columbia Recording Company 215
Columbia Records 17, 92, 213, 215
Columbia Symphony Orchestra 303
Columbia Workshop 142, 226
Columbo, Russ 30
Command Performance 63, 85, 277, 279
Commercial advertising 320–321
Community Sing 286
Como, Perry 30, 54, 213, 264, 281–282
Conan, Bob 193
Condie, Richard P. 274
Congress Cigar Company 246
Congress Hotel, Chicago 23
Conley, Eugene 113, 299, 304, 311
Conlon, Jud 52
Connee Boswell Presents 279
Conner, Nadine 113, 261, 265–267, 299, 303–304
Conniff, Ray 48
Conqueror Record Time 197
Conqueror records 197
Conservatoire de Musique, Paris 12
Conservatorio de Musica, Valencia, Spain 12
Considine, Bob 164
Constitution Hall, Washington, DC 10
Contact men 28

The Contented Hour 295
The Contented Program 238
Conti Castille shampoo 285
The Conti Castille Show 285
Contino, Dick 132
Conway, Bill 47
Conway, Julie 129
Cook, Mary Lou 52, 65
Coon, Carleton 18
Coon-Sanders Nighthawks 19
Coon-Sanders Orchestra 18, 296
Cooper, Emil 113
Cooper, Gary 72, 198
Cooper, Stoney 177
Copas, Lloyd T. "Cowboy" 177
Copeland, Alan 318, 334
Copper-Glo cleaning agents 280
Corey, Jill 130, 318, 326, 334
Corn Products Refining Company 222, 279, 285
Cornelius, Corky 38
Cornell, Dale 41
Cornell, Don 41
Cornwall, J. Spencer 274
Coronet magazine 213
Coronet on the Air 213
Correll, Charles 54, 77, 152
Costello, Lou 57, 245
Cotner, Carl 192
Cottingham, Ruth 164
Cotton, Helen Strauss 98
Cotton, Larry 132, 263
Cotton Club 27, 38
Coughlin, Bunny 245, 317
Coulter, Douglas 261
Country Style 131
Courtney, Del 29, 150
Courtney, Diane 81, 126
Cousin Minnie Pearl 186, *187*
Cousin Willie 213
Cowan, Louis G. 130
Cowan, Tommy 107
Cox, Wally 134
Cracker Barrel Old Country Store 184
Craig, Don 164
Craig, Edwin 180–181, 188–189
Crane, Malcolm 49
Crawford, Jack 224
Crazy Water Crystals 227
Crenna, Richard 80
Cresta Blanca 218
The Cresta Blanca Carnival of Music 218
Crime detective mysteries 230–231
Crime Photographer 214
Cronk, Billy 34, 35
Crook Brothers 177, 186

Crooks, Richard 299, 302, 304–306
Crosby, Bing 3, 31, 49, 51–80, *71*, 251
Crosby, Bob 66, 69, 282–283
Crosby, Everett 57–58
Crosby, Gary 79
Crosby, Harry Lowe 55
Crosby, John 257, 307
Crosby, Lou 192, 193
Crosby Research Foundation 75
Cross, Glenn 229, 238, 309
Cross, Maury 41
Cross, Milton J. 81–88, 103, 109, 112–117, *114*, 126
The Croupier 221
Crow, Bill 38
Crowley, Jim 245
The Cuckoo Hour 213
Cugat, Xavier 21–25, 29, 33–34, 45, 312, 315
Cullen, Bill 130, 142, 143, 161
Culley, Fred 164, 165
Culley, George 165
Cummings, Lucille 3
Cummins, Bernie 29
Curley, Leo 193
The Curt Massey Show 223
Curt Massey Time 290
The Curt Massey–Martha Tilton Show 290
Curtis, Mert 44
Curzon, Clifford 3, 7
Cutrer, T. Tommy 177
Cutshall, Cutty 39
Cyrano de Bergerac 118
Czech State Opera 311

Dae, Donna 164
Daley, Cass 25
Daly, John 312
Daly, William 299, 303
Dame, Donald 228, 236
Damon Runyon Cancer Fund 321
Damone, Vic 134
Damrosch, Walter 107, 118, 181, 194
Dana, Richard 317
Dangerous Assignment 213
D'Annolfo, Frank 47
The Danny Kaye Show 225
Danny O'Neil and His Guests 214
Danny O'Neil Show 214
The Danny Thomas Show 225
Dashanska, Hulda 109
A Date with Duchin 37
A Date with the Duke 38
Daum, Margaret 228, 236
David Rose Orchestra 223

The David Rose Show 223
Davidson, Stanley 52, 62
Davies, Ben 44
Davis, Agnes 3
Davis, Al 39
Davis, Beryl 318
Davis, Elmer 245
Davis, Ennis 174
Davis, Janette 128
Davis, Joan 140
Davis, Johnny "Scat" 165
Davis, Kay 38
Davis, Maude 245
Davis, Peter 305
Davis, Sammy, Jr. 264
Davis, Skeeter 177
Dawson, Ken 193
Day, Dennis 210, 312
Day, Doris 30, 261, 265, 268, 318, 326
A Day in the Life of Dennis Day 213
Dean, Eddie 192
Death Valley Days 226
Decca records 54, 172, 224
December Bride 219
Defense Attorney 221
De Forest, Lee 106–107, 111, 301
DeFranco, Buddy 35, 48
DeHaven, Gloria 30
Dehner, John 202
Dekker, Albert 202
DeLeath, Vaughn 299, 301
Della Casa, Lisa 113
Della Chiesa, Vivian 3, 96, 121, 228–229, 236, 240–241, 261
Delmar, Kenny 317
Del Monaco, Mario 113
Delmonico Club, New York 283
Del Monte Corporation 227
DeLong, Tom 45, 112, 123, 274, 315
de los Angeles, Victoria 3, 113
Delugg, Milton 335
Delys, Gogo 318, 324
Demarest, William 140
Dengler, Clyde 271
Dengler, Hunt 271, 272
De Reszke, Jean 11
DeSair, Skippy 40
The Desert Song 268, 269
Design for Happiness 218, 226
Desmond, Johnny 318, 326
Destinn, Emmy 106
De Sylva, Buddy 151
Detroit Symphony Orchestra 209
Deutsch, Emery 208
Devine, Ott 177
De Vol, Frank 38, 207, 215
de Witt, George 143

De Wolfe, Billy 67
The Diamonds 134
Diaz, Rafael 107
DiCarlo, Tommy 49
Dick, Edith 318
The Dick Haymes Show 220, 287
Dick Haymes Society 287
Dickens, Little Jimmy 177
Dickenson, Hal 47
Dickenson, Jean 117, 228, 236
Dickey, Annamary 261
Dictograph Corporation 292
Diddley, Bo 158
Dietrich, Marlene 66
Digby, Noel 177
Dillagene (Carlson) 40
Dillon, Jim 44
The Dinah Shore Show 85, 215
D'Ippolito, Hugo 44
Disc jockeys 28, 31, 32, 144–163
di Stefano, Giuseppe 113
Distinguished Volunteer Service Award 291
Dixieland Little Symphony 83
Dixieland Octet 89
The Dixieland Song Shop 282
Dixon, Joe 35
Dobkin, Larry 202
Dobson, Bert 192
The Doctor Fights 226
Dr. I. Q. 130
Dr. Lyons tooth powder 241
Dr. Pepper Bottling Company 224
Dole Cannery 224
Dolph, Jack 164
Domingo, Placido 113
Don Donnie's Orchestra 235, 242
Donahue, Al 21, 29
Donahue, Sam 35, 49
Donna and the Don Juans 132
Don't Forget 115
Doolittle, John 209
The Doris Day Show 215, 294
Dorothy Warenskjold Musical Theater 266
D'orsay, Fifi 242
Dorsey, Jimmy 29, 31–35, 49–52, 59, 64–65, 210
Dorsey, Tommy 24–29, 31–36, 49, 81–84, 150, 287
The Dorsey Brothers Orchestra 34, 36
Dosh, Joe 318
Double Danderine shampoo 240
Double Everything 278
Double or Nothing 61, 130
Dough Re Mi 131

Douglas, Mike 129, 264, 265
Douglas, Paul 164
Downes, Olin 114
Downey, Morton 49, 56, 151, 251, 283–284
Dragon, Carmen 262
Dragonette, Jessica 90, 96–101, 247, 262
Drake Hotel, Chicago 20, 130, 132
A Dream Comes True 215
Drene shampoo 41, 215, 298
The Drene Show 298
Drew, Ellen 140
Dru, Joanne 287
Dubin, Al 329
Dubonnet 33
Dubow, Marilyn 3
Duchin, Eddy 29, 36–37, 69, *71*, 154, 210
Duchin, Peter 37
Dudley, Paul 317
Duey, Phil 243
Dumont, Paul 229, 239
Dumont Television 137
Duncan, Todd 3
Dunham, Edwin L. 299
Dunham, Sonny 29
Dunn on Discs 151
Dunning, John 152
Dunninger, the Mentalist 213
Durante, Jimmy 72, 229, 238, 264
Durbin, Deanna 210
Dutton, Mike 164

Earhart, Amelia 95
Earl Carroll Theatre 5
Earl Carroll's Club, Hollywood 214
Eastman, Mary 229, 240
Easton, Florence 106
Eastvold, Donald W., Sr. 293
Eberle, Bob 34, 160
Eberle, Ray 30, 47
Eckstine, Billy 30
Ed Wynn, the Fire Chief 37
The Eddie Cantor Show 61, 85, 210, 280, 284
Eddie Dowling's Elgin Revue 39
Eddie Duchin Orchestra 37
The Eddie Duchin Show 284
The Eddie Fisher Show 284
Eddy, Nelson 3, 6–8, 10–11, 66, 266–267, 299
Eden Liquid Dry shampoo 47
Edgar Bergen and Charlie McCarthy Show 61, 63, 66, 209
Edgewater Beach Hotel, Chicago 224
Edison, Thomas A. 302

The Edison Hour 94
Edna W. Hopper (Hopper's White Clay Pack) 296
The Edward Everett Horton Show 222
Edward Maguiness and His Band 137
Edwards, Douglas 253
Edwards, Jack 203
Edwards, Joan 49, 87, 261, 318, 325–328
Edwards, Ralph 325
Edwards, Vince 80
E.I. Dupont Company 6, 213
Eileen Farrell Sings 12
Eldridge, Jean 38
Eldridge, Roy 39, 41, 49
Eleanor Roosevelt 118
Eleanor Steber Music Foundation 307
Electric Autolite Company 220, 222, 287
Electric Cooperative 289
The Electric Hour 11, 40, 213
The Electric Hour Summer Series 289
Electrical transcription 69, 76, 126
Elgart, Les 29
Elgin Watch Company 23, 39
Elias, Rosalind 113
Elitch's Gardens, Denver 22
Elizabeth Arden, Inc. 37
Ellington, Duke 21–29, 31, 37–38, 49, 151
Ellington, Maria 38
Ellington, Mercer 38
Elliott, Richard 274
Ellis, Herb 34
Ellis Island 10
Ellis Island Medal of Honor 297
Elman, Ziggy 35, 39
Elmo, Cloe 3
Emerson, Joe 272
Emerson Drug Company 217, 220, 285
Empire Builders 262
Encore 227
Encore Society 308
Encores from The Bell Telephone Hour 4, 13–14
Endorsed by Dorsey 36
Energine cleaning fluid 240
Energine Shoe-White polish 240
Enesco, Georges 109
Engelbach, Dee 81
Engineers, broadcast 27–28
Engle, Vic 49
Enna Jettick Melodies 213
Enna Jettick shoes 213

Ennis, Skinnay 29, 30
Erlenborn, Ray 192
Errol, Leon 261
Erwin, Peewee 35, 47
Erwin, Trudy 129
Escape 219, 226
La Escuela de Musica de Maria Jordan 12
Esty, William 183
The Eternal Light 213
Ethel and Albert 245
The Ethel Merman Show 217
Evangelista, Lucia 310
Evans, Chuck 49
Evans, Dale 30, 193, 200–201
Evans, Richard L. 274
Evening in Paris 93, 224, 284, 291
Evening Melodies 235, 242
The Eveready Hour 93, 223, 280
Eversharp Company 33, 279, 280
Everyman's Theater 220
Everything for the Boys 220, 287
Ex-lax 297
Eyes Aloft 220

Fairbanks, Douglas, Jr. 66
Fairfax, Lee 3
Faith, Percy 76, 315
Fame and Fortune 35, 133, 295
Family Hotel 218
Family Service Association of America 137
Fan Hartesfeldt, Fran 193
Fanchon-Marco vaudeville circuit 132
Farber, Bert 128
Farnsworth Radio & TV, Inc. 104
Farr, Hugh 193
Farrell, Eileen 3, 8, 12, 229, 241, 299
Faso, Tony 49
Fatool, Nick 39
Faust 269
Faye, Alice 25, 30, 109
Faylen, Carol 80
Fazola, Irving 47
The FBI in Peace and War 211
Feather, Leonard 151
Federal Bureau of Investigation 9
Federal Communications Commission 153, 160
Federal Radio Commission 172
Federation of American Music Clubs 303
Feldkamp, Elmer 46
Feldman, Victor 40
Fels Naphtha 225, 278

Felton, Happy 130, 142
Ferretti, Andy 35
Ferrier, Jack 47
Festival of Music 126
Festival of Song 126
Feuer, Cy 226
Fibber McGee and Molly 54, 66, 210, 221, 281
Fiedler, Arthur 315
Field, Marshall 125
Fields, Shep 21
Fields, W.C. 66, 268, 280, 318, 323
Fiesta 216, 219
Fifteen Minutes with Bing Crosby 53
Fifty-One East Fifty-First 214
Fina, Jack 46
Finch, Dee 160
Finegan, Bill 35, 47
Finian's Rainbow 269
Finke, Jacques 317
Finkelstein, Norman 106
Fio Rito, Ted 21, 223
The Fire Chief 5
Firestone, Elizabeth 312, *313*
Firestone, Harvey S., Jr. 315
Firestone, Mrs. Harvey S. 299, 305, 312
Firestone, Harvey S., Sr. 300–302, 307, 314
Firestone Chorus 312
The Firestone Hour 300–301
Firestone Symphony Orchestra 301
Firestone Tire and Rubber Company 300
First broadcast of a dance band 17
Fish Pond 137
Fisher, Eddie 54, 264, 284
The Fitch Bandwagon 25, 139, 215, 296
Fitzgerald, Barry 67
Fitzgerald, Ella 30
Flagstad, Kirsten 12, 106, 109, 113
Flagstaff jellies 246
Flanagan, Ralph 41, 281
Flashgun Casey 214
Flatt, Ernie 323
Flatt, Lester 177, 184, 289
Fleischer, Editha 112
Fleischer, Leon 3
The Fleischmann Hour 298
Fletcher's Castoria 240
The Flit Soldiers 286
Flores, Chuck 40
Florida Citrus Growers 165, 227
Florida Philharmonic 116
Florsheim Company 285

Florsheim Frolics 285
Flory, Med 40
Foggy Mountain Boys 177, 184
Foley, Clyde Julian "Red" 177 186, 203, 272, 289
Folies Bergere of the Air 235
Folies de Paree 235
Fonda, Henry 66
Fontana, Carl 40
Food Industries of Philadelphia 217
For America We Sing 242
Ford, Art 159–160
Ford, Benjamin Francis "Whitey" 177 186, 272
Ford, Mary 66, 192
Ford, Tennessee Ernie 151, 264
Ford Motor Company 35, 53, 78, 165–173, 217, 224–227, 282, 291-295
The Ford Show 85
The Ford Showroom 227
The Ford Summer Hour 5, 226, 291
Ford Sunday Evening Hour 226
Ford V8 Revue 282
Forever Tops 50
Forman, Bill 129
Forrest, Helen 30, 38, 48
Forty-Five Minutes in Hollywood 142
Fosdick, Dudley 44
Foster, Chuck 29
Foster, Kay 38
Foster, Stephen 12, 270
Foster, Stuart 334
The Four Clubmen 226
Fourestier, Louis 113
Fowler, Wally 177
Foy, Eddie 70
Francescatti, Zino 3
Francis, Arlene 131
Francis, Connie 134
The Frank Fontaine Show 217
Frank Parker Show 93
Frank Sinatra Show 61
Frankhauser, Charlie 40
The Frankie Laine Show 289
Franklin, Aretha 158
Frasier, Charlie 34
The Fred Allen Show 209, 217, 294
The Fred Brady Show 220
The Fred Robbins Show 151
Fred Waring and His Pennsylvanians 312
Fred Waring Choral Workshops 174
The Fred Waring Show 164–176
Fred Waring U.S. Chorus 175
Freddy Martin Orchestra 46–47

Freddy Rich's Rhythm Kings 246, 250
The Free Company 226
Free World Theater 85, 220
Freed, Alan 146–147
Freeman, Bud 35, 39
Freeman, Hank 47, 49
Freeman, Jerry 242
French Mignon Trio 235, 242
Friday, Pat 193
Friday Night Frolics 188
Frigidaire 218
Frizzell, William Orville "Lefty" 177
Froman, Jane 87, 266, 284–285, 312
Frontier Gentleman 219
Frost, David 264
Fruit Jar Drinkers 177, 186
Fulton, Jack 49, 59
Fun Valley 224
Funk, Larry 290
F.W. Fitch Company 25, 215, 226, 296

Gable, Clark 203
La Gaiete Parisienne 235, 242
Gale, Tony 245
Gallaher, Eddie 156–157
Gallop, Frank 109
Gangbusters 158
Garber, Jan 21, 25, 210
Gardella, Tess 242
Gardner, Ava 49
Gardner, Kenny 30, 44
Gargan, William 67, 140
Garland, Beverly 80
Garland, Judy 66, 72–73, 140, 198
Garrett, Kelly 335
Garry, Al 245
Gaslight Gaieties 294
Gateway to Hollywood 218
Gatti-Casazza, Giulio 9, 103, 106, 111
Gaunt, J.L. 166
Gaye, Marvin 158
Gaynor, Mitzi 67, 152
Gearhart, Livingston 165
Gedda, Nicolai 3
Gelinas, Gabe 47
Gem blades 225
Gems of Melody 235, 242
Gene Autry, Inc. 196–197
Gene Autry Blue Jeans 192
Gene Autry Film and Music Festival 199
Gene Autry Oklahoma Museum 199
Gene Autry's Melody Ranch 192–193, 197, 200

General Cigar Company 44
General Electric Corporation 53, 78, 80, 219, 224
General Electric Hour 224
The General Electric Show 52, 54, 78
The General Electric Theater 63, 219
General Foods, Inc. 193, 214–219, 223–227, 246, 252, 279, 285-294
General Mills, Inc. 213, 219, 221–225, 272, 296
General Motors Concerts 106, 115, 224
General Motors Corporation 105, 215, 220, 224, 288
General Motors Corporation Buick Division 50
General Motors Family Party 224
The General Motors Family Party 91
Geneva Conservatory 13
Gennaro, Peter 323
Gentry, Chuck 39, 47
George, Tom 131
The George Burns and Gracie Allen Show 44, 49–50, 61, 93, 210, 227
George D. Hay Foundation, Mammoth Spring, Arkansas 189
George D. Hay Music Hall of Fame Theater 189
The George Jessel Show 210
Georgian Court Convent 97
Germanic Museum, Harvard University 273
Gershwin, George 92, 151, 259, 262
Gerun, Tommy 292
Getz, Stan 39, 40
Giannelli, Tony 49
Gibbs, Georgia 30, 48, 87, 318, 326
Gibbs, Terry 35, 40
Gibson, Barbara 3
Gibson, Fredda 48, 318
Gibson, Hoot 204
Gibson, Virginia 318, 334
The Gibson Family 5
Gilbert, Doris 192, 245
Gilbert and Sullivan 10, 263
Gillespie, Dizzy 29
Gillette Company 128, 219, 286, 297
Gilliland, Jim 167
The Ginny Simms Show 215, 223, 293
Giuffre, Jimmy 40

Give and Take 130
Givor, George 165
Glade, Earl J. 274
Gladys Swarthout 213
Glamour Manor 294
Gleason, Jackie 32, 35, 264, 265
Glen Island Casino 24
Glenn, Carroll 3
Glenn, Wilfred 92
Glenn Miller Orchestra 48, 278
Glow, Bernie 40
Gluskin, Lud 207, 215–217
Gobel, George 65
God Bless America Foundation 257
Godfrey, Arthur 54, 93, 128, 134, 158, 161
Going Places 46
Gold Seal Company 214
Golden, Milt 35
"Golden Memories of Radio" 125
The Golden State Blue Monday Jamboree 227
Golden Treasury of Song 93
Goldman, Edwin Franko 90–91, 94, 223
The Goldman Band Concert 91
Goldovsky, Boris 114
Goldstein, Chuck 47
Golenpaul, Dan 331
Gonsalves, Paul 38
Gonzaga University 55
Good News of 1938–1940 227
Goodman, Al 207, 217, 317, 324
Goodman, Benny 3, 7, 13–16, 21, 38–40, 137, 142, 150–154, 287–288
Goodman, Gordon 164
Goodman, Harry 39
Goodman, Irving 39
The Goodrich Silvertown Orchestra 279
Goodson, Mark 130, 245
Goodyear Tire and Rubber Company 193, 221
Gordon, Mack 329
Gordon Jenkins Orchestra 220
The Gordon MacRae Show 214, 263
Gorin, Igor 3, 269, 299, 304, 311
Gorman, Ross 49
Gorme, Eydie 30
Gosden, Freeman 54, 77, 152
The Gospel Singer 272
Gould, Morton 137, 207
Goulet, Robert 134
Gowans, George 44
Gozzo, Conrad 34, 49
Grable, Betty 30

The Gracie Fields Show 225
The Gracie Fields Victory Show 225
Graham, Ross 90, 93
Grammy Lifetime Achievement Award 296
Grams, Martin 211
Granada Café, Chicago 19
Grand Central Station 118
Grand Ole Opry 15, 62, 85, 177–191
Grand Ole Opry House 185, 190
Grand Slam 131
Grand Street Follies 97
Grand Terrace, Chicago 27
Grandstaff, Olive Kathryn 79
Granger, William W. 114
Grant Park, Chicago 9, 98
Grapevine Rancho 216
Grauer, Ben 97, 117–118, 317
Gray, Glen 24, 27, 29, 154, 210
Gray, Jerry 47, 48, 49, 207
Gray, Wardell 39
Grayson, Kathryn 140
"Great Artists" series 5, 8
The Great Atlantic & Pacific Tea Company 246, 294
Great Depression 16, 21, 24, 56, 95, 111
The Great Gildersleeve 63, 213, 222
Great Northern Railroad 262
Great Personalities 92
Greco, Buddy 39
Green, Johnny 29, 317
Green, Marie 318
Green, Urbie 40
The Green and White Quartet 90, 93
Greer, Sonny 38
Grey, Carolyn 40
Grey, Charles C. 115
Grier, Jimmie 293
Griffin, Chris 39
Griffin, Merv 30, 46, 264
Grill Room of the Hotel Taft 46
Grofé, Ferde 25, 49, 151, 210
The Groucho Marx Show 213
Grove Laboratories, Inc. 165, 289
Guarnieri, Johnny 34, 39, 49, 263
Guedel, John 76
Guerra, Freddy 47
Guest Star 223, 225, 281
Guizar, Tito 3
Gulf Headliners 93, 217, 291
The Gulf Musical Playhouse 285
Gulf Oil Corporation 217, 226, 278, 285, 291, 292
Gunsmoke 208, 211, 221

Guy Lombardo and his Royal Canadians 22, 47
Guy Lombardo Orchestra 44–45
Gwinn, Bill 140

Hackett, Bobby 47, 132
Haenschen, Gustav 207, 212, 228, 236–238, 243, 303
Hagen, Earle 35
Hager, Clyde 245
Hain, William 3
Haines, Connie 30, 35, 133
Haley's M-O 240
Hall, George 21
Hall of Fun 220
Hallmark Greeting Card Company 223
The Hallmark Hall of Fame 202
Hallmark Playhouse 223
The Halls of Ivy 63
Hamilton, Bob 225
Hamilton, Gene "Dr. Gino" 81, 83, 86, 88, 126
Hamilton, Jimmie 38
Hammerstein, Oscar 263
Hammerstein, Ted 243
Hammerstein Music Hall 235, 238, 243
Hampton, Lionel 29, 39, 84, 154
Hancock, Don 130
Handy, W.C. 83
Hanlon, Tom 192
Hanna, Jack 40
Hannon, Bob 229, 238, 240, 241
Hansel and Gretel 112, 269
Hanserd, Tom 177
Hanson, Howard 121
Hap Hazard 220, 222
The Happiness Boys 285–286
Happiness Candy Stores 286
The Happy-Go-Lucky Hour 224
The Happy Wonder Bakers 94
Hardwick, Toby 38
Hare, Ernie 285
Hargis, Tom 193
Harmon, Dave 164
Harold Sanford's Orchestra 243
Harrel, Scotty 192
Harrell, Mack 266
Harrington, Bill 318
Harriott, Nicole 3
Harris, Bill 39, 40
Harris, Phil 25, 33, 67, 210, 293
Harry Horlick and the A&P Gypsies 207
Harry Sosnik Orchestra 224
Harry Walsh's Dixieland Band 242
Hart House String Quartet 27
Hartt School of Music, Hartford, Connecticut 12

Harvest of Stars 92, 94, 268
Harvuot, Clifford 3
Haskell, Jack 130, 141
Haskins, Virginia 261, 269
Hasselmans, Louis 113
Hatch, Wilbur 207, 218–219, 226
Hatfield, Lansing 3
Haupt, James 228, 236
Hauser, Johnny 318, 324
Hausner, Jerry 192
Hawaiian Pineapple Company 278
Hawk Durango 219
Hawk Larabee 219
Hawkins, Coleman 25, 29
Hawkins, Harold F. "Hawkshaw" 177
Hawkins, Hoyt 178
Hawthorne TBA 213
Hay, George Dewey 177, 179–181, 189, 194
Hayes, Gabby 193
Hayes, Harvey 262
Hayes, Helen 247
Hayes, Peter Lind 140
Hayes, Richard 134, 248
Hayloft Jamboree 190
Haymer, Herbie 34
Haymes, Dick 30, 35–38, 54, 286–287, 318, 326
Haymes, Joe 36
Haynes, Harry 178
Hayton, Lennie 52, 58, 317, 324
Hayworth, Rita 33, 287
Heart Fund 289
Hefti, Neal 40
Heidt, Horace 21–29, 130–133, 173, 215, 263
Heifetz, Jascha 3, 6–9, 61, 106
Heigh Ho Club 298
Heinz Magazine of the Air 226
Helbros Watch Company 45
Heller, Benny 39
The Hellman Mayonnaise Troubador 292
Hellman's Salad Bowl Revue 210
Hemingway, Frank 193
Henderson, Fletcher 21, 23, 29, 35–39
Henderson, Horace 38
Hendricks, Ray 38
Henley, Art S. 245
Henning, Paul 289
Henry, Bill 245
Henry, Frances 44
The Henry Morgan Show 118
Herbert, Victor 97, 263
Here Comes Elmer 224
Here's to Romance 287
Herfurt, Skeets 35

Herman, Woody 24, 29–32, 40–41
The Hermit's Cave 221
Herrick, John 243
Herry Reser and the Cliquot Club Eskimos 207
Hess, Dame Myra 3
Hibbler, Al 38
Hiestand, Bud 129
Higby, Mary Jane 58–59
Highways in Melody 84, 91–94, 101, 238, 266, 309
Higman, Fred "Derf" 44
Hildegarde 222
Hildegarde's Radio Room 225
Hildegarde's Raleigh Room 225
Hill, George Washington 317, 320–333
Hill, Teddy 39
Hill, Tiny 29
Hilliard, Harriet 30
Hillsboro Theater, Nashville 183
Hilman, Roc 34
Himber, Richard 317
Hines, Earl 21, 27, 29, 81
Hines, Jerome 3, 113, 299, 304, 309–310, 313
Hines, John Henderson 317
Hires Root Beer 127, 222, 297
Hirsch, Bernard 228, 236
Hirt, Al 132, 263
Hit Paraders 318, 324, 326
Hit the Jackpot 131, 217
Hite, Earl 29
H.J. Heinz Company 226
HMS Pinafore 268, 269
Hobby Lobby 225
Hodges, Johnny 38
Hoff, Carl 317
Hoffman, Josef 3, 109
Holiday, Billie 30, 48, 49
Holiday for Music 223, 290
Holiday Inn 268
Holland Furnace Company 39
Hollander, Lorin 3
Holloway, Jean 57, 245, 262
Holloway, Sterling 261
Holly, Buddy 134
Hollywood Bowl 311
Hollywood Bowl Orchestra 222
Hollywood Hotel 222
Hollywood Mardi Gras 222, 292
Hollywood Nights 231, 243
Hollywood on the Air 291
Hollywood Palladium 41
Hollywood Playhouse 225
Hollywood Rendezvous 279
Hollywood Showcase 216, 267
Holm, Celeste 67
Home Is What You Make It 118

Homer, Louise 115
Homer and Jethro 178
Hometown Jamboree 190
Honey and the Bees 164
Honeymoon Lane 248
Honolulu Bound 278
Hoover, Herbert 302
Hoover Sentinels 97
Hope, Bob 54–59, 66–67, 72, 85, 93–97, 215
Horace Heidt and His Musical Knights 130
Horace Heidt Show 127–128, 132
Horace Heidt's Alemite Brigadeers 127
Hormel Company 49, 226
Horn, Art 167
Horn and Hardart Automat 284
The Horn and Hardart Children's Hour 284
Horne, Lena 30, 48, 81, 89, 140, 324
Horner, Chuck 128
Horse operas 192–205
Horton, Edward Everett 70, 139
Hot Springs National Park 93
Hotel Commodore, New York 42
Hotel Pennsylvania 17, 27
Hotel Pennsylvania Orchestra 17
Hotel Pennsylvania's Madhattan [sic] Room 23
Hotel Roosevelt Grill, New York 19, 22, 23
The Hour of Charm 238
Hour of Romance 37
House of Squibb 226
The House of Wrigley 92
Household Finance Corporation 219
Housewarming Time 39
Howard, Eugene 242
Howard, Frank 49
Howard, Willie 242
The Howard Miller Show 161
Howe, Louis McHenry 95
How'm I Doin? 142, 290
Hucko, Peanuts 39, 47
Hudson Company 225
Hudson-Terraplane Motor Car Company 246
Hufsmith, Fred 243
Hughes, Buddy 34
Hughes, Marjorie 334
Hughes, Randy 178
Hull, Warren 317, 324
The Human Side of the Record 50, 150
Hummert, Anne 12, 95, 117
Hummert, Anne and Frank 228–244

Hummert, Edward Frank, Jr. 12, 59, 95, 117–118, 230–231
The Hummert Musicales 212
The Humming Birds 309
Hunt, Arthur Billings 271–272
Hunt, Frances 38
Hunt, Lois 299
Hupfer, Nick 40
Hurley's Bar 22
Hurst, Jack 188
Husing, Ted 151, 259
Huskey, Ferlin 178
Hutton, Betty 30, 45
Hutton, Ina Ray 32
Hutton, June 30
Hutton, Marion 30, 45, 47, 261
Hyams, Margie 40
Hymns of All Churches 272

I Fly Anything 287
I Love Adventure 221
I Love Lucy 219
"I Remember Radio" 125
I Sustain the Wings 48
I Want a Divorce 223
I Was There 216
Ice Box Follies 222, 296
Igoe, Sonny 39
Illinois Glass Company 165
The Imperial Hollywood Band 235, 243
In Person, Dinah Shore 85, 220
Indiana University's School of Music 12
Information Please 115, 118, 130, 331
Ingram, Gail 317
Inside Story of Names That Make News 11
Institute of Radio Engineers 75
Intellectual property 144–145
International Novelty Orchestra 223
International Silver Company 47, 222
The Interwoven Pair 286
Interwoven Sock Company 286
The Intimate Hour 285
The Intimate Revue 217
Intrigue 216
The Iodent Program 285
Iodent toothpaste 285
The Ipana Troubadours 34, 35, 39
Ironized Yeast 240
Irwin, Pee Wee 35
It Pays to be Ignorant 130, 245
It's a Great Life 219
It's Showtime from Hollywood 47
Iturbi, Jose 3, 7, 8, 12–13, 109

Ives, Burl 76

J. Walter Thompson advertising agency 60–61
Jack Armstrong, the All American Boy 296
Jack Benny Program 92–94, 118, 210
Jack Berch and His Boys 278
The Jack Berch Orchestra 278
The Jack Berch Show 278
The Jack Carson Show 47
The Jack Kirkwood Show 216
Jack Okie's College 39
The Jack Pearl and Mimi Benzell Show 267
The Jack Pearl Show 35, 218
The Jack Pepper Show 214
The Jack Smith Show 85, 215, 293, 294
Jackson, Allan 157
Jackson, Chubby 40
Jackson, Mahalia 312
Jackson, Stonewall 178
Jacobs, Dick 317
Jaffe, Henry 14
Jagel, Frederick 3
Jamboree USA 190
James, Dennis 137
James, Ed 192
James, Harry 25–39, 81, 84, 287
James, Hugh 299, 311–314
James, Lewis 92
The James Melton Show 217
Jamison Bedding Company 184
The Jane Froman and Don Ross Show 285
The Jane Froman and Jan Peerce Show 285
The Jane Froman Show 285
Jane Froman's U.S.A. Canteen 285
The Jane Pickens Show 94, 291
Jane Pickens Theatre 291
The Janette Davis Show 214
Janke, Helen 271, 272
Janssen, Herbert 113
Jarvis, Al 153–154
The Jeddo Highlanders 115
Jefferson Island salt 184
Jeffries, Fran 287
Jeffries, Herb 30, 38
The Jell-O Summer Show 285
Jenkins, Gordon 40, 97, 207, 220, 287
Jenkins, Les 49
Jenney, Jack 34, 49
Jepson, Helen 3, 59, 113, 242
Jerome, Henry 29
Jerome, Jerry 39, 47
The Jerry Mann Voices 229, 239

Jewish Theological Seminary 213
Jimmy Dorsey Orchestra 34
The Jimmy Durante Show 289
The Jo Stafford Show 295
The Joan Brooks Show 214
Joan Davis Time 216
Joanie's Tea Room 216
Jobin, Raoul 3
The Joe Cook Show 5, 217
The Joe E. Brown Show 225
Joe Emerson Choir 272
Joe Emerson's Hymn Time 272
The Joe Penner Show 210
Johanessen, Grant 3
The Johnny Mercer Music Shop 295
Johnny Presents 294
Johnny Presents Ginny Simms 293
Johnson, Betty 134
Johnson, Edward 103, 117
Johnson, Howard 245, 250
Johnson, Jay 164
Johnson, Johnny 287
Johnson, Kenneth M. 196
Johnson, Raymond Edward 4
Johnson Family Singers 159, 196
Jolson, Al 59, 66, 70, 72, 287–288
Jones, Billy 285
Jones, Buck 204
Jones, Dick 48
Jones, George 178
Jones, Isham 21, 30, 221
Jones, Louis M. "Grandpa" 178
Jones, Shirley 101, 264
Jones, Spike 53, 65, 72, 312, 315
Jordan, Jim 54
Jordan, Marian 54
The Jordanaires 178
Joy, Dick 4
Joyce, Vicki 34
Jubilee USA 190
Jud Conlon's Rhythmaires 52, 71
The Judge 226
The Judy Canova Show 213, 220
Judy, Jill and Johnny 142
Juke Box Jury 151
Julliard School of Music 94, 266, 307
"Jumping" Bill Carlisle and the Carlisles 177
Juno and the Paycock 118
Jurist, Edward 245
Just Entertainment 278
Juvenile adventure series 230

Kabibble, Ish 129, 139, *140*
Kahn, Otto 112

Kallen, Kitty 30, 34, 48
Kallir, Lillian 3
Kaminsky, Maxie 49
Kamuca, Richie 40
Kanter, Hal 52, 72, 76
Kapell, William 4
Karloff, Boris 139
Kassell, Art 29
Kate Smith and Her Swanee Music 245, 246, 251
Kate Smith Calling 247
The Kate Smith Hour 294
The Kate Smith Show 142, 212, 245–260
Kate Smith Sings 246, 247, 250
Kate Smith Speaking Her Mind 247
Kate Smith Speaks 247, 251–254
Kate Smith's A&P Bandwagon 246, 251, 294
Kate Smith's Coffee Time 246, 251, 294
Kate Smith's Column 247
Kate Smith's Hour 246, 251
Kate Smith's Matinee Hour 246, 251
Kate Smith's New Star Revue 246, 251
Kate Smith's Serenade 247
Kated Corporation 249
Kaufman, Irving 243
Kay Kyser Orchestra 129
Kay Kyser's Kollege of Musical Knowledge 118, 129, 138–140, 221, 293
Kay Kyser's Orchestra 293
Kay Thompson Show 214
Kaye, Carol 40
Kaye, Danny 67
Kaye, Milton 126
Kaye, Sammy 21, 25, 27, 41–42, 133
Kaye, Sharri 40
Kazebier, Nate 34, 39
KDKA, Pittsburgh 272
Kearns, Joey 208
Keel, Howard 312
Keep 'em Rolling 218
Keepsakes 225, 266
Keller, Nelson 167
Kelley, Welbourn 81–82, 88
Kelly, Gene 140, 261, 268
Kelly, Grace 67
Kelly, Paula 47, 48
Kemp, Hal 21, 24–29, 65, 138
Kemper, Ronnie 132, 263
The Ken Christie Chorus 90, 94
Ken Christie Mixed Chorus 4
Ken Lane Chorus 318, 326
The Ken Murray Program 216
Kennedy, Ethel 86

Kennedy, Tom 143
Kent, Atwater 93
Kenton, Stan 29
Kentucky Club, New York 38
KEPT, Salt Lake City 273
Kern, Betty 49
Kern, Jerome 49, 263
Kessel, Barney 49
KFBW, Los Angeles 279
KFEQ, St. Joseph, Missouri 92
KFI, Los Angeles 63, 220
KFRC, San Francisco 224, 227, 285
KFWB, Hollywood 150, 151, 153
KHJ, Los Angeles 287, 295
KHL, Los Angeles 267
Kiefer, Ed 40
Kiefer, Peter T. 166, 171
Kielber, Erich 109
Kiffe, Earl 34
Kilgen, Noel 49
Kilgore, Wyatt Merle 178
Kimberly-Clark, Inc. 214, 293
Kinard, Spencer 274
Kincaide, Dean 35
King, B.B. 158
King, John Reed 264
King, Louise 318
King, PeeWee Frank 178
King, Wayne 19, 27, 29, 42–43, 76
King and His Court 289
King Cole Trio Time 289
King Features 33
The King Sisters 129, 132, 192, 263
The King's Henchman 107
King's Row 82
Kingsbridge Armory, Bronx 107
Kirby, Durward 161
Kirk, Andy 29
Kirkwood, Charles 174
Kirsten, Dorothy 4, 66, 96, 101, 113, 261–266, 299
Kiss Me Kate 268
Kitsis, Bob 49
Kitt, Eartha 312
KLAC, Los Angeles 152
Klauber, Edward 56
Klein, Manny 35, 47
Klemperer, Otto 109
Klink, Al 47
KLRA, Little Rock 190
KMBC, Kansas City, Missouri 190, 203, 289
KMOX, St. Louis, Missouri 220
Knight, Evelyn 263
Knight, Felix 117, 228, 236, 238, 309
Knight, Frank 124–126
Knight, Gladys 158

The Knightsbridge Chorus 230
KNX, Hollywood 161, 266
Knowlton, Bill 190
Kodak Company 224
The Kodak Weekend Hour 224
KOIN, Portland, Oregon 267
Kolster Radio Company 45
Koppers Coke Company 37
Korean conflict 52
Kostelanetz, Andre 9, 106, 315
Koury, Rex 129, 207, 208, 220–221
Kraft, J.L. 68
Kraft Foods Company 34–37, 50–53, 59–61, 68–70, 213, 222–225, 279–289, 298
Kraft Music Hall 11, 34–37, 50–53, 58–72, 202, 210–213, 222, 266–267, 279–289
The Kraft Program 288
Kramer, Alex 318, 335
Kreisler, Fritz 4, 7, 7
Kreitzer, Fritz 44
Kremel shampoo 37
KRLD, Dallas 190
Krueger, Bennie 30
Krupa, Gene 24, 30, 35, 39, 41
Krupp, Roger 52, 228, 229, 236, 239
KTHS, Hot Springs, Arkansas 93
KTUL, Tulsa, Oklahoma 156
Kuhl, Cal 52, 60, 65
Kullmann, Charles 4
KVOO, Tulsa 197
KWBU, Corpus Christi, Texas 190
KWKH, Shreveport, Louisiana 161, 190
KWTO, Springfield, Missouri 190
KXLA, Pasadena 190
KYW, Chicago 107, 218, 287
Kyser, Kay 21–27, 129, 138–141, *140*, 173, 292

La Brun Sisters 245
LaCentra, Peg 38, 48
Lady Esther Cosmetics Company 42, 43, 44, 47, 219
The Lady Esther Screen Guild Theater 219
Lady Esther Serenade 42
LaForge, Frank 305
Lahr, Bert 229, 238
Laine, Frankie 154
Lair, John 272–273
Lake, Bonnie 48
La Martinique, New York 287
Lamb, Bobby 40
Lambert, Scrappy 318

Index

Lambert Pharmacal Company 104
Lamond, Don 40
Lamour, Dorothy 30, 67
Lancaster, Burt 86
Lane, Abbe 30, 34, 312
Lane, Kathleen 40
Lane, Kitty 47
Lane, Muriel 40
Lane, Priscilla 170
Lane, Rosemary 170
Lane, Vera 242
The Lane Sisters 164
Lang, Eddie 49, 53, 58
Lang, Harry 192
Langan, Tom 317
Langendorf bread 213
Langford, Frances 30, 66, 198, 261
Lanin, Howard 239
Lanin, Sam 30
Lanny Ross and His State Fair Concert 292
The Lanny Ross Show 292
Lanny's Log Cabin Inn 292
Lanphere, Don 40
Lanson, Snooky 183, 318, 326–328
LaPorta, John 40
La Rocca, Nick 88
LaSalle Style Show 37
La Scala, Milan 9
Lasker, Albert 321
Lathrop, Jack 47
Laughlin, Lucy 243
Lavalle, Paul 81–84, 90–95, 126, 312, 315
Lavender and Old Lace 237, 243
Lawrence, Elliot 208
Lawrence, Jerome 262
Lawrence, Jerry 262
Lawrence, Lucile 317
Lawrence, Marjorie 4, 109
Lawrence, Steve 134
The Lawrence Welk Show 13
Lawson, Yank 35
Layton, Skip 34
Lazy Dan, the Minstrel Man 243
L.C. Smith Corona Typewriter Company 294
Lebieg, Earl 167
Ledbetter, Huddie "Leadbelly" 81
Lee, Bob 245
Lee, Brenda 178
Lee, Dixie 55, 79–80
Lee, Don 141, 215, 222
Lee, Loretta 318
Lee, Peggy 30, 38, 52, 65, 160, 288–289
Lee, Robert 262

Lee, Ruth 49
Lee, Wilma 177
Leeman, Cliff 40, 49
Lehar, Franz 263
Lehn & Fink Products 217
Leinsdorf, Erich 113
Leith Stevens Harmonies 226
Leith Stevens Orchestra 226
Lennox, Elizabeth 228, 236, 238, 242
Leonard, Harlan 30
Leonard, Jack 35, 160
Leonard, Richard 123
Leonetti, Tommy 318, 334
Lerner, Alan Jay 317, 323
Les Brown Orchestra 215
Lescoulie, Jack 161
Lester, Jerry 53, 65
LeSueur, Larry 157
Let's Be Charming 224
Let's Dance 21–23, 25, 33, 39
Let's Go to Town 214
Let's Pretend 208, 209
Levant, Oscar 4, 7, 114
Lever Brothers Company 50, 213–222, 226, 288, 293
Levine, Henry "Hot Lips" 81–82 88–89, 126
Lewis, Forrest 193
Lewis, Jerry 12
Lewis, Mort 4
Lewis, Robert Q. 156
Lewis, Shari 134
Lewis, Ted 21, 27, 30, 250
Lewis-Howe Company 127, 224
Lewisohn Stadium, New York 11
Lieberfeld, Daniel 228, 236
The Life of Riley 63
Life with Luigi 216, 219
The Lifebuoy Program 216, 288
Liggett & Myers Tobacco Company 24, 42, 48–58, 77–78, 165, 173, 214–215, 221–227, 278–289, 295–297
Light, David 192, 198
Light Up Time 266
Lights Out 226, 296
Liliom 118
Lillie, Beatrice 229, 238, 242
Lincoln Center 110
Lincoln Memorial, Washington, DC 10
Linit Bath Club Revue 210
The Linit Show 285
Linkletter, Art 152, 264
Lionel Hampton Quartet 81
Lipkin, Seymour 4
Lipkins, Steve 47
Lipman, Joe 34, 48, 49
Little Ol' Hollywood 220

Little Orphan Annie 296
Little Richard 158
Live audiences, and Bing Crosby 60
Live Like a Millionaire 134
Liversidge, Herbert 115
Livingston, Fud 34
Lockhard, Gibby 290
Lockheed Corporation 216, 219, 220
Lodice, Don 35
Loesser, Frank 329
Loftus, Nadea Dragonette 99
The Log Cabin Bar Z Ranch 289
The Log Cabin Dude Ranch 289
The Log Cabin Inn 292
Lombardo, Carmen 19, 43, 44
Lombardo, Guy 19, 25–30, 43–45, 76, 151, 210
Lombardo, Lebert 19, 44
Lombardo, Rose Marie 19, 44
Lombardo, Victor 19, 44
Lombardoland USA 44
London, George 4, 8, 113, 299, 303
London, Julie 312
London Merry-Go-Round 236, 243
The Lone Wolf 221
Long, Johnny 30
Longhurst, John 274
The Longines Symphonette 76, 105, 106, 124, 125
Longines Symphonette Society of Larchmont, New York 125
Longines-Wittnauer Watch Company 105, 124, 126
Lopez, Vincent 17, 21, 25, 45–46, 298
Lord and Thomas ad agency 231, 322
Lorenzo Jones 158
Lorraine, Kay 81, 126, 318
Lorre, Peter 139
Los Angeles Philharmonic Orchestra 222, 309
Los Angeles Symphony 303
Louella Parsons 222
Louise Massey and the Westerners 289
Louisiana Hayride 190
Louisville Orchestra 116
The Louvin Brothers 178
Love Notes 118
Lowe, Jim 161
Lowell, Eugene 126
Lowell Mason Award 6
Lowell Thomas and the News 311
Lowrey, Fred 132, 263
Luboff, Normon 262
Lucas, Nick 250

Lucky Pierre 151
Lucky Strike cigarettes 320–335
Lucky Strike Dance Orchestra 25, 217, 320, 322
The Lucky Strike Hour 218
The Lucky Strike Music Hall 115
Lucky Strike Orchestra 324–325
The Lucky Strike Program 283
Lud Gluskin Orchestra 216
Lugosi, Bela 139
Luke Slaughter of Tombstone 219
Lunceford, Jimmie 21, 30
Lunch with Mimi 267
Luncheon at the Waldorf 142
Luncheon with Lopez 45–46
Lund, Anthony C. 274
Lund, Art 30, 38
Lupino, Ida 67
Luther, Frank 243
Lux Radio Theatre 63, 198, 213, 270, 314
Luxor 43
Lyman, Abe 207, 212, 228–229, 236–243, 317, 325
Lyn Murray Chorus 318, 326
Lynch, Christopher 299, 303, 307
Lynch, Peg 245
Lyon, Charles 192, 195, 196
Lyons, Eugene 108, 122
Lyons, Ken 128
Lyric Opera, Chicago 12, 116
Lytell, Park 167

The Mac McGuire Show 151
MacDonald, Fred 210
MacDonald, Jeanette 10, 11, 261, 268, 312
Mace, Tommy 49
MacGregor, Chummy 47
MacGregor, Evelyn 117, 228, 229, 236, 240, 241
MacGregor, Kenneth W. 177
Mack, Charles 165
Mack, Floyd 4
Mack, Nila 208
Mack, Ted 129, 137
MacKenzie, Gisele 318, 326, 328
MacKenzie, Murdo 52, 65, 71
Macon, Uncle Dave 182
MacRae, Gordon 30, 132, 261, 263–265, *269*
MacRae, Meredith 265
MacRae, Sheila 265
Madame Butterfly 269
Madeira, Jean 113
Madriguera, Enrico 30
The Magic Hour 279

The Magic Key 115, 118, 224, 289, 291
Magill, Wallace 3, 5
Magnante, Charles 278
Magnetic tape recording 75–76
Magnetophon machines 74–75
Maguiness, Edward *see* Mack, Ted
Maher, Wally 192
Mahler, Gustav 65
Mahoney, Frank 192
Major Bowes' Capitol Family 129
Major Bowes' Capitol Theater Concert 129
Major Bowes' Original Amateur Hour 117, 128–129, 135–137
Major Bowes' Shower of Stars 137
Make Believe Ballroom 85, 153–154
Malats, Joaquin 12
Malbin, Elaine 261, 299, 303
Maltin, Leonard 196
Man About Hollywood 218
The Man Called X 220
Mangano, Mickey 35
Manhattan Merry-Go-Round 93, 117, 229–239, 309
Manhattan Opera Company 107
Manhattan Soap Company 278
Mann, Peggy 318
Manners, Lucille 90, 101
Mannes College of Music 308
Manning, Irene 261
Manone, Wingy 25
Mansfield, Irving 128
Mansfield, Saxey 40
Manski, Dorothee 112
Marcellino, Muzzy 207
March of Dimes 280
The March of Time 6, 12, 303
Maria Certo's Matinee 292
Mariani, Hugo 299, 303
Marino, Joe 164
Mario, Queena 112
Markle, Fletcher 192, 198
Markowitz, Marky 40
Marlowe, Charles "Corn Horn" 83
Marlowe, Marion 93
Marlowe, Sylvia 82, 84
Marmarosa, Dodo 49
Marowitz, Sam 40
Marrow, Macklin 125
Marsh, Arno 40
Marsha, Jack 290
Marshall, Peggy 128
Martha White Foods 184
Martin, Dean 264
Martin, Frank 113

Martin, Fred 192
Martin, Freddy 21, 32, 46–47
Martin, Lewis "Freckles" 83
Martin, Mary 52, 65
Martin, Ricardo 106
Martin, Tony 210, 312
Martinelli, Giovanni 113
Martino, Al 134
Marvin, Dick 183
Marvin, Frankie 192
Marx, Groucho 12, 70, 76–77, 261, 268
The Marx Brothers 222
Mason, Nancy 192
Mason, Sully 129, 139–140, *140*
Massey, Curt 203, 289–290
Massey, Louise 261
Masters, Frankie 25
Mastren, Carmen 47
Mather, Jack 192
Matinee at Meadowbrook 142
Matinee Melodies 235, 243
Matteson, Don 34
Matthews, Dave 34, 39, 40
Matthews, Neal 178
Matzenauer, Margaret 11
Maxwell, Jimmie 34, 39
Maxwell, Marilyn 30, 52, 65, 140
Maxwell, Marvel (Marilyn) *see* Maxwell, Marilyn
Maxwell, Richard 272
Maxwell House Coffee Time 227
The Maxwell House Concerts 5
The Maxwell House Ensemble 292
The Maxwell House Showboat 5, 217, 227, 289, 292
May, Billy 30, 47, 65
Mayer, Louis B. 10
Maynor, Dorothy 242
Mayor of the Town 220
MCA *see* Music Corporation of America (MCA)
McCall, Mary Ann 40
McCarthy, Albert 132
McCarthy, Charlie 11, 54
McCarthy, Jack 81
McCarty, Jerry 192
McClellan, Eleanor 12
McClelland, Stanley 229, 241
McClennan, Rodney 229, 238, 309
McClintock, Poley 165, 166
McCormack, Franlyn 43
McCormack, John 307
McCormick, Col. Robert R. 269
McCoy, Clyde 21, 30
McCoy, Jack 134
McCrae, Margaret 38, 318
McDonough, Dick 47

McEachern, Murray 39, 49
The McFarland Twins 165
McGarity, Lou 39
McGarry and His Mouse 142
McGee, Kirk 178
McGee, Sam 178
McGeehan, Pat 193
The McGuire Sisters 134
McHugh, Edward 272
McHugh, Frank 66, 80
McHugh, Jimmy 329
McIntyre, Hal 30, 47
McKay, Cheri 318
McKenna, Marty 41
McKenzie, Red 49
McKinley, Ray 30, 34, 47, 48
McLean, Mack 52, 72
McLeod, Elizabeth 152
McLeod, Vic 52, 62
McManus, Marian 117, 229, 238, 309
McMichael, Joe 52, 65, 318
McMichael, Judd 52, 65, 318
McMichael, Ted 52, 65, 318
McMickle, Dale 47
McMurtrie, Burt 52, 59
McNamee, Graham 90, 95
McNaughton, Pat 49
McNeill, Don 204, 209, 264, 271
McPartland, Marian 134
McVey, Tyler 192
Meakin, Jack 81, 84, 126
Medbury, John 164
Medbury, J.P. 165
Meeder, William 243
Meet Corliss Archer 61, 63, 219
Meet Me at Parky's 289
Meet the Press 118
Meland, Ted 312
Melchior, Lauritz 4, 106, 113, 269, 299
Mele, Vi 34
Melis, Jose 134
Mello Men 193
Melodiana 235, 243
Melody and Madness 49, 216
Melody Highway 115
Melody Puzzles 131
Melody Ranch Six 192
Melton, James 4–5, 8, 90–95, 113, 269, 299–303
Mel-Tones 48, 296
The Men About Town 90, 93, 229, 239
Mendez, Ralph 72
Mengelberg, Willem 109
Menjou, Adolphe 139, 261, 268
Menotti, Gian Carlo 114
Menuhin, Lotte 106
Menuhin, Yehudi 61, 106

Mercer, Johnny 30, 49, 318, 326, 329
Mercer, Mary Ann 242
Mercer, Tommy 30
Mercurio, Walter 35
Meredith Willson Orchestra 227
Meredith Willson's Music Room 227
Meredith Willson's Musical Revue 227
Merman, Ethel 66, 67, 151
Meroff, Benny 30
Merrill, Robert 113–117, 121, 137, 267, 299, 303–304
Merriman, Nan 121
The Merry Macs 52, 65, 71, 318, 326
The Merry Widow 268, 269
Mert's Record Adventures 151
Messner, Johnny 30, 45
Metro-Goldwyn-Mayer 67, 243, 267
Metropolitan Opera 15, 103–106, 110–112, 115
Metropolitan Opera Association 111
Metropolitan Opera Auditions on the Air 93, 104–106, 115, 117, 265, 306–308
Metropolitan Opera Company 5–9, 12, 109, 112, 223
Metropolitan Opera House 106
Metropolitan Theater, Los Angeles 55, 167
Metz, Ed 282
Meynante, Charles 238, 309
MGM Radio Movie Club 231, 243
Michaels, Buss 49
The Midnight Dance Party 158
Midweek Hymn Sing 271
Midwestern Hayride 190
The Mikado 268, 269
Milanov, Zinka 113
Miles Laboratories, Inc. 180, 193, 289–290
Miley, Bubber 38
Milk Foundation, Inc. 221
Milkman's Matinee 159
Miller, Ann 140
Miller, Bill 242
Miller, Glenn 24–27, 30–31, 36, 45–48, 137, 173
Miller, Howard 160–161
Miller, Jack 207, 212, 245, *258*
Miller, Marvin 193, 262, 268, 270
Miller, Mildred 4, 8, 303
Miller, Mitch 281
Millpond Playhouse, Roslyn, Long Island 265

Mills, Billy 207, 211, 221–222
Mills, Verlye 317
Mills Brothers 52, 56, 59, 67, 251
The Milton Cross Opera Album 115
Mince, Johnny 35, 47
Minneapolis Standard Oil 288
Minneapolis Valley Canning Company 165
Minnesota Mining and Manufacuring Company (3M) 76
Minute Maid Corporation 53
The Minute Men 6
The Miracle 97
Miracle Whip 59
Miramar Hotel, Santa Monica 138
Miss America Pageant 142
Mr. and Mrs. North 211
Mr. Chameleon 82
Mr. Chameleon 118
Mr. District Attorney 118
Mr. First Nighter 204
Mr. Gallagher and Mr. Shean 231, 243
Mr. Keen Tracer of Lost Persons 118, 211
Mitchell, Dolly 49
Mitchell, Paul 35
Mitchell, Sue 40
Mitropoulos, Dimitri 11, 109, 121
Mix, Tom 202, 204
The Mixed Chorus 242
Mobil Oil Company 216
The Mobil Oil Concert 92
Modern Minstrels 226
The Modernaires 49; *see also* Paula Kelly and The Modernaires
Moffo, Anna 313
Mole, Miff 39
Molinari, Bernardino 109, 121
Molle Merry Minstrels 226
Molle shaving creme 226
Monarch, Inc. 214
Monday Merry-Go-Round 236, 243
"Monday Night of Music" 4, 102, 299, 310
The Monday Night Show 279
Mondello, Pete 40
Mondello, Toots 39
Monroe, Bill 178
Monroe, Lorne 4
Monroe, Lucy 228–229, 236, 238, 240, 243, 309
Monroe, Vaughn 25, 30, 47, 160, 290
Montana Corporation 293

Montemezzi, Italo 113
Monteux, Pierre 121
Moody, Ralph 193
Moody, Robert 318
Moon River 281
Moondial 156
Mooney, Harold 34
Mooney, Joe 49
Moonlight Serenade 48
Moore, Frank 164
Moore, Garry 204, 264
Moore, Grace 4, 8, 103, 106, 113
Moore, Victor 261
Moran, George 165
Morgan, Frank 66, 69–70
Morgan, George 178
Morgan, Helen 242
Morgan, Henry 141
Morgan, Russ 17, 25, 30, 46
Morgan, Tommy 39
Morgenthau, Henry, Jr. 123
Morini, Erica 106
Morison, Patricia 261
Morley, Virginia 165
Mormon Tabernacle Choir 15, 273
Morris, Willie 318
Morrow, Bill 52, 72, 77
Morrow, Buddy 35, 36, 284
Morse, Ella Mae 34
Morse, Lee 21
The Morton Downey Show 283
Morton Downey's Studio Party 283
Morton Gould Orchestra 218
Most, Abe 35
Mostel, Zero 81, 84
Mother Maybelle Carter and the Carter Sisters 177
Mott, Robert L. 73, 198
Much Ado about Doolittle 226
Muehlbach Hotel, Kansas City 18
Mueller, William 242
Mullican, Moon 178, 186
Mulligan, Gerry 38
Mullin, John 74–75
Mulsified Coconut Oil shampoo 240
Mundy, Jimmy 38, 49
Munn, Frank 93, 228, 229, 236–238, 242, 243
Munsel, Patrice 113, 117, 261, 268, 299, 303
Murder and Mr. Malone 221
Murphy, George 53, 65, 261, 268
Murphy, Horace 192
Murphy, Lambert 225
Murray, Dave 177
Murray, Jan 134

Murray, Kel 21, 22
Music America Loves Best 222
Music and the Spoken Word from the Crossroads of the West 15, 273–275
Music Appreciation Hour 181, 194
Music by Goodman 217
Music Corporation of America (MCA) 19, 22
Music Festival 39
Music for Today 218
Music from America 13
The Music Maids and Hal 52, 65, 71
The Music Man 142
Music That Satisfies 52–53, 224, 279, 285, 297
Musical Americana 115, 222
Musical Autographs 44
Musical Headliners 291
Musical identification contests 138–143
Musical instruments 31
Musical Mock Trial 85, 131
The Musical Revue 231, 243
Musical Treasure Chest 131
Musico 131
Musicomedy 222
Musso, Vido 35, 39, 40
Mutual Broadcasting System 253
Muzzillo, Ralph 34
My Favorite Husband 219
My Friend Irma 216
My Little Margie 217
Myrt and Marge 221
"Mystery Melody" 142

NAB *see* National Association of Broadcasters (NAB)
Nachman, Gerald 131, 325
Name That Tune 143
Name the Place 118
Names of Tomorrow 266
Nance, Ray 38
Nash Motors 45, 223, 225
The Nash Program 45
Nash-Kelvinator Corporation 278, 285, 290
"Nashville Sound" 179
Nashville's Music Row 179
National Amateur Night 134
National Association of American Composers and Conductors 303
National Association of Broadcasters (NAB) 149
National Barn Dance 180, 190, 197, 203, 272, 289
National Biscuit Company 21, 214

National Biscuit Company (NBC) 22, 28
National Brewer's Association 279
National Broadcasting Company 89, 91, 107–108, 115, 183, 271
National Broadcasting Company Concert 292
National Brotherhood of Christians and Jews 289
National Carbon Company 223
National Farm and Home Hour 197, 204
National Ice Advertising Company 213
The National Juke Box 151
National Life and Accident Insurance Company 180
National Life Building 182
National Radio Auditions 308
The National Radio Fan Club 151
The National Radio Pulpit 273
National Vespers 273
The Natural Bridge Revue 213
Natural Bridge shoes 213
Nature's Remedy 35, 295
Naughty Marietta 268, 269
Naumburg Orchestra 92
NBC Artists Service 118
NBC Bandstand 143
NBC chimes 63–64
NBC Hollywood 227
The NBC String Symphony 106
NBC Symphony Orchestra 9, 222
The NBC Symphony Orchestra 12, 93, 94, 105–106, 118–121
Neagley, Clint 39
Nelson, Ozzie 25, 207, 210
Nelson, Skip 47
The Nelson Eddy Show 11, 267
Nesbitt, John 4
Nevada Opera 116
New England Conservatory of Music 307
The New Mel Torme Show 297
The New Old Gold Show 11, 41, 213
New Year's Eve 19
New York City Opera 311
The New York Philharmonic Children's Concerts 110, 117
New York Philharmonic Orchestra 13, 303, 305
The New York Philharmonic Orchestra 5, 12, 103, 106, 110
New York Philharmonic Symphony 98, 106, 223, 227
The New York Philharmonic Symphony 115, 117

New York Symphony Orchestra 107
Newell, Lloyd 274
Newman, Jimmy C. 178
Nichols, Bobby 47
Nichols, Red 21, 137
Night Club of the Air 243
Nightbeat 213
Nikolaidi, Elena 4
Niles, Ken 129
Niles, Wendell 192
Niles and Prindle 296
Nilsson, Birgit 113
Nine to Five 294
The 1937 Radio Show 294
Ninety-Nine Men and a Girl 222
Nistico, Sal 40
Nixon, Richard 190
The N–K Musical Showroom 278, 285, 290
No, No Nanette 268, 269
Noble, Ray 207, 210
Nobles, Gene 158
Nolan, Bob 193
Non-Spi Company 297
Norge home appliances 223
Norman, Lloyd 261
Norman, Loulie Jean 52, 72
Norman, Lucile 261, 265–266
Norman, Patricia 318
Norman Luboff Choir 262
Norvo, Red 39
Novak, Frank 226
Novotna, Jarmila 4, 261
Noxema 220
NTG and His Girls 61

O'Brien, Larry 48
O'Brien, Pat 66
O'Connell, Helen 30, 34, 35
O'Connor, Dick 229, 238, 309
O'Connor, Donald 67
O'Connor, Frank 129
O'Day, Anita 30, 40
Off and On the Record 151
Ohio State University 42
Ohman, Phil 30
O'Keefe, Dennis 139, 140
Oklahoma! 268
Old Dominion Barn Dance 190
The Old-Fashioned Revival Hour 273
Old Gold cigarettes 25
The Old Gold Hour 49
The Old Gold Program 216
The Old Gold Show 40
Old Hickory Singers 178, 186
Old Kentucky Barn Dance 190
The Old Plantation Sextet 242
Oliver, Sy 35

Olsen, George 21, 215
Olsen and Johnson 224
On a Sunday Afternoon 157, 219
On the Town 36
The Ona Munson Show 216
One Man's Family 63
The Open House 216
Opera Arts Training Program 11
Opera News on the Air 114
Opera Quiz 114
Opryland USA 190
Orech, Carl 49
Organists 274
Original Amateur Hour 267
Original Dixieland Jazz Band 88
Ormandy, Eugene 103, 315
Orson Welles' Almanac 216
The Orson Welles Theater 216
Osborne, Will 21, 288
The Osborne Brothers 178
Oscard, Marty 41
Otis, Fred 40
Ottley, Jerrold 274
Otto Gray's Oklahoma Cowboys 186
Our Gal Sunday 142, 158
Our Miss Brooks 219
Owen, Larry 44
Owens, Johnny 49
Owens-Illinois Glass Company 219
The Oxydol Show 293, 294
Ozark Jubilee 190

P. Ballantine & Company 282
P. Lorillard, Inc. 39–41, 49–50, 128, 130, 165, 173, 213–216, 282–289, 295
Paar, Jack 264
Pabst Brewing Company 213, 223, 225, 280, 284
Pacific Borax Company 226
Packard, Elon 52, 62
The Packard Hour 6, 222, 292
Packard Mardi Gras 63
Packard Motor Car Company 222, 292
Paducah Plantation 289
Page, Hot Lips 25, 49
Page, Patti 30, 38
Pagliacci 106
Paige, Raymond 58, 207, 222
Paley, William S. 19–20, 56–58, 77, 108–112, 250–253, 297
Palmieri, Remo 214
The Palmolive Beauty Box Theatre 92, 99–101, 217, 224, 262, 285, 307–308
The Palmolive Hour 92, 94, 238, 301

Palomar Ballroom, Los Angeles 16, 22, 23, 39
Panizza, Ettore 113
Papi, Gennaro 113
Paramount Studios 58, 67
Paramount Theater, New York 26, 51, 222, 281
Paris Conservatoire 9
Paris Night Life 231, 235, 243
Park Central Hotel, New York 21
Parker, Frank 76, 90–99, 98, 99, 210, 228, 237, 242
Parker, Lew 66
Parks, Bert 130, 141–143, 183, 245
Parks, Larry 288
Parlato, Charlie 52, 72
Parodying, of music 82–89
The Passing Parade 63
Passport for Adams 216
Pastor, Tony 48, 49, 281
The Patti Clayton Show 214
Paul, Charles 207
Paul, Les 66, 165, 170
Paul Lavalle Orchestra 95
Paul Warmack and His Gully Jumpers 182
Paul Weston Orchestra 295
The Paul Whiteman Buick Program 291
Paul Whiteman Concerts 50
The Paul Whiteman Hour 50
Paul Whiteman Orchestra 50
Paul Whiteman Presents 50, 85
The Paul Whiteman Program 50
The Paul Whiteman Record Club 50, 150
Paul Whiteman Varieties 50
Paul Whiteman's Musical Varieties 284
Paul Whiteman's Teen Club 50
Paula Kelly and The Modernaires 47
The Pause That Refreshes on the Air 285, 293
Payne, Virginia 266, 284
Payola 28–29, 145–148
Peabody Award 13
Pearl, Jack 25
Pearl, Minnie 62
Pearl Harbor 123
Pearson Company 216
Pebeco toothpaste 280
Peck, Nat 48
Peerce, Jan 113, 121
The Peggy Lee Show 289
Peggy Marshall and the Holidays 128
Pelletier, Wilfred 113, 117, 299, 303, 315
Pellettieri, Vito 177

Pennario, Leonard 4
The Pennsylvanians 167, 173
Penthouse Party 290
Penthouse Serenade 47
Penzoil 224
The Penzoil Program 224
People Are Funny 130
Pepper, John "Wings" 83
Pepsodent Company 35–37, 215–219, 224, 295
Perkins, Bill 40
Perkins, Luther Monroe 178
Perkins, Ray 134
Perlea, Jonel 113
Perrin, Vic 203
Perron, Mac 164
Perry, Ron 49
The Perry Como Show 214, 281
Pet Milk Company 184, 221
The Pet Milk Show 283
Peter Potter's Platter Parade 151
Peters, Ken 193
Peters, Roberta 113, 299, 303
Peterson, Chuck 35, 49
Peterson, Pete 49
Petina, Irra 261
Petrillo, James Caesar 147–148
Pettiford, Oscar 38
Pfiffner, Ralph 40
The Phil Baker Show 278
Philadelphia Philharmonic Orchestra 13
The Philco Hour Theatre of Memories 97, 99
Philco Radio Corporation 50, 53, 70
Philco Radio Hall of Fame 50
Philco Radio Time 52, 54, 71–75, 78, 288
Philip Morris Company 25, 127, 132, 216, 219, 223, 246, 280, 293–298
The Philip Morris Playhouse 216
The Philip Morris Show 294
Phillips, Flip 40
Phillips, Irna 234
Phillips Milk of Magnesia 180, 229
The Piano Playhouse 115
Piastro, Mishel 76, 124–125
Piatigorsky, Gregor 4, 7
Piazza, Marguerite 266
Pick and Pat 45
Pickens, Jane 37, 81, 229, 241, 290–291
Pickens Party 291
The Pickens Sisters 291
Pickett, Wilson 158
The Pied Pipers 35, 295, 318, 326
Pierce, Nat 40

Pierce, Webb 178
Pierson, Al 45
Pillsbury Mills, Inc. 129, 214, 221, 297
Pillsbury Pageant 297
Pinafores 192
Pingatore, Mike 49
Pinza, Claudia 4
Pinza, Ezio 4, 9–10, 103, 113, 299, 309
Pious, Minerva 245
The Pirates of Penzance 268
Pittsburgh Symphony 116, 222
Plantation Jubilee 290
Plantation Party 289
Platterbrains 151
The Playboys 16
Plays for Americans 220
Plaza Hotel, New York 291
The Pleasure Hour 279
Pleasure Island 44
Pleasure Time 165
Plough, Inc. 44
Poetic Melodies 221
Polk, Lucy Ann 129
Pollack, Ben 21, 30, 39, 48, 137, 282
Pompeian Cosmetics Company 279
Pompeian Makeup Box 279
Pons, Lily 4, 8, 9, 113, 137
Ponselle, Carmela 242
Ponselle, Rosa 12, 107, 113
The Pontiac Hour 50, 285
Pontiac Motor Car Company 50, 285
The Pontiac Parade 285
Poole, Bob 155
Poole's Paradise 155–156
Porgy and Bess 268
Porter, Cole 329
Pot 'o' Gold 118, 128, 130–132
Potter, Peter 151–152
Poulsen, Valdemar 75
Powell, Jane 261, 265, 267–268, 269
Powell, Mel 39, 48
Power, Tyrone 37
Prado, Perez 34
Presenting Al Jolson 288
Presenting Bing Crosby 53
Presenting Mark Warnow 284, 292
Presidential Medal of Freedom 257
Presley, Elvis 47, 134
Preston, Robert 101
Previn, Andre 154
Price, Bob 48
Price, Leontyne 113
Price, Ray 178

Priddy, Jimmy 48
Prima, Louis 25
Prime, Harry 30
Privin, Bernie 35, 39, 48, 49
Procter & Gamble Company 47, 184, 215, 220–223, 254, 287, 292–296
Professor Quiz 131
Prohibition 21
Promoting Priscilla 225
The Prudential Family Hour 12, 93, 217, 294, 308
Prudential Insurance Company 217, 278, 294
Pryor, Arthur 223
Psychological behavior of bandleaders 31
Pure Oil Company 42
The Pure Oil Company Program 91
The Purple Heart 293
Pursuit 226
Purtill, Maurice "Moe," 48

Quaker Oats Company 193, 296
Quebec Academy of Music 92
Quinn, Carmel 134
Quintet, Scott 317
The Quiz Kids 130

Rabin, Michael 4
"Race music" 18
Rachmaninoff, Sergei 61, 170
Radio as marketing tool 320–321
Radio Bible Class 273
Radio City 98, 118
Radio City Music Hall 218, 222
Radio City Music Hall of the Air 106
Radio City Music Hall Orchestra 95
Radio Corporation of America 36, 108, 208, 222–227, 314
Radio Frankfurt 74–75
Radio Hall of Fame 277, 279
Radio Luxembourg 295
Radio Music Box 108
Radio Singer of the Year 283
"Radio wires" 19
Radisson Hotel, Minneapolis 288
Rae, Nan 245
Rafferty, Frances 140
The Railroad Hour 4–11, 85, 102, 126, 261–270, 308
Rainbow Court 296
Rainbow Ranch Boys 178
Rainbow-RKO 67
Rainger, Ralph 329
Raising Your Parents 115

The Raleigh Cigarette Program 223
Raleigh cigarettes 25
The Raleigh Room 225
The Raleigh-Kool Program 35, 218, 295
Ralf, Torsten 4
Ralph Carmichael Orchestra 202
Ralston Purina Company 184, 188
Ramona 49, 59
Ranch Boys 204
Randall, Bill 177
Randolph, Amanda 242
Rapee, Erno 106
Raphael, Sidney 208
Rarig, John 262
Rasey, Uan 39
Rathbone, Basil 4, 7
Ravazza, Carl 30
Ravinia Opera Company, Chicago 310
Rayburn, Gene 160
Rayburn, John 199–200
Raye, Martha 264
The Raymond Paige Orchestra 115, 222
Raymond Scott Orchestra 294
Rayve shampoo 41
RCA Magic Key 94
RCA Radiotrons 94
RCA Victor 47, 223
The RCA Victor Show 222
Rea, Virginia 228, 236, 238
Reader's Digest Association 246
Reagan, Ronald 257
Realsilk Hosiery Mills 225
The Realsilk Program 225
Red Horse Tavern 224
Red Ryder 213
The Red Skelton Show 223
Redding, Otis 158
Redman, Don 34, 49
Reese, Gail 47
Reeves, Chick 40
Reeves, James Travis "Jim" 178
Refreshment Time 279
Reichman, Joe 150
Reid, Kit 49
Reid, Neil 40
Reiner, Fritz 106, 113
Reinhardt, Max 97
Reisman, Leo 37, 317
The Remarkable Miss Tuttle 226
Renard, Jacques 207
Renfrew of the Mounted 142
Renfro Valley Barn Dance 190, 272–273
Renfro Valley Sunday Mornin' Gatherin' 273

Reno, Don 178
Reno Club, Kansas City 27
Republic Pictures 199
Request Performance 226
Rethberg, Elisabeth 113
Reuss, Allan 39
Reveille Round-Up 289
Revel, Harry 329
The Revelers 90, 92–94, 98, 301
Revue de Paree 235
Rexall Drug Company 43, 152, 289
The Rexall Drug Program 289
Rey, Alvino 132, 192, 215
Reynolds, Burt 86
Reynolds, Debbie 268, 284
Reynolds Metals Company 221, 227
Rhapsody in Rhythm 289
Rhymo 131
Rhythm at Eight 217
Rhythm Boys 49, 51, 55
Rice, Gladys 299, 302
Rice, Grantland 90, 95–96, 99
Rich, Buddy 35, 49
Rich, Freddie 30, 317, 325
Rich, Larry 277
Richard Hellman, Inc. 286, 292
Richard Hudnut, Inc. 41, 216
Richards, Johnny 30
Richbourg, John 157–158
Richfield Oil Company 219, 226
Richman, Boomie 35
Richman, Harry 164
Richmond, June 34
Rickey, Al 207
Riddle, Nelson 35, 64, 207
Riders of the Purple Sage 193
Ridges, Joseph 274
Riedel, Karl 113
Riggio, Vincent 317, 327
Riggs, L.A. "Speed" 317 332
Rigoletto 269
Riley, Mike 30
Rinker, Al 49, 55
The Rinso Program 216, 288
Rio, Rosa 273
Rio Grande Oil Company 218
The Risë Stevens Show 308
Rittenberg, Milton 90, 96
Ritter, Tex 203
R.J. Reynolds Tobacco Company 23, 33, 39, 178, 183, 216–226, 279–283, 290–293
Robbins, Marty 178
Robert Burns Panatella Cigar Company 19
Robert Shaw Chorale 121
Roberts, Barry 229, 238, 309
Roberts, Lynn 35
Robertson, Guy 242

Robertson, Rae 109
Robin, Leo 329
Robin, Ruth 30
Robinson, Les 39, 49
Robison, Willard 207
Roche, Betty 38
Rochester Philharmonic Orchestra 13
Rodgers, Harry 48, 49
Rodgers, Richard 174, 263, 270, 329
Rodin, Gil 282
Rodney, Red 40
Rodriguez, Willie 49
Rodzinski, Artur 109, 121
Roger and Gallet perfume 282
Rogers, Billie 40
Rogers, Elizabeth 40, 41
Rogers, Roy 193, 199–203
Rogers, Shorty 40
Rogers, Will 197, 203, 280
Rogers of the Gazette 217, 219
Rogue's Gallery 226
Roland, Will 128
Rolfe, B.A. 21, 25, 320
Rollini, Arthur 39
Roma Wine Company 216
Romance, Rhythm and Ripley 287
The Romance of Helen Trent 296
Romay, Lina 33
Romberg, Sigmund 263
Romeo, Bob 49
Rooney, Andy 128
Rooney, Mickey 140
Roosevelt, Eleanor 10, 247
Roosevelt, Franklin Delano 16, 148, 257, 280, 311, 327
Roosevelt Grill, New York 45
Rosario Bourdon Orchestra 92
Rose, Dave 48
Rose, David 207, 222–223
Rose, George 39
Rose, Ralph 193
Roseland Ballroom, New York 40
The Rosemary Clooney Show 281
Rosenbloom, Max "Slapsie Maxie" 140
Ross, David 164, 297
Ross, Hugh 121
Ross, Jack 204
Ross, Lanny 242, 267, 291–292, 318, 326
Rosten, Norman 4
Rothier, Leon 107
Rounseville, Robert 299, 303, 313
Roxy and His Gang 92, 93, 115

Roxy Symphony Theater of the Stars 231, 243
Roxy Theater, New York 220, 243
Roxy Theater Concert 165
The Roy Rogers and Dale Evans Show 202
Roy Rogers Radio Show 193
Roy Rogers Show 193–194, 200
Royal, Ernie 40
Royal, John F. 56, 119
Royal, Marshall 38
Royal Air Force, Great Britain 74
The Royal Gelatin Hour 298
Rubinowich, Sam 40
Rubinstein, Arthur 4, 7, 109
Rudolf, Max 113
Rudy Vallee and His Connecticut Yankees 298
The Rudy Vallee Fleischmann Sunshine Hour 250
Rudy Vallee Orchestra 298
The Rudy Vallee Show 61, 210, 215, 298
Ruffo, Tito 107
Rush, Art 193
Rushing, Jimmy 30
Rushton, Joe 133
Russell, Andy 318, 325, 328
Russell, Jane 30
Russin, Babe 34, 35, 39
The Ruth Etting Show 224
Ruysdael, Basil 317, 332
Ruzzillo, Ralph 39
Ryan, Dennis 229, 238, 309
Ryan, Jack 34
Ryan, Tommy 41
Ryman Auditorium 183, 184
Rysanek, Leonie 113

Sachs Furniture Company 286
The Sachs Program 286
Sacred Song Concert 272
St. Leger, Frank 113
St. Louis Browns 12
St. Louis Symphony 11
St. Petersburg Conservatory 125
Sal Hepatica Revue 210
Salt Lake City Tabernacle Choir 273
Salter, Harry 130, 141, 317, 325
Salute to Youth 118, 222, 267
Sam Lanin and the Ipana Troubadors 207
Sam 'n' Henry 152
Sammy Kaye Orchestra 41–42
Sammy Kaye Sunday Serenade 41–42
Sammy Kaye's Cameo Room 42
Sammy Kaye's Sylvania Serenade 42

Sampson, Edgar 38
San Carlo Opera, Tampa, Florida 12, 266, 311
San Francisco Girls Chorus 11
San Francisco Opera 12, 116
San Francisco State University 11
San Jose Symphony 116
Sanders, Joe 18
Sannella, Andy 229, 239
Sara's Private Caper 213
Sarnoff, David 108–112, 208, 314
Sarnoff, Dorothy 261
Saturday Night 131
Saturday Night Party 291
Saturday Night Serenade 100
The Saturday Night Swing Club 25, 226
Saturday Nite Shindig 190
Saturday Review 226
Sauter, Eddie 38
Savage, Muriel 272
Savitt, Buddy 40
Savitt, Jan 25, 30, 208
Savoy Company 10
Sayao, Bidu 4, 8, 11, 113
S.C. Johnson & Sons 165, 220–222, 227, 281
Scandals and Vanities 5
Scheff, Fritzi 243
Schelling, Ernest 110
Schenley Laboratories 226
Schick blades 226
Schmidt, Joseph 106
Schonberg, Harold 305
Schorr, Friedrich 113
Schreiner, Alexander 274
Schultzendorf, Gustav 112
Schumann, Walter 207
Schumann-Heink, Ernestine 225
Schuster, Josef 126
Schutter Candy Company 290
Schutz, Buddy 34, 39
Schwartz, Julie 39
Schwartz, Wilbur 48
Scott, Martha 202
Scott, Raymond 208, 317, 325
Scott, Will S. 83
Scott, Willard 156
Scranton Lace Company 246
The Screen Guild Theater 85
Scripps-Howard newspaper syndicate 86
Scripteasers 131
Scroggins, Jerry 192
Scruggs, Earl 177, 184, 289
The Sea Has a Story 216
Seagle, John 90, 92
Sealtest Corporation 215
Sealtest Dairies 291, 298

The Sealtest Show 298
The Sealtest Sunday Night Party 118
The Sealtest Village Store 215
Searchey, George 165
Sears, Al 38
Sears, Roebuck and Company 75, 197
Seberg, George 35
Second Honeymoon 142
Second Husband 158
Seefried, Imrgard 4
Segal, Vivienne 229, 240
Segovia, Andres 4
Seiberling Singers 92
Selinsky, Vladimir 207
Sellers, Charles 165
Selvin, Ben 21, 207, 286
Sensation and Swing 41
Sensation cigarettes 41
Senter, Boyd 30
The Sentimentalists 35
Serafin, Tullio 113
Serkin, Robert 109
Service with a Smile 118
Seymour, Dan 133, 263
Shake the Maracas 46
Shand, Terry 46
Shannon Four 301
The Shannon Quartet 92
Shapiro, Artie 49
Sharbutt, Del 317
Shavers, Charlie 35
Shaw, Artie 17, 25–26, 30–31, 45–49, 210
Shaw, Elliott 92
Shaw, Oscar 242
Shaw, Robert 164, 170, 174
Shefter, Bert 218
Shell Chateau 288
Shell Oil Corporation 127, 288
Shepard, Jean 178
Sheralee 335
Sheridan, Ann 152
Sheridan, Frank 109
Sherin, Leo "Ukie" 52 62
Sherock, Shorty 34, 133
Sherrill, Joya 38
Sherry, Diane 80
Shertzer, Hymie 39
Sherwin-Williams Company 104, 214
Sherwood, Bobby 30
Shields, Larry 88
Shilkret, Jack 207
Shilkret, Nathaniel 207, 223–224, 303
Ship of Joy 127, 133, 227
Shirley, Tom 4, 245, 259
Shore, Dinah 30, 81–88, *87*, 126, 261–268, 318, 326

Shore, Frances Rose "Fanny" *See* Shore, Dinah
Show Boat 267
Show Business Old and New 280
Showboat 210, 217, 227, 268, 289
Shower of Stars 129, 218
Showland Memories 243
Shut-In Hour 271
Siepi, Cesare 113, 299, 303, 313
Sies, Luther 272
Sigmund Spaeth's Music Quiz 131
The Signal Carnival 220, 227
Signal Oil Company 218, 220, 227
Silhouettes in Music 95
Sills, Beverly 113, 137, 267, 299
Sills, Paul 192
The Silver Summer Revue 222
Silvers, Phil 66
Simmons, Bob 318
Simmons, Kermit 40
Simmons, Robert 90, 93
Simms, Ginny 30, 129–140, 155, 261–268, 292–293, 318
Simms, Hal 130
Simms, Lu Ann 134
Simon, George 48, 133
Simon, Joe 158
Sims, Zoot 35, 40
Sinatra, Frank 30–35, 54, 66–70, 133–137, 151, 160, 266–267, 318, 325–328
Sinatra, Ray 317
Sinfonietta 106
Sing for Your Dough 137
Sing for Your Money 137
Sing It Again 133
The Singing Bee 131
Singing cowboy 194
Singo, Rhymo, Jimgo 294
Singo, Songo 131
Siravo, George 48
The $64 Question 130
Skelton, Red 12, 54, 77, 140, 223, 264
Skyline Roof 214
Slack, Freddy 34
Slamaggi Opera Company 311
Sleep No More 118
The Slumber Hour 115
Smalle, Ed 92
Smith, Carl 178
Smith, Ethel 317, 318
Smith, Floyd 89
Smith, Frank 193
Smith, Howard 48
Smith, Jack 54, 293–294
Smith, J.S. 261
Smith, Kate 8, 56–57, 67, 79, 86, 101, 151, 245–260, *258*

Smith, Robert W. "Wolfman Jack," 161
Smith, Verne 129, 193
Smith, Willie 38
Smith Brothers 130, 220, 224
The Smith Brothers Program 224
The Smoky Mountain Boys 177
The Smoothies 164
Snow, Clarence Eugene "Hank," 178
Snow Village Sketches 245
So You Want to Lead a Band 41, 42, 133
Soap operas 194, 230, 253–254
Socony Oil Company 39, 224
Socony Vacuum Oil Corporation 103, 105
Soconyland Sketches 11
Sodero, Cesare 113
Sommers, Jay 81
A Song Is Born 133
The Song of Norway 268
Song of the City 296
Song pluggers 28
Song scouts 322–323
The Song Shop 267
Songs America Sings 227
Songs by Dinah Shore 85
Songs by Eddie Fisher 284
Songs by Morton Downey 284
Songs for Sale 134, 281
Songs of the B-Bar-B 203
Songs of the Century 12
Songs You Love 224
The Songsmiths 318, 326
Songwriters 328–329
Sons of Italy 281
Sons of the Pioneers 193, 199–200, 202, 204
Sosnik, Harry 25, 40, 207, 224–225, 317, 325
Sousa, John Philip 94, 223, 227
Southern Cruise 216
Southern Regional Opera Company 11
Sparkle Time 227
Speaks, Margaret 299, 302, 309
Speaks, Oley 309
Specht, Paul 17
Speidel 130
Spellman, Francis Cardinal 101
Spenser, Tim 193
The Spike Jones Show 85
Spitalny, Phil 27
Spivak, Charlie 35
The Sportsmen 262
Spotlight Bands 25
Spotlight on Music 219
Sprudel Salt Company 283
Squires, Bruce 34

Stacy, Jack 34
Stacy, Jess 39
Stafford, Hanley 318, 323
Stafford, Jo 30–35, 76, 87, 261–268, 294–295, 312
The Stafford Sisters 295
Stage Door Canteen 222, 279, 285
Stage Door Canteen, Hollywood 139
Staley Corporation 214
Standard Brands, Inc. 36, 50, 128, 213–222, 280, 298
Standard Candy Company 184
Standard Oil Company 44, 286
Stapp, Jack 177, 183
Starr, Kay 30
Stars in Khaki 'n' Blue 131, 284
Stars of the Milky Way 221
Stars on Parade 277, 281
Star-Spangled Vaudeville 222
State Fair 268
Steamboat Jamboree 292
Steber, Eleanor 113–117, 299, 303, 306–307, 313, *313*
Steck, Steve 48
Steel Pier, Atlantic City 281
Steffe, Edwin 4
Steidry, Fritz 113
Stein, Jules 19
Steinberg, William 121
Stella and the Fellas 164
Stella Dallas 118
Stepping Out 281
Sterling, Jack 161
Sterling Drugs, Inc. 180, 214, 228–230, 238, 240
Stern, Isaac 4
Stevens, Connie 284
Stevens, Leith 207, 225–226
Stevens, Lynne 40
Stevens, Risë 4, 67, 103, 113–114, 262–268, 299–313
Stevens, Sheila 263
Steward, Herbie 40
Stewart, Jimmy 48, 66
Stewart, Phil 43
Stewart, Rex 38
Stock market crash of 1929 18
Stoker, Gordon 178
Stokes, Leonard 318
Stokowski, Leopold 109, 123, 151
Stoll, Georgie 52, 59
Stone, David 177
Stone, Eddie 46
Stone, Ezra 245
Stoneburn, Sid 35
The Stony Mountain Cloggers 178, 186
Stoopnagle and Budd 226

Stop the Music! 130, 141–143, 209
Stordahl, Axel 35, 317, 325, 327
The Story of the Sea 216
Storz, Todd 161–162
Stoska, Polyna 4
The Stradivari Orchestra 95
Straeter, Ted 259
Strahorn, Lee 317
Straight, Bobby 30
Strand Theater, New York 26
Strand Theatre, Newport 291
Stravinsky, Igor 109
Strayhorn, Billy 38
The Street Singer 297
Streich, Rita 4
Strike It Rich 130, 136–137
Striker, Ernie 49
The Student Prince 97, 268, 269
Studio bands 206–227
Stulce, Fredy 35
Styne, Jule 329
Sullivan, Brian 4–8, 113, 299, 303, 313
Sullivan, Ed 264
Sullivan, Joe 88
Sullivan, Johnny 178
Sullivan, Rollin 178
Summer Hotel 286
Summer Pastime 35, 295
Summer Playhouse 36
Summer Serenade 36
Summey, James C. 178
Sunday at the N— K Ranch 290
Sunday Down South 183
Sunday Morning Revue 128
Sunday on the N.K. Ranch 225
Sundelius, Marie 107
Sundial 156
Sunkist Growers 222
Sunset Serenade 48
The Sunshine Hour 298
Surprise Party 129, 293
Suspense 85, 211, 216, 218
Sutherland, Joan 113
Svanholm, Set 4
Swan Lake 268
Swarthout, Gladys 4–8, 103, 113, 242, 262–268, 299–302, 310–311
The Sweeney and March Program 216, 219
Sweet and Rhythmic 220
Sweetest Love Songs Ever Sung 235, 237, 243
Sweetheart Serenade 278
Swift & Company 224
Swope, Earl 40
Swor, Bert 165
Sylvania Corporation 42
Symphony of the Air 94

Szell, George 113
Szigeti, Joseph 109

Tageman, Nell 262
Tagliavini, Ferrucio 4
Take It or Leave It 130, 280
Talent Search 131
Talent Theater 293
Tangee 41
Tangee Varieties 41
Tanner, Elmo 158
Tanner, Paul 48
Tape recording radio programs 68–69, 75
Tassinari, Pia 4
Tastyeast Bakers 286
The Tastyeast Jesters 286
Tauber, Richard 106
Taylor, Davidson 12
Taylor, Deems 59, 107, 109–110, 112–113, 123
Taylor, Elizabeth 284
Taylor, Tommy 38
The Taystee Loafers 286
Teagarden, Charlie 34, 49, 82, 84
Teagarden, Jack 25, 31–32, 49, 82–84, 150–151
Teatro Hidalgo, Mexico City 13
Tebaldi, Renata 4, 113
Ted Mack and His Band 137
Ted Mack's Original Amateur Hour 129, 135
Ted Straeter Chorus 245
Teen Town 131
Television 32
Templeton, Alec 4
Tennessee Barn Dance 190
Tennessee Capitol Building 182
Tennessee Travelers 178, 186
Terry, Clark 38
Tetley, Walter 318, 323
Tex, Joe 158
Tex Ritter's Camp Fire 203
The Texaco Opera Quiz 131
Texaco Star Theater 92, 198, 217, 263, 285, 294
Texaco Town 280
Texas Barn Dance 190
Texas Company 37, 104, 116, 217, 263, 280–285, 294
The Texas Playboys 203
Texas Troubadors 178
Textor, Keith 164
Textor, Sylvia 164
Teyte, Dame Maggie 4
That's Life 220
Thaxter, Phyllis 264
Thebom, Blanche 4, 8, 11, 113, 262, 268
Theme songs of bands 29–30

Theme songs of Hummert musicales 244
Thibault, Conrad 229, 238, 241, 269
This Is Bing Crosby 54
This Is New York 226
This Is Nora Drake 59
This Is Your FBI 115
Thomas, Cliff 177
Thomas, John Charles 4, 8, 106, 113
Thomas, Thomas L. 93–96, 117, 229–239, 243, 269, 299, 303–313
Thomas J. Lipton, Inc. 128, 214
Thompson, Blanche 164
Thompson, Henry William "Hank" 178
Thompson, Kay 164, 165, 170, 318, 324
Thompson, Marian 164
Thompson, Uncle Jimmy 181
Thorborg, Kerstin 113
Thornhill, Claude 24, 30, 46, 48, 49
Three Ambassadors 245, 293
Three for the Money 137
The Three GirlFriends 164
Three Little Maids from Pixie 291
Three Ring Time 44, 282
Three Sheets to the Wind 63
Through the Years 291
Tibbett, Lawrence 4–6, 103, 113, 118, 299–306, 318, 326–328
Tiberi, Frank 40
The Tide Show 294
Tilton, Martha 30, 34, 38, 262, 318, 326
Tim and Irene 6
The Time, the Place and the Tune 266
Time to Smile 280
Tizol, Juan 38
Tobacco auctioneers 332
Tobin, Louise 38
Todd, Dick 318, 328
Tom Mix 203–204
Tommy Dorsey, Inc. 36
Tommy Dorsey Orchestra 35–36, 295
The Tommy Dorsey Show 36, 287
Tommy Dorsey's Playshop 36
Tommy Dorsey's Variety Show 36, 295
Tommy Riggs and Betty Lou 215
Tone Syllables techniques 166
Tonight on Broadway 279
Torme, Mel 30, 48, 151, 295–297

Torme Time 297
Toscanini, Arturo 9–12, 103–109, 119–124, *122*, 208, 227, 241
Touff, Cy 40
Tough, Davey 34, 35, 39, 40, 49
Tourel, Jennie 4
Town Hall, New York 10
Town Hall Tonight 294
Tozzi, Giorgio 4, 113
Tracy, Arthur 67, 297
Trade and Mark 224
Traubel, Helen 4, 6, 8, 11–12, 113, 299
Travelers Aid Society 136–137
La Traviata 269
Treasury of Stars 225
Treasury Star Parade 217
Tremaine, Paul 30
Trendler, Robert 269
Trotter, John Scott 52, 64–65, 71, 73, 78, 212
The Troubador of the Moon 292
Trout, Robert 157, 245, 259
True Name Society 266
True Story 118
Truman, Margaret 262, 268
Trumbauer, Frankie 49
Truth or Consequences 130, 325
Tubb, Ernest Dale 178
Tubb, Justin Wayne 178
Tucker, Orrin 27, 30, 173, 317
Tucker, Richard 113
Tucker, Sophie 250
The Tuesday Night Party 216, 288
Tums 291
Tums' Treasure Chest 128
Tune-based quiz programs 131
Tune In 4
Tune Twisters 285
Turner, Grant 177, 184
Turner, Ike 158
Turner, Lana 49
Turner, Nicholas M. 101
Turner, Tina 158
Twelve Players 219
Twentieth Century Concert Hall 304
Twentieth Century Fox 281, 284
Twenty Thousand Years in Sing Sing 118
The Two Black Crows 165
Two Boys and a Piano 55
Two in the Balcony 213
Twombly, Gene 192
The TwoTon Baker Show 151
Tydol Oil Company 46

Uggams, Leslie 134

Uncle Ed Poplin and His Old Timers 182
United Artists 67
United Press International 252
U.S. Army 289
U.S. Army Reserve 82
U.S. Office of Emergency Management 218
U.S. Rubber Corporation 103
U.S. Tire and Rubber Company 222, 291
U.S. Treasury Department 42, 217, 223, 225, 242
University of Maine 12
University of North Carolina 138
Uppman, Theodor 4, 113
Usifer, Joseph *see* Lavalle, Paul

Vacation Serenade 118
Vacation with Music 225
The Vagabond King 268, 269
Valdengo, Giuseppe 4
Valdes, Miguelito 33
Vale, Jerry 137
Valetti, Cesare 313
Vallee, Rudy 19–20, 30–31, 45, 56, 62, 70, 98, 151, 262–268, 297–298
Vallee Varieties 298
Valli, June 318, 326
Van, Betty 38
Van Alexander's Orchestra 265
Vanderbilt University 85, 92
Van Dyke, Leroy 178
Van Epps, Bobby 34
Van Eps, Johnny 35
Van Hartesveldt, Fran 261
Van Heusen, Jimmy 329
Van Steeden, Peter 207, 317, 325
The Variety Show 279
Vaughan, Sarah 30
The Vaughn Monroe Show 290
Vause, George 271, 272
The V-8 164
Venetia, Joe 49
Ventura, Charlie 284
Venuti, Joe 49
Vera-Ellen 67
Verplanck, Billy 34, 35
Verplanck, Marlene 35
Vichey, Luben 4
Vick Chemical Company 47
Vicks Open House 11, 47
Victor Arden's Orchestra 243
The Victor Borge Show 39, 222
Victor Hour 223
Victor phonograph records 17
Victor Salon Orchestra 223
Victor Talking Machine Company 92

Victory Parade of Spotlight Bands 25
Victory Tunes 165
Videotape recording (VTR) 75–76
Vienna Conservatory of Music 311
Vienna Opera Company, Chicago 310
Vincent Lopez Orchestra 45–46
Vocalian records 197, 199
Vocalists 30–31
Voice of America 118
Voice of Democracy 295
The Voice of Eileen Farrell 12
The Voice of Firestone 4–15, 92–102, 126, 212, 238–239, 266–267, 299–316
Volstead Act 21
Von Deyn, Hyatt Robert 293
Voorhees, Donald 3–6, *7,* 13–15, 21, 137, 207–212
Vox Pop 118

WAAT, Newark, New Jersey 142
Wabash River, Indiana 17
WABC, New York 125, 147, 154, 298
Wade, Stuart 30, 46
Wages of bands 26–27
Wagner, Robert 152
Wagon Masters 178
Wagoner, Porter 178
Wahl, Enrico 238
Wain, Bea 48, 151, 243–245, 318, 325–328, 333–334
Wakefield, Henrietta 112
Waldorf Astoria Hotel, New York 33, 107
WAMO, Pittsburgh 190
WASH, Washington, D.C. 157
WAVY, Portsmouth, Virginia 159
WBBM, Chicago 19, 161, 224
WBIR, Knoxville, Tennessee 159
WBT, Charlotte, N.C. 158–159, 190, 196
WBZ, Boston 223, 272
WCBS, New York 161
WCCO, Minneapolis 156
WCFL, Chicago 161
WCKY, Cincinnati 190
WCOP, Boston 190
WDAF, Kansas City 18
WDAY, Fargo, North Dakota 288
WDY, Roselle Park, New Jersey 280
WEAF, New York 95–97, 107, 118, 203, 223, 271, 280–286

WEBH, Chicago 224
WENR, Chicago 296
WFAA, Dallas 190
WFBM, Indianapolis 161
WFBR, Baltimore 134, 223
WFIL, Philadelphia 161
WGH, Newport News, Virginia 92
WGN, Chicago 19, 130, 152, 161, 190, 268, 296
WGST, Atlanta 142, 183
WHAS, Louisville 190
WHIL, Medford, Massachusetts 190
WHN, New York 135, 161, 243
WHP, Harrisburg, Pennsylvania 92, 223
WIND, Chicago 160–161
WINS, Manhattan 146–147
WIP, Philadelphia 214
WIRE, Indianapolis, Indiana 92
WJAR, Providence, Rhode Island 223
WJJD, Chicago 161
WJR, Detroit 190
WJSV, Washington, D.C. 134, 161
WJW, Cleveland 146
WJZ, New York 17, 93, 107, 115, 148
WJZ, Newark 286, 291, 309
WKBN, Youngstown 278
WLAC, Nashville 157–158, 188
WLS, Chicago 180, 190, 197, 272, 279
WLW, Cincinnati 190, 272, 278, 281, 284
WMAL, Washington, D.C. 134, 223
WMAQ, Chicago 152, 161
WMC, Memphis 179
WMCA, New York 21, 214, 297
WMGM, New York 161
WMTA, Charleston, S.C. 158
WNBC, New York 161, 267
WNEW, New York 85, 154, 155, 159, 160, 271
WNOX, Knoxville 190
WNTA, New York 159
WOR, Manhattan 101, 107, 154, 161, 203, 298, 309
WOR, Newark, New Jersey 218, 278
WPRO, Providence, Rhode Island 223
WRC, Washington, D.C. 134, 156
WRG, Buffalo 223
WRJN, Milwaukee 190
WRVA, Richmond 190
WSB, Atlanta 190
WSM, Nashville 85–86, 92, 178–186, 188–194, 203
WSMB, New Orleans 279
WTOP, Washington, D.C. 156, 157
W2XAB, New York 259
WWBM, Chicago 241
WWDC, Washington, D.C. 157
WWJ, Detroit 17
WWVA, Wheeling, West Virginia 190

XERF, Cuncino, Mexico 161

www.ingramcontent.com/pod-product-compliance
Lightning Source LLC
Chambersburg PA
CBHW081535300426
44116CB00015B/2635